"Liederbach and Lenow provide a robust survey of Christian ethics. The discussion of theology's interaction with metaethics and normative ethics is especially helpful."
—**J. Alan Branch**, Professor of Christian Ethics, Midwestern Baptist Theological Seminary

"*Ethics as Worship* is a most intriguing title. In our world, ethics is often a manipulative game to justify what our group wants to do. Basing ethics on our relationship with the Lord of Exodus 34:6–7, however, is a graciously firm foundation. Thus, ethics is not about specific choices but about what makes the character of our Lord visible in our deeds, which flow from our loving him with our heart, soul, mind, and strength. Since he is Lord of all, that sort of ethic will guide every part of our lives as individuals and in community. The unique foundation, careful metaethical development, and wise application in the most difficult issues make this a magnificent contribution to worshipful living."
—**Gerry Breshears**, Professor of Theology, Western Seminary

"*Ethics as Worship* is a theologically framed, deeply informed, and richly integrated guide to thinking and living—each day—as a disciple of Jesus Christ. Liederbach and Lenow instruct and invite, equipping and inspiring the reader to both 'be' and 'live' ethics as worship."
—**W. David Buschart**, Professor of Theology and Historical Studies, Denver Seminary

"*Ethics as Worship* is an excellent and comprehensive work that orients and overlays ethics as an expression of worship to the glory of God. As I teach seminary worship classes, I emphasize the place of corporate gathered worship in equipping the people of God and transforming them into greater Christlikeness in a way that is lived out missionally between Sundays in all of life as worship. *Ethics as Worship* has great potential to introduce, enhance, and bring this focus into the field of ethics, including substantial application to eleven presenting issues that we as the people of God face in our day-to-day lives."
—**Mark Dalbey**, President and Professor of Applied Theology, Covenant Theological Seminary

"As our world spirals further into confusion with every passing day, the study of ethics has never been more important. This excellent volume by Mark Liederbach and Evan Lenow is exactly the kind of book that we need for this moment. Drawing from biblical and theological foundations, it demonstrates that, rightly understood, ethics is about worship of the one true God. Christians of every perspective will want to read and digest this book."

—**Jamie Dew**, President and Professor of Christian Philosophy, New Orleans Baptist Theological Seminary

"Too often the discipline of ethics focuses on minutiae that can become overwhelming to students and generalists. *Ethics as Worship*, however, focuses on the glory of God and the alignment of God's will, God's Word, and the behavior of God's people. The result is a mixture of exaltation and practicality, orthodoxy and orthopraxy, as Liederbach and Lenow carefully unfold their approach with wisdom and discernment."

—**Gene C. Fant Jr.**, President and Professor of English, North Greenville University

"Right behavior is one of the most important ways in which gospel-transformed people worship their Creator. We must grasp this insight or our gospel will remain too narrow to change our lives, and our ethics will remain either permissive or legalistic. *Ethics as Worship* zeroes in on this essential issue for a church that desperately needs to reconnect ethics with religious experience."

—**Greg Forster**, Director, Oikonomia Network

"This book is an important contribution to the field of Christian ethics and ultimately to Christian discipleship. Mark Liederbach and Evan Lenow get to the heart of ethics by articulating something that is often missed in other resources: the end of ethical living is the worship of God. They not only present a good big picture of ethics as worship to God, but also provide areas of application in ways that challenge us how to think rightly about Christian morality. Their work is an asset to the field of Christian ethics and will be a valuable resource for years to come."

—**RaShan Frost**, Executive Director, 1 Charleston; Lead Pastor/Church Planter, The Bridge Church, Charleston, South Carolina; Adjunct Professor of Christian Studies, Charleston Southern University

"*Ethics as Worship* is the book that I have been waiting for. Authors Liederbach and Lenow approach ethics in a way that is biblically faithful, philosophically robust, and accessible to students. By framing ethics as worship, this book brings issues of applied ethics into the realm of discipleship where it belongs. Not only will readers grow in their understanding of ethics, but, more importantly, they will grow in their love of Jesus and in faithfulness to him."

—**Adam Groza**, Associate Professor of Philosophy of Religion and Vice President of Enrollment and Student Services, Gateway Seminary

"In *Ethics as Worship*, Liederbach and Lenow connect conservative Christian theology and biblical interpretation to the call for Christians to live out our worship of Jesus in a variety of life's most challenging situations. This volume grounds its ideas in a clear, mature, and nuanced framework that provides a balanced biblical perspective that will challenge Christians on both sides of our current political divide to love Jesus more deeply. Christians who engage this text will consider their actions and life more clearly, ponder their motivations and outcomes more sincerely, and recognize more urgently the need to worship Jesus now and forever."

—**Peter Link Jr.**, Associate Professor of Christian Studies, Charleston Southern University

"This important book tells us to ascribe to the God of the Bible all he deserves from the entirety of our holistic selves as an act of loving devotion. Once ethics as worship becomes our regular orientation, we can tackle all the sticky cultural issues of our day. Please use this very helpful resource in your classrooms, in your churches, and with your families."

—**Dwayne Milioni**, Pastor, Professor, and Board Chairman, Pillar Church Planting Network

"In classical ethical theories, ethics is about the actor, the character of the person making the virtuous choice. In modern ethical theories, ethics is about the action, the choice that the person makes. Mark Liederbach and Evan Lenow demonstrate clearly from Scripture that ethics is about God and our whole-person worship of him. This volume is God-centered, biblically rigorous, pastorally helpful, and delightfully refreshing. Read it as an act of worship."

—**C. Ben Mitchell**, Graves Professor of Moral Philosophy (ret.), Union University; former editor, *Ethics and Medicine: An International Journal of Bioethics*; Senior Fellow, Academy of Fellows of The Center for Bioethics & Human Dignity

"In a time and context when Christians need to rethink both their private and public ethical approaches, Liederbach and Lenow's *Ethics as Worship* is both timely and helpful. The text assists Christians in navigating difficult topics by viewing them through a biblical lens and by reconsidering ethical behavior as worship through an expression of love and care for neighbor. Given a long history of evangelical Christian approaches to slavery, the civil rights movement, abuse, and even modern justice struggles, this text should help believers navigate a complex modern world. *Ethics as Worship* will help seminary students, college students, and all others who want to more deeply consider their ethical framework as Christians living for the kingdom."

—**Otis W. Pickett**, Associate Professor of History, Mississippi College

"Yes! An understanding of ethics that centers on God, is saturated with the gospel, and is inextricably tied to the mission that Jesus has given his church to make disciples of all nations. *Ethics as Worship* provides desperately needed ballast for our souls amid a sea of ethical confusion that surrounds us in this world."

—**David Platt**, Pastor, McLean Bible Church, McLean, Virginia; author, *Radical*, *Follow Me*, and *Counter Culture*

"In an age when orthodoxy is too often severed from orthopraxy, the church needs a work such as *Ethics as Worship: Moral Discipleship to the Glory of God*, which puts right belief and right action back together again. This comprehensive text not only has a firm biblical foundation but fairly and effectively engages with our broader cultural context and its countervailing perspectives. This is a work of serious scholarship and of immense worth in practical application."

—**Karen Swallow Prior**, Research Professor of English and Christianity and Culture, Southeastern Baptist Theological Seminary; author, *On Reading Well: Finding the Good Life through Great Books*; coauthor, *Cultural Engagement: A Crash Course in Contemporary Issues*

"As the leader of an organization dedicated to inspiring and equipping Christians to become better stewards of their lives and the world that God has given us, I enthusiastically offer my endorsement to *Ethics as Worship* by Liederbach and Lenow.

"This text is refreshing in that it develops the biblical foundations for *why* before explaining the biblical commands that guide our *what* and *how*. Too often, discussions of ethics fall on the side of moralistic legalism or vague calls to love one another. This text, however, avoids both extremes, seeking instead to place the entire ethical enterprise in context of loving worship of God, which in turn guides our obedience to the commands of Scripture. By focusing on both the Old and New Testament themes of worship, the authors show how pursuit of the person of Christ ought to both drive a passionate devotion to God and result in transformative flourishing in individuals and society as a whole. In this way, the discipline of ethics is transformed from an enumeration of duties to an adventure of joy that ends in human flourishing under the lordship of Christ.

"This book is a well-ordered, biblically sound, and theologically satisfying exploration of the discipline of ethics."

—**Matthew Sleeth**, Executive Director, Blessed Earth

"Liederbach and Lenow fill a void that has long been missing in the study of Christian ethics by beautifully balancing a classic deontological ethic with a biblically informed virtue ethic. Their well-researched treatment of contemporary ethical issues is biblical, pastoral, and missional. They show that ethics flows more from a life of discipleship than from an application of rules."

—**John K. Tarwater**, Associate Professor of Finance, Cedarville University School of Business Administration

"It is common to think of ethics as merely an exercise in abstract navel-gazing. What Mark Liederbach and Evan Lenow have done is the opposite: situating ethics as an expression of our love for God—and there's nothing abstract or dispassionate about loving God. We're told by Christ to love God with all our heart, soul, and mind. Add to that *ethics*. I look forward to seeing this book make an impact in the wider evangelical orbit."

—**Andrew T. Walker**, Associate Professor of Christian Ethics, The Southern Baptist Theological Seminary; author, *Liberty for All*

"Mark Liederbach and Evan Lenow have made a wonderful contribution to the field of Christian ethics. *Ethics as Worship* offers fresh insights for Christian moral reasoning on contemporary issues ranging from metaethical foundations to emerging issues in applied ethics. Liederbach and Lenow's extensively researched, nuanced, and charitable treatment of each issue sets an example of what evangelical ethics should be."

—**Tim Yonts**, Instructor, Christian Ethics; Associate Director of LU Serve, Liberty University

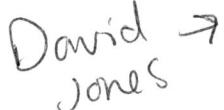

ETHICS

AS WORSHIP

ETHICS
AS WORSHIP

The Pursuit of Moral Discipleship

Mark D. Liederbach
Evan Lenow

P&R
PUBLISHING
P.O. BOX 817 • PHILLIPSBURG • NEW JERSEY 08865-0817

Unless otherwise indicated, all Scripture quotations are from the New American Standard Bible®. Copyright © 1960, 1962, 1963, 1968, 1971, 1972, 1973, 1975, 1977, 1995 by The Lockman Foundation. Used by permission.

Scripture quotations marked (NKJV™) are taken from the New King James Version®. Copyright © 1982 by Thomas Nelson, Inc. Used by permission. All rights reserved.

Italics within Scripture quotations indicate emphasis added.

Printed in the United States of America

978-1-62995-262-8 (hardback)
978-1-62995-263-5 (ePub)

Library of Congress Cataloging-in-Publication Data

Names: Liederbach, Mark, author. | Lenow, Evan, author.
Title: Ethics as worship : the pursuit of moral discipleship / Mark Daniel
    Liederbach and Evan Lenow.
Description: Phillipsburg, New Jersey : P&R Publishing, [2021] | Includes
    bibliographical references and index. | Summary: "Ethics as Worship
    examines the foundations and application of Christian ethics, offering
    an ethical system that emphasizes the worship of God as motivation,
    method, and goal of the ethical endeavor"-- Provided by publisher.
Identifiers: LCCN 2021008271 | ISBN 9781629952628 (hardback) | ISBN
    9781629952635 (epub) | ISBN 9781629952642 (mobi)
Subjects: LCSH: Worship. | Christian ethics.
Classification: LCC BV10.3 .L54 2021 | DDC 241--dc23
LC record available at https://lccn.loc.gov/2021008271

For our students

Contents

Part 4: The Application of Ethics as Worship

Illustrations

Figures

Tables

Foreword

MANY OF US live in a society in which sexual orientation and gender identity, climate change and care for the environment, capital punishment and criminal justice reform, racism and poverty, abortion, euthanasia, and physician-assisted suicide are hotly debated and polarizing issues. Who would have thought they were all about worship? Allow me to explain.

Christians believe that two aspects of worship are very important for the believing life: congregational worship and worship in all of life. In congregational worship (which is sometimes called *corporate worship or public worship*), God's people gather on the Lord's Day to meet with God and give him the glory due his name according to his Word, as his Word is read, preached, prayed, and sung, and as baptism and the Lord's Supper (his "visible words," Augustine called them) are administered. This aspect of worship (public worship) actually disciples Christians in how they are supposed to live the rest of their lives (worship in all of life).

Worship in all of life is what Paul is especially talking about in Romans 12:1–2: "Present your bodies as a living sacrifice, holy and acceptable to God, which is your spiritual worship. Do not be conformed to this world, but be transformed by the renewal of your mind, that by testing you may discern what is the will of God, what is good and acceptable and perfect." This passage begins an extended treatment of ethical issues in Romans 12–15. There, Paul is especially exhorting us about our whole manner of life, what we do in the totality of our thoughts, desires, speech, and actions. In other words, he is calling us to live our whole lives as worship to God. He wants believers to approach their lives by viewing themselves as living, breathing, walking, talking offerings to God (hence "living sacrifices"). To say it yet another way, Paul wants us to give our whole selves, the whole of our lives, to God as an act of worship. This means that how we live *is* worship. It shows our ultimate allegiance and our highest priority. It reveals our deepest convictions.

This is why Elizabeth Payson Prentiss, in her novel disguised as a journal, *Stepping Heavenward*, has Ernest say to Katy, "Every act of obedience is an act of worship." What we believe, desire, say, and do are all expressions of worship. Hence, ethics is worship—the very thing that the writers of this book, *Ethics as Worship*, are considering. Personally, I believe that this aspect of the work, in and of itself, is worth the price of admission. They ask us to consider all our conduct, private and public, internal and external, individual and corporate, as worship.

And so whether we are considering justice and social engagement, race, ethnicity, and kingdom diversity, wealth and poverty, creation care and environmental stewardship, capital punishment, war, abortion, euthanasia, physician-assisted suicide, and end-of-life decision-making, sexuality, marriage, divorce, and remarriage, contraception, birth control, and reproductive technologies, and the like, it's all about worship. Whom we worship, from the heart, according to his instruction, in all of life, will show itself in our ethics. In fact, Liederbach and Lenow define Christian ethics as "a Christ-centered response of thanksgiving, rightly ordered by Scripture to be a service unto God in obedient love that is formed and embodied in a discipleship that is oriented missionally, such that all creation might once again do what it was created to do: maximally render unto God all the praise, honor, and glory that he is due."

The very first course I taught as a newly minted systematic theology professor at Reformed Theological Seminary was Pastoral and Social Ethics. I wish I had had this volume to help me put that course together. Numerous features in this book stand out to me. For one, the tables sprinkled throughout the book are especially useful, for students and teachers alike, and I can see this volume as providing great assistance to both.

Their discussion of worldview (an idea that has undergone a serious cross-examination in the last few years) in relation to ethics is very helpful. Their inclusion of topics sometimes overlooked in evangelical ethical discussion (racism, societal justice, culturally embedded sin patterns, etc.), and their clear, calm, careful treatment of them, would make many of our current arguments better. I love their embrace and deployment of the threefold aspect of the law, and of the so-called third use of the law, as well as their gracious and compelling articulation of complementarianism, biblical sexuality, and more.

Liederbach and Lenow also engage knowledgeably and widely with the historic Christian tradition's teaching on ethics and with the Protestant confessional legacy, thus grounding their consideration of Scripture in the wisdom of the church's reading of the Scriptures. At some points, I would go in a little different direction from the one that they chart out. For instance, concerning marriage, divorce, and remarriage, my views are those of Westminster Confession of Faith chapter 24, helpfully elaborated by the PCA Study Committee Report on Divorce and Remarriage (1992)—but this does not take away at all from the help and clarity that I get from their treatment of even that topic.

This is a volume that I will use myself and commend to others for use in seminaries, universities, schools, and churches. Pastors, in particular, looking to disciple Christians in order that they would obey all that Jesus has commanded (Matt. 28:20) will be edified and equipped by this volume.

May your careful reading of this book help you to become a more grateful and faithful hearer and doer of God's Word (Matt. 7:24), and so to worship God.

Ligon Duncan
Chancellor and CEO, Reformed Theological Seminary
John E. Richards Professor of Systematic and Historical Theology
Jackson, Mississippi

A Word from Daniel L. Akin

I HAVE BEEN in the world of Christian ministry and education for more than four decades. I have been a part of the Southern Baptist Convention for all my adult life. I have ministered and preached in churches and have taught and led in various schools and institutions of higher learning. I have interacted with men and women from many different denominations and religions, and I have had the privilege of speaking of the name of Christ around the globe. Throughout all these experiences, I have seen evangelism strategies come and go. I have seen religious ideas and fads ascend in popularity and then rapidly decline. I have seen many seasons when particular moral issues have garnered heated attention and then faded from prominence. And I have read many books on ethics that have followed these strategies, addressed the hot topics of the day, been popular for a season, but ultimately disappeared because they lacked staying power.

But amid the flowing tides of culture, the changing demands of ministry circumstances, and the coming and going of various moral debates, some books on ethics remain as 'must-reads.' Over the years of serving our Lord, I have come to realize that a few things must always remain constant and must always anchor our souls to historical orthodoxy: a high view of God, a clear understanding and articulation of the gospel of Jesus Christ, and a total commitment to the Great Commission. Books that capture these elements and set them as foundational stones are the books that tend to last and be treasured on the shelves of any worthy library. Because they manage to keep those things that are central to the story they tell, they have the potential to outlast the fads and cultural tides. This is what I believe Mark Liederbach and Evan Lenow have done, and done well, in *Ethics as Worship*.

First, they speak clearly and biblically to many of the pressing issues and concerns of our day. Second, they adeptly shed light on the complexities of these modern moral issues, bringing greater clarity and understanding. Third, they direct us to see the One from whom light comes and then look at the issues with his light. They have reminded us that only in and through Jesus Christ's penal substitutionary atonement can we be restored to a place where ethics is transformed from mere obedience to joyful worship. Fourth, they have highlighted our desperate need to rely on the Holy Spirit's empowerment to become in practice what God created and redeemed us to be as his image-bearers. Fifth, they have cast the entire ethical endeavor in the context of God's mission to make disciples of every people, tribe, tongue, and nation so that he receives all the glory, praise, honor, and worship that he is due.

This book is not a discourse in dos and don'ts. Nor is it a book about rights and wrongs or goods and evils. While it certainly speaks to these things, this is ultimately a book about God, his worthiness, and the praise that he is due. It is a book about the person and work of Jesus Christ and the whole-life response we ought to have to his wondrous gospel. It is a book that focuses our attention not on our actions, character, or circumstances, but on the wonder of the Holy Trinity and the joys awaiting us as we live in light of God's eternal plan and for his eternal purpose. It is a book about finding our small story caught up in God's eternal and infinite story. It is a book about worship in every waking moment because God is a God worthy of each of those moments.

I have known Mark and Evan for many years. My love and respect for both is difficult to put into words. They walk with integrity and live gospel-saturated lives. I have looked forward to the publication of this work, and now that it is here, I hope and pray that it will become a standard in the field of ethics for years to come—it is that well done. Bravo, brothers! You have served our Savior well in your labor of love."

Daniel L. Akin
President and Professor of Preaching and Theology,
Ed Young Sr. Chair of Preaching,
Southeastern Baptist Theological Seminary

Preface: Worship and Ethics

"Whether, then, you eat or drink or whatever you do, do all to the glory of God."
—1 CORINTHIANS 10:31

*"The integrity of Christian ethics is better described as derived from a
certain shared faith about the nature of God as Ultimate Reality and
man's proper response to him."*[1] —WALDO BEACH AND H. RICHARD
NIEBUHR, Christian Ethics: Sources of the Living Tradition

Morality: Invented, Proclaimed, or Discovered?

When we are asked what we do for a living, our reply that "we teach ethics" often meets with interesting responses. Some people respond with a puzzled "what's that?" look. Others say, "I'm glad somebody is out there to help set all those lawyers and politicians straight." But an increasing number of folks we interact with express a level of skepticism about the discipline as a whole. One particular interaction highlights much of the attitude that we believe increasingly reflects the moral sentiment of contemporary culture. Several years ago, Mark's wife, Harriette, was getting her hair done by a local stylist. In the course of conversation, the stylist asked, "What does your husband do for a living?" When she replied, "He's a professor of ethics," the stylist immediately (and seriously) responded, "Oh, so he can do whatever he wants and know how to justify it."

Contrast this with what we commonly experience in our introductory ethics classes. Both of us teach ethics at Christian higher education institutions (college and seminary). Our classes are the first introduction to the formal study of ethics that most of our students experience. It is very common for these students

---

1. Waldo Beach and H. Richard Niebuhr, eds., *Christian Ethics: Sources of the Living Tradition*, 2nd ed. (New York: John Wiley & Sons, 1973), 5.

to show up with the preconception that *ethics* is just a fancy term for *moralism*. That is, they expect that the class will be some kind of glorified rehashing of rule-keeping—"Don't drink or chew or go with boys or girls who do!"—for college or graduate-school credit. Typically, the novice ethics student has been preconditioned by our evangelical subculture's tendency to package morality into oversimplistic bumper-sticker formulas such as "God said it, I believe it, that settles it."

Both these perspectives demonstrate in their own way why studying ethics is so important. On the one hand, the stylist's reply captures the cultural ethos gaining momentum around the globe: *morality is invented,* From this point of view, the study of ethics is really just a study of preferences and morality is relative to one's own perspective. Whether or not the hairstylist realizes it, an unholy trinity of ideas undermines any sense of ultimate values. The embrace of self-determinism, the commitment to moral autonomy, and an underlying sense of life's meaninglessness lead to an ethic that is nothing more than an ode to personal expression. Tragically, this *morality is invented* perspective is all too often further fueled by a pop psychology that abandons common sense. It is normally accompanied by a demand for absolute "tolerance" of any lifestyle—except, of course, those lifestyles that claim that there is something called *absolute good and evil* or *right and wrong*.

On the other hand, regarding our Christian college and seminary students, while there is a presumption that they hold an underlying belief system tying ethics to a more lasting foundation, too often that foundation is underdeveloped. As a result, the connections between morality, God, and his commands are weak. Thus, while the students do not believe that morality is merely invented, they often perceive—rather tepidly—that *morality is proclaimed*. At first blush, this may not seem like such a bad perspective. At least this perspective begins with respect for the Bible and God's revelation. The problem, rather, relates to an improper view of the God who does the proclaiming. It involves the tendency to relegate the instructions given by God to a domain of systematic legalism and thereby miss both the nature of God and the goodness of his divinely given commands. When people do so, they also misunderstand the deeper purposes of morality, its connection to God's character, the manner in which he created humans to flourish through abiding in the Word, and the deeply ingrained purpose of worship written into the very fabric of the universe.

The unfortunate reality is that these erroneous perceptions inevitably result in the belief that the discipline of ethics is primarily concerned with keeping the rules of a divine taskmaster who functions like an authoritarian school principal (or dean of students). Our duty (and therefore our ethic) is to obey the rules as best we can and hope God either grades on a curve or overlooks our inadequacies. Ethics, then, becomes little more than a rigid structure of behaviorism and a guilt inducing accountability system enforced by a divine Judge eager to show us where we have gone wrong.

Interestingly, both these perspectives on ethics are tragically wrong for similar reasons. The former is wrong because of its *radical misdirection* about the shape and purpose of the universe as well as the God who created it. The latter is wrong because of its *anemic and impotent understanding* about the shape and purpose of the universe and the God who created it. Both miss the heart of morality and ethics.

Rightly understood, *morality is a discovery*. It is first and foremost a discovery of the God who is to be treasured above all things. It is a discovery of a God who marvelously spoke the universe into existence. It is a discovery of the One who graciously designed it to function maximally when it is properly centered on him. It is a discovery of the One who came to live, die, and rise again to make it possible to have an abundant life on this planet. And it is a discovery of the Helper who indwells us and empowers us to worship God with all that we are.

Not only is it a discovery of God, but it is also a discovery of the indescribable wonder of what it means to be a human created in God's image and for his purposes. It is a discovery of what it means to be transformed at the depth of our character. It is a discovery of guiding principles, commands, and exhortations that God has revealed to help us maximally live in his world. And it is a discovery of the everlasting opportunity to experience the inexhaustible love of an eternal God and to explore his infinite nature forever into the future.

The Heart of Christian Ethics

The study of ethics, then, is not *primarily* about choices, acts, results, or even obeying the commands of Scripture (though we believe that doing so is crucial). Ethics is about God. It is about maximally adoring him and rendering to him all that he is due from all that he has made. And it is about our doing so both individually and corporately.

It follows that the primary purpose of a rightly framed ethical system must be to direct us in the *whys, whats,* and *hows* of rendering unto God all the praise and honor he is due. A rightly framed ethical system must be concerned that we worship maximally in every moment, by every choice and act, from every square inch of his created order, and ideally with every person who ever lives. Not only must it be concerned with our actions, but it must also press us to become the kind of people whose character is so shaped to be like Jesus Christ's that we do these things reflexively, constantly, obediently, lovingly, joyfully, and missionally. This is the heart of Christian ethics.

Simply put, we must live worshipfully because we have become true worshipers. For only such an effort would be worthy of an eternal and infinite God.

Studying ethics is the joyful discovery of what it means to live a life of *worship*. Making this discovery is both the premise and purpose of this book.

What Do We Mean by *Ethics as Worship*?

So what do we mean by the phrase *ethics as worship*? While we will develop the concept more robustly throughout the book, here we offer a brief discussion and definition not only of what worship is but of how it relates to the discipline of ethics.

When modern Christians hear the word *worship*, all too often our thoughts turn primarily to a consideration of the singing that takes place during our Sunday morning church services. While certainly this can be an aspect of what it means to worship, the Bible gives us a much richer and more comprehensive picture. Linguistically speaking, the biblical words most often translated into English as "worship" carry with them the connotations of bowing down or prostrating oneself before God in humility as well as our rendering service to him. For example, in regard to bowing down before God, the Hebrew verb *shachah* (translated in the King James Version ninety-nine times as "worship") literally carries the meaning of bowing down or prostrating oneself in the presence of a superior.[2] Similarly, in the New Testament, the Greek verb *proskuneo* (translated sixty times in the King James Version as "worship") bears the identical idea of kneeling down or prostrating oneself before one of superior rank.[3] In regard to offering our service to God, in the Old Testament the word *abad* can literally be translated as "work" or "serve" but is also translated as "worship" (see, e.g., Ex. 3:12). Similarly, in the New Testament the Greek word *latreia* is also alternatively translated as "service" or "worship" (Rom. 12:1).

Now, certainly we need to do more than evaluate possible word meanings to establish a firm idea of what these words imply about worship. But we can be sure that it includes humbling oneself before God as well as offering him our services and work as a part of our worship patterns.[4]

If we are not careful, it is also possible to conclude from this word study that proper worship entails only an outward display without ever getting to an interior expression of love for, and faith in, God. But as the greatest commandment clearly states, God desires us to love him with all our heart, soul, mind, and strength (Deut. 6:4–5; Mark 12:28–31). Obviously, then, worship involves more than good works. Mere external behaviors do not capture the total picture.

Therefore, while it is beyond the scope of this introductory chapter to fully

---

2. Strong's, 7812, https://www.biblestudytools.com/lexicons/hebrew/kjv/shachah.html.

3. Strong's, 4352, https://www.biblestudytools.com/lexicons/greek/kjv/proskuneo.html.

4. Daniel I. Block, *For the Glory of God: Recovering a Biblical Theology of Worship* (Grand Rapids: Baker, 2014), 9, 17–18. See also Strong's, 5647, https://www.biblestudytools.com/lexicons/hebrew/nas/abad.html.

develop the following ideas, we believe that worship that is acceptable minimally requires of us five key elements:[5]

1. The correct God must be worshiped (Gen. 1:1; Ex. 3:14; 20:2–3; Matt. 28:18–20; Heb. 1:1–3).
2. Worship must come interiorly from the heart as an expression of thanksgiving and love for God and in response to his grace (Deut. 6:4–5; Mark 12:29–31; John 14:6; Rom. 10:9).
3. Worship must take the proper form as God gives us instruction (John 14:15, 31; Rom. 14:17–18).[6]
4. Worship is comprehensive in nature; it requires all aspects of our selves and our lives (Mark 12:29–31; Rom. 12:1; 1 Cor. 10:31).
5. Worship is both individual and corporate in nature (Heb. 10:24–25; Rev. 4–5).

Put simply, worship requires that we give to the *correct God* (the one true God) all the praise, honor, and glory he is due *from the heart*, as he *instructs*, in *every aspect* of our existence, both *by ourselves and corporately* with all people created in his image.[7] See diagram below (fig. P.1).

In an attempt to pull these ideas together, we offer the following working statement as a baseline for understanding as we move into the chapters that follow:

> Ethics as worship begins with the acknowledgment of the greatness of God's nature and character, his preeminence over all things, and his gracious creation and redemption accomplished through Christ. It is best expressed through the humble, willing, faith-filled, and loving response of image-bearers who submit all aspects of

5. We are indebted here to Daniel Block's work. Though we nuance our definition differently, we would be remiss not to credit him both for the influence that his work has had on our understanding and in relation to the adjoining diagram. See Block, *For the Glory of God*, chap. 1, esp. pp. 9, 17–18, 26.

6. As David Peterson rightly points out, the Bible depicts both acceptable and unacceptable forms of worship (e.g., Rom. 12:1–2; 14:17–18; Heb. 12:28–29; and 13:16 vs. Gen. 4:3–7; Ex. 32; and Isa. 1). He comments that "acceptable worship does not start with human intuition or inventiveness, but with the action of God." He also notes that we cannot simply determine for ourselves what we believe is honoring to God. Instead, acceptable worship "is a matter of responding to God's initiative in salvation and revelation, and doing so in the way that he requires." David Peterson, *Engaging with God: A Biblical Theology of Worship* (Downers Grove, IL: InterVarsity Press, 1992), 17, 26, 19.

7. Our English word *worship* (*worth* + *ship*), which literally means "to ascribe worth to something," is an attempt to capture this richness in one word. It carries the connotations of recognizing the worth of something and then responding to that worthiness with a sense of honor, reverence, respect, and adoration. In relation to God, this involves recognizing his infinite and therefore supreme worthiness and thus also making an offering of appropriate response—which in light of his nature requires all that we have, all that we are, and all that we do both individually and corporately.

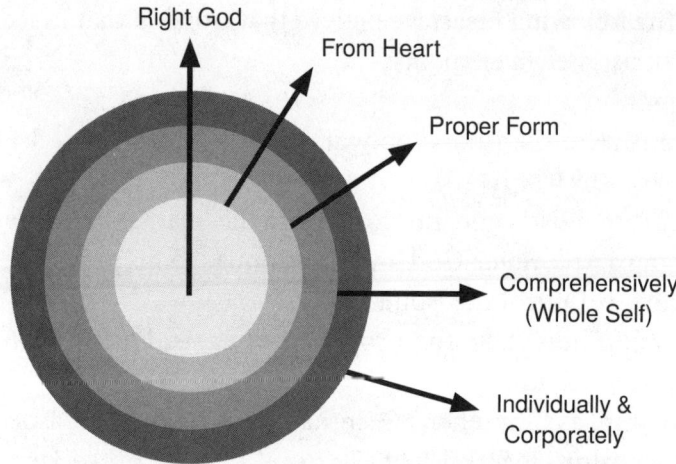

Fig. P.1. Elements of Proper Worship

themselves (both individually and corporately) to him—on his terms, in all ways, at all times, in all places, for his glory, and in a manner that promotes his fame throughout all creation. It is enabled by grace, engaged in faith, motivated by thanksgiving, pursued in love, guided by Scripture, and empowered by the Spirit, and results in joy.

Building on these premises, we will use Scripture as our inerrant, infallible, and sufficient source of authority to argue that because God is the sovereign and holy King who created all things, he is then also the bright and glorious center of the universe. He is both the source of all things that exist and the ultimate goal for which they exist. Because he is the Lord God Almighty, the way we live and move and have our being (both as individuals and together as a human society) must be determined in light of his majestic nature and its accompanying authority. But most importantly, because God creates and orders the universe out of an eternal love between the three persons of the Trinity (Father, Son, and Holy Spirit), the very nature of all things is flavored by God's love, and all things were created and ordered to move in and through the energy of this same eternal love.[8] All that we are and all that we do are meant to be done and ordered through a love toward and unto that which is most lovely—God himself.

We will argue that when rightly formed, a methodology of ethics is:

1. Centered on God and not us.
2. Motivated preeminently, fully, and finally by a virtuous love for God.

---

8. For a fuller discussion of this rich concept, see Michael Reeves, *Delighting in the Trinity: An Introduction to the Christian Faith* (Downers Grove, IL: InterVarsity Press, 2012).

3. Shaped by a full obedience to God's commands.
4. Appropriately nuanced in light of the context.
5. Cognizant of anticipated and potential consequences.
6. Sensitive to the impact our moral choices and stances will have on our relationships with fellow image-bearers

God designed ethics to be both a personal and corporate embodiment of a life of worship. Only in and through the saving work of Jesus Christ can the worship of sinners be rightly ordered to God in obedient love now and forevermore. This happens positionally by grace through faith in Jesus Christ, progressively throughout life as the Holy Spirit works cooperatively with us, and in accord with our created nature as image-bearers.

Our purpose and desire is to take our readers with us on an exploration into the nature and character of God, the world he created, and the people he created to steward it in his name. In so doing, we hope to discover together from his Word how best to honor him as God, steward the world he created to flourish, and be the kind of people he created us to be. Our hope is that as we take this journey together, it will become evident that the discipline of ethics requires of us a serious pursuit of and commitment to *discipleship* and *disciple-making*. That is, the practice and embodiment of ethics as worship involve the hard work of disciplining the loves, worship patterns, and practices of image-bearers in every aspect of life such that we become a people who take the gospel and all it entails to the ends of the earth. Ethics as worship requires us to shape our character and discipline our conduct in light of God's mission to make disciples of all nations. Ultimately, it is concerned that all the earth be filled with the knowledge of the glory of the Lord as the waters cover the sea (Gen 1:27–28; Hab. 2:14; Matt. 28:18–20).

If there is to be any hope that our students (or any other Christians) can discover the wonder of God and the richness of his plan for their lives, and they in turn can help the local hairstylist (and the countless others who share her worldview) discover this same God, who is the beginning and end of all things, then it is imperative that our students (and all the rest of us) grow in our own understanding of ethics as worship. Further, because God loves the world he created, it is also imperative that every Christian learn to communicate the hope of the gospel and the fullness of ethics as worship from a theological perspective of clarity, conviction, cultural relevance, and joy.

This is both our prayer and our hope.

The Outline of the Book

In order to accomplish our purpose, we have divided the book into four parts. In part 1, we provide a basic introduction to the discipline of ethics in general.

In chapter 1, we discuss the personal and cultural relevance of studying ethics, demonstrate the importance of understanding how underlying worldview assumptions affect one's perspective on the prevailing moral issues of the day, introduce the concepts of metaethics, normative ethics, and applied ethics as the necessary elements to develop a well-formed ethical system, and then identify the distinctive nature of a particularly Christian ethic.

In part 2, we develop the biblical and theological foundations (metaethics) for ethics as worship by exploring the metanarrative of Scripture through a four-fold paradigm of creation, fall, redemption, and restoration. We also explore what Jesus means by stating that God is looking for worshipers who worship him "in spirit and truth" (John 4:23–24). This part of the book reflects our conviction that the Bible guides proper worship by first revealing an underlying metaphysical reality about the way things *are* (*revealed reality*). Further, we believe that it is only after one identifies and understands this underlying design and moral structure that a discussion of normative ethics—the way things ought to *be*, and what we must *do*—can rightly take place (*revealed morality*).

In chapter 2, we focus our attention on Genesis 1–2 as the primary text from which to develop the creation portions of the biblical narrative. Our goal is to highlight the theocentric nature of all reality, the created design of human beings as God's image-bearers, and the nature of human beings as both worshipers and a people on mission to shape the entire cosmos to maximize the glory of God. Chapter 3 continues the discussion by exploring the reality of human sin and the fall, God's gracious work to redeem and reclaim the fallen world, and the Lord's work to restore his people to their original design and intended purpose. In particular, our interest is to develop the ethical implications not only of Christ's *saving* work but also of the *restoration* to abundant life and eternal hope that accompanies that saving work and that takes place through the process of discipleship and disciple-making.

In keeping with this, the following two chapters develop Jesus' teaching about true worshipers who "worship in spirit and truth" (John 4:23–24). Our purpose here is to highlight the *means* by which God intends to empower and guide his people to maximize his glory through their ethical choices and behaviors. These two chapters serve as a bridge between our metaethical discussion and the development of our normative ethical method. Chapter 4 focuses on the role that the Holy Spirit plays in the ethical formation and virtuous character development of a Christian disciple. The focus here is on the shaping within the believer of a "heart of worship" that is rightly ordered to God and that is reflexively active in the life of a believer. This naturally moves into a discussion in chapter 5 of why the Bible as the "Word of God" must be the Christian's primary source of truth and thus the chief and final authority for ethics, moral formation, and moral decision-making.

In this chapter, we emphasize that it is Jesus, the "Word of God," who through the Holy Spirit gives us Scripture as the "Word of God" such that we might be able to shape our behaviors and character in accord with God's eternal wisdom and the moral design.

Whereas the concern of part 2 of the book is to understand metaethics through what Scripture tells us about the way that things are (*revealed reality*), the focus of part 3 is to understand and develop a normative ethical method (*revealed morality*). In chapters 6 and 7, which should be read as a single unit, we pull together the biblical and theological ideas discovered in the previous chapters to assemble the normative methodological structure of ethics as worship. We begin by first recognizing the key link between our stated beliefs and loves and our actual practices. We then identify six domains of ethical assessment that factor into every moral situation, illustrate how various moral theories emerge when any one of these domains is made the primary or exclusive element in moral evaluation, discuss the biblical precedence for considering each domain, and describe how they should be employed together as a normative pattern for ethical decision-making.

In chapter 8, we bring closure to the normative part of the book by dealing with the problem of moral dilemmas. We recognize that while in an ideal world the process of shaping character and identifying moral norms should lead us directly from an understanding of the commands of Scripture to a flawless application in the context of life and practice, in a fallen world such application is often very difficult. Our discussion in this chapter, then, focuses on how to make ethical decisions that worship and glorify God when it appears that we can do so only by breaking the commands of God or choosing a "lesser evil." We use the story of Rahab from Joshua 2 as the foundational text for this discussion.

Finally, in part 4, our discussion moves from the metaethical foundations developed in part 2 and the normative methodology developed in part 3 to a discussion of how the concepts developed in ethics as worship relate to decision-making regarding particular issues we face in contemporary life and society. Chapter 9 serves as a bridge from our normative method to our application. The point of discussion is the concept of justice and a discovery of how best to think about justice in the social context in which we all seek to live out our ethical convictions. A key point of the chapter highlights the fact that all ethical issues involve a quest for biblical justice. This doctrinal point is a particularly important notion to clarify in light of the contemporary confusion and division that exist among evangelicals regarding the term and concept of *social justice*. For some, the term simply expresses God's heart for societies to reflect his just character in and through their laws and social systems. For others, the term and concept is inextricably linked to liberal/Marxist agendas. We seek to clarify the language and concepts in order to avoid unfortunate misrepresentation of how the gospel of Jesus Christ relates to the issues of seeking justice in the society of humanity as God desires.

Chapters 10–12 then focus on three particular issues related to gospel-centered justice: race, wealth and poverty, and creation care. Chapters 13–16 focus on issues most commonly described as relating to life and death (capital punishment, war, abortion, euthanasia). Chapters 17–19, finally, focus on issues most commonly described as relating to marriage and sexuality (biblical sexuality and disordered sexuality, divorce and remarriage, and contraception, birth control, and reproductive technologies).

Acknowledgments

MARK WOULD LIKE to thank Brad Holloway, John Hare, Kyle Smith, Walter Strickland, Ronjour and Annie Locke, James White, Missie Branch, RaShan Frost, Jesse Parker, Drew Ham, Jake Hatfield, Dave Phillips, Kelsie Berry, and Keverly Dyson for their invaluable ideas, corrections, and graphics, as well as their patience and encouragement to carry on. True friendship is a gift that defies my ability to say "thank you" well enough to give the honor that is due. You people are amazing. I love each of you and am a better man because of you. A special thanks goes to my children, Daniel, Hannah (and her Daniel), and Katherine, and my amazing grandchildren. "Liederbachs may fail . . . but they never quit." Thank you all for pressing me to remember and stick to what I tried to teach you! Certainly, there is no proper way to express my love, devotion, and thankfulness for the tireless encouragement and support from my best friend and amazing wife, Harriette. Life with you just keeps getting better every day! Your selfless love, over-the-top service, and joyful laughter make the idea of chasing the Infinite One with you for eternity an incredibly rich, joyfully hopeful, and exciting expectation. Let's enjoy the wonder of God together with the saints in an increasing manner forever!

Evan would like to thank Paul Morrison, Madison Grace, Bill Goff, Chris Taylor, Sterling Sellman, Emily Jones, and Otis Pickett for pushing me to articulate my ideas more clearly, serving as a sounding board, and checking references. I am especially grateful to Mark Liederbach—my professor, mentor, and friend—for inviting me to be a part of this project. When I stepped into your ethics class my first semester in seminary more than twenty years ago, I did not realize the friendship that would grow between us and the trust you would have in me to put on paper the ideas that you imparted to me beginning in that class. I am also thankful for Blake Thompson, who encouraged me to continue working on this project after I arrived on the campus of Mississippi College. My family deserves a special place of recognition as well. My parents, Ed and Marge Lenow, lovingly asked for updates on the progress of my writing throughout the process. My children—Molly, Elizabeth, William, and Laurel—have encouraged me with their love and smiles as they watched me work at the office and at home. You may not be quite ready to read this book, but you have been an inspiration to me. Finally, my wonderful wife, Melanie, has been by my side since before these ideas ever started percolating in my head. She has listened to my ideas and evaluated my arguments. I could not have done this without you. You are my favorite!

Abbreviations

AID	artificial insemination donor
AIH	artificial insemination husband
APA	American Psychological Association
ART	assisted reproductive technology
BDAG	Frederick William Danker et al., eds., *A Greek-English Lexicon of the New Testament and Other Early Christian Literature*, 3rd ed. (Chicago: University of Chicago Press, 2000)
BibSac	*Bibliotheca Sacra*
CDC	Centers for Disease Control and Prevention
CMDA	Christian Medical & Dental Associations
ET	embryo transfer
GA	graded absolutism
GIFT	gamete intrafallopian transfer
HA	humble absolutism
IA	ideal absolutism
IUD	intrauterine device
IUI	intrauterine insemination
IVF	in vitro fertilization
JAMA	*Journal of the American Medical Association*
JBMW	*Journal for Biblical Manhood and Womanhood*
JETS	*Journal of the Evangelical Theological Society*
MCR	*Military Chaplains' Review*
NAC	New American Commentary
NASB	New American Standard Bible

NCA	nonconflicting absolutism
NEJM	*New England Journal of Medicine*
NKJV	New King James Version
PAS	physician-assisted suicide
PNTC	Pillar New Testament Commentary
SBJT	*Southern Baptist Journal of Theology*
SWJT	*Southwestern Journal of Theology*
WCF	Westminster Confession of Faith
WLC	Westminster Larger Catechism

PART 1

An Introduction to Ethics

1

What Is Christian Ethics?

"You shall love the Lord your God with all your heart, and with all your soul, and with all your mind, and with all your strength. . . . You shall love your neighbor as yourself." —JESUS CHRIST, MARK 12:30–31

"Biblical ethics begins with God and ends with him."[1] —WALDO BEACH AND *H. RICHARD NIEBUHR*, Christian Ethics: Sources of the Living Tradition

The Central Importance of Ethics: Life's Most Enduring Questions

Gay marriage and gender identity, global warming and environmental stewardship, capital punishment and war, racism and poverty, abortion, euthanasia, and physician-assisted suicide. All these topics reside at the center of society's most intense debates. And they are all issues of morality and ethics.

The fact that questions of morality and ethics play such a crucial role in society should not surprise us. Indeed, it would not be hard to argue that humanity's most enduring questions have always been "How should I live my life?" and "How should we live our lives together?" For this reason, some twenty-five hundred years ago, Socrates famously stated that the "unexamined life isn't worth living."[2] He knew then what is still evident today—that moral clarity is required for human fulfillment.

Socrates has not been alone in his desire to link the value and shape of our lives to a deeper purpose. Indeed, some of the most influential thinkers in history— Plato, Aristotle, Moses, Confucius, Buddha, Jesus, Augustine, Aquinas, Luther, Calvin, Hobbes, Kant, Mill, and Nietzsche—all in their own way admonished

---

1. Waldo Beach and H. Richard Niebuhr, eds., *Christian Ethics: Sources of the Living Tradition*, 2nd ed. (New York: John Wiley & Sons, 1973), 15.

2. Plato, *Apology*, 38a, in *A Plato Reader: Eight Essential Dialogues*, ed. C. D. C. Reeve (Indianapolis: Hackett, 2012).

their followers to examine themselves and the choices they make in life. Each offered answers to the questions "How should I live my life?" and "How should we live our lives together?" Simply put, for the vast majority of human history, some of the greatest efforts of religious, philosophical, and sociopolitical inquiry have revolved around the quest for meaning and morality. That is, they have revolved around ethics.

Obviously, then, ethics is an extremely important and relevant discipline of study. It is in the realm of ethics that we not only explore *how* we should live, but also examine—as Socrates admonished—the reasons *why* we (as individuals or society) choose to live the way we do. How one arrives at an answer to these questions, how one justifies the answers, and how one seeks to apply them in his or her own daily life (and how society does so as a whole) is the concern of the discipline of ethics.

For this reason, the purpose of this first chapter is to introduce the foundational questions and concepts necessary to properly understand the discipline of ethics with a particular emphasis on *Christian* ethics. Three questions guide our discussion:

1. What are worldviews, and how are they foundational to morality and ethics?
2. What is the relationship between a person's worldview and how one practices ethics?
3. What are the distinguishing marks of Christian ethics?

What Are Worldviews, and How Are They Foundational to Morality and Ethics?

Is Morality Invented or Discovered?

Whether we know it or not, all of us have already adopted a moral and ethical framework. When one considers the list of topics that reside at the center of cultural debate, not only are personal preferences and liberties on the line, but so also are tax dollars, cultural norms, and national policies. Indeed, the blood of armies is ultimately spilled over convictions about right and wrong, good and evil.

This is why it is critically important to recognize that the study of ethics does not concern itself with the question whether it is appropriate to legislate morality. The question is not *whether* we should legislate morality, but always *whose morality are we going to legislate?* At a fundamental level, every decision related to human behavior—from putting up a speed-limit sign on a road (in order to protect and save lives) to providing legal recognition for people of the same gender to marry—is a reflection and assertion of some moral point of view. Indeed, human society itself is by default a form of corporately legislated morality.

It follows that if we are going to live according to one morality or another, then questions of justification not only must be taken seriously, but need to be moved to the center of the debate. That is, we are going to have to decide why one moral theory or vision is superior or preferable to another. Re — Read

This is, in fact, why Socrates admonished his followers to examine themselves. Having good reasons to justify why one has chosen to live as one has is a part of what it means to live wisely. But the choice of why one might live one way versus another requires us to consider what reasons justify or legitimize any particular moral system over and above another. Ethical examination is necessary if one desires to actually live a life worth living.

Perhaps the most direct way to begin this examination is to ask, "Where does morality come from?" or "What is the source of morality?" For example, if morality is simply *invented*, then persons and societies are free to choose whatever relative values they want. Ultimately, there is no absolute standard of right and wrong, good or evil. Rather, the roots of our morality are grown in the soil of personal choice, public values, cultural likes or dislikes, political agreement, or authoritarian power. Moral authority resides in the individual's conscience, in the collective thought of a culture, or in the will of a society's most powerful agents. Morality is fluid, right and wrong are merely sentiments, and ethical systems are a matter of convention.

If morality is *discovered*, then a completely different set of ideas and grounding assumptions come into play regarding the formation of personal and cultural morality. If morality is discovered, then this means that there exists an objective standard that is not dependent on human ingenuity or whim. Rather, there is a moral authority independent of humans to which all will be held accountable. And for this reason, then, wisdom directs each of us individually —and the human race as a whole—to use all our strength and ingenuity to discover it.

Further, if there is an objective standard of moral behavior that can be discovered and to which we are all beholden, then it certainly follows that we would be wise to ask whether that standard was put in place by God. If so, then it follows that the God who made the world and designed us to live in it knows how we ought to best live our lives and maximally flourish in his creation. Obviously, then, this debate about the source and justification of morality has much to do with the question of God. While it is possible to build an ethical system on the assumption that God does not exist, the question of God's existence (or not) plays a central role in the examination of a life worth living. If he does exist, then building an ethical system on the assumption that he does not would be the extreme example of human foolishness and arrogance. This is why the question of God and his existence (and how it is answered) will always play a key role in the formation of any and all ethical systems. Drop the mic

Either way, something profound should come into focus as we pursue this line of reasoning. That is, whether or not one realizes it, the opinions, values, and ideas that *anyone* holds regarding *any* moral issue ultimately rest on some underlying assumptions about God, what the world is like, and how one believes morality should be legislated. There are no morally neutral points of view. Our opinions about morality and moral issues do not arise from a vacuum. Whether someone can clearly state his or her underlying assumptions has little to do with the fact that such assumptions are there. At some level, consciously or unconsciously, deeper assumptions and ideas about God and the nature of the world drive competing visions of morality.

What Is a Worldview?

The name typically given to these "deeper assumptions" and foundational beliefs is *worldview*. It is vitally important to understand that *everyone* has a worldview—even if he or she does not know it, does not realize it, or is unable to articulate it. Indeed, this is the very thing that Socrates was trying to push his followers to understand when he admonished them to examine themselves. While he did not use the term *worldview*, Socrates understood that everyone's moral choices are in some very important way connected to—and directed by—one's underlying assumptions, beliefs, or affinities. This is why they *must* be examined. If someone wants to live a life that is worth living, then he or she must dig down deep and take a closer look to see whether the choices being made actually align with what is held in the highest esteem or believed to be most important. From a Christian point of view, this idea is carried even further. It is important not only to be *aware* of one's worldview assumptions but also to examine oneself to see whether these foundational loves and ideas actually *align with what God reveals about himself and the way he ordered the world*. As the apostle Paul exhorts believers in 2 Corinthians 13:5: "Test yourselves to see if you are in the faith; examine yourselves!"

The term *worldview* was first introduced into philosophical discussion through the work of Immanuel Kant (1724–1804), who employed the German word *Weltanschauung* to capture the idea of how our minds function in light of a deeper abiding sense, understanding, or "intuition of the world" around us.[3] Then, as David Naugle demonstrates, the concept was brought into Christian philosophy and parlance in the late 1800s primarily through the initial work and influence of James Orr (1844–1913) and Abraham Kuyper (1837–1920).[4] According to Orr, a *Weltanschauung* (or, as it was translated into English, *worldview*) functions as "the

---

3. Immanuel Kant, *Critique of Judgment: Including the First Introduction*, trans. and intro. Werner S. Pluhar (Indianapolis: Hackett, 1987), 111–12.

4. David K. Naugle, *Worldview: The History of the Concept* (Grand Rapids: Eerdmans, 2002), 5–25.

widest view that the mind can take of things in the effort to grasp them together as a whole from the standpoint of some particular philosophy or theology."[5] For Kuyper, it represented a "life-system" that involved a "comprehensive vision of reality engendering the worship of God and submission to His will in all things."[6]

Regardless of its origins, the importance of understanding this "comprehensive vision" or "life-system" by which to "understand the whole" cannot be overstated. Worldviews are vitally important for shaping and orienting how each of us lives and functions in the world. As Al Wolters explains:

> A worldview, even when it is half unconscious and unarticulated, functions like a compass or road map. It orients us in the world at large, gives us a sense of what is up and what is down, what is right and what is wrong in the confusion of events and phenomena that confronts us. Our worldview shapes, to a significant degree, the way we assess the events, issues, and structures of our civilization and our times.[7]

We understand a worldview to involve all parts of the self in the manner in which we perceive our world. This includes not only our minds but also our loves and wills. Thus, we define *worldview* as a *conceptual framework made up of our fundamental beliefs and loves that then functions as the means by which we perceive, interpret, and judge reality and that also drives how we behave in it.* Metaphorically, it might be helpful to think of a large jigsaw puzzle. Each of our lives has thousands of little pieces: choices, ideas, contexts, loves, interests, people, emotions, and situations that we face each day. We are constantly working to "put it all together" in a coherent fashion. But how difficult is it to put together a massive puzzle with no comprehensive picture to help guide how we ought to put each piece into its proper place? Thus, a worldview functions much as the puzzle's box top in that it is meant to serve as a guide in order to see, orient, and then place each piece in the proper position.

It is commonly held that a worldview is primarily concerned with only the rational part of the self and functions solely in the realm of ideas, truth claims, or

5. James Orr, *The Christian View of God and the World as Centering in the Incarnation* (Edinburgh: Andrew Eliot, 1893), 3.

6. Naugle, *Worldview*, 17; see also David K. Naugle, "Worldview: History, Theology, Implications," 8, http://www3.dbu.edu/naugle/pdf/WV-HistyTheolImplications.pdf. Naugle also cites the work of R. D. Henderson, "How Abraham Kuyper Became a Kuyperian," *Christian Scholars Review* 22, no. 1 (1992): 22, 34–35. Kuyper's discussion can be found in Abraham Kuyper, *Lectures on Calvinism* (Grand Rapids: Eerdmans, 1931), 11. Kuyper particularly addresses this in his first lecture, "Calvinism a Life-System." See http://www.reformationalpublishingproject.com/pdf_books/scanned_books_pdf/lecturesoncalvinism.pdf.

7. Albert M. Wolters, *Creation Regained: Biblical Basics for a Reformational Worldview*, 2nd ed. (Grand Rapids: Eerdmans, 2005), 5.

stated beliefs.[8] But in agreement with St. Augustine, we affirm that "when there is a question as to whether a man is good, one does not ask what he believes, or what he hopes, but what he loves."[9] Human beings are both rational and affective. They both think and desire. Both elements are crucial to understanding human choices, behaviors, and character, and ultimately how each person will embody these things in and through the person's morality and ethics. Because our loves are so central to the people we are and the choices we make, it is imperative to recognize the connection of our affections and desires to our worldview and consequently our moral choices. James Sire rightly notes that a worldview is "a fundamental orientation of the heart."[10]

It is appropriate, therefore, to understand that a person's worldview relates not only to the rational part of the self or the mind, but also to the affective or desiring parts of the self. David Naugle captures this idea well when he points out that a worldview involves a "vision of God, the universe, our world, and ourselves rooted and grounded in the embodied human heart as the seat and source of our worship and spirituality, ideas and beliefs, loves and affections, and decisions and actions."[11] Since worldviews relate to the whole self, the shaping of a worldview must involve the formation of the whole self—heart, soul, mind, and strength (Mark 12:29–31).

Five Components of a Worldview

In his book *Life's Ultimate Questions*, Ronald Nash identifies five components or "clusters of beliefs" that form a person's worldview. These involve what a person believes to be true about metaphysics, epistemology, anthropology, theology, and axiology.[12] Each one plays a significant role in how each of us understands the

8. See, for example, James K. A. Smith's otherwise outstanding book *Desiring the Kingdom*, in which he identifies a worldview primarily in terms of "beliefs, ideas, and doctrines" and relegates it to the realm of gaining information. James K. A. Smith, *Desiring the Kingdom* (Grand Rapids: Baker, 2009), 17–18. Indeed, it is easy to see how one might reach such a conclusion, considering the influential definition of *worldview* from such excellent scholars as J. P. Moreland, who writes: "A person's worldview contains two important features. First, it includes the set of beliefs the person accepts, especially those about important matters such as reality, God, value, knowledge and so on. But a worldview is more than just a set of beliefs. . . . A worldview includes the rational structure that occurs among the set of beliefs that constitute it." J. P. Moreland, *Kingdom Triangle: Recover the Christian Mind, Renovate the Soul, Restore the Spirit's Power* (Grand Rapids: Zondervan, 2007), 33.

9. Augustine, *Enchiridion*, CXVII. See *The Enchiridion on Faith, Hope, and Love* (Washington, DC: Regnery Gateway, 1961), 135.

10. James Sire, *The Universe Next Door: A Basic Worldview Catalog*, 4th ed. (Downers Grove, IL: InterVarsity Press, 2004), 17.

11. David K. Naugle, "Worldview: Definitions, History, and the Importance of the Topic," 4, http://www3.dbu.edu/naugle/pdf/Worldview_defhistconceptlect.pdf.

12. Ronald H. Nash, *Life's Ultimate Questions: An Introduction to Philosophy* (Grand Rapids: Zondervan, 1999), 14–15. Nash actually uses the word *ethics* for his fifth component, but we have opted for the term

world in which we live, why we love the things we do, and consequently how we choose to act in the world. So they are vitally important for understanding the discipline of ethics.

Metaphysics has to do with how one understands the nature of reality. It has to do with questions about first things and being. That is, it is an inquiry into how things come into existence, as well as an exploration of a thing's essential nature. It seeks to answer questions such as these: Is there a God? Is the universe all there is? Is there such a thing as a spiritual realm? How did the universe come into existence? Are miracles possible?

Epistemology is the study of the theory of knowledge. It deals primarily with how one can know and what one claims to know. It seeks to answer questions such as these: Can we have accurate knowledge of the world we live in? Are there ideas that are objectively true, or is all knowledge merely opinion? Can we trust our senses? Can we trust our conscience? Is there a connection between faith and reason?

Anthropology considers what it means to be human. When we speak of anthropology in the realm of medicine, we might think of studying the biological systems of human beings, such as the circulatory system and the nervous system. But when we speak of anthropology as it relates to worldviews, we are looking into the nature of human beings in a different way. In regard to ethics, we are concerned with questions such as these: What can we know about human nature? Are human beings made up of anything more than clustered molecules? Do human beings have souls? If so, how do the body and soul interact? Do humans have free will? Does death conclude our existence, or do humans live on in an afterlife?

Theology has to do with the study of the nature of God. Whereas metaphysics asks whether God exists, theology is concerned with questions such as these: If God exists, what is God like? Is there one God or many? Is God a personal being or a powerful life force? Did God cause the universe and design it? If God is a personal being, what attributes does he have? Does God reveal himself to humans? If so, how?

Finally, when we speak of *axiology* as a component of a worldview, we explore why and how we value things as we do. More specifically, we are examining why and how we value moral choices and actions as we do. Here the questions relate to whether there are actions that are objectively or universally right or wrong or whether things are inherently good, evil, or neutral. If there is such a thing as right or wrong, good or evil, in what way is an individual human responsible to know and act in light of these realities? To what degree are human societies responsible

---

axiology ("the study of value") to avoid confusion when drawing a distinction between worldview components and our overall project in *Ethics as Worship*.

to uphold goodness and justice? For example, if a person were asked to give an opinion on abortion or homosexuality, the answer would relate directly to the person's underlying beliefs or assumptions held about the nature of morality. Or, for a second example, one might ask whether someone such as Adolf Hitler should have been held morally accountable for his actions in World War II. If so, why? How? On what authority? By what standard? Moral inquiry is concerned with whether someone's opinions are just personal preferences, are culturally held preferences, or are in alignment with objective moral facts.

Now, while it is possible and appropriate to identify and speak of each of these worldview components or areas of belief separately, it is better to consider them as overlapping and interacting categories of ideas and beliefs. In some ways, each of these areas or clusters of beliefs is dependent on the others. For example, a person's belief about what God is like (theology) is dependent on whether God exists (metaphysics) and how we might know that he does exist (epistemology). Likewise, to understand whether abortion is wrong or gay marriage is permissible, one would have to engage not only the category of ethics but also the nature of human persons (anthropology), whether God would be pleased about it (theology), and how we might know those answers (epistemology). Thus, while we can conceive of them separately, and while we can discuss them separately, it is in holding them together that we best recognize the fundamental role they play in shaping our thoughts and desires (beliefs and loves). This brings us directly to the question of how worldviews and ethics are related.

Table 1.1. Five Components of a Worldview

Metaphysics	Inquiry into the nature of reality
Epistemology	Study of knowledge: how we know things
Anthropology	Study of the nature of human beings
Theology	Study of the nature and character of God
Axiology	Inquiry into the nature and practice of good and evil/right and wrong

What Is the Relationship between Worldviews and Ethics?

To understand the relationship between worldviews and ethics, we must first make a distinction between the terms *morality* and *ethics*. While these words have important areas of overlap and are sometimes even used interchangeably, there is actually an important difference. In *An Introduction to Biblical Ethics*, David W. Jones makes the point nicely:

The word *ethics*, which comes from the Greek term *ethos*, is a broad term that refers to a manner of living. The word *morals*, which is derived from the Latin word *mos*, is a more focused term that is used in reference to specific customs, habits, or conduct. In other words, ethics emphasizes an entire belief system and gives a general perspective; morality emphasizes individual acts and gives specific principles.[13]

As it is normally used, *morality* relates to the prevailing values of a given culture and refers more to the particular acts or behaviors of a person or people in a given context or situation. As Scott Rae simply puts it, "Technically, morality refers to the actual *content* of right and wrong, and ethics refers to the process *of determining*, or discovering, right and wrong."[14]

Table 1.2. Ethics and Morality

Ethics	Morality
The reasons I do something	What I actually do
Asks questions such as: 1. Why should I do this? 2. Are there binding rules? 3. Where do the rules originate? 4. What type of person do I want to be? 5. How do I determine right versus wrong, good versus evil?	Asks questions such as: 1. What should I do? 2. What are the rules? 3. What behavior is expected or required? 4. What can I do to become a good person? 5. What do most people do?

When one studies *ethics*, therefore, one is attempting to go deeper and to discover and develop a foundational, systematic, and applied understanding of the nature of morality. This involves asking *why*, *what*, and *how* questions about morality:

- Why do we believe something to be moral?
- What standards of behavior or character traits are morally valuable, and what are the methods for employing them?
- How do we actually apply them in real-life contexts?

When rightly developed, the study of ethics is concerned with understanding how these elements ought to relate to, and inform, one another. Typically, ethicists divide the field into three branches or subcategories that specifically relate to these

13. David W. Jones, *An Introduction to Biblical Ethics* (Nashville: B&H Academic, 2013), 5–6.

14. Scott B. Rae, *Moral Choices: An Introduction to Ethics*, 4th ed. (Grand Rapids: Zondervan, 2018), 19–20.

why, *what*, and *how* questions. These are *metaethics*, *normative ethics*, and *applied ethics*, respectively.[15]

Metaethics

Metaethics is the subfield in the discipline of ethics that focuses on the question *why?* It is foundational and thus the most important subfield of ethics because it seeks to discover and establish the origin and basis by which one might assess something to be right or wrong, good or evil. It is concerned with discovering or establishing the basic grounding or justification for claiming why one view of morality should be accepted as superior (or at least preferred) to another.[16] Ultimately, it provides the moral motivation or *why* that drives or undergirds how one chooses to live, act, and behave in the world.

Thus, in the discipline of ethics, when one discusses the idea of developing a metaethical foundation, he or she is at the most foundational level using the same categories that shape a person's worldview. As Benjamin Wiker describes it, "Every distinct view of the universe, every theory about nature, necessarily entails a view of morality; every distinct view of morality, every theory about human nature, necessarily entails a cosmology [or worldview] to support it."[17] One's underlying worldview assumptions about metaphysics, epistemology, anthropology, theology, and axiology shape our deepest beliefs and our metaethical point of view and therefore the entirety of our personal moral decision-making process.

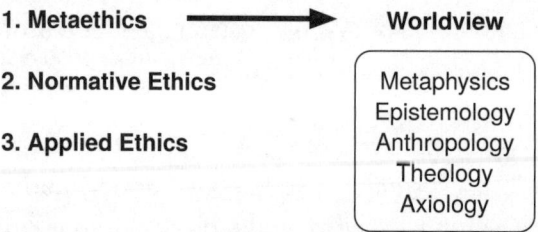

Fig. 1.1. Metaethics

15. In addition to these three, two other branches of ethics should be mentioned: *descriptive ethics* and *professional ethics*. The concern of descriptive ethics is not to identify how people *ought* to act, think, or value things but simply to identify and report how people *do* act. It is, then, very similar to the discipline of sociology in its descriptive contribution to recognizing how individuals and societies act, think, or value things. The concern of professional ethics is identifying the personal or corporate standards or guidelines that are established within a particular profession or field of industry that should guide behavior within that sector of society.

16. James Fieser, *Metaethics, Normative Ethics, and Applied Ethics: Historical and Contemporary Readings* (Belmont, CA: Wadsworth, 2000), 1. For a related discussion, see Louis P. Pojman, *Ethics: Discovering Right and Wrong* (Belmont, CA: Wadsworth, 1990), 2.

17. Benjamin Wiker, *Moral Darwinism: How We Became Hedonists* (Downers Grove, IL: InterVarsity Press, 2002), 22.

a life worth living!
why

Unfortunately, *metaethics* is typically the area most neglected in a person's system of morality because it involves deeper theological and philosophical thinking and development. Metaethics requires the hard work of constructing a thorough understanding of the five components of one's worldview identified above, and a careful evaluation and ordering of one's ideas and beliefs as they relate to each component. It is our conviction that developing a biblically informed and consistent metaethical framework is the most important element in becoming an ethical person. This is so because when one has a properly formed personal metaethics, it provides the basis for justifying one's normative standards, which in turn can and ought to lead to consistent moral application. Though difficult, we believe Socrates would tell us that it is through examining one's metaethical foundations that one can have a life worth living. More importantly, we believe it is the foundational piece to understanding what Jesus described as the "abundant life." For it is what we believe and love at the deepest levels of ourselves that will give rise to why and how we do the things we ultimately decide to do.

When a person has a well-developed metaethics (worldview), it enables him or her to:

1. Understand the *whys* that undergird the drive toward character formation and moral decision-making.
2. Have the conviction necessary to explain and hold on to the person's moral standards through the various contours of daily life.
3. Develop a moral perspective that is consistent across a broad spectrum of moral issues.

Normative Ethics *what*

While having a clear and consistent metaethical foundation is vital for understanding the *whys* of ethics, by itself metaethics does not directly translate into clarity on how one should behave in the various moral situations we face each day. A fully orbed moral system must also articulate *what* beliefs and convictions arise from those *whys*. The next step in ethics is to develop a *normative theory* consisting of guidelines, or *norms*, to order one's character and behaviors in a manner consistent with one's underlying metaethical framework or worldview.

Because morality is concerned with the kind of person we become in both our character and our behavior, normative ethics seeks to identify and articulate norms that shape both what kind of people we seek to become and what kinds of things we should do. It is concern with character and actions, being and doing. Ethicists often refer to development of norms of character with terms such as *virtue*, *righteousness*, and *godliness*. They refer to norms of behavior with terms such as *rules*, *principles*, and *commands*. From a distinctly Christian point of view, the goal in normative ethics is to develop our character such that we become "conformed to the image of [Christ]" (Rom. 8:29b). The path toward developing a person who is conformed to the image of Christ is through obedience to Christ's commands. Character arises from obedience. *Normative ethics*, then, is the name given to the subfield of ethics that is concerned primarily with the systematic identification and development of the virtues and norms necessary to shape morally good character and guide morally right decision-making in light of the circumstances, consequences, and relationships present in a given context.

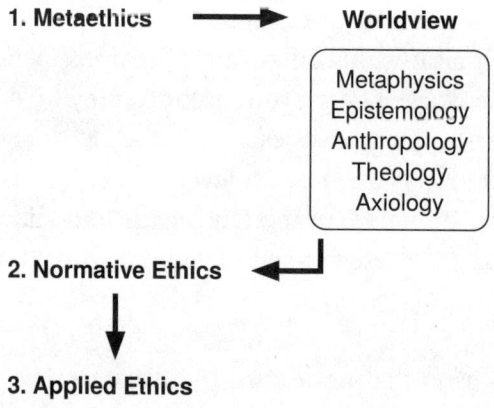

1. Metaethics ⟶ **Worldview**

Metaphysics
Epistemology
Anthropology
Theology
Axiology

2. Normative Ethics ⟵

3. Applied Ethics

Fig. 1.2. Normative Ethics

Applied Ethics From theory to action

Finally, while metaethics provides clarity on why we regard certain things as morally good and right and others as evil and wrong, and normative ethics provides a system of norms to guide character development and moral decision-making, one still needs to know how to act in a given situation. The subfield of *applied ethics* seeks to move from theory to action in a particular context. Applied ethics moves us from the deeper *whys* discovered in metaethics through the *whats* of normative ethics to answer this question: "How am I (or are we) to behave in this particular situation?"

In sum, if we think of living the ethical life as a journey that God invites us to enjoy with him, we could think of *metaethics* as our ethical compass, *normative ethics* as our map, and *applied ethics* as the places and events we experience along the journey. The *whys* shape the *whats*, which in turn inform the *hows*. From an evangelical perspective, the only way to give sure guidance about how one should act is by appealing to deeper realities about the way that God ordered the world and what his instructions are for how best to live in it. Since difficult situations requiring ethical insight are often unpredictable, the best time to study ethics and develop this kind of moral clarity is before one faces a challenging situation.

Consider the following case study to understand how each of these subfields comes into play in a real-life situation. Suppose that during your sophomore year of college, two of your friends who have been dating for the past eleven months come to you and tell you that they just found out they are pregnant. They are scared and uncertain what to do, and ask you if you think they should get an abortion. What should you do? What advice should you give?

This case demonstrates the importance of having well-founded and clear convictions at the deepest levels of one's worldview (metaethics). The natural flow and ordering of these three subfields of ethics should guide you as you give your friends help and advice. Ideally, you would have taken the time to discover and develop foundational metaethical beliefs and convictions about why certain things are right or wrong, good or evil. Also, you would have explored things such as God's design and purposes for sexuality, the nature of human life and its inherent value, the true nature of human flourishing, and the value of trusting and obeying God in hard places. Then from these foundational convictions, you would have explored and identified moral norms of behavior to guide your advice as well as the moral character to give the advice with an attitude of faith, hope, and love. From this normative ethic you would be able to move with wisdom and confidence into the vitally important task not only of advising these dear friends how to make the right decision, but also of helping them live with the consequences of choosing to honor God and protecting the innocent life of the child even in such a life-altering circumstance. See table 1.3 below.

Table 1.3. Subfields of Ethics

Subfield of Ethics	Driving Question	Foundational Answer	Metaphor
Metaethics (worldview)	*Why* is something right or wrong, good or evil?	Human beings are image-bearers, and therefore their lives are sacred from the moment of conception to the point of death.	Compass
Normative Ethics	*What* norms of behavior or character should guide the way I should behave right and be good and avoid behaving wrong or becoming evil?	Love God and neighbor (Mark 12:29–31). You shall not murder (Ex. 20:13).	Map
Applied Ethics	*How* do I apply the norms of behavior and character in the real-life situations and contexts I face?	Honor the Lord, the baby, and yourselves by not having an abortion.	Journey

All of us are still in the process of moral development. Jesus Christ is the only morally perfect human being to have ever lived. For the rest of us, being and becoming an ethical person involves a long process of growth and maturing in real-life contexts in which obedience is sometimes hard—but still best. Indeed, this reality highlights the very reason it is so important to study ethics. Not only does it help us answer the centrally important questions "How should I live my life?" and "How should we live our lives together?," it helps us have confidence that Socrates would affirm that ours is both a well-examined life and thus a life worth living.

What Are the Distinguishing Marks of Christian Ethics?

If having a consistent, well-formed ethical system is all that is necessary to receive the blessing of Socrates, why is it important to study Christian ethics? What is a particularly *Christian* ethic? What makes it distinctive?

To answer these questions, it is important to understand that one does not need to be religious or believe in God to develop or live by a system of ethics. It is possible to live an internally consistent life with the basic assumptions that God does not exist. Indeed, history is littered with examples of ethical thinkers and ethical methods that do not rely on the existence of God or his revelation for the formulation of any part of their ethical systems. Epicurus, David Hume, and Friedrich Nietzsche are all examples of men who developed ethical systems that expressly denied either God's existence or the ability for human beings to have clear guidance from God in determining how best to live life. In each case, the thinker's ethical system was meticulously developed and internally consistent from the metaethical foundations to the point of application.

While it is possible to have a system of ethics that is logically coherent and internally consistent without a religious foundation or appeal to God, coherence and consistency alone do not necessarily mean that the ethical system is either good or right. One could have a belief that the moon is made of cheese and develop an internally coherent and consistent plan to mine the moon for cheese. But if the moon is not made of cheese, then the coherence and consistency of the plan make little difference in the grand scheme of things. It is only when our metaethical foundations are *rightly* ordered in accord with ultimate reality, when our normative convictions are *properly* formed in accord with God's moral revelation, and when our method of application *has as its end the worship and glorification of God* that we can rest in the faith and hope that we are following Jesus on the path to the abundant life. The goal of Christian ethics is not to receive Socrates' blessing, but God's.

What are the distinguishing marks of Christian ethics? While many could be listed, we believe the following six elements particularly distinguish Christian ethics from all other systems of ethics.

The Christocentric Nature of Christian Ethics

The first and most important distinguishing element is ethics' Christocentric nature. Christian ethics is not merely an alternative system of ethics that one can pick and choose from among a vast array of options. Christian ethics is *Christian* precisely because it recognizes the unique nature of the second person of the Trinity, who became incarnate in the person of Jesus Christ in order to live a perfect and sinless life, die to make penal substitutionary atonement for sinners, and rise again as the conquering King who triumphed over death and hell, so that he could be the Savior of all who will call on his name. The person Jesus, not just his moral teaching, is the essential center point and focus in Christian ethics. The entire ethical task must be pursued with an explicit reference to him as the orienting principle of all elements of the ethical endeavor from start to finish.

- Christ is the *beginning and ground of ethics* because he is the principal agent of creation who, in accord with the Father and the Holy Spirit, designed and oriented all things to the glory of God (Gen. 1:1; Col. 1:16).
- Christ is the *means of ethics* because after human beings sinned and fell short of the glory of God (Rom. 3:23), he makes it possible to live the abundant life that we are created for through his death and resurrection as well as his teachings that guide our restoration (5:8).
- Christ is the *end and consummation of ethics* because he is the object of love, obedience, emulation, and worship as well as the One to whom we will be conformed when we finally meet him face to face (1 John 3:2).

Response of Thanksgiving Not a Means to Salvation

In light of the fact that Jesus is the answer to the *why*, *what*, and *how* questions of ethics, it is good and right to also recognize, second, that the entire discipline of Christian ethics differs from all other ethical systems in that it is not a means to salvation but a response of thanksgiving and love in light of Christ's saving work. Indeed, in the shadow of the cross, the ethical endeavor changes from a mere method for guiding behavior to an ethic that entails rendering all of ourselves, in all areas of life, at all times unto God in a posture of gratitude.[18]

This thanksgiving-motivated reorientation, then, properly involves:

18. For a very helpful discussion on the importance of gratitude as a core motivation for ethics, see Douglas B. Ponder, "Thanks Be to God: Exploring the Nature and Place of Gratitude in Christian Ethics" (ThM thesis, Southeastern Baptist Theological Seminary, 2020), 59.

- A combination of right thinking *about* and genuine love *for* God (meta-ethics);
- Good and right behavior properly ordered in us *by* God (normative ethics); and
- Living life in the context of all life situations *unto* God (applied ethics).

To say it another way, Christians who are properly motivated by thankfulness step from *orthodoxy* into *orthopraxy* for the purpose of *doxology*. Rightly formed and ordered beliefs (orthodoxy) give rise to rightly formed and ordered principles of life and practice (orthopraxy). These principles then shape good and virtuous disciples who live out their lives in God-glorifying thanksgiving and praise (doxology).

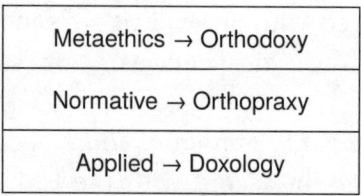

| Metaethics → Orthodoxy |
| Normative → Orthopraxy |
| Applied → Doxology |

Fig. 1.3. Ethics as a Response of Thanksgiving

Scripturally Ordered

A third distinguishing mark of Christian ethics is its commitment to Scripture as the primary source of authority. Whenever a person makes a moral choice, he or she will have knowingly or unknowingly done so on the basis of an appeal to a source of authority. Generally speaking, people appeal to one of four sources of authority in order to inform their choices: Scripture, tradition, reason, or experience.[19]

The way that one prioritizes and orders these sources of authority will go a long way in determining what kind of normative ethic the person develops. For example, if someone believes that the Bible should serve as his or her chief source of authority, then the person's normative system will likely be shaped by the content of Scripture. From our perspective, this would include an emphasis on both developing virtues in hopes of conforming to the character of Jesus Christ and obeying objective moral standards that God reveals in the form of commandments. If a person appeals to experience as his or her chief source of

---

19. Historically, these are referred to as the "Wesleyan Quadrilateral." See Donald A. D. Thorsen, *The Wesleyan Quadrilateral* (Grand Rapids: Zondervan, 1990; repr., Lexington, KY: Emeth, 2005); Thomas C. Oden, *The Living God*, vol. 1 of *Systematic Theology* (Peabody, MA: Hendriksen, 2008), 330–39.

authority, then that person's normative system will likely downplay the role of absolutes and commands and opt instead for an ethic that maximizes personal autonomy and freedom from rules. What a person appeals to as the means to justify behavior will reflect his or her underlying worldview assumptions and ideas about what we can know and will in turn shape the way that he or she believes we should live.

A distinctly Christian ethic understands that the Bible guides the development of our thinking about obedient love in two categorical ways: *revealed reality* and *revealed morality*.[20] First, as *revealed reality*, Scripture gives an accurate and foundational understanding of the nature of reality and the way things *are*. It provides for us a metaphysical (and therefore metaethical) framework by which to understand our world. The Bible opens to us a window through which we can glimpse the underlying reality of the nature of all things and how those revealed realities ought to shape how we perceive, understand, and bring judgments to the world in which we live (worldview). In giving us this picture of reality, it also indicates to us those goods and ends that are worthy of being the objects of our love, desires, and affections.

Second, Scripture as *revealed morality* provides norms, principles, rules, guidelines, and moral examples for us to become the kind of people that he designed and created us to be, and then to act in accord not only with our designed nature but also with the original design of the world as God created it. In this way, revelation guides both our love for God and our obedience to God, that we might be rightly conformed to his character and rightly ordered to loving obedience, and thus experience the abundant life that Christ promised (John 10:10). It provides us with the normative action guides, or moral map, to live in the world that God created and reveals to us. Oliver O'Donovan is correct when

---

20. Here we are adopting and adapting the language of James M. Gustafson, who originally (and influentially) employed these terms to identify two very distinct ways in which Christian ethicists tend to use the Bible to develop their moral theories. On the one hand, according to Gustafson, there is a tendency for some to see the Bible as a revelation of God's will through the assertion of commandments and deontological requirements (duties). This understanding of revealed morality he attributed primarily to conservative, evangelical Protestants. On the other hand, he sees Karl Barth as the key figure representing a revealed-reality approach because Barth emphasized that the Bible's purpose was to reveal God and his activity in the world, not merely standards of behavior. In so doing, then, human moral agents were responsible for an appropriate response to the living God, not the abstract requirements of law or list of commands that may be found in Scripture. While Gustafson saw these as distinct and perhaps even competing ideas, our purpose here is to demonstrate that these categories must function in unison and in a mutually reinforcing relationship in order for Christian ethics to faithfully reflect the design of God and thus properly be an ethic of worship. See James M. Gustafson, "Christian Ethics," in *Religion*, ed. Paul Ramsey (Englewood Cliffs, NJ: Prentice-Hall, 1965), 309–16. See also James M. Gustafson, "The Place of Scripture in Christian Ethics: A Methodological Study," *Interpretation* 24, no. 4 (1970): 430–55, reprinted in James M. Gustafson, *Theology and Christian Ethics* (Philadelphia: Pilgrim, 1974), 121–45.

he asserts that purposeful action must be determined in light of what is true about the world in which we live, love, and act.[21]

Embodied by Obedient Love

Obedient love is the fourth distinguishing mark of Christian ethics. With Christ as the center, thankful Christ-followers who recognize Scripture as their primary source of authority will then be compelled to embody and practice their ethical system in light of God's commands to both love him and obey him. Jesus, then, is held to be not only one's Savior, but also one's Lord, who is *the* way, *the* truth, and *the* life (John 14:6).

When Jesus was asked which of the commandments was the most important, he highlighted the idea of love—love of God and love of neighbor. In Mark 12:28–31, we read:

> One of the scribes came and heard them arguing, and recognizing that He had answered them well, asked Him, "What commandment is the foremost of all?" Jesus answered, "The foremost is, 'Hear, O Israel! The Lord our God is one Lord; and you shall love the Lord your God with all your heart, and with all your soul, and with all your mind, and with all your strength.' The second is this, 'You shall love your neighbor as yourself.' There is no other commandment greater than these."

According to Jesus, the gravitational center and chief imperative of Christian ethics is *love*. Love is first and foremost directed to God, and then directed toward neighbor. This love requires total commitment of the self in a holistic and fundamental ordering to God that includes one's affections, beliefs, thoughts, and actions—everything about us. For Jesus' disciples, nothing else is more central or more important. Christian ethics is flavored from top to bottom by God's command to his people to love in a manner that shapes the totality of who we are to *be*, as well as what we are to *do*. Love, in Christian ethics, is both the central virtue to develop and the chief duty to perform. Jesus tells his disciples that it is precisely this kind of Christian love that they are to be known for (John 13:35).

If it is true that love is the chief imperative of Christian ethics, then the most important follow-up question we can ask is this: How? How do we love God with all we are? How do we act in love toward others? The answer that Jesus gives us is *obedience*. In John 14:15, he asserts, "If you love Me, you will keep My commandments." Then a few verses later, he reverses the order and declares, "He who has My commandments and keeps them is the one who loves Me" (v. 21). Obedience to

---

21. Oliver O'Donovan, *Resurrection and Moral Order: An Outline for Evangelical Ethics*, 2nd ed. (Grand Rapids: Eerdmans, 1994), ix.

God's commandments provides the norms of behavior that help us both develop the virtue of love and express that virtue in our actions.

Love and obedience are to serve in a dynamic relationship with each other to mutually reinforce the manner in which we give thanks to God and worship him as the Scripture guides us. As the apostle Paul asserts in Romans 13:10, "love is the fulfillment of the law," and in Galatians 5:6, we find "faith working through love." Paul Ramsey states that "instantaneous, total obedience to the demands of God's reign and perfect love for man are in fact precisely the same thing. Obedience means no more than love and love fulfills every legitimate obedience."[22] Similarly, Waldo Beach and H. Richard Niebuhr observe, "Christian ethics says in many different ways that the Christian life consists in the response of obedient love to God in whatever he wills."[23]

The dynamic relationship between love and obedience informs all other questions about how we are to live our lives ethically unto God and in the service of our neighbors. While Christian ethics is concerned with questions of justice, rights, obligations, duties, sins, and the like, all of these can become clear only when obedient love first forms the shape of Christian ethics.[24]

Discipleship-Focused

The fifth distinguishing element that shapes the context of Christian ethics follows logically from the first. Because Christ is the Creator, the Redeemer, and the One to whom our lives must conform (Rom. 8:29), a focus on discipleship is at the heart of living ethically. It is a quest to become like him in all the ways that we can, to live in accord with all his instructions for us, and thereby to experience the abundant life that he came to give (John 10:10). It is imperative to understand that the study of Christian ethics is not merely or even primarily interested in discovering or developing a system of rules for behavior modification. For the Christian, ethics is about shaping our lives to conform to Christ, who is our Creator, moral exemplar, Savior, and object of worship. Thus, the ethical context for understanding and embodying obedient love is one of discipleship.

Missionally Oriented

Finally, a contextual element of a distinctly Christian ethic is its missional orientation. In Matthew 28:18–20, we find that Jesus' final words to his disciples before he ascended to heaven provide crucial (though often-overlooked) instructions about the missional nature of Christian ethics:

22. Paul Ramsey, *Basic Christian Ethics* (New York: Charles Scribner's Sons, 1951), 34.

23. Beach and Niebuhr, *Christian Ethics*, 5.

24. Ramsey, *Basic Christian Ethics*, xi. Ramsey comments to this end: "this concept [of obedient love, which is] basic to any understanding of the Christian outlook with the demands it places upon moral action, gives

> And Jesus came up and spoke to them, saying, "All authority has been given to Me in heaven and on earth. Go therefore and make disciples of all the nations, baptizing them in the name of the Father and the Son and the Holy Spirit, teaching them to observe all that I commanded you; and lo, I am with you always, even to the end of the age."

Jesus desires that his disciples—those who follow him in obedient love—express their love by telling their neighbors (local and global) the good news about himself, and then teaching them to obey his commandments in like manner.

Not only is Christian ethics about learning and growing a *personal* love for God and obedience to him; it is also concerned that our neighbors (both local and global) know and love God and learn to obey his commands. Through the lenses of the Great Commission (Matt. 28:18–20), we learn that the Great Commandment (Mark 12:28–31) is vitally linked to both the proclamation of saving faith in Christ (evangelism) and the embodiment of that faith in ethical practices that shape issues of society and culture in all nations. Jesus came not only to seek and to save the lost (Luke 19:10), but also to preach the gospel to the poor, release those who are in captivity, heal the blind and lame, and set free the oppressed (Luke 4:18).[25]

It is through understanding this connection between the *Great Commandment* and the *Great Commission* that we discover that Christian ethics is concerned that human beings from every people, tribe, tongue, and nation would obediently love him, such that "the earth will be filled with the knowledge of the glory of the LORD, as the waters cover the sea" (Hab. 2:14). In this sense, Christian ethics is a means for social impact precisely because it is a Great Commission ethic. The missional element of Christian ethics has as its final goal the proper worship of God by the entirety of human society and all creation.

What is Christian ethics? In sum, it is a Christ-centered response of thanksgiving, rightly ordered by Scripture to be a service unto God in obedient love that is formed and embodied in a discipleship that is oriented missionally, such that all creation might once again do what it was created to do: maximally render unto God all the praise, honor, and glory that he is due.

---

us the clue essential to understanding certain other ideas, such as 'justice,' 'right' or 'obligation,' 'duties to oneself,' 'vocation,' 'virtues' or moral character, 'sinfulness' and the 'image of God,' which in turn are of crucial importance in elaborating a theory of Christian ethics."

25. For a helpful discussion on the relationship between the mission of the church to proclaim the gospel and the ethical implications of the gospel, see Kevin DeYoung and Greg Gilbert, *What Is the Mission of the Church? Making Sense of Social Justice, Shalom, and the Great Commission* (Wheaton, IL: Crossway, 2011), 91–113.

Table 1.4. The Distinguishing Marks of Christian Ethics

1. Christocentric Foundation
2. Response of Thanksgiving
3. Scripturally Ordered
4. Embodied by Loving Obedience
5. Discipleship-Focused
6. Missionally Oriented

Conclusion

We began this chapter by listing many of the prevailing ethical issues of the day and considering how they relate to some of humanity's most enduring moral questions. We then considered how the manner in which we address any and all moral issues will be shaped by underlying worldview assumptions that every one of us has, even if we don't know it or are unable to articulate them. From there, we showed how worldview assumptions connect to the discipline of ethics through the branch of ethics known as *metaethics*, and how these in turn shape how we form our normative ethical systems, and ultimately apply our ideas, beliefs, and convictions to real-world situations. We then moved to a discussion of Christian ethics and attempted to identify its most distinctive elements.

By way of conclusion, we can summarize the main points of this chapter by offering five reasons why it is important to engage wholeheartedly in the study of Christian ethics.

First, studying ethics is important because ethics helps us answer life's *most enduring questions*: How should I live my life? How should we as a society live our lives together? Of course, these general questions can be broken down into more common ones that we face each day: How should I treat my friends? How should I treat my family? Should I respect those in authority over me? Why should I obey a speed limit? Can I cheat on my test to get ahead? Are there limits to sexual expression? Should people's skin color or ethnicity affect how I think of them or treat them as image-bearers? When properly understood, the discipline of ethics provides the means to address all the questions that we face daily, from the most mundane to the most problematic.

Second, it is important to study ethics because the discipline of Christian ethics deals with the questions that are *most important* to human life: What is the meaning of life? How can I be happy? Is there such a thing as right and wrong that transcends my own preferences? Is there such a thing as ultimate good and evil? How should the answers to these questions shape my life? Do my choices relate to anything more than this life on earth? Do my moral decisions matter for eternity? When properly understood, the discipline of ethics depends first and foremost on Scripture to provide a rich understanding of, and answers to, these questions.

A third reason is the reality that *everyone is already an ethicist, but not everyone realizes it.* That is, every person has opinions on moral matters, and everyone's opinions on these moral matters come from a deeper frame of reference that we identified as worldview assumptions or *metaethics.* Sadly, however, while most of us will have had training in how to perform a science experiment, produce a well-written paper, or play an instrument, very few will have had any comparable training in how to understand morality and ethics. Thus, studying ethics not only helps us understand and form our own convictions and opinions, but also helps us navigate important discussions with understanding and consistency.

Fourth, developing skills in ethical thinking and living helps *guide us through the labyrinth of "real life" in a consistent and meaningful way.* It helps us understand why people think as they do, why nations react as they do, why our hearts have the longings they do. It helps us understand how others are approaching subjects of great importance and why they may or may not hold differing opinions. It gives us criteria by which to evaluate our own point of view, as well as the views held by others. Ultimately, it serves to guide our daily actions and decisions in a manner consistent with our most deeply held beliefs and ideas.

Finally, the study of ethics is important because it *enables us to live a life that maximizes God's glory* in accord with the way he created the universe and with the moral guidelines he placed within it, and in anticipation of an ever-increasing life of joy with God in eternity. In other words, the study of ethics is important because, when done rightly, it is the path to our becoming the kind of worshipers that Jesus is looking for: "true worshipers" who worship God "in spirit and truth" (John 4:23–24).

Table 1.5. Five Reasons Why Studying Christian Ethics Is Important

1. Because ethics deals with the questions that are most *enduring* to human life.

2. Because ethics deals with the questions that are most *important* to human life.

3. Because everyone acts and thinks from an *ethical framework*. Working to understand ethics and intentionally shaping one's own view enables wise navigation in important moral discussions.

4. Because developing skills in ethical thinking and living helps *guide* us through the labyrinth of "real life" in a consistent and meaningful way.

5. Because having a biblically faithful ethical foundation and system enables us to live a life that *maximizes God's glory*.

Key Terms and Concepts

anthropology

applied ethics

doxology

epistemology

flourishing

inherent value

metaethics

metaphysics

morality is discovered

morality is invented

normative ethics

obedient love

orthodoxy

orthopraxy

penal substitutionary atonement

revealed morality

revealed reality

worldview

Key Scriptures

Genesis 1:1

Habakkuk 2:14

Matthew 28:18–20

Mark 12:28–31

John 10:10

John 14:6

Romans 3:23

Romans 5:8

Romans 8:29

2 Corinthians 13:5

Colossians 1:16

1 John 3:2

Study Questions

1. Central to the discussion and study of ethics is the question "Is morality discovered or invented?" Why is this question so foundational? How does the way in which a person answers this question impact the way that he or she will approach any ethical issue? Consider the topic of homosexuality, for example. How might the way in which one answers this question affect the way that the person reaches a conclusion regarding the morality of same-sex marriage?

2. What is a worldview, and how is it related to a person's ethical decision-making?

3. Distinguish between metaethics, normative ethics, and applied ethics. How are they related? How are they distinct?

4. In this chapter, the authors list six distinguishing marks of Christian ethics. What are those six, and how does each one set Christian ethics apart from other religious- or secular-based ethical systems?

5. How is Christian ethics related to discipleship? How is it related to the Great Commission?

For Further Reading

Davis, John Jefferson. *Evangelical Ethics: Issues Facing the Church Today*. 4th ed. Phillipsburg, NJ: P&R Publishing, 2015.

Feinberg, John S., and Paul D. Feinberg. *Ethics for a Brave New World*. 2nd ed. Wheaton, IL: Crossway, 2010.

Geisler, Norman L. *Christian Ethics: Contemporary Issues and Options*. 2nd ed. Grand Rapids: Baker Academic, 2010.

Grudem, Wayne. *Christian Ethics: An Introduction to Biblical Moral Reasoning*. Wheaton, IL: Crossway, 2018.

Jones, David W. *An Introduction to Biblical Ethics*. Nashville: B&H Academic, 2013.

Magnuson, Ken. *Invitation to Christian Ethics: Moral Reasoning and Contemporary Issues*. Grand Rapids: Kregel, 2020.

Mitchell, C. Ben. *Ethics and Moral Reasoning: A Student's Guide*. Wheaton, IL: Crossway, 2013.

O'Donovan, Oliver. *Resurrection and Moral Order: An Outline for Evangelical Ethics*. 2nd ed. Grand Rapids: Eerdmans, 1994.

Rae, Scott B. *Moral Choices: An Introduction to Ethics*. 4th ed. Grand Rapids: Zondervan, 2018.

PART 2

Revealed Reality:
The Metaethical Foundations
of Ethics as Worship

2

Revealed Reality: Ethics as Worship through the Lens of Creation

"The intention of Moses in beginning his Book with the creation of the world is to render God, as it were, visible to us in his works."[1]
—JOHN CALVIN, Commentary on Genesis

"Christianity is not primarily about lifestyle change: it is about knowing God."[2]
—MICHAEL REEVES, Delighting in the Trinity

Introduction

It is our purpose in part 2 to develop the metaethical foundations for ethics as worship. To do so, we first consider what Scripture reveals to us about the nature and character of God and then proceed to explore the metanarrative story line of Scripture through a paradigm of creation, fall, redemption, and restoration. That is, we will consider God's design of the world in creation (*creation order*), the impact of the fall on all creation, God's plan for the redemption of his created order (focusing on humans in particular), and the restoration of all things partially in the here and now, and fully in the eschatological reality of our union with Christ for all eternity.

Our reason for laying out the metaethical foundations in this manner is our conviction that in order to properly develop a Christian ethic, we must first understand the nature of how things ought to be and how they actually are before we can best understand how we ought to live. We want to explore what Scripture

---

1. John Calvin, *Commentary on the First Book of Moses Called Genesis* (Grand Rapids: Baker, 2005), 58.
2. Michael Reeves, *Delighting in the Trinity: An Introduction to the Christian Faith* (Downers Grove, IL: InterVarsity Press, 2012), 10.

reveals about the nature of reality (*revealed reality*) so that we can better understand why he has given us the instructions he has and why it is important to follow them (*revealed morality*). Our ultimate goal in this part of the book is to argue that when the discipline of ethics is properly grounded on a creation-order foundation with God at the center of all that we think and do, then every moment of life—from the most mundane, repetitive action to the highest pinnacle of loving contemplation—rightly becomes an opportunity to glorify God as an act of worship.

In keeping with this theme, the purpose of this chapter in particular is to explore the first element of the paradigm of creation, fall, redemption, and restoration. In this chapter, we begin with a discussion of what God has revealed to us about himself, the nature of the universe, the reason for its existence, and the universal context of worship that permeates all reality. Next, we move to a discussion of the nature and purpose of human beings as God created us to live and lead within the created order. Finally, before bringing the chapter to a conclusion, we explore the missional calling that God gives to his image-bearers to fill the earth with worship and consider the ramifications of this created design and calling for understanding the discipline of Christian ethics within the context of worship.

Creation and the Universal Context of Worship

The Theocentric Basis of All Reality (Gen. 1:1)

The first step to building a worthy Christian ethic is to begin where all good theology does: with an inquiry about the nature of God and his purposes for the world. As Dietrich Bonhoeffer put it, ethics must give priority to the question of *Who* over *how*, and the proper way to understand *how* must be determined in light of *Who*.[3] A. W. Tozer made a similar point in his classic work *The Knowledge of the Holy*:

> A right conception of God is basic not only to systematic theology but to practical Christian living as well. It is to worship what the foundation is to the temple; where it is inadequate or out of plumb the whole structure must sooner or later collapse. I believe there is scarcely an error in doctrine or a failure in applying Christian ethics that cannot be traced finally to imperfect and ignoble thoughts about God.[4]

Unfortunately, however, it is our observation that most ethical discussion in our culture begins not with an investigation into the nature and character of

3. Dietrich Bonhoeffer, *Christology* (London: Collins, 1971), 37–39.
4. A. W. Tozer, *The Knowledge of the Holy* (San Francisco: HarperCollins, 1961), 2.

God, but with the felt needs and experiences of daily life. This, in turn, often leads believers to look to Scripture as a source of commands and rules to govern behaviors and guide decisions as felt needs arise. While certainly we applaud any move to seek wisdom from God concerning morality and ethical decision-making, our concern is that this approach ultimately relegates the rich counsel of Scripture to little more than a rule book and diminishes the discipline of ethics to little more than behavior modification.

Ethics, however, is not primarily about actions, character, results, or responses to situations—it is about God. Our actions, character, results, and responses take on proper context only when, first, we understand that God, not humans or their life situations, is the central question that ethics is meant to pursue. Simply put, the Christian life will be properly applied only after it is properly grounded.

In order to see this point, consider the opening words of the very first verse of the Bible: "In the beginning God created the heavens and the earth" (Gen. 1:1). While we often take them for granted, these first words, "in the beginning God," are vitally important for the development of a biblical ethic because they press us into asking questions about *who* this God is that exists "in the beginning" and what his existence demands of us as we live in his created order.

Regarding *who* this God is, Scripture first reveals to us that the God who is "in the beginning" is an eternal Being. As Psalm 90:2 declares, "Before the mountains were born or You gave birth to the earth and the world, even from everlasting to everlasting, You are God." God has always been and will always be. By his very nature, he has always existed and depends on nothing else for his existence. Sometimes theologians refer to this attribute of God as his *aseity* (self-existence). In Exodus 3:14, God identifies himself to Moses as "I AM WHO I AM" (YHWH)—a phrase that indicates his complete independence from need of anything else. Put in more philosophical terms, the great I AM is completely unique and prior to all things that exist. His existence does not depend on anything else except himself. Thus, he is the Uncaused Cause and the Unmoved Mover that even Aristotle recognized but could not ultimately describe. God exists by the virtue of his very own nature.[5] He is the one *noncontingent* Being on whom everything else that exists depends (or is contingent) for existence. All other things that exist do so because God created them and gave them being. For this reason the apostle Paul will later argue, while preaching to the philosophers on Mars Hill in Athens, that only in this God do we "live and move and have our being" (Acts 17:28 NKJV).

Not only is this God the eternal, self-existent ground of all things, but we also learn from the phrase "in the beginning God" that God is meant to be the center

---

5. Wayne Grudem, *Systematic Theology: An Introduction to Biblical Doctrine* (Grand Rapids: Zondervan, 1994), 161.

of the story of the universe and all existence. To highlight this point, consider a question that we often place before our college and seminary students to help them grasp the importance of these concepts: "What are the first two chapters of the Bible about?" The most common answer we receive is "creation." But a simple evaluation of the grammar in Genesis 1:1 helps unearth a far more profound answer.

We understand that in the English language, a proper sentence has a subject, verb, and direct object. Considering Genesis 1:1, we see that "created" is the verb; it tells us what God did. "The heavens and the earth" are the direct objects; they tell us what God created. And this, in turn, leaves "God" as the subject of the sentence. In other words, the English translation of the original Hebrew is structured to point out the main focus of the text. God is the center of the story. He is the subject. That which is created has been created in order to give testimony to the greatness of the Creator. The introductory words that God uses to reveal the beginning and nature of all things do not put the creation in the place of prominence. Nor is humanity given the seat of primacy. The story is about God.

"In the beginning, *God*!"

If there are any doubts about this theocentric understanding of Scripture and particularly the God-centered nature of the creation narrative of the first chapter of the Bible, one need only scan the rest of Genesis 1 to see how this God-centered reading unfolds in the text. Almost every verse draws attention to God with phrases such as "then God said . . . ," "and God saw . . . ," "God separated . . . ," "God called . . . ," "God made . . ." Over thirty times in Genesis 1, a direct reference is made to God and how he is crafting the world.[6] It is as though Moses were shouting through the ages to us from the very first words of the Bible: "if the *creation* is incredible, how much more stunning is the *Creator*!"

This is a vitally important point for ethics. If we do not grasp the centrality of God in the creation narrative, we will tend to read the story as though that which is created is the central point of the story and thus the story revolved around us.Such a reading will then, in turn, lead us to wrongly conclude that the story revolves around us. But when we see that from the beginning God is the eternally preexistent ground of all being and the center point of the universe, it follows that not only *is* he the Lord of all things, but he *ought to be recognized as such* by everything else that exists. As the psalmist puts it, "the earth is the LORD's, and all it contains" (Ps. 24:1). The more we contemplate this simple but profound truth, the more import it has for our lives. The more we learn to appreciate the fact that God is both Creator and Owner of all things, the more it will

6. Gen. 1:1, 2, 3, 4 (twice), 5, 6, 7, 8, 9, 10 (twice), 11, 12, 14, 16, 17, 18, 20, 21 (twice), 22, 24, 25 (twice), 26, 27 (twice), 28 (twice), 29, 31.

Responded to live

help us understand how we ought to appropriately respond to him and live our lives before him. As Gordon Lewis and Bruce Demarest state, "consciousness of the Most High ideally results in a sense of ultimate dependence on him and obligation to him, and awesome worship of him as the Almighty and praise to him as the Creator."[7]

As to how all this relates to our lives and our ethics, a very simple but ultimately profound point must shape our worldviews and metaethical foundations. The simple fact is that God is God and we are not. He is the ground of all existence. All things that exist do so because he chose to make them. He owns all things, and he is the central focal point of all that exists. This God who is "in the beginning" is by his very nature the Owner and Master. He is our Lord. Based on this fact, regardless of whether a person acknowledges it, we owe him our total allegiance. Truly and simply, based on who he is, it is right that we would serve and obey him because he is God. Obedience to God is the duty of all created beings.

Now, if this were the only thing that God revealed to us about his nature and character through Scripture—that he is the ultimate Owner and Ruler of the universe—we would have enough to set the foundations for a clear ethical system. Our ethics would involve receiving the commands of God and following them in submission as our duty. It would be right to work hard to obey God's commands simply in light of the "Godness of God." In such an ethic, duty and obligation would be the basis of our efforts to please God. And our hope of salvation would likely depend on our ability to do and accomplish what God commands.

Additionally, if this were the only thing that God revealed about himself—if all we knew about God was that he is the eternal center, Owner, and Ruler—then we would have no certainty about whether the God we would be serving was a good or loving being. It could very well be that the raw duty-based obedience required of us would be rendered unto a tyrannical, whimsical god who simply ruled his minions through power and lust. *Right* and *wrong* would be defined only in terms of doing what the master required, no matter what he might require on any given day.

Thankfully, however, this is not the only thing we know about the character of the God of the Bible. Scripture also reveals to us that God is majestically good (Ps. 86:5). Scripture teaches us that God is merciful, gracious, and kind (Pss. 33:4–7; 103:8; 121; 145:8; Eph. 2:4–9). It also teaches that he is a holy God who has all knowledge, and is entirely wise in all he does (Ps. 139:1; Isa. 6:3; 1 Cor. 1:20–26).[8]

---

7. Gordon R. Lewis and Bruce A. Demarest, *Integrative Theology*, vol. 1 (Grand Rapids: Zondervan, 1987), 233.

8. For a great devotional read and study of the attributes of God, see Tozer, *Knowledge of the Holy*. Another classic study of the nature of God that is accessible for the layperson is J. I. Packer, *Knowing God* (Downers Grove, IL: InterVarsity Press, 1973).

His justice, therefore, is always perfect in both its assessment and its application (Ps. 96). In addition to these (and the many other splendid attributes that we did not mention), the Bible also emphasizes that God is a God of love. Indeed, 1 John 4:8 simply tells us that "God is love." Wayne Grudem describes this attribute of God as meaning that God is "eternally giving of himself to others" and that it is "part of his nature to give of himself in order to bring about blessing or good for others."[9]

These additionally revealed attributes of God radically alter the nature of Christian ethics. Instead of raw obedience offered up to a divine Owner and taskmaster, we have revealed for us in Scripture a picture of a God who elicits from us not just duty and obedience, but a loving response based on the fact that among all his other many and splendid attributes, God is ultimately a "loving Father."

This attribute of God as loving Father takes on a particularly fascinating quality for ethics when one sees it in light of the Trinity. As Michael Reeves points out in his book *Delighting in the Trinity*, Jesus himself tells us in John 17:24 that before the creation of the world ("in the beginning," Gen. 1:1), the Father was eternally loving the Son. Indeed, "before he ever created, before he ever ruled the world, before anything else, this God was a Father loving his Son."[10] Thus, Jesus tells us, the most foundational way for us to understand God—more foundational for Christian living than understanding God as the preexistent ground of all existence, or the Creator of all things—is to see him not only as a God of love but as a *loving Father.*

> Since God is, before all things, a Father, and not primarily a creator or ruler, all his ways are beautifully fatherly. It is not that this God "does" being a Father as a day job, only to kick back in the evenings as plain old "God." It is not that he has a nice blob of fatherly icing on top. He is Father. All the way down. Thus all that he does he does as Father. That is who he is. He creates as a Father and he rules as a Father; and that means the way he rules over creation is most unlike the way any other God would rule over creation. . . . It is only when we see that God rules his creation as a kind and loving Father that we will be moved with delight in his providence.[11]

---

9. Grudem, *Systematic Theology*, 199.

10. Reeves, *Delighting in the Trinity*, 21.

11. Reeves, *Delighting in the Trinity*, 23. This is an important point even for those who have experienced hardship and pain at the hands of their earthly fathers precisely because the heavenly Father perfectly embodies and infinitely exceeds all the things we most long for from our finite and fallen fathers. Rather than being a stumbling block for those who have been let down by their earthly fathers (as all of us have in one form or another), God chooses in perfect wisdom to reveal himself as Father precisely because he alone can satisfy our deepest longings.

From eternity past, the Father, the Son, and the Holy Spirit have shared a perfect mutual love, fellowship, and community with one another. Unlike Allah, or the Brahman of Hinduism, "the fact that God is three persons yet one God means that there was no loneliness or lack of personal fellowship on God's part before creation."[12] In fact, the love shared among the three persons of the triune God is and always will be far more perfect than humans can share with one another or with God.[13] And this, in turn, means that he creates not out of neediness for human fellowship, but out of the fountain of his love that pours forth into life and giving in order to bring about blessing to all things that he creates. *

Now, as we pursue the question about what the God of Genesis 1:1 is like, not only do we discover from Scripture that his attributes are many and splendid, but two closely related points help us further see the wonder of the God who is the foundation of a Christian ethical system. First, it is important to point out that when the Bible describes God by listing his different attributes, it never intends to single out any one of them as more important than any of the others. Rather, there is an assumption that every attribute ascribed to God is completely true of God all the time. Theologians call this idea the *simplicity of God* or the *unity of God*. It implies that God's nature is not divided into parts, as though he could be loving without being totally just, or he could be just without also being totally loving. Grudem notes: "God's whole being includes all of his attributes: he is entirely loving, entirely merciful, entirely just, and so forth. Every attribute of God that we find in Scripture is true of all God's being, and we therefore can say that every attribute of God also qualifies every other attribute."[14]

Second, because God's being is infinite, his attributes should be understood as infinite in nature as well. That is, in each and every one of his perfections, God is unbounded and has no limits in his ability to express and display them. Not only does he embody mercy, grace, kindness, goodness, holiness, knowledge, wisdom, justice, and love, there is no limit to the extent to which he can express them or pour them forth in keeping with his own nature. God is good not because there is something outside himself that is good to which he is beholden. He is the expression of infinite goodness in his own being, and thus he always acts in every situation in light of what is most good. Again Tozer is helpful:

Whatever God is and all that God is, He is without limit. . . . He is measureless. . . . His love is measureless. It is more: it is boundless. It has no bounds because it is not a thing but a facet of the essential nature of God. His love is something He is,

12. Grudem, *Systematic Theology*, 161.
13. Grudem, *Systematic Theology*, 161.
14. Grudem, *Systematic Theology*, 179.

and because He is infinite that love can enfold the whole created world in itself and have room for ten thousand times ten thousand worlds besides."[15]

The Purpose and End of All Creation Is Worship

What does this exploration into the nature of the God who is "in the beginning" have to do with building our metaethical foundations? Everything! Not only was this God "in the beginning" before creation, but as the rest of Genesis 1:1 tells us, this God also *created* the heavens and the earth. So the preexistent God reveals himself as the eternally preexisting great I AM and is also a loving Father of many splendid attributes who causes the universe to exist, shaping and directing it as he wishes. God not only designed the world and gave it its form, but also ordered it toward a final goal.

What is the design and final goal of all things? As we have seen, Scripture plainly teaches that God is the Creator. We also learn from Scripture that the whole earth is full of God's glory (Isa. 6:3). While we will point out in the next section that humans have a special role in giving God the worship and honor he is due, the worship of humans by no means provides the sum total of worship in the universe. Noel Due declares: "God's decision to create the universe is the effective cause of worship. He creates and that which springs into being through his Word and Spirit as a result of his creative will worships."[16] Every element of creation, simply because it *is* his creation, is meant to reflect back to God the glory he is due. As Jonathan Edwards affirms, the glory of God is the chief end of *everything*.[17] Or as Charles Hodge simply put it, "the final cause of all God's purposes is his own glory."[18] Metaphorically, we could say that creation serves as the great symphony hall built for worship in which the whole of creation is meant to sing a song of worship to the great and loving God who created it and desires for it to maximally flourish.

The idea that the universe was created to glorify God is true for both the inanimate and animate aspects of creation alike. This takes place because even the nonsentient elements of creation exist according to God's will, and merely by their existence they speak of the greatness and mercy of God. As Psalm 19:1 proclaims, simply by their existence, "the heavens are telling of the glory of God; and their expanse is declaring the work of His hands." Psalm 148 likewise indicates that it is the right and proper disposition of all creation to praise the Lord.

15. Tozer, *Knowledge of the Holy*, 44–47.

16. Noel Due, *Created for Worship: From Genesis to Revelation to You* (Fearn, Ross-shire, Scotland: Christian Focus, 2005), 35.

17. Jonathan Edwards, *A Treatise concerning Religious Affections*, accessed May 8, 2020, http://www.jonathan-edwards.org/ReligiousAffections.pdf. See sections 2.3.142, 2.4.221, 5.10.238–39, 7.264–85.

18. Charles Hodge, *Systematic Theology*, vol. 1 (Grand Rapids: Hendrickson, 2003), 535.

Even Jesus during his triumphal entry into Jerusalem states that if human beings did not praise God as they ought, even the stones would cry out in worship (Luke 19:40). Now, one may not want to go so far as to interpret Jesus' words about stones to mean that they would literally find voices and shout praises, but the larger point remains that human worship of God is not the full extent of worship that takes place in the universe. This point is even more strongly affirmed when one realizes that Scripture indicates that in heaven the seraphim, cherubim, living creatures, and elders all render to God the praise that he is due (Ps. 99:1; Isa. 6:2; Rev. 4:4–9).

We are wise to realize that worship does not begin with humans. "Worship begins with God. By virtue of his very being as God and by virtue of his act of creation, God is the initiator of worship. It begins with God, and it was evident in the celestial and terrestrial creation before human beings were brought into existence."[19] In other words, before the creation of humankind, God wove the very fabric of creation with the thread of praise and worship. Reality itself is a mosaic of worship with God as the centerpiece not because he is somehow needy, but because he is the fountain of all life, love, and joy. He is the one Being who is wholly worthy of all worship. All creation will maximize its existence as it does what it is created to do—glorify God and enjoy him forever.

Returning to Bonhoeffer's point with which we began this part of the discussion, if theology and ethics rightly begin with a discussion of *Who* over *how*, then we emphasize that the *how* of ethics can take on proper formulation and application only when we discover that the very nature of the universe we inhabit not only was created and designed by God, but is centered on him, and ultimately exists by and for the One who is the *Who*. Reality itself exists as an environment of theocentric worship. As Paul declares in Romans 11:36, "For from Him and through Him and to Him are all things. To Him be the glory forever. Amen."[20]

If we miss this point, we are in danger of missing what is arguably the single most important element for understanding not only the discipline of ethics but also perhaps even the entire point of the Bible. For only from this perspective can one begin to rightly understand the purpose of humanity in the grand scheme of the universe. The reality is that when God created the human race, Adam and Eve "came into a worship-filled creation. By implication their existence was also to be taken up in worship."[21] For this reason, any discussion of how humans ought to behave (ethics) must be pursued from the framework and context of the greater purpose for which all creation exists: the worship and glory of God.

---

19. Due, *Created for Worship*, 37.
20. See also 1 Cor. 10:31; Col. 1:16; 3:17.
21. Due, *Created for Worship*, 37.

The Nature and Purpose of Humans in a Universe of Worship

The Nature of Human Beings

Having considered the worthiness of God, we now consider the place that human beings have in the grand symphony hall of worship that we call the universe. Genesis 2:7 helps us see that the basic nature of human beings has both a material and an immaterial component: "Then the LORD God formed man of dust from the ground, and breathed into his nostrils the breath of life; and man became a living being." Earlier, in Genesis 1:9–10, Scripture indicates that God initially created the "dust" and "ground" as "land" and that he declared it to be good. Now this verse tells us that God is using that good matter to purposefully design, form, and bring to life a human being. The Hebrew words describing God's actions here are interesting.

In the original language, the text indicates that God "formed man [*'adam*] of dust from the ground [*'adamah*]." That is, Adam, "the man of the earth," is literally made of the earth (dust, ground) that God declared to be good. From this small point, we see an important idea in Christian theology. God created all physical matter, and because God created it, we know it is good, for he declared it to be so.[22] God further affirms the goodness of the created realm when he uses the dirt he created to create Adam. From this we can see that God affirms not only the physical nature of the world, but also the physical body of human beings. Scripture indicates that God intended the human body to be enjoyed and celebrated as a part of his creative grace.

Human beings, however, are more than simply physical bodies. Genesis 2:7 also tells us that God breathed the breath of life *into* the human body and thereby transformed the mere body into a "living being." As such, human beings are composed of both a material part (the body) and an immaterial part (the soul). The body and soul become integrated into a unified whole, sometimes described by theologians and philosophers as a *psychosomatic unity* or *dualistic holism*.[23] Christian ethicists normally describe the united nature of human beings with the term *embodied selves* or *embodied souls*. The important part for our discussion is to understand that Scripture rejects any form of dualism like that present in ancient Greek philosophies, in which the immaterial soul was considered to be good while the body was evil. Instead, the human person is a unified whole that includes both body and soul.[24]

---

22. Gen. 1:4, 10, 12, 18, 21, 25, 31.

23. Here we are making a distinction between human nature as *dualistic* and what is more commonly understood by the word *dualism*. *Dualism* is normatively used in a manner that not only recognizes two distinct substances (material and immaterial parts of the self) but also affirms a relationship of these parts as opposed or divided fundamentally from one another. Such a mind/body dualism was the position held by Plato and Descartes.

24. For a more in-depth discussion of this concept, see James R. Beck and Bruce Demarest, *The Human*

Scripture also indicates that in one sense human beings are "living beings" just like other plants and animals. But humans also possess a unique quality that sets them apart from the other living things. Alone among the created beings on earth, they bear the image and likeness of God. Genesis 1:26–28 reads:

> Then God said, "Let Us make man in Our image, according to Our likeness; and let them rule over the fish of the sea and over the birds of the sky and over the cattle and over all the earth, and over every creeping thing that creeps on the earth." God created man in His own image, in the image of God He created him; male and female He created them. God blessed them; and God said to them, "Be fruitful and multiply, and fill the earth, and subdue it; and rule over the fish of the sea and over the birds of the sky and over every living thing that moves on the earth."

A look at the grammatical structure of these verses can again be helpful for understanding what God intends for us to learn from them. Note the ordering of ideas in Genesis 1:26–27:

A. God creates human beings in his image and likeness.
B. God creates human beings as male and female.

Then in verse 28:

B'. He instructs humans to be fruitful and multiply and fill the earth.
A'. God instructs humans to subdue and rule.

This ordering, known as a *chiasm* (A, B, B', A'), highlights the essential functions that humans are to carry out related to the nature of what they are. That is, because humans are made in the image and likeness of God (A), they are tasked with the function to subdue and rule (A'). Similarly, because humans are created male and female (B), the corresponding function is to be fruitful and multiply and fill the earth (B').

Table 2.1. The Chiastic Ordering of Genesis 1:27–28

A—God creates humans in his image and likeness → A'—subdue the earth and rule over the earth
B—God creates human beings as male and female → B'—be fruitful and multiply, fill the earth

Person in Theology and Psychology: A Biblical Anthropology for the Twenty-First Century (Grand Rapids: Kregel, 2005), 119–54.

While the exact nature of what it means to be an *image-bearer* has long been under debate, several important scholars have recently suggested that understanding the term (at least in part) relates to how ancient Near Eastern monarchs used statues to represent their authority in a given realm. By placing a statue or image of himself in a region, the king was establishing his authority and right to rule that part of the kingdom even in his absence. Thus, when God declares human beings to be his image-bearers, he is establishing the fact that they are to be his visible representatives in the created world. As such, they are to function with a derived authority to act as God would act and rule over the created order as God himself would.[25]

When we look further into the meaning of "image" and "likeness" as a paired set of words, a beautiful picture of God's intentions for humans in the world becomes clearer. Peter Gentry and Stephen Wellum highlight the key idea:

> Given the normal meanings of "image" and "likeness" in the cultural and linguistic setting of the Old Testament and the ancient Near East, "likeness" specifies a relationship between God and humans such that *'adam* can be described as the son of God, and "image" describes a relationship between God and humans such that *'adam* can be described as a servant king. Although both terms specify the divine-human relationship, the first focuses on the human in relation to God and the second focuses on the human in relation to the world. These would be understood to be relationships characterized by faithfulness and loyal love, obedience and trust. . . . In this sense the divine image entails a covenant relationship between God and humans on the one hand, and between humans and the world on the other.[26]

The main point as far as it concerns our exploration of metaethics is that human beings who are embodied selves (physical and spiritual wholes) and made in the image and likeness of God are specifically designed and uniquely qualified to play a dual role in the created order. In one sense (*likeness*), they are similar to God and have a position of authority over the rest of the created order. Thus, they are created and designed to be God's representatives and carry out his wishes and commands to the rest of creation. In this sense, we could say that they are "over" creation and are thus tasked to act as God's representatives "down" to the rest of creation. In this role, they are to ensure that God's designs for the world are fulfilled and his instructions communicated and implemented.

In another sense (*image*), human beings are made of the dust of the earth and set in place by God. They are both a part of the created order and embedded

---

25. Gordon J. Wenham, *Story as Torah* (Grand Rapids: Baker Academic, 2000), 25–26. See also William J. Dumbrell, *Covenant and Creation* (Flemington Markets, New South Wales, Australia: Paternoster, 1984), 31–34.
26. Peter J. Gentry and Stephen J. Wellum, *Kingdom through Covenant: A Biblical-Theological Understanding of the Covenants* (Wheaton, IL: Crossway, 2012), 194.

within it. As image-bearers, they still carry an authority over the rest of creation, but in this role they use their position and authority to rally and guide the created order back up to God. They are set apart as part of creation to govern it, care for it, shape it, use it, and ultimately present it back to him. As the diagram below illustrates (see fig. 2.1), God uniquely designed humans to play the role of mediator between God and nature.

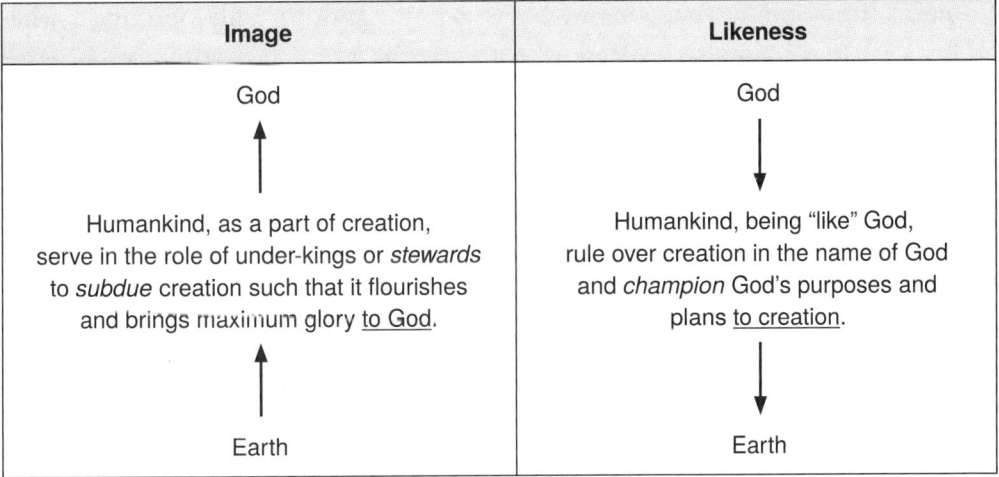

Image	Likeness
God	God
↑	↓
Humankind, as a part of creation, serve in the role of under-kings or *stewards* to *subdue* creation such that it flourishes and brings maximum glory to God.	Humankind, being "like" God, rule over creation in the name of God and *champion* God's purposes and plans to creation.
↑	↓
Earth	Earth

Fig. 2.1. Image and Likeness of God

Understanding this unique positioning of human beings gives us the context to properly appreciate the nature of the instructions that God gave to Adam and Eve when he commanded them to "subdue" and "rule" over the earth. The Hebrew word translated into English as "subdue" is *kabash*. The word connotes the use of strength or force to bring something under control or to subjugate it. The Hebrew word translated into English as "rule" is *radah*. This word also has a strong connotation of a ruler's having dominion over a kingdom. Depending on the context of the passage in which these Hebrew words are used, understanding of how the strength or dominion is exercised can vary. It can be positive or negative, caring or harsh. In this particular context of Genesis 1, the instructions are given in a prefall world to nonfallen humans. The obvious implication is that the ones made in the image of God are designed to be a part of the created order and use the authority and strength they have to shape or *subdue* the earth in a manner that is in keeping with the nature and moral character of God.[27] They are *stewards* of the Great King who care for all the things of God in order to return them to him for his honor and glory.

27. For an example of how this might look, consider Psalm 104.

Likewise, the ones who go out in the likeness of God should *rule* over the earth in such a way that their governance rightly represents the wishes of God toward the created order. They are *champions* of God, going forth in his name to herald his good cause to all the earth. When rightly done together, the humans then subdue and rule creation as mediators between God and the rest of creation in such a way that God receives from it all the glory, honor, praise, and worship that can be mustered from each and every aspect of the created realm.[28]

Four direct implications arise from this point and not only pertain to what humans are *to do*, but also indicate who they *are* as image-bearers.

First, by design, God embedded humans in the creation order when he made them from the dust of the ground, yet at the same time uniquely gave them authority over creation. They not only are in and of the creation, but also are created to be leaders over it. Simultaneously, they have both full solidarity and identification with the rest of creation as created beings themselves and also a special affinity with God as his image-bearers and are given headship over creation. By nature, they are *embedded heads* in and over the creation order.[29]

A second implication that we glean from the text is that humans are by definition *missional*. In this case, because of how God designed them as image-bearers and embedded them in headship over creation, it is their nature to represent God to the world and represent the world to God. God not only made them to go into the world, but created them as *goers* by design. They express the fundamental nature of their humanness by going forth from God and in the name of God to champion forth to the world the things of God. Humankind is created to be on mission to cultivate a flourishing world full of praise and glory to God. Therefore, this is not merely their "mission" in the sense of its being merely something to "do." Rather, it is a part of *who they are*. God created them to be *missional* by nature.

Third, human beings are *worshipers* by nature as well. As missional beings embedded in the created order, humans go forth into creation as God's *champions*, acting in his name in order to lead a created order that is flourishing as though God himself were leading and nurturing it. In so doing, they are loving God, honoring God, and returning to him what he is due. Indeed, "from the perspective of our relationship to God as our Creator-Father, in whose image we have been made, worship is natural to us. . . . We have been made by the Triune God to reflect his internal self-giving love, and to participate in the action of honouring

---

28. For further investigation of these ideas, see J. I. Packer, *Concise Theology* (Wheaton, IL: Tyndale, 1993), 71–76. See also Francis Schaeffer's discussion of this dual mediatorial role of human beings in *Pollution and the Death of Man* (Wheaton, IL: Crossway, 2011), 48.

29. For a fuller discussion of this, see Mark Liederbach and Seth Bible, *True North: Christ, the Gospel, and Creation Care* (Nashville: B&H Academic, 2012), 72–79.

him above all things."[30] Human beings are not merely created *to* worship, nor are they created simply *for* worship. Describing them in either of these ways would suggest that somehow the act of worshiping could be separated out from their nature or relegated to a specific subcategory of their nature. Rather, humans are best understood as worshipers by the very nature of their constitution. As Harold Best aptly put it, humans were created as worshipers who are "continuously outpouring" worship simply because we were created in that condition. The very nature of being *imago Dei* means to be a worshiper.[31]

Finally, a fourth implication is that by creating human beings in this unique fashion, God has given them a special status that imbues them with a beautiful and unique *dignity*. Ultimately, a human being's value is not dependent on his or her actions, but is grounded in the God who created and designed the person and put him or her into the world as his representative. All humans have an *inherent* value given to them by God.

Table 2.2. Four Implications That Arise from Image-Bearing Status

1. Humans are embedded heads in and over creation by design and nature.
2. Humans are missional beings by design and nature.
3. Humans are worshipers by design and nature.
4. Humans have an inherent dignity by design and nature.

The Purpose of Humans in a Universe of Worship

Having considered God's creative design of human beings, we now consider the purpose, final goal, or *telos* for which he created them. Given what we have learned above, it should come as no surprise that a human being's purpose is directly related to his or her nature. That is, God designs the human person such that what he or she *is* perfectly coincides with what he or she *ought* to do. Or, said another way, God tasks humans to fulfill through their *doing* the very things he created them to *be*. A closer look at Genesis 2:15 helps us see this beautiful link between our nature and our purpose: "Then the LORD God took the man and put him into the garden of Eden to *cultivate* it and *keep* it."

After creating Adam as an embodied self, God then took him, placed him into the garden of Eden, and gave him a task. Because of how most English versions translate the original Hebrew words in this verse, it is possible to conclude that Adam's primary task was to be a gardener. Indeed, in a manner of speaking, this would be an accurate understanding. There is no question that God wanted him

---

30. Due, *Created for Worship*, 39.
31. Harold Best, *Unceasing Worship* (Downers Grove, IL: InterVarsity Press, 2003), 23.

to cultivate the garden, look after it, and cause it to flourish. Keeping in mind, however, what we learned above about the nature of God and how he designed his image-bearers, it should come as no surprise that when we take a more nuanced look at this verse and the passage it sits within, a richer meaning and understanding springs forth. Adam's cultivating and keeping of the garden was meant to be a part of—and means to—a life fully on mission, rightly ordered to God in worshipful obedience so that the whole earth ultimately offers to God maximally all the glory that he is due.

To understand this, consider the phrase "cultivate it and keep it" in Genesis 2:15. The Hebrew words translated into English are *'abad* ("cultivate") and *shamar* ("keep"). There are several very interesting things about these words both as they are considered individually and as they appear in relation to each other in the Old Testament. In regard to *'abad*, depending on both the immediate context and the larger context of the passage in which it falls, it can be translated as "cultivate," "work," "serve," or "worship." For example, in Exodus 3:12, Moses uses this word when he asks Pharaoh to let the Israelites leave Egypt in order to "serve" or "worship" God in the wilderness. *Shamar,* again depending on context, can be rendered "keep," "watch," "preserve," "care for," or "obey." For example, in Deuteronomy 5:10, this word is used to express the blessing that comes when God's people "keep" or "obey" the Sabbath.

In the immediate context of Genesis 2:15, we see that God placed Adam into the garden of Eden. From this, many translators focus the translation of the two words with direct reference to the garden. From this point of view, because God put Adam into a garden, the words *'abad* and *shamar* must refer to the garden and Adam's responsibilities as they directly relate to that place. Thus, the words are often translated "cultivate" and "keep."

While this approach to the verse is not without merit, we believe that such an interpretation is too narrow. It does not pay enough attention to the grammatical structuring of the words in the larger surrounding context of the creation narrative in which it sits, nor does it account well for the larger canon of Scripture. Consider, for example, the context of what is taking place in the creation narratives.[32] We have already seen that *in the beginning* the Bible depicts a theocentric universe

---

32. While two distinct narratives are clearly represented in Genesis 1 and 2 (Gen. 1:1–2:4; 2:5–25), it is important to keep this in tension with the reality that the editors of the Torah placed them together with the purpose of providing a full depiction of a single event. As Gentry and Wellum state, "the pattern of Hebrew literatures is recursive, resumptive, and holographic. Gen. 1 goes round the topic of creation, and Gen. 2 goes round the topic again from a different perspective. Put the two together and you have a hologram of the creation." Gentry and Wellum, *Kingdom through Covenant*, 215. Richard Bauckham concurs and comments that the narratives "have been combined by editors who surely did not simply cut and paste them, but brought them together intelligently into what they perceived as a coherent whole." Richard Bauckham, *The Bible and Ecology: Rediscovering the Community of Creation* (Waco, TX: Baylor University Press, 2010), 20.

where a loving God is the center of the story and worthy of all praise. In keeping with this idea, a growing number of influential Old Testament scholars, such as Meredith Kline, Greg Beale, Gordon Wenham, and William Dumbrell, have pointed out that the Genesis 1 and 2 narratives are heavily laden with language picturing the created order as a temple of worship for the King of the universe.[33] Adam's life in the garden was to be lived out in the presence of God. The garden was to be a sort of holy sanctuary in which Adam worshiped the Lord in, and by, the daily tasks he performed in the Lord's presence.[34]

Consistent with this idea is the grammatical structuring of the verse. Within the larger context of the Old Testament canon, an interesting pattern emerges when considering the manner in which the words *'abad* and *shamar* appear together in the text. When these words are found in combination in the Old Testament, they form what linguists call a *collocation*, a grouping of words that appear together consistently and that convey a greater meaning when they appear together than they might otherwise convey when used separately.[35] For example, one might find the words *precious* and *stone* placed together in Hebrew to give the meaning of "piece of jewelry."

The key point is this: when *'abad* and *shamar* appear together elsewhere in the Old Testament, they *never* convey an agricultural meaning. They do, however, commonly refer to the service and guardianship that Levitical priests would provide in the care for Israel's temple (Lev. 18:5; Num. 3:7–8; 8:25–26; 18:5–6; 1 Chron. 23:32). They convey a meaning rich with honoring God and the keeping of his commands in a posture of worship.[36]

33. Meredith G. Kline, "Creation in the Image of the Glory-Spirit," *Westminster Theological Journal* 39, no. 2 (Spring 1977): 250–72. See also Meredith G. Kline, *Images of the Spirit* (Grand Rapids: Baker, 1980), 20–26. For further investigation of this point, see G. K. Beale, *The Temple and the Church's Mission* (Downers Grove, IL: InterVarsity Press, 2004); T. Desmond Alexander, *From Eden to the New Jerusalem: An Introduction to Biblical Theology* (Grand Rapids: Kregel Academic, 2008); Gordon J. Wenham, "Sanctuary Symbolism in the Garden of Eden Story," in *Proceedings of the Ninth World Congress of Jewish Studies, Division A: The Period of the Bible* (Jerusalem: World Union of Jewish Studies, 1986), 19–25; Dumbrell, *Covenant and Creation*; John M. Frame, *The Doctrine of God* (Phillipsburg, NJ: P&R Publishing, 2002), 291; Christopher J. H. Wright, *The Mission of God* (Downers Grove, IL: IVP Academic, 2006), 415.

34. Robert Jamieson, A. R. Fausset, and David Brown, *Commentary Critical and Explanatory on the Whole Bible* (Oak Harbor, WA: Logos Research Systems, 1998).

35. *Encyclopedia of Hebrew Language and Linguistics*, accessed May 24, 2018, http://referenceworks .brillonline.com/entries/encyclopedia-of-hebrew-language-and-linguistics/collocation-modern-hebrew -EHLL_COM_00000796#d4760123e68.

36. The *Theological Lexicon of the Old Testament* points out that translating *shamar* with the meaning of keeping of commandments, statutes, and instructions of God "dominates the entire semantic field in the religious realm. It appears in almost all portions of the OT with widely varying expressions, grammatical constructions, and addressees." Ernst Jenni and Claus Westermann, *Theological Lexicon of the Old Testament* (Peabody, MA: Hendrickson, 1997), 1381–82. See also Umberto Cassuto, *A Commentary on the Book of Genesis* (Jerusalem: Magnes, 1978), 122; John H. Sailhamer, "Genesis," in *Genesis, Exodus, Leviticus, Numbers,*

So how does this discussion of Hebrew grammar help us understand the meaning of Genesis 2:15 and its relationship to the field of ethics? While technically the Hebrew words *'abad* and *shamar* can refer to the task of cultivating and keeping the garden, we believe there is more to their meaning when we consider:

1. The immediate context of the verse.
2. The God-centered context of the creation narratives in which this passage falls.
3. The creation order as a *temple of worship* motif identified by key scholars.
4. The possible range of meaning that each of the words can carry.
5. The grammatical structure of these two words in the Old Testament as a whole (collocation).

The proper way to understand Genesis 2:15 is that God placed Adam into the garden to *worship and obey God in and through the cultivation and keeping of the garden.*

Table 2.3. Meaning of the Language in Genesis 2:15

Genesis 2:15	Hebrew	Other Passages Where the Word Is Used	Various Possible Meanings
Cultivate (Work)	*'abad*	Exodus 3:12	Work Serve Worship
Keep (Till)	*shamar*	Deuteronomy 5:10	Keep Watch Preserve Care For Obey
Cultivate and Keep	*'abad* and *shamar* (collocation)	Leviticus 18:5; Numbers 3:7–8; 8:25–26; 18:5–6; 1 Chronicles 23:32	Serve and Protect Work and Care Worship and Obey

Thus, in interpreting Genesis 2:15, we discover that while God did indeed place Adam in the garden of Eden to literally take care of it, the full context indicates that Adam's caretaking also had a higher ordering. It was meant to be an act of loving and worshipful obedience in which he guarded, protected, and brought

---

ed. Frank E. Gaebelein, *Expositor's Bible Commentary 2* (Grand Rapids: Zondervan, 1990), 45; Gentry and Wellum, *Kingdom through Covenant*, 212.

to flourishing the natural sanctuary where God had placed him. The garden of Eden, then, was created by God as a sort of *whole-life temple* in which Adam worshiped God and was daily employed in the offering of his life in thanksgiving and praise. The passage is meant to convey something about what Adam was created and tasked to *do*, but it tells us this in light of what God created him to *be*. Adam was to care for God's creation and rightly order it to God's glory as only a missional worshiper can. In the words of Old Testament scholar John Sailhamer: "Man is put in the garden to worship God and to obey him. Man's life in the garden was to be characterized by worship and obedience."[37]

Here we find a crucial connection between the God who created the universe, the nature of the universe, the nature of human beings, the task God gave to human beings, and the discipline of ethics. When Genesis 2:15 tells us that "God took the man and put him into the garden of Eden to cultivate it and keep it," we learn that Adam's task was to *embody worship by obeying God's command for him to cultivate and keep the garden*. The primary sign and expression of worship was fundamentally ethical in nature. Caring for the garden is what Adam was told to *do* in obedience, but the work he did was done in fulfillment of his nature as a worshiper—and thus for the *purpose of worship*. Because Adam was created as a worshiper, his God-assigned work was to always be both a duty and a joy-filled act of praise. He was designed and tasked to live a life of *orthopraxy and doxology*.

Therefore, Adam's entire existence was designed to be one of worship. Who he was created to be, the action he performed, and the praise he offered were all designed to perfectly and harmoniously overlap as he worshiped the God who was his loving Father. Adam's duty to render unto God the glory he was due would be experienced and ordered as an offering of loving worship both in response to the character of God and in fulfillment of who he was created to be.[38] In light of this, it would come about that as he lived a life of worshipful obedience, Adam would both express the fullness of his humanity and reach the highest expression of his nature: that is, he would be *fully human* and *fully alive*. Noel Due captures the idea of worshipful obedience well:

> [We] should see humanity as being brought into, and existing in, a matrix of worship. The primal couple did not exist for themselves, or by themselves, but they existed for God, at the head of creation yet to be brought into its full glory. We see

37. Sailhamer, "Genesis," 45.

38. John Murray captures this point nicely: "The biblical ethic, as it would have been exemplified in a sinless world and as it is exemplified in redeemed humanity, knows no antithesis between duty performed in obedience to commandment and love as the fulfillment of the law." For his full discussion of worship and ethics in the prefall context, see John Murray, *Principles of Conduct: Aspects of Biblical Ethics* (Grand Rapids: Eerdmans, 1957), 37–39.

that the primal couple was given a mandate, to "fill" the earth, and "subdue" it and "rule over" it (Gen. 1:26), and a task to "cultivate and keep" the Garden (Gen. 2:15). To engage in such tasks and to fulfill the mandate was to be their expression of worship. Their communion with God, the joy of his nearer presence, the offering of praise and adoration to him, were not to be set in some compartmentalized fashion away from their daily activity, but the daily activity was their service to God.[39]

The Mission of Filling the Earth with Worship

So far in this chapter, we have been setting the metaethical foundations for ethics as worship by exploring what Scripture teaches us about the nature and character of God, the design and purpose of the created order, and the corresponding nature and function of human beings. Our attention now turns to a consideration of the missional task that God assigned to humans before the fall. We will consider this task in light of God's nature, the manner in which he created the world, and how he fashioned humans as worshipers.

A "Helper" in Worship[40]

When God placed Adam into the garden to worship and obey, he did not intend for Adam to be alone. Rather, God's grand design included the creation of Eve so that she could partner with Adam in accomplishing the great and final goal for which all creation was formed. By exploring Genesis 2:18–20 and Genesis 1:27–28, we discover how God designed these two equally valuable, yet crucially distinct, image-bearers to complement each other as together they set out to accomplish God's grand mission for his creation. Genesis 2:18–20 reads:

> Then the LORD God said, "It is not good for the man to be alone; I will make him a helper suitable for him." Out of the ground the LORD God formed every beast of the field and every bird of the sky, and brought them to the man to see what he would call them; and whatever the man called a living creature, that was its name. The man gave names to all the cattle, and to the birds of the sky, and to every beast of the field, but for Adam there was not found a helper suitable for him.

Several key elements in the passage are particularly relevant to our discussion. First, the text indicates that God identifies the solitary nature of Adam in the garden as something that is "not good." Interestingly, the passage does not stress an

---

39. Due, *Created for Worship*, 40.

40. A version of this section was originally published in Mark D. Liederbach and Alvin L. Reid, *The Convergent Church: Missional Worshipers in an Emerging Culture* (Grand Rapids: Kregel, 2009), 122–24.

emotional state of loneliness for Adam. Nor does it suggest that Adam was some-how pining away or sulking in the garden as he looked around to find a compan-ion. Indeed, he appears to be largely unaware of any need, since the text indicates that it is God, not Adam, who identifies the problem of Adam's being "alone." It would certainly be unwise to suggest that Adam, in perfect harmony and fellow-ship with God, was somehow "lonely" in the sense of emotional neediness. He experienced perfect relationship with the most fulfilling Being in existence—God himself. Even in light of Adam's relational harmony with God, however, there is something about Adam's being the only image-bearer in the garden that God determines to be "not good."

To remedy this situation, God first does something a bit unexpected in the flow of the text. That is, after declaring that it was "not good" for Adam to be alone, instead of immediately creating Eve, the text tells us, God first forms the beasts of the field and birds of the sky so that Adam might name them. Apparently, then, it was in the midst of this job of naming the animals that Adam began to realize that there was not a "helper suitable" for him. Perhaps in naming the animals, he saw that each had a corresponding mate but that he did not. We cannot know for sure what caused Adam to realize that there was no "helper suitable" for him because the text does not directly tell us. Regardless, only after this realization awoke in Adam did God set out on the task of creating a "helper suitable" to be Adam's wife. He created the first woman to be the perfect complement to the first man. The human male-female binary is God's perfect design to accomplish his purposes in the world.

A second and related point is that the text indicates that Adam was "alone" before God created Eve. He was not "lonely." Why is this important? Recogniz-ing that Adam was "alone" and not lonely helps us avert the unfortunate sugges-tion that God created women for the sake of solving some kind of "loneliness problem" for men. Adam's contentment was to be found in God. As we pointed out above, before Eve was created, Adam had a perfect, unblemished relationship with God, who is the most fulfilling Being that exists. In the presence of God, Adam could hardly be "lonely." Indeed, Jesus teaches us in the Gospel of Matthew that in heaven there will be neither giving nor taking of wives (Matt. 22:30). Why? Because we will each find our fullest joys in the presence of God. If fellowship with God is enough to satisfy us emotionally for eternity future, then certainly it was sufficient for Adam in the garden. This is not to say that God did not give a special grace of companionship to Adam and Eve when he gave them to each other as husband and wife. Indeed, the unitive and relational aspect of God's provision of marriage is a great good that should be identified as a crucial aspect of marriage. We will address this point in chapter 18. Here, however, the point of emphasis is that Adam's relational neediness was not God's primary motive for creating Eve.

As beautiful as it is for Eve to be Adam's wife, God's purposes for creating her are caught up into something even more profound than being his companion.

A third key element to explore in this passage relates to these questions: Why was it "not good" for Adam to be alone? For what purpose did Adam need a "helper suitable for him"? To best answer these questions, we need to return once more to a consideration of Genesis 1:27–28. Recalling the chiastic structure of the passage, we have already seen that in being made in the image and likeness of God, Adam and Eve were created to subdue the earth and rule over it as they worshiped and obeyed God by causing the garden to flourish. The part of the passage that we have not yet considered is the second part of the chiasm. From this we see that in being made as "male and female," Adam and Eve were created to "be fruitful and multiply, and fill the earth."

Table 2.4. Implications from the Chiastic Ordering of Genesis 1:27–28

God creates humans in his image and likeness → subdue the earth and rule over the earth
God creates human beings as male and female → be fruitful and multiply, fill the earth

As we look at Genesis 1:27–28 in this light, it becomes clearer why God would identify why it was "not good" for Adam to be "alone." Certainly, it would be impossible for Adam to be fruitful and multiply by himself. Thus, a procreative element is tied into the purposes of marriage. God designed the male-female, husband-wife relationship to be, at least in part, the means by which his purposes for the world would be accomplished. But while affirming this procreative element of marriage, we must again be careful not to regulate God's special depiction of Eve as a "helper suitable" as merely some type of baby factory to help Adam populate the earth. While being a wife and motherhood are both beautiful and praiseworthy aspects of womanhood, neither by themselves nor even together do they capture the fullness of God's design and intent for Eve.[41]

So why does God point out that it was "not good" for Adam to be alone? Why does God create a "helper suitable" for Adam? Simply put, it is because God desired that their relationship and fruitfulness would result in a world full of worshipers who would together maximize the glory of God being made manifest throughout

---

41. It is important to point out that if we reversed the flow of the conversation, we would come to the same conclusion for men. That is, if Eve had been created first, we would say the same thing for her: "how could she be fruitful and multiply without Adam?" Likewise, we would point out that certainly Adam's role would not be simply understood as that of a seed-producer to make babies. Finally, while we would certainly want to honor the high and glorious calling for the man to be a husband and father, we would likewise say that neither by themselves nor both together would they capture the fullness of God's design or intent for Adam.

all creation. Part of the fundamental purpose of marriage is to perpetuate the mission of God. The children born of Adam and Eve's union, as worshipers in their own right, were to take up the mission of God as well and champion forth the things of God by going into the created order and filling the earth with the knowledge of the glory of the Lord. They, like their parents, were to steward the creation in such a profound manner that it would manifest the glory of God and give marvelous testimony to the Creator's awesome and grand love. In short, through their complementary roles, Adam and Eve were designed to lead worship. We will address several of these points again in more depth in chapter 12 on creation care and environmental stewardship and in chapter 18 on marriage and divorce.

Table 2.5. Man and Woman as Creation's Worship Leaders

1. Men and women are equal in value and dignity as image-bearers.
2. Men and women have distinct, yet complementary, roles that they were designed to fulfill.
3. Each of the complementary roles is vitally important to accomplish the mission of God.
4. The value that God assigned to each of their roles is therefore equally lofty.

A Worship Mandate and a Great Commission

Finally, then, we can say that *if* Adam and Eve had not sinned, *if* they had remained pure, *if* they had obeyed God and fulfilled the task that God created them for, *then* they would have filled the earth with sinless worshipers united in one purpose: to subdue and rule the world in the name of God, for the glory of God.

Together the man and woman were to be fruitful and multiply. *Together* they were to fill the earth. *Together* they would raise their offspring to flourish before the One who had created all things and given them a purpose and order. *Together* they were designed to use all the gifts that God had given them to create cultures and societies of wonder—each human individually, and all humans corporately, maximizing all that they had been created to be so as to live abundant and flourishing lives together *for something much greater than themselves.* God remedied Adam's aloneness not so much because Adam was "lonely," but because remaining "alone" would make it impossible to complete the task that God meant for both Adam and Eve to accomplish: filling the earth, subduing the earth, and ruling the earth, all for the glory of God.

In sum, God designed human beings as missional worshipers and then embedded them in the created order so as to cause it to maximize his praise and glory throughout all the earth. As the first parents, they were designed and instructed to seed and shape the world and all the various cultures that would inevitably result from their choices, behaviors, and values as societies of worship. This is why

Genesis 1:27–28 is not only a *cultural mandate* but also a *worship mandate*. God gave Adam and Eve a *great commission* to fill the earth with people who called on God as their Lord, obeyed him in all their ways, and flourished as they worshiped through every thought and deed.

Conclusion: The Creation Order and Ethics as Worship

Having explored the creation narratives for guidance in understanding God and his design for the world, we can now pull these ideas together as the key building block for understanding the metaethical foundations of Christian ethics. We began the chapter with the premise that to properly understand Christian ethics, it is imperative that we first consider *Who* before we study the *how* of ethics. In this vein, we discovered from Scripture that God is the unique, eternal, self-existent, noncontingent Being who, through his many and splendid attributes, created all things as a loving Father and designed all things to express and experience the wonder of his glory. Into this grand symphony hall of worship that is our universe, God then created human beings in his image and likeness. He designed them to represent himself to the rest of creation, as well as to subdue and rule it as his champions of worship. In keeping with this, God tasked humans to do that which was most in keeping with who they had been created to be when he placed them in the garden of Eden to cause it to flourish as an ongoing act of worshipful obedience.

It is specifically at this point that the connection between ethics and worship should now be evident. Because God is the ground of all existence and because he is the One who, through his Word, reveals the nature of how things really are, then we can wholeheartedly agree with Oliver O'Donovan's assertion that "the way the universe *is*, determines how man *ought* to behave himself in it."[42] Morality is discovered, not invented.

Therefore, if ethics involves (1) the process of discovering right and wrong or good and evil, (2) the shaping of one's character to be able to desire to accomplish the proper behavior in every situation we face, and (3) evaluating and determining proper behavior, then, in the person and nature of God, we find the ultimate source of evaluation and the ultimate motive for behavior. God not only lovingly

---

42. Oliver O'Donovan, *Resurrection and Moral Order: An Outline for Evangelical Ethics*, 2nd ed. (Grand Rapids: Eerdmans, 1994), 17. It is precisely the point that this understanding of ethics overcomes the *naturalistic fallacy* (*is/ought fallacy*) because God is the source of both ontology and epistemology, and he reveals both when he reveals to us how things really are and then how we ought to live in light of them. Of course, the existence of God and the veracity of his revelation are key assumptions in this formulation that are not addressed in this book. But given these assumptions, which are foundational to the Christian faith, the so-called naturalistic fallacy is overcome.

created the universe with a design and order that reflects his own nature and character, but also designed human beings to live in that created universe and lead it to flourish through obedient worship in accord with his design and instruction. God is both the First Cause of all things and the final point of culmination of all things. This *exitus et reditus* ("exit and return") understanding of the being and function of the universe recognizes that God is "the Alpha and the Omega, the first and the last, the beginning and the end" (Rev. 22:13). As Peter Kreeft nicely puts it, "God is the ontological heart that pumps the blood of being through the arteries of creation into the body of the universe . . . and receives it back through the veins of man's life of love and will."[43]

From this perspective, it is a simple step to understand that the purpose of ethics is to guide the image-bearer not merely *to* worship—because we are worshipers by nature—but to be properly shaped and ordered as a worshiper who worships *well*. The discipline of ethics finds its center precisely on this point. Christian ethics is at its deepest roots a discipline that guides the image-bearer to appropriately, and increasingly, reflect back to God the glory he is due in and through every aspect of our lives.

By using a compass metaphor, we might depict this idea as follows:

TRUE NORTH
God

Image-Bearer

Fig. 2.2. Properly Ordered Worship

The image-bearer naturally wants to worship, but a proper understanding of Christian ethics helps to point our worship in the right direction. Getting our worship just slightly out of alignment can result in worshiping improperly or worshiping an improper vision of God. This is why *revealed reality* and *revealed morality* must be understood to work together in unison. Together they ensure that we are worshiping God *as he reveals himself* and *in the way he reveals for us to worship*.

---

43. Peter Kreeft, *A Shorter Summa: The Most Essential Philosophical Passages of St. Thomas Aquinas' Summa* (San Francisco: Ignatius, 1990), 15.

Thus, we come to the realization that A. W. Tozer was right when he wrote, "What comes into our minds when we think about God is the most important thing about us."[44] What we think and believe about God will shape our loves, our values, our thoughts, our actions, and our lives. It will also shape our ethics. For this reason, "the gravest question before the Church is always God himself, and the most portentous fact about any man is not what he at any given time may say or do, but what he in his deep heart conceives God to be like."[45]

In terms of how we understand ethics, our lives cannot possibly find proper ordering until we apprehend in the core of who we are that only one Being has the immensity and grandeur to send forth a universe from his glory as well as the gravity of self to pull it all back unto his praise. Therefore, every thought, love, motive, and deed is not primarily about us. It never has been. It never will be.

The apostle Paul clarifies the entire project of Christian ethics when he reminds us in 1 Corinthians 10:31, "Whether, then, you eat or drink or whatever you do, do all to the glory of God." Only when we come to grips with this foundational starting point for ethics do we begin to see the truly amazing nature of the entire discipline of ethics. Far more than a system of legalistic moralism, ethics is designed by God to be the good and right means, as well as the proper expression, for image-bearers in completing their mission of causing the entire created order to flourish through their obedient worship. It has an ever-outward-reaching momentum to fill the earth with God's glory and an ever-upward thrust to return to him all the praise, glory, and honor that he is due. When we finally get it, when we see that God stands at the center of all things, worship and ethics forever find their harmonizing point. It is in the One who composed the music of eternity.

The heart of ethics as worship is the simple fact that God is the center of the story. *How* can be rightly determined only in light of the One *Who* was "in the beginning." This is the most important fact of ethics. It is all about him. Always has been. Always will be.

Key Terms and Concepts

attributes of God	cultural mandate
champion	dignity
chiasm	dualism
collocation	dualistic holism
complementarianism	embedded headship
creation order	embodied self

44. Tozer, *Knowledge of the Holy*, 1.
45. Tozer, *Knowledge of the Holy*, 1.

exitus et reditus

Godness of God

helper suitable

I AM

imago Dei

metanarrative

missional worshiper

noncontingent Being

psychosomatic unity

revealed morality

revealed reality

steward

telos

temple of worship

worship mandate

Key Scriptures

Genesis 1:1

Genesis 1:26–28

Genesis 2:7

Genesis 2:15

Genesis 2:18–20

Psalm 19:1

Psalm 24:1

Romans 11:36

1 Corinthians 10:31

Revelation 22:13

Study Questions

1. Early in the chapter, the authors make the statement that "the Christian life will be properly applied only after it is properly grounded." Explain what this means. How does understanding God's design and purpose for the world help shape your own understanding of your life and purpose in the world?

2. Why is Genesis 1:1 such a crucial verse for understanding the foundations of Christian ethics? How should the first four words of the English Bible shape the way in which we understand the purpose of creation?

3. How should the realization that the glory of God is the final goal of creation shape how we understand our own moral choices and the entire discipline of ethics?

4. In this chapter, the authors make the argument that human beings are "embodied selves." What do they mean by this, and how ought it to shape our understanding of the goodness of both our bodies and our souls? Of our physical life and our spiritual life?

5. How is Genesis 1:26–28 related to Matthew 28:18–20? What are the implications for this as it relates to how a Christian ought to understand his or her mission in life?

For Further Reading

Due, Noel. *Created for Worship: From Genesis to Revelation to You*. Fearn, Ross-shire, Scotland: Christian Focus, 2005.

Dumbrell, William J. *Covenant and Creation*. Flemington Markets, New South Wales, Australia: Paternoster, 1984.

Gentry, Peter J., and Stephen J. Wellum. *Kingdom through Covenant: A Biblical-Theological Understanding of the Covenants*. Wheaton, IL: Crossway, 2012.

Reeves, Michael. *Delighting in the Trinity: An Introduction to the Christian Faith*. Downers Grove, IL: InterVarsity Press, 2012.

Tozer, A. W. *The Knowledge of the Holy*. San Francisco: HarperCollins, 1961.

Wenham, Gordon J. *Story as Torah*. Grand Rapids: Baker Academic, 2000.

Wright, Christopher J. H. *The Mission of God*. Downers Grove, IL: IVP Academic, 2006.

3

Revealed Reality: Ethics as Worship in Light of the Fall, Redemption, and Restoration

"The essence of idolatry is the entertainment of thoughts about God that are unworthy of Him."[1] —A. W. TOZER, The Knowledge of the Holy

"A gospel that is only about the moment of conversion but does not extend to every moment of life in Christ is too small. . . . A gospel that rearranges the components of your life but does not put you personally in the presence of God is too small."[2]
—FRED SANDERS, The Deep Things of God

Introduction

In the previous chapter, we set the foundation for understanding ethics as worship by arguing that from the beginning of creation, God designed ethics and worship to enjoy a complete overlap in the practice and experience of his image-bearers. We made this argument by developing five points:

1. The universe—everything and everyone in it—was created by a loving God and for God's own glory.
2. God created human beings in his image and likeness as *missional worshipers.*
3. When God placed Adam in the garden, he purposed him to worship and obey (Gen. 2:15).
4. God created Adam and Eve in a complementary fashion so that together, through their respective roles, they would lead all creation in worship.

1. A. W. Tozer, *The Knowledge of the Holy* (San Francisco: HarperCollins, 1961), 3–4.
2. Fred Sanders, *The Deep Things of God: How the Trinity Changes Everything*, 2nd ed. (Wheaton, IL: Crossway, 2017), 112.

5. Because living for God, and unto God, involves both who we are and what we do, then by divine design, ethics and worship were intentionally and integrally united by the Creator as one and the same thing.

The purpose of this chapter is to continue building our metaethical foundations for ethics as worship by exploring the next three aspects of the biblical metanarrative: fall, redemption, and restoration. Four questions will guide us along the way: How do sin and the fall impact our ability to live ethically and worship God rightly? How does the redeeming work of Jesus Christ impact our ability to live ethically and worship rightly? What does the doctrine of sanctification have to do with our ability to live ethically and worship rightly? And finally, by way of conclusion, what is the relationship between discipleship and ethics as worship?

How Do Sin and the Fall Impact Our Ability to Live Ethically and Thereby Worship God Rightly?

Moral Vertigo (Gen. 3:1–7)

As our discussion in the previous chapter about the *imago Dei* suggested, the crucial question that each person faces in life is not *whether* one is worshiping, but *whether one's worship is directed to the right end* and done *in the right way*. Discovering that the universe, and each of its elements, was designed and intended for the harmonious and total worship of God does not mean that this is what actually takes place. As Genesis 3 indicates, Adam and Eve's sin plunged not only themselves but the entire human race into a fundamental disordering. Consider Genesis 3:1–7:

> Now the serpent was more crafty than any beast of the field which the LORD God had made. And he said to the woman, "Indeed, has God said, 'You shall not eat from any tree of the garden'?" The woman said to the serpent, "From the fruit of the trees of the garden we may eat; but from the fruit of the tree which is in the middle of the garden, God has said, 'You shall not eat from it or touch it, or you will die.'" The serpent said to the woman, "You surely will not die! For God knows that in the day you eat from it your eyes will be opened, and you will be like God, knowing good and evil." When the woman saw that the tree was good for food, and that it was a delight to the eyes, and that the tree was desirable to make one wise, she took from its fruit and ate; and she gave also to her husband with her, and he ate. Then the eyes of both of them were opened, and they knew that they were naked; and they sewed fig leaves together and made themselves loin coverings.

When considering the impact of sin and the fall of the human race into rebellion, it is important to recognize the nature of Satan's deception as he tempted Adam and Eve to disobey God. One of the great ironies of this passage has to do with Satan's promise to Adam and Eve that by eating of the fruit they could become "like God" (Gen. 3:5). As we learned in the previous chapter, God had already created them in his "image" and "likeness" (1:26–27). They already possessed in their nature the moral alignment to know that it would be good to obey God and not to obey evil. The serpent's promise was not to give them something new and better, but to give them a false and inferior version of what they already possessed—the likeness of God (compare 1:27 with 3:5). Finding this desirable, they disobeyed the command that God had explicitly given to Adam in Genesis 2:16–17:

> The LORD God commanded the man, saying, "From any tree of the garden you may eat freely; but from the tree of the knowledge of good and evil you shall not eat, for in the day that you eat from it you will surely die."

When Eve plucked the fruit from the tree and gave it to her husband, who was standing "with her" (Gen. 3:6), they willfully rebelled against their good and loving Father. In so doing, they did not merely break a command, but shifted the direction of their love and worship away from the only One worthy of it. They traded a rightly ordered existence for a love focused on themselves.

Scripture indicates that this sinful choice, and the associated transference of worship, had devastating consequences. First and foremost, Adam and Eve's relationship with God was broken. Through this initial fall from grace, all humans (with the exception of Jesus Christ) have joined Adam and Eve in their sin. Romans 3:23 indicates that like our first parents, "all have sinned and fall short of the glory of God." Romans 6:23 goes on to state that the penalty of our sin is "death," or eternal separation from God (the truest definition of *death*).

As bad as this is, in terms of ethics, the fall also brings with it other consequences that greatly impact our ability to live morally as God designed. Scripture indicates that the fall also impacts our worldview, how we shape our cultures and societies, our very reasoning ability, and ultimately our understanding of morality itself. Indeed, as we will see from Scripture, the effects of sin so upend our perspective on the shape and nature of both reality and morality as to inevitably plunge each of us into what we might describe as *moral vertigo*.

To understand what we mean by this term, consider that the physical condition of vertigo is also known by the term *spatial disorientation*. In short, this phenomenon can happen to pilots when (for any number of reasons related to gravity, lack of visual stimuli, or the sense of balance in the inner ear) they experience a conflict between what their instruments are telling them about their position in space and what their own sense of perception leads them to believe. That is, the instrument panel on a plane may say one thing, but the pilot's self-perception of his position in space is telling him something else. When this type of disorientation happens, and the pilot experiences vertigo, he can actually think or perceive that he is flying right side up when in actuality he is flying upside down. Obviously, this is extremely dangerous. The choices that a pilot makes may "feel right" while in vertigo, but unless he reorients himself in light of reality, those choices will ultimately lead to disaster.

When we use the term *moral vertigo*, we employ the idea as a metaphor to explain what happens to human moral perception because of the darkening effects of sin on our minds and hearts. Moral ideas or decisions may *feel* right, but this does not necessarily mean that they *are* right. If morality is discovered and not invented (as we argued in the previous chapters), then like a good pilot we need to trust what our instruments are telling us more than our perceptions or intuitions. In Christian ethics, the instrument panel that we need to learn to trust is the Bible.

Scripture indicates that because of our sin, our ability to see the world and God's design for it is seriously compromised. Consider the following passages to make the point:

> For even though they knew God, they did not honor Him as God or give thanks, but they became *futile in their speculations*, and *their foolish heart was darkened*. Professing to be wise, they became fools. (Rom. 1:21–22)

> But a natural man does not accept the things of the Spirit of God, for they are foolishness to him; and *he cannot understand* them, because they are spiritually appraised. (1 Cor. 2:14)

> So this I say, and affirm together with the Lord, that you walk no longer just as the Gentiles also walk, in the *futility of their mind, being darkened in their understanding*, excluded from the life of God because of the ignorance that is in them, because of the hardness of their heart; and they, having become callous, have given themselves over to sensuality for the practice of every kind of impurity with greediness. (Eph. 4:17–19)

Morally and spiritually, human beings created by God to know him and live in worshipful obedience now find themselves living in *futility*. As a result of sin, our understanding about God and his design for the world is now *darkened* (Eph. 4:17–18). Our perceptions about the nature of reality have in turn become merely foolish speculations (Rom. 1:21–22). In this postfall "natural state," we have become so blind to God's design and laws that we *cannot* even understand or rightly "appraise" them (1 Cor. 2:14).

As hard as this might be to believe about ourselves, these Scriptures indicate that our inner moral and spiritual insight is so dramatically affected that our very perception of right and wrong has become distorted. Our worldview—the means by which we perceive, interpret, and judge reality—is askew.

In daily life, this means that sin makes it impossible for both individuals and societies to rightly discern all the ethical and moral patterns that God placed in the world. This means not that we never see God's moral patterns, but that they are wrongly interpreted, ignored in favor of personal preferences, or outright rejected. Worse still, Scripture tells us that we also have a proclivity (both as individuals and as entire societies) to exchange the truth for a lie and foolishly adopt alternative moral and spiritual ideas as our means of worship. This is no minor sin. As Paul tells us in Romans 1:23, we have "exchanged the glory of the incorruptible God" for something far inferior. And in so doing, we have exchanged the truth for a lie and have "worshiped and served the creature rather than the Creator, who is blessed forever" (Rom. 1:25).

As this moral vertigo becomes entrenched in our own hearts, it also begins to impact the moral patterns of the societies we form and the cultures we create. Not only do individuals seek to call that which is evil in the eyes of God "good," we also find that a certain "moral momentum" begins to gather within those societies, which in turn presses the culture as a whole to adopt moral standards that are in direct opposition to the ways of God. Whether it be laws legalizing abortion, euthanasia, same-sex marriage, slavery, or the glorification of morbid forms of entertainment, human societies as a whole can find themselves passing laws or adopting standards that stand in direct opposition to God's moral design and the instructions he gives to enable us to flourish. As the Scripture puts it, we not only choose to do what is right in our own eyes, but also gather to ourselves others who are in like-minded rebellion (Judg. 17:6; 21:25; Rom. 1:32; 2 Tim. 4:1–5). When this type of cultural momentum couples with moral vertigo, even the good news of the gospel is perceived as nothing more than a foolish tale (1 Cor. 1:18–25), and the moral values that God created for our flourishing will often be both shunned and mocked (2 Tim. 4:3–4). Morally and spiritually, we are "flying upside down" and headed for disaster.

When we look to Scripture, we can see these effects of sin on both individuals and societies in the chapters immediately following the description of the fall in Genesis 3. It is not long before those whom God designed as worshipers, who were also commissioned to be on mission as his champions to fill the earth with cultures of rightly ordered worship, instead find themselves killing one another and creating cultures of depravity. Instead of causing life and flourishing, they are in immediate need of instruction and warning not to shed one another's blood (Gen. 4:1–16; 9:6). Instead of "ruling" and "subduing" the earth in such a way that God's glory is maximized, sinful humans more often than not introduce forms and patterns of oppression and domination such that creation itself groans and longs for redemption (Rom. 8:22–24).

Returning to the compass metaphor that we introduced in the previous chapter, we can say that while Adam and Eve were originally created for—and oriented toward—*true north*, after sin their worshipful moral nature and orientation became fundamentally disoriented. Created to worship and obey, they did not cease their worship and morality, for it was inherent to the kind of creature they were. Rather, their worship and morality became disordered and was now directed to false ends. The image-bearers whom God created to know him and live for his glory are now separated from him, live for their own pleasures, and invent their own moral rules and social patterns in hopes of justifying their rebellion. As John Calvin so poignantly puts it, sin has turned our hearts into "idol factories."[3] Building on a previous illustration (see fig. 2.2), the following diagram (see fig. 3.1) illustrates the point.

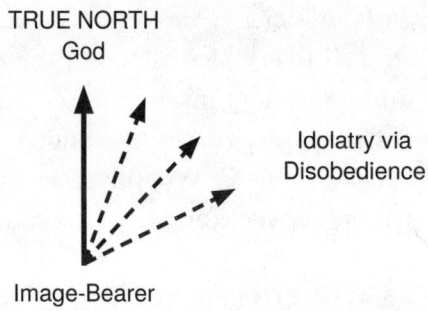

Fig. 3.1. Proper Worship versus Disordered Worship

As a result, we who were once perfectly aligned with God's will, and who were commissioned to create societies and cultures throughout the world that would fill the created order with ever-greater symphonies of praise, now live in a state of final futility. As individuals and as a society, we have become alienated from our four most basic relationships: our relationship with God, ourselves, one another, and the rest of creation. Instead of God's image-bearers' experiencing the ever-increasing fullness of our humanity through an everlasting life, Adam—and all of us since—has chosen *uncreation*. That is, we have chosen in

3. John Calvin, *Institutes of the Christian Religion*, ed. John T. McNeill, trans. Ford Lewis Battles, 2 vols., Library of Christian Classics 20–21 (Philadelphia: Westminster Press, 1960), 1.11.8.

our sinful state to move contrary to God's design in favor of moral degradation and everlasting death. Far from the original champions that God created, we have become hollow shadows of our original glory as we morally and spiritually fly upside down.

Ethics as Disordered Worship

Visually we can diagram the ethical trajectory of the human race after sin by referring to the diagram below (see fig. 3.2). The top line in the diagram represents the trajectory for which God originally created humans. He designed them to flourish for eternity future, in an ever-increasing journey of joy. They were to perpetually grow and enjoy his presence as they matured in their humanity through worshipful obedience. After the fall, these same image-bearers continue to worship, but their relationship with God is broken, the trajectory of their existence is disordered, and thus their moral worship is ordered to false ends. In this state, those on the bottom line of the diagram can conceive of the reality with only a partial knowledge or a *darkened understanding* of God's larger design for the world. In such a state, even the best deeds of sinners appear as nothing more than "filthy garments" before God (Isa. 64:6).

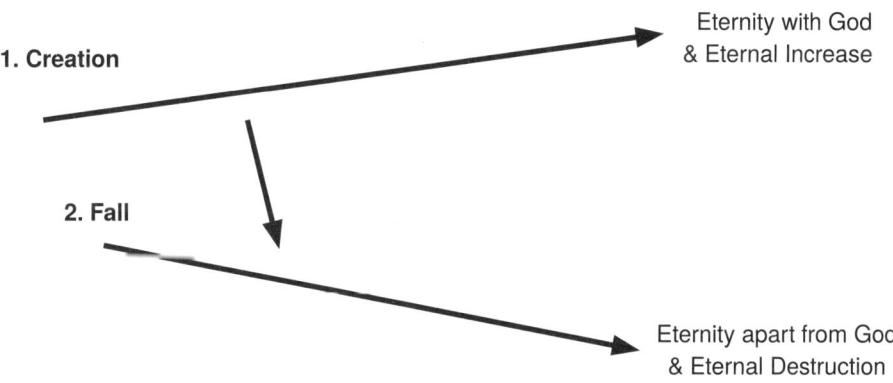

Fig. 3.2. Man's Trajectory Impacted by the Fall

The reality of these two trajectories raises the question whether a person could be *ethical* without being properly oriented to God. The answer depends on how one understands and uses the word *ethical.* If by this word one simply means behaving in a manner that flows from an internally coherent and consistent justificatory system within the frame of reference of the bottom line of the two-line diagram (see fig. 3.2), then the answer is "yes." Throughout the ages, humans have developed many ethical systems by which one could motivate and justify patterns of behavior beneficial to the human race within that frame of reference. Though the creation groans from sin, the inherent patterns and moral order still remain in reality. The moral fabric is still intact. Oliver O'Donovan captures this idea in his *Resurrection and Moral Order*:

> We are not so visited with the fruit of our moral disorder, that we find ourselves converted, like Odysseus' sailors, into swine. In this sense it is true to say that the image of God is "defaced" but not "lost" and thus some semblance of morality can be had by those apart from saving knowledge in Christ.[4]

While this defacing does not erase our moral worth as image-bearers, it does, tragically, include an ultimate disordering of both our acts and our character from the final *telos* for which God created us. Thus, in Adam, human beings are now relationally and spiritually "lost" and morally disordered.

If, however, one were to replace such an anemic understanding of the word *ethics* with the more biblically founded notion of ethics as worship that we have been exploring in this and the previous chapter, then the answer to the question "could one be ethical without being properly oriented to God?" would be "no." Apart from a right ordering to God, neither a person nor his or her moral choices could be *ethical* in the fullest and right sense of the word. The reason for this is that ethics is not merely about action or behavior; it is primarily about rendering to God what he is due: worship. It is only when someone is first properly related to God that the possibility exists for choices and behavior to be rightly and finally placed within a full context in which the behavior both aligns with God's moral design and is rendered unto him as acceptable worship. Only then could it be fully described as *ethical*. Any action or character trait that was not also aligned with God's initial design and final purposes would ultimately be judged as insufficient and disordered.

Likewise, any ethical system that did not hold God and his glory as the final purpose for moral behavior—even if it had good elements—would need to finally be assessed as fundamentally misdirected.[5] As O'Donovan puts it:

> If the Creator is not known, then the creation is not known *as creation*; for the relation of the creation to its Creator is the ground of intelligibility as a created universe. If one term of that relation is obscured, the universe cannot be understood.

4. Oliver O'Donovan, *Resurrection and Moral Order: An Outline for Evangelical Ethics*, 2nd ed. (Grand Rapids: Eerdmans, 1994), 88.

5. As O'Donovan puts it, the knowledge of God "is something from which we can turn away, refusing to glorify God as God. And in that case the universe confronts us as something which might have been understood but has in fact been misunderstood, giving rise to various kinds of idolatry in which the creature is regarded as absolute." O'Donovan, *Resurrection and Moral Order*, 88.

. . . Knowledge of the moral order is a grasp of the total shape in which, if anything is lacking, everything is lacking.[6]

St. Augustine makes a similar point in *City of God* when he argues that the apparent virtues modeled by the Romans and their empire were actually not virtues at all because "there is no reference to God in the matter." He argues that any moral activity or character quality that is not properly ordered to its final end is nothing more than "a splendid vice."[7]

Returning to the two-line diagram (see fig. 3.2), then, it is right to conclude that for the unbeliever—a person whose life is ordered by the bottom line in the diagram—it is impossible to be truly *ethical* in the fullest sense of what we are describing here with the notion of ethics as worship. Apart from God's saving work to rescue us and restore us back to his created design, the best we can attain is *ethics as disordered worship*. Apart from God's saving grace, even our best deeds and highest moral achievements fall desperately short.[8]

How Does the Redeeming Work of Jesus Christ Impact Our Ability to Live Ethically and Thereby Worship Rightly?

If the foundation of ethics as worship is God's *creation grace* (i.e., *first grace*) by which he designed and ordered the entire universe and caused it to exist, then after the fall ethics as worship relies on God's *saving grace* (i.e., *second grace*) to rightly order it to its final end. To understand this, we now turn to a brief consideration of the ethical foundation driving the central teaching on ethics in the Old and New Testaments.

Ethics in the Old Testament: God, Salvation, and Worship

When one turns to the central ethical teaching of the Old Testament—the Decalogue (the Ten Commandments) in Exodus 20—it is interesting to see that

---

6. O'Donovan, *Resurrection and Moral Order*, 88–89.

7. Augustine, *City of God*, 19.25, trans. Marcus Dods (New York: Modern Library, 1993), 707. Calvin also touches on this point in *Institutes*, 1.1.2. For a further rich discussion of this, see Waldo Beach and H. Richard Niebuhr, eds., *Christian Ethics: Sources of the Living Tradition*, 2nd ed. (New York: John Wiley & Sons, 1973), 108–9.

8. At this point, one might question why the believer strives to engage culture on points of ethical debate. Once again, it is vital to be clear on the distinction we are making. The fullest and most proper understanding of the word *ethics* is "that which properly worships God." The value of moral debate, then, has several points of overlap with general culture. First and foremost, morality debate in the culture should function in a manner consistent with Martin Luther's description of the first use of the law: to show us our need for Christ through its condemning action. Second, moral debate in culture should also function like the second use of the law: to restrain the culture from being as bad as it would otherwise be. Here we emphasize that the development

the passage begins neither with an imperative to moral action nor with the listing of the commands, but rather with a reminder of the saving work of God. Exodus 20:1–2 reads, "Then God spoke all these words, saying, 'I am the Lord your God, who brought you out of the land of Egypt, out of the house of slavery.'"

As we discussed in the previous chapter, God is the eternally preexistent Creator on whom the entire universe depends for its existence. When God self-identifies to Moses with the words "I am the Lord your God," he is reminding Moses and the people receiving the commandments that the One giving the commands—not the commands themselves—is the center point of focus. God is the ontological ground of everything. He is the source of existence. He is the source of morality. Only in him can the people created in his image flourish. These words are a reminder to Moses and the people that they ought to worship and obey simply because of who God is. In addition to this, we see in the remainder of the verse that God also reminds them that he is a good and gracious God. God is the One that brought them out of slavery. God is not just their Creator; he is also their *Savior*.

The point is both simple and profound: God, the One who was "in the beginning," is also their loving, kind, and gracious Savior. God is reminding the people with this preamble to the Decalogue that the commands they are about to receive come to them from the One who both designed them and saved them. It is out of God's kindness, mercy, and grace that the commands are given, and it is in light of God's kindness, mercy, and grace that they should be obeyed.

Before the fall, God's *first grace*, or *creation grace*, to create them as he did was the foundation for the harmonious overlap between ethics and worship. God designed them to be and live a certain way. If they had done so, they would have maximally flourished and worshiped. Now, after the fall, the *second grace* or *saving grace* of God becomes the point of a renewed harmony of ethics and worship. The ethical demands of the Ten Commandments were never meant as a means to earn God's favor. Rather, they are given to guide the people's proper response of thanksgiving, love, and worship to the God who rescued them from slavery.

Interestingly enough, this response of loving worship is even reflected in the ordering of the commandments themselves. The two tablets of the Decalogue are commandments establishing a comprehensive summary of the will of God for his people. The first tablet, which includes the first four commandments, guides how God's people ought to properly love him. The first four commands provide a proper final ordering of our ethics to God himself ("love God"). The remaining six commands instruct us on how to behave toward one another ("love others"). In other words, the Ten Commandments themselves are reflective of what Jesus

---

of virtues has a positive effect on humanity, but such virtues are really only "splendid vices" when viewed in light of the nonbeliever's position.

will affirm as the heart of the Old Testament law: to love God with all our heart, soul, mind, and strength (Matt. 22:37; cf. Deut. 6:4–5) and to love our neighbors as ourselves (Matt. 22:39) (see fig. 3.3).[9]

In sum, the central ethical teaching of the Old Testament establishes a clear connection between God's created order, God's saving grace, and our worshipful response to him, which in turn drives our treatment of those in society around us. David Peterson's comments summarize the point nicely:

> Decisive for understanding the Old Testament view of worship is the idea that the God of heaven and earth had taken the initiative in making himself known, first to the patriarchs of Israel and then, through the events of exodus from Egypt and the encounter on Mount Sinai, to the nation as a whole. . . . The whole system of worship . . . was designed to be a means of acknowledging and living in relation to God's royal and holy presence. Obedience to God in [religious] observance was to go hand in hand with obedience in matters of everyday life.[10]

Thus, we see that in the Old Testament, the ethical requirements of the people of God not only were grounded in the person of God but demanded an interlacing of both worship and obedience to the Creator, who had also rescued them from captivity. The created pattern of reality is both assumed and affirmed throughout the ethical teachings. After the fall, the work of God to bring salvation to his people drives the moral impetus of his followers. Faith in God, love for God, obedience to God, and worship of God together make up the proper shape of moral motivation for God's people.

The entire ethical system that God revealed in the Old Testament ultimately carried with it a future hope of final fulfillment. The sacrificial system, the moral teachings, and social structures all looked forward to a day when a perfect Prophet, Priest, and King would come and bring final rest to the people. The entire system looked forward to the coming of a Messiah, who would bring hope of a more perfect future redemption.

Looking back through the eyes of the New Testament and the teaching of Paul on this, we learn from Galatians 3:15–29 that the law and moral codes given to Israel were ultimately given to function as a tutor to help them see their need for salvation and lead them to Christ—the fulfillment of the law. The book of Hebrews teaches that the entire system of religious ceremony, moral practices, and ritual sacrifices was only a shadow of the future hope that God would bring in Christ

9. David W. Jones, *An Introduction to Biblical Ethics* (Nashville: B&H Academic, 2013), 110. Used with permission of the author.

10. David Peterson, *Engaging with God: A Biblical Theology of Worship* (Downers Grove, IL: InterVarsity Press, 1992), 48.

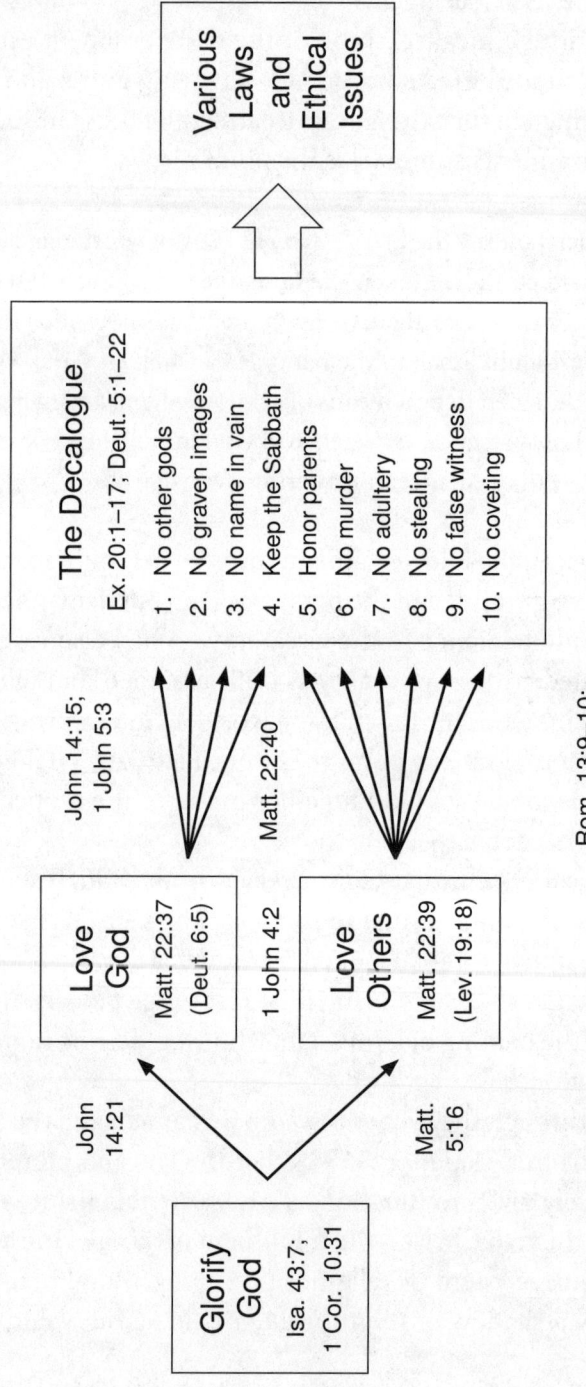

Fig. 3.3. The Structure of Biblical Ethics

(Heb. 7:18–29). The rituals and laws were meant to provide order and direction for a life of worship that would ultimately be superseded by a more perfect means that would allow for restoration of the created purpose of God's people.[11]

Ethics in the New Testament: God, Salvation, and Worship

As we turn to the New Testament, we discover once again that God's *saving grace* serves as the basis for a proper ethical response to God. The New Testament's teaching linking morality and ethics to the saving work of Christ is clearly on display in Ephesians 2:1–10. In Ephesians 2:1–3, Paul summarizes the devastatingly clear truth regarding the image-bearer's position or standing before God (*coram Deo*) apart from saving knowledge in Christ:

> And you were dead in your trespasses and sins, in which you formerly walked according to the course of this world, according to the prince of the power of the air, of the spirit that is now working in the sons of disobedience. Among them we too all formerly lived in the lusts of our flesh, indulging the desires of the flesh and of the mind, and were by nature children of wrath, even as the rest. (Eph. 2:1–3)

This passage indicates that the innate postfall direction of the human soul, apart from the redemptive atonement of Christ, is fundamentally disordered in every sinful human being. Referring back to our two-line diagram (see fig. 3.2), all sinful human beings find themselves on the bottom line—fallen from grace and destined to spend eternity apart from God. Sinners are not merely disordered away from God; in their sin, they have aligned themselves with Satan ("prince of the power of the air") and stand against God.

It is important not to underplay the potency of this situation. Paul is teaching the Ephesian believers (and all of us) that when humans fell from grace in the garden, they did not stop worshiping. Rather, their worship became disordered. It was inverted. They were flying upside down in moral and spiritual vertigo. Our sinful disposition of maleficent worship left us "dead in [our] trespasses and sins." Rather than filling God's magnificent symphony hall with praise and glory, the human soul now sings a song of filth and discordant blasphemy.

As the passage indicates, this fallen condition places all who have sinned (all of us!) in the horrific position of being an enemy of God whose worship is given over to Satan. No wonder Paul tells us that God now considers sinners to be "children of wrath."

In a contrast that could not be starker, however, Ephesians 2:4–9 reveals to us the amazing kindness and grace of God even toward these same sinners. The

---

11. David Clyde Jones, *Biblical Christian Ethics* (Grand Rapids: Baker, 1994), 109.

passage begins with what we can only describe as the most beautiful "but" in Scripture. Paul uses this word of contrast to emphasize the oppositional and like-wise unimaginable riches that God so lavishly heaps on those who would become children who are saved by his grace through faith in Christ:

> But God, being rich in mercy, because of His great love with which He loved us, even when we were dead in our transgressions, made us alive together with Christ (by grace you have been saved), and raised us up with Him, and seated us with Him in the heavenly places in Christ Jesus, so that in the ages to come He might show the surpassing riches of His grace in kindness toward us in Christ Jesus. For by grace you have been saved through faith; and that not of yourselves, it is the gift of God; not as a result of works, so that no one may boast. (Eph. 2:4–9)

Note that the passage begins with an affirmation of the central role that God plays. The possibility of change and restoration rests not on a person's own abilities or efforts, but first on God and his good works on our behalf. Particularly, it is based on God's work of *justification* on our behalf that Paul is emphasizing the same point we saw in Exodus 20 regarding the foundations of the Ten Commandments. It is God's first and preemptive work of grace to save us that becomes the foundation of ethics.

By *justification* we mean God's judicial act of pardoning sinners, making them righteous, and accepting them as justified such that their relationship and standing with himself is permanently made right.[12] It is God's declaration that a sinner has been made righteous in the eyes of God on the basis of grace alone and taken advantage of by faith alone.

Consider the list of graces that mark the believer's new position *coram Deo* ("before the face of God") because of Christ's justifying work. Those who were once dead are made alive, and furthermore, those who were destined to experience the wrath of God are now *raised up*. Those who were followers of Satan are now *seated* with Christ in the heavenly places. Although they were destined to spend eternity apart from God, they will now be shown the *surpassing riches of grace* in perpetuity.

Not only is this a picture of what has been accomplished regarding the forgive-ness of our past sins, but it is a declaration of triumphal hope that accompanies every believer as he or she faces any given situation. In terms of our ethical motiva-tions to live for God and pursue Christian maturity and moral formation, we must lock onto the reality that as a good Father, God took the initiative to find us, and at great cost he has welcomed us home. Because of Christ, we have actually been adopted by God and have become children of the King of the universe (Gal. 4:5).

---

12. J. I. Packer, *Concise Theology* (Wheaton, IL: Tyndale, 1993), 164.

And because of this adoption, Christ's disciples have been granted the remarkable privilege to cry out to God, "Abba! Father!" and can know that he will call back to each of us as his children "son!" or "daughter!" as he literally delights over us (Zeph. 3:17; Rom. 8:15–16). J. I. Packer gets it right: "The New Testament gives us two yardsticks for measuring God's love. The first is the cross; the second is the gift of sonship."[13]

Table 3.1. Positional Truths

Before Saving Faith (Eph. 2:1–3)	After Saving Faith (Eph. 2:4–9)
Dead in trespasses	Recipients of mercy
Walking according to the ways of the world	Objects of love
Following the prince of the power of the air	Made alive with Christ
Sons and daughters of disobedience	Saved by grace
Living in the lusts of our flesh	Raised by grace
Living in the lusts of our minds	Seated with Christ in heaven
Children of wrath both individually and societally	Recipients of surpassing riches of grace
	Recipients of surpassing riches of kindness

This "gift of sonship" that Packer refers to not only involves the fact that in Christ we are restored to a relationship with God as our Father, but also implies even more remarkable spiritual blessings. As Romans 8:17 indicates, if we have become children of God, then we have also become God's heirs with Christ. Scripture tells us that we become partakers with Christ in the fullness of what he accomplished through his birth, death, and resurrection.

- Galatians 2:20 tells us that we have been *crucified* with Christ.
- Romans 6:4 tells us that we have been *buried* with him through baptism into his death.
- Romans 6:4 also tells us that we have been *resurrected* with him into life.
- Ephesians 2:6 tells us that we are *raised* with Christ.
- Ephesians 2:6 also tells us that we are *seated* with Christ in the heavenly places.

In other words, we have been co-crucified, co-buried, co-resurrected, co-raised, co-ascended, and co-seated with Christ in heaven next to the throne of God,

---

13. J. I. Packer, *Knowing God* (Downers Grove, IL: InterVarsity Press, 1973), 214.

where Jesus our Savior then "always lives to make intercession for [us]" to the Father (Rom. 8:34; Heb. 7:25).

Truly this is a gift that is not only undeserved but so stunning in nature that it should cause us to rejoice and respond in thanksgiving and love for eternity future. When rightly understood, the dramatic transformation pictured ought to drive us to ask, "What kind of God would love me in such a way?" Or as the New King James translation captures the idea: "Behold what manner of love the Father has bestowed on us, that we should be called children of God!" (1 John 3:1 NKJV).

This leads to a clear recognition, understanding, and appreciation of Paul's placement of the ethical imperative as the climactic point of application in the Ephesians 2:1–10 passage:

> For we are His workmanship, created in Christ Jesus for good works, which God prepared beforehand so that we would walk in them. (Eph. 2:10)

Paul sees a necessary link between the saving grace of God in Christ's atoning work and the Lord's call to a life of obedient worship. In light of God's gift of salvation, one's view and practice of morality and ethics ought to be radically transformed. *Out* with cold legalism or calculating moralism. *In* with a passionate desire to worship such an amazing God with every fiber of our being and every breath that is in us.

Two points must be made explicit if one is to understand the importance of the good news expressed in the previous verses and their relationship to the ethical instruction given here. First, it is crucial to note that "good works," moral effort—ethics—are to come on the heels of salvation. In other words, the good works in Ephesians 2:10 are mentioned only after verses 1–9—*after* Paul's explanation of the gospel and also *after* our conversion. Obedience is a result of salvation, not the work to achieve it. Second, Paul directly links the good news of the gospel to God's design to obey and do good works that were put in place "beforehand," that is, *in the beginning*. Here we see in the life, death, resurrection, and ascension of Christ an affirmation of the purposes of the universe embedded by God into the created order. We were built for good works ("His workmanship") and designed to "walk in them." Ethics overlaps with worship and mission. As it was in the beginning, so now it can be once again in Christ.

The following diagram (see fig. 3.4) builds on the earlier one (see fig. 3.2) to illustrate the point. The atoning work of Jesus Christ through his life, death, and resurrection (the gospel) rescues us from the penalty of the fall and once again places us on the ethical (worshipful) trajectory that we were created for. Ethics as worship, then, is not only theocentric in nature, but radically Christocentric.

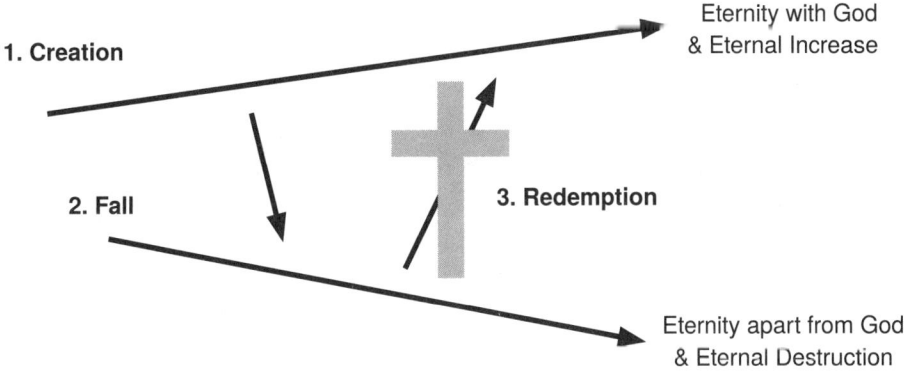

1. Creation

Eternity with God
& Eternal Increase

2. Fall

3. Redemption

Eternity apart from God
& Eternal Destruction

Fig. 3.4. Man's Trajectory through Redemption

What Does Sanctification Have to Do with Our Ability to Live Ethically and Thereby Worship Rightly?

While the metaethical foundations of ethics as worship are grounded in God's *creation grace* and restored to their final end through God's *saving grace*, it is through God's *sanctifying grace* that image-bearers can once again rightly order their ethics and worship to God.

Sanctification

For the person saved by the grace of God through faith in Jesus Christ and restored to right relationship with the Father, *sanctification* is the process in and by which new believers become in both their character and their deeds what God has initially designed them to be and now has saved them to be. It is what happens *after* a person believes, and it involves the transformation of both character and behavior. The work of sanctification in the life of a Christian is heavily dependent on the work of the Holy Spirit to reshape the life of the image-bearer such that the believer becomes "conformed to the image of [Christ]" (Rom. 8:29).

Crucial for the discussion of ethics as worship, it is important to distinguish between justifying grace and sanctifying grace, but we must be careful to never separate them. Together these doctrines help save us from the erroneous view that our moral and ethical behavior can possibly serve to make us favorable to God. No, only Christ can do that for us through justification. Our morality and ethics are a means of worship after we have been rescued and believe. On the other hand, they also help save us from the idea of *cheap grace* in which a believer who has been justified may be tempted to think that because of Christ's saving work he or she need not worry about obedience. No, while we are saved by grace alone, saving grace is never alone. Love for God is best demonstrated by obedience to God (John 14:15). Wayne Grudem summarizes the distinctions between justification and sanctification in the following table[14] (see table 3.2).

Table 3.2. Distinctions between Justification and Sanctification

Justification	Sanctification
Legal standing	Internal condition
Once for all time	Continuous throughout life
Entirely God's work	We cooperate
Perfect in this life	Not perfect in this life
The same for all Christians	Greater in some than in others

The New Testament word translated from the Greek into English as "sanctification" is *hagiasmos.*[15] This word is based on the same root word from which we get our English word *holiness.* A common assumption that often accompanies these English words *sanctification* and *holiness* is that they denote the idea that something is to be "set aside" in order to keep it morally pure and unstained by the vain things of this world. Certainly, this is true, but if this is all that is understood about *hagiasmos*, then we have done the concept an injustice. When a person is set free by the gospel, he or she is not only set free *from* the power of sin and death, but also set free *to* pursue the fullness of what God created the person to be and do. In the words of Paul: "It was for freedom that Christ set us free" (Gal. 5:1).

Thus, it is important to highlight that sanctification is not merely the process of being removed or separated from sinful tendency; it involves a fervent pursuit of the things of God. It rests on a believer's being saved *from* the power of sin and death and being *made holy* through the work accomplished by Jesus (justification), and then applied to the person by the Holy Spirit. In addition, it denotes a wholehearted devotion to *pursuing* and *becoming* in order to embody the great benefits of what it means to be a child of God rescued by Christ and regenerated by the Holy Spirit.[16] As Peter Gentry puts it, "holiness should not be defined as moral purity, but rather purity is the result of being completely devoted to God."[17]

---

14. Wayne Grudem, *Systematic Theology: An Introduction to Biblical Doctrine* (Grand Rapids: Zondervan, 1994), 747.

15. Frederick William Danker et al., eds., *A Greek-English Lexicon of the New Testament and Other Early Christian Literature*, 3rd ed. (Chicago: University of Chicago Press, 2000) (BDAG), s.v. "ἁγιασμός."

16. Jonathan T. Pennington, *The Sermon on the Mount and Human Flourishing: A Theological Commentary* (Grand Rapids: Baker, 2016), 74.

17. Peter J. Gentry, "The Meaning of 'Holy' in the Old Testament," *BibSac* 170, no. 680 (2013): 400–417.

In the language of ethics, sanctification is the key doctrinal foundation for the development of rightly ordered and shaped character and *virtues*.[18] We can define *sanctification*, then, as *the work of the Holy Spirit to help disciples of Jesus Christ to become in character and practice what God has declared them to be in truth.* It involves understanding three distinct stages: (1) what has been accomplished in and by Christ and applied to us by the work of the Holy Spirit; (2) what still needs to be accomplished in us in terms of our character and practices as the Holy Spirit matures us into conformity with Christ; and (3) the final transformation into Christlikeness that will happen on that day when we stand before him and see him face to face (1 John 3:2). We can therefore speak of three stages of sanctification—*positional*, *progressive*, and *final* or *perfect*. We will address each stage, and along the way continually refer to their importance for the process of moral formation.

Positional Sanctification

Positional sanctification has much in common with the doctrine of justification and is often confused with it. When we speak of this aspect of sanctification, we are addressing the Holy Spirit's work to apply the benefits of justification to our lives. It begins by understanding that when the Holy Spirit regenerates a person and he or she confesses sin, asks forgiveness, and places his or her faith in Jesus Christ, God's grace saves that person through his or her faith. Paul teaches us in 2 Corinthians 5:21 that this involves God's making Jesus (who knew no sin) to be sin for us, so that in Jesus we might have the full righteousness of God *imputed* to us. By *imputation* we mean that the righteousness lived out by Jesus is placed on those who believe, and it is credited to our account. Our sinfulness, on the other hand, is placed on Jesus and credited to his account. He lived the life that we should have lived, and he died the death that we should have died. As a result, God's work in Christ and through the Holy Spirit dramatically changes our standing before God. Whereas before we were enemies of God lost in sin, now we have become righteous before God. As John Calvin states:

> We are justified before God solely by the intercession of Christ's righteousness. . . .
> Man is not righteous in himself but because the righteousness of Christ is communicated to him by imputation. . . . For in such a way does the Lord Christ share his righteousness with us that, in some wonderful manner, he pours into us enough of his power to meet the judgment of God.[19]

---

18. John Frame makes a similar argument in the concluding chapter of his extensive volume on ethics, *The Doctrine of the Christian Life*. He entitles the chapter "Growing in Grace." See John M. Frame, *The Doctrine of the Christian Life* (Phillipsburg, NJ: P&R Publishing, 2008), 911–29.

19. Calvin, *Institutes*, 3.11.23.

Once this "great exchange" takes place, Scripture teaches us, a definite moral change occurs within us. Believers literally and actually are made righteous before God because we have been given the righteousness of Christ. And based on this, we literally and actually are "sanctified" by the Holy Spirit as he applies the work of Christ to our lives. As Paul puts it in 1 Corinthians 6:11: "Such were some of you; but you were washed, but you *were sanctified*, but you were justified in the name of the Lord Jesus Christ and in the Spirit of our God." Here Paul's language looks back on our salvation and sanctification as a completed event.[20] And again in Titus 3:5, he indicates that the application of this great work of sanctification to our lives is due to the agency of the Holy Spirit on our behalf: "He saved us, not on the basis of deeds which we have done in righteousness, but according to His mercy, *by the washing of regeneration and renewing by the Holy Spirit.*"

For this reason, the first stage of our sanctification is often referred to as a forensic, relational, or *positional sanctification.* The emphasis is on the permanent state of being that we enjoy in Christ. As both the righteous Judge and the redeeming Savior, he declares us justified and reconciled to himself, and establishes us secure in our position with him in light of the righteousness he imputes to those who call on his name in faith. This positional sanctification focuses on identifying *whose* we now are because of the gospel.

At least five elements of positional sanctification are particularly important for *our moral formation*. The first of these relates to God's *declaration regarding our sins*. Romans 8:1 tells us that "there is therefore now *no condemnation* for those who are in Christ Jesus." For this reason, once the Spirit applies salvation to us and sanctifies us, we actually stand before God justified. The words "not guilty!" resound in heaven around the judgment seat of God for those who have believed in Christ. We are legally—forensically—declared by God to be completely innocent. Because of this pronouncement, we can have confidence to live boldly for God as we make moral decisions.

Second, as we discussed earlier related to our justification, we can know that at the moment of genuine faith, a person's *position* before God as a sinner who deserves hell shifts dramatically. Not only does God declare us not guilty, we are now made citizens of his kingdom with all the rights and privileges that go with it. Colossians 1:13–14 tells us that "He rescued us from the domain of darkness, and transferred us to the kingdom of His beloved Son, in whom we have redemption, the forgiveness of sins." This initial stage of sanctification moves us from being far off as aliens to citizens of the kingdom of God. We have motivation to pursue holiness and conformity to Christ as good subjects of the King.

Third, positional sanctification restores the *relational* beauty of our standing

20. Grudem, *Systematic Theology*, 747.

before God. Specifically, because of the work of Christ to accomplish our salvation and of the Holy Spirit to apply it to our lives, God adopts us and makes us his sons and daughters. John 1:12 tells us that "as many as received Him, to them he gave the right to become children of God, even to those who believe in His name."

Fourth, because all these great truths regarding our positional sanctification have been applied to us by the Holy Spirit, Christ's followers are now actually "dead to sin" and in contrast "alive to God in Christ Jesus" (Rom. 6:8–18). Morally this means that because sin is no longer our "master," we have been "freed from sin" and no longer *have to* sin. We have become free (as Adam was before the fall) to not sin. As Grudem writes: "To be dead to the ruling power of sin means that we as Christians, by virtue of the power of the Holy Spirit and the resurrection life of Christ working in us, have power to overcome the temptations and enticements of sin. Sin will no longer be our master, as once it was before we became Christians."[21]

This is not to suggest that we will achieve a sinless life here. We will not reach a point of moral perfection in this lifetime.[22] Nor does it imply that we will even have immediate release from all temptation. Rather, it means that sin no longer *rules* over us. To understand this, we want to take care to make a distinction between the words *capacity* and *ability*. In Christ, our capacity to avoid sin has been restored, but in our practice we still need to work on strengthening our ability to avoid sin. This strengthening of our ability to avoid sin and live for Christ is the goal of *progressive sanctification.* By God's grace, we will find that our ability to avoid sin gets stronger with each day we walk with Christ, but the lingering effects of sin are so potent in our lives that we will not see this ability fully realized until we experience our final and perfect sanctification in the presence of Christ. We will address this more fully in chapter 4.

Fifth, as we mentioned above, often when we speak of "salvation," the focus is on what we have been *saved from.* Given our conversation about sin and the punishment we have earned, this is totally appropriate. But in light of our larger conversation about ethics, it is just as important to point out that the biblical idea of salvation is not only about salvation from sin; it also implies return to a healthy relationship with God and realignment to his eternal plan. As Al Wolters notes, "virtually all of the basic words describing salvation in the Bible imply a *return* to an originally good state or situation. Redemption is a good example. . . . The point of redemption is to free the prisoner from bondage, to give back the freedom he or she once enjoyed."[23]

21. Grudem, *Systematic Theology*, 747.

22. For a helpful discussion on the possibility of moral perfectionism, see Grudem, *Systematic Theology*, 750–52.

23. Albert M. Wolters, *Creation Regained: Biblical Basics for a Reformational Worldview*, 2nd ed. (Grand Rapids: Eerdmans, 2005), 69–70.

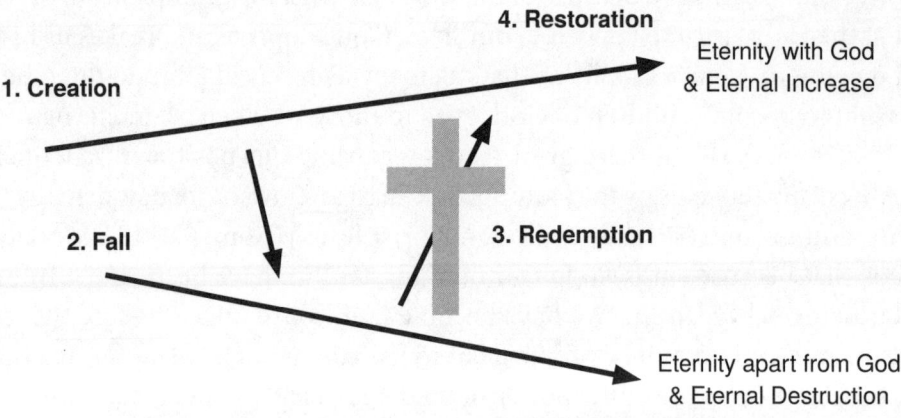

Fig. 3.5. Man's Trajectory Restored

Wolters goes on to point out:

> In a very significant sense this restoration [through the gospel] means that salva-
> tion does not bring anything new. Redemption is not a matter of an addition of
> a spiritual or supernatural dimension to creaturely life that was lacking before;
> rather, it is a matter of bringing new life and vitality to what was there all along. . . .
> The only thing redemption adds that is not included in the creation is the remedy
> for sin, and that remedy is brought in solely for the purpose of recovering a sinless
> creation. . . . Grace restores nature, making it whole once more. . . . If the whole
> creation is affected by the fall, then the whole creation is also reclaimed in Christ.[24]

Saving grace enables us to once again pursue that which we were created to
pursue. God's saving grace enables us to once again pursue the end for which we
were created: flourishing in the presence of God and to the glory of God. "We
must go beyond thinking of redemption as *mere* restoration, the return of a status
quo. The redemption of the world, and of mankind, does not serve only to put us
back in the Garden of Eden where we began. It leads us on to that further destiny
to which, even in the Garden of Eden, we were already directed."[25] Saving grace
puts us back on our mission of worship (position 4 on figure 3.5).

Freed from sin by Christ, we are brought back into right relationship with
God in that we are freed to become more like him as the image-bearers that he
created us to be. *In Christ*, we are restored to the joyful task of knowing him and
making him known. *In Christ*, we are restored to worshiping him and extending

24. Wolters, *Creation Regained*, 71–72.
25. O'Donovan, *Resurrection and Moral Order*, 55.

that worship to the ends of the earth and every people, tribe, tongue, and nation (Rev. 5:9; 7:9). *In Christ*, we are restored to obeying him and calling all humanity and the created order to render to him the obedience of faith that he is worthy of.

Table 3.3. Great Commissions

Old Testament Great Commission (Gen. 1–2)	New Testament Great Commission (Matt. 28:18–20)
In the beginning God (Gen. 1:1)	All authority is given to Jesus
Be fruitful and multiply, fill the earth (Gen. 1:28)	Go . . . and make disciples of all the nations
Image-bearer who is like God (Gen. 1:27)	Baptize disciples (total identification with Christ)
Worship and obey (Gen. 2:15)	Teach disciples to obey all that Jesus commands
Ethics is worship	Ethics is worship

In this we see once again the complete overlap of the initial *worship mandate* that God issued to Adam and Eve in Genesis 1:26–28 with the Great Commission that Christ gave to his disciples in Matthew 28:19–20. Restoration involves a reengagement of the missional aspect of our nature and purpose that should have impact on the world and cultures we live in. After the life, death, and resurrection of Jesus Christ, the means of the mission take on a new form. Evangelism is the means of inviting God's image-bearers back to their created purpose (2 Cor. 5:18). Discipleship is the means by which God's children are to be fruitful and multiply and fill the earth with worshipers (Matt. 28:18–20; 2 Tim. 2:1–2). Likewise, cultural engagement for the purpose of creating cultural patterns that honor God and of transforming society is now the means by which God's restored image-bearers are to rule the earth and subdue it for his glory (Luke 4:18–19; Rom. 13:4; Col. 1:20). As the Christmas hymn "Joy to the World!" proclaims, God's project of reclamation extends *as far as the curse is found*.

Humankind, which botched its original mandate and the whole creation along with it, is given another chance in Christ; we are reinstated as God's managers on earth. The original good creation is to be restored. . . . Marriage should not be avoided by Christians, but sanctified. Emotions should not be repressed, but purified. Sexuality is not simply to be shunned, but redeemed. Politics should not be declared off-limits, but reformed. Art ought not to be pronounced worldly, but claimed for Christ. Business must no longer be relegated to the secular world, but must be made to conform again to God-honoring standards.[26]

Every sector of human life must be claimed back *for* and *to* the glory of God. Table 3.4 summarizes the relationship between positional sanctification and ethics as worship.

Table 3.4. The Importance of Positional Sanctification for Ethics as Worship

Benefits of Positional Sanctification	Related Importance for Ethics as Worship
Forgiveness	Confidence to live boldly
Citizenship in the kingdom of heaven	Life orientation directing our actions
Adoption into "sonship"	Love for the Father as moral motivation
Dead to sin	Freedom from sin as our master and ability to choose not to sin
Restoration to original created purpose and toward the final *telos*	Reengagement of missional component of ethics as worship

Progressive Sanctification

The second stage of sanctification has to do with the ongoing process of experiencing in our daily practices and attitudes the truth of what God has declared to be true of us because of the finished work of Christ. This is frequently described as *moral* or *progressive sanctification* whereby we work in cooperation with the Holy Spirit to constantly, and increasingly, become more conformed in our character and our practices to the person of Christ. It is a critical part of understanding and living out ethics as worship because it focuses on knowing *who we are to become in light of the gospel.*

Christ has fully accomplished the work of our justification, and there is nothing that we need do (or could do) to bring about our own salvation. But having

---

26. Wolters, *Creation Regained*, 70–71. Here we also want to point our readers to an important discussion of the relationship between God's mission for the church and the function of Christian ethics as it relates to the proclamation of the gospel through evangelism and discipleship and the good works of Christians personally and in society as the embodiment of Christianity. See Kevin DeYoung and Greg Gilbert, *What Is the Mission of the Church? Making Sense of Social Justice, Shalom, and the Great Commission* (Wheaton, IL: Crossway, 2011), 91–113.

been saved by God's grace, we must pursue being made holy in our character and in our practices. For while it is true that the gospel saves us from our sins, it does not remove us from the context of a sinful world (1 John 2:15–17). It does not automatically remove our sinful desires (Gal. 5:16). And there is still an adversary in the devil who seeks to morally derail us and even kill and destroy us (John 10:10a; 1 Peter 5:8).

While it is true that the work of redemption is finished and the whole of creation is *reclaimed* in Christ, between *this* day and *that* day when we finally see God face to face and all things are finally and completely made new, we still live in a broken world that is bent in on itself. We live, as it were, in a "time between the times." Our sanctification has the flavor of being in a state of the *now and not yet*. In light of both our positional sanctification and the reality of the broken world that we currently inhabit, our discipleship must involve a *resting* in and on the truths of the gospel, and also a *striving* to live out who we should be as children of God.

In this vein, it is right to understand that when Scripture instructs us to "work out [our] salvation with fear and trembling" (Phil. 2:12), it is giving us a rather demanding call to whole-life discipleship. It implies that we stand firm on the truths of our positional sanctification and aggressively seek to rightly order our worship unto God through both character formation and daily obedience in our everyday moral practices. This is how virtues are developed in a true worshiper of Jesus Christ. Progressive sanctification involves the disciplined shaping of every area of our lives so that we worship the Lord rightly at all times and thereby devotedly embody our image-bearing status as we were created to be *in the beginning*, and rescued to be in Christ.

What does it mean to "work out [our] salvation"? Philippians 1:6 tells us that it begins with the promise that "He who began a good work in you will perfect it until the day of Christ Jesus." And Philippians 2:13 tells us that it involves God himself, "who is at work in you, both to will and to work for His good pleasure." Indeed, this is why the Holy Spirit's role is so important. For as the third person of the Trinity, the Holy Spirit "works within us to change us and sanctify us, giving us greater holiness of life."[27] But it also involves each of us working with and in accord with the Holy Spirit to become in character and practice what God has declared us to be in truth. We will discuss the process of progressive sanctification again in chapter 4 as we return to these ideas within the context of understanding the Holy Spirit's role in transforming us into "true worshipers" who worship God "in spirit and truth" (John 4:23–24).

---

27. Grudem, *Systematic Theology*, 754.

Table 3.5. Categories of Sanctification

Positional Sanctification	*Whose* we are by God's gracious work and declaration: "I have been saved"
Progressive Sanctification	Becoming *who* we have been declared to be: "I am being saved"
Perfect Sanctification	*Whose* we are and *who* we are in perfect harmony forever: "I will be saved"

Perfect Sanctification

The third stage of sanctification has to do with the final experience of our transformation in the presence of God when our practices and attitudes fully align with the finished work of Christ. For this reason, it is often referred to as our *future sanctification* because it will take place in heaven. It is also known as our *final sanctification* because it will restore us fully to the image and likeness of God. Perhaps it is best described as our *perfect sanctification*, for it will mark our perfect conformity to the image of Christ. Ultimately, it concerns the full realization of our positional status as *true worshipers* who worship God in spirit and truth (John 4:23–24). It focuses on the complete harmonization of *whose we are* with *who we will be* in heaven.

We can more fully develop the concept of perfect sanctification by exploring the meaning of 1 John 3:2:

> Beloved, now we are children of God, and it has not appeared as yet what we will be. We know that when He appears, *we will be like Him, because we will see Him just as He is.*

This passage teaches that for Christians, there is a day in our future when we will stand before God and "we will see Him just as he is." The language that theologians use to describe this event is *beatific vision*. The word *beatific* describes something ecstatic, joyful, rapturous, exalted, or glorious. This phrase literally means the "blissful sight" of God.

When Christ's disciples finally behold the beautiful glory of God, this encounter will immediately generate two all-consuming loves that will transform them forever. First, they will find their highest joy and deepest love because they are in the presence of the only One worthy of all their love. In his majestic and splendid character, God alone will be clearly revealed as the one perfect and glorious object of love and devotion. In the light of his presence, everything else will become obviously and immeasurably inferior to his infinite splendor. Second, because

God is the one perfect and glorious object of love and devotion, humans will find their highest joy in loving him—and this will in turn somehow redound to their loving him even more. They will love him because he is the source of joy, and they will love him because loving him makes them so joyful. He is worthy of our love, and it is joyful to love him.

Not only does 1 John 3:2 tell us that we will see God, but it also tells us that because we will see him, we will be *made like him*. In the Old Testament, when Moses begged the Lord to show him his glory, God replied that if any mere mortal were to look upon him, the vision would kill him (Ex. 33:18–20). So the Lord hid Moses behind a cleft in a rock and covered his eyes so that he could see only a mere glimpse of the divine. God did this to spare his life. The awesome nature of God's glory would literally have killed Moses if God had not mediated the vision. But in heaven, because the Holy Spirit applies God's sanctifying grace to us, not only does Christ's work provide us with the permission to be there, the Spirit's application of grace also strengthens and enables us to actually thrive in the presence of God. Because of Christ, no longer will this encounter *kill* us—rather, it will *transform* us.

When the Bible tells us that we will "be [made] like Him," this does not mean that we will become divine in our nature. God alone is God. Our essential nature will always be distinct. The text is teaching us that we will be similar to him as the image-bearers that we were created to be before Adam and Eve sinned. Therefore, the transformation that is initiated by the life, death, and resurrection of Christ, and then applied to us through the working of the Holy Spirit, is God the Father's means of placing things back in order. In the presence of God and through the grace of God, we once again finally and without blemish will become like him—as he created us to be.

Christ's disciples will finally taste what they were made for *in the beginning*, what they have longed for all their lives, and what they have finally found in the welcoming eyes of their Savior.[28] Theologians describe this as the *summum bonum* or ultimate good for which all things strive.

What Is the Relationship between Discipleship and Ethics as Worship?

Between the *now* of our lives and the *not yet* of this glorious future, ours is the long road of struggle and growth as we seek to fill out and embody that which God designed for us in the beginning and redeemed us to in Christ. This is why Christian ethics must be understood in terms of discipleship. Put in the form of

---

28. Mark Liederbach, *Chasing Infinity: Discipleship as the Pursuit of the Infinite Treasure* (Orlando, FL: Cru Press, 2017), 164–67.

a question, we might at this point ask: "If through the saving work of Jesus Christ God has made it possible for us to live worshipful lives as we were designed, how do we best do so?" The answer is found in discipleship.

What Is a Disciple?

Why is understanding discipleship important for our metaethical understanding of ethics as worship? When rightly understood, the word *discipleship* captures the essence of God's plan for his image-bearers and their quest (now struggle) to live a moral life as God designed from creation into eternity. To see this, reflect once again on the words of the Great Commission:

> Go therefore and make *disciples* of all the nations, baptizing them in the name of the Father and the Son and the Holy Spirit, teaching them to observe all that I commanded you; and lo, I am with you always, even to the end of the age. (Matt. 28:19–20)

In the English language, a simple, straightforward reading of the text seems to put emphasis on the word "go" as the primary command of the passage. Yet this is not the case in the original Greek from which we get our English translations. In the original language, the main verb and command imperative of the sentence is actually the term "make disciples" (*mathēteuō*), based on the root word for "disciple," which is *mathētes*. What is a disciple?

In classical Greek culture, ancient philosophers such as Plato and Aristotle used the term *mathētes* to describe "one who is a diligent student." But for the Greeks, this did not merely imply someone who gathers and memorizes information. Rather, the "Greek philosophers generally understood that the disciple's life involved apprenticeship, a relationship of submission, and a life of demanding training."[29] It was a relationship that included the disciple's commitment to the mentorship of the teacher for an extended period, normatively in the group context and involving both formal elements of instruction and passive and informal elements of instruction as the disciples followed, observed, and participated in informal situations and contexts of the teacher's daily life and routine.[30]

When used in the New Testament, the word carries a very similar meaning. Technically speaking, the word derives from a term meaning "to learn." Thus, a disciple of Jesus is one who learns from him as the Master Teacher. But again, the English word *learner* (or even *student*) does not capture the fullness of the

---

29. Bill Hull, *The Complete Book of Discipleship: On Being and Making Followers of Christ* (Colorado Springs: NavPress, 2006), 53.

30. Sylvia Wilkey Collinson, *Making Disciples: The Significance of Jesus' Educational Methods for Today's Church* (Eugene, OR: Wipf & Stock, 2004), 24.

meaning. *Mathētes* indicates not merely someone who gains information, but also one who intentionally "follows" and "conforms" his or her life to the patterns and character of the one whom he or she is following. The learning is holistic and involves the shaping of the disciple's acts, choices, attitudes, behaviors, desires, and affections. The goal is that the disciple will eventually become so much like the one whom he or she is emulating that his or her very life begins to reflect the same characteristics and purposes of the one being followed. One could say that one is to become conformed to the image of the one whom he or she is following.

This conforming of one's whole life requires study, practice, effort, repetition, and persistence through time. This is why the English word *disciple* is rooted in the idea of discipline. A *disciple* is someone who *disciplines* himself or herself to become like the one being followed. This includes both life practices and purpose. The Scriptures bear this idea out. For example, Jesus tells his disciples to "abide" or "remain" in him (John 15) and be *"fully trained"* (Luke 6:40). Paul also exhorts Christ-followers to *imitate* Christ (1 Cor. 11:1), *discipline* their bodies (1 Cor. 9:27), *put off* old behaviors and *put on* new ones (Col. 3), and *train* in godliness (1 Tim. 4). ⟶ *thankyou Jesus!*

Hence, restoration of one's own life—being conformed to the image of God as a disciple of Jesus Christ—involves hard work and discipline over time. Even in recognizing this fact, the experience of being a Christian disciple is meant to be one of joy precisely because of the One to whom a disciple is conforming his or her life. We are called by God to become like Jesus, who, as Colossians 1:15 tells us, is the "image of the invisible God." Christian discipleship is the process of restoration that involves pressing on to become more like Jesus in all aspects of our humanity. The goal for all disciples is to rightly display the image of God as we were created to do in the beginning and as Jesus did perfectly while on the earth (Rom. 8:29).

Disciple-Making and Ethics

Of course, as we have been discussing throughout these chapters, ethics is not merely a personal journey of worship and the transformation of our own lives. It also involves the restoration of all things to God for their joy and God's glory. That is why it is important to understand that in Matthew 28:18–20 the command imperative of the passage is not to "be a disciple" but to "make disciples" (*mathēteuō*). Jesus not only wants us to pursue our own discipleship, not only wants us to live ethically, but desires restoration to extend to all nations and *as far as the curse is found*. As it has been from the beginning, the Lord wants all the earth to be filled with worshipers.

By putting disciple-making as the point of emphasis, Jesus made a direct connection for the disciples between what they had experienced for the past three years as they lived and walked with him and what they were commanded to do for others. Having walked with Jesus, learned from him, and conformed their lives to his, they were now ready to embark on the mission to reach the nations with the hope of the gospel. The time had come for them to "go out into the world and win others who would come to be what they themselves were—disciples of Christ."[31]

While the instruction to "make disciples" is the central point of the command, within the passage are also three other words that in the English appear to have the power of command themselves: "go," "baptize," and "teach." In the original Greek language, these phrases are actually not commands in and of themselves, but participles that are connected to the main verb "make disciples" (*mathēteuō*). This is important because when the meanings of the participles "go," "baptize," and "teach" are hinged to the central commanding verb, they both shape the command and take on its force. In other words, Jesus is commanding his disciples to:

1. Make disciples as they *go* to the nations.
2. Make disciples and *baptize* them in the name of the Trinity.
3. Make disciples, being sure to *teach* them to obey everything he commanded.

By stating the Great Commission in this fashion, Jesus not only provided a command for us to obey, but also gave us the criteria by which to know whether we are obeying the command. One can determine whether he or she understands the missional component of ethics by evaluating how well one carries out each of these elements. Our lives, in other words, are meant to show the quality of our discipleship, and our involvement in God's mission (or not) helps us evaluate whether we understand the missional purpose of ethics as worship. Therefore, taking a closer look at the meaning of each of these participles is important.

The Greek participle translated into English as "go" comes from the verb *poreuomai*. The participle carries with it the sense of continuing or pursuing a quest that one has already started ("as you go about your everyday affairs") as well as carrying command force that one should set out and pursue the task of making disciples.[32] When attached to the verb "make disciples," it conveys that there should be intentionality about making disciples that pervades all the rhythms of a Christ-follower's life. Everywhere a Christian goes, regardless of where or how he or she earns a paycheck, the believer is to be about the task of making disciples.

---

31. Robert Coleman, *The Master Plan of Evangelism* (Old Tappan, NJ: Spire, 1963), 108.

32. For a discussion of this dependent participle and its implied imperatival force, see D. A. Carson, "Matthew," in *Matthew, Mark, Luke*, ed. Frank E. Gaebelein, Expositor's Bible Commentary 8 (Grand Rapids: Zondervan, 1984), 595.

Further, because a Christian is to be intentional about making disciples, he or she ought to look at going to places both locally and among the nations where there currently are no disciples. The Lord wants his followers in every waking moment to be about the business of his kingdom work—making disciples.

The word translated "baptize" in the English comes from the Greek word *baptizō*. This word literally means to "dip" or "submerge" something. Baptism symbolizes the death, burial, and resurrection of Jesus Christ. As disciples are baptized, they are identifying with (or being conformed to) the person of Christ. The whole self belongs to the Father, Son, and Holy Spirit. Whether one is eating or drinking, in every thought or deed, everything is to be done in the name of God and thus according to his will and plan. Ethical living is part and parcel of the Great Commission. In this sense, it builds on the word "go" because when people are totally identified as Christ-followers, they can't help but bear witness both actively and passively anywhere they "go." It also anticipates the need for teaching because in order for one to demonstrate a total identification, he or she must know the commands to obey and model them for all to see.

The third Greek participle, translated into English as "teach," is *didaskō*. This word literally means "to cause to learn" and relates to the imparting of knowledge from one person to another. In this sense, it implies that the commands of Christ are *known and followed* by the Christian, and that it is normative for the Christian to *instruct others* in the commands of Christ in such a way that they learn it, live it, and impart it to others. By connecting "teach" to "make disciples," Jesus is indicating that anyone who claims to be his follower must be eager and purposeful to *learn and follow* Jesus' commands, but will be just as eager and purposeful to *teach* others to do likewise.

What does all this have to do with developing a normative framework for ethics as worship? Everything! From the beginning, God created humans to worship him, obey him, and make his glory manifest throughout all creation. In Christ's final words, he instructed his followers to make disciples who would obey all his commands and teach others, who would totally identify with him in all of life, and who would seek to make his glory manifest throughout all creation. In both life and mission, from the beginning and then again in Christ, all of human life is to be about not only personal worship of God, but seeing that the glory of God is manifest throughout creation.

In sum, we see that our understanding of ethics—because it is concerned both with *who* we are to be and with *what* we are to do—is directly connected to how we understand Jesus' call on us to be his disciples. It has a missional outward thrust, it has an emphasis on character and behavior, and it seeks to instruct others to go and do likewise.

Ethics is both personal and missional.

Summary and Conclusion

In the previous chapter, we began an exploration of the metanarrative story line of the Bible (creation, fall, redemption, restoration) in order to set the meta-ethical foundations for ethics as worship. In this chapter, we continued in that theme by focusing on the final three elements of that story line: fall, redemption, and restoration. We then turned our attention to the topic of discipleship in order to understand the connection between the discipline of ethics, worship, and God's mission to make disciples of all nations.

Having reached this point in our discussion of the metaethical foundations for ethics as worship, we believe it is now helpful to list and summarize the meta-ethical foundations that we have discussed in this and the previous two chapters. We offer the following list by way of summary:

1. As the eternally preexistent loving Creator, God created all things and designed all things to find their highest flourishing in him and return to him all the glory he is due. This *exitus et reditus* ("exit and return") understanding of the being and function of the universe recognizes that God is the Alpha and Omega of all things.
2. Everything, including ethics, has its source in God. He is the ground of all being, the Creator of the universe, and the architect of how the universe functions.
3. Because ethics is grounded in God and reflective of his nature, it is both objective and universal. Morality is to be discovered, not invented.
4. By creating human beings in his image, God uniquely designed them as image-bearers who by nature are designed to champion—and tasked with championing   forth God's glory to the rest of the created order and to steward the created order such that it would ever-increasingly display God's glory and return it back to him. Ethics, then, is both missional in nature and directly related to evangelism.
5. As image-bearers, all humans are by nature worshipers, and therefore their actions are always acts of worship. The question is never *whether* they worship but rather *who or what* they worship and whether the worship is *in accord with* God's design.
6. Because of the way in which God designed both creation as a whole and image-bearers in particular, human beings will flourish most excellently when they live according to the nature God gave them in alignment with the patterns of morality he embedded into creation.
7. In choosing to sin, human beings did not cease worshiping; they disordered it. As a result, not only is their relationship with God broken,

but their role of leadership in the created order is likewise fundamentally disoriented and in antithesis with God's good design as their worship is given over to lesser things.

8. After the fall and because of their sin, human beings experience brokenness in all parts of their nature. Their minds, wills, and affections are all now darkened and incapable on their own of ordering moral choices to the ultimate final end.

9. Christ's redeeming work of atonement is necessarily the only basis for human beings to once again be rightly ordered to God both relationally and morally.

10. Between the *now* of justification and the *not yet* of final glorification, we walk the road of progressive sanctification by living as disciples who are conforming our lives to Christ's and are engaged in his mission. Sanctification is the ongoing process of becoming in our character and practices what God has declared us to be in truth through the gospel.

Ethics as worship is not primarily about actions, behaviors, character traits, or consequences. Ethics is about God and his glory. Ethics as worship is grounded on God's first *creation grace* and is rescued and restored by God's *saving grace* that reorients image-bearers to their appropriate expression of loving, obedient worship and mission. Ethics begins with God, our moral lives are lived out *for* God, our ethics are rendered *unto him*, and ultimately they culminate *in* God. To put it simply, ethics as worship is the application of vibrant, orthodox, worshipful theology to loving, obedient, missional living. It is a quest of discipleship that began in the garden of Eden, was restored at Calvary and through the open tomb, and will reach its zenith when we see God face to face and pursue his infinite wonder for eternity future.

For this reason, it is entirely appropriate to build our normative methodology for an ethic of worship from within the framework of Christian discipleship and particularly in light of Jesus' Great Commission to "make disciples of all the nations" as given in Matthew 28:18–20. Discipleship and the discipline of ethics are interwoven pathways on which we must walk if we are to live lives of worship and see to it that the earth is filled with Christ-centered, God-honoring worshipers. Both *ethics* and *discipleship* can be defined as "the disciplining of our worship patterns (both individually and corporately) so that we can love God and maximize the manifest glory of God throughout the earth." Ethics as worship requires discipleship as its shaping framework. Discipleship requires ethics as worship as its material content and guidance on how to accomplish its mission.

In this light, it is now appropriate to consider as the final stage of understanding our metaethical foundations the means that God makes available to us such that we might worship him fully through our ethical endeavors. In the next two chapters, we will consider the ethical implications of Jesus' statement that the Father is looking for worshipers who will worship him "in spirit and truth" (John 4:23–24). It is to this discussion that we now turn.

Key Terms and Concepts

adoption	justification
beatific vision	moral formation
capacity versus ability	moral vertigo
conformity to Christ	obedience of faith
creation grace	positional truth
curse	redemption
darkened understanding	restoration
death	sanctification, perfect
Decalogue	sanctification, positional
discipleship	sanctification, progressive
disordered worship	sin
fall, the	sonship
first grace	submission
flourishing	true north
idol factory	uncreation
imputation	

Key Scriptures

Genesis 1:26–28	Romans 5:8
Genesis 3:1–7	Ephesians 2:1–10
Matthew 28:18–20	Ephesians 4:17–18
Romans 1:21–22	1 John 3:2
Romans 3:23	

Study Questions

1. According to Romans 1:21–22 and Ephesians 4:17–18, human sinfulness results in a "darkened" understanding of the world. Why is this an important concept for understanding why ethics must be gospel-centered? How does the reality of this "darkening" of our minds relate to the need for ethics to have an external source of authority (such as the Bible) to guide moral behavior?

2. In this chapter, the authors claim that the Ten Commandments were not given as a means to earn God's favor. Rather, they were given to guide a proper response of thanksgiving, love, and worship to God. How does Exodus 20:1–2 set up the context of the giving of the Ten Commandments that follow in Exodus 20:3–17?

3. Ephesians 2:10 is a key verse for understanding the connection between God's first grace in our lives, his second grace in our lives, and the importance of ethics for discipleship. Read over the verse and explain how it connects ethics to God's plan "in the beginning" (Gen. 1:1).

4. What is the beatific vision, and why is it important for motivating Christian ethics (1 John 3:2)?

5. How is Christian ethics related to both the cultural mandate and the Great Commission? Citing the "Creation, Fall, Redemption, and Restoration" diagram in the chapter, explain the connection between Genesis 1:26–28 and Matthew 28:18–20.

For Further Reading

Hull, Bill. *The Complete Book of Discipleship: On Being and Making Followers of Christ*. Colorado Springs: NavPress, 2006.

Liederbach, Mark. *Chasing Infinity: Discipleship as the Pursuit of the Infinite Treasure*. Orlando, FL: Cru Press, 2017.

O'Donovan, Oliver. *Resurrection and Moral Order: An Outline for Evangelical Ethics*. 2nd ed. Grand Rapids: Eerdmans, 1994.

Packer, J. I. *Knowing God*. Downers Grove, IL: InterVarsity Press, 1973.

Pennington, Jonathan T. *The Sermon on the Mount and Human Flourishing: A Theological Commentary*. Grand Rapids: Baker, 2016.

Peterson, David. *Engaging with God: A Biblical Theology of Worship*. Downers Grove, IL: InterVarsity Press, 1992.

Wolters, Albert M. *Creation Regained: Biblical Basics for a Reformational Worldview*. 2nd ed. Grand Rapids: Eerdmans, 2005.

4

Worship in Spirit and Truth: The Role of the Holy Spirit in Ethics as Worship

"The essence of the Christian religion consists in this, that the creation of the Father, ruined by sin, is restored in the death of the Son of God, and re-created by the grace of the Holy Spirit into a kingdom of God."[1]
—HERMAN BAVINCK, Reformed Dogmatics

"If we live by the Spirit, let us also walk by the Spirit."
—GALATIANS 5:25

Introduction: The Kind of Worshipers That God Is Looking For

In the previous two chapters, we have explored the metaethical foundations for ethics as worship. By studying the metanarrative story line of the Bible through a paradigm of creation, fall, redemption, and restoration, we were able to see that God created us as worshipers on mission to see the earth filled with his glory. Each of our lives (and all our lives together) was meant to be lived in accord with God's design and instruction. Our sin, however, disordered our worship, our ethics, and our sense of mission (individually and corporately). Because of sin, even our best efforts to live morally fall short of God's perfect standards and his glory (Isa. 64:6; Rom. 3:23). But God, being rich in mercy, sent the second person of the Trinity, Jesus Christ, to live a sinless life, die a death that he did not deserve, and triumphantly rise from the dead, that we might be saved by grace through faith in him and his atoning work. In terms of ethics, we discovered that this redemptive work of Christ not only provides salvation *from* our sin, but also paved the way for us to be saved (or restored) back *to* God's

---

1. Herman Bavinck, *Reformed Dogmatics*, vol. 1, *Prolegomena* (Grand Rapids: Baker Academic, 2003), 112.

original design and ultimate *telos.* Using the language of the Westminster Larger Catechism, we might say that Christ made it possible once again for his disciples to shape their ethics in order to live maximally toward their chief end: to glorify God and enjoy him forever.[2]

Having established this theological baseline for ethics as worship, we now want to complete our discussion of metaethics by exploring the means by which God desires his disciples to worship him fully and enjoy him maximally. In question form, we are asking: "What provision has God made for his followers to maximize their worship and thereby mobilize their lives for his glory and their own good?" Or: "By what means has God made it possible for his disciples to embody and live out ethics as worship?" Thankfully, Jesus tells us the answer. In John 4, he declares:

> An hour is coming, and now is, when the true worshipers will worship the Father in spirit and truth; for such people the Father seeks to be His worshipers. God is spirit, and those who worship Him must worship in spirit and truth. (John 4:23–24)

If it is the task of this book to explain why and how Christian ethics ought to be understood and pursued by and through a disposition of worship, then it is imperative that we explore what Jesus means when he teaches that "true worshipers" must worship God in both "spirit" and "truth." D. A. Carson's comments are helpful toward this end. He writes that "spirit" and "truth"

> are not two separable characteristics of the worship that must be offered: it must be "in spirit and truth," i.e. essentially God-centered, made possible by the gift of the Holy Spirit, and in personal knowledge of and conformity to God's Word-made-flesh, the one who is God's "truth," the faithful exposition and fulfillment of God and his saving purposes [Jesus Christ].[3]

---

2. WLC 1, http://www.pcaac.org/wp-content/uploads/2012/11/LargerCatechismwithScriptureProofs1.pdf.

3. D. A. Carson, *The Gospel according to John*, PNTC (Grand Rapids: Eerdmans, 1991), 225. There is some debate as to what exactly Jesus means by the terms "spirit" (*pneuma*) and "truth" (*aletheia*). A common means of translating this phrase is to place emphasis on having a proper inward and outward disposition toward God. See, e.g., Andreas J. Köstenberger, *John*, ed. Clinton E. Arnold, Zondervan Illustrated Bible Backgrounds Commentary (Grand Rapids: Zondervan, 2002), 48. F. D. Brunner, however, agrees with Carson's rendering when he offers a strong rebuttal to this common translation that places emphasis on our inward and outward disposition. Brunner writes: "No! Spirit, *pneuma* in the Gospel of John, is in its majority usage not our 'inwardness' but the reality of the Holy Spirit. And 'truth' in the Gospel of John is not one of Plato's Forms or Ideas; no, it is the person of the Lord Jesus Christ ('I am the Way, the Truth, and the Life,' Jesus famously says at John 14:6). The Holy Spirit will even be called 'the Spirit of Truth,' in Jesus' closet teaching, the Discipleship Sermons (14:17; 15:26; 16:13)." Frederick Dale Brunner, *The Gospel of John: A Commentary* (Grand Rapids: Eerdmans, 2012), 262–65. See also Craig S. Keener, *The Gospel of John: A Commentary*, vol. 1 (Grand Rapids: Baker Academic, 2003), 619; Graham A. Cole, *He Who Gives Life: The Doctrine of the Holy Spirit* (Wheaton, IL: Crossway, 2007), 83, 236; John F. Walvoord and Roy B. Zuck, *The Bible Knowledge Commentary, New*

The driving purpose of this chapter and the next is to finish laying the meta-ethical foundations for ethics as worship by exploring what Jesus means when he tells us that we must "worship in spirit and truth." In short, we will argue in this chapter that worshiping God in *spirit* depends on the working of the Holy Spirit to restore us by shaping our character, that we might be conformed to the image of Christ. In the next chapter, we will argue that worshiping God in *truth* depends on Jesus—the One who is both "the truth" and the living "Word"—to provide us with the Scriptures as our authoritative guide for all areas of our life and practice (John 1:1; 14:6; Heb. 4:12). It is through the guidance of Scripture that our actions are rightly shaped, such that whatever we do, in word or deed, we do all to the glory of God. Attending to each of these in turn will enable a more robust understanding of the distinctively Trinitarian nature of ethics as worship, as well as set our future discussions regarding normative and applied ethics within the appropriate context of what it means to be a disciple who worships God in "spirit" and "truth."

Specifically as relating to this chapter, five questions guide us along the way: Why is understanding who the Holy Spirit is important for ethics as worship? Why is understanding the Holy Spirit's role as a Paraclete important for ethics as worship? What are the means of transformation that the Holy Spirit uses to shape our character? What does the process of the Holy Spirit's shaping us into true worshipers entail? What are the results of the Holy Spirit's work as they relate to ethics as worship?

Why Is Understanding Who the Holy Spirit Is Important for Ethics as Worship?

The Divine Personhood of the Holy Spirit

The first step of understanding the Holy Spirit's work in transforming us into the kind of "true worshipers" who can embody ethics as worship is to understand his nature both as God and as a person. In regard to his divine nature, the New Testament clearly sets him forth as the third divine person of the Trinity, who, like the Father and the Son, has the attributes, nature, and authority of the one true God. One of the clearest examples of this in Scripture is found in the Great Commission, where Jesus commands his apostles to go and make disciples of all nations, baptizing them in the name of the Father, Son, and Holy Spirit (Matt. 28:19), and thereby equating the Spirit with himself and the Father. Another example that demonstrates the Scriptures' testimony to the divine nature of the Holy Spirit is in the book of Acts when Peter confronts the sin of Ananias and Sapphira:

Testament Edition (Colorado Springs: David C. Cook, 1983), 286.

> But Peter said, "Ananias, why has Satan filled your heart to lie to the Holy Spirit and to keep back some of the price of the land? While it remained unsold, did it not remain your own? And after it was sold, was it not under your control? Why is it that you have conceived this deed in your heart? You have not lied to men but to God." (Acts 5:3–4)

Peter understood that lying to the Holy Spirit was a lie to God himself and therefore an offense of ultimate proportion.[4]

These two passages are merely representative of the witness given throughout the New Testament where the Father, Son, and Holy Spirit are linked together in unity and all three are given the status of equal divinity (e.g., 1 Cor. 12:4–6; 2 Cor. 13:14; Eph. 1:3–13; 1 Peter 1:2). According to R. C. Sproul: "The Bible so clearly represents the Holy Spirit as possessing divine attributes and exercising divine authority that since the fourth century his deity has rarely been denied by those who agree that he is a person. Though there have been many disputes concerning the question of whether the Spirit is a person or an impersonal 'force,' once it is admitted that he is indeed a person, the fact that he is a divine person falls easily into place."[5]

Sproul's comment is helpful because when we discover that the Holy Spirit is God, we also discover from the witness of Scripture that he is indeed a person who shares the same divine essence as the other two persons of the Trinity, yet is distinct from both the Father and the Son. To be clear, what makes him distinct is his divine personhood. Like Jesus and the Father, he is God, and like Jesus and the Father, he is also a person. One of the clearest and simplest ways in which we see Scripture distinguish the Holy Spirit from the other two persons while also affirming his personhood is the use of personal pronouns to reference him and his work. Scripture always refers to the Holy Spirit in terms of "He" and not "it" (see, e.g., John 15:26; 16:5–8).

In addition to these personal references, Scripture records that the Holy Spirit hears, speaks, leads, guides, commands, teaches, intercedes, and can be grieved—all of which are the actions or responses of a personal being.[6] For this reason, J. I. Packer is emphatic: "So I plead: never think or speak of the Holy Spirit in less than personal terms! . . . For you cannot understand the Spirit's ministry till you have grasped the fact of his personhood."[7]

---

4. Millard J. Erickson, *Christian Theology*, 3rd ed. (Grand Rapids: Baker Academic, 2013), 297.

5. R. C. Sproul, *The Mystery of the Holy Spirit* (Fearn, Ross-shire, Scotland: Christian Focus, 1990), 21. See also Cole, *He Who Gives Life*, 69–72. Cole further develops the idea that the biblical presentation of the attributes of the Holy Spirit is that they are the same attributes typically attributed to God.

6. See John 14:26; 15:26; 16:7–15; Acts 2:4; 8:29; 13:2; 16:6–7; Rom. 8:14, 16, 26–27; Eph. 4:30.

7. J. I. Packer, *Keep in Step with the Spirit: Finding Fullness in Our Walk with God*, 2nd ed. (Grand Rapids:

Paraclete

Understanding the fact that the Holy Spirit is the third divine person of the Trinity is important because it sheds light on how he carries out his role as our *Helper*. On the night of the Last Supper, knowing that he would soon be crucified, Jesus addressed his disciples to encourage and comfort them. In this context, he promised that he would send the Holy Spirit:

> I will ask the Father, and He will give you another Helper, that He may be with you forever; that is the Spirit of truth, whom the world cannot receive, because it does not see Him or know Him, but you know Him because He abides with you and will be in you. (John 14:16–17)

What did Jesus mean when describing the Holy Spirit with the term "Helper"? The word that Jesus used in the original Greek is *Paraclete* (*paráklētos*). While there have been many attempts to translate the meaning of this term into an English equivalent (as the New American Standard Bible has done with the word "Helper"), it is difficult to find an exact English parallel that captures the meaning of the term. The word is derived from the prefix *para-*, meaning "to come alongside" or "close beside," and the root word *kalien*, meaning "to make a call." It can mean "helper," "comforter," "champion," "counselor," or "intercessor." In fact, many scholars choose not to attempt a translation and simply stick with the transliteration ("Paraclete") because of the richness of its meaning.[8] Importantly, however, the implication of the word in its historical context can, in addition to the meanings given above, indicate a person called to come alongside as an advocate or helper as in a court of law.[9]

This leads us to an important nuance as it relates to understanding ethics as worship. While it is commonplace among Christians to speak only of the Holy Spirit as *the* Paraclete, Jesus actually describes him as "*another* Paraclete." Jesus is clearly indicating that the Holy Spirit is not the only One who helps us experience the fullness of God's design for us. The Holy Spirit is not the only "Helper" that God sends to assist his disciples. By stating that he would send "another Helper," Jesus was indicating that the help he was sending "would be another of the same sort as he."[10] Jesus, then, is properly described as the *first Paraclete,* the Holy Spirit as the *second Paraclete.* The Holy Spirit was to come and continue Jesus' own work on behalf of his followers by empowering them and bringing them to maturity in the faith. This point is of particular importance because it not only helps us

---

Baker, 2005), 55. See also Cole, *He Who Gives Life*, 65–69.

8. For example, Cole, *He Who Gives Life*, 184–85; Packer, *Keep in Step with the Spirit*, 54.

9. Strong's, 3875, accessed June 5, 2020, *HELPS Word-studies* http://biblehub.com/greek/3875.htm.

10. Cole, *He Who Gives Life*, 67, 185.

understand the unity of mission between Jesus and the Holy Spirit, but also helps us understand both the distinct yet continuous nature of their work as it relates to ethics as worship.

To understand this important point, consider what the Scripture teaches us about Jesus' ministry. Luke tells us that God in Christ came to seek and to save the lost (Luke 19:10). John tells us that Jesus serves as our "Advocate" or *parákletos* who advocates like unto a lawyer who stands on our behalf before God the righteous Judge and pleads our case for our redemption and forgiveness (1 John 2:1). In accomplishing our salvation by dying and rising from the dead, Jesus played the foundational role of achieving the salvation initiated and ordained for us by the Father. In doing so, Jesus fulfilled the foundational role of *Paraclete* in the life of the believer. Sproul comments that the "role of Jesus as our Advocate before the Father is so important that we dare not let it be obscured in our understanding of the ministry of the Holy Spirit as Paraclete."[11]

This, then, sheds light on the Holy Spirit's role because in working as our "Helper" he is personally picking up the redeeming and restoring work begun by Jesus, who saved us, in order that the saving work of Christ is then "worked out" into the ethical life of the believer. As Paracletes working on our behalf, the second and third persons of the Trinity are fulfilling the will of the Father by moving us along an arc of continuation all the way from the day of salvation to the final point of our glorification. In other words, the Holy Spirit's role is to personally shepherd us from the moment of salvation into the glory of God by helping each one of us personally walk well along the way. The Holy Spirit is the "second Paraclete," who is constantly at work in us to point us to the "first" or "original Paraclete," who is the One in whom our salvation is both founded and ultimately completed.[12]

Why Is Understanding the Holy Spirit's Role as a Paraclete Important for Ethics as Worship?

To Shine a Floodlight on Christ

This leads us to ask, "Why is understanding the Holy Spirit's role as a Paraclete important for ethics as worship?" The first reason is that the Holy Spirit is at work to focus our attention on Christ and to help us to become like him. Scripture tells us that the Holy Spirit's task is to bear witness to Jesus (John 15:26–27) and to glorify Christ (16:14). His job is to help us focus our attention on Christ and place our hope in him, the author and perfecter of our faith (Heb. 12:2). As Packer puts it, the Holy Spirit's distinctive role is a self-effacing one in which he is

---

11. Sproul, *Mystery of the Holy Spirit*, 151.
12. Packer, *Keep in Step with the Spirit*, 58.

constantly "directing all attention away from himself to Christ and drawing folk into the faith, hope, love, obedience, adoration, and dedication, which constitute communion with Christ. . . . The Holy Spirit's distinctive new covenant role, then, is to fulfill what we may call a 'floodlight ministry' in relation to the Lord Jesus Christ."[13]

While the Spirit brings disciples to life by causing them to be born again (John 3:1–8), and while he drives and empowers their lives of ethical worship (Acts 1:8; Eph. 5:18), it is not his role or desire to receive worship.[14] Nowhere in Scripture do we see him seeking attention for himself or encouraging the adoration of God's people.[15] Rather, the focus is on the person and work of Christ, to whom our lives must be conformed if we are to have fullness of life (Rom. 8:29). As Daniel Block puts it, "True Christian worship focuses particularly on Christ, through whose sacrificial death and justifying work sinners are qualified for worship, and through whose resurrection they hope in eternal life and worship in the presence of God."[16]

To Transform Us into True Worshipers

The role of the Spirit is particularly important for ethics as worship because by focusing our attention on Jesus Christ, the Spirit is working to make us the "true worshipers" that Jesus referenced in John 4:23–24 (those who will worship "in spirit and truth"). In order to develop this thought, consider again Jesus' words:

> An hour is coming, and now is, when the true worshipers will worship the Father in spirit and truth; for such people the Father seeks to be His worshipers. God is spirit, and those who worship Him must worship in spirit and truth. (John 4:23–24)

The context of the passage involves Jesus' talking with a Samaritan woman who in the midst of a discussion engages Jesus in what would have been an ongoing debate between the Jews and the Samaritans regarding the proper place of worship. While Samaritans believed that true worship must take place on Mount Gerazim in the region of Samaria, the Jews argued that it was in Jerusalem at the temple where the worship of God must take place. Jesus, however, cut through

---

13. Packer, *Keep in Step with the Spirit*, 56–57.

14. This should not be taken to imply in any way that there is an essential or ontological distinction between the three persons of the Trinity. Rather, it is a manner of distinguishing the eternally generated, mutually determined roles of the three persons of the Trinity. So in a sense, we can say that as the Holy Spirit is God, he receives worship. But as a person of the Trinity, he has as his role the shining of a light on the work of Christ to the glory of the Father.

15. Daniel I. Block, *For the Glory of God: Recovering a Biblical Theology of Worship* (Grand Rapids: Baker, 2014), 50.

16. Block, *For the Glory of God*, 53.

this debate by referencing the need for "true worship." He would not allow the discussion to center on the *location* of worship. Instead he moved the discussion to the *person* who should be the *object* of worship.[17] The passage continues:

> The woman said to Him, "I know that Messiah is coming (He who is called Christ); when that One comes, He will declare all things to us." Jesus said to her, "I who speak to you am He." (John 4:25–26)

By so directly centering true worship on himself, Jesus helps us understand that while we can say that the foundation of true worship is grounded in the way that God created human beings and initially oriented them to himself and his mission to fill the earth and subdue and rule it in his name, the restoration of true worship comes through the person and work of Christ. But note here that in John 4:24 Jesus indicates that because God is Spirit, true worshipers must worship him in both "spirit" and "truth." That is, not only must it be *God* who is truly worshiped, but God must be worshiped *in a certain manner.*

What, then, does it mean to worship "in spirit and truth"? With regard to "spirit," Peterson is helpful here:

> "Spirit" and "truth" are closely connected in John's portrait of Christ. No-one can see the kingdom of God or experience the blessings of the End-time without being born-again by the Spirit (3:1–8). . . . The Father begets true worshipers through the Spirit. . . . The primary reference in John 4:23–24 is not to the human spirit but to the Holy Spirit, who regenerates us, brings new life, and confirms us in the truth (cf. 15:26–27; 16:13–15).[18]

Regarding "truth," D. A. Carson is likewise helpful when he points out that in John's Gospel,

> Jesus appears as the *true* vine, the *true* manna, the *true* Shepherd, the *true* temple, the *true* Son—to worship God "in spirit *and in truth*" is first and foremost a way of saying that we must worship God *by means of Christ*. In him the reality has dawned and the shadows are being swept away (cf. Heb. 8:13). Christian worship is new covenant worship; it is gospel-inspired worship; it is Christ-centered worship; it is cross-focused worship.[19]

---

17. David Peterson, *Engaging with God: A Biblical Theology of Worship* (Downers Grove, IL: InterVarsity Press, 1992), 98.

18. Peterson, *Engaging with God*, 99.

19. D. A. Carson, "Worship under the Word," in *Worship by the Book*, ed. D. A. Carson (Grand Rapids: Zondervan, 2002), 37.

Ethics as worship requires the work of both the first Paraclete and the second Paraclete if it is going to be rightly ordered to the Father as *true worship.*

If this is a correct understanding of Jesus' teachings about worship in spirit and truth, and we should understand this phrase to be a referent to the second and third persons of the Trinity, then we can begin to see the vitally important role that the Holy Spirit plays in our transformation into true worshipers. In regard to our salvation, it is the Father who initiates it and the Son who accomplishes it, but it is the Holy Spirit who applies it to our lives (Eph. 1:3–13). Likewise, in our growth as disciples and the moral formation we need to undergo, it is the Spirit who enables us to move our thoughts and deeds toward God in accord with the truth given to us in the person and Word of Jesus Christ. Only through the conjoined work of the first Paraclete with the second Paraclete can we hope for our lives to be transformed such that we offer to God that which we were created and redeemed for: worshiping God in spirit and in truth.

What Are the Means of Transformation That the Holy Spirit Uses to Shape Our Character?

This brings us to our next question: What are the means of transformation by which the Holy Spirit shapes our character and thereby helps us become the true worshipers that God created and redeemed us to be? Here we identify ten ways in which the Holy Spirit works in believers to shape their character and enables them to be the kind of people who reflexively seek to maximize worship in and through their ethical behavior.

Conviction

First, John 16:8–11 tells us that Jesus sends us the Holy Spirit to bring *conviction*:

> And He, when He comes, will convict the world concerning sin and righteousness and judgment; concerning sin, because they do not believe in Me; and concerning righteousness, because I go to the Father and you no longer see Me; and concerning judgment, because the ruler of this world has been judged.

The Holy Spirit brings conviction regarding sinful actions as people compare their deeds to God's moral standards as they are revealed through both the written Word and the deeper testimony of that which is written on the heart (Rom. 1–3). This leads to a crucial conviction that has to do with a lack of belief in Jesus himself, who is the only hope for the restoration of souls and the transformation of our lives. Further, it also leads to a conviction about Christ's just or righteous place as Lord and Judge over all creation, as well as a conviction regarding the just condemnation of Satan.

Regeneration

When this conviction takes place, the second means of transformation that the Holy Spirit uses to make us true worshipers is the application to our lives of the atoning work of Christ by bringing us from death to life through *regeneration*. As Jesus puts it in John 6:63, "It is the Spirit who gives life; the flesh profits nothing." And Romans 8:11 likewise teaches us that it is the Spirit of God who gives us life: "But if the Spirit of Him who raised Jesus from the dead dwells in you, He who raised Christ Jesus from the dead will also give life to your mortal bodies through His Spirit who dwells in you."

Only as a person is "born again" through the Spirit can he or she hope to enter the kingdom of God (John 3:1–8). As Daniel Block puts it, "In the New Testament the Holy Spirit's role is to animate sinners who are dead in trespasses and sins and effect their adoptions as sons and daughters of God."[20] And likewise, R. C. Sproul comments that in regard to our salvation, "the first step, the step of regeneration by which a person is quickened to spiritual life, is the work of God and of God alone. The initiative is with God, not with us. . . . It is to the Holy Spirit of God that we are debtors for the grace of regeneration and faith. He is the Gift-giver, who while we were dead made us alive with Christ, to Christ, and in Christ."[21]

Indwelling

The third means of transformation that takes place in the life of a believer is the remarkable gift of the Holy Spirit's indwelling us and making our bodies his temple (1 Cor. 6:19). In referring to the *indwelling* of the Holy Spirit, this means that when a person receives Christ as his or her Savior and the Holy Spirit generates new life in the new believer (Titus 3:5), the Holy Spirit then lives *with* us and *in* us, as Jesus tells us:

> I will ask the Father, and He will give you another Helper, that He may be with you forever; that is the Spirit of truth, whom the world cannot receive, because it does not see Him or know Him, but you know Him because He abides *with* you and will be *in* you. (John 14:16–17)

Therefore, the language of the *indwelling* of the Holy Spirit is meant to indicate the permanence of the redemptive relationship that each Christian has with Christ

---

20. Block, *For the Glory of God*, 50n65.
21. Sproul, *Mystery of the Holy Spirit*, 87, 93.

from the moment of conversion.[22] Romans 8:9-11 helps us see the vital importance of this truth:

> However, you are not in the flesh but in the Spirit, if indeed the Spirit of God dwells in you. But if anyone does not have the Spirit of Christ, he does not belong to Him. If Christ is in you, though the body is dead because of sin, yet the spirit is alive because of righteousness. But if the Spirit of Him who raised Jesus from the dead dwells in you, He who raised Christ Jesus from the dead will also give life to your mortal bodies through His Spirit who dwells in you.

Paul helps us understand that if we are Christians, we have indeed "received" the Spirit, who adopts us and makes us God's children. Thus, the Spirit "dwells" in us. If the Spirit does not dwell in us, then we are not believers. This is important for ethics because if indeed the Holy Spirit indwells us, then we can have assurance that we belong to God and are spiritually alive. Further, as the Spirit lives in us, we begin to experience the leading of the Spirit to put to death sinful actions and live our lives more and more as an act of worship to God, who is our loving Father. That is to say, because the Spirit indwells us, we have a real hope that moral and ethical transformation can take place not merely at the behavior level, but at the level of *character.*

Sanctification

This point leads us to the fourth means of transformation that the Holy Spirit uses to help us become true worshipers: the process of *sanctification*. In the previous chapter, we discussed this doctrine at length, so we will not repeat that discussion here. By way of simple reminder, we can rest assured that God is transforming us to complete the good work he began in us by Jesus Christ (Phil. 1:6). This takes place not only because in Christ we have been saved *from* sin, but also because we have been set aside *to* live for God and enjoy his fellowship forever. Sanctification involves the Holy Spirit's helping Christ's disciples to become in character and practice what God has declared them to be in truth. This work is dependent on Christ's work of justification, and it has an eye toward the final glorification we will experience when we see the Lord face to face (1 John 3:2).

Sealing

The fifth means of transformation that the Holy Spirit uses to help us become true worshipers is the *sealing* of believers, which guarantees their status as God's

---

22. Gordon R. Lewis and Bruce A. Demarest, *Integrative Theology*, vol. 3 (Grand Rapids: Zondervan, 1994), 211.

redeemed treasure to the praise of his glory.[23] Ephesians 1:13–14 states that in Christ, "you also, after listening to the message of truth, the gospel of your salvation—having also believed, you were sealed in Him with the Holy Spirit of promise, who is given as a pledge of our inheritance, with a view to the redemption of God's own possession, to the praise of His glory."

This passage teaches us that it is the Father's good pleasure to make our salvation completely secure through the work of Christ and by the sealing of the Holy Spirit. Scripture tells us that because Jesus and the Father are one, and the work of Jesus on the cross paid for all sins (past, present, and future), no one can take us out of God's hand (John 10:27–30). In fact, no one can even bring a charge against God's children because he has himself justified them (Rom. 8:33). In light of this, we can rest assured that *nothing* can separate one of God's children from him. Indeed, if such a thing were possible, it would mean either that God was incapable of completing his saving work or that he was somehow acting in a manner that denied his own character (Rom. 8:38–39; 2 Tim. 2:13). Scripture tells us, however, that the Father is delighted also to *seal* us in our salvation by giving us the Holy Spirit as a promise and a pledge of our inheritance, and to demonstrate that we are now his own possession, rescued for the praise of his own glory. By doing so, as was the case with our positional sanctification discussed above, the Holy Spirit in this beautiful work provides the basis from which the believer can have confidence to work hard in his or her moral formation, knowing that his or her salvation is secure in Christ. It also provides a basis of security on which a believer can step out in boldness evangelistically, knowing that fear of human rejection should fade to nothing in light of the glorious approval and love of Christ.

Uniting

The sixth means of transformation that God uses to help us become true worshipers is *uniting* the believers through the corporate indwelling of the Spirit in the body of Christ—the church. In 1 Corinthians 3:16, we see Paul reminding the Corinthian believers of this very fact as he admonishes them to live in a manner that seeks the glory of God over their own desires: "Do you not know that you are a temple of God and that the Spirit of God dwells in you?" D. A. Carson points out, in reference to this verse, that unlike 1 Corinthians 6:19–20, where Paul uses the temple as a metaphor for our individual bodies, here the context is actually in reference to the church. The corporate body of Christ in its local expressions is a visible manifestation of the larger body of Christ as a whole. Here we learn that the Spirit not only indwells individuals but also dwells in all of us together. This, in turn, not only means that the Spirit is the basis of our unity or oneness as the

---

23. Block, *For the Glory of God*, 50n65.

body of Christ, but is a further reason to pursue holiness and sanctification both individually and corporately.

The fact is, our moral choices and behaviors have both personal and corporate consequences (for better or worse). Therefore, caring for our own moral growth and spiritual formation is a form of neighbor love in that it helps the entire body become more of what God desires it to be. The gathering of the people of God in the local church is the place God designed and created for his people to learn how to *become* true worshipers, *be* true worshipers, *practice* true worship together, *display* the beauty of true united worship, and *invite* others to join with them in true worship.

Gifting

The seventh means of transformation that the Holy Spirit uses to help us become true worshipers is the *gifting* that he gives both to individuals and to the body of Christ for the purpose of edification, encouragement, and the good works of ministry. Three central passages that discuss gifts of the Spirit in the New Testament are Romans 12:3–13, 1 Corinthians 12, and Ephesians 4:7–11. While a full discussion on the impartation, types, and extent of the gifts of the Spirit available to the church today is beyond our scope here, a few important points must be drawn forth in relation to spiritual formation and the shaping of Christ's disciples into true worshipers.

J. I. Packer's engagement on this topic is particularly helpful as he places the discussion within the larger framework of the purpose for which God gives gifts and then defines them as spiritual (or not), not primarily in terms of their form or the fact that one possesses an ability, but rather in light of their usage for the purpose for which God bestows them. In this light, he distinguishes spiritual gifts from natural endowments that enable a person to be skilled on the one hand (such as a musical talent or oratory skills) and what he describes as "supernatural novelty" abilities on the other hand (speaking in tongues, healing, and the like). He defines them as "enrichments" given by Christ and received by believers (which may include things such as the "supernatural novelty abilities" mentioned above), but crucially he links the definition of a "spiritual gift" to the purpose of edifying or building up the body of Christ.[24] He writes that

> [according to Paul], edification is precisely a matter of growing in depth and fullness of one's understanding of Christ and all else in relation to him and in the quality of one's spiritual relationship with him, and it is not anything else. So spiritual gifts must be defined in terms of Christ, as actualized powers of expressing,

24. Packer, *Keep in Step with the Spirit*, 70.

celebrating, displaying and so communicating Christ in one way or another, either by word or deed. This would not be edifying otherwise. . . . The truth we must grasp here is that our exercise of spiritual gifts is nothing more nor less than Christ himself ministering through his body to his body, to the Father, and all mankind.[25]

Therefore, what makes a gift spiritual is not the mere possession of an ability (even if it is supernaturally endowed), but the purpose for which it is employed. If it is not used to edify the body, it is not actually functioning as a spiritual gift (Greek, *charisma*). Again, Packer is helpful:

When, therefore, Christians are said to "have gifts" (Rom. 12:6), the meaning is not that they are in any respect outstandingly brilliant or efficient (they may be, they may not; it varies), but rather that God has observably used them to give edification in specific ways already, and this warrants the expectations that he will do the same again. We need to draw a clear distinction between man's capacity to perform and God's prerogative to bless, for it is God's use of our abilities rather than the abilities themselves that constitute *charismata*. If no regular, identifiable spiritual benefit for others or ourselves results from what we do, we should not think of our capacity to do it as a spiritual gift. . . . You cannot define a *charisma* [spiritual gift] as performance alone; the definition must include the relational factor of God-given edification in Christ through the performance.[26]

In sum, regarding the means of transformation that the Spirit uses to shape believers into true worshipers, Packer helps us see something very important about the gifts that God gives his church. What constitutes and identifies a spiritual gift is not merely the form or possession of the gift, but the use of it to bring the blessing of God into building up the body of Christ.[27] If it is not used to shape us and grow us in depth and fullness of our understanding and worship of God, then it is not actually a gift that we would call spiritually useful. On the other hand, regarding our transformation into true worshipers both individually and corporately, when the Spirit uses the gifts to encourage believers to become more like Christ in and through the mutual building up of the body, then these divinely given "enhancements" are certainly *charismata*. By and through them we can serve one another, love one another, worship with one another, and invite others to join with us in doing the same—all the while seeking to build one another up in Christ and worship God in spirit and truth.

25. Packer, *Keep in Step with the Spirit*, 71.
26. Packer, *Keep in Step with the Spirit*, 72.
27. Packer, *Keep in Step with the Spirit*, 72.

Prayer

The eighth means of transformation that the Holy Spirit uses to help us become true worshipers is *prayer*. Romans 8:26–27 tells us:

> In the same way the Spirit also helps our weakness; for we do not know how to pray as we should, but the Spirit Himself intercedes for us with groanings too deep for words; and He who searches the hearts knows what the mind of the Spirit is, because He intercedes for the saints according to the will of God.

In these verses, we learn not only that the Holy Spirit assists our prayer and helps us pray better and more appropriately than we know how to do on our own, but also that he prays to God on behalf of believers (the "saints").

One of the incredible facts related to this is that Scripture teaches that not only does the Holy Spirit pray on our behalf, but Jesus "always lives to make intercession for [us]" (Heb. 7:25), and according to Romans 8:34, he is currently seated at the right hand of God, praying for us. Once again, we see the conjoined work of the first and second Paracletes, helping us to become worshipers in spirit and truth by assisting us to pray, as well as praying on our behalf. "Just as we enjoy two Advocates with the Father, so also do we have two Intercessors with the Father. The Holy Spirit assists us in praying properly to the Father."[28]

Guidance

The ninth means of transformation that the Holy Spirit uses to help us become true worshipers is his *teaching and guiding influence* in our lives. In John 14, as Jesus seeks to comfort his disciples and prepare them for ministry after his death, he begins to teach them about the role of the Holy Spirit and says to them: "These things I have spoken to you while abiding with you. But the Helper, the Holy Spirit, whom the Father will send in My name, He will teach you all things, and bring to your remembrance all that I said to you" (John 14:25–26). Likewise in John 16:13, Jesus went on to encourage his disciples by assuring them that "when He, the Spirit of truth, comes, He will guide you into all the truth; for He will not speak on His own initiative, but whatever He hears, He will speak; and He will disclose to you what is to come."

So how should we understand what the Lord means here by the Spirit's teaching us "all things" and guiding us "into all the truth"? The first thing to keep in mind to answer this question is that the Holy Spirit's task, as we discussed above, is first and foremost to glorify Jesus and magnify his ministry by shining a floodlight on his work of reconciliation. Thus, when we see these statements about "all

---

28. Sproul, *Mystery of the Holy Spirit*, 151.

things" and "all the truth," we should interpret them to mean not that the Spirit will give us unlimited information about everything, but rather that he will give to us all we need to know about Christ and remind us of all the things Christ taught. The promise to "disclose . . . what is to come" also has as its referent the person and work of Christ. Instead of our thinking in terms of unlimited predictive prophecy, this statement is best understood to mean that the Spirit would give the disciples clarity on all the things that were about to happen to Christ (his death, resurrection, future glory, and so on).[29]

The focus of these passages is to give comfort to the disciples by assuring them that the Holy Spirit would be with them, would lead them, and would guide them in the continuation of the gospel ministry in which Jesus himself had been training them for years. What does this guidance entail? Paul's discussion of the transformation that takes place through the work of the Spirit in 1 Corinthians 2:12–16 helps give us a sense of what the Spirit's guidance is and how it functions in the life of a disciple:

> Now we have received, not the spirit of the world, but the Spirit who is from God, so that we may know the things freely given to us by God, which things we also speak, not in words taught by human wisdom, but in those taught by the Spirit, combining spiritual thoughts with spiritual words.
>
> But a natural man does not accept the things of the Spirit of God, for they are foolishness to him; and he cannot understand them, because they are spiritually appraised. But he who is spiritual appraises all things, yet he himself is appraised by no one. For who has known the mind of the Lord, that he will instruct Him? But we have the mind of Christ.

Note, first of all, that Paul is making a contrast here between a natural understanding that comes merely through human reason ("the spirit of the world") and a spiritual understanding that is enabled by the Holy Spirit. In context, he is helping the Corinthian believers recognize that rational, scientific, and philosophical thought reaches its proper place only when it is properly ordered spiritually and theologically. Without the working of the Holy Spirit, such knowledge is ultimately inferior, not because it gets facts or ideas wrong, but because it is limited by its frame of reference. In our modern context, this means that if one does not accept the possibility of a spiritual reality, then anything pertaining to the spiritual world will appear nonsensical to that person's point of view. Those things discovered about the physical universe are not understood in terms of the larger reality and final ordering of all things.

29. Packer, *Keep in Step with the Spirit*, 56.

In this light, Paul goes on to contrast the "natural man," who does not accept the teachings given by the Spirit of God that relate to the spiritual realities of God and his created universe, and the spiritual man ("he who is spiritual"), who does. For the former (natural man), spiritual ideas and discussions about the gospel appear as foolishness because he has already rejected the possibility of their reality. But for the latter person (spiritual man), he or she is able to "[appraise] all things" even if no one else believes them, because the Holy Spirit has regenerated the person's life and mind to be able to accept and comprehend the things of God. There is a difference between a natural understanding of the world and a spiritual understanding because "a person cannot discern spiritual [truths] until that person is first made alive to spiritual things by the Spirit of God. It is the Spirit's work of regeneration, or spiritual rebirth, that enables us to have spiritual discernment."[30]

In reference to the diagram below (see fig. 4.1, which we introduced in the previous chapter), we might say that there is a qualitative difference between how one perceives and knows the world depending on where one finds oneself in his or her spiritual journey. Because the "natural man" that Paul describes would find himself at point 2 (fall), his ability to see and understand the things of God would be limited to the vantage point of the bottom line. For that person, it would appear as though the top line did not even exist. On the other hand, the "spiritual man" would be positioned at point 4 (restoration) and would have the capacity to see what the entire diagram is attempting to depict, and thus discern a larger perspective of reality.

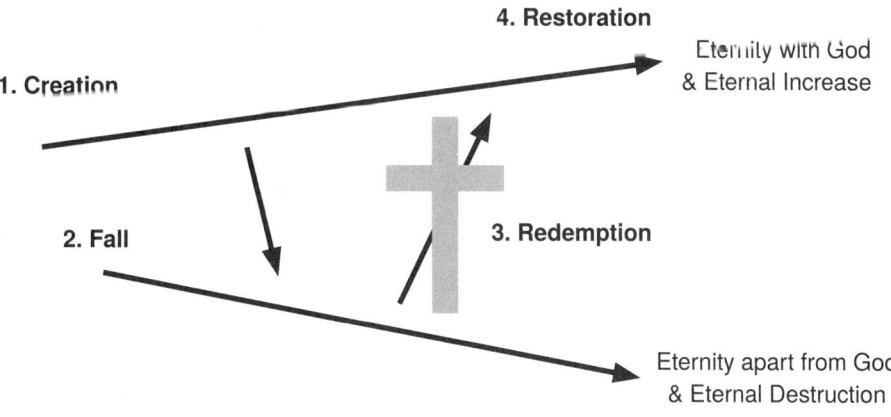

Fig. 4.1. Man's Trajectory Restored

30. Sproul, *Mystery of the Holy Spirit*, 14.

So again, the question is not necessarily one of raw data recollection, logical reasoning, or becoming aware of new teachings never before given. Instead, the spiritual person is guided by the Holy Spirit to discern the spiritual nature and condition of the world, the hope that the gospel of Jesus Christ brings, and the intended final ordering of all things, both material and spiritual.

We must be careful at this point to recognize that the discernment given to the "spiritual man" does not automatically or immediately mean that a Christian has perfect discernment at the point of conversion. No, for while we can see from the last phrase in the 1 Corinthians 2:14–16 passage that we have been given "the mind of Christ," the New Testament speaks of the need for us to have our minds renewed so that we might follow Christ wisely and walk well in his teachings (Rom. 12:1–2). Hence, like moral sanctification, there is also an important element of mental sanctification that enables us to rightly discern Christ's teachings. That is, while we can say *positionally* that we have been given the mind of Christ, we must also recognize our need to *progressively* grow in our ability to discern as well as yield our wills to the instructions of the Lord.

This leads us back to the question of how the Holy Spirit leads and guides us as we seek to live out ethics as worship. Sproul answers the question well when he simply says that "in the process of sanctification the Spirit is our Teacher. His textbook is the Bible."[31] Helpfully, he goes on to say:

> The Holy Spirit is the Author of Sacred Scripture. He is the only One who inspired the original writings. He is the One who illumines the Word for our understanding. He is the One who uses the Word to bring us under conviction. The Holy Spirit may be distinguished from the Word, but to separate the Word and the Spirit is spiritually fatal. The Holy Spirit teaches, leads, and speaks to us through the Word and with the Word, not apart from or against the Word.[32]

This is the Holy Spirit's job in giving us the mind of Christ. As Fred Sanders remarks, "what we need is the miracle of being able to see our own situation from an infinitely higher point of view. We need to start our thinking from a center in God, not in ourselves."[33] And it is precisely here that the Spirit of God uses Scripture to provide this proper frame of reference as well as the particular moral instructions to guide us into true worship that comports with the manner in which God shaped and ordered the universe. In our study and meditation on the Word of God, our heart's cry should align with David's: "From the end of the

31. Sproul, *Mystery of the Holy Spirit*, 99.
32. Sproul, *Mystery of the Holy Spirit*, 101.
33. Fred Sanders, *The Deep Things of God: How the Trinity Changes Everything*, 2nd ed. (Wheaton, IL: Crossway, 2017), 107–8.

earth I call to You when my heart is faint; lead me to the rock that is higher than I" (Ps. 61:2).

Once this perspective is in place and we recognize that the process of having a renewed mind chiefly involves conformity to the teachings of Scripture about the nature of reality and morality, then much of the Spirit's leading relates to the shaping of our attitudinal disposition to submit ourselves under the teaching of the Word given by the first and second Paracletes for our growth, guidance, and edification toward becoming true worshipers. We will return and address the role of Scripture in ethics in much more depth in the next chapter.

power
dunamis

Empowering

Finally, the tenth means of transformation that God uses to help us become true worshipers is the *empowerment* he provides through the Holy Spirit. In the final words we have from Jesus before he ascended to heaven, he told his disciples that "you will receive power when the Holy Spirit has come upon you; and you shall be My witnesses both in Jerusalem, and in all Judea and Samaria, and even to the remotest part of the earth" (Acts 1:8). The Greek word from which the English word *power* is derived is *dunamis*.[34] The connotation of the word implies the strength, potency, and ability to do marvelous—even spectacular—works for the glory of God.

In the book of Ephesians, Paul gives the congregation instructions to "be filled" with the Holy Spirit. The concept of being "filled" (Greek, *plēroō*) has to do with making something complete or making something amply supplied for the need at hand. The believer—and the church corporately—is charged to look to the Spirit for fulfillment and completion and nothing else. In context of the entire passage, we see that Paul is using this concept to make a distinction between getting drunk with wine and being filled with the Holy Spirit. In Ephesians 5:18, Paul instructs the believers not to get drunk with wine because that leads to reckless wastefulness. Instead, he commands the believers to "be filled with the Spirit."

The contrast with wine and the filling of the Spirit harks back to Acts 2 and the day of Pentecost. In that context, when the Holy Spirit came upon the believers, they began to speak the message of the gospel in the various languages of the crowd present in Jerusalem. Onlookers who did not understand what was happening began to mock the Christians as if they were drunk. But of course they were not. The Holy Spirit was empowering them to proclaim the gospel message (Acts 2:13–41).

---

34. Frederick William Danker et al., eds., *A Greek-English Lexicon of the New Testament and Other Early Christian Literature,* 3rd ed. (Chicago: University of Chicago Press, 2000) (BDAG), s.v. "δύναμις." For further information, see Packer, *Keep in Step with the Spirit,* 23.

When Paul teaches about the *filling* of the Spirit in Ephesians 5:18 and contrasts it with the idea of getting drunk, he is illustrating two important points. The first is that *filling* relates to what has control over a person. Paul is teaching us that allowing alcohol to have control is a waste of time and that it foolishly mocks what God wants to do through the filling of the Holy Spirit. This is why Christians are commanded not to get drunk. The second is that in contrast to alcohol, which needs to be poured in from the outside, because the Holy Spirit already dwells in us, we already have the resources available to be filled. Filling is something that happens from the inside out. The Holy Spirit takes over (or fills out) all aspects of our lives.

Paul teaches that if the Spirit has control, something amazing can happen—as it did in the book of Acts. Paul does not specify in that passage all the particulars of what can happen through the filling of the Holy Spirit, but he indicates that the filling is crucial for living the Christian life. It is through the work of the Holy Spirit that we have the power to control our lives for the proper worship of God in and through our ethics. This is why Paul gives us the imperative to "be filled."

The fact that the Holy Spirit indwells us completely at the moment of salvation should not imply that we are from that point on also fully submitted to the work of the Spirit. As we discussed in the previous chapter, *progressive sanctification* is largely about disciples of Jesus Christ increasingly yielding so that the Holy Spirit gets more of us. It is an ongoing experience. As J. I. Packer rightly cautions, any talk that suggests that once we become Christians, God's power in us will immediately cancel our defects of character and make our lives easy is "so unbiblical as to be positively dishonest." He goes on to say that "certainly God sometimes works wonders of sudden deliverance from this or that weakness at conversion . . . ; but every Christian's life is a constant fight against the pressures and pulls of the world, the flesh, and the devil; and his battle for Christlikeness . . . is as grueling as it is unending."[35]

Part of the ongoing battle that is progressive sanctification is that sinners who have been saved by grace too often still love their sin and sin patterns. Because of this, we frequently hold onto old sins and sin patterns as though they would somehow lead us to flourishing. But God is kind to us in spite of our foolishness. As Hebrews 4:15 tells us, by living a fully human life Jesus experientially faced all the categories of temptations that humans face, yet he was able to face them without sinning. God not only understands our temptations, but actually sympathizes with us about them, and through the work of the Holy Spirit he desires to help us conquer them as we consistently yield to his working in our lives.

The empowerment that comes through the filling of the Holy Spirit is an

---

35. Packer, *Keep in Step with the Spirit*, 26.

important means by which God enables us to progress in the Christian life. But it is not only God's means to provide strength for each of us individually; it is also meant to help all of us corporately to live ethically as his representatives and be on mission for him as we take the gospel message to the world.[36]

Table 4.1. The Means by Which the Holy Spirit Helps

The Means by Which the Holy Spirit Helps	Scripture
He convicts us and the world of sin	John 16:8–11
He regenerates us	John 3:3–7; 6:63; Ephesians 2:5
He indwells us	1 Corinthians 3:16
He sanctifies us (positionally, progressively, perfectly)	1 Corinthians 6:11; 2 Thessalonians 2:13
He seals us in Christ	Ephesians 1:13
He unites us to the body of Christ	Ephesians 4:1–6
He provides us with divine gifts and callings	1 Corinthians 12:1–31; Ephesians 4:11–16
He prays with and for us	Romans 8:26–27
He guides us into truth	John 16:13
He empowers us for holy and missional living	Acts 1:8; Ephesians 5:18

What Does the Process of the Holy Spirit's Shaping Us into True Worshipers Entail?

What does the process of Holy Spirit–driven moral formation and transformation into true worshipers look like in actual practice? While obviously the process of moral formation and life transformation will look different in each person's life context, it is possible to mark out the contours of what it may look like in general categories. Here, we will focus on four of these categories that we believe to be crucial: inviting the Lord to change us through prayerful yielding, diligently striving, keeping in step with the Spirit, and abiding in Christ. We will address each in turn.

36. For further discussion of how the Spirit empowers, see Packer, *Keep in Step with the Spirit*, 23–27, 51.

Prayerful Yielding

The first step of moral and spiritual transformation involves an attitude of humble submission or yielding that can be expressed at the very least through a prayer of invitation for God to change us. While our prayers need to be accompanied by real desire for change and a willingness to yield, it is important to keep in mind that each member of the Trinity is a person. As Jesus taught his disciples to pray, he taught them to address God the Father in personal terms (e.g., "our Father," Matt. 6:9). It is fully appropriate for us to prayerfully ask the Father to bring change and transformation into our lives through the working of the Holy Spirit within us.

As we learn from the life of Jesus, this is not always an easy request, for even as he was in the garden of Gethsemane on the night before his death, he cried out to the Father: "My Father, if it is possible, let this cup pass from Me; yet not as I will, but as You will" (Matt. 26:39). The crucial element of the prayer of Jesus is that even as he was experiencing intense personal anguish, he yielded his own will to the Lord and worshiped through submission to the eternal plan of the Trinity. Conforming our lives to Christ's involves a disposition of willing submission, and expressing that to God through prayer is a great first (and ongoing) step in the transformation process.

Diligent Striving (Holy Sweat)

A second crucial element in the process of transformation into a true worshiper involves diligently striving to put off the habits and vices of the old self while also working hard to put on the virtues and character traits (such as the fruits of the Spirit) that Scripture identifies as key markers of spiritual maturity. In Ephesians 4:22–24, Paul encourages this very thing. He writes to the believers:

> In reference to your former manner of life, you lay aside the old self, which is being corrupted in accordance with the lusts of deceit, and . . . be renewed in the spirit of your mind, and put on the new self, which in the likeness of God has been created in righteousness and holiness of the truth.

We trust that the parallel with our earlier discussions related to sanctification and the term *holiness* is self-evident through Paul's instructions in this passage. The language of "laying aside the old self" and "putting on the new self" directly corresponds to the idea that holiness requires both a setting of something aside *from* impurity and sin and also a setting apart *to* the life and joy that God desires for his people. True human freedom comes not merely through abstaining from sin but in moving into the full life of Christ (Gal. 5:1).

This is no task for the lazy or fainthearted! As was pointed out in our discussion

we rest on the promises of the gospel

of progressive sanctification in the previous chapter, this conforming of our character and practices requires that we *rest* on the promises of the gospel regarding our salvation, but also that we *strive* with the help of the Spirit to become in character and practice what God has proclaimed us to be in truth.

While the truest thing about us is that which God declares us to be (and makes a reality in us through Christ), because we live in a world marred by sins and sinfulness, our lives will involve struggle and toil. While our chief purpose and task is to pursue God, in our own lives and the world around us we still experience the effects of the fall. Through the structures of the world around us, the wayward desires of our flesh, and enticing lies of the devil, who still prowls about this world like a roaring lion, seeking to devour, we are still vulnerable and often stumble.

This is why progressive sanctification, through the empowerment of the Spirit, requires active participation on our part. It requires effort—yes, sometimes even aggressive effort. If our lives and souls are to flourish as God designed us and as he desires for us, then the practical application of the great positional truths must be developed through disciplined practice and exercise in all areas of our lives.

It requires holy sweat.

Passivity in our walk with Christ is not the way of a worshiper. Scripture uses terms such as "strive," "be diligent," "resist the devil," and "prepare your minds for action" to convey this very point (1 Tim. 4:10; 2 Tim. 2:15; Heb. 4:9–11; James 4:7; 1 Peter 1:13). We must never allow ourselves to be deceived about this. It is true that God has done beautiful things in and for us and that our justification and positional sanctification is 100 percent based on his work and merit. Yet, at the same time, because the context of the world is still broken, the desires of our flesh still wage war within us, and an adversary is trying to kill us along the way. Sanctification also requires work, toughness, and aggressiveness. God desires us to aggressively pursue him with all the resources that he has provided for us. In this way, we can experience the fullness of his grace as well as have abundant joy in our daily life as we live as an act of worship unto him.

This is why, in 1 Corinthians 9, Paul uses the metaphor of running a race to describe the Christian life. He writes:

> Do you not know that those who run in a race all run, but only one receives the prize? Run in such a way that you may win. Everyone who competes in the games exercises self-control in all things. They then do it to receive a perishable wreath, but we an imperishable. Therefore I run in such a way, as not without aim; I box in such a way, as not beating the air; but I discipline my body and make it my slave, so that, after I have preached to others, I myself will not be disqualified. (1 Cor. 9:24–27)

The phrase "discipline my body" in 1 Corinthians 9:27 is vitally important to our discussion of ethics as worship. It points to the reality that change and progress take discipline. In some translations, the phrase is rendered as "buffet my body" (as in "beat," "batter," or "strike a blow to"). Sadly, too often, we as Christians pursue our discipleship and worship patterns as though this word meant "buffet our body" (as in "all you can eat").

By saying this, we do not mean to simply bring conviction about our physical fitness (although that could certainly be appropriate). We do mean to point out that as Christians, we far too often have a self-indulgent "all you can eat" kind of attitude about our lifestyle, our morality, and therefore our worship as well. We allow ourselves to be self-indulgent in relation to sin and are too nonchalant about the amount of effort we put into following Christ. Paul clearly had something else in mind for the Christian disciple. This is why in Romans 12:1–2 he urges Christians not to be *conformed* to this world but to be *transformed* by presenting their bodies as "living and holy sacrifice[s]" to God as a "spiritual service of worship."

Shaping the character of a true worshiper who worships in spirit and truth requires our cooperation with the Holy Spirit by his power that fills us through a practiced obedience extended through time. Yes, practice. Decision after decision. Choice by choice. Act by act. One by one, time after time, deciding, choosing, and acting to walk in Spirit-filled obedience to the Word of God. This is how virtuous character is both built and exercised (strengthened).

Keeping in Step with the Holy Spirit

This leads us directly to the next important element in the process of spiritual formation and life transformation. Diligent striving to become a true worshiper happens not merely through Spirit-empowered effort, but through Spirit-empowered effort that moves in the proper direction. Thus, our transformation into true worshipers not only involves practice, but involves practiced obedience. Yes, obedience. This is how we conform our loves and shape our character to be like that of Jesus Christ. As we have seen, Jesus himself emphasized the importance of obedience for the shaping of our lives and our loves in the following passages:

If you love Me, you will keep My commandments. (John 14:15)

He who has My commandments and keeps them is the one who loves Me; and he who loves Me will be loved by My Father, and I will love him and will disclose Myself to him. (John 14:21)

Obedience demonstrates our love for God. It never earns God's love for us. In addition to demonstrating our love, it also makes us into *lovers of God* when our

Obedience

rightly ordered intentions are matched with rightly ordered behaviors. When our hearts and our minds are wedded to our wills, then we move as whole persons step by step, choice by choice, act by act to grow habits—and eventually virtues—that reflect and embody our loves.

This is why in Galatians 5:25 Paul admonishes us, "If we live by the Spirit, let us also walk by the Spirit." The word he uses here for "walk" in the original Greek is *stoicheō*, which has a very different connotation from merely meandering along as one might do on an afternoon stroll. Quite the contrary, it has more in common with a military march and more literally means "walking in strict accordance with the rule" or "keeping in step."[37] The idea that Paul is communicating by choosing this word is that life transformation requires us to keep in step with the Holy Spirit, who is guiding us to demonstrate that we live our lives for Christ by obeying his commandments. This is how one walks into the exceedingly full (abundant) life that Jesus promised and wants true worshipers to experience (John 10:10).

Abiding ; a long obidence)

The fourth step of transformation involves what might best be described as a long obedience in the same direction, or *abiding* (John 15:7). Change happens through the arc of time, when our behaviors remain consistently pointed in a similar direction. Quietly when no one is watching, and publicly while all the world is aware, we make choices, we commit acts, and little by little, for better or worse, we become a certain kind of person. A person depicted by love for God. A person who is identified by a love for God. A person who embodies love for God. When this takes place, "this transformation will mean that we do indeed 'keep the rules'—though not out of a sense of externally imposed 'duty,' but out of the character that has been formed within us."[38]

Any basketball player will tell you that in order to become an excellent scorer, you can't shoot just one jump shot and expect to be great. You have to shoot thousands of jump shots. And such is the case with the practice of the Christian faith. It doesn't take just one act of obedience to become excellent in your faith. It doesn't take just one moral choice to have the virtues of Christ. It takes thousands. But it is also not enough in basketball to simply shoot thousands of jump shots. You have to shoot thousands of *excellent* jump shots. They need to be the right form and need to be aimed at the right target. Again, it's the same in the Christian faith. We must commit our actions or make our choices in an excellent manner. They must conform to God's instructions and be aimed at the right target: the glory of God.

Sometimes this is easy, and sometimes it takes grit, perseverance, courage,

---

37. Packer, *Keep in Step with the Spirit*, 16–17.
38. N. T. Wright, *After You Believe: Why Christian Character Matters* (New York: HarperOne, 2010), 26.

and holy sweat. But little by little, the choices shape who we become. N. T. Wright captures the idea well:

> Virtue, in this strict sense, is what happens when someone has made a thousand small choices, requiring effort and concentration, to do something which is good and right which doesn't "come naturally"—and then, on the thousand and first time, when it really matters, they find that they do what's required "automatically," as we say. On that thousand and first occasion, it does indeed look as if it "just happens"; but reflection tells us that it doesn't "just happen" as easily as that. . . . Virtue is what happens when wise and courageous choices have become "second nature." . . . Like an acquired taste, such choices and actions, which started off being practiced with difficulty, ended up being, yes, "second nature."[39]

This, then, is how character is formed. This is how we become like Jesus. This is how we become true worshipers . . . or not. For it is a sad reality that when we remain in step with our sin patterns and repetitively fall into them through time, they likewise shape our character. But instead of producing virtues, these behaviors produce vice. Thus, abiding requires diligence to be sure that we are abiding in and keeping in step with the right rule of life and practice.

Abiding in Christ involves the recognition and choice to make every act (and therefore the next act) an opportunity to glorify God. It involves making every choice (and therefore the next choice) an opportunity to worship. Abiding requires us to recognize that every decision (and therefore the next decision) is an opportunity to become like Jesus and advance toward becoming a true worshiper. As C. S. Lewis puts it, "Every time you make a choice you are turning the central part of you, the part of you that chooses, into something a little different from what it was before."[40] The following diagrams (see fig. 4.2) help illustrate the process as choices shape habits and in turn form character dispositions for either better or worse (virtue or vice).

Keep in mind that while it may take thousands of acts and choices to become more like Jesus, it begins with just one. And then after you make the first choice, it requires just the next choice. Each choice is vital, but the next choice is the only one that the Lord is asking you to focus on. He sent the Holy Spirit to help empower you to make the right choice one at a time. Abiding is the discipline that brings about character formation and the development of virtues. Act by act, choice by choice, minute by minute, day after day . . . a long obedience in the same direction. Empowered by the Holy Spirit. Holy sweat.

---

39. Wright, *After You Believe*, 20–21.
40. C. S. Lewis, *Mere Christianity* (New York: Touchstone, 1996), 87.

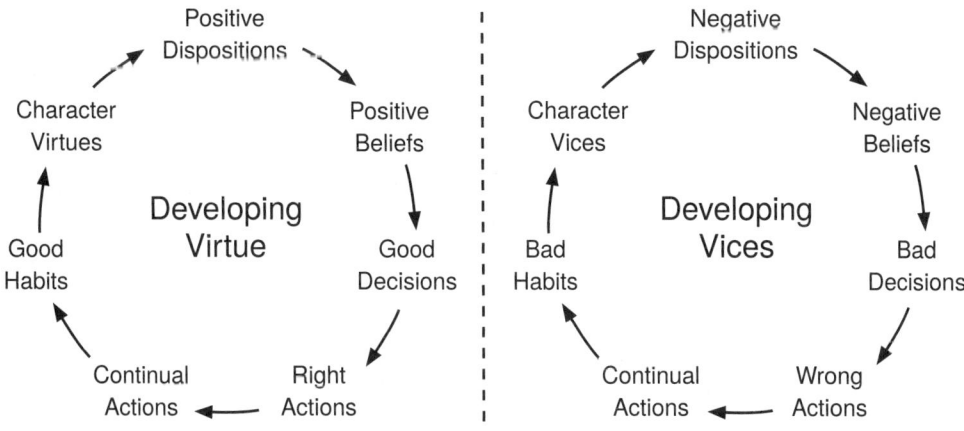

Fig. 4.2. Developing Virtue versus Developing Vices

It has been popularly said that we often overestimate what we can accomplish in a year, but frequently underestimate what we can accomplish over five years. Separating ourselves from old sinful habits and patterns can take time. Likewise, developing new habits to replace the old ones takes time. But with steady practice, rightly ordered habits, and a clear eye looking toward the One who is our Hope and Life, the Spirit of God, the second Paraclete is in the business of making real change take place. Deep inside we become renewed to that image-bearer whom God designed us to be and that person conformed to the image of Christ whom Jesus saved us to be.

What Are the Results of the Holy Spirit's Work as They Relate to Ethics as Worship?

Fully Human (*Teleios*) Perfect

What results may one expect as the Holy Spirit transforms us into true worshipers? The first and most obvious answer is that we can expect to see the fruit of the Spirit form in our lives and eventually become that which depicts our character. Paul lists these character traits most famously in Galatians 5:22–23:

> But the fruit of the Spirit is love, joy, peace, patience, kindness, goodness, faithfulness, gentleness, self-control; against such things there is no law.

Beyond (or perhaps behind) the manifestations of these virtues in our lives, we recall from our earlier discussion that it is the task of the second Paraclete to perfect or complete in us the work that the first Paraclete began (Phil. 1:6). Scripture tells us that while we as sinners have been conformed to the image of Adam, the Holy Spirit's goal is to help us conform to the image of Christ (Rom. 8:29)—the One who Colossians 1:15 tells us "is the image of the invisible God" and who Hebrews 1:3 tells us is "the radiance of [God's] glory and the exact representation of His nature." In other words, as our lives begin to conform to the image of Christ through the work of the second Paraclete, we are once again being restored to the fullness of what God created us to be in the beginning: humans made in the image of God (Gen. 1:26–27).

One might say that as the Holy Spirit transforms us into true worshipers, he is actually making us become what God intended for us to be all along: fully human. God through the Holy Spirit is restoring us through the gospel to be the image-bearers of God that he initially created us to be in all the fullness of what that remarkable description means.

To be clear, when we suggest that the work of the Holy Spirit results in our being fully human, we are not speaking in terms of ontology or about the essence of one's being. For all humans bear the image of God, and even as fallen sinners each of us still retains the image of God along with the inherent dignity and worth that comes with that status. Rather, we are speaking of both the final ordering and the full expression of what it means to be an image-bearer. This is the distinction between having the *status of* being human and the proper expression or fulfillment of *how one ought to live* as a human being.

Scripture uses several different concepts and words to capture this idea of how the gospel and the work of the Holy Spirit are meant to restore us to the fullness of what God originally created us to be as human image-bearers. In 1 Corinthians 2:14–15, Paul makes a clear distinction between those whom he describes as "natural" or "men of the flesh" and those who are "spiritual" (Greek, *pneumatikos*). In 1 Peter 1:13–19, we are admonished to "be holy" as God himself is holy (Greek, *hagios*). In 1 Timothy 4, Titus 2, and 2 Peter 1 and 3, believers are encouraged to embody "godliness" (Greek, *eusebeia*) in their life and practice.

While differing in nuance, all these terms not only carry a notion of deep devotion and directional focus that is oriented Godward, but also imply that such a perspective is a settled disposition of one's character. They imply mature and virtuous character. They depict not merely what a person does but who a person has become. Perhaps not flawlessly, but certainly consistently. And they also imply a fullness of what it means to become once again that which God intended for us to be from the beginning in creation and are now able to be restored to because of the gospel. As Wright puts it: "The key to it all, though, is that the Christian vision of virtue, of character that has become second nature, is precisely all about discovering what it means to be truly human—human in a way most of us never imagine."[41]

---

41. Wright, *After You Believe*, 25.

Perfect

With all of this in mind, we can say that as the Holy Spirit works in us to guide us, direct us, and restore us back into conformity to the image of God in Christ, the desired result is that we would become and embody what Jesus depicts in the Sermon on the Mount when he teaches that his followers are to be "perfect, as your heavenly Father is perfect" (Matt. 5:48). The word translated as "perfect" in this crucial text is the Greek word *teleios*. Unfortunately, no single one English word captures well the idea of *teleios*. As Jonathan Pennington rightly points out in his excellent work on the subject, *The Sermon on the Mount and Human Flourishing*, the word "perfect" is insufficient because it tends to lead us to the conclusion that the fullness that Jesus is advocating here is primarily about rule-keeping and moral perfectionism. In fact, the word has a far richer connotation in which the person depicted as *teleios* embodies a whole-life devotion to the things of God in character, disposition, and action such that he or she is mature, complete, lacking in nothing spiritually.[42]

Other crucial passages that use this word to depict the maturity of a Christ-follower are Romans 12:1–2, Colossians 1:28, and James 1:4, where the fully mature *teleios* behavior and disposition of the disciple of Christ are explicitly linked to the proper worship of God. One could say that the Christ-follower who embodies *teleios* is one who has the enduring quality of living a life that reflects the characteristics of Christ and thus maximizes worship in and through his or her life. In actuality, it would be totally appropriate to describe a person who embodies Christlikeness as *perfect* in the sense that the person is *fully human as God* created him or her to be.[43]

Table 4.2. Scripture Passages about Maturity in Christ

Matthew 5:48	Therefore you are to be **perfect**, as your heavenly Father is **perfect** [*teleios*].
Romans 12:1–2	Therefore I urge you, brethren, by the mercies of God, to present your bodies a living and holy sacrifice, acceptable to God, which is your spiritual service of worship. And do not be conformed to this world, but be transformed by the renewing of your mind, so that you may prove what the will of God is, that which is good and acceptable and **perfect** [*teleios*].
Colossians 1:28	We proclaim Him, admonishing every man and teaching every man with all wisdom, so that we may present every man **complete** [*teleios*] in Christ.
James 1:4	And let endurance have its perfect result, so that you may be **perfect** [*teleios*] and complete, lacking in nothing.

42. Jonathan T. Pennington, *The Sermon on the Mount and Human Flourishing: A Theological Commentary* (Grand Rapids: Baker, 2016), 67–85, esp. p. 70.

43. For clarity, perhaps it is wise to distinguish between the words *totally* and *fully*. Whereas the former has to do with what one is (i.e., all the parts of a person are human), the latter has to do with what one does with what one is. That is, *fully* relates to the expression, function, and flourishing of a thing.

Fully Alive (*Makarios*)

But it is not only the task of the Holy Spirit to glorify Christ through the life of a disciple by guiding him or her into the full expression of human wholeness and maturity, it is also his task to enable a transformed worshiper to experience the accompanying joy that results from being in that state. Scripture teaches that when a person lives in the wholly devoted mature pattern of life unto God depicted by *teleios*, an expected result of the Spirit's work is that the restored image-bearer will enjoy the correlated experience of *flourishing* as a human being.

One of the clearest places where this idea is depicted in the New Testament is once again found in Jesus' teaching in the Sermon on the Mount. In Matthew 5:3–12, Jesus lists a series of beatitudes depicting this state of flourishing: "Blessed are the poor in spirit, . . . blessed are those who mourn, . . . blessed are the gentle," and so forth. Each of these verses begins with the Greek word *makarios*, which is most typically translated into English as "blessed" or "happy." But once again, these English renderings fall short of the full concept that *makarios* represents. Indeed, in its context the word *makarios* is meant to capture the two contributing conceptions of both the Hebrew word *shalom* and the Greek *eudaimonia*.

The Hebrew word *shalom* relates to the inner harmony, wholeness, or sense of completeness of the human being that results from living a life rightly ordered to God in the manner that he designed. Likewise, the Greek term *eudaimonia* can literally be translated as "good spirits," but the concept depicts much more than a psychological state of mind or emotion. Rather, it depicts the objective observable state of something that is fulfilling that which it is designed or created to be.

Makarios is meant to depict or describe, based on observation, the flourishing of a human life as a result of how one is living. If one is living rightly ordered to God in the manner he designed and in accord with the person's essential nature as *imago Dei*, then his is a life of *makarios*—a flourishing human life.[44]

Putting these ideas together, then, we can understand that in the Sermon on the Mount, Jesus is painting a picture of not only what it means to be most fully human, but also how people can most fully experience what Jesus promised he would give in John 10:10—the exceedingly full life: "The thief comes only to steal and kill and destroy; I came that they may have life, and have it abundantly." Thus, we note that as the Spirit transforms us into the true worshipers that God is seeking, living "the good life" is not the goal. Worshiping and glorifying Christ is. The crucial role that the Holy Spirit plays in living for this ultimate purpose is to complete the good work that God begins in us through salvation by guiding us into

---

44. For a full discussion of these words and concepts, see Pennington, *Sermon on the Mount and Human Flourishing*, 41–67.

teleios (Phil. 1:6). When this happens, according to Jesus, the result is a life that is truly abundant and flourishing (*makarios*).

In sum, we can put these ideas together to say that it is the role of the One who gives life—the second Paraclete—to glorify the Lord Jesus Christ by helping image-bearers most fully embody what it means to bear the image of God (*teleios*). Thus, not only will Christ be magnified, but the image-bearers will also flourish in light of who they are and what they were created to be. The Holy Spirit's role is to grow each of us into a person who embodies Christlikeness and thus form us to be *fully human* (*teleios*) and *fully alive* (*makarios*).

Conclusion

As we near the end of this chapter, it is good to once again consider the words of Jesus in John 4:23–24:

> An hour is coming, and now is, when the true worshipers will worship the Father in spirit and truth; for such people the Father seeks to be His worshipers. God is spirit, and those who worship Him must worship in spirit and truth.

The purpose of this chapter has been to explore how the ministry of the Holy Spirit as the second Paraclete, who is tasked to complete the good work begun in us by the first Paraclete (Jesus Christ), works in us to produce the kind of moral and spiritual formation that will allow us to once again become the kind of followers that God desires: true worshipers who worship him in spirit and truth.

By way of conclusion, we can all give thanks to the Father and the Son for sending us the Spirit, that he might continue the work that was begun in us through our first Paraclete, Jesus Christ. For it is by the work and ministry of the Holy Spirit—the second Paraclete—that each of us is being transformed moment by moment, degree by degree, step by step until we finally become in character and practice what God has declared us to be in truth. Far more than merely rearranging the components of our lives, the Spirit is at work in us precisely for the purpose that we may come into the presence of God in every thought and deed (Col. 3:17). It is through the work of the One who gives life that each moment of life can be transformed, and every moment of life enjoyed in the presence of God.

Perhaps if we abide, if we yield, if we let the author of life have his way in us, then maybe, just maybe, we will taste and see that the Lord is indeed good as he uses us to take part in his glorious mission to maximize the worship and glory of God in every waking moment, through every thought and deed, to every square inch of the created order, such that the knowledge of the glory of the Lord covers the earth as the waters cover the sea. May it be that he who gives life—the Holy

Spirit—will help us to become *fully human*, *fully alive*, and *fully on mission* as we seek to become the kind of worshipers that God is seeking: those who worship God in spirit and truth. This is what ethics as worship is all about!

Having addressed here the meaning of worshiping God in *spirit*, it is to a consideration of what it means to worship God in *truth* that we now turn.

Key Terms and Concepts

abiding	Paraclete, first
Advocate	Paraclete, second
charismata	perfect
edification	reconciliation
eudaimonia	regeneration
flourishing	sanctification
fully alive	sealing
fully human	*shalom*
glorification	spirit and truth
Holy Spirit, filling of	spiritual formation
Holy Spirit, indwelling of	spiritual man
holy sweat	striving
makarios	*teleios*
mind of Christ	transformation
natural man	true worshipers

Key Scriptures

Matthew 5:3–12	Romans 8:29
Matthew 5:48	1 Corinthians 2:14–3:3
John 4:23–24	Galatians 5:22–23
John 10:10	Galatians 5:25
John 14:16–17	Ephesians 5:18
John 15:26–27	Colossians 1:28
John 16:8–11, 14	Hebrews 12:2
Romans 8:9–11	1 Peter 1:13–19

Study Questions

1. What did Jesus mean when he said in John 4:23–24 that God is looking for "true worshipers"?
2. What do the authors mean by the term *holy sweat*? How does hard work

and practice in the Christian life fit in with the idea that we are saved by Christ alone, by grace alone, and through faith alone?

3. Consider John 14:15 and 21. How is obedience tied to loving God? What does a lack of obedience tell us about our love for God?

4. What does it mean to "be filled" with the Holy Spirit? Why is this important for the Christian trying to worship God well through his or her ethics and morality?

5. In this chapter, the authors discuss the process of Christian disciples' becoming "fully human" and "fully alive" through the work of the Holy Spirit. What do they mean by becoming "fully human"? What do they mean by becoming "fully alive"? How do these ideas relate to Christian ethics?

For Further Reading

Block, Daniel I. *For the Glory of God: Recovering a Biblical Theology of Worship*. Grand Rapids: Baker, 2014.

Carson, D. A. "Worship under the Word." In *Worship by the Book*, edited by D. A. Carson, 11–63. Grand Rapids: Zondervan, 2002.

Cole, Graham A. *He Who Gives Life: The Doctrine of the Holy Spirit*. Wheaton, IL: Crossway, 2007.

Packer, J. I. *Keep in Step with the Spirit: Finding Fullness in Our Walk with God*. 2nd ed. Grand Rapids: Baker, 2005.

Pennington, Jonathan T. *The Sermon on the Mount and Human Flourishing: A Theological Commentary*. Grand Rapids: Baker, 2016.

Sanders, Fred. *The Deep Things of God: How the Trinity Changes Everything*. 2nd ed. Wheaton, IL: Crossway, 2017.

Sproul, R. C. *The Mystery of the Holy Spirit*. Fearn, Ross-shire, Scotland: Christian Focus, 1990.

Wright, N. T. *After You Believe: Why Christian Character Matters*. New York: HarperOne, 2010.

Worship God & enjoy him forever :)

5

Worship in Spirit and Truth:
The Role of the Bible in Ethics as Worship

*"In the beginning was the Word, and the Word was
with God, and the Word was God." —JOHN 1:1*

"Jesus not only taught the truth, he is the truth."[1]
—GORDON R. LEWIS AND BRUCE A. DEMAREST, Integrative Theology

Introduction: The Kind of Worshipers
That God Is Looking For: Worshipers in Truth

If God is preeminently worthy of our worship, if human beings have been created as his worshipers, and if the chief end of humankind is to worship God and
enjoy him forever, then understanding and rightly applying Jesus' words asserting
that God is looking for true worshipers who will worship him in *spirit* and *truth* is
the most important quest of human existence.[2] This is the heart and soul of ethics
as worship.

In the previous chapter, we engaged this quest by examining John 4:23–24 and
concluding that when Jesus stated that true worshipers must worship "in spirit
and truth," he was referring to the second and third persons of the Trinity: himself
and the Holy Spirit. We then focused our discussion on exploring what it means
to worship God in *spirit*. The discussion in that chapter centered on the person
and work of the Holy Spirit as the *Helper* or *Paraclete* tasked to complete the good
work begun in us by Jesus Christ. Ultimately, the role of the Holy Spirit in ethics

---

1. Gordon R. Lewis and Bruce A. Demarest, *Integrative Theology*, vol. 1 (Grand Rapids: Zondervan,
1987), 47.

2. WLC 1, http://www.pcaac.org/wp-content/uploads/2012/11/LargerCatechismwithScriptureProofs1.pdf.

is to enable us to *become conformed to the person of Christ* and empower us to maximally worship God in all aspects of life.

In this chapter, we continue our quest by focusing our attention on what Jesus means by true worshipers' worshiping God in *truth*. Here we give our attention to Jesus as the "Word of God" made flesh and as the One who gives us perfect instruction on how to rightly align our worship in, and through, the Bible. Proper worship requires not only that we seek to develop good character but that we do so according to the instructions that Jesus gives us about how to discern right and wrong and live accordingly. As Carl F. H. Henry puts it, "the question of right and wrong elbows itself into prominence wherever human beings exist."[3] Because this is true, our goal in this chapter is to understand how the Bible functions as our living guidebook on how to *rightly order our lives* and behaviors so that we can become the kind of worshipers that God is looking for.

Four questions will guide our discussion: What is revelation, and how does it relate to the Bible? What is the nature of Scripture as it relates to understanding ethics as worship? How does Scripture function as the guidebook for ethics as worship? How are we able to best understand Scripture as our guidebook for ethics as worship?

What Is Divine Revelation, and How Does It Relate to the Bible?

What Is Divine Revelation?

"Christianity differs from religion, commonly understood, in that it involves God's gracious quest for the person rather than the person's groping search for God. Central to the Christian way is the claim that God has taken the initiative and has, in intelligible ways, disclosed himself to people."[4] This disclosure of himself is known as *divine revelation*. In Scripture, the Greek root word for "revelation" is *apokaluptō*, which carries the meaning of revealing something that is hidden or making something fully known.[5] Therefore, when we speak of *divine revelation*, we mean that God is actively making himself and his will known to those who would otherwise be unable to see or know these things.

Christianity is a revelation-based faith. God lovingly condescends to reveal truth to us. Humans are able to understand what God communicates because he created us in his "image and likeness" such that there is an "analogy of being" between God and humans.[6] As Millard Erickson states, "Because humans are

---

3. Carl F. H. Henry, *Christian Personal Ethics* (Grand Rapids: Baker, 1957), 21.

4. Lewis and Demarest, *Integrative Theology*, 1:61.

5. Frederick William Danker et al., eds., *A Greek-English Lexicon of the New Testament and Other Early Christian Literature*, 3rd ed. (Chicago: University of Chicago Press, 2000) (BDAG), s.v. "ἀποκαλύπτω."

6. Graeme Goldsworthy, *Gospel-Centered Hermeneutics: Foundations and Principles of Evangelical Biblical*

finite and God is infinite, if they are to know God, that knowledge must come about by God taking the initiative to make himself known."[7]

Throughout history, God has revealed himself to humans in a number of different ways. He has spoken to—and through—patriarchs, kings, and prophets. Most graciously and profoundly, he revealed himself in the person of Jesus Christ. Further, as a means of love, guidance, and hope, he has also revealed himself through the Scriptures in order to give his followers everything they need for both life and practice. As J. I. Packer puts it: "Christianity is the true worship and service of the true God, humankind's Creator and Redeemer. It is a religion that rests on revelation. . . . God and godliness are the Bible's uniting themes."[8]

Because revelation has its source in God, we can have confidence that anything that God reveals about himself and the world he created will always be completely true. Not only this, but God's revelation will also have a perfect unity and will never be contradictory. If God chooses to reveal truth about himself via the natural created order, the words of a prophet, the person of Christ, the internal witness of conscience, or Scripture, his revelation will always be both true and consistent because it comes from his eternal mind and reflects his perfect nature. Hence, we can say that any form of revealed truth that comes from God is a subset of the infinite, inexhaustible, and perfect moral knowledge of our omniscient and good God.[9]

It follows that we can also know with confidence that if there is any *perceived* error or inconsistency, either between one's own perspective on truth and revelation from God or between one form of revelation and another, then the problem

---

Interpretation (Downers Grove, IL: IVP Academic, 2006), 34–35. Language functions to communicate ideas in three ways: univocally, equivocally, and analogically. Univocal communication means that there is only one basic possible meaning of a term. Equivocal communication means that there are multiple possible meanings of a term. Analogical communication means that communication about something is done through analogy because it is impossible to describe God exactly as he is. Thus, our language falls short in its ability to describe God perfectly because he is infinite and we are not. But this does not mean that our language is inaccurate or meaningless; rather, it simply recognizes limits to how much it can capture. As image-bearers, we are different from God but uniquely analogous to him. Thus, we are created uniquely able to receive communication from him. Because humans are "like" God, we can perceive things about him and describe him in ways that no other creature on earth can.

7. Millard J. Erickson, *Christian Theology*, 3rd ed. (Grand Rapids: Baker Academic, 2013), 122.

8. J. I. Packer, *Concise Theology* (Wheaton, IL: Tyndale, 1993), 3.

9. When we say "any form of revealed truth," we actually mean anything that is true. Thus, even things such as mathematics could (and rightly should?) be understood as a part of the moral law in the sense that it is a part of how we understand the basic structures of the world—the revealed reality in which we must function to live ethically unto God in worship. Thus, it is not a category shift to move from scientific/rational categories about the structure of the universe to moral categories if all the universe is created by God and for his glory. Understanding ethics as worship from a revealed-reality and revealed-morality perspective provides the unifying link. For a further development of these ideas, see Thomas Aquinas's discussion on the nature and types of law in his *Summa Theologica*, I.II.93.1. See also our previous discussion in chapter 1 footnote 20.

lies not with the divine revelation itself, but with our perception, interpretation, or understanding of it. Even if something in Scripture *appears* to be in contradiction to our finite and fallible minds, there will never be an *actual* contradiction. As Scripture teaches us, because of sin, our hearts are rebellious, our minds are darkened, and our wills are weakened (Rom. 1:18–24; Eph. 4:18; Heb. 4:15; cf. Matt. 26:41). In itself, however, God's revelation will always be true, good, beautiful, united in theme, and noncontradictory—like God himself. Our inability to rightly perceive, know, and act on truth does not negate the perfect unity of God's revelation. It merely shows us the depth of our own brokenness and highlights the great need we have for God to reveal himself to us, that we might know our sin and discover his plan for our rescue.

Two Kinds of Divine Revelation: General Revelation and Special Revelation

How does God reveal himself to us? There are two kinds, or categories, of divine revelation: *general revelation* and *special revelation*. They are both important to how we worship God in truth.

General Revelation

General revelation refers to any and all knowledge that God reveals about himself and that is available to be discovered "generally" by God's image-bearers—be they his disciples or not. More simply put, "General revelation is God's communication of himself to all persons at all times and in all places."[10] Scripturally, the clearest discussion of the universal availability of God's self-revelation is found in Romans 1:18–21:

> For the wrath of God is revealed from heaven against all ungodliness and unrighteousness of men who suppress the truth in unrighteousness, because that which is known about God is evident within them; for God made it evident to them. For since the creation of the world His invisible attributes, His eternal power and divine nature, have been clearly seen, being understood through what has been made, so that they are without excuse. For even though they knew God, they did not honor Him as God or give thanks, but they became futile in their speculations, and their foolish heart was darkened.

The term *general* as we are using it here, then, is referencing who this type of revelation is available to. In the words of Lewis and Demarest, "*General revelation* refers to the disclosure of God in nature, in providential history, and in the moral law within the heart, whereby all persons at all times and places gain a

---

10. Erickson, *Christian Theology*, 122.

rudimentary understanding of the Creator and his moral demands."[11] Demarest also adds elsewhere, "General revelation, mediated through nature, conscience, and the providential ordering of history, traditionally has been understood as a universal witness to God's existence and character."[12]

Within the larger discussion of general revelation, there is considerable debate among theologians, philosophers, and ethicists regarding the extent to which accurate knowledge about God and his moral standards can be discovered and properly applied to life and practice by those who have not been saved by God's grace.[13] The term *natural theology* is often used to refer not to what God has generally revealed, but to how much of God's general revelation can be perceived by sinners apart from the Bible.[14] The term *natural moral philosophy*, likewise, is the attempt to develop moral systems apart from reliance on Scripture. And the term *natural law* can also refer to attempts to discover moral standards and patterns in the natural world through human reason unaided by God's special revelation. From a particularly Christian point of view, however, given that God created the world and the humans who inhabit it, we should more precisely understand the term *natural law* to refer to those moral principles that are woven into the fabric of the universe by God's design and to which all humans are accountable—whether they discover them or not, or whether they attribute them to God or not.

It is beyond the scope of this book to explore these debates fully. For the purposes of our discussion, however, we simply point to passages such as Psalm 19, Acts 17, and Romans 1–3 that indicate that all humans have access to at least a minimal threshold of knowledge about both God's existence and his moral laws.

11. Lewis and Demarest, *Integrative Theology*, 1:61.

12. Bruce A. Demarest, *General Revelation: Historical Views and Contemporary Issues* (Grand Rapids: Zondervan, 1982), 14.

13. Lewis and Demarest provide a helpful discussion on this topic that captures much of our thoughts on the matter. Here we quote them at length: "The reality of natural theology, though devalued or denied in some Barthian and Reformed thinking, is explicitly and repeatedly taught in Scripture. . . . The texts often used by Barth and Reformed theologians to deny the actuality of a natural knowledge of God fail to take sufficiently into account the two kinds of knowledge of God required by the respective contexts: knowledge of a moral theism and knowledge of God's redemptive plan. Passages of Scripture that state that people do not know God deny, not a knowledge of theism, but a knowledge of God's redemptive plan in the incarnate, crucified, and risen Christ. . . . Although no one is by nature a spiritually reborn child of God, everyone is by nature a child of the Creator, deriving life and breath from him (Acts 17:28). The lack of redemptive sonship does not deny the reality of a metaphysical creaturely sonship. Does the teaching that some truth can be known through the creation contradict the teaching that depraved minds cannot understand the things of God apart from faith in Christ (1 Cor. 2:14)? Again, the context has to do with redemptive truth—the message of the Cross (1 Cor. 1:18), Jesus Christ and him crucified (1 Cor. 2:2)." Lewis and Demarest, *Integrative Theology*, 1:75–76.

14. Lewis and Demarest, *Integrative Theology*, 1:75. See also Graham A. Cole, *He Who Gives Life: The Doctrine of the Holy Spirit* (Wheaton, IL: Crossway, 2007), 260. We are indebted to Cole for his discussion and clarity in defining each of these terms.

In Psalm 19:1, we learn that the heavens themselves "are telling of the glory of God." In Acts 17, we see that even the pagan Gentiles acknowledge that some form of deity exists, and Paul, in Romans 1–3, indicates that both God's existence (Rom. 1:20) and basic moral standards (v. 32) are "evident" (v. 19) even if denied. Thus, in regard to general revelation, Scripture plainly teaches that there is a basic universal human accountability regarding both God's existence and his moral standards. Having acknowledged this, however, when it comes to guiding our ethical quest to worship God in truth, the value of general revelation and natural law is limited. General revelation is not sufficient to communicate God's plan of redemption. In terms of ethics, it is limited to the rudimentary recognition that there is indeed a God and a moral standard to which we are accountable, and that general revelation in turn works to bring conviction of sin and thereby shows our great need for redemption.

Recognizing these limitations, however, is not to suggest that all human efforts toward a discovery of morality by nonbiblical or non-Christian writers is fully wrong or without value. If there is a basic unity of revelation and if there is some rudimentary ability of human beings to reason that remains intact after the fall, then it would follow that a touch point of basic moral knowledge is shared by believers and unbelievers alike. This is true not only of the discovery of things such as basic mathematics, but also of some basic moral knowledge that may enable non-Christians to order society. As Carl F. H. Henry puts it: "A point of continuity does exist between biblical and nonbiblical ethical writers, if not in their respective systems. The Christian ethical ideal is not to be defined entirely apart from the ethical ideal of all humanity. If Truth is one, and if the Good is one, and if God is everywhere with a witness—and these are basic Christian assertions—then such a connection must be insisted upon. Christianity stresses the unity of Truth, and the universal validity of the Good and Right, and the universality of rational norms."[15]

With this in mind, we can go a bit further to suggest that there should be no fundamental debate or rivalry between the disciplines of theology, philosophy, and ethics in regard to the discovery and application of truth. For if all revelation and truth has its grounding in God, then however it is discovered, it remains a gift of a kind God to humanity. Henry again gives proper perspective:

> The Christian emphasis is that revelation supplies philosophy with its only secure presuppositions and that a coherent philosophy is the handmaid rather than the jealous rival of theology. In that Christianity recognizes that the special moral revelation of the Bible authoritatively enlarges the general revelation in man's

15. Henry, *Christian Personal Ethics*, 148–49.

conscience, Christian ethics may be considered a species of philosophical ethics. This is provided the latter term is not arbitrarily restricted to speculative ethics and thus made to exclude an ethical content derived from supernatural disclosure. . . . The tension between Christian and speculative ethics rises from the fact that the latter term usually designates those movements that erect a standard for the will through rational speculation, independent of any appeal to special revelation. . . . But this is due to arbitrariness of philosophical definition and bias.[16]

When properly understood, then, because all true knowledge and true moral principles are grounded in the nature of God and given by his grace in revelation, any discovery of truth—regardless of how it is discovered—is a testimony to the fact that God created the world according to his eternal wisdom and plan. It is the *first grace* of God's creating and giving material, spiritual, and moral order that is being discovered. Nothing that is actually true is independent from God. Claims to the contrary do not negate the validity of what truths may be discovered through general revelation; they merely demonstrate human sinful arrogance.

Special Revelation

Because of this human sinfulness and arrogance, God in his kindness has offered a further grace toward us in regard to how he reveals himself. *Special revelation* refers to "God's manifestation of himself to particular persons at definite times and places, enabling those persons to enter into a redemptive relationship with him."[17] When we speak of this revelation as being *special*, we are referring to both the fact that God commonly used *supernatural* means to communicate about himself and the fact that it is only through special revelation that a person can gain saving knowledge. As John Frame rightly explains, "God has given us Scripture, or 'special revelation,' both to supplement natural revelation (by adding to it the message of salvation) and to correct our misuses of natural revelation."[18]

In this regard, one could say that special revelation works much like a pair of glasses that God gives to humans so that they can see God's world rightly. John Calvin famously introduced this metaphor to explain the function of Scripture as special revelation:

Now in describing the world as a mirror in which to behold God, I would not be understood to assert either that our eyes are sufficiently clear-sighted to discern

16. Henry, *Christian Personal Ethics*, 149.
17. Erickson, *Christian Theology*, 144.
18. John M. Frame, *Apologetics to the Glory of God* (Phillipsburg, NJ: P&R Publishing, 1994), 23. See also Aquinas, *Summa Theologica*, I–II.91.5.

what the fabric of heaven and earth represents, or that the knowledge we thereby derive suffices for salvation. As a matter of fact, because the Lord invites us to himself by means of created things but with no effect except thereby to render us inexcusable, he has added (as was necessary) a new remedy, or at any rate mitigated the coarseness of our disposition by means of other assistance. For with Scripture as our guide and teacher, not only does he make plain those things that would otherwise escape our notice, he virtually forces us to behold them, as if he had assisted our dull sight with eyeglasses.[19]

Throughout redemptive history, God has revealed truth via special revelation through various means (e.g., casting lots, dreams, visions, the Urim and Thummim, prophets, theophanies, angels). But the preeminent means by which he has done so is through the Word of God—Jesus Christ and the Bible.

The Word of God as Special Revelation

Graeme Goldsworthy is correct to point out that when we talk about God's Word, "we have something of a dilemma. There are two distinct, if related ways of identifying God's word. We speak of both Jesus Christ and the Bible as God's word. Putting an upper-case W on Word when we speak about Jesus as the Divine Word may remove some ambiguity, but we need to understand the relationship between the two."[20]

The Word of God Incarnate

In order to gain this understanding, first consider what we mean by Jesus as the incarnate Word of God. John begins his account of the life of Christ with the assertion, "In the beginning was the Word" (John 1:1). Later, John declares that the "Word" then "became flesh" as the person of Jesus Christ and "dwelt among us, and we saw His glory, glory as of the only begotten from the Father, full of grace and truth" (v. 14; cf. v. 17). The Greek term translated in John's Gospel as "Word" is *Logos*. This word is rich in meaning and represents a synthesis between both Hebrew and Greek Stoic thought. It refers to both God's eternal wisdom in divine communication and the "divine power that undergirds rational and moral life."[21] In using it, John is attempting to shed light on the fact that the second person of the Trinity became incarnate as Jesus Christ, but also the basis by which Jesus is "the true Light which, coming into the world, enlightens every man" (v. 9).

Thus, at the very heart of Christianity is the belief that the person Jesus Christ,

---

19. John Calvin, *Institutes of the Christian Religion*, ed. John T. McNeill, trans. Ford Lewis Battles, 2 vols., Library of Christian Classics 20–21 (Philadelphia: Westminster Press, 1960), 1.6.1.

20. Goldsworthy, *Gospel-Centered Hermeneutics*, 35.

21. Lewis and Demarest, *Integrative Theology*, 1:71.

as the living Word of God, is the ultimate revelation to humankind of God himself. For as Paul tells us, "In [Christ] all the fullness of Deity dwells in bodily form" (Col. 2:9). Likewise, the opening words in the book of Hebrews teach us that Jesus Christ is the epitome of God's love displayed through his willingness to reveal himself to humanity:

perfect example

> God, after He spoke long ago to the fathers in the prophets in many portions and in many ways, in these last days has spoken to us in His Son, whom He appointed heir of all things, through whom also He made the world. And *He is the radiance of His glory and the exact representation of His nature*, and upholds all things by the word of His power. (Heb. 1:1–3)

Additionally, John tells us that Jesus the Word of God incarnate is also the embodiment of truth and the only way to the abundant life. As John 14:6 tells us, "Jesus said to him, 'I am the way, and the truth, and the life; no one comes to the Father but through me.'" When we consider Jesus' proclamation that God is seeking true worshipers who will worship him in spirit and truth, we find that Jesus as the incarnate Word of God is the very embodiment of truth. So through his life, death, and resurrection, we not only see truth displayed in its clearest form, but also are truly provided with access to right relationship with God.

The Word of God Inscripturated

So how, then, does understanding Jesus as the incarnate Word of God and the embodiment of truth relate to our understanding of Scripture as the Word of God? The first key element in discerning the answer to this question relates to what Jesus taught his disciples about the nature of truth as its relationship to his teachings and commandments. For example, John 8:31–32 points out that Jesus told his disciples, "If you continue in My word, then you are truly disciples of Mine; and you will know the truth, and the truth will make you free." Here the Greek text uses the same term (*Logos*) that identifies Jesus as the "Word" in John 1:1. While simply using the same terminology does not by itself establish the correlation between Jesus and the Bible, Jesus himself understood that his instructions were the means by which his disciples would be rightly related to himself both spiritually and ethically.

For example, in the same chapter in which Jesus tells his disciples that he is "the way, and the truth, and the life" (John 14:6), he also instructs them about the written Word of God and the important role of the commandments in ordering their worship. Consider again John 14:21: "He who has My commandments and keeps them is the one who loves Me." And immediately following this he reasserts the point by saying:

> If anyone loves Me, he will keep My word; and My Father will love him, and We will come to him and make Our abode with him. He who does not love Me does not keep My words; and the word which you hear is not Mine, but the Father's who sent me. (John 14:23–24)

Clearly, Jesus' assumption is that his commandments are the truth that will set them free. Obedience to his commandments is the pathway to loving worship of God.[22]

Elsewhere in the New Testament, we see that Jesus gave similar instructions to his disciples as part of his Great Commission:

> And Jesus came up and spoke to them, saying, "All authority has been given to Me in heaven and on earth. Go therefore and make disciples of all the nations, baptizing them in the name of the Father and the Son and the Holy Spirit, *teaching them to observe all that I commanded you*; and lo, I am with you always, even to the end of the age." (Matt. 28:18–20)

J. I. Packer is on point as he makes the connection for us: "Since the Father has now given the Son executive authority to rule the cosmos on his behalf (Matt. 28:18), Scripture now functions precisely as the instrument of Christ's lordship over his followers."[23] It is then through the written Word of God, the Scriptures, that the disciples would learn how to worship God in truth. Lewis and Demarest capture the idea well: "The function of the written Word is to teach Christ, the living Word."[24] Perhaps this is why Jesus prayed for his disciples in his High Priestly Prayer that the Father would "sanctify them in the truth; Your *word* is truth" (John 17:17).

Both Paul's and Peter's teaching about the nature of Scripture makes the point even more explicit. In 2 Timothy 3:16–17, Paul writes:

> All Scripture is *inspired* by God and profitable for teaching, for reproof, for correction, for training in righteousness; so that the man of God may be adequate, equipped for every good work.

---

22. It is important to note here that Jesus' commandment to love is not distinct from the moral commandments found in the Bible (such as the Ten Commandments). Rather, here he connects the two intimately. That is, love for God and love of neighbor are summary expressions of what the Ten Commandments are aiming for. Similarly, the Ten Commandments are meant to guide the proper expressions of love. Jesus' discussion of several of the Ten Commandments in the Sermon on the Mount (Matt. 5–7) demonstrates this exact point.

23. Packer, *Concise Theology*, 16.

24. Lewis and Demarest, *Integrative Theology*, 1:136.

The Greek word translated as "inspired" is *theopneustos*, which literally means "God-breathed." Paul uses this distinct word to show us that the Scripture is literally God's Word given to humans through a cooperative process in which he gives us in writing the truths we need as his disciples for rightly ordered faith and ethics. Peter affirms this teaching when he writes in 2 Peter 1:21 that "no prophecy was ever made by an act of human will, but men moved by the *Holy Spirit spoke from God.*" Scripture, then, is God's special revelation to his disciples that has come to us from the mouth of God.[25] Literally, it is the Word of God. It is God's eternal wisdom given through divine communication. The Bible's source is God, and it reflects perfectly (not exhaustively) the character of God.

In asserting that the Bible is *inspired*, we mean that ultimately God has the primary role in authorship. He worked *concursively* with human authors, meaning that he allowed for their human personalities and wills to be involved, yet he carried them along in the process such that they wrote exactly what he wanted to communicate. Thus, in one sense, we can say that each book of the Bible is authored both by its human writer and by God. In another sense, however, while we recognize that human authors penned the words onto the original manuscripts, the Word written ultimately "originated as an action of God who breathed it out."[26] It is the result of divine power and influence, and it reveals exactly what God desired to reveal of himself and his eternal, infinite mind. As Robert Plummer puts it, God "superintended the process that every word written was also the exact word [God] wanted to be written."[27] The idea of *superintended* means that God used a guiding process that at times was very direct, at other times less so, but one in which, as the writers composed the text of Scripture, God both guided and guarded their words such that they would be exactly as he desired them to be in the original manuscripts.[28] B. B. Warfield captures the idea when he writes that "the Bible is the Word of God in such a sense that its words, though written by men and bearing indelibly impressed on them the marks of their human origin, were written, nevertheless, under such an influence of the Holy Ghost as to be also the words of God, the adequate expression of His mind . . . and will."[29]

In sum, we can assert that "the God of revelation is no mime who simply acts to create and redeem but leaves his creatures to grope for interpretation. God has made himself known in prophetic word, gospel word, and supremely the

---

25. Calvin, *Institutes*, 1.18.4.

26. Charles C. Ryrie, *Basic Theology* (Wheaton, IL: Victor, 1986), 69.

27. Robert L. Plummer, *40 Questions about Interpreting the Bible* (Grand Rapids: Kregel, 2010), 32. See also Millard Erickson's helpful discussion in *Christian Theology*, 189–91.

28. Ryrie, *Basic Theology*, 71.

29. B. B. Warfield, "The Real Problem of Inspiration," in *Revelation and Inspiration*, vol. 1 of *The Works of Benjamin B. Warfield* (Grand Rapids: Baker, 2003), 173.

incarnate Word. The crystallization of such revelation is found in the scriptural word."[30] When we speak of special revelation and consider the two primary means by which God reveals himself specially to his people, we understand that "only God can make God known" and that "God reveals himself through himself."[31] And as he does so, we understand that "Jesus not only taught the truth, he is the truth."[32]

Summary

In sum, there are two big takeaway points from the discussion thus far about the nature of truth and its importance for developing our ethical methodology. First, we must begin by recognizing that *truth is a person*.[33] Worshiping God in truth is not merely—or even primarily—about identifying a standard or list of rules to adhere to, but rather, it is the pursuit of a relationship with the Creator God who made us and loves us enough to reveal himself to us, that we might have fellowship with him and abide with him in joy forever.

Second, not only has God revealed himself perfectly through the Word *incarnate*, he has also revealed himself to us through the *written Word*. In doing so, he provides a perfect means to communicate to us his enduring instructions for how to be rightly restored to him and then live rightly as worshipers. In relation to understanding morality and ethics, these written instructions found in Scripture are indeed God's standard for us. But they are not merely standards; they are his expression of himself. Therefore, when we read these divinely revealed truths, they are also meant to lead us not merely to an ethical lifestyle, but to the One who is truth. They are given so that in obeying them we might be conformed to his image as we were created to be in the beginning.

Tying this discussion to the larger question of how one becomes a worshiper in spirit and truth that we began in the previous chapter, we can now say that it is through the *written Word* containing commands, principles, guidelines, and stories that the *incarnate Word* supernaturally gifted to his followers the means by which we might reach maturity (*teleios*) and flourish (*makarios*) as the Spirit enables us. In short, the Spirit of God in perfect harmony with the Word of God incarnate has given us the Scriptures, that we might become the kind of worshipers that God the Father is looking for: those who worship him in spirit and truth (John 4:23–24).

30. Cole, *He Who Gives Life*, 260.

31. Kevin J. Vanhoozer, "Holy Scripture," in *Christian Dogmatics: Reformed Theology for the Church Catholic*, ed. Michael Allen and Scott R. Swain (Grand Rapids: Baker, 2016), 39.

32. Lewis and Demarest, *Integrative Theology*, 1:47.

33. For a helpful discussion of this point, see Calvin, *Institutes*, 1.13.7.

What Is the Nature and Character of Scripture as It Relates to Understanding Ethics as Worship?

Infallible, Inerrant, Immutable, and Clear

In light of the previous discussion, it is proper to also point out that because God is the ultimate author of the Bible and has divinely superintended the inspired writing of the Bible, we can expect that not only has he had sovereign control of every word recorded in the Bible, but he is also the protector of its truthfulness. God's "supernatural influence upon divinely chosen prophets and apostles" is the means by which "the Spirit of God assures the truth and trustworthiness of their oral and written proclamations."[34] We can expect that Scripture has a particular nature and characteristics that distinguish it from any other book or source of moral authority.

Infallible

First, because the ultimate author of the Bible is God, then it logically follows that the Scriptures that God has "breathed out" would reflect his nature and character. Because he is perfect, we can expect his words to be perfect. This is the testimony of Scripture itself: "The law of the Lord is perfect, restoring the soul" (Ps. 19:7). Thus, it is right to speak of Scripture as *infallible.* By the term *infallible*, we mean that the words of the Bible are "incapable of being wrong" in the matters they speak to—particularly regarding faith and doctrine. As the Chicago Statement on Biblical Inerrancy states:

> Holy Scripture, being God's own Word, written by men prepared and superintended by His Spirit, is of *infallible* divine authority in all matters upon which it touches: it is to be believed, as God's instruction, in all that it affirms; obeyed, as God's command, in all that it requires; embraced, as God's pledge, in all that it promises.[35]

The Bible can be trusted to guide us to accomplish the ends for which it was given. Scripture will never lead our ethical practice or worship astray.

Inerrant

Not only is the Bible infallible, but again, because it is "God-breathed," it logically follows that it is also free from all error, falsehood, fraud, or deceit. That is,

---

34. Carl F. H. Henry, *God, Revelation, and Authority*, 6 vols. (Waco, TX: Word, 1976–83), 4:129.

35. International Council on Biblical Inerrancy, "The Chicago Statement on Biblical Inerrancy," accessed June 1, 2020, https://library.dts.edu/Pages/TL/Special/ICBI_1.pdf (emphasis added).

Wholly true

it is *inerrant*. While this word carries with it many of the same connotations as *infallible*, the assertion here is that not only will it not fail because it is incapable of error (like God himself), it is also wholly true. As Wayne Grudem explains, "the inerrancy of Scripture means that Scripture in the original manuscripts does not affirm anything that is contrary to fact. . . . The definition in simple terms just means that the Bible always tells the truth, and that it always tells the truth concerning everything it talks about."[36] The *Evangelical Dictionary of Theology* is likewise helpful: "Inerrancy is the view that when all the facts become known, they will demonstrate that the Bible in its original autographs and correctly interpreted is entirely true and never false in all it affirms, whether that relates to doctrine or ethics or to the social, physical, or life sciences."[37]

If God is the author of Scripture who inspired its content, wouldn't it logically follow that because he is God and incapable of error, there would be no error in the words he gave to his people?[38] We can agree with St. Augustine, who wrote in a letter to Jerome: "I believe most firmly that not one of those authors has erred in any respect in writing."[39] Thus, even when we find ourselves questioning ideas or facts about reality or morality presented in the Bible, we can have confidence that its assertions are never in error.[40]

---

36. Wayne Grudem, *Systematic Theology: An Introduction to Biblical Doctrine* (Grand Rapids: Zondervan, 1994), 90.

37. Paul Feinberg, "Bible, Inerrancy and Infallibility of," in *Evangelical Dictionary of Theology*, ed. W. A. Elwell, 2nd ed. (Grand Rapids: Baker, 1984), 142. Obviously, this quote raises questions related to accuracy in transmission of the text from early manuscripts to our modern Bible translations as well as interpretive methods. For further study see International Council on Biblical Inerrancy, "The Chicago Statement on Biblical Inerrancy."

38. This is not to say that there are not some places in the Scriptures where there is difficulty explaining the exact nature of how the Bible is inerrant. Descriptions of such things as the "sun rising" may run into claims of falsehood or error, but to make such claims would be to misunderstand the nature of inerrancy as well as the nature and genre of the text of Scripture where such phrases are used. For the doctrine of God's inspired Word as being *inerrant* includes consideration of the various purposes of authors as they write, the varied genres of different portions of Scripture (e.g., poetic literature often uses illustrative language to express a point), and the context of the everyday language patterns that the original hearers of the text would have understood. While a fuller discussion of this point is beyond our scope here, both Robert L. Plummer and Wayne Grudem are helpful sources for those who may want to explore the question more fully. See Plummer, *40 Questions about Interpreting the Bible*, 41–45; Grudem, *Systematic Theology*, 90–104. See also "Chicago Statement on Biblical Inerrancy," art. XIII.

39. Augustine, *Letter* 82.3, quoted in Lewis and Demarest, *Integrative Theology*, 1:136.

40. St. Augustine has a fascinating perspective on perceived errors: "I have learned to yield this respect and honour only to the canonical books of Scripture: of these alone do I most firmly believe that the authors were completely free from error. And if in these writings I am perplexed by anything which appears to me opposed to truth, I do not hesitate to suppose that either the manuscript is faulty, or the translator has not caught the meaning of what was said, or I myself have failed to understand it." Augustine, *Letter* 82.3, accessed January 11, 2019, http://www.newadvent.org/fathers/1102082.htm. Millard Erickson likewise takes an approach that trusts the character of God to deliver infallible teaching even when personal understanding

Eternal and Immutable

Third, following the logic that "truth is a person" and that the person of God has revealed himself through the Word of God, then because he is both eternal and immutable in his essential character, we should also expect that the moral principles he reveals in Scripture would likewise have an eternal and immutable character. And indeed, Scripture itself testifies to this reality:

> Forever, O LORD,
> Your word is settled in heaven. (Ps. 119:89)

> The grass withers, the flower fades,
> But the word of our God stands forever. (Isa. 40:8; 1 Peter 1:24–25)

> But it is easier for heaven and earth to pass away than for one stroke of a letter of the Law to fail. (Luke 16:17)

> You have been born again not of seed which is perishable but imperishable, that is, through the living and *enduring* word of God. (1 Peter 1:23)

With regard to ethics as worship, we can rest in the assurance that the moral principles God reveals are not capriciously given. Nor will they change from era to era or circumstance to circumstance. While application of the principles may be nuanced to different contexts or situations, and while some of the civil and ceremonial laws given to Israel for its time and context have been fulfilled in Christ, we can have confidence that as God does not change in his essential nature, neither will his moral instructions change.[41] Because that which God reveals through Scripture reflects his eternal and omniscient mind, as well as his unchanging character, his instruction *endures through time and every circumstance*. There is nothing he does not know, and he is never taken by surprise. Thus, because he created the world and gave instructions on how best to live in it, we can have confidence that he knew what he was doing and saying. God's instructions are eternally valid and trustworthy because he is eternally good and true. The Bible's moral instruction doesn't change, but the moral instruction in the Bible is certainly meant to change us.

---

is lacking: "We must, then, continue to work at the task of resolving whatever tensions there are in our understanding of the Bible. . . . Rather than giving fanciful explanations, it is better to leave difficulties unresolved in the confidence, based on the doctrine of Scripture, that they will be removed to the extent that additional data become available." Erickson, *Christian Theology*, 205.

41. For a fuller discussion on the divisions of the law between civil, ceremonial, and moral, see David W. Jones, *An Introduction to Biblical Ethics* (Nashville: B&H Academic, 2013), 56–63.

Clear

Finally, in addition to Scripture's being infallible, inerrant, and immutable, we also understand that God, in his kindness, is both willing and able to make his self-revelation through Scripture *clear*. This idea, sometimes called the *perspicuity of Scripture*, means that the fundamental story line and message of the Bible can be understood—at least intellectually—by ordinary readers.

Indeed, the Bible attests to its own clarity. In the Old Testament, we see that after giving the law to the Israelites, Moses reminds God's people: "These words, which I am commanding you today, shall be on your heart. You shall teach them diligently to your sons and shall talk of them when you sit in your house and when you walk by the way and when you lie down and when you rise up" (Deut. 6:6–7). The ability to teach the commands of God to children presupposes that they can be clearly understood and transferred between old and young. Later, in Psalm 19:7, David affirms this very point when he proclaims that "the testimony of the LORD is sure, *making wise the simple*."

This is not to say that each passage is equally clear. For example, even Peter acknowledged that some of Paul's writings were difficult to understand (2 Peter 3:15–16). And indeed, one need only read the prophecies of Ezekiel or the book of Revelation to recognize that there are difficult passages and puzzling ideas. Nor, as we will discuss below, is it meant to imply that proper interpretation is necessarily easy.

Instead, the point is that it would be wrong to think of the Bible as a secretive book that only a special class can understand. Its fundamental story line and meaning are not full of hidden meanings and allegories that take years of special training to unravel. Certainly, training can help unravel the more puzzling passages, and like any other life skill, growing in wisdom in accomplishing a task such as Bible interpretation is advantageous both for the self and for the church as a whole. But here, as we emphasize the perspicuity or clarity of the Bible, the big idea is that the main story line and the main plot of Scripture are discernible to the ordinary reader. This is the case because of the grace of God to condescend to the level of human interaction and kindly provide a source of knowledge and truth. As such, the Bible gives us clearly everything necessary to understand, believe, and follow both for salvation and for our ethical living. As Graeme Goldsworthy helpfully writes, "despite the many and varied interpretations of certain details, and despite the many difficult texts, the humble believer will not be led astray in the reading of the Bible's essential message, and spiritual sustenance will be delivered to young and old, to the uneducated and the sophisticated alike."[42]

---

42. Goldsworthy, *Gospel-Centered Hermeneutics*, 17.

Authoritative

Four Reasons Why We Should View Scripture as Authoritative

Following from these ideas, then, we can also understand that the Scriptures are meant by God to function authoritatively as our guide to living a life of ethics as worship before God. We speak of the authority of the Bible in several senses. First and most importantly, Scripture is authoritative because it has its source in God. It is his words. And thus, merely based on the nature of who God is, his instructions and his commands should be obeyed. He is God and we are not. Hence, fully apart from the question whether we perceive his instruction as "good" or "right," there is a sense in which we should understand that the *Godness* of God alone requires us to bow down in submission to his instruction. "Thy will be done" is always a good response when your conversation partner is God.

Second, and closely related, Scripture carries authority simply because it comes from God as an expression of his love and grace. The remarkably good news is that God's instructions in Scripture are given for our benefit and to provide the right and good path to life, joy, and flourishing. As John puts it famously in his Gospel, "For God so loved the world, that He gave His only begotten Son" (John 3:16). Therefore, in love God gives us his revelation, and through this revelation we find abundant life (10:10). As Jesus states in relation to his teachings, "If you continue in My word, then you are truly disciples of Mine; and you will know the truth, and the truth will make you free" (8:31–32).

Third, and again closely related, when we speak of Scripture as being authoritative, we do so because it is ultimately trustworthy. Throughout his life and ministry, Jesus himself relied on and trusted Scripture as his authoritative guide for life and practice (see Matt. 4:4, 7, 10; 5:17–18; 19:1–9; John 16:12–15; 17:18; 20:21). His view of Scripture should shape our view as Christ's disciples. We should hold the instructions given in the Bible authoritatively as he did.[43]

Fourth, then, building on these previous ideas, we hold Scripture as authoritative in regard to the nature of its content. Scripture addresses life's most important questions. It deals with eternal matters, not merely or only temporal problems. It relates to the very nature of what it means to be human. It speaks to how we might best flourish. It addresses the question of life, death, and our eternal state.

Authority in Relation to Other Sources (Four Sources of Authority)

Finally, we addressed this point in chapter 1, but it is worth reiterating here. In relation to other possible sources of moral authority, because Scripture is

---

43. For a helpful discussion of this point, see Sinclair B. Ferguson, "How Does the Bible Look at Itself?," in *Inerrancy and Hermeneutic: A Tradition, A Challenge, A Debate*, ed. Harvie M. Conn (Grand Rapids: Baker, 1988), 58–59.

grounded in God's eternal character and mind and is given to us infallibly by his mercy and grace, it is then to be understood as the supreme source of authority as it pertains both to human salvation and to ethical living. Grudem notes, "If the Bible alone is the Word of God written for our benefit and given to us, then we must count it a higher authority than all other sources of authority in ethical discussions."[44]

What the supremacy of special revelation means for salvation is that there are no other writings of equal value to Christian Scripture as historically received in the canon. It also means that no other revelation is necessary, beyond the historically received canon of Scripture, to understand the good news of salvation in Christ alone, through faith alone, and by grace alone.

In terms of ethics, the supremacy of Scripture means that emphasis should always be placed first and foremost on what God has revealed in Scripture to guide any and every moral situation. This includes placing an appeal to Scripture above any form of tradition, human reason, or experience as the primary basis for moral decision-making.[45]

Table 5.1. Sources of Authority ("Wesleyan Quadrilateral")

| Scripture |
| Tradition |
| Reason |
| Experience |

We see this principle lived out in the life of Jesus himself: he often appealed to Scripture as the highest and final source of authority during his life and ministry. For example, in Matthew 7:12, he appeals to the Law and the Prophets as the basis for his understanding of how to fulfill the commandment to love one's neighbor as oneself. In Matthew 19, he appeals to the creation narrative of Genesis to

44. Wayne Grudem, *Christian Ethics: An Introduction to Biblical Moral Reasoning* (Wheaton, IL: Crossway, 2018), 89.

45. *Scripture, tradition, reason,* and *experience* are commonly referred to as the "Wesleyan Quadrilateral." John Wesley himself never used this phrase. Albert C. Outler coined the phrase and later regretted that it had been misconstrued. See Albert C. Outler, "The Wesleyan Quadrilateral in Wesley," *Wesleyan Theological Journal* 20, no. 1 (1985): 16–17. Wayne Grudem notes two other sources of authority, both of which also fall under Scripture in priority. Those are expected results and subjective impressions. See Grudem, *Christian Ethics*, 90.

ground his teaching on divorce and remarriage. And in the Sermon on the Mount in Matthew 5, his understanding of the Old Testament both grounds and drives his moral instruction. "Jesus, God incarnate, viewed his Bible (our Old Testament) as his heavenly Father's written instruction, which he no less than others must obey."[46]

This is not to say that these other categories of moral authority are unimportant or that they should be dismissed. On the contrary, they can and often do prove helpful to provide a basis for logical consistency in how one thinks through a moral situation, for wisdom from the history of Christian thought on how best to apply moral norms, or for helping gather information pertaining to how a moral act might affect oneself or others. But while important information can be garnered from these other sources, in a distinctly Christian ethic they never take a place of primacy. Scripture is always the *primary* source in shaping the character traits that govern our loves, our desires, and the decision-making processes by which we determine a right or wrong moral action. And to be clear, it is Scripture that is primary—not necessarily any individual's interpretation of it. Sin impacts our view of Scripture, and thus we need great wisdom and the work of the Holy Spirit as we approach Scripture such that we handle it accurately. This is why the hard work of wise interpretation is necessary. We will return to this point below.

For our purposes in this section, we are simply stating that *Scripture is the norming norm*. Nothing supersedes it. Other sources may affirm and aid Scripture in assessing moral behavior, but nothing can take its place. Even when a believer faces a complex moral situation in which it appears that it would be "better" to break a commandment in order to bring about an anticipated or projected "good" result, it would be better to obey the command and leave the results in the hands of God. The reason for this is that Scripture is objectively authoritative, while a projected consequence is based on a subjective judgment or prediction of what *might* happen. In such cases, a commitment to Scripture as the chief source of moral authority recognizes the objectively binding nature of the moral norms revealed in Scripture.

To put it another way, the circumstances of the case and the predicted outcomes are only *prima facie* binding (they hold an apparent binding force), while scriptural norms are *actually* binding. Therefore, while circumstances or projected outcomes in complex moral contexts may tempt us to disobey a command in order to bring about a good result (e.g., telling a lie because one believes that in doing so it may save a life), true love is demonstrated by obeying God's commandments (John 14:15). We will return to this conversation in chapter 8.

---

46. Packer, *Concise Theology*, 4.

Sufficient

Finally, as we consider the nature and character of Scripture in regard to how we worship God in truth, it is important to consider how all the previous elements help us recognize the *sufficiency* of Scripture as it pertains to both our faith and our ethics. Because all revelation—both general and special—is grounded in the nature and character of the God who designed, created, and formed the world, it is right to say that both are equally authoritative when properly discerned. Historically, however, orthodox Christians have always understood that only God's special revelation is considered *sufficient* for faith and ethics.

This relates to the problem of human sin and the impact of the fall on both our relational standing before God and our moral condition. As we pointed out earlier in this book, even before they sinned, Adam and Eve needed God's special revelation to guide them. God did not create them as omniscient beings. While they were sinless, they still needed to learn. As finite creatures, they needed to be disciplined (in the positive sense of the word) into all they were created to be so that they could cause the entire world to flourish. So God's discipleship of them before the fall included special revelation primarily for the purpose of guiding them into all that they had been designed, created, and formed to be (see Gen. 2:16–17).

After they sinned, however, their need for special revelation exponentially expanded. Now they would need God's special revelation not merely because they were finite and in need of maturation, but because they were broken and disordered. They would need a special grace from God to instruct them in how they might be restored to him relationally as well as how to see their moral capacities to worship through their life practices realigned. In short, it is not the generally revealed or natural moral fabric of the universe that is lost; we are.

This is why in his kindness and grace God then gives us special divine revelation. For "only through the written Word, that testifies to Christ, the living Word, does the sinner gain knowledge of God as Redeemer."[47] It is in the message of the Bible that we discover how to be rightly restored to him relationally through the work of Jesus Christ in his crucifixion and resurrection, and also how to be restored morally and ethically to the good works for which he originally created us (Eph. 2:10). While God's general revelation still exists and while the natural moral law is still in place, neither is sufficient to instruct us in how to be saved "by grace . . . through faith" (vv. 8–9). Since humans have become darkened in their understanding, God deemed it necessary to provide special revelation to properly guide believers once again to live a rightly ordered worshipful obedience.

Therefore, when we say that only special revelation is sufficient for faith and ethics, we recognize that while fully consistent with the natural moral law

---

47. Lewis and Demarest, *Integrative Theology*, 1:100.

and general revelation, special revelation goes beyond general revelation in two important ways. First, it is only by God's special revelation that human beings learn how they can be saved from the penalty of sin by God's grace through faith in the person and work of Jesus Christ. Second, it is only through God's special revelation that our darkened minds can gain clarity on how to once again live as we were designed to live in regard to the development of our character as well as our choices and actions. As Grudem puts it, "the sufficiency of Scripture means that Scripture contained all the words of God he intended his people to have at each stage of redemptive history, and that it now contains all the words of God we need for salvation, for trusting him perfectly, and for obeying him perfectly."[48] Likewise, Carl F. H. Henry is correct when he asserts that "there is actually no ethical decision in life which the biblical revelation leaves wholly untouched and for which, if carefully interpreted and applied, it cannot afford some concrete guidance."[49]

Scripture is meant to have impact on—and provide guidance for—all areas of life. This is as true for the plumber or accountant as it is for the preacher or missionary. In saying this, however, we also recognize that its influence and impact may happen in different ways. In some contexts of life, it will have direct and immediate instruction, while in others its impact will be more indirect. For example, we don't look to Scripture to teach us how to fix a leaky sink. But the attitude and integrity by which I go about fixing a leaky sink absolutely must be shaped by Scripture. Thus, sufficiency should not be understood to be exclusionary of other sources of truth because plain common sense shows us that God has not given us Scripture to work like a plumbing manual.[50] Scripture is, however, authoritative in how it shapes all of life, and it is also sufficient to give us all we need to pursue life and godliness as a whole act of worship.

In sum, we can say that Scripture is *sufficient* in two primary ways. First, it contains all the words of God necessary for salvation. Second, it contains all the foundational instruction necessary to live a life of worshipful obedience unto him.[51] As the apostle Paul puts it in 2 Timothy 3:15–17:

> From childhood you have known the sacred writings which are able to give you the wisdom that *leads to salvation through faith which is in Christ Jesus.* All Scripture is inspired by God and profitable for teaching, for reproof, for correction, for training in righteousness; *so that the man of God may be adequate, equipped for every good work.*

48. Grudem, *Systematic Theology*, 127.
49. Henry, *Christian Personal Ethics*, 339.
50. Ferguson, "How Does the Bible Look at Itself?," 60–61.
51. Grudem, *Systematic Theology*, 127–38.

How Does Scripture Function as the Guidebook for Ethics as Worship?

Having discussed the nature and character of Scripture as God's revealed truth, we find it natural to turn to a discussion of how Scripture functions as our sufficient guide for faith and ethics. As we pointed out in chapter 1, Scripture as God's crystallization of special revelation guides and directs us by providing for us two fundamental frames of reference by which to see the world and order our lives. Scripture first provides us with God's revelation about the nature of reality and then as a mark of God's kindness. It also provides for us moral instruction on how to live maximally in the reality that he created. That is, Scripture functions as a guide to faith and practice because it is a book of both *revealed reality* and *revealed morality*.[52] As *revealed reality*, it gives an accurate and foundational understanding of the nature of reality and the way things *are*. As *revealed morality*, it provides for us norms, principles, rules, and guidelines to become the kind of people that he designed and created us to *be*, and it does so by using these norms, principles, rules, and guidelines to instruct us regarding what is good and right for us to *do*. This is the focus of our current discussion.

The interconnection between these foundational categories helps us understand Christian ethics first and foremost as a loving relationship with God and the pursuit of understanding and embodying the proper worship of him. Since this is the case, it follows that our ethical relationship with God must fit within the paradigm that he has revealed to be true about the world he created, and in accord with the instructions he gave about how to live in it. Therefore, along with the relationship comes both a worldview and moral instruction: *revealed reality* and *revealed morality*.

The Threefold Division of the Law

In order to understand how Scripture functions as *revealed morality* and thus as our guide for life and practice, it is helpful to first make an important distinction between different types of laws that appear in Scripture. This is particularly important when attempting to understand the various types of commands given in the Old Testament. Much confusion about God's moral instructions can be avoided by recognizing these categories.

Historically, both Catholic and Protestant thinkers have recognized three distinct categories of laws: civil (or judicial), ceremonial, and moral.[53] *Civil laws*

---

52. Refer back to our discussion of this topic in chapter 1 for an extensive footnote discussion on these terms.

53. Among Protestants, the most classic example of this threefold division can be found in Calvin, *Institutes*, 2.7.1–17; 4.20.14–16. But even before Calvin, Thomas Aquinas recognized these same categories in his *Summa Theologica*, I–II.99.1–4. As Aquinas stated, "We must therefore distinguish three kinds of precept

were given to the nation of Israel to guide the people in governing their particular theocratic society. These laws included such things as penalties for crimes and instructions for treating sojourners who traveled or dwelt among the Israelites. The primary use of these laws was to help the people of that era and time apply God's moral standards to their particular context. Underlying each civil law is a deeper, more abiding moral law, but the civil law relates to practices that are specific to the time and context. For example, consider a law such as Leviticus 20:13:

> If there is a man who lies with a male as those who lie with a woman, both of them have committed a detestable act; they shall surely be put to death. Their blood-guiltiness is upon them.

Here we see both a moral principle and a civil application, each of which is directly related to the practice of homosexual behavior. Because the civil portion of the verse relates directly to that particular cultural time and context, to ask whether the command to put someone engaging in homosexual behavior to death should be applied in a modern context signals a misunderstanding of the nature of civil law. The underlying moral law, however, because it reflects the abiding nature of God, endures beyond the particulars of context and time. David W. Jones clarifies the idea well: "While God's moral standards do not change, their application (and penalty for violation) in each time and culture is unique and ever changing."[54] Thus, if someone accuses a Christian of "cherry picking" verses in the Bible and obeying only half of them, as is often the case as it relates to this particular verse, what is actually taking place is that the person making the accusation is demonstrating a lack of understanding of the nature of Scripture, the laws found therein, and the proper rules of interpreting ancient texts.

In addition to the civil laws found in Scripture, *ceremonial laws* are those that God gave to the Israelites in order to establish them as a distinct people religiously. The ceremonial laws dealt with such things as dietary codes, bathing and cleansing rituals, and the regulation of temple worship. Most importantly, they included instructions to guide the people's worship as they offered sacrifices for the atonement for sin. Again, Jones is helpful:

---

in the Old Law; viz. 'moral' precepts, which are dictated by the natural law; 'ceremonial' precepts, which are determinations of the Divine worship; and 'judicial' precepts, which are determinations of the justice to be maintained among men." Indeed, as early as Irenaeus (*Against Heresies*, 4.15.1; 4.16.5) and Augustine (*Reply to Faustus the Manichaean*, 6.2), the distinction between different types of law and the distinct purposes were being identified to explain how and why certain Old Testament laws apply in the Christian context and why others do not. See also Jones, *Introduction to Biblical Ethics*, 56–60.

54. Jones, *Introduction to Biblical Ethics*, 59.

While there are numerous ceremonial laws in the Old Testament, a commonality among them is that they all relate to the Israelites' approach to and right standing before God. The ceremonial laws are designed to communicate that God is holy, that man is unclean and unrighteous, and that redemption is on God's terms. In retrospect, it is evident the ceremonial laws prefigure the redemptive work of Jesus. . . . Moreover, the New Testament is clear that the ceremonial laws were fulfilled—not abrogated—by the advent and work of Christ.[55]

In keeping these laws, the people of Israel would demonstrate not only their devotion to God but also the distinct nature of their worship from the surrounding nations and cultures. Many of these laws were fulfilled completely in Christ and therefore are no longer binding in the same way they were for the Israelites.

Table 5.2. Three Divisions of the Law

Civil	Time- and context-bound laws for governing a theocracy	Leviticus 20:13b
Ceremonial	Laws regulating religious ceremonies, many of which have been fulfilled in Christ	Acts 10:11–16
Moral	Enduring laws reflecting the moral character of God	Exodus 20:1–17 Leviticus 20:13a

Finally, the *moral laws* are those that are "based on, reflect, and demand conformity to God's own moral character. As such, since man is made in God's image, the moral laws are written on men's hearts and are timeless (cf. Rom 2:14–15)."[56] The Ten Commandments (the Decalogue) are an example of these types of laws. Importantly, a careful study of Scripture indicates that humans were held accountable to these moral laws before God gave the law to Moses on Mount Sinai, and they are reaffirmed in the New Testament (cf. Matt. 5:27–30). In other words, while the *civil laws* may be time-bound and *ceremonial laws* find their fulfillment in Christ, the *moral laws* endure beyond context and time. They are as enduring as God himself, and they are meant to teach us how to conform to his image in both character and action. "As a revelation of God's character, the moral law is timeless, unchanging, and the standard by which God judges man."[57]

55. Jones, *Introduction to Biblical Ethics*, 57–58.
56. Jones, *Introduction to Biblical Ethics*, 59.
57. Jones, *Introduction to Biblical Ethics*, 60.

Three Uses of the Moral Law

Having identified these distinct categories or divisions of the law, we can now focus our attention particularly on the moral laws and ask how they function to guide our ethics. Historically, Christians have recognized three distinct uses or functions for the moral law: condemning, restraining, and guiding.[58]

We can see a clear example of the first function or use of the law—its *condemning use* in Romans 3:19–20:

> Now we know that whatever the Law says, it speaks to those who are under the Law, so that every mouth may be closed and all the world may become accountable to God; because by the works of the Law no flesh will be justified in His sight; for through the Law comes the knowledge of sin.

In this capacity, Scripture sets forth the moral law of God plainly and clearly such that all humans understand that they have "sinned and fall short of the glory of God" (Rom. 3:23). As J. I. Packer notes, this "first function is to be a mirror reflecting to us both the perfect righteousness of God and our own sinfulness and shortcomings."[59] By revealing to us how far short we fall of God's perfect holiness, the Bible then becomes our teacher in that it shows us our need for the gospel and leads us toward repentance and faith in Christ for salvation. Again, as Paul states, "Therefore the Law has become our tutor to lead us to Christ, so that we may be justified by faith" (Gal. 3:24).

The second way that God uses Scripture as *revealed morality* relates to its power and influence to limit both individuals and society as a whole from being as bad as they would otherwise be. Considering what Scripture reveals to us about the nature of human persons after the fall who are "dead in [their] trespasses and sins" and who walk through life "according to the course of this world, according to the prince of the power of the air" (Eph. 2:1–2), it is amazing that we do not all constantly live in a state of total moral chaos. The reason that individuals and human society as a whole do not sink to this level is that God's generally given grace and moral law "restrains" us from being as wicked or immoral as we might otherwise be. For this reason, this use of the law is often referred to as the *restraining use* of the moral law.[60]

While the moral principles that God reveals cannot in themselves change a person's heart, they often function to limit negative moral behavior through an implicit threat or judgment that is connected to the mere presence of the law. If

---

58. These three uses are most clearly and explicitly laid out by Calvin in *Institutes*, 2.7.

59. Packer, *Concise Theology*, 94.

60. Jones, *Introduction to Biblical Ethics*, 60.

there is a law, then it follows that there is also likely a lawgiver who has authority to judge one's behavior. In this sense, Scripture functioning as *revealed morality* can "to some extent inhibit lawlessness by its threats of judgment, especially when backed by a civil code that administers present punishment for proven offenses. . . . Thus it secures some civil order and goes some way to protect the righteous from the unjust."[61] This is true whether God's moral laws are recognized by means of general or special revelation.

Table 5.3. Three Uses of the Law

Condemning	Shows people their state of *condemnation* due to their sinfulness and thereby awakens their need for the gospel.
Restraining	*Restrains* sinful people and society from being as bad as they would otherwise be.
Guiding	*Guides* Christians into both a rightly ordered worship and a maximum expression of that worship through both the shaping of character and the guiding of behaviors.

John Calvin describes the third way that God uses Scripture as the most important way because it is most closely connected to Scripture's original and final purpose.[62] God uses Scripture as *revealed morality* in order to teach and guide Christians how to live once again in a manner that maximizes what they were originally created for, which will in turn maximize the glory of God throughout the earth and bring maximum joy to them as they do so. This is the *guiding use* of the law. Scripture is useful as our primary guide to worshipful living because as Psalm 19:7–8 tells us:

The law of the LORD is perfect, restoring the soul;
The testimony of the LORD is sure, making wise the simple.
The precepts of the LORD are right, rejoicing the heart;
The commandment of the LORD is pure, enlightening the eyes.

Thus, Scripture can serve to light the path before Christians as they pursue daily character formation and life choices that maximize their worship of the living God (Ps. 119:105).

61. Packer, *Concise Theology*, 94.
62. Calvin, *Institutes*, 2.7.12.

In terms of forming our character and the shaping of who we should *be*, Scripture as *revealed reality* and *revealed morality* functions to guide the believer by first ordering our efforts toward character formation to the right end and then also telling us the behaviors and practices that will shape our character in the right way. In other words, right intentions to love God and love our neighbor as expressions of worship must be guided by proper action guides so that they embody and reflect God's moral character. Said another way, right actions in keeping with God's *revealed morality* are the necessary means by which we form good and right character.

The task of Christian ethics is to be conformed to the person of Christ. Therefore, as we discussed in the previous chapter, the focus in character formation is not merely on forming virtues for their own sake, but on forming virtues that conform us to Christ in the way he prescribes. While a society or culture may claim the same names of virtues, such as *compassion* and *kindness*, it is Scripture that actually gives content, description, and boundaries to the formation of the virtues that God desires us to embody. Henry provides a helpful illustration on how Scripture is to shape a distinctive Christian virtue: "A Jonathan apple tree produces apples because of the distinctive nature of the tree. . . . Even so the Christian life produces ethical virtues that are distinctive and characteristic of the Christian life alone. There may be imitations of Christian virtues, but they are no more the real thing than a crab apple is a Jonathan apple."[63] The moral commands of Scripture ensure that our virtues are actually fruits of the Spirit of God.

Similarly, with regard to what we must obey or *do*, Scripture provides action guides to properly order our behaviors in the form of rules, laws, principles, and even moral examples. From Scripture we have "the idea of a unitary biblical ethic, of one coherent and consistent moral requirement, that lays claim on all [humans] at all times."[64] And Scripture provides us with "objectively revealed precepts, institutions, commandments which are the norms and channels of human behavior."[65]

But again, we stress that the larger context in which these commands are given presumes a disposition of love for God and neighbor that motivates and drives our conformity to God's commands. This is why it is vitally important to see Scripture in the sense of the third use of the law—our guide. What God desires us to *be* must always be shaped by his understanding and instruction regarding what we should *do*. Similarly, what he desires us to *do* must always be understood and practiced in light of what he is shaping us to *be*.

---

63. Henry, *Christian Personal Ethics*, 472.

64. Henry, *Christian Personal Ethics*, 236.

65. John Murray, *Principles of Conduct: Aspects of Biblical Ethics* (Grand Rapids: Eerdmans, 1957), 24.

The diagram below (see fig. 5.1) illustrates how this third use of the law functions to guide ethics as worship. Scripture shows us how best to love and worship God by guiding both our actions and our loves (attitudes/motives), and as it does so, it also shapes our character as those who obey and love God.

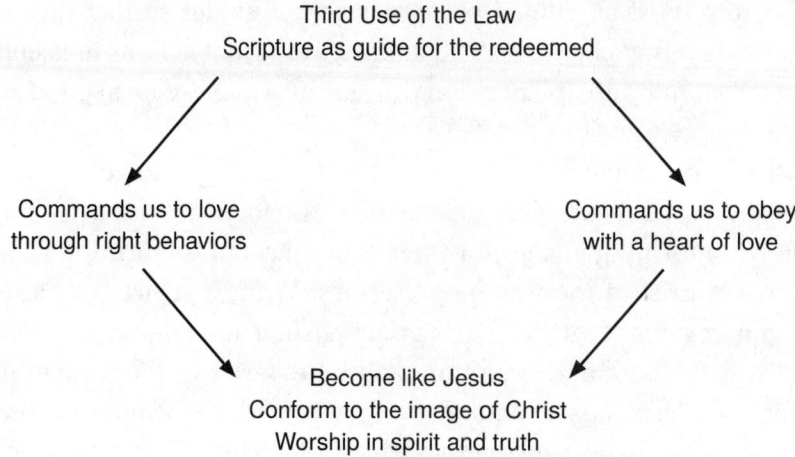

Fig. 5.1. The Third Use of the Law

Exitus et Reditus

Finally, we can see the beauty of how *revealed morality* functions as our guide for ethics when we consider the *exitus et reditus* ("exit and return") pattern of God's moral commands. Earlier in the book (chapter 2), we highlighted and expanded on the idea not only that God created the universe as an outflow of his eternal character, love, and kindness, but also that in having its existence, it would return back to him the glory that he is due. In a similar fashion, God created human beings as his image-bearers and placed them in the world to "cultivate it and keep it" (or "worship and obey") as they ruled over it and subdued it (Gen. 2:15; 1:27–28), such that through the created order they might return to God all the glory, honor, praise, and worship they could rouse from the creation. Now we see that Scripture is meant to function in the same way.

Consider, for example, Jesus' instructions to his disciples when he commands them, saying, "A new commandment I give to you, that you love one another, even as I have loved you, that you also love one another" (John 13:34). Here we can see a downward flow of love that originates with God, is given to humans, and is commanded to flow outward toward others. Beautifully, though, not only does God first love us and make his love the ground by which he commands us to love others, he also reveals to us that if we obey his commands to love our neighbor, we are actually loving him:

Truly I say to you, to the extent that you did it to one of these brothers of Mine, even the least of them, you did it to Me. (Matt. 25:40)

God in his kindness aligns his commands to our created purpose so that we might—through our obedience—maximize our expression of loving worship to him. The beauty of the Word is that it guides us to understand that God is both the source and the end of our love. As such, he is also the source and the end of our ethics, and thus, he is ultimately the source and the end of our worship.

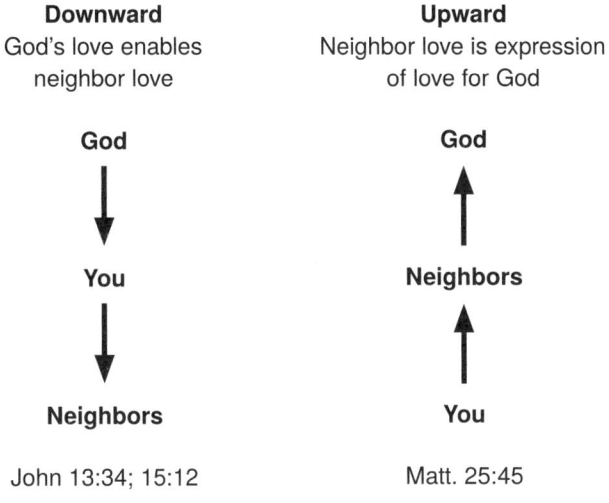

Fig. 5.2. Loving God and Loving Neighbors

How Do We Best Understand Scripture as Our Guidebook for Ethics as Worship?

Having defined *revelation*, identified the nature of Scripture, and discussed how the Bible functions as our guide to live ethically as an act of worship, we now consider how to best understand Scripture so as to make proper ethical application. While the discipline of hermeneutics (proper understanding and interpretation of Scripture) requires an entire study in its own right, our goal here is much more modest. It is our purpose to lay out basic contours of biblical interpretation particularly as it relates to moving from the written instructions for moral living given in Scripture to ethical application in the daily contexts of life. We begin by identifying six basic rules to guide our understanding and interpretation (hermeneutics). Then we discuss briefly the doctrine of illumination and the important role that the Holy Spirit plays in making application of truth to our lives and ethical contexts.

Six Basic Rules of Hermeneutics for Ethics as Worship

In 2 Timothy 2:15, Paul admonishes Timothy, "Be diligent to present yourself approved to God as a workman who does not need to be ashamed, accurately handling the word of truth." If ethics as worship is to take Scripture seriously as its primary source of authority, then mastering basic skills of interpretation is a necessary part of what it means to "be diligent" such that we handle God's Word accurately. So while it is true that the basic story line is clear and able to be understood (perspicuous), it is likewise true that proper interpretation and application requires both careful work and interpretive skill. J. P. Moreland's comments toward this end are insightful:

> Because of the Bible's nature, serious study is needed to grasp what it says. Of course, the Scripture contains easily grasped portions that are fairly straightforward. But some of it is very difficult, intellectually speaking. In fact, Peter once said that some of Paul's writings were intellectually challenging, hard to understand, and easily distorted by untaught (that is, uneducated in Christian theology) and unstable people (2 Peter 3:16). Anyone who has tried to grasp the theological depths of Romans or Ephesians will say "Amen!" to that. The more a person develops the mind and the understanding of hermeneutics (the science of interpreting Scripture), the more he or she will be able to understand the meaning and significance of Scripture.[66]

Christ-Centered Reading—Godward Worship Orientation

The first and most important rule of proper interpretation for ethics as worship is to keep the main point of the Bible clearly in view from start to finish. And that main point of the Bible—the central plot of Scripture from beginning, to middle, to end—is the person and work of Jesus Christ. Jesus understood this to be true, and for this reason we as his disciples must also understand this point. In Jesus' own words, "You search the Scriptures because you think that in them you have eternal life; it is these that testify about Me. . . . If you believed Moses, you would believe Me, for he wrote about Me" (John 5:39, 46; cf. Luke 24:25–27).

So how should a Christ-centered reading guide our attempts to understand the Bible? Robert Plummer makes the point that "if we read or teach any part of the Bible without reference to Jesus the Savior, we are not faithful interpreters."[67] Gordon Fee and Douglas Stuart build on this idea and point out that the reason for making such a strong claim is that God's loving and gracious work of "atonement and the subjection of all creation to Christ is the climax of the plot," and that thus all the various stories, commands, passages, lineages, and instructions

---

66. J. P. Moreland, *Love Your God with All Your Mind* (Colorado Springs: NavPress, 1997), 26.
67. Plummer, *40 Questions about Interpreting the Bible*, 96–97.

ultimately point to this climax. The "Scriptures in their entirety bear witness to him and focus toward his loving lordship."[68]

This does not necessarily mean that every passage and every book will refer to Jesus in the same way, or that it will be easily evident how every verse and chapter relates to Jesus. Rather, the idea is to point out that Jesus and his redemptive work is the hermeneutical key that unlocks the treasure trove of meaning that can and ought to be found in every portion of Scripture.

Context of the Passage Is Vital

The second guiding principle for proper interpretation relates to placing the passage that is being studied in its proper context. When we approach the text of Scripture for the purpose of gleaning ethical insight, we cannot simply find a verse we like and use it as a proof text for determining behavior. Because we believe that Scripture is inspired by God and that his divine fingerprints of authorship are all over the text, we must take into account how all the Scriptures are woven together. Not only are the words themselves inspired, but the biblical authors were inspired to construct the text in the way they did as well.

When we speak of understanding the context of a passage, it is important to consider two categories. The first relates to having some understanding of the historical context in which the book was written. While we have already made a case for the clarity or perspicuity of Scripture and would therefore contend that the basic meaning of the text can be found within the text, having some knowledge of the author's historical and cultural assumptions can go a long way toward deepening one's understanding of a passage or book. For example, in Matthew 20:1–16, Jesus tells a parable that involves paying workers a denarius for their wage. While knowing the exact worth of a denarius may not be crucial to understanding the parable, the justice and grace sought and demonstrated in the parable take on a richer meaning and depth when one understands that a denarius was equivalent to a full day's wage.[69]

The second and more important sense in which we speak of context has to do with the *literary context*. "Essentially, the literary context means first that words only have meaning in sentences, and second that biblical sentences for the most part only have clear meaning in relation to preceding and succeeding sentences."[70] When we are seeking moral guidance from Scripture, then, it is important to take into account the context of the verse, passage, chapter, book, and entire Bible. As Plummer notes, this is so important because attempting to "understand or apply

---

68. Gordon D. Fee and Douglas Stuart, *How to Read the Bible for All Its Worth*, 3rd ed. (Grand Rapids: Zondervan, 2003), 91–92.

69. Fee and Stuart, *How to Read the Bible for All Its Worth*, 26.

70. Fee and Stuart, *How to Read the Bible for All Its Worth*, 27.

a particular biblical phrase or verse without reference to the literary context is virtually guaranteed to result in distortion."[71]

For example, consider for a moment the familiar story of King David and his relationship with Bathsheba. In 2 Samuel 11, we learn of David's wicked plot to sexually exploit Bathsheba and then have her husband killed. But in 2 Samuel 12, we learn that Bathsheba gives birth to Solomon, who eventually becomes the great king of Israel. If one were not careful, one could arrive at the conclusion that because God blessed David with the birth of Solomon through his relationship with Bathsheba, it must have been permissible for him to sexually exploit her and commit adultery. Now, obviously, such an interpretation is far-fetched, but without placing the various events within the context of their passages, considering the genre of literature involved (historical account), or the larger teachings about adultery, lying, murder, and divine grace found in the entirety of Scripture, all kinds of fanciful interpretations could be rendered. By necessity, it is important that we not take a verse or passage out of context to prove what we want to say. Rather, the goal is to find out what the original author intended the reader to understand in the original context.[72]

This is an extremely important point with regard to ethics because the discipline of ethics pertains not just to the facts we understand about a passage, but also to what the passage may demand of us in regard to how we actually live our lives. If we are honest, the temptation of every human heart is to justify our own behaviors and look for ways to affirm our passions, loves, and choices even when we sense that they are wrong. It is not hard to imagine a person in an adulterous relationship saying, "It worked out okay for David, so it can't be so bad"—not because the sin isn't obvious, but because we try so hard to justify our sins. Indeed, our sinful tendencies will be to look at a command that prohibits what we love, or demands something that is hard, and try to explain it away or twist it in such a way that our situation becomes an exception to a rule, or the command somehow does not apply to us. Proper hermeneutics, however, helps us take this tendency captive by driving us to see what the text meant as it was written and delivered. As Fee and Stuart rightly put the point, "a text cannot mean what it never meant"— or, to say it differently, "the true meaning of the biblical text for us is what God originally intended it to mean when it was first spoken."[73] Once we discover this meaning, then we are confronted with the bald reality that we must either change

---

71. Plummer, *40 Questions about Interpreting the Bible*, 104.

72. The wrongful twisting of Genesis 9 and the curse given by Noah to Ham and his son Canaan in order to justify the enslavement of people of African descent is a powerful and tragic example of the importance of this principle. A second example involves the twisting of 1 Samuel 18 to suggest the relationship between David and Jonathan may have been homoerotic.

73. Fee and Stuart, *How to Read the Bible for All Its Worth*, 30.

or continue in sin. But we cannot use Scripture wrongly to justify choices contrary to God's will. In sum, before we move to a determination of what a passage or command may mean *to me*, we must first be diligent and honest to discover what it first meant to its original audience.

Clearer Passages Must Be Used to Shed Light on Less-Clear Passages (Analogy of Scripture)

A third basic rule of interpretation for ethics is sometimes referred to as the *analogy of Scripture*. In simple terms, this is the idea not only that Scripture should be used to interpret Scripture (as the discussion above about context implies), but that clearer and plain-to-understand texts should clarify unclear texts.

Not all Scripture passages are created equal. As the J. P. Moreland quote above pointed out, not every passage of Scripture lends itself to a simple interpretation. Some passages are straightforward and lead to direct application in life. Other passages are difficult to understand but can be interpreted with some diligent work. Still other passages are extremely difficult to understand and require diligent work just to discover a few possible interpretations.

If we believe that God spoke the Scriptures and has given us his words for life and ethics, then we can expect that those divine words will never contradict one another. We can also expect that "passages of Scripture that are less clear can be interpreted with reference to those that are transparent in meaning."[74] Accordingly, a helpful interpretive principle when we encounter difficult passages is to interpret the more difficult ones in light of those that have a clearer and simpler (or more plain) meaning.

Often, this principle is extremely helpful in interpreting narrative sections of Scripture that report an activity that appears to be sinful, but that the immediate context nowhere states was wrong. For example, we learn in Scripture that David and Solomon both had many wives. Often the immediate contexts discussing these relationships do not clarify God's moral valuation. They simply report data about the relationships. But when these narrative descriptions are seen in light of other passages such as Genesis 1–2 and Deuteronomy 17:17, where God instructs the king "not [to] multiply wives for himself, or else his heart will turn away," or Ephesians 5, one can gain clarity on the practice of polygamy.

St. Augustine's comments summarize the point well:

When we have made ourselves to a certain extent familiar with the language of Scripture, we may proceed to open up and investigate the obscure passages, and in doing so draw examples from the plainer expressions to throw light upon the more

---

74. Plummer, *40 Questions about Interpreting the Bible*, 97.

obscure, and use the evidence of passages about which there is no doubt to remove all hesitation in regard to the doubtful passages.[75]

Scripture Drives Theology, and Then Scripture-Driven Theology Shines Light on Less-Clear Texts

Fourth, it is often the case in ethics that we run into issues and scenarios that are not *directly* addressed by Scripture. Examples are not hard to find. Consider such things as cloning and stem-cell research. If one were to explore a concordance in the back of a Bible, looking for the word *cloning*, disappointment would result. While cloning is not mentioned, this does not mean that the Bible is silent in relation to how we make moral determinations about things (such as cloning) that are not explicitly mentioned in the text of Scripture. Indeed, the Bible is sufficient to guide us morally even when a new issue or context arises.

In these cases, the move from Scripture to issues begins with a two-step process that involves gaining an understanding of the nature of the issue and identifying relevant moral principles that may relate to different aspects of the issue. For example, on the issue of stem-cell research, one would need to learn where the stem cells are being harvested from. If, as has sometimes been the case, the source of stem cells is human embryos, and if the removal of stem cells requires the killing of babies, then the moral standards related to murder and the sacredness of human life applies. If, however, the stem cells are taken from non-life-threatening sources, then the moral proscription does not apply.

The point is that moving from Scripture to moral evaluation of issues requires proper hermeneutics to develop and understand moral principles revealed in Scripture, and then properly apply them to situations and contexts that we have worked hard to understand. Situations and contexts don't determine morality, but our understanding of them must shape the application of morality (a point that we will highlight in part 3 of this book).

The Desired Interpretation Leads to Behavior That Maximizes Our Response of Worship, Not That Which Is Merely Possible or Permissible

A fifth principle of hermeneutics relates closely to the first rule in terms of its application. Because we concluded that Jesus is the center point of the biblical revelation, it follows that maximizing his worship ought to be the aim of our understanding of Scripture. In terms of biblical interpretation, if there are various ways to understand an ethical principle (or, more to the point, various ways to apply a biblical moral principle), then the interpreter's attitude ought to be motivated by

---

75. Augustine, *On Christian Doctrine*, 2.9.14, accessed January 11, 2019, https://www.ccel.org/ccel/schaff /npnf102.v.v.ix.html.

maximizing the worship and glory of God. This involves shaping our character not merely to find a lowest-common-denominator solution that may satisfy the letter of the law, but to seek its full intent.

Obviously, this is a nuanced aspect of biblical interpretation, but ethically it has important ramifications because it deals not just with understanding the technical meaning of a text and our obedience to it, but also with the motivations of our hearts as we obey. Ethically speaking, we can say that as we understand commands that require our obedience, we should also always keep in mind that raw, wooden obedience is not the final goal. Instead, Jesus—the person who is truth—is seeking conformity of our lives to himself not merely in what we do but in who we are and are becoming.

We see this principle in play all throughout Jesus' moral teachings in the Sermon on the Mount as he instructs about obedience to the commandments. Murder is not merely about not literally taking a life; it is about becoming the kind of person who does not even speak badly of others (Matt. 5:21–26). Adultery is not merely about not literally having sexual intercourse outside marriage; it also includes becoming the kind of person who does not lust (vv. 27–30). Ethical interpretation of the biblical commands includes an attempt to seek not just obedient actions but "going the extra mile" (vv. 38–42). As we put it in the previous chapter, the ultimate goal is to become the kind of person who is "perfect" (*teleios*) and as a result "is blessed" (*makarios*).

Read the Bible in Community

Sixth and finally, Robert Plummer is exactly right when he writes:

> We live in an individualistic age. Yet God created us to live and worship and grow spiritually together in community. . . . Reading the Bible with fellow believers helps us to gain insights that we would otherwise miss. Also, our brothers and sisters can guard us from straying into false interpretations and misapplications.[76]

The final of our six rules to guide biblical interpretation for ethics as worship is to read and interpret the Bible in the context of the larger community of God's church. This means not only the local church body that one may be a part of, but also the body of Christ through time. Not only should our reading be under the authority of the pastor and elders in our local church, we must also be careful to honor the teaching handed down through time (Jude 3) that the great cloud of witnesses in heaven (Heb. 12:1–2) are cheering for us to abide by. One ought to be wary of any idea or interpretation that has never been heard of or adopted by the

---

76. Plummer, *40 Questions about Interpreting the Bible*, 105.

church before. Likewise, because very few things (indeed, nothing) are "new under the sun" (Eccl. 1:9), any interpretation of Scripture that has been deemed heretical by the saints on whose shoulders we now stand and abide with via the great creeds of the church must also be rejected. Fee and Stuart are correct:

> Let it be said at the outset—and repeated throughout—that the aim of good interpretation is not uniqueness; one is not trying to discover what no one else has ever seen before. . . . Unique interpretations are usually wrong. . . . The aim of good interpretation is simple: to get to the "plain meaning of the text."[77]

Practically speaking, as an example, faithful followers of Christ ought to be both alarmed and spurred into deeply diligent study to "present [themselves] approved to God" in "handling the word of truth" when the church wholeheartedly adopts moral standards and practices that have been seen as sinful and heretical for millennia (2 Tim. 2:15). One need only consider contemporary attitudes in many of our churches and denominations regarding issues related to sex, sexuality, and gender for rather poignant examples.

Table 5.4. Six Hermeneutical Rules in Using Scripture to Guide Ethics as Worship

1. Ensure that reading is Christ-centered.
2. Context of passage is vital.
3. Clearer passages must be used to shed light on less-clear passages (*analogy of Scripture*).
4. Scripture drives theology, and then Scripture-driven theology shines light on less-clear texts.
5. The desired interpretation leads to behavior that maximizes our response of worship, not that which is merely possible or permissible.
6. Read the Bible in community.

The Illuminating Role of the Holy Spirit

When we consider Paul's admonition to diligently study Scripture to make sure that we "accurately [handle] the word of truth" (2 Tim. 2:15), it is right and good to approach the task of interpreting and applying Scripture with great humility. As we have repeatedly discussed throughout this book, human sin impacts all areas of our lives: our loves are disordered, our minds are darkened, and our wills are weakened. Therefore, even when we identify and attempt to follow proper rules of

77. Fee and Stuart, *How to Read the Bible for All Its Worth*, 17–18.

interpretation to move from the teachings of Scripture to ethical application, it is likely that we will still bump into our own sinful tendencies and inabilities.

Thankfully, as we seek to rightly understand and apply Scripture, we can take comfort that we do not approach the text alone. Jesus is our Word of Truth, and the Holy Spirit is the One who helps bring about our proper understanding of it. As Jeannine Brown rightly puts it, as Christians "we believe that even in our fallible and finite interpretations, God's Spirit somehow works and moves. . . . We have the promise that the Holy Spirit is with us as we read God's word, just as we have the promise of God's presence in all of life."[78]

When we discuss the role of the Holy Spirit to help us understand and apply truth to our lives, we are touching on the *doctrine of illumination*. Simply put, the doctrine of illumination relates to the work of the Holy Spirit in the life of a believer to gain both a greater mental/cognitive *understanding* of a text as well as *willingness to receive* the teachings and *abide* by them.

Understanding

Regarding how the Holy Spirit helps us in our understanding of Scripture, it is helpful to touch once again on Paul's contrast between the natural man and the spiritual man in 1 Corinthians 2:6–16. As we saw in chapter 4, Paul teaches in this passage that the "natural man" (a non-Christian) "does not accept the things of the Spirit of God, for they are foolishness to him; and he *cannot* understand them, because they are spiritually appraised." Something has happened to such a person's cognitive abilities such that making a proper assessment of the world in which we live is impossible without God's help. This coincides with Paul's teaching elsewhere in the New Testament where he identifies sinfulness as having significant impact on how humans see and understand the world in which we live.[79] This depiction of the natural man sits in stark contrast to the picture he paints of the spiritual man, who is a Christian filled with the Holy Spirit and abiding in the things of God. This person, the apostle says, "appraises all things" and has been given "the mind of Christ" (1 Cor. 2:15–16).

Scholars often disagree on the exact meaning of "the mind of Christ" in relation to being able to "appraise all things." Yet as we pointed out in the previous chapter, there is general consensus that Paul is not implying that we pick up

78. Jeannine K. Brown, *Scripture as Communication* (Grand Rapids: Baker, 2007), 128.

79. Recall that in Romans, Paul tells us that in sin humans "suppress the truth" by our wickedness and that as a result we become "futile in [our] speculations" and "darkened" in our hearts (Rom. 1:18, 21). Likewise, in Ephesians 4:17–18, Paul describes the mind of the unbeliever as "darkened" and "futile" in regard to understanding spiritual realities. And in 2 Corinthians 4:4, he explains that "the god of this world has blinded the minds of the unbelieving so that they might not see the light of the gospel of the glory of Christ, who is the image of God."

IQ points simply because we have become Christians. One does not immediately become a master Bible interpreter simply because he or she has faith in Christ. In fact, we freely admit that even an atheist who has developed skill in the interpretation of ancient texts could produce a highly accurate description of Pauline thought superior to the interpretation of many Christians.

In this text, what Paul is speaking about has to do with one's overall vision of and perspective on reality. He is emphasizing that "because the Bible's view of reality clashes with the way people, apart from the work of the Holy Spirit, want to see things, its message will therefore be regarded as foolishness."[80] The emphasis seems to be on the fact that the Holy Spirit brings a greater ability both to understand the meaning of the truths revealed in Scripture and as a result to better understand the world in which we live. This makes sense when we consider how Scripture functions as both *revealed reality* and *revealed morality*. When God rescues us and the metanarrative story line of creation, fall, redemption, and restoration clarifies our understanding of the world, and when our worldviews in due time are shaped to see the world in light of God's revelation, it follows that we would see and "appraise" all things from a new perspective—one that is like Christ's (i.e., "the mind of Christ," 1 Cor. 2:16). It is through the work of Jesus— who is the truth—to redeem us, and through the regenerating and sanctifying work of the Holy Spirit working in conjunction with the inspired Scriptures, that our minds can be renewed (cf. Rom. 12:1–2).

Having acknowledged this illuminating work of the Spirit to help us see the world rightly and morally appraise all situations, we are wise not to underestimate the hard work that is still involved in properly interpreting and applying Scripture. We have no guarantee that we will not still misunderstand or misapply God's words. The impact of sin that remains on our cognitive abilities even after we have been saved by grace is significant. As Paul put it, we still "see in a mirror dimly" (1 Cor. 13:12).

Therefore, regarding our mental/cognitive understanding of Scripture, we must be careful not to assume that the Holy Spirit's illumination is equivalent to an "I feel it is right, so it must be right" perspective on biblical interpretation and ethical application. "There is no one-to-one correspondence between personal piety and correct interpretation, although this conviction is sometimes used as a trump card for interpretative correctness (i.e., 'I prayed and God told me that this passage means . . .')."[81] We must be careful to not use an appeal to the Holy Spirit's

80. Daniel P. Fuller, "The Holy Spirit's Role in Biblical Interpretation," in *Scripture, Tradition and Interpretation.*, ed. W. Ward Gasque and William Sanford LaSor (Grand Rapids: Eerdmans, 1979), 189–98. Or *International Journal of Frontier Missions* 14, no. 2 (April–June 1997): 92, accessed February 15, 2019, https://ijfm.org/PDFs_IJFM/14_2_PDFs/14_2%20Fuller%20Holy%20Spirit.pdf.

81. Brown, *Scripture as Communication*, 128.

leading as justification for making the text of Scripture mean anything that we may want it to mean. Instead, because the Holy Spirit's teaching cannot contradict itself, and it is the Spirit that inspired Scripture, the Spirit's help for us will come as we do the diligent work of "discovering the original intent and in his guiding us as we try to faithfully apply that meaning to our own situations."[82] As Packer writes, "the way to benefit fully from the Spirit's ministry of illumination is by serious Bible study, serious prayer, and serious response in obedience to whatever truths one has been shown."[83]

Receive and Abide

This leads us to the second aspect of the illuminating work of the Holy Spirit, namely, the willingness to receive (or welcome) the teachings and abide by them. Returning to Paul's discussion of the "natural man" in 1 Corinthians 2, we see that such a person "does not *accept* the things of the Spirit of God, for they are foolishness to him; and he *cannot* understand them, because they are spiritually appraised." The Greek word translated here as "accept" is *dechomai*, which can alternatively be translated as "welcome" and which has reference not so much to the mind, but to the heart. A crucial aspect of the Spirit's work of illumination, then, is not only to assist our cognitive understanding but also to enliven our longings and willingness to welcome the truths taught by God about *revealed reality* and *revealed morality*. The Spirit helps us receive these truths in a manner much like greeting dear friends who are knocking at the door.[84] We are eager to open our lives to them and welcome them in. It is the Spirit's job to help us believe and trust in the teachings of Scripture on a very personal and existential level.

In Scripture, we see numerous examples of the Holy Spirit's doing this kind of work so that people gain not just a *cognitive understanding* of the divinely revealed truth, but also a *heart understanding* or a *faith-based understanding* and trust. We think of the disciples on the road to Emmaus after Jesus' resurrection (Luke 24:13–35), of Paul and the scales that fell from his eyes so that he could see both spiritually and physically (Acts 9:18), and of Lydia, the first convert in Europe, of whom it is recorded that "the Lord opened her heart to respond to the things spoken by Paul" (Acts 16:14). For each, something more was in play than mere technical understanding of facts.

In these texts, we see the Holy Spirit at work, bringing the truth as it is revealed in Scripture into clarity in at least two ways. First, the Spirit provides a mental/cognitive frame of reference by which to see the world and gain proper

---

82. Fee and Stuart, *How to Read the Bible for All Its Worth*, 30.
83. Packer, *Concise Theology*, 155–56.
84. Cole, *He Who Gives Life*, 274.

understanding of it. Second, the Spirit works to enliven one's affections to welcome and abide by the truths that Scripture reveals.

In sum, John Piper captures the overall idea of how the Holy Spirit aids our understanding of the text, that we might be able to move toward ethical application:

> When we pray for [the Holy Spirit's] help, we do not pray that he will spare us the hard work of rigorous reading and reflection. What we pray is that he would make us humble enough to welcome the truth. The work of the Spirit in helping us grasp the meaning of [Scripture] is not to make study unnecessary but to make us radically open to receive what our study turns up, instead of twisting the text to justify our unwillingness to accept it. . . . We must soak all of our study in prayer that his Spirit would humble us to submit to every truth and commandment in it. The work of the Holy Spirit is to make us say from the heart as we take up the [Bible], "Far be it from me that I should glory except in the cross of our Lord Jesus Christ, by which the world was crucified to me, and I to the world." If our pride has not been crucified by the Holy Spirit, the Bible will be a wax nose and we will call it foolish or mold it to fit our own natural desires.[85]

Conclusion: Worshiping God in Spirit and Truth

In the previous chapter, we began an exploration of what Jesus meant when he made the statement in John 4:23–24:

> An hour is coming, and now is, when the true worshipers will worship the Father in spirit and truth; for such people the Father seeks to be His worshipers. God is spirit, and those who worship Him must worship in spirit and truth.

In that chapter, we argued that Jesus' reference to worshiping God in this manner was actually Trinitarian and that the "spirit" and "truth" referred to were actually the third and second persons of the Trinity, respectively: the Holy Spirit and Jesus. The focus of the previous chapter was to develop what it means to worship God in "spirit," with particular emphasis on the Holy Spirit's role to shape our character and virtues in such a way that we grow to maturity as image-bearers conforming to the nature of Christ.

It has been our task in this chapter to continue along the same theme by exploring what it means to worship God in "truth." Here our emphasis has been on God's revelation of himself as the embodiment of truth both in the person of

---

85. John Piper, "How the Spirit Helps Us Understand," May 20, 1984, accessed February 15, 2019, https://www.desiringgod.org/messages/how-the-spirit-helps-us-understand.

Jesus Christ, who is the Word of God made flesh, and through the written Word of God—Scripture—which 2 Timothy 3:16 tells us is "inspired" (God-breathed) and thus profitable for guiding us into "every good work."

Bringing our findings from these two chapters together, we can now state that the role of the Holy Spirit is to point us to Jesus, who is the truth, as well as to work in us to shape us into the kind of people that God designed and rescued us to be. In addition, this Jesus, who saved us from our sins by his work of penal substitutionary atonement, also gives us a special form of revelation in Scripture such that the character and worship patterns being formed in us by the Holy Spirit can be rightly guided in accord with God's nature, design for the world, and revealed will. The Spirit of God takes the very words of God and uses them to guide us into becoming the true worshipers that he created us to be. And by his doing so, we find that we become fully human and fully alive.

By way of conclusion to both this chapter and our entire discussion in part 2 on the metaethical foundations for ethics as worship, we would agree with Carl F. H. Henry when he argues that it is "the severance of ethics from fixed values and standards" that has brought us to a place of "moral chaos."[86] As we pointed out in chapter 1, when the standards of ethics are left to human invention and have no foundation other than personal whim, cultural preference, or social convention, it should come as no surprise that "doing what is right in our own eyes" will eventually be the theme song that captures the spirit of the age.

As we have discovered through our study in part 2, we can give thanks to God because he has not left us without hope in the world. Not only has he shaped the world according to his design and ordered it toward a final end, he has also redeemed it and set forth for us a path of restoration so that we might maximize his glory and in so doing find abundant life. In his kindness, God has sent the Holy Spirit to shape us into the kind of people that he designed us to be. Likewise, truth became incarnate in the person of Jesus Christ and has been revealed to us in the living words of Scripture. With Spirit and truth to save us, shape us, and guide us, we have hope of becoming in our character and behavior the kind of worshipers that God is looking for: true worshipers who worship "in spirit and truth" (John 4:23–24). Without the Spirit and the truth to rescue us and guide us, humans will be trapped in a state of moral vertigo.

Ultimately, we can rest in the knowledge that obedience to God's moral law is not an empty practice of moralism, but an adventure of growing in obedient love with the infinite triune God, who created us to know him, love him, find ever-increasing joy in him, and flourish as his disciples as we live out ethics as worship.

---

86. Henry, *Christian Personal Ethics*, 13.

Key Terms and Concepts

appraise

authority, objective

darkening of the mind

God-breathed

Godness of God

hermeneutics

illumination

immutable

inerrant

infallible

inspiration, concursive

inspiration, superintended

Law and the Prophets

literary context

Logos

natural law

natural theology

norming norm

obedient love

perspicuity of Scripture

prima facie

principles

revelation, divine

revelation, general

revelation, natural

revelation, special

sources of authority

sufficient

three divisions of the law

three uses of the law, condemning

three uses of the law, constraining/
    restraining

three uses of the law, guiding

truth is a person

Key Scriptures

Psalm 19:1

Psalm 119:105

Matthew 25:40

John 1:1–17

John 4:23–24

John 14:6

John 14:15–24

Romans 1:18–21

Romans 3:19–20

1 Corinthians 2:6–16

1 Corinthians 13:12

2 Timothy 2:15

2 Timothy 3:16–17

2 Peter 1:21

2 Peter 3:15–16

Study Questions

1. What is the grounding source of both general revelation and special revelation? How are God's nature and character related to both general revelation and special revelation? Based on this, can there ever be an ultimate conflict between them?

2. When the Bible asserts that Scripture is "inspired" (God-breathed), what does this mean? How does this relate to the trustworthiness of Scripture for moral guidance as well as moral accountability?

3. The authors describe Scripture as both *revealed reality* and *revealed morality*. Define these terms and distinguish them from each other, and explain why each is important for understanding Christian ethics.

4. The authors suggest that a crucial element of faithful biblical interpretation is seeking to maximize our worship and not merely seeking what may be permissible. Explain this idea, and discuss why it is important for Christian discipleship and ethics.

5. What is the doctrine of illumination, and how does it simultaneously protect us from subjectivism and also allow for personal application?

For Further Reading

Brown, Jeannine K. *Scripture as Communication*. Grand Rapids: Baker, 2007.

Fee, Gordon D., and Douglas Stuart. *How to Read the Bible for All Its Worth*. 3rd ed. Grand Rapids: Zondervan, 2003.

Ferguson, Sinclair B. "How Does the Bible Look at Itself?" In *Inerrancy and Hermeneutic: A Tradition, A Challenge, A Debate*, edited by Harvie M. Conn, 47–66. Grand Rapids: Baker, 1988.

Goldsworthy, Graeme. *Gospel-Centered Hermeneutics: Foundations and Principles of Evangelical Biblical Interpretation*. Downers Grove, IL: IVP Academic, 2006.

Moreland, J. P. *Love Your God with All Your Mind*. Colorado Springs: NavPress, 1997.

Osborne, Grant R. *The Hermeneutical Spiral: A Comprehensive Introduction to Biblical Interpretation*. 2nd ed. Downers Grove, IL: InterVarsity Press, 2006.

Plummer, Robert L. *40 Questions about Interpreting the Bible*. Grand Rapids: Kregel, 2010.

PART 3

REVEALED MORALITY:
THE NORMATIVE FORMULATION
OF ETHICS AS WORSHIP

6

The Normative Methodology for Ethics as Worship: Part 1

"If you love Me, you will keep My commandments." —Jesus Christ, John 14:15

"Biblical ethics begins with God and ends with him. In this it is distinguished from those types of ethical thought which begin with requirements of human nature or define human happiness or perfection as the final goal. Such interests are not absent from Biblical ethics but they are not primary."[1]
—Waldo Beach and H. Richard Niebuhr, Christian
Ethics: Sources of the Living Tradition

Introduction

In part 1 of this book, we offered a general introduction to the discipline of ethics by exploring the nature and importance of worldviews for developing a robust and coherent ethical theory that moves from clear metaethical foundations to the development of a normative method so that we could then have a consistent approach to applied ethics. Building on this, in part 2 we developed the metaethical foundations for ethics as worship by exploring the relevant biblical and theological doctrines related to the creation, fall, redemption, and restoration story line of the Bible. We also explored the vital and foundational role that the Holy Spirit and the Scriptures play in the development of the type of people that God is looking for: "true worshipers" who worship "in spirit and truth" (John 4:23–24). Our purpose in doing so was to establish the *why* of ethics before exploring the *what* and *how to* of ethics.

---

1. Waldo Beach and H. Richard Niebuhr, eds., *Christian Ethics: Sources of the Living Tradition*, 2nd ed. (New York: John Wiley & Sons, 1973), 15.

With our having accomplished these goals, our purpose in part 3 is now to specifically develop our *normative* formulation of ethics as worship. The task before us is to explore how we are to shape our understanding of ethics such that in all we think, love, say, and do we can maximally glorify God as true worshipers who love and behave:

1. In accord with the patterns and purposes that he established "in the beginning";
2. By grace through faith trusting in the atoning work of Jesus Christ for both salvation and sanctification;
3. As disciples of Jesus Christ on mission with him to fulfill the Great Commission;
4. In hopes of looking into the eyes of our Savior and hearing him say the words "well done";
5. As image-bearers who are growing toward being fully human and fully alive because we are empowered by the Holy Spirit and being shaped in our character to become like Christ; and
6. In submission to the Word of God (Scripture) as our chief source of authority to guide our life and practices.

As we described in chapter 1, *normative ethics* is the name given to the subfield of ethics that is primarily concerned with the systematic identification and development of the virtues and norms necessary to shape morally good character and guide morally right decision-making in light of the circumstances, consequences, and relationships present in any given context. With this definition in mind, then, our purpose in part 3 is to draw on the biblical and theological ideas explored in the previous chapters in order to develop the normative methodological form and structure of ethics as worship.

To accomplish this goal, this chapter begins with a discussion of how normative ethics serves as the link between our underlying beliefs and our actual practices. We then identify six *domains of ethical assessment* that Christian disciples must take into consideration in every moral event. In the remainder of this chapter, we focus our attention on the first three of the domains (*telos*, agent, act) to discuss their nature and importance and the biblical rationale for including and ordering each one in the development of our normative methodology for ethics as worship. In the following chapter, we continue in the same vein of discussion by focusing on the remaining three domains of ethical assessment (circumstances, consequences, and relational responses), and then proceed with a discussion of how all six domains must function together as the normative criteria for ethics as worship.

Normative Ethics as the Link between Stated Beliefs and Actual Practices

Stated Beliefs and Actual Practices

In Philippians 1:27, Paul encourages Jesus' disciples to conduct themselves "in a manner worthy of the gospel of Christ." His concern was that their lives, choices, and moral behaviors would be consistent with the underlying gospel message. He was also concerned that how they lived their lives would serve as a testimony to the hope of that gospel before a watching world.

Paul understood something that would be wise for all of us to give heed to: *the way in which we live our lives and the choices we make display what we believe and what we love at the deepest levels of our hearts and minds.* As Jonathan Edwards stated in his classic *Religious Affections*: "Scripture plainly teaches that practice is the best evidence of the sincerity of professing Christians; so reason teaches the same thing. Reason shows, that men's deeds are better and more faithful interpreters of their minds than are their mere words."[2] If this is true, then we have bumped into a very powerful idea as it pertains to our discipleship, our ethics, and therefore our worship. Paul tells us that it is through an evaluation of how we conduct ourselves (normative ethics) that we can identify our deepest loves and beliefs (metaethics/worldview).

We pointed out in chapter 2 that our growth as disciples is crucially linked both to our metaethical understanding about the manner in which God made the world and to the deeds that we do in the world. Therefore, in order to live consistently as Jesus' disciples and worship well in and through our ethics, it is important that we learn how to match our underlying beliefs about God and the way he made the world with our actual practices. This is exactly where normative ethics becomes relevant. By developing our understanding of normative ethics, we can put in place a methodology that assists us in making all the daily decisions that flow from—and are consistent with—what we believe to be true about God and the moral patterns he wove into creation for his glory and our good. As we worded it earlier, ethics as worship is the application of vibrant, orthodox, worshipful theology to loving, obedient, missional living. Normative ethics serves as the link between our theology and our practice. It serves as the bridge from orthodoxy to doxology by providing for us a God-glorifying orthopraxy. Put most simply, normative ethics guides us in how to live our daily lives in light of what we claim to believe as Christians.

If we were to put this idea into a formula, we could express it in the following way: (1) everyone has a set of stated beliefs and proclaimed loves, and (2) when

---

2. Jonathan Edwards, *A Treatise concerning Religious Affections*, 3.12.1, accessed May 8, 2020, http://www.jonathan-edwards.org/ReligiousAffections.pdf.

those beliefs or loves are evaluated in light of one's actual practices, then (3) we can discover what one truly believes or loves (see fig. 6.1).

Stated Belief + Actual Practice	Proclaimed Love + Actual Practice
= Actual Belief	= Actual Love

Fig. 6.1. Formula for Normative Ethics

If this is true, then it should be obvious that is it wise not only to dig deeply into identifying what beliefs and loves we hold and which ones are worthy of our most profound allegiances, but also to consider what conduct is most in keeping with these beliefs and loves so that our lives proclaim a message consistent with our words. Or if we were to reverse the process, then we could begin by evaluating our actual practices and ask what they are telling us about what we truly believe or truly love. Either way, faithful discipleship and actual Christian growth demands that we pay close attention to both our worldview assumptions and our normative ethical decision-making process. The goal of normative ethics is to bring consistency between what we claim to believe and love with our daily practices and choices.

The Domains of Normative Ethical Assessment

Recognizing the connection between our actual practices to our underlying worldview assumptions should make it obvious how important it is to develop a normative system of ethics to properly order our loves and actions to God as worship. Discovering, understanding, and living in accord with a distinctly Christian ethical system, however, is a more complex endeavor than many at first realize. It involves much more than merely identifying a list of rules and seeking to abide by them as though other factors (such as one's character or motives) were irrelevant.

As a case in point, consider Jesus' rebuke of the religious leaders of his day. Although the scribes and Pharisees were experts at keeping the law, Jesus described them as "whitewashed tombs" (clean on the outside, but dead on the inside) because of their tendency to reduce morality to rule-keeping alone (Matt. 23:27). Jesus wanted them, and all his disciples, to understand that a properly formed ethic requires more than mere rule-keeping. In order for it to be truly worshipful, the moral endeavor must be situated in a larger frame of reference, and every moral choice must be engaged in light of its relationship to the grand story of creation, fall, redemption, and restoration.[3] Then, as the moral event is viewed in light of the grand story, other elements (such as a proper heart motivation, the development of personal character, and a wise understanding of the context) are also necessary to consider so that one's choices and acts maximally glorify God through proper moral application.

To highlight the importance of the different morally relevant factors of ethical decision-making, consider the following scenario. Suppose that Dan, Hanna, and Katy are all graduating seniors taking their last final exam. Further suppose that all three need to pass the test in order to graduate. As they take their seat in the classroom and glance over the exam, each of them realizes in horror that he or she studied the wrong material. Each realizes that he or she has no realistic probability of passing the test without cheating. In the heat of the moment, each considers the options.

Dan is initially panicked and uncertain of what to do. There is obviously a lot riding on his test score, and he is tempted to cheat. But then, at a deeper level, something else begins to sway his moral evaluation. Even though he knows that cheating can "get him out of a jam," deep in his heart he is concerned what kind of person he will become if he chooses to cheat. In the end, his character wins out, and he decides not to cheat. Inwardly, he whispers to himself: "Dan, you are not the kind of person who cheats, and you are not going to start down the path to becoming one today!" Being a good person and pursuing character formation is the most important factor in his ethical formulation.

Hanna's approach to moral evaluation in this situation has a very different flavor. For her, the situation is black and white. Not only is cheating "against the rules," but she believes it is actually equivalent to stealing. Questions about consequences and character barely even come into the picture. Based on her clear sense of right and wrong, she never even considers cheating as an option. So even though Hanna reaches the same moral conclusion, the manner of moral evaluation is fundamentally rule- and act-based.

Finally, for Katy, while she has general convictions about being a person of character as well as convictions about rules of right and wrong, what really rises to the level of priority in her moral evaluation are the factors relating to her particular context of life. In her immediate context in the classroom, the teacher is sitting nearby, making "sneaking a peek" at a neighbor's paper difficult. She is afraid of getting caught and suffering the disciplinary consequences for breaking the honor code. But in her larger life context, she is even more concerned with how her family, her friends, and even the school officials would feel about her if

3. Oliver O'Donovan, *Resurrection and Moral Order: An Outline for Evangelical Ethics*, 2nd ed. (Grand Rapids: Eerdmans, 1994), 77–79.

she were caught. Frustrated, she briefly wishes that she were part of a different family with more relaxed values. In the end, she also decides not to cheat. Yet for her, the decision is not primarily about character or rules, but a consideration of the possible consequences or relational costs that could result from her choices.

Notice that in this case, all three persons faced the same situation, and all reached the same conclusion, but each determined a course of action by focusing on different morally relevant factors. Dan's primary concern was with what kind of person he should *be* or *who he might become*. Hanna and Katy both focused on what they should *do*. But while Hanna and Katy shared a focus on what to *do*, the way in which they came to their conclusions was very different. One's evaluation was on the nature of the act itself and whether it was inherently right or wrong, while the other focused on the factors of the surrounding context—negative consequences or negative responses of people she loves.

This fictional case study illustrates that moral and ethical evaluation is not as simple as it may first appear. In this case, we see that there are multiple morally relevant factors, distinct aspects of morality, or what we label in this book as *domains of ethical assessment* that must be taken into consideration. That is, a concern for character of the agent, a concern about the nature of the action itself, and a consideration of context, possible consequences, and even the relational responses of others all played an important role in the moral evaluation of the people involved.

In addition, this case demonstrates that when any one of these factors is raised to the place of primacy, the method of moral evaluation and decision-making can radically change. In our fictitious story, the three students all ended up arriving at the same conclusion. But just as easily, their justification for behavior based on these various "domains" of assessment could have led to very different conclusions. Dan could have valued achievement over honesty, Hanna could have relegated rules of right and wrong to mere suggestions, and Katy could have determined that the outcome of getting a passing grade was well worth the risk. She could just as easily have decided that the ends (graduation) justified the means (cheating).

We are wise to give careful concern when formulating a normative ethical methodology not only to identify *which* domains of ethical assessment the Lord deems crucial for moral decision-making, but also to carefully consider how those domains of assessment ought to be valued, ordered, and interacted with. Ultimately, every moral act, decision, or behavior (*actual practice*) will not only reflect an underlying worldview, but also result from a pattern of decision-making that prioritizes in one way or another these domains of ethical assessment. How these domains are prioritized and ordered has much to do with what one ultimately believes to be true and what (or who) one ultimately loves most highly. Any and every moral act, choice, or behavior reflects in some way an explicit or implicit identification and valuation of the domains of ethical assessment. Similar to a conclusion we reached in chapter 1, just as everyone has a worldview—even if the person is unaware of what his or her worldview is—so also does everyone function from a normative ethical system—even if he or she is unable to articulate what that normative ethical system is.

Therefore, for Christians to grow morally and be consistent and deliberate in their daily life and faith choices, it is wise not only to understand how these domains impact every moral choice we make, but also to consider how we should rightly order them to maximally glorify God in each and every moral situation. Our first task, then, is to consider which domains of ethical assessment are important for constructing a distinctly Christian approach to normative ethics.

Historically, Thomas Aquinas identified three parts of morality and argued that all three must be rightly ordered for any moral behavior to be judged a morally good act. The three that he identified are: (1) the act itself (the object chosen), evaluated objectively in light of God's revealed moral laws; (2) the intention of the agent, evaluated subjectively in terms of what motivates the person acting; and (3) the situation or circumstances surrounding the act, which are relative factors to each situation.[4] Similarly, C. S. Lewis describes three parts of morality, which he refers to as: (1) relations between man and man; (2) the things inside each man; and (3) relations between man and the power that made him.[5] More recently, John Frame has employed the term *triperspectivalism* in an attempt to highlight three aspects of morality that he describes as: (1) the normative perspective; (2) the existential perspective; and (3) the situational perspective.[6] David W. Jones likewise adopts a threefold methodology that identifies (1) conduct, (2) character, and (3) goals as the three key aspects of biblical ethics.[7]

Interestingly enough, while there has been historical precedence within Christian ethics to identify three key elements of moral evaluation, and while unquestionably all these systems seek to incorporate similar elements of morality, the three domains chosen by any given author do not necessarily capture the same elements as those chosen by another, nor do they speak of the importance of the various morally relevant factors in the same way. The following diagram (see table 6.1) illustrates the points of emphasis in various Christian methodologies.[8]

---

4. Thomas Aquinas, *Summa Theologica*, trans. Fathers of the English Dominican Province (Notre Dame, IN: Christian Classics, 1981), I–II.18.3–4. See also the Catechism of the Catholic Church, http://www.vatican.va/archive/ccc_css/archive/catechism/p3s1c1a4.htm.

5. C. S. Lewis, *Mere Christianity* (New York: Touchstone, 1996), 69–73.

6. John M. Frame, *The Doctrine of the Christian Life* (Phillipsburg, NJ: P&R Publishing, 2008), 33–36.

7. David W. Jones, *An Introduction to Biblical Ethics* (Nashville: B&H Academic, 2013), 20–26.

8. See also WCF 16.7; Cornelius Van Til, *Christian Theistic Ethics* (Phillipsburg, NJ: Presbyterian and Reformed, 1980), 125; O'Donovan, *Resurrection and Moral Order*, 5; Wayne Grudem, *Christian Ethics: An Introduction to Biblical Moral Reasoning* (Wheaton, IL: Crossway, 2018), 149–51. Admittedly, our depiction of each of these systems in the chart above is a bit oversimplistic. We have done so, however, to approximate

Table 6.1. Various Ethical Methods and the Domains of Ethical Assessment

	Telos	Agent	Act	Circumstances	Consequences	Relationships
Aquinas		X	X	X		
Frame		X	X	X		
Jones	X	X	X			
Grudem	X	X	X		X	
Lewis	X	X				X
O'Donovan	X		X	X		
Van Til	X	X	X			
Westminster Confession	X	X	X			

In light of these differences, it seems that the most significant point of debate is how to factor in a discussion regarding both the final end or *telos* toward which our moral choices should be accounted for and how to allow for contextual factors to shape normative ethics. In fairness, we point out that within each of these various systems identified in the preceding chart is an attempt to identify and account for many various domains in one way or another. But this mere fact, to some degree, highlights the possibility that choosing three elements is in actuality an attempt to force a pattern that does not cleanly match the biblical data of what factors Scripture highlights as morally relevant.

In light of what we discovered in our metaethical analysis (part 2), there are things that God has revealed about himself and about the world (*revealed reality*) that should give us clarity not only on which domains of assessment are important to direct and shape our normative ethical methodology, but also on how to order these domains and to properly guide our behaviors. For example, we know that because the universe is theocentric in nature, the most important element of any ethical choice or moral behavior is whether the moral agent aims to love God and glorify God, thus making the *telos* the most important domain. Likewise, because humans are made in the image of God and are commanded to be conformed to the image of Christ as persons, giving priority to the domain concerned with the

and highlight as easily as possible how each system chooses to use three categories (with the exception of Grudem). In particular, Aquinas and O'Donovan in the chart above are a bit misleading because Aquinas explicitly includes the category of consequences into his discussion of circumstances. In the case of O'Donovan, our own position most closely aligns with his depiction that identifies an "objective order," a "subjective order," and a final end.

agent and his or her character is also vital. We know that because God tells us that our obedience demonstrates our love, then the domain concerned with the nature of the *act* is also a priority.

Again, when properly understood from the larger framework of the narrative of creation, fall, redemption, and restoration, it is apparent that these three domains of ethical assessment are meant to function in such a way that a concern for who we are and who we are becoming (*being*), as well as how we behave and what actions we choose (*doing*), must be prioritized. But as important as each of these elements of morality is, both of them must fall under an ultimate concern to do that which we were both created and saved to do: glorify God through whole-life worship (*goal*). Taken together, these three domains serve to give an objective ordering to our normative moral methodology. For this reason, we will refer to these three together as the *theological/normative domains.*

While these three domains are primary, however, and while they rightly set the upward trajectory as well as the boundaries of ethical decision-making and moral behavior, they must also confront the subjective world in which we live. In this way, they can be appropriately applied so that we can live within the world that God created for us to make flourish. For this reason, the first three domains do not exhaust all the aspects of moral decision-making that God wants us to give attention to.[9] Scripture also indicates that God is concerned that our moral evaluations take into consideration the *context* or situation in which a moral event takes place, the *consequences* that result from the conduct chosen, and the *relational response* of those who feel the impact of the conduct chosen. We will, then, refer to this second set of three domains as the *pastoral/contextual domains* as we consider them together.

Table 6.2. The Six Domains of Normative Ethical Assessment for Ethics as Worship

Theological/ Normative	1. The goal, final purpose, *telos* (end) toward which all our behaviors are oriented. 2. The *agent*, or *character* of the person(s) or agent(s), who is involved in the moral event. 3. The *act* or *conduct* of the person(s) or agent(s) involved in the moral event.
Pastoral/ Contextual	4. The *circumstances* or *context* or situation in which a moral event takes place. 5. The *consequences* that result from the conduct chosen. 6. The *relational response* of those who feel the impact of the conduct chosen.

9. O'Donovan, *Resurrection and Moral Order*, 101.

The Theological/Normative Domains of Ethical Assessment

Domain #1: The *Telos*—Purpose, Goal, Intention

The Greek word *telos* means "ultimate end" or "final purpose." When we use the word in the study of ethics, we are referring to the highest goal or final purpose toward which a behavior is ordered and that normally serves as the primary motivation for behavior. When we speak of the *telos* as a domain of assessment for moral evaluation, we mean that we are looking to discover not merely *what* a person has as his or her final goal, but also *why* someone has chosen a particular *telos* as *whether or not* that final goal or *telos* is a good or appropriate one. Teleological ethics, in other words, is concerned not so much with the consequences or results of a moral choice, but with one's intention to act toward a final goal.

The evaluation of the *why* that motivates someone to act toward any particular ultimate end presses us back into the discussion of that person's worldview and his or her underlying value system. The evaluation of *whether or not* the final *telos* is good or appropriate relates to what can be discovered or what one believes about the nature of the universe in which we live.

For this reason, it should come as no surprise that evaluating the *telos* is often considered the most important of all the domains of assessment for ethics. What a person ultimately desires to achieve will not only reflect, but also demonstrate what he or she believes to be most important in the world. It is the key element that connects the desires and ideas of the heart and mind to the final end (or *telos*) that the agent wants to accomplish.

To help illustrate this idea, consider the fictitious case of two men named Stuart and Sam who each donate $10,000 to a local charity. On the surface, the actions look identical and praiseworthy. But when motive is considered, it turns out that Stuart gave the money as a way to honor the Lord by helping the needy in the community, but Sam gave the money only to get a tax deduction. While Stuart's goal or motive was pointed toward God, Sam's was pointed toward himself. Clearly, the act of giving the money can have a positive effect regardless of motive. As this illustration demonstrates, however, one's final purpose and ultimate motivation play a pivotal role in how the person assesses any given moral event. While the two acts may be identical on the surface, one is judged morally praiseworthy, while the other is morally tepid or even blameworthy, depending on how the act was motivated by the final *telos*.

Properly understanding the place and role of the *telos* as a domain of assessment requires seeing its connection to what one believes about the nature and design of the universe and the final purpose for all things. For example, if one believes that the universe has no ultimate design or final purpose, then motive becomes merely an interior drive related to one's personal desires. Ultimately, there is no clear objective standard by which to determine whether it is good or bad, right or wrong. On the other hand, if there is a clear design and purpose for the universe and all things within it, then a person's internal motivation can be judged in light of how closely it aligns with that ultimate design or purpose.

Consider once again the case of Stuart and Sam. If the universe had no ultimate purpose or design, then one could say that Stuart's motivation to give was "nice" or that people "liked it," but it would be much more difficult to say that it was *objectively* "right" or "good." Likewise with Sam, while one could say that his action was "inferior" or "selfish," it would be hard to judge it as *objectively* "wrong" or "evil." Without a transcendent source of morality, there would be great difficulty in establishing a clear objective standard of right and wrong, good and evil. The moral evaluation would be a mere reflection of opinion or sentiment.

On the other hand, if God designed the universe, shaped human nature, and revealed that the chief goal of every action and choice ought to be to glorify God, then Stuart's motivation could be judged to be good or right to the degree that it was ordered to this highest goal. Likewise, Sam's could be evaluated as bad or wrong to the degree that his motives did not match up with God's ultimate design and purpose for all things. Even when both men's actions look the same, where the act is ultimately pointed (toward God or toward self) makes a profound difference in how God evaluates it.

In a very important sense, then, we would say that every moral action is in some way *teleological*—ordered toward a final end. As we pointed out in chapter 1, this is precisely why no action can be said to be morally neutral. Every choice that could be made will reflect an underlying value system, and every method of decision-making will reflect what one deems to be most important at the worldview or metaethical level. For the same reason, we could also make the case that every action is also an act of worship in the sense that it is ordered toward a final or ultimate end. Whatever end it is ordered toward serves as a *functional god*—be it the self, others' opinions, the environment, or the God of the Bible.

This is precisely why it is so important to identify the *actual telos* that motivates and orders one's moral behavior—in terms not merely of what one states to be his or her purpose or goal, but also of what is actually motivating at the deepest level of the self. Even if one has never clearly done the hard work to determine a chief end or *telos*, all of us will function as though we had. We will reflexively and instinctively make choices in light of that which we believe or love most truly. Our actual practices will ultimately reflect our deepest values, whether we are explicitly aware of them or not.

What kinds of ethical systems develop when consideration of the *telos* is given the place of primacy in moral evaluation? Consider the following chart to help illustrate the ideas. The left-hand column represents various possible ends (*telos*) that might be given highest priority at the worldview level. The adjacent column then identifies the final ordering principle that serves as the metaethical foundation for the ethical system that begins to emerge in light of the final *telos*. The third column indicates the likely manner in which the moral status of persons or things will be evaluated by that system. The column on the far right identifies that person or thing that takes the place of the object of worship or *functional god*.

For example, if a person ultimately acts to maximize his or her own personal pleasure, then we can say that the corresponding ethical system will by default be egocentric in nature. As a result, it is likely that such an ethical system will give priority to the self in terms of who or what should be considered most valuable (i.e., *moral status*) when determining how to make moral decisions. It would be appropriate to suggest that the *self* (one's own goals, desires, pleasures, profits, and so on) serves as this person's *functional god*.

Table 6.3. Ethical Systems Based on *Telos*

Telos (the Ultimate Goal, Purpose, Motive Driving Ethical Behavior)	Corresponding Metaethical Foundation	Who or What Has Moral Status	Functional Object of Worship
Personal pleasure/ satisfaction	Egocentric	Self has ultimate moral status. Everything else has lesser or instrumental value.	Self
Care for humans	Anthropocentric	Humans have ultimate moral status. Everything else has lesser or instrumental value.	Human race
Care for all living things	Biocentric	All living things have ultimate moral status. Everything else has lesser or instrumental value.	The biosphere
Care for all living things and their environment	Ecocentric	The environment as a whole has ultimate moral status.	The environment
Glorifying God (Christian)	Theocentric	God has ultimate moral status. Everything else is given inherent value (to varying degrees) by him.	God

While not all ethical theories will cleanly fit into the categories of this chart, the point is to show that whichever one a person chooses (or acts on by default) as the driving *telos* of his or her ethic will greatly impact the person's moral evaluation. Of course, there will always be mixed motivations and goals in any moral event. These categories are not meant to imply that each motive is necessarily mutually exclusive of the others. A Christian worshiper of God, for example, should certainly want to care for the world that God created as well as the people that God put into that world. Rather, our goal is to identify the ultimate or chief end (*telos*) for which a moral behavior is chosen.

With this in mind, we see that the chart helps illustrate several important points relating to how a distinctly Christian ethic ought to differ from other ethical systems that are built on the various alternative metaethical assumptions. First, notice that as one moves down the list and the *telos* becomes more comprehensive in nature, the previous lines on the chart are encompassed in the latter. For example, if one's chief concern or *telos* is with the self, then only the self is of ultimate concern. But if one is ultimately concerned with the biosphere, then all living things—including the self—are of importance, and so on down the list.

Second, the chart highlights the reality that all ethical systems can be identified as a system of worship in some manner or another. The question is not really *whether* something is being worshiped, but *what* is being worshiped. Whatever one focuses on as the final or highest goal or value becomes a *functional god*. For example, if the environment as a whole serves as the chief *telos*, then caring for it becomes primary and all other moral actions (as well as political policies) are oriented through the grid of how to best honor and care for the environment. In such a case, environmentalism could be said to be functioning as a form of religion. It becomes the standard for how one views the world and the primary determinant of how we should act in it.

This, then, leads to the third point. While many different possible functional gods can take the place of a highest and final *telos*, the most important question of ethics is "which one is worthy of holding the place of highest honor?" From a distinctly Christian point of view, only the triune God of the Bible is worthy of holding the place of the final *telos*. And it is only in honoring the one true God, and orienting all things toward him as he instructs, that the preceding categories of concern (persons, human race, biosphere, environment, and anything else) will ultimately be rightly cared for and governed.

The Bible is full of illustrations relating to the importance of identifying, valuing, and properly ordering one's moral choices toward God as the final and ultimate end. Both the Old and New Testaments place the love of God as the ultimate ordering principle for life and practice:

> Hear, O Israel! The LORD is our God, the LORD is one! You shall love the LORD your God with all your heart and with all your soul and with all your might. (Deut. 6:4–5; cf. Mark 12:29–31)

Jesus also gave clear instruction to his disciples indicating the importance of ordering one's behaviors to God as the proper *telos*. One example of his moral teaching in this regard can be found in Matthew 6:1–18. In this passage, Jesus teaches his followers how to properly order charitable giving, prayer, and fasting. In each case, he warns his followers not to practice their righteousness in front of others in order to be seen by them. Instead, the acts are to be done "in secret" so that only God the Father can see them. When they are properly ordered to God, Jesus teaches, then these same actions will be worthy of divine approval. Ultimately, according to Jesus, the ethical assessment of these apparently good acts of obedience (giving, praying, fasting) depends to a large degree on the final end to which they are ordered and the motive of the person performing them.

Perhaps, however, the Bible is nowhere clearer about the role and importance of the *telos* as the chief domain of ethical assessment than in the following New Testament verses:

> Whether, then, you eat or drink or whatever you do, do all to the glory of God. (1 Cor. 10:31)

> Whatever you do in word or deed, do all in the name of the Lord Jesus, giving thanks through Him to God the Father. (Col. 3:17)

These verses communicate the two reasons that the *telos* should be the chief domain of ethical assessment: scope and direction.

Scope
First, consider the *scope* of life that is identified in these passages. Both these verses insist on a universal understanding that all our actions—even the most mundane—are important to God. Notice that nothing is excluded in either verse. Indeed, with statements such as "do *all* to the glory of God" and "do *all* in the name of the Lord Jesus," these verses include the whole of our lives. First Corinthians 10:31 is interesting because it gives specific examples of just how much the simplest and most repetitive things we do in life matter to God. Apparently, whether or not I eat a peanut-butter sandwich matters to God. Whether or not I drink a soda matters to God. Colossians 3:17 likewise identifies universal categories ("word or deed") of things we are doing all the time and often without giving them a second thought. Apparently, the simple jokes I make every day matter

to God. And whether I tie my shoes or not matters to God. Every word. Every deed. All our life choices matter to God, even the smallest and seemingly most insignificant choices. God wants our worship in spirit and truth to encompass everything.

Direction

Second, and perhaps more directly related to this part of the discussion, both verses tell us about the orientation, final ordering, or *direction* of where all the various things we do, think, or say in life should be oriented. Not every ethical decision is rightly oriented toward God as the final ultimate end, but every act is ordered to *some* ultimate end. As we noted above, it is not always the case that our actual practices match up with our stated beliefs. But these verses clearly indicate that all our actions *should* be oriented to God as the final end goal and rendered to him as acts of worship. Glorifying God is the ultimate end for Christian morality, and it is therefore the most fundamental and important aspect of morality.

Because this is true, these passages also indicate that all the choices and actions we make in life have a spiritual dimension. Everything we do is ultimately a choice and action of worship. God desires each one of them to be ordered and rightly directed to him. In light of our discussion in part 2 of the book, this direction should now come as no surprise. God built us to worship. He created us to do all things for the purpose of filling the earth with the knowledge of his glory, and these verses tie together the nature of morality with the ultimate purposes for which all things exist. John Frame notes that "when God commands us to glorify him in all things (1 Cor. 10:31), *everything* we do ought to be an application of that command. *Everything* we do is either a fulfillment or a violation of that obligation. In that sense, all our actions are ethical. They are either good or bad, depending on whether they glorify God or not."[10]

Ethics *is* worship. The real question is not *whether* we are worshiping in everything we do, but *who* or *what* we are worshiping. This is why the *telos* is the most important domain of ethical assessment.

Domain #2: Character of the Agent

The second domain of ethical assessment relates to the person or *agent* who is involved in a moral event. Whereas the primary concern in our discussion of the *telos* was with the final ordering or goal of the behavior, an evaluation of the *agent* emphasizes a person's character. The question is not primarily about the person's *purpose* or *motive* (though, as we will see, this remains very important), nor is

---

10. Frame, *Doctrine of the Christian Life*, 17 (emphasis added).

it primarily concerned with determining what someone should *do* (although a good moral act is certainly desired). Rather, the primary question of moral evaluation relates to discovering whether the person in question embodies the types of character qualities or virtues that enable him or her to most fully be what he or she ought to *be*. That is, what character traits or virtues ought to depict a person in order for that person to be described as a good or godly person who embodies the values of a true worshiper? And how ought those virtues to direct that "good person" toward good moral conduct?

To understand these ideas, consider another fictional case. Imagine that two men (this time named Lawrence and Robert) each donate $10,000 to a local charity. On the surface, both actions appear morally praiseworthy. Imagine, however, that although Lawrence is a millionaire and has plenty of discretionary income, he actually had no internal desire to donate the money. In fact, further imagine that he intensely resents his wife for volunteering their funds to the charitable cause. Internally, he has no love for the people who will benefit, he does not care about their plight, and if he had his way, he would never be involved in charitable giving again. His only reason for giving in this scenario is that he felt obligated to do so because his wife put him in an awkward position by volunteering his assistance. Robert, on the other hand, is an underpaid minister who barely makes enough to get by. But because he has great concern for the people who will benefit from the charitable contribution, he patiently saves the money over a two-year period. After much sacrifice and penny-pinching, he finally reaches his goal of $10,000 and joyfully gives the money away. How should we evaluate each man's behavior?

In this situation, even though both men performed the same action, there is obviously something very different in relation to the character of each of them. Lawrence's greed and lack of care for his fellow man taint the moral quality of the donation. Robert, on the other hand, is marked by a disposition of benevolence, generosity, and love. Thus, even though the action of giving $10,000 to charity is the same between the men, Robert's donation is the one that is actually morally praiseworthy when a consideration of his moral character is factored into the conversation.

In the discipline of ethics, discussions relating to the evaluation and formation of character typically utilize the language of *virtue*. The English word *virtue* comes from the Latin root word *virtus*, referring originally to the ancient Roman understanding of the qualities of "manliness" that were sought after in an excellent soldier (bravery, strength, skill, wisdom, and so forth). With time, the term came to refer more generally to the qualities of excellence in any person. The classical Greek counterpart for *virtus* is the word *arête*, meaning "excellence." A simple understanding of the term *virtue*, following these linguistic roots, is *an ingrained character trait or reflexive disposition that enables or assists an individual to live life in an excellent manner and thereby flourish as a human being.*[11]

Obviously, then, determining whether an ingrained disposition or character trait is actually a virtue depends to a large degree on who gets to define what "living life in an excellent manner" or living a "good life" actually consists of. This, then, relates to how we define what kind of thing a human being *is*. For example, if human beings are the mere product of an evolutionary process in which chance and time are the primary factors in our existence, then it is possible to conclude (as many philosophers have) that there is no such thing as a universal "human nature" and that we all must determine for ourselves what kind of thing we want to be.[12] According to this view, as autonomous creatures with no necessary accountability to God or others, each person is a moral blank slate who is capable and free to determine his or her own self in line with whatever he or she desires.

Having a "good" character, in this frame of reference, means nothing more than having the character traits that one personally likes or that fit in well with a given society's chosen values. A pirate, for example, can have the character traits that make him a good pirate and thus morally praiseworthy within his own community. Thus, even though gluttony, lust, and villainy are the traits that mark him, if there is no God, then these character traits are evaluated as "good" in light of his own self-determination or because they are the values applauded by his community.

Historically, however, it has been important to recognize that having an ingrained and reflexive character trait that is socially acceptable is *not* necessarily the same thing as having a *moral virtue*. A pirate may have a reflexive pattern of behavior to kill or rape when an opportunity arises. But while his fellow pirates may applaud this disposition, and while these character traits may make him an excellent pirate, from an almost universally accepted point of view, one would hardly describe these behaviors as morally praiseworthy. Rather, for the vast majority of human history it has been understood that in order to describe a person as morally virtuous, that person's life and behaviors must align with the nature of what that person is created to be as determined by God's design and in

11. In keeping with this, Alasdair MacIntyre defines *virtue* as "an acquired human quality, the possession and exercise of which tends to enable us to achieve those goods which are internal to practices and the lack of which effectively prevents us from achieving any such goods." Alasdair MacIntyre, *After Virtue: A Study in Moral Theory*, 3rd ed. (Notre Dame, IN: University of Notre Dame Press, 2007), 191. Similarly, Wyndy Reuschling defines *virtues* as "human qualities and characteristics that can be labeled 'good' and to which humans aspire *because* these qualities are good and crucial to living a good life." Wyndy Corbin Reuschling, *Reviving Evangelical Ethics: The Promises and Pitfalls of Classic Models of Morality* (Grand Rapids: Brazos, 2008), 121.

12. Examples are Nietzsche, Camus, Sartre.

light of God's eternal moral law. It would therefore be a mistake to assume that virtuous behavior is that which is merely socially approved.[13]

Once again, we see the importance of one's metaethical assumptions as they relate to the overall moral evaluation of a person and his or her character. If the focus on the agent's character is tied to a metaethic that assumes that God *does not* exist, then the character traits deemed valuable could (and likely would) be very different from those in a culture or context that believes that God *does* exist and has revealed his moral instructions to us through Scripture. One culture could describe *virtues* as those character dispositions that maximize self-interest (i.e., "greed is good"), while another would maximize service to others (i.e., "neighbor love"). Thus, as was the case with understanding the *telos* as a domain of assessment, properly understanding the place and role of the *agent* as a domain of assessment also requires seeing the connection between what one believes about the nature and design of the universe and the final purpose for all things.

If there is a final purpose for the universe and the persons who live in it, then a person would be wise to develop the character traits that will enable him or her to fulfill that purpose and live maximally toward his or her final end. The same would be true of human society as a whole. The virtues that we value corporately ought to enable us to live together in a manner that facilitates communal flourishing. But if there is no ingrained nature, no basic form, no design or God-given purpose, *how* we seek to develop ourselves as human moral agents ultimately depends on one's personal desires and self-determination. To put it simply, understanding why, focusing on the character of the agent, and then determining which character traits one ought to develop as a moral agent are intimately connected to discovering our created purpose and design.

Recalling our discussions about the created purpose and design for human beings in part 2 of this book, we learned that God originally designed and created us as worshipers who—before sin—were rightly aligned to the eternal moral patterns that he wove into the fabric of creation. Tragically, however, human sin and the fall impacted all of us such that our worship is now fundamentally disordered. Therefore, in order for any of us to rightly order our conduct to God and then rightly act morally, God must radically transform the agent.

This transformation has two closely related elements. As John 1:12 indicates, we must first *become* children of God through saving faith in Jesus Christ. Then, Scripture teaches, we need to have our character conformed to the image of Christ so that we can once again embody in our character and dispositions the kind of persons that God created us to be as his image-bearers (Rom. 8:29; Eph. 4:13). The

---

13. Tom L. Beauchamp and James F. Childress, *Principles of Biomedical Ethics*, 4th ed. (New York: Oxford University Press, 1994), 63.

core of moral discipleship, then, requires that each of us as a moral agent must strive in all aspects of life to become more like Jesus Christ through development of certain character traits and virtues that enable us to be more like him.

Put in terms of theology, we would say that whereas the lived doctrine of *justification* requires the infusion of *theological virtues* (i.e., positional truths) into our lives by grace through faith, the lived doctrine of *sanctification* requires the development of *moral virtues*. Passages such as Galatians 5:16–24 emphasize the importance of developing our character as the Holy Spirit grows in us the "fruit of the Spirit" so that our lives might be characterized by virtue. Indeed, Paul sets up a contrast between dispositions that mark sinful worldliness and those that reflect godly character. The desires of the flesh include such sinful vices as immorality, strife, jealousy, and anger, which in turn result in deeds (or actions) of the flesh (vv. 19–21). By contrast, the one who walks in the Spirit exhibits the fruit of the Spirit—love, joy, peace, patience, kindness, goodness, faithfulness, gentleness, and self-control (vv. 22–23).

In chapters 4 and 5, we discussed the process of character formation and virtue development in much greater detail. For our purposes here, we simply want to highlight that acquiring the moral virtues necessary to conform to the image of Christ involves the work of the Holy Spirit to empower the process of becoming in character and actual practice what God has made true of us through Christ's atonement. This involves growing into maturity (Col. 1:28; 4:12; Heb. 6:1–3), exhibiting in our character the fruits of the Spirit (Gal. 5:22–23), and embodying a life of "godliness" (1 Tim. 4:8; 6:6; 2 Peter 1:5–8). Primarily, the life of a true worshiper is to be marked by the virtue of love.

Throughout the Gospels, Jesus repeatedly centralized the importance of his disciples' being marked by the virtue of love. We see his emphasis on this no more clearly than in his response to the scribe who asked him which of the commandments was the greatest. Interestingly, he answered with a command to be the kind of person who loves God with the whole self and who also loves one's neighbor:

> The foremost is, "Hear, O Israel! The Lord our God is one Lord; and you shall love the Lord your God with all your heart, and with all your soul, and with all your mind, and with all your strength." The second is this: "You shall love your neighbor as yourself." There is no other commandment greater than these. (Mark 12:29–31)

The greatest commandment in the Bible is a command to be a virtuous person: to love God and neighbor with excellence (virtue). It is from this character formation in the moral agent that loving acts of obedience will then rightly flow. The person we become through the development of character and virtues is shaped by what we do, and what we do is shaped by the person we have become in character.

Character formation, then, is closely linked with obedience in our conduct. This then leads us to a discussion of the next domain of ethical assessment.

Domain #3: The Act/Conduct—Determining an Objective Standard for Conduct Worthy of the Gospel

In addition to rightly ordering all that we are and do toward its proper end (*telos*), and becoming the right kind of person by cultivating virtues and character, ethics as worship requires instructions and standards by which to evaluate whether the actions we choose rightly align with God's eternal moral design for all things and the character he desires for us to have. Thus, the third most important domain of ethical assessment for ethics as worship is a consideration of our particular *actions* and *conduct*. This domain pertains to identifying the criteria necessary to determine whether an action undertaken is inherently good or bad, right or wrong. This is typically done by evaluating the act in question in light of whatever laws, rules, or principles are said to be morally binding in a given situation.

As was the case with understanding both the *telos* and the *agent* as domains of assessment, properly understanding how to evaluate the *act* requires seeing the connection between what one believes about the nature and design of the universe and the final purpose for all things. As we highlighted in our discussion of the *telos* earlier in the chapter, if the assumption that God does not exist is the basis of one's metaethical assumptions, then it follows that the idea of discovering a morality that is objective and universal in nature is difficult to sustain. Moral laws, rules, or principles indicating whether a particular act is always right or always wrong would seem nonsensical—or at least hard to prove. Making universal moral claims in a world that precludes God immediately raises the question of how those rules got there, why they are morally binding, and what type of accountability exists if one breaks them.[14]

On the other hand, if God does exist, and if he did design the universe, then it follows as a logical possibility that the moral patterns that God wove into the world will be discoverable and discernable (at least to some degree). If so, these patterns (sometimes called *natural* or *general revelation*—see chapter 5) could be used to discern objective standards for governing behavior. Likewise, it is also plausible that God could more directly communicate laws, rules, principles, or guidelines for how people ought to act or behave in the world (most often described as *special revelation*). These laws, then, would be good for humans to obey because not only would they align with God's ultimate design and purpose, they would also

---

14. For an interesting discussion, see C. S. Lewis's argument related to the existence of morality and law as a proof for the existence of God. Lewis, *Mere Christianity*, 17–39.

provide clear objective standards by which to evaluate the rightness or wrongness of any given act.

When the act itself is under evaluation as the primary category of ethical assessment (apart from consideration of the final purpose or character of the agent), the types of ethical systems that emerge are often described as *deontological*. The word *deontology* finds its roots in the Greek term *deon*, which carries the meaning of "duty" or "obligation." Deontology, then, is the study of moral obligation. A deontological system of ethics, likewise, is one that emphasizes a person's duty or obligation to do a particular action simply because it is the "right thing to do" in and of itself without any consideration of other factors, such as the character of the agent, the ultimate purpose, or other possible contextual factors that may apply. Once a rule, law, or principle of behavior (e.g., the Ten Commandments) is identified as morally binding, then it becomes one's duty to obey by keeping those rules, laws, or principles as obediently as possible. It is the "letter of the law" that matters.

To highlight the general concept, consider yet another case, in which two men named Seth and Travis both make a $10,000 donation to charity, but each does so for completely different reasons. Seth makes his donation with an altruistic desire to benefit those in need, while Travis makes his contribution based solely on the desire to impress his girlfriend, Elizabeth. While a moral evaluation based on virtue ethics would rank Seth's action as better than Travis's, in a purely act-based or deontological assessment, because the focus is on the act itself and not the motive or character, the act of each would be considered equal in terms of its moral praiseworthiness.

Or consider the opposite approach to highlight the nature of act-based systems. Let's say that Mandy slowly embezzles $10,000 from her workplace so that she can buy a beautiful wedding dress. Stephany, on the other hand, slowly embezzles the same amount of money to buy medicine that she could not otherwise afford in order to take care of her sick child. In a purely act-based system of ethics that understands a commandment such as "thou shalt not steal" to be morally binding, both acts would be considered equally wrong regardless of the attending context and motives. The only thing that matters in such systems is an evaluation of whether the act itself aligned with whatever specified rule is said to be morally binding in that case.

In the simplest terms, we can say that deontological systems focus on evaluating the rightness or wrongness of the act itself in light of whatever moral rules are considered authoritative to govern behavior. This, then, leads to a discussion about the nature and function of moral rules within action-based ethical systems.

Many act-based moral systems differentiate between various types of moral rules that ought to govern behavior and their related *moral weightiness*. With regard to the type of rules, we can distinguish between *objective rules* and *subjective rules*. By *objective rules* we mean rules that exist and stand independent of someone's opinion about them—including one's own. That is, they are not influenced by one's personal belief or feelings; rather, they are said to exist objectively. These can be contrasted with *subjective rules* that are derived from or heavily influenced by one's own beliefs or feelings rather than being based on facts or commands that arise external to oneself. These rules are said to be matters of one's own opinion. Most deontological systems maintain that moral laws, rules, or principles are objective in nature.

In addition to the type of rules, it is also important to consider the strength or *weightiness* that is assigned to the rules in question. On one end of a spectrum, rules might be recognized as good ideas, but be given very little binding power. They would function more like guidelines or suggestions. For example, a guideline such as "never ask a woman if she is pregnant" might be a good social guideline, but while we might call someone "stupid" for breaking it, we would likely not call him "immoral." On a more serious note, someone may consider a rule such as "never tell a lie" to be a generally good idea, but when pressed into a hard place, the person may consider telling a "little white lie" to be acceptable when it can get him or her out of a tight spot. The rule acts as a helpful guide but not a binding norm.[15]

On the other end of the spectrum, rules might be considered to have absolute binding power or weight. By *absolute* we mean that they are binding at all times regardless of the motive, circumstances, or potential consequences. These types of rules would carry maximum weight. For example, a command such as "thou shalt not murder" would mean that under no circumstances would the intentional taking of innocent human life be without fault or moral guilt. Likewise, "lying is wrong" would mean that under no circumstances would it be justifiable to tell a lie without incurring moral guilt.

Between these two ends of the spectrum, there is a third type of rule that is often identified in ethical discussions as one that is *prima facie* ("at first glance") binding.[16] While normatively such rules would function as binding at all times—as absolutes—there may be rare situations in which they come into conflict with other absolutes that may override them in a particular circumstance. For example, consider a situation in which Jerry makes a promise to meet his friend Anne at 7 P.M. to help her study for a philosophy exam. While Jerry is on the way, however, he notices that a little old lady has fallen down in the street and requires immediate medical attention. In this case, while Jerry believes that he should always keep his promises, he is confronted with a situation in which the

15. Kyle D. Fedler, *Exploring Christian Ethics: Biblical Foundations for Morality* (Louisville: Westminster John Knox, 2006), 24.

16. Philosopher W. D. Ross (1877–1971) is often credited with coining this phrase. See W. D. Ross, *The Right and the Good* (Oxford: Oxford University Press, 1930), 21.

woman will likely die if he does not intervene. What is he to do? If he breaks his promise to Anne, will he be doing something that is morally wrong even though he is striving to save a life? Will he be sinning? On the other hand, if he decides to keep his promise to Anne and simply leave the woman to die, has he neglected his duty to honor human life? Will Jerry be sinning?

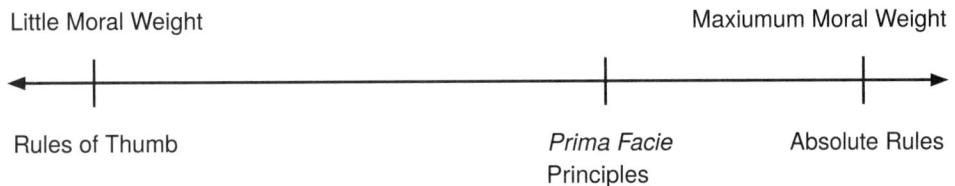

Fig. 6.2. Moral Weightiness of Rules

In this case, unless one is willing to suggest that Jerry somehow incurs moral guilt for breaking his promise while helping to save the lady's life, some ethicists consider that it is best to describe the commands as *prima facie* binding instead of absolutely binding. The reason for this is that the term *absolute* implies no exceptions. Thus, lest one do damage to the language and meaning of the term *absolute*, the term *prima facie* serves as a way to retain the notion that the command normatively holds an absolute weightiness unless or until it comes into conflict with an equally weighty command and both cannot be kept simultaneously. While most Christian ethical systems will refer to biblical commands as absolute moral norms, some deontological systems of ethics will adopt the language of *prima facie* principlism in order to accommodate for morally complex situations in which a choice must be made between what might otherwise be considered two absolute commands. We will return to this discussion, often described as the problem of *moral dilemmas* or *tragic moral choices*, in chapter 8.

Returning to our immediate discussion of how to evaluate the nature of an act itself as a domain of ethical assessment in Christian ethics, consider once again our discussion of the great commandments to love God and neighbors from the preceding section. Recall that when Jesus commands us to be the kind of people who love God and neighbor, he is commanding us to *be* virtuous. Having been given this command, however, we are still left with the question of how we are to know whether we are actually loving God in our actions. After all, if our actual beliefs and actual loves are best identified by our actual practices, then a concern for what we *do* must also be given a position of priority in our normative ethical method.

In other words, having been given the command to love God and neighbor, we are still left with the question of how a person is to know whether his or her actions are actually consistent and in keeping with the kinds of virtues that God has commanded him or her to embody. How are we to know whether we are actually loving our neighbor as God desires? Is the answer merely dependent on our sentiment, feelings, or emotions to make the determination? Does it depend solely on my own perceptions of how I like to be treated? Consider, for example, that the Scripture tells me to "love my neighbor as myself." Does this mean that the way I love my neighbor is ultimately subject to my own preferences? If so, what does this mean if I like to be slapped? What if I like it when people punch me? What if I like to harm myself? Would the command to "do unto others as I would like them to do unto me," then, allow me to slap, punch, or harm others?

The question regarding our conduct seems to be this: How do we evaluate whether the actions we take in the name of a virtue such as love are actually loving actions? Ronald Nash is correct when he states that "love is insufficient in itself to provide moral guidance for each and every moral action. It requires the further specification of principles or rules that suggest the proper ways in which love should be manifested."[17] It requires knowledge of what commands, principles, rules, and guidelines God has revealed to us in the Bible to evaluate our conduct.

As we highlighted in previous chapters, Scripture gives us the answer in the way in which Jesus connected virtues to standards and norms of actions. Recalling once again John 14:15, Jesus says, "If you love Me, you will keep My commandments." And then again in John 14:21 he says, "He who has My commandments and keeps them is the one who loves Me; and He who loves Me will be loved by My Father, and I will love him and will disclose Myself to him." Accordingly, we see in the first of these verses that the virtue of love is to be evaluated and determined by biblical commandments that instruct us more particularly about which actions are right or wrong, good or evil.

Love has a particular shape that is defined not by subjective feelings and desires but by the instructions and commands God gives to guide our choices, acts, and behaviors. It is only as we allow those action commands and instructions to shape particular choices and behaviors in a repeated manner over time that our desires and character traits will be rightly ordered. In this way, we discover that our feelings don't drive us, but that we shape our feelings and desires in light of God's commands through a long obedience in the same direction. Then, when our desires and feelings have been harnessed, shaped, and properly ordered to God in a worship-maximizing way, we will know that we are truly loving God and neighbor. This is what the psalmist means when he tells us to "delight yourself in the LORD; and He will give you the desires of your heart" (Ps. 37:4).

---

17. Ronald H. Nash, *Worldviews in Conflict: Choosing Christianity in a World of Ideas* (Grand Rapids: Zondervan, 1992), 45–46. In our chapter on justice and social engagement, we will highlight the formal and material principles of justice in a similar manner.

In sum, we can see how important an evaluation of the act itself is for the shaping of a normative methodology of ethics as worship. Neither the final ordering nor the motive by itself justifies the action. The inherent value of the act itself must be considered before the moral event can be judged good or evil, right or wrong. From God's commands, principles, rules, and action guides we learn how to actually behave like virtuous disciples of Christ, and from obeying these commands we also become virtuous people who love God.

The Affinity and Interaction of the Theological/Normative Domains

Having explored the nature and importance of these first three domains of ethical assessment, we are now at an important juncture in the formulation of the normative aspects of ethics as worship. As we consider building an ethical methodology that helps us in knowing how to live, we must now pause before concluding this chapter and consider how these first three domains work in concert with one another to help shape our ethical decision-making. That is, having offered reasons for *why* each domain is important, we now move to a discussion of *how* they function together in the shaping of the normative aspect of ethics as worship.

With regard to these first three domains—*telos*, *character*, and *act*—we noted that the focus of each pertains primarily to how we are to rightly order our morality and ethics to God. To use a spatial or directional metaphor, these three domains are primarily concerned with ordering, shaping, and aligning the *vertical dimension* of ethics as worship in light of all we discovered in part 2 of this book regarding the creation, fall, redemption, restoration story line of the Bible (*revealed reality*). Scripture plainly teaches that as God's image-bearers, we are to order all things to God, become lovers of God, and choose righteous actions that align with God's laws of love. Thus, we note that these categories tend to be more theologically ordered and objective in nature, and can be dealt with more abstractly as dispositions of the image-bearer who considers the best way to worship the Lord. They are therefore concerned with discovering the principles of character that guide our loves as well as principles of conduct that shape our actions so that our ethics can be properly aimed in a Godward direction.

The second thing to note is how the three domains relate to, interact with, and rely on one another in order to ensure the proper vertical ordering of our ethics. As we have argued throughout the book, worshiping and glorifying God is of utmost importance (*telos domain*). But in order to do this well, the *telos* domain must be shaped by one's character (*virtue domain*) and obedience to God's commands (*act/conduct domain*). In the language of ethics, one might describe ethics as worship as a Christ-centered, deontological virtue ethic. That is, God desires his image-bearers to glorify him through habituated obedience that flows reflexively through our transformed character.[18] The following diagram (see fig. 6.3) illustrates both the priority of the *telos* and the interactive dependence of these domains one to another.

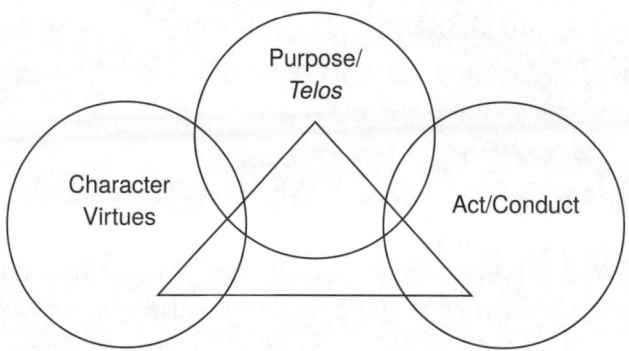

Fig. 6.3. The Priority of *Telos*

In order to further explain and clarify the interdependent relationship between these domains in the proper shaping and ordering of our ethics unto God as worship, consider once again a situation in which a student is tempted to cheat. Suppose Michelle sits down at her computer to take an online closed-book final exam in her ethics class. Upon opening the exam, she realizes that she did not study well for the questions the professor is asking. What should she do? At one level, she could simply address the issue by looking at the instructions on the test that say, "This is a closed-book exam." The test rules forbid her from opening her books. Thus, there is a rather surface-level manner in which to address the "what should I do" aspect of her situation. In this sense, the immediate, closest, or most *proximate* aspect of her decision has to do merely with whether or not she will break the rules of the professor and cheat.

There are, however, more elements to the moral decision-making process. The other theological/normative domains help us to see the deeper nature of the moral choice facing Michelle. First, she needs to realize that if she does cheat, she is not merely breaking the professor's classroom rules. By doing so, she will also be disrespecting authority, being dishonest, and taking someone else's answers as her own, and in so doing she will behave in a manner that dishonors the name *Christian* that she claims as a Christ-follower. In other words, in regard to the act domain alone, her choice to cheat in this context would break at least four of the Ten Commandments (third, fifth, eighth, ninth).

18. J. Douma, *Responsible Conduct: Principles of Christian Ethics* (Phillipsburg, NJ: P&R Publishing, 2003), 26.

Further, as we consider the domain of virtues, clearly because Michelle is breaking commands, she is also not able to embody true love for her teacher, who is her neighbor; her fellow students, who have worked hard to take the exam honestly; or the Lord, who has given her instruction not to disobey his commands. In addition, if she does cheat, she is negatively reinforcing through her choice a lack of character in relationship to the virtues of honor, integrity, honesty, and self-control. On the other hand, if she chooses to honor the commands and resist the temptation to cheat, not only has she chosen the right act, she has also reinforced the character traits of a godly person (love for God and neighbor).

When we consider the situation from the most important or *ultimate* aspect of ethics, Michelle's choice is ultimately a choice of what (or who) will be her object of worship as she decides whether or not to cheat. Her primary question is not "should I cheat?," nor is it "am I the kind of person who cheats?," but "is it possible to rightly worship God and move toward conformity to Christ's character by cheating?" Stated more positively, Michelle's primary question is "will I choose to be the kind of person who glorifies God through my obedience in this particular situation?" If we are to worship God in spirit and truth, the ethical task requires us not only to direct our worship toward God, but to do so in a good and right manner.

Conclusion

In this chapter, we identified six domains of ethical assessment present in any moral event that are called on to make moral decisions and evaluations. We then focused our attention on three of these domains: the *telos*, the *agent*, and the *act*.

It is important to note as we draw this portion of the discussion to a conclusion that by identifying these first three domains together and giving primacy to them in the moral decision-making process, the resulting ethical method will have as a strength a high fidelity to God's Word as the shaping source of authority that determines the Christian's perspective both on his or her metaethical assumptions (*revealed reality*) and on his or her normative method (*revealed morality*), which includes a focus both on character formation and on obedience to God's moral commands. Scripture both orients the moral decision to its right and proper end and provides transcendent and objective norms to shape our character and guide our actions. That is, these three theological/normative domains guide ethics as worship by providing both foundational justification for the moral decision-making and the normative guiderails to properly direct our moral decision in a Godward direction.

As important as these three are, however, an ethical system must also consider how best to apply the moral data discovered from these first three domains to real-life contexts. For this reason, we must now consider how the particular circumstances a person faces, the potential consequences that might result from a person's behavior, and the relational responses of those we interact with ought to influence the way that we apply what we have learned from the normative domains to those real-life contexts. It is to this discussion that we now turn.

Key Terms and Concepts

agent	moral weightiness
anthropocentric	normative ethics
autonomy	pastoral/contextual domains
biocentric	principles, absolute
character formation	principles, *prima facie*
conduct	reflexive pattern of behavior
deontology	rules, objective
domains of ethical assessment	rules, subjective
ecocentric	stated beliefs and loves versus actual
egocentric motive	practices
final purpose	teleological ethics
functional god	theological/normative domains
moral dilemmas	virtues, moral
moral status	virtues, theological

Key Scriptures

Exodus 20:2–3	1 Corinthians 10:31
Deuteronomy 6:4–5	Galatians 5:22–23
Mark 12:29–31	Philippians 1:27
John 14:15	Colossians 3:17
John 14:21	1 Timothy 4:8
Romans 8:29	

Study Questions

1. What is the relationship between our stated beliefs and what we actually do in practice? How do our moral choices and ethical practices shed light on what we truly believe about God and his world?
2. Why is it important in Christian ethics for a person to know and understand what his or her ultimate *telos* is?
3. Why is a focus on a moral agent's character an important domain of eth-

ical assessment? How does spiritual and moral formation relate to ethical decision-making?

4. Why is a focus on the actions one chooses an important domain of ethical assessment?

5. How do the first three domains of ethical assessment relate to one another and shape the vertical aspect of our ethics to be a proper form of love for God?

For Further Reading

DeYoung, Rebecca Konyndyk. *Glittering Vices: A New Look at the Seven Deadly Sins and Their Remedies*. Grand Rapids: Brazos, 2009.

Frame, John M. *The Doctrine of the Christian Life*. Phillipsburg, NJ: P&R Publishing, 2008.

Jones, David W. *An Introduction to Biblical Ethics*. Nashville: B&H Academic, 2013.

Lewis, C. S. *Mere Christianity*. New York: Touchstone, 1996.

MacIntyre, Alasdair. *After Virtue: A Study in Moral Theory*. 3rd ed. Notre Dame, IN: University of Notre Dame Press, 2007.

Reuschling, Wyndy Corbin. *Reviving Evangelical Ethics: The Promises and Pitfalls of Classic Models of Morality*. Grand Rapids: Brazos, 2008.

7

The Normative Methodology for Ethics as Worship: Part 2

"I have fought the good fight, I have finished the course, I have kept the faith;
in the future there is laid up for me the crown of righteousness, which the Lord,
the righteous Judge, will award to me on that day; and not only to me,
but also to all who have loved His appearing."
—APOSTLE PAUL, 2 TIMOTHY 4:7–8

"Our freedom as agents depends upon our acting in accord with reality.
Reality is the point on which both freedom and authority rest,
and at which they complement each other."[1]
—OLIVER O'DONOVAN, Resurrection and Moral Order

Introduction

In the previous chapter, we began our discussion and development of the normative method for ethics as worship by first demonstrating the link between our underlying beliefs and loves and our actual practices. Our purpose for doing so was not only to highlight the need for clarity regarding one's underlying worldview or metaethical assumptions, but also to demonstrate the importance of developing a normative ethical methodology to guide our moral behavior in a manner consistent with our metaethical commitments. We then identified six domains of ethical assessment that ought to shape and guide how a Christian formulates his or her moral decision-making process. In the remaining bulk of the chapter, we then explored the nature, importance, and biblical rationale for how the first

---

1. Oliver O'Donovan, *Resurrection and Moral Order: An Outline for Evangelical Ethics*, 2nd ed. (Grand Rapids: Eerdmans, 1994), 109.

[handwritten margin notes: telos, act, agent, act]

three of those domains—which we refer to collectively as the *theological/norma-tive domains*—ought to shape our normative methodology for ethics as worship.

In this chapter, we pick up the same thread of conversation, but shift our focus to the remaining three domains of ethical assessment: the *circumstances* in which the moral event takes place, the *consequences* that result from the moral event, and the impact on crucial *relationships* that occurs in relation to the moral event. Collectively, we refer to these as the *pastoral/contextual domains.* Upon comple-tion of this discussion, we then explain how all six of the domains should function together to shape the moral decision-making process in ethics as worship. Finally, before bringing the chapter to a conclusion, we offer a generalized procedure or model for making decisions from the perspective of ethics as worship.

The Pastoral/Contextual Domains of Ethical Assessment

[handwritten margin notes: Circumstances, Consequences, relationships]

While a focus on the theological/normative domains of ethical assessment seeks to ensure the proper vertical ordering of our love and worship to God, a consideration of the remaining domains seeks to ensure the proper horizon-tal application of our ethics by guiding the way in which we love and serve our neighbors. If the normative methodology of an ethical system is built on any of these three domains without first grounding them in the theological/normative domains, then those ethical systems will invariably turn out to be subjective and relativistic in nature. When they are first grounded in the theological/normative domains, however, they help us move Christian moral decision-making out from the so-called world of the "ivory tower" where abstract ideas dwell and into the "real-life" scenarios where circumstances, relationships, and consequences all come to call. This is why we describe them as the *pastoral/contextual domains.* When they are rightly applied and ordered under the authority of the theological/ normative domains, they not only help us to avoid the charge of being "so heav-enly minded that we are no earthly good," but also provide the relevant moral data to enable us to love in a manner most fitting to the situation at hand.

Domain #4: Circumstances—The Situation in Which Moral Events Take Place

The fourth domain of ethical assessment and the first of the pastoral/contex-tual cluster we consider concerns the *circumstances* in which a moral event takes place. By *circumstances* we mean those factors relevant to the moral decision other than a consideration of the *telos*, the character of the agent, or the objective gov-erning rules discovered in God's Word. When the circumstances are brought into the moral decision-making process, consideration is given to the conditions sur-rounding the situation at hand. For example, one might say that killing a human being is wrong in general, but that in specific circumstances (such as war or as a penalty for a capital crime) it may be justified. Domain #4, then, is concerned with giving attention to a consideration of other data, such as economic, age, gender, ethnicity, location, community values, timing, or other mitigating factors, that may be relevant to a given context.

When the circumstances of the moral event are given the place of primacy in moral evaluation, each situation is addressed on its own terms, and only the various particulars of each individual circumstance are taken into consideration for moral evaluation. Moral systems that then emerge will typically appeal to the right values of compassion and mercy, but usually also lack clarity on how to know whether a particular act is actually compassionate or merciful and will therefore usually end up to be systems of moral relativism.

Consider, for example, a famous literary case to help understand this point. In Victor Hugo's famous work *Les Misérables*, the protagonist of the story, Jean Valjean, is arrested and ends up serving a nineteen-year prison sentence after stealing a loaf of bread. The complicating and relevant circumstantial factor in the story is the reason *why* he stole the bread. His sister's child was starving, and he believed that stealing the bread was the only means by which he could save her life.

If one were to approach Jean Valjean's choice to steal bread from a strict perspective of deontology, the moral conclusion would be simple and clear. It was an act of stealing, it was wrong, and he should be judged. And indeed, this is the perspective depicted in the famous novel by the relentlessly pursuing police officer named Javert. From his perspective, Jean Valjean's act was categorically wrong regardless of any mitigating factors.

Now, to be fair to those who hold a purely deontological perspective on morality, holding to moral clarity on the wrongness of Jean Valjean's crime does not require either the harshness or the length of punishment that Victor Hugo depicts of the Napoleonic government era in which the story falls. The antagonist, Javert, represents an extreme version of a rule-keeping moralist that would not normatively characterize a deontological ethic. But for Hugo's famous story, as well as for the purposes of the point we are highlighting here, Javert's extreme legalism is an effective point of contrast to a circumstantially driven ethic.

In contrast to a strictly law- or rule-driven ethic, when Jean Valjean's scenario is evaluated from an ethical perspective that places the circumstances as the main element of the moral decision-making process, the case does not appear so cut-and-dried. While the deontologist would interpret the behavior by running it through the lens of a given rule, someone who gave primacy to context would run the rules through the lens of the situation. The former would determine that because a rule was broken, a wrong was done. The latter would consider the child who is starving, the mother who has no money, the fact that Jean Valjean is the uncle, the economic disparity in the country at the time, and so on, and likely conclude that not only was stealing the bread the "right thing to do," but the enforcing of the law—and perhaps the law itself—was unjust.

Situationalism

This is not to say that the other domains are totally irrelevant in most versions of the ethical theories that arise from placing circumstances first. But the other domains play only a subordinate role and can rightly be applied only when situational factors are given ethical primacy and authority. From this point of view, rules would be given only the moral weight of general guidelines and would never be considered absolutely binding. They function as "rules of thumb" or, as Joseph Fletcher describes them in his *Situation Ethics*, "illuminators" that may have some relevance but that certainly should not function as determiners.[2] Human experience in the midst of the context carries the greatest weight. Indeed, an appeal to human experience is often how such an act is justified. One can imagine a debate over Jean Valjean's situation in an ethics classroom and expect to hear a student say by way of justification, "If you were in the same position, you would likely do the same thing."

How, then, does one arrive at a decision when the circumstantial factors are elevated to the place of primacy in moral evaluation? The emphasis is placed on the autonomous, free moral choice of each moral person who is acting or making the moral judgment in the given situation. While there is a significant resistance to relying on objective rules such as "thou shalt not steal" to reach a conclusion, one should not conclude that moral reasoning is abandoned. Rather, some form of moral reasoning is used in an attempt to determine what course of action is most "appropriate" or "fitting" given the existential and particular circumstances and context.

But it is precisely at this point where the biggest questions arise for those who want to view circumstances as the primary domain of ethics. Ultimately, that manner in which one makes a decision and arrives at a conclusion that a particular course of action is "fitting" or "appropriate" will still reflect some internal grid of valuation. That is, it will reflect one's underlying worldview, one's understanding of right and wrong, and one's internal moral compass (or lack thereof). While internal intuition seems to be relied on, intuition does not function in a void. Something will guide the decision-making process. Ideas and values shape intuitions. Thus, we are still forced to ask questions such as these: What underlying values form the moral grid of the person evaluating the circumstances? If one should not appeal to externally derived moral rules, what should one appeal to? Personal intuition? Unrecognized cultural norms that have shaped the person's

---

2. Joseph Fletcher, *Situation Ethics: The New Morality* (Philadelphia: Westminster Press, 1966), 26.

ideas? Personal selfish motivations to maximize pleasure? Influences of religion that undergird one's moral framework? What makes one frame of reference, or in this case an unspecified frame of reference, better than one that is rationally predetermined or divinely revealed? How one answers these questions will go a long way in shaping the particular flavor of a moral methodology that emphasizes the primacy of circumstances in moral decision-making.

To a large degree, the particular shape of a circumstantially based moral system will depend on what level of moral weightiness is given to circumstances over and above an appeal to externally derived rules and norms.[3] The chart below (see table 7.1) identifies five different types of moral theories and the relationship that exists between how one weighs moral rules versus the circumstances that arise in a given context. The first two represent rule-based systems, while the latter three represent circumstantially based systems. As will become clear as we move on with the chapter, our own system of ethics as worship seeks to incorporate the high view of moral authority presented in Scripture in a manner similar to an absolutist deontology but with an overt attempt to incorporate contextual factors in a subordinate role when making ethical application of moral rules in real-life situations.

Evaluating the Proper Role of the Circumstances Domain

Interestingly enough, in Victor Hugo's *Les Misérables*, neither the strict legalist morality nor a purely circumstantially driven morality is ultimately championed. Rather, *Les Misérables* is a story of redemption that depicts a man who was both guilty of breaking the law and also unjustly treated, who is redeemed by grace, and who is transformed into a man of godly character and action. The ethic that emerges in the story is not one that disregards the law, but rather one in which a man who has tasted mercy and who is transformed by grace then rightly abides by the law and applies it so that he can use his position of authority to bring proper justice to the communities he encounters.

This is instructive for us as we consider how the given circumstances of a particular situation in which moral decision-making takes place ought to influence our ethical process. The simple fact of the matter is that all our moral encounters take place in concrete situations. Ethics is not merely a theoretical endeavor. Real people bump into real situations that require real choices. For this reason, whenever one considers what to do or how to behave, the details related to the situation at hand must be considered as a significant factor in how one makes the final determination of what behavior will most please the Lord.

---

3. For a helpful and concise discussion of this point, see P. Helm, "Situational Ethics," in *Encyclopedia of Biblical and Christian Ethics*, ed. R. K. Harrison, rev. ed. (Nashville: Thomas Nelson, 1992), 384.

Table 7.1. Relationship between Moral Theories and Rules

System of Ethics	Weightiness of Rules	Weightiness of Circumstances	
Absolutist Deontology	Absolute: Rules are unaffected by circumstances.	Lowest (none): Circumstances are nonfactors in obeying rules.	Absolutism Objective
Prima Facie Principlism	High: Rules have heavy, but not absolute, moral weight.	Low: Circumstances are determinate considerations only in tragic moral choices.	
Communitarian Ethics Narrative Ethics Liberation Theology (Critical Race Theory)	Low: Rules may have power within a tradition or narrative, but they stand as artifacts of past ethical systems that carry little weight outside a particular narrative.	High: The experience and "situatedness" of particular persons and peoples carry greater weight than past rules or interpretations of morality given by other narratives.	
Situation Ethics (Fletcher)	Low: Rules have little moral weight, serving as advice, suggestions, or "illuminators," but not "determiners."	High: Circumstances are the determining factor, with some influence of external guidelines and social mores.	
Antinomianism (Nietzsche, Foucault)	Lowest (none): Rules have no weight.	Highest (absolute): Circumstances are the only morally relevant factor.	Relativism Subjective

For example, even as I (Mark) sit here and write this morning, I have received a series of emails from a young man who is asking me for a recommendation about where to send a female friend for counsel regarding an unplanned pregnancy. The email indicates that the pregnant woman is uncertain whether she wants to keep the baby, put the baby up for adoption, or seek an abortion. On one level, I have clarity on how to respond because I know that Scripture tells me that intentionally and directly taking the life of an innocent person is wrong ("You shall not murder," Ex. 20:13). Because of the truth of Scripture, I know right off the bat that it cannot be a loving thing to give a recommendation toward taking the life of an innocent unborn child. It could never actually be compassionate or merciful to do so. The compulsion to embody the virtues of love and mercy are not enough in themselves. The proper expression of love and mercy must be guided by the moral principles that God gives in Scripture to illuminate for us what types of actions and behaviors are actually loving and merciful. Because God tells us that the purposeful and intentional taking of innocent human life is evil, I therefore know that abortion is not a loving or merciful option. But I still do not have a lot of information that might shape the kind of advice I ultimately give as I seek to also keep Jesus' commandment to love my neighbor. What I don't know about the situation is whether the woman in question is married or single. I don't know whether she is in good health or has ovarian cancer. I don't know whether she is forty years old or fifteen years old. I don't know whether she has a good support system in a home or through a church, or whether she is all on her own. I don't know whether a husband or a boyfriend is pressing her to have an abortion or keep the child. Nor do I know whether she is pregnant because she was raped. Without knowing more specifics of the woman's real-life situation, giving more specified advice on how to care for the woman in question becomes much more difficult.

The reason why specific data from the particular circumstance play such a big role in moral decision-making is not that the commands of Scripture are not sufficient for every moral event. Rather, in order to be sufficient for every moral event, many of them have been given by God to us in the form of more generally formulated principles that can apply universally, instead of in specified rules that govern all the details of all situations.

In his classic *Worldviews in Conflict*, Ronald Nash helpfully explains the difference between commandments in the form of principles versus commandments in the form of rules:

> Much confusion surrounding ethics results from a failure to observe the important distinction between principles and rules. Let us define moral principles as more general moral prescriptions, general in the sense that they cover a large number of instances. Moral rules, on the other hand, will be regarded as more specific moral prescriptions that are, in fact, applications of principles to more concrete situations.[4]

In Scripture, we find that God gives us moral commands both in the form of general principles and in the form of specific rules. For example, the Ten Commandments function at the more general level of principles. They are grounded in the nature and character of God; therefore, without question they are absolute, universally binding, and timeless. Yet they do not give specifics on how they are to be applied in every scenario.

---

4. Ronald H. Nash, *Worldviews in Conflict: Choosing Christianity in a World of Ideas* (Grand Rapids: Zondervan, 1992), 42–43.

Consider, for example, the sixth commandment ("You shall not murder," Ex. 20:13). The more generally formulated principle tells us that murder is wrong, but we know that in places in the Bible, God clearly commands his people to kill other human beings (Deut. 20:16–18). Is God not beholden to his own rules? Or does the context help us understand how the command is appropriately applied? Here we see again the importance of the particular circumstances. The command against murder relates to the unjustified and direct taking of innocent life as opposed to killing in general. Depending on the situation (e.g., killing a child through abortion versus killing an enemy soldier in a just-war scenario), the application of the command allows for very different conclusions. We discuss these ideas in much more depth in several of our applied chapters in part 4 of this book.

Or consider God's command against adultery in Exodus 20:14 as a universally binding principle. A more specific formulation of that command is given to us in Matthew 5:27–28:

> You have heard that it was said, "You shall not commit adultery"; but I say to you that everyone who looks at a woman with lust for her has already committed adultery with her in his heart.

In this passage, Jesus puts the command into a specific situation or set of circumstances and turns it into a more detailed rule for governing particular behaviors: "If you don't want to break the seventh commandment, do not look lustfully at women."

We will return to a more detailed discussion of both war and abortion in chapters 14 and 15. For now, we are simply attempting to show the important role that knowing the details of a specific context plays in determining which action most glorifies the Lord.

Domain #5: Consequences—The Results of the Conduct Chosen

The fifth domain of ethical assessment involves a consideration of the outcomes, or *consequences*, that result from the behavior chosen in a moral event. As we pointed out in our discussion above about the importance of considering the circumstance in ethical evaluation, morality happens in concrete situations in which real people bump into real situations that require real choices. Now we consider the related fact that in these real concrete situations and circumstances, the choices that are made also result in real consequences. This is why paying attention to the anticipated, projected, likely, or even merely possible consequences that may result from a moral decision is also an important factor to consider in building a normative ethic. As is the case with all three of the pastoral/contextual domains, recognizing the importance of potential consequences helps keep ethics as worship out of the merely abstract realm of ideas and concepts by embedding it in real-life consideration of the impact of our moral decisions. Indeed, Jesus tells us that it is wise for a disciple seeking to live worshipfully to "count the cost" of his or her choices and actions as a part of his or her moral methodology.

Consequentialist theories of ethics are those theories suggesting that actions are right or wrong based on their good or bad *outcomes*. The right behavior in a given context is the one that produces the best overall result *after the moral behavior takes place* in relation to whatever one is seeking to maximize. Thus, when determining what one ought to do, a system of ethics that makes a consideration of consequences the primary point of moral evaluation requires that one make a *prediction* of future outcomes that are most likely, and then weigh them against a similar prediction of the outcomes from other alternative possible actions. In such systems, determining the morally right thing to do is a function of how well one can accurately predict what will happen as a result of one's choices as well as how one assigns value (or disvalue) to those future outcomes.[5] Likewise, if an action has already taken place, the sole basis for judging its moral value is by considering how the positive results compare to the negative results.[6]

Utilitarianism

Utilitarianism is the modern name given to the most common form of an ethical theory that places a consideration of consequences as the primary domain of ethical assessment. Historically, it was developed in ancient Greece by Epicurus (341–270 B.C.), and later in the Enlightenment it was revived and reformulated by Jeremy Bentham (1748–1832) and, most famously, by John Stuart Mill (1806–73).

---

5. James Rachels and Stuart Rachels, *The Elements of Moral Philosophy*, 9th ed. (New York: McGraw-Hill Education, 2019), 120–24.

6. Given this definition, two points of clarification are helpful to make at this point. First, technically speaking, one could look at virtue theories as a form of consequentialism because virtue theories seek to maximize good character as a result of choices and habituated practices. Second, because an evaluation of the consequences relates to a consideration of "*end* results," some moral philosophers and ethicists tend to attach the language of *teleology* to consequentialist theories. While it is not logically contradictory or linguistically wrong to consider virtue theories as consequentialist or to think of consequentialist theories in light of an evaluation of a *telos* or end result, we do believe that using the language of consequentialism in either manner is ultimately unhelpful for the discipline of ethics. We believe this because using the language in such ways unnecessarily confuses the primary area of focus for each of the domains we are discussing. Normatively speaking, when the language of *consequentialism* is employed to discuss ethical theories, it is primarily concerned with the results that come from actions and the amount of happiness or pleasure they result in while simultaneously limiting suffering, pain, or harm. Teleology, on the other hand, not only considers what happens, but does so after both focusing attention on the design or inherent purpose of the moral agent and evaluating the appropriateness of the behavior in light of both the created nature and the final goal that ought to be sought after. This is why we believe that it is better to speak of consequentialist theories not in terms of teleology, but rather either simply as consequentialist theories or perhaps with reference to the most prominent version of consequentialism: *utilitarianism*.

Similar to the previous domain we discussed in which the *circumstances* played the major role in moral evaluation, utilitarianism also seeks to take into consideration the importance of the context and the particular concrete circumstances that are in play. It differs from a purely circumstantial-based approach to ethics, however, in that it holds that one normative moral principle should always be in place in order to evaluate the circumstances: *the principle of utility*. This principle, in the words of Mill, is described as follows:

> The creed which accepts as the foundation of morals, Utility, or the Greatest Happiness Principle, holds that actions are right in proportion as they tend to promote happiness, and wrong as they tend to produce the reverse of happiness.[7]

In simpler terms, utilitarianism can be—and often is—best summarized with slogan phrases such as "the greatest good for the greatest number of people," or "the good of the many outweighs the good of the few," or "the ends justify the means." Ultimately, it is a moral form of a cost-benefit analysis in which the good outcomes of a moral decision are placed in a balance and weighed against the bad outcomes. The moral action that is said to be the "right" one causes the highest or greatest benefits while simultaneously producing the fewest negatives.

One could look at virtually any morally controversial topic today and see that the controversy often stems from a conflict between those who hold to some form of ethic that values the place of transcendent moral laws (such as deontology) and those who hold to a consequence-based ethics (such as utilitarianism). We have already seen examples in some of our previous case studies relating to cheating in class and giving money to charity. We saw how each of these cases can be evaluated differently depending on which approach to ethics one takes. But to highlight the distinction more clearly here, consider the following scenario. Suppose that you are the mayor of a city. You are contacted by a terrorist organization that tells you that it has planted bombs in several highly populated areas, one of which includes the daycare center where your children are cared for. The terrorists plan to detonate the bombs and kill thousands of people in the next five minutes unless you meet their demands to kill the chief of police, who is standing with you in the office. Assume for the sake of clarity that the bombs are real and will kill your children. Also assume for the sake of clarity that if you do kill the chief of police, the terrorists will not detonate the bombs and will never again threaten your city. What would you do? What do you believe to be the "right" course of action?

If at this point you are thinking that it would be wrong to kill the chief of police because it would be a form of murder to do so, then you are thinking much

---

7. John Stuart Mill, *Utilitarianism* (London: Longmans, Green, 1897), 8.

like a deontologist. Remember that deontology is the moral system that evaluates the nature of the act itself and claims that certain acts (such as intentionally killing an innocent chief of police) are inherently right or wrong without consideration of the consequences. If, on the other hand, you are doing mathematical equations in your head and comparing the cost of one life to the cost of many lives lost in the city, or even just comparing the cost of one chief of police to the cost of the life of your own children, then you are thinking along the lines of a utilitarian. Utilitarians contend that the action (in this case, the killing of the chief of police) should not be evaluated by some notion that the act is inherently right or wrong. Rather, they would argue that primary consideration should be given to the consequence or results that killing the chief of police would produce.

Or consider another case that relates to healthcare. Suppose that a person named Scott has an otherwise very healthy twenty-seven-year-old brother named Ryan who is involved in a terrible car accident. Upon arrival at the hospital, Scott learns that Ryan has experienced severe trauma to the brain and that though it is possible that he will survive, Ryan will be in a permanently vegetative state for the rest of his life. He will be able to breathe on his own and all his body functions will work without medical intervention, but he will never regain consciousness. Yet there is a complicating factor. In the same accident, two other family members were also injured, and their lives hang in the balance. One needs an immediate heart transplant; the other needs an immediate liver transplant. The doctors tell Scott that his brother's organs are compatible with each of the other family members, but that if they harvest Ryan's organs to save the other family members, Ryan will die. On the other hand, if they don't harvest the organs and attempt the transplants, the other two will die. Because Scott is the next of kin and the decision needs to be made immediately, he must decide now. What should he do?

Again, note the moral implications and the way that the evaluation may take place. On the one hand, there is a question regarding Ryan's life. Is it sacred? Would it be inherently wrong to sacrifice his life for his family members without Ryan's consent? Or does the possibility of saving two lives at the cost of one life tip the scales in favor of harvesting the organs? What if only one family member could be saved but could expect a full recovery? Should the fact that Ryan will live in a long-term permanently vegetative state affect how his life should be valued? How should his life be compared in value to the other family member who might make a full recovery? Both the cases above serve to highlight the issues raised when a consideration of the consequences rises to the place of primacy in moral evaluation.

In comparison to deontological ethics, which emphasizes having the right means, without consideration of the results, utilitarianism reverses the equation.

What matters is only the end result, not the means. Let's revisit a previous case in which our friends Stuart and Sam each make charitable donations of $10,000 to help the needy in their community, but now let's change the elements of the case a bit. Let's say that this time, Sam donates money he has earned through hard work with a motive to care for the poor. Stuart, on the other hand, donates stolen money, and his motive is to earn votes for an upcoming election. From a strictly utilitarian evaluation, even though the manner in which the money was obtained and the motivations for donating were vastly different, the moral evaluation of the actions of both men to give to charity would be considered equally positive because the outcome of the acts is equal. The ends justify the means.

As each of these cases illustrates, several significant problems ultimately prohibit the Christian from placing the domain of consequence in the place of moral primacy. First, despite the efforts to make the principle of utility applicable, there is a significant problem related to who gets to determine what is ultimately considered a positive outcome and what is a negative outcome. If it is left up to the practical wisdom of a particular person or even the majority sentiment of a culture, then the moral results will ultimately be relative to that person's or that community's sense of value.

From a particularly Christian point of view, who gets to define what constitutes the "greater good" or the potential "harm" is vitally important to the way that one approaches the world. The values assigned will ultimately reflect the deeper worldview assumptions about right and wrong, good and evil that occupied our discussions in the early chapters of this book. For example, if the person or persons in charge of determining the greater good do not believe that God exists and that there is no ultimate moral design to the world or divinely revealed moral rules, then the "greater good" would be fully subject to personal opinion, cultural sentiment, or perhaps the whims of those in positions of power. For example, what if a society believes that homosexuality is an acceptable alternative lifestyle based on the general sense of happiness in a culture but at the same time that moral evaluation is directly opposed to the revelation of Scripture? With such a moral calculus, the likely outcome is that utilitarianism will result in a public law that is directly at odds with the Christian faith.

A second significant problem with utilitarianism is that it requires virtual omniscience to properly employ. This is the case because of the vast complexity of any moral event. Consider, for example, what it takes to evaluate all the consequences of Jean Valjean's stealing a loaf of bread to feed someone's family. At one level, the consequences seem to relate to the man stealing the bread and the starving child. But what about the breadmaker's family? What if they are also starving? Then consider what happens if the father is put in jail. The kids grow up without a father, and perhaps they live in poverty all their lives even though the famine ended a year later. Then consider whether one of those kids growing up in poverty ends up getting hooked on drugs and murdering someone for drug money. You see the point. How do we know where the limit to all the relevant consequential factors lies? How many circles of influence count? How many generations?

The dropping of atomic bombs on Hiroshima and Nagasaki in World War II, for a real-life example, is normatively evaluated in the number of lives saved from avoiding an invasion versus the lives lost in the bombing. What about all the emotional, social, and political costs to the Japanese families? What about all the noncombatants living in these areas who were not a part of the war effort? What about the future generations of people who will experience the long-term impact of the bombs for generations to come? What about the billions of dollars that would ultimately be spent on nuclear détente? On what basis are they not considered?

In order to calculate the greatest good for the greatest number, one must be able to accurately predict the level to which all people might be affected by a particular action or set of actions. As J. Budziszewski describes the problem, utilitarianism is practically impossible because the utilitarian must do seven things:

1. Identify all the possible courses of action.
2. For each course of action, identify all the persons affected, however remote the effects on them may be.
3. For each person, identify every pain or pleasure likely to result from the course of action under consideration.
4. Assign each of these pains and pleasures a numerical value.
5. Calculate the net gain or loss for each person.
6. Sum up these gains and losses to arrive at a grand total for each course of action or each governing rule—its utility.
7. Carry out the course of action with the highest utility.[8]

As one can see, accomplishing all seven steps requires virtual omniscience and the capability to carry out each step perfectly. It seems that only God could actually be a utilitarian and make it work. For the rest of us, utilitarianism is in actuality impossible to implement with any certainty. Ultimately, it is based on a rather arrogant perspective about our ability to predict the future with enough breadth and accuracy. It presupposes that we—in our finite minds—are somehow able to measure all the relevant consequences and secondary effects that result from our choices.

---

8. J. Budziszewski, *Written on the Heart: The Case for Natural Law* (Downers Grove, IL: InterVarsity Press, 1997), 145–46.

Another significant problem is that utilitarianism can ultimately lead to what most of us would believe to be massive forms of injustice toward those who are in the minority positions in society. For example, consider the historical case of slavery in the United States. From a strictly utilitarian principle, one could make the claim that enslaving people of African descent attained the greatest good for the greatest number of people. What deontology would prohibit, consequentialism could justify. The rights of freedom for individuals in this case would disappear because there is no basis for them outside the utility principle. Thus, individuals and minority perspectives could be trampled for the gain of the majority because the good of the many was determined to be worthy of the sacrifices of the fewer. Without other guiding principles, those who are adversely affected have no recourse for correcting the pain. Raw consequentialism can create what ethicists sometimes refer to as a *tyranny of the majority*.

In conclusion, these problems that are inherent to utilitarianism and reflective of consequential-based systems of ethics demonstrate that the domain of consequences cannot be elevated to the primary place of moral consideration. From a theological perspective, they do not adequately consider either the finite abilities of humans to predict the future accurately or all the necessary contingencies. They also do not account for the realities of the fall and human sinful frailty. But perhaps most importantly, they relegate God's moral instruction and commands that comport with the nature of reality and that are given to instruct us about the nature of morality to subordinate roles. Scripture and God's moral commands are placed behind experience and reason as sources of moral authority.

Evaluating the Proper Role of the Consequence Domain

Having pointed out that a consideration of consequences should not be put in the place of primacy in moral evaluation does not mean that there is not an important role for this domain to play in the development of a robust Christian ethic. Indeed, Scripture indicates that when properly understood and ordered, a consideration of consequence (both temporal and eternal) should play an important role in Christian moral reasoning.

First, weighing the cost against the benefits on the front side of a decision helps the person making the decision be clear about what is at stake in any given situation and can thereby aid a believer in enduring in faith when hardship comes. Consider Jesus' teaching about the importance of counting the costs of being his disciple in Luke 14:27–33:

> Whoever does not carry his own cross and come after Me cannot be My disciple. For which one of you, when he wants to build a tower, does not first sit down and calculate the cost to see if he has enough to complete it? Otherwise, when he has

laid a foundation and is not able to finish, all who observe it begin to ridicule him, saying, "This man began to build and was not able to finish." Or what king, when he sets out to meet another king in battle, will not first sit down and consider whether he is strong enough with ten thousand men to encounter the one coming against him with twenty thousand? Or else, while the other is still far away, he sends a delegation and asks for terms of peace. So then, none of you can be My disciple who does not give up all his own possessions.

The context of this passage is Jesus' helping his potential followers recognize the cost of being one of his disciples. He uses two illustrations to make his point: one about a builder and one about a king heading to battle. In both illustrations, Jesus points out that if the agent making the choice is wise, he will evaluate his resources and consider the likely outcome before he begins to either build or fight. Otherwise, he is likely to be found foolish in the endeavor.

Now, in both scenarios, while a consideration of the possible outcomes plays an important role, notice that Jesus is evaluating not whether following him is the right thing to do, but whether the potential disciples have the wherewithal to endure. Thus, while a consideration of the possible end results plays an important role in determining whether one can follow, in neither case was the end result meant to be the primary factor in determining the right thing to do: follow Jesus.

Therefore, in ethics as worship, consideration of consequences plays a subordinate role in the final determination of moral conduct, but *subordinate* does not mean "unimportant." A properly oriented action that moves from a right motive and that comports with God's commandment can still be deficient if it lacks wisdom in the application. As J. Douma correctly points out, "counting the cost is part of wisdom."[9]

A second reason to acknowledge the importance of evaluating possible consequences is that not only does it help a disciple *endure* hardship, but a consideration of results can also *spur on greater fervency* in the development of moral virtues as one anticipates the future rewards to be received in heaven. Consider, for example, the powerful teaching of Paul in 2 Corinthians 4:

Therefore we do not lose heart, but though our outer man is decaying, yet our inner man is being renewed day by day. *For momentary, light affliction is producing for us an eternal weight of glory far beyond all comparison.* (2 Cor. 4:16–17)

Similarly, in Philippians 3:12–14, he writes:

9. J. Douma, *Responsible Conduct: Principles of Christian Ethics* (Phillipsburg, NJ: P&R Publishing, 2003), 25.

> Not that I have already obtained it or have already become perfect, but I press on so that I may lay hold of that for which also I was laid hold of by Christ Jesus. Brethren, I do not regard myself as having laid hold of it yet; but one thing I do: forgetting what lies behind and reaching forward to what lies ahead, *I press on toward the goal for the prize of the upward call of God in Christ Jesus.*

In both these cases, Paul finds tremendous motivation to pursue Christ more fervently *precisely because of the results.* Not the least of these is hearing the words "well done, good and faithful slave" when he finally sees Christ face to face (Matt. 25:23).

Indeed, some of the last recorded words we have from Paul in the New Testament drip with anticipation of positive eternal consequences:

> I have fought the good fight, I have finished the course, I have kept the faith; in the future there is laid up for me the crown of righteousness, which the Lord, the righteous Judge, will award to me on that day; and not only to me, but also to all who have loved His appearing. (2 Tim. 4:7–8)

In this passage, we see that while the first two phrases are largely related to the development of virtues such as endurance and hope, the third phrase demonstrates that a consideration of consequences is important for ethics related to the putting off of vices. Scripture is filled with passages that use a consideration of future judgment as a means to dissuade immorality and sinful actions (e.g., Gen. 2:17; Matt. 10:28; Rom. 2:6–10; 2 Cor. 5:10; Gal. 6:7; 2 Thess. 1:9). Therefore, while we affirm that loving and obeying God in order to maximally worship him is the best means for determining moral behavior in a properly formed Christian ethics, Scripture clearly shows us that a negative threat of punishment can also serve as a key motivating element for shunning sinful behaviors and the subsequent development of sinful vices.

In sum, consequentialist systems of ethics sound appealing because we want to ensure positive results. The fact that Jesus himself utilized a version of consequentialist reasoning as he taught his disciples to "count the cost" is important to consider. Yet while there is a place for consequentialist consideration within a Christian ethic, given its deficiencies as a moral system, it would be a mistake to put it in the place of primacy for moral evaluation. Given humans' limited ability to assess all the elements and outcomes of any given moral context, its reliability for ethical evaluation is limited.

Having acknowledged these reasons why a consideration of possible future consequences is important for ethics, as it relates to actually playing a determinative role in what is the right thing to do, this domain has real but subordinate

✓ amen

value. One needs to trust in the wise counsel of Scripture over and above predictions about future possible outcomes.

Domain #6: Relational Response—The Reactions of Those We Impact by the Conduct Chosen

The final domain of ethical assessment involves a consideration of what ethical behavior would be the most fitting or appropriate *relational response* in light of any particular moral context in which one finds oneself. It begins with the understanding that human beings are not primarily autonomous individuals who stand alone and apart from other persons. Rather, it recognizes that when God created human beings in his image to steward the creation in his name, he created them as social creatures. As such, he embedded and enmeshed his image-bearers in a network of harmonious and mutually beneficial relationships:

- Humans with God;
- Humans with others;
- Humans with themselves; and
- Humans with the world that God created.

It presses us to consider the fact that morality not only happens in the context of concrete circumstances that result in real consequences, but also takes place in the midst of real relationships. Like the two preceding pastoral domains, it provides an important humanizing element to the ethical task by recognizing the fact that all our decisions affect and are influenced by the relationships that we are situated in. This domain of ethical assessment, therefore, is concerned with understanding *how caring for these relationships ought to shape our moral choices, acts, and behaviors.*

Consideration of this domain presses us to consider how relationships function as part of the metaethical grid through which morality must be understood. That is, it forces us to remember that moral concern for others is not merely a rational function of the fact that others are "ends in themselves" (i.e., Kant) or rights-bearers (i.e., Locke), or utility maximizers (i.e., Mill). Rather, this domain helps us remember that those we encounter in moral situations and whom our ethical choices involve and concern are real people. They are "Beth" or "Mary" or "Fred" or "John." They are real people, who are in real contexts, whom we are called to love, and for whom Christ died. As Jewish philosopher/theologian Martin Buber might describe it, because life finds meaning in the context of relationships, we are to encounter others not as though we were entering an "I-It" relationship, but rather with the type of genuine dialogue that can happen only in an "I-Thou" relationship.[10]

---

10. Martin Buber, *I and Thou*, trans. Ronald Gregor Smith (New York: Scribner Classics, 2000).

The concern of this domain has particular relevance to how we think of ethics in any and all helping professions—such as medical ethics and ministerial ethics—for it speaks not merely to what healthcare professions and ministers *do* (care for persons, care for souls), but also to *how* they are supposed to do it. The patient or the parishioner is a *person* who ought to be given personal attention and care. In the language of medicine, this domain speaks to the "bedside manner" of the caregiver. In the language of ministry, this domain speaks to wisely administering "pastoral care" to the hurting.

Clearly, care and concern for others is an important aspect that should impact ethical evaluation and determination. Jesus, for example, demonstrated such care when he entered into the pain and anguish of his friends Mary and Martha and wept with them over the death of their brother Lazarus (John 11:35). But while we recognize that consideration of this domain plays a vital role in applying ethics, as we saw with the previous two domains, when this domain is elevated to the *primary* point of concern in ethical evaluation, an important and dangerous shift takes place. The locus of moral decision-making moves into a subjective realm in which an otherwise proper drive to be concerned with and care for the well-being of the "other" becomes the only or primary factor in ethical evaluation. When this takes place, care and concern for others and the relationships we are embedded in do not merely influence our *application* of ethical principles, but become the *determining* element of morality while ethical commands and principles are reduced to the level of guiding rules of thumb.

This is not to suggest that there is a general abandonment of principles, but they are considered helpful only if they "allow room for discretionary and contextual judgment. At the same time, . . . defenders of [this type of ethic] do find principles often irrelevant, unproductive, ineffectual, or unduly constrictive in the moral life."[11] Care for persons and relationships takes precedence over care for principles and rules. Likewise, while there is great concern with this domain for the virtues that help one care for the persons involved, the primary focus of the domain is the relationships and not the character of the agents.[12] Thus, when the domain of *relational response* is raised to the level of primacy in moral evaluation, an entirely distinct ethical methodology emerges. This ethical methodology has come to be known as the *ethics of care*.

11. Tom L. Beauchamp and James F. Childress, *Principles of Biomedical Ethics*, 6th ed. (New York: Oxford University Press, 2009), 37.

12. Here we are inclined to agree with Virginia Held's argument for a distinction between ethics of care and virtue ethics. See Virginia Held, *The Ethics of Care: Personal, Political, and Global* (New York: Oxford University Press, 2006). Yet we agree with Beauchamp and Childress that one should not make too sharp a distinction, since there is important overlap between the two domains. See Beauchamp and Childress, *Principles of Biomedical Ethics*, 59n19.

The Ethics of Care

The language of *ethics of care* was born out of a study done by a psychologist named Carol Gilligan. In her landmark book *In a Different Voice*, Gilligan demonstrated that when various people attempt to evaluate morally complex situations, they do not always perceive and evaluate the situations in the same manner.[13] In fact, she argued, there are two primarily distinct ways in which people tend to make moral evaluations: one from the perspective of *justice* and one from the perspective of *care*.[14]

Consider the following case study that Gilligan used to demonstrate her findings.

> A man named Heinz has a wife who is dying from cancer. Doctors tell him there is a new drug that can save his wife but it costs much more than Heinz can afford. After trying to raise the money by working hard and appealing to friends and family to help, he still cannot afford it. Heinz, then, has to decide whether or not to steal the drug in order to give his wife the cure she needs and save her life. What should Heinz do?[15]

Through her research, Gilligan noticed that the way in which certain groups of people answered this question tended to fall into two distinct categories, typified by two children named Jake and Amy.

When asked whether the man should steal the medication, Jake, on the one hand, concluded that Heinz should steal the medicine because the wife's life was more important than keeping the rule against stealing. Further, he concluded that a judge would likely agree with his position because laws can have mistakes and cannot cover every contingency. In this sense, Jake approached the moral situation as if it were a math problem that needed a solution.

Amy, on the other hand, concluded that Heinz should not steal the medicine.

---

13. Carol Gilligan, *In a Different Voice* (Cambridge, MA: Harvard University Press, 1982).

14. According to Gilligan, it is normative that the "justice" approach is typically also the male approach, while the "care" approach is typically the approach of women. Crucially, however, she does not suggest that this is an absolute category distinction. Many men will engage from a care perspective and many women will engage from a justice perspective. Gilligan's study was also instrumental in demonstrating that the highly influential work on moral formation done by Lawrence Kohlberg was inherently biased toward the justice perspective and should not be considered as the normative manner for evaluating moral development between boys and girls. For the full discussion, see Carol Gilligan, "Moral Orientation and Moral Development," in *Justice and Care: Essential Readings in Feminist Ethics*, ed. Virginia Held (Boulder, CO: Westview, 1995), 31–46.

15. Gilligan, *In a Different Voice*, 25. This was the case that Lawrence Kohlberg used before Gilligan to identify and evaluate the difference in moral development between boys and girls. It was his conclusion that because girls reasoned this out differently, their moral development was weaker than and inferior to that of the boys at the same age. Gilligan, who was Kohlberg's student, reasoned to a different conclusion.

While she was also concerned to solve the problem, her method of moral evaluation took a different route. She believed that Heinz should not steal the medicine because if he got caught and went to jail, there would be no one to look after his wife. Amy's approach to solving the dilemma was for Heinz to go back to the pharmacist and try to work out a bargain whereby he could attain the medicine and pay for it later. She figured that if the pharmacist understood the situation better, he would work with Heinz to find a solution.

Therefore, Amy's approach did not address the question of the law or its fairness, but rather addressed the case based on the impact that the husband's actions might have on the wife. As Gilligan puts it:

> Seeing in the dilemma not a math problem with humans but a narrative of relationships that extends over time, Amy envisions the wife's continuing need for her husband and the husband's continuing concern for his wife and seeks to respond to the druggist's need in a way that would sustain rather than sever the connection. Just as she ties the wife's survival to the preservation of relationships, so she considers the value of the wife's life in a context of relationships.[16]

Amy's approach to the problem is concerned not with the rights of those involved but rather with helping those involved each figure out how to provide the proper care for the wife.

Gilligan notes that the two children are really answering two different questions. Whereas Jake answered the question "should Heinz steal the medicine *or not*?," Amy answered the question "should Heinz steal the medicine *or something else*?" Gilligan explains:

> Thus in Heinz's dilemma these two children see two very different moral problems—Jake a conflict between life and property that can be resolved by logical deduction, Amy a fracture of human relationship that must be mended with its own thread. Asking different questions that arise from different conceptions of the moral domain the children arrive at answers that fundamentally diverge.[17]

Gilligan concluded from this that Jake's judgments reveal a sophisticated understanding of logic and justification that depict a "justice approach" to ethics. "He abstracts the moral problem from the interpersonal situation, finding in the logic of fairness an objective way to decide who will win the dispute."[18] Amy, on the

---

16. Gilligan, *In a Different Voice*, 28.
17. Gilligan, *In a Different Voice*, 31.
18. Gilligan, *In a Different Voice*, 32.

other hand, had an equally sophisticated—but different—approach that "led her to see those involved in the situation not as opponents in a contest of rights but as members of a network of relationships. . . . With this shift, the moral problem changes from one of unfair domination, the imposition of property over life, to one of unnecessary exclusion, the failure of the druggist to respond to the wife." In sum, Amy's moral judgments—in contrast to Jake's justice approach—illustrate the elements of what Gilligan describes as an "ethic of care."[19]

From this study, Gilligan goes on to suggest that while in the past the discipline of ethics has largely been approached singularly from the perspective of justice, she believes not only that both approaches are equally valid, but that both are necessary. This is so because humans are relational beings who are connected to those around them in a morally real and important way. Individual autonomy is an illusion and thus problematic, for it can breed both an inability to see the totality of the moral event and indifference to the needs or concerns of others. This, in turn, can hinder the moral agent's ability to properly discern the key interpersonal elements of a moral event and miss the clues necessary to act, behave, or respond appropriately in context.[20]

It is important to note here that Gilligan's study not only identified two distinct tendencies in how people approach ethical situations (justice and care), but also noted that these distinct perspectives tended to fall along the lines of gender—with men being more justice-oriented and women more care-oriented. Up to this point we have not mentioned this because if these perspectives are indeed various ways in which humans approach moral questions, then in one sense the gender association is irrelevant. The various perspectives would need to be considered on their own merits apart from the question whether either was associated with a particular gender. And indeed, Gilligan herself points out that the association of one perspective to a male point of view and the other to a female point of view is not categorical or absolute. They are tendencies.

At this point in the discussion, however, we bring attention to this gender distinction because following Gilligan's work, an entire field of feminist ethics emerged in part as a reaction to her conclusions.[21] As Nel Noddings, an influential

---

19. Gilligan, *In a Different Voice*, 30–32.

20. Gilligan, "Moral Orientation and Moral Development," 36.

21. By using the word *feminist*, we are making a distinction between *feminine* and *feminist* in that the former term typically denotes the dispositions and characteristics that are associated with females. The latter term, however, moves beyond this and focuses on the rights, duties, validations, and so on that should be afforded to women as women. While a full investigation of this discussion is beyond the scope of our purposes here, for those interested in pursuing the conversation further, we recommend Virginia Held's edited work entitled *Justice and Care: Essential Readings in Feminist Ethics* (Boulder, CO: Westview, 1995) for a breadth of primary-source articles that shaped the field. We also recommend chapters 5 and 6 from Rebecca Merrill Groothuis's book *Women Caught in the Conflict* (Grand Rapids: Baker, 1994). While we do not agree with all

author and advocate of relationally based ethics of care, has correctly stated, "if a substantial segment of humankind approaches moral problems through a consideration of the concrete elements of situations and a regard for themselves as caring, then perhaps an attempt should be made to enlighten the study of morality in this alternative mode."[22] One could certainly argue that if the perspective of half the population has been neglected (a point that not all agree on), then certainly we are late in giving heed to this aspect of moral evaluation.

Feminist approaches to ethics certainly did blossom following (and in part as a response to) Gilligan's efforts. While a full investigation of feminist ethics is beyond the scope of our study, here we simply note that not only did part of the feminist movement begin to assert that the care perspective was a distinct and helpful way to evaluate a moral event, but some have also asserted that it is a superior perspective and should become normative or replace justice-oriented approaches. Nel Noddings, for example, argues that this compunction to care should become the fundamental point of view from which any and all moral choices should be determined. As such, it should also occupy the most important role in determining how one should behave in any given context and thereby replace a reliance on externally discovered or derived principles with a "disposition to care" at the heart of ethics.[23] All moral decisions then become a question of how relationships and caring for persons in the network of relationships in which we live should define and delimit our moral conclusions.

As a result, according to those who hold this perspective, a question about a moral issue—such as abortion—is not to be determined by asking whether the action is right or wrong in some objective sense; it is not about the value of human life or the concept of the sanctity of life. Rather, according to Noddings and other feminists, the moral question primarily concerns the state of the relative relationships and what would constitute the most caring thing to do for those involved in a moral context. According to this point of view, the moral question for something such as abortion revolves around whether having an abortion in a particular situation is the most caring option for those involved in the context.

Evaluating the Proper Role of the Relational-Response Domain

While we will identify many positive and important elements about this domain below, because the relational-response domain casts us back on a similar problem we discussed when we considered the previous domain (consequences), we begin with critique. As was the case when we considered consequentialism,

---

her conclusions, we found Groothuis's analysis of the feminism movement in these chapters to be outstanding.

22. Nel Noddings, "Caring," in *Justice and Care: Essential Readings in Feminist Ethics*, ed. Virginia Held (Boulder, CO: Westview, 1995), 8.

23. Noddings, "Caring," 9.

perhaps the single biggest problem with focusing on relational care as the most important domain of ethical evaluation is the question of who gets to decide what is actually "caring" in a given context. If it is left up to the practical wisdom of a particular person or even the majority sentiment of a culture, then the moral results will ultimately be relative to that person's or that community's sense of value. The basis for ethical decision-making will shift from ultimate reliance on objectively determined and revealed moral norms given by God and instead rely on subjective human sentiment and intuition. The ethical methodology will shift from an "ethics from above" perspective to an "ethics from below" point of view. The primary source of moral authority will be experience, not revelation.

While some might laud the "freedom" to act situationally with a motive of care, without some guiding principles to help us know what care actually is beyond a sentiment or feeling, we are left in a place with virtually no basis for moral accountability that is not arbitrarily imposed. We face the same problem we discerned in relation to other domains when they are not guided by the theological/normative domains. In the name of relational care, person A could look at a particular situation and decide to euthanize a patient, and person B could fight to keep the person alive. There would be no clear guiding principle to know whether either did something wrong.

Likewise, one could affirm transgenderism in a six-year-old child, while someone else could resist that affirmation in the same child—both based on a motive of care. Underneath each claim lies a series of metaethical precommitments that drive the understanding of what is most caring. Without any externally normative principles to shape morality, the system devolves into a battle of dueling consciences, competing preferences, or even moral relativism. Civil accountability and laws would be nothing more than power-based preferences of which group of lawmakers gets elected and makes the laws. Social affirmation or disapproval would merely reflect majority opinion created in media-driven echo chambers.[24]

As we have noted with each of the previous domains, how one formulates and understands metaethics plays a critical role in the formation of one's ethical methodology. There is no exception here. From a particularly Christian point of view, the question of who gets to define what constitutes the "most caring response," or which response is most sensitive to the given relationships involved, is directly related to the question whether God exists and whether he has given instructions to guide all subordinate relationships. Once again, we are cast back to one of the central questions of ethics: Is morality invented or discovered? As we

---

24. This is also the danger of the recent trends to adopt so-called Critical Theory as a basis for deconstructing moral systems and adopting intersectionality as the basis for determining moral action. Without a firm, transcendent foundation, the ethical process becomes a battle for power to invent morality instead of a discovery of what God has fixed and revealed about the nature of reality and morality.

have repeatedly seen, the values we assign to make our decisions will ultimately reflect the deeper worldview assumptions about God, how we are to have a right relationship with him, and how that ought to shape our perspective and moral choices concerning all our other relationships.

Ethics as worship recognizes that the preeminent relationship that we must be concerned with is our relationship with God. With this in view, attending to that relationship first puts guardrails around how we think of all the other relationships. That is, only as we love God first can we properly love, care for, and show compassion to our neighbors, ourselves, and the rest of the created order. Likewise, only as we obey the Lord as a demonstration of our love for him can our actions to care for others take proper form. The good and right motives of compassion and care remain formless virtues until they are guided with instructions that God gives us in Scripture to teach us what actions truly and properly embody rightly ordered compassion and care. That is, motivation to have compassion and care for someone does not legitimize any action that follows. The presence of strong feelings and sentiments of compassion and care is not enough to legitimize a moral action, choice, or behavior. Those feelings and sentiments must be ordered to a right end, shaped by right character, and guided by God's moral commands.

With these critiques having been made, however, when a concern for relational response is not moved to the place of primary concern in ethical evaluation and instead plays a subordinate role in shaping our ethical response, then it is an invaluable element of normative ethics because it gives ethical data that appropriately help shape the way that a Christian ought to love and care for his or her neighbor. Scripture clearly indicates the importance of this domain in ethical decision-making. Consider, for example, how Jesus modeled the importance of relational care in the way that he attended to real people in real places who were experiencing real joys and real pains. He provided wine for a wedding to care for a couple and their guests (John 2:1–12); he crossed ethnic and gender barriers to minister to a Samaritan woman (John 4:3–26); he healed a woman on the Sabbath who had suffered for eighteen years (Luke 13:10–17); he stopped on his way to visiting an important dignitary in order to recognize the healing faith of a downtrodden woman who had been sick for years (Matt. 9:18–26). Time and again, he demonstrated the importance of emotion and care as a part of the moral process.

Paul likewise gave clear instruction pertaining to this domain by the way in which he shaped his ministry and message so that he did not unduly offend his listeners in order to model integrity and maintain doctrinal purity in and through his moral and theological message. Consider 1 Corinthians 9, where he expresses his willingness to lay down his rights and freedoms, and conform the parts of his ministry that are not absolutely bound to a particular form by the commands of Scripture for the sake of those he is ministering to:

For though I am free from all men, I have made myself a slave to all, so that I may win more. To the Jews I became as a Jew, so that I might win Jews; to those who are under the Law, as under the Law though not being myself under the Law, so that I might win those who are under the Law; to those who are without law, as without law, though not being without the law of God but under the law of Christ, so that I might win those who are without law. To the weak I became weak, that I might win the weak; *I have become all things to all men*, so that I may by all means save some. (1 Cor. 9:19–22)

Paul understands that his care and compassion for those he is ministering to matters greatly. Yet he also orders this care and compassion to a higher ultimate end. He desires to love them ultimately not merely by showing deference to their opinions and preferences; he wants to love them by introducing them to faith in God.

Similarly, Paul shows deference and care for those he is ministering to by being aware of the likely negative responses of those he hoped to minister to if he was unwilling to give up his freedom to eat certain foods. Paul instructs us in several passages that our concern for another person's *conscience* should be a grid through which we filter our moral choices. In both 1 Corinthians 8:4–13 and Romans 14:13–23, he makes a specific appeal to the weaker consciences of others as an important factor in determining our actions. Specifically related to whether it is permissible to eat meat sacrificed to idols, Paul writes:

But take care that this liberty of yours does not somehow become a stumbling block to the weak. For if someone sees you, who have knowledge, dining in an idol's temple, will not his conscience, if he is weak, be strengthened to eat things sacrificed to idols? For through your knowledge he who is weak is ruined, the brother for whose sake Christ died. And so, by sinning against the brethren and wounding their conscience when it is weak, you sin against Christ. Therefore, if food causes my brother to stumble, I will never eat meat again, so that I will not cause my brother to stumble. (1 Cor. 8:9–13)

Even though Paul rightfully argues that meat sacrificed to an idol is not inherently wrong, he also recognizes that some fellow Christians may take offense when they see him eat such meat. Therefore, appealing to the need to appropriately care for the others, Paul determines that it is best not to eat the meat sacrificed to idols in order to protect their consciences. He concludes his similar argument in Romans 14 by saying, "Do not tear down the work of God for the sake of food. All things indeed are clean, but they are evil for the man who eats and gives offense. It is good not to eat meat or to drink wine, or to do anything by which your brother stumbles" (vv. 20–21). Therefore, care and concern for the potentially offended party plays an important role in the ethical assessment of the moral context and the determination of the most appropriate behavior.[25]

This willingness to forgo personal freedoms in order to honor another person's conscientiously held moral standards demonstrates that in an ethic of worship, consideration of the responses of those we interact with is important and needs to play a role in how we wisely go about caring for others with whom we interact.

The Interaction of the Pastoral/Contextual Domains

As we did with the first three theological/normative domains, it is now helpful to pause and consider how these three pastoral/contextual domains work in concert with one another to help shape our ethical decision-making. Having offered reasons for *why* each domain is important, we now move to a discussion of *how* they function together in the shaping of the normative aspect of ethics as worship.

Regarding the second three domains—*circumstances, consequences,* and *relational response*—we noted that each respectively pertains to the concrete situation that one faces, the outcomes that result from one's choices, and the impact that one's decisions make on the individuals and relationships that he or she is associated with in the context of the moral event. Data derived from a consideration of each, then, can change from event to event. They are therefore more subjective in nature but remain vitally important for consideration on how best to apply our virtuous and obedient behaviors in specific contexts.

While ethics as worship requires clear, objective, unchanging principles to rightly order moral behavior to their proper end, in order to properly apply those virtues and principles in any given context, we need wisdom and discernment in determining which data are relevant to the case at hand as well as in how to process the information and apply it to moral decision-making in context. These three domains of ethical consideration help us worship God well by shaping our love for God and neighbors in a manner that is most appropriate and fitting to the specific context. The information gathered from a consideration of these domains enables moral persons to make the most appropriate applications of the biblical commands in the situations, contexts, and lives of those they come in contact with.

In addition to having an affinity to one another, the contextual domains interact with one another in an important manner as well. The circumstance domain is of most importance in this cluster because it concerns the context in which the

---

25. Paul offers a similar line of reasoning in his taking Timothy to be circumcised for the sake of the Jews (Acts 16:3) but refusing to have Titus circumcised (Gal. 2:3–5).

event actually takes place. It concerns a consideration of the details in any particular context in which moral decision-making must take place. The other two domains are primarily concerned with providing data related to an evaluation of how any given behavior might affect the moral situation or what things might result from a chosen course of action. The relational domain and consequence domain each provide key information to help a moral agent consider the larger possibilities and potential effects of his or her behavior in the specific situation that he or she faces.

In sum, in addition to being an ethics of habituated obedience, ethics as worship must be incarnationally aware of the full context in which the moral choice, act, or behavior must take place. Giving appropriate attention to the pastoral/contextual domains makes this incarnational worship possible.

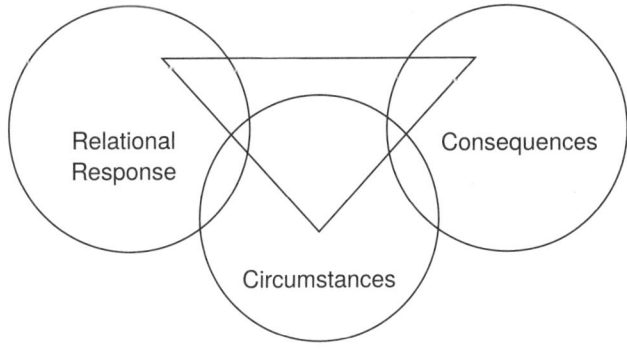

Fig. 7.1. Pastoral/Contextual Domains of Ethical Assessment

The Six Domains of Ethical Assessment and the Normative Criteria for Ethics as Worship

The Prioritization of the Domain Clusters in a Moral Event

With our having recognized the interdependent relationships between the domains in each cluster, it is now also important to consider how best to prioritize each of the clusters when a moral agent moves toward ethical decision-making. Because the theological/normative domains are the defining elements of what it means to do "Christian ethics," they are without question the most foundational and important domains at play in a moral event. Indeed, they must also hold the position of priority so that we may do as Jesus bids and "seek first [God's] kingdom" (Matt. 6:33).

While the context, the predicted consequences, and the potential relational responses of the pastoral/contextual cluster ought to inform moral decision-making, in order for an ethic to be truly Christian, they can *never* be allowed to override the goals, virtues, and standards of the theological/normative cluster that God reveals for us to apply in any moral context. While considerations of the context, the relational responses, and the predicted consequences are *important* factors, they are never *absolutely binding* factors. Contextual, relational, and consequential factors are only *prima facie binding*, while the focus on glorifying God, the command to be Christlike, and the standards of obedience are absolutes. The teachings of Scripture regarding who we are to be and what we are to do must hold sway over our circumstances and not vice versa. Scripture holds the place of preeminence as our source of authority, not our experience or projected ideas about the contextual domains. This allows for proper contextualization of the moral commands while also ensuring to guard against syncretism or the subjugation of biblical commands to inferior worldview assumptions.

On a very pragmatic level, this point is of great importance because of what we pointed out in the previous chapter—*the way in which we live our lives and the choices we make display what we believe and what we love at the deepest levels of our minds and hearts*. Every moral situation provides an opportunity to reveal by our response what we actually believe to be true about God's commands to us and what we actually consider to be worthy of our greatest love and commitment. Every moral decision places us in a moment of decision about what we choose to believe and how we will express our deepest affections. Every time we face a temptation, we are actually facing a crisis of both our beliefs and our loves. What loves will most shape us? Do we believe that the words of Scripture are truer than our predictions of possible consequences? Do we choose holiness over the fulfillment of fleshly pleasure because we are willing to trust God and believe his promises to be better than what appears incredibly tempting at a given moment? What ideas will we believe when God's Word leads us in a direction that we do not like? What loves will compel us when obedience to Scripture seems counterintuitive? Will we believe those words of Scripture over and above our fallen intellectual and broken consciences? Will we choose to love and obey God even when we are uncertain of the outcomes and costs that come from loving and obeying him? Even when we are afraid?

For a poignant example of why the theological/normative domains must hold the place of priority in ethics as worship, consider the example of King Saul in 1 Samuel 13. As the king of Israel, Saul had an army of three thousand men at his command when he faced a Philistine army of thirty thousand chariots, six thousand horsemen, and "people like the sand which is on the seashore in abundance" (1 Sam. 13:1–5).[26] Faced with these overwhelming odds, the Israelite army begins to abandon Saul as he waits on the prophet Samuel to come and seek the Lord for

---

26. Some translations read "3,000 chariots."

instruction on how to proceed. But when the prophet does not show up in the time Saul expects, the king chooses to disobey the commands of God. He performs a sacrifice that he is not authorized to perform in order to seek the Lord's favor in battle. At that moment, the prophet Samuel arrives on the scene and confronts King Saul about what he has done. Saul then replies:

> Because I saw that the people were scattering from me, and that you did not come within the appointed days, and that the Philistines were assembling at Michmash, therefore I said, "Now the Philistines will come down against me at Gilgal, and I have not asked the favor of the LORD." So I forced myself and offered the burnt offering. (1 Sam. 13:11–12)

Note that in this situation, it was through an evaluation of the pastoral/contextual domains that Saul chose to act as he did. He looked at the situation, he saw the number of enemy warriors, and he predicted consequences of defeat and destruction. With these thoughts in mind, he reasoned that the relational cost with the prophet would not be as bad as the defeat of his army, so he then "forced himself" to disobey and offer the sacrifice.

In this light, consider the reply of the prophet Samuel:

> Samuel said to Saul, "You have acted foolishly; you have not kept the commandment of the LORD your God, which He commanded you, for now the LORD would have established your kingdom over Israel forever. But now your kingdom shall not endure. The LORD has sought out for Himself a man after His own heart, and the LORD has appointed him as ruler over His people, *because you have not kept what the LORD commanded you*." (1 Sam. 13:13–14)

Here we see that while God desired the king's obedience as a demonstration of properly ordered love for God, Saul chose a decision-making process based on circumstantial reasoning and fear of possible consequences. As a result, not only did Saul earn God's disfavor, God ultimately removed Saul from his position as king of Israel. As Samuel will later tell the king after he makes a second and similar decision to disobey the commands of God, "to obey is better than sacrifice" (1 Sam. 15:22).

What we learn from Saul's choice to disobey God's clear commands in light of pressing circumstances is that God desires for us the type of virtuous character that is willing and quick to obey even in the face of overwhelming odds. The circumstances that we face in life—no matter how dire they seem—are not to rule over our obedience to God because God's commands will always lead us to maximum worship even if they come at great cost. God wants us to understand that the theological/normative domains hold sway over the pastoral/contextual moral factors even when it appears that obedience may lead to defeat and death. This is the cost of discipleship as it relates to ethical decision-making.

On a much more personal level, all of us are vulnerable to similar choices when we face temptations and trials. Whether it be contexts in which we face extremely potent temptations (such as a desire for an extramarital affair or pornography) or when a difficult situation faces us (an unwanted pregnancy, a difficult marriage, or the potential to fail a final exam), all of us are prone to King Saul's error. All of us are prone to base our decisions on what we believe will provide immediate pleasure or relief even when it is contrary to true love for God and obedience to his commands. It is precisely at these times when God wants us to walk by faith and not by sight (2 Cor. 5:7). The fact of the matter is that it is often at the times of trial and temptation that what we ultimately decide will both *reflect* and *shape* us at the level of our deepest loves and beliefs. Each decision comes from the heart, and each decision will further shape the heart. As we pointed out in our discussion of the Holy Spirit's role in bringing about sanctification (chapter 4), every choice one makes impacts the central part of who we are and who we are becoming.[27] This is why God wants us to recognize the primacy of the *telos*, the character, and the action commands of the theological/normative cluster. They are God's merciful means to orient us, help us endure, and protect us in the face of temptation, fatigue, and lack of faith.

The Interaction of the Domain Clusters in a Moral Event

Having recognized the place of priority and authority of the theological/normative cluster, we now want to once again emphasize that these two clusters must not function separately from each other. While the pastoral/contextual cluster is not as authoritative, it is vital. To have the first three domains in order without the influence of the pastoral/contextual cluster would greatly diminish the compassionate quality, the personal sensitivity, and the warm humanness that should mark Christian morality. Consideration of any one domain "apart from the others will provide insufficient information in order to engage in informed, responsible, ethical evaluation."[28]

Both clusters and all six domains together highlight not only the vital parts of ethics as worship but the entirety of the ethical method as a whole. They provide the normative criteria that we might love God and neighbor well (Mark 12:29–31), and they help us be the kinds of worshipers that Jesus is looking for, those who worship "in spirit and truth" (John 4:23). The following diagram, then, serves

---

27. C. S. Lewis, *Mere Christianity* (New York: Touchstone, 1996), 87.
28. David W. Jones, *An Introduction to Biblical Ethics* (Nashville: B&H Academic, 2013), 22.

to highlight how all six domains function together to shape and direct the holistic act of ethical worship.

In sum, if one is to make God-honoring moral decisions that are both rightly ordered to God and incarnationally sound, then the normative method of decision-making must simultaneously take into consideration the transcendent and timeless guidance given by God on the one hand and the contextual factors relative to the given situation on the other. Any truly Christian ethic must attend to how one rightly orders both these ends of morality into one unified act of worship in any moral event.

Making Moral Decisions

In light of the preceding discussion about identifying the domains of a moral event, why they are important, and how to order them, it is now time to suggest a procedure for how one might go about making moral decisions. It is not our intent here to provide either a rigid formula or an exhaustive step-by-step process. Rather, our intent is to broadly outline key elements in the process of applying ethics as worship in a live situation.[29] We will divide our methodology into two general categories: (1) things that should be in place before one faces a moral event, and (2) key elements to consider when in the midst of a moral event.

Let's once again consider the plight of a student who is tempted to cheat on an exam. Suppose that Michelle, upon starting the exam, realizes that she did not study properly and is not prepared to answer the questions. She needs to pass this exam to graduate, but now she realizes that she has no chance of passing unless she cheats. How would processing her situation through the normative methodology of ethics as worship help her decide what to do?

Before the Situation Arises

As we frequently remind our ethics students, the best time for a person to settle his or her convictions about an ethical issue is *before* he or she has to face it. This mitigates the need to have to do the moral calculus necessary in the heat of the moment when the pressures of the circumstances, potential consequences, and possible relational responses are all bearing down in a given context. In relation to Michelle's decision, this would mean that while she will feel the pressures

29. We are indebted to Scott Rae at this point for his example suggesting a simple and clear model for making moral decisions. Our model is not exactly the same in order or detail, but the two are akin in many aspects. Rae's model lists the following elements: (1) gather the facts, (2) determine the ethical issues, (3) determine what virtues/principles have a bearing on the case, (4) list the alternatives, (5) compare the alternatives with the virtues/principles, (6) consider the consequences, and (7) decide. See Scott B. Rae, *Moral Choices: An Introduction to Ethics*, 4th ed. (Grand Rapids: Zondervan, 2018), 111–13.

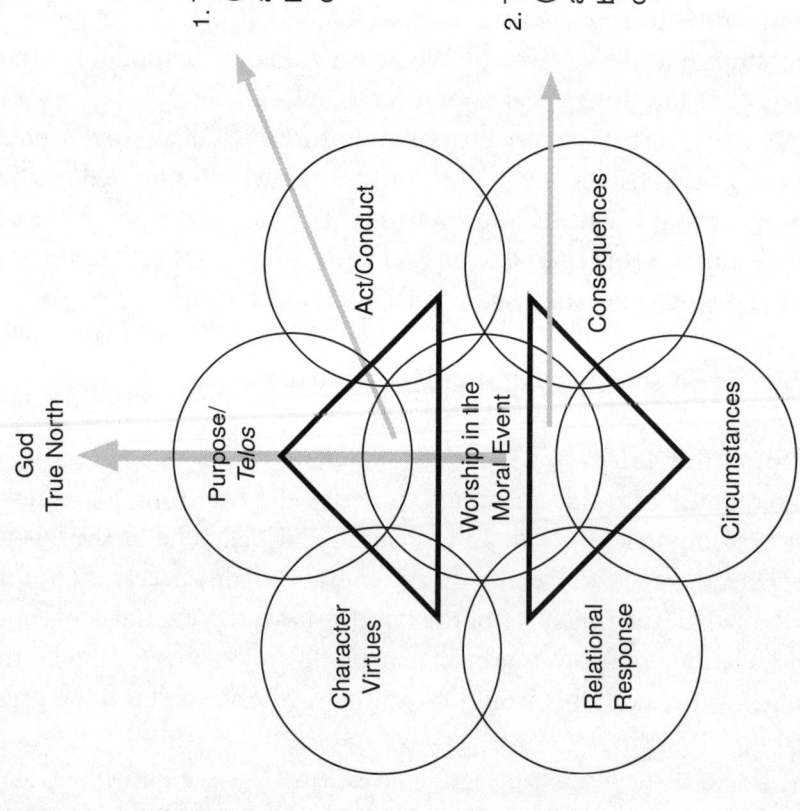

God
True North

1. The Theological/Normative Domains
   (Ordering, Motivating, Guiding & Guarding)
   a. God-Ordered
   b. Character-Based
   c. Command-Guided

2. The Pastoral/Contextual Domains
   (Nuancing, Not Determining)
   a. Circumstantially Discerning (Situationally Aware)
   b. Consequence-Perceptive
   c. Interpersonally Caring

Act/Conduct

Consequences

Purpose/
Telos

Worship in the
Moral Event

Circumstances

Character
Virtues

Relational
Response

Fig. 7.2. Six Domains of Ethical Assessment

in a given moment in time, in actuality, how she behaves will involve a process that has been in play for a long time. Thus, a decision-making process actually has two categories that we must consider: (1) what has been taking place before the situation arises, and (2) how to make a choice in a given situation. We begin with two crucial elements related to what should take place before facing a moral decision-making context.

Examine Yourself to See Whether You Are of the Faith (2 Cor. 13:5)

Faith in Christ is the key element of transformation to rightly order an act to its final end. Those who are not of the faith cannot rightly worship the triune God. Therefore, Michelle first needs to have settled the matter of her faith in her heart. In 2 Corinthians 13:5, Paul admonishes his readers to test themselves and see whether they are in the faith. The right time for Michelle to do this is not while sitting in the classroom in the midst of her exam. Long before stepping foot into that room, she needs to know where her faith resides. Does she know Christ? Has she passed the test of true faith that Paul mentions in 2 Corinthians? Passing the test of faith is far more important than passing a final exam in chemistry. Of course, the particular circumstance may press the person to a moment of eternal significance, but in terms of the moral formation necessary to make a God-honoring decision, it would obviously be best for Michelle's questions of faith commitment to be settled before facing the situation.

Pursue Spiritual Formation as a Part of Ongoing Discipleship (Phil. 2:12–13)

More than simply knowing the state of one's soul, the Christian needs to pursue spiritual formation through the process of discipleship. It is through discipleship that virtues are cultivated and we become the type of persons that God has called us to be. It is neither likely nor wise to expect new moral character to show up at a moment of crisis and point of decision-making. Virtues do not magically appear when they are most needed. In Philippians 2:12–13, Paul writes, "So then, my beloved, just as you have always obeyed, not as in my presence only, but now much more in my absence, work out your salvation with fear and trembling; for it is God who is at work in you, both to will and to work for His good pleasure." Working out our salvation entails discipleship and growth in our faith so that we can become like Christ (Phil. 2:5).

Ideally, Michelle would already be on the road of discipleship and maturing in her faith so that this moment of testing could be addressed not from panic but from a perspective of faith. Ideally, she would be equipped to see the entire moral event through the eyes of faith, with the larger grand narrative of reality in view (*revealed reality*), and with a disposition above all to honor and please the Lord, who created and is in control of all things.

When Confronted by a Moral Event

Now we reach the moment of decision. For many people, this is the point at which they believe ethics comes into play. As we identified above, however, this is merely the moment of decision. Ethics as worship has started long before this point through faith and discipleship. Yet when confronted by a moral event, we must act in real time with a real context and in real relationships. Michelle is now confronted with her moment of decision, and she has several steps to determine what action will honor God through her worship.

Identify the Issue

In some respects, this is the easiest part of the process. What is the presenting issue, problem, or choice that one is facing? For Michelle, her problem is that she did not adequately prepare for the exam, and her future (as she sees it) depends on a passing grade. Therefore, she is faced with the question of cheating. Should she cheat to pass the exam and thus pass the class in order to graduate?

Sometimes the scenario is not so clear-cut. There may be complicating factors in the context that blur the decision. Perhaps there are more than two alternatives. Most of our decisions will be fairly straightforward, but that is not always the case. When the situation is more complex, if possible, it is best to set the decision aside in order to clarify what relevant moral factors are in play. We will address more complicated scenarios in the following chapter.

Prayerfully Submit Yourself and the Situation to the Lord

Prayer is vitally important to the moral decision-making process. Unfortunately, many of us are prone to bypass this step out of neglect. In a world where we want to be self-sufficient, we neglect to recognize our dependence on the Lord in prayer. The most important part of submitting ourselves and the situation to the Lord in prayer is to pray for a heart to first of all honor the Lord. This is more important than praying for wisdom or direction in the situation. We should pray for those as well, but the submissive heart is crucial to making a God-honoring decision. Ultimately, this discipline helps us bring the entire moral event into alignment with the first domain.

At this point of decision, Michelle needs to pause and submit her heart to God and seek the Lord's guidance. It is best not to move to a decision without first lifting her situation up to the Lord and recognizing his lordship over her life and circumstances. In Philippians 4:6, we read, "Be anxious for nothing, but in everything by prayer and supplication with thanksgiving let your requests be made known to God." Recognizing through prayer that God's goodness is not contingent on her grade, Michelle can begin to set aside the anxiety of her situation and can call out to God in prayer to help her submit to divine wisdom regardless of the cost.

Identify the Relevant Data from the Theological/Normative Cluster

Now that Michelle knows the issue and has submitted her heart to the Lord in prayer, it is time to identify the data from the theological/normative cluster. This includes identifying the *telos*, *virtues* (character), and *commands* that relate to the act of cheating. The *telos* is always clear, no matter the situation. We must desire to glorify God and worship him rightly in all things. Can she maximize the worship and glory of God by cheating?

In regard to the *character* domain, the peripherally appropriate character traits and virtues may vary from situation to situation, but in every case the moral agent must be primarily concerned with cultivating his or her love for God above all else as well as seeking practical wisdom to guide one's actions in context. In Michelle's case in particular, she needs to determine whether she can simultaneously love God with primacy and cheat. Is her love for God stronger than her love for a good grade? Is her love for God stronger than her desire for her friends and family to be proud of her good marks?

Similarly, assuming that Michelle's love for God is primary and she desires to honor him through her moral behavior, she must then have the courage to make the decision to forgo cheating as well as the self-control to resist temptation. While, as we noted a moment ago, these character traits will not miraculously appear if she has not been cultivating them before this moment of decision, it is the case that what she decides here will play a role in what kind of person she becomes going forward. She needs to ask herself whether the decision she makes will help her become more conformed to the image of Christ. What will she do when no one is looking? Will she steal the answers simply because she can get away with it? Or does the fact that whatever action she chooses will impact her character (one way or another) matter enough to her?

Finally, Michelle needs to consider the *act* domain and identify any commands or biblical instructions that relate to her situation. She can do this by asking, "Is the choice I am about to make clearly in accord with the commands of Scripture?" At the outset, she may not at first identify the fifth commandment relating to honoring authority, the eighth commandment relating to stealing, or the ninth commandment relating to lying and deceit as relevant. Indeed, the relevance of the fourth commandment ("You shall not take the name of the LORD your God in vain," Ex. 20:7) and what it means to bear the name *Christian* may not even be on her radar. But as she considers the situation and understands these commands, ideally she will come to realize that cheating is a form of stealing, it is a form of lying, and it does represent the Lord's name poorly because her choice to disobey (actual practice) would reflect poorly on her claim to be a Christian (stated belief). In addition to these commandments, Scripture is replete with verses that commend truthfulness and integrity (Prov. 10:9; 11:3; 12:22; Eph. 4:25; Col. 3:9).

If Michelle has been hiding God's Word in her heart as part of the process of discipleship, then the Holy Spirit will bring verses such as these to mind, and then she will clearly know what shape love for God, self-control, and courage should take as she moves into a consideration of her particular context. Table 7.2 summarizes these first three steps in question form.

Table 7.2. Three Key Questions Related to the Theological/Normative Domains

1. What does maximally worshiping God in this context look like? (*telos* domain)

2. Will this choice help me to become more conformed to the image of Christ? (character domain)

3. Is the choice I am about to make clearly in accord with the commands of Scripture? (act domain)

Consider the Data Relative to the Pastoral/Contextual Cluster

Having worked through the theological cluster, however, does not mean that contextual factors do not matter. This cluster gives Michelle more specific details about her exact situation and helps her recognize the impact that her decision will make one way or the other. Identifying the relevant data from this cluster will help her know how to apply the principles from the theological/normative cluster, count the cost to her grades, and consider the impact that her choices might have on the relationships with all those involved. Beginning with the circumstances, she is wise to consider all the various elements of the situation she is facing. She knows that her situation is difficult: If she does not pass the exam, she will not pass the class. If she does not pass the class, she will not graduate. There could also be a host of other complicating factors, such as a scholarship that is tied to a particular GPA or her parents, who are paying tuition for college. Or perhaps other non-school-related factors must be taken into consideration as well. For example, what if she had been sick for the three days before the exam and couldn't study? What if a family member had unexpectedly passed away?

Recognizing these circumstances helps her see how complicated her situation really is. It helps her accurately take into consideration the likely consequences and relational responses that would come to bear regardless of her final choice. It also helps her consider whether there are other options to discuss with the professor.

The consequences of cheating could be passing the class and graduation if no one discovers her deception. But it could also result in failure and discipline by her university if she is caught.

The relational response could be unaffected with her teacher, family, and friends at least on the surface—if she is not caught cheating; but she may have difficulty looking her professor in the eye and being honest with the classmate from whom she cheated. If she is caught, relationships with her professor, her university, her classmates, and even her parents will likely be damaged. More importantly, what about her relationship with God? Even if she doesn't get caught, she already knows that her conscience will zing her and that she will need to repent if she wants to continue in a healthy relationship with the Lord. Is the good grade worth that relational pain? The risk is high for negative outcomes, but facing all the contingencies helps her realize the cost of her discipleship and helps her evaluate how much she wants to love and serve God even when it is tough.

List Possible Alternatives

While in most situations there are many possible alternatives that one could consider, Michelle's decision is fairly straightforward. She can choose to cheat or choose to take the exam on her own. But beyond these initial alternatives, there are secondary choices that the pastoral/contextual cluster can help her consider and prepare for. For example, if the reason that she did not study for the exam was that a family member died or that she was sick with a sudden bout of the flu, a third alternative of talking to the professor and seeking an extension could be in order. On the other hand, if she is unprepared simply because she was out late with friends and forgot about the test, then she may think through ahead of time how she will interact with her parents, or perhaps talk to the professor to see whether there is some way to earn extra credit. While the simplicity of the initial decision (cheat or not) is straightforward, consideration of the contextual cluster may work to mitigate against possible negative consequences as well as unearth possible alternative solutions.

Submit the Alternatives to the Data Gathered from the Theological/Normative Cluster

As we reach the moment of decision, we need to look back to the theological/normative cluster one last time, knowing the possible alternatives. This is not always an easy step because the choice may not be clear, but it is necessary because the theological/normative cluster must take priority. For Michelle, she knows what her options are and she needs to ask whether cheating fits within the theological/normative cluster as a viable option. Based on the desire to glorify God and an understanding that God commends integrity, it seems clear that Michelle must not cheat. Her options, then, seem to be to find another solution by working with the professor or to follow the expectations of Scripture and worship God with her moral decision while trusting the Lord to work out the consequences. Table 7.3 summarizes these latter three steps in question form.

Table 7.3. Three Key Questions Related to the Pastoral/Contextual Domains

1. What mitigating circumstances am I facing in this situation? (circumstance domain)

2. What likely outcomes (both short- and long-term) will result from this action or decision? (consequence domain)

3. How will the people involved in the situation be impacted by my action or decision? (relational domain)

Make a Decision

Of course, if possible, it is wise to take extended time to seek the Lord's wisdom as well as the counsel of faithful Christians before any morally complicated or demanding decision is made. In best-case scenarios, this would become a normative practice. Ideally, over time, the process would become more reflexive and "second nature."

As this case illustrates, however, taking a lengthy time to arrive at a decision is not always possible. This is why we reiterate that morality is a long-range process and that the best time to become ready to make a moral decision is long before one has to do so. In this way, even though these steps may seem long and arduous as they are read and thought about, when they become a part of one's character as a worshiper, they can be addressed relatively quickly in context.

Ultimately, the final step is to make the decision. As for Michelle, after working through these steps, it becomes clear to her what she must do if she is going to love and worship God as he instructs. She must refuse to cheat, do the best she can, turn in her exam, and then perhaps appeal to the professor afterward in light of the situation. All that is left now is for her to do it. It would be both appropriate and wise here for her to pray for courage as the moment of decision arrives and she finally acts.

Conclusion

It has been our goal in this chapter and the previous one to develop a normative methodology for ethics as worship from within a context of discipleship. We first discussed the important role that normative ethics serves in bridging metaethics to applied ethics by highlighting the relationship between our underlying beliefs and our actual practices. Then we explained the six domains of ethical assessment from a particularly Christian point of view and suggested both a logical and a hierarchical ordering. Next, we discussed how the six domains ought to function together in two clusters. The first, the *theological/normative cluster*, includes the *telos*, *virtue* (character of the agent), and *act/conduct* domains. The second *pastoral/contextual cluster* grouped the circumstance, consequence, and relationship domains as the normative criteria for ethics as worship. Finally, we offered a general procedure for making moral decisions from the perspective of ethics as worship and then modeled how it might function by applying it to a rather simple but useful case.

Of course, "simple but useful" cases are not always the types of situations we face as we seek to live ethically before the Lord. In fact, sometimes the moral situations we find ourselves in appear to be so complex that we hardly know how to escape them without sinning in one way or another. Therefore, before we move to the final applied ethics section of the book in which we address particular issues, it is important that we consider how to navigate more complicated situations, sometimes described as *moral dilemmas*. It is to this topic we turn in the following chapter.

Key Terms and Concepts

antinomianism

circumstances

consequences

fittingness

"greatest happiness" principle

I-thou

justice versus care

moral relativism

principle of utility

relational response

situational ethics

tyranny of the majority

utilitarianism

Key Scriptures

1 Samuel 13:1–14

1 Samuel 15:22

Luke 14:27–33

Romans 14:13–23

1 Corinthians 8:4–13

1 Corinthians 9:19–22

2 Corinthians 4:14–17

2 Corinthians 5:7

2 Corinthians 13:5

Philippians 2:12–13

Study Questions

1. How does a recognition of the pastoral/contextual domains of ethical assessment help to properly order our neighbor love?

2. The idea of "the greatest good for the greatest number of people" is perhaps the most influential ethical idea in modern secular culture. Explain why it is not wise for a Christian to make this the primary element of moral reasoning. In other words, what are the reasons why Christian ethics is not utilitarian?

3. What does the concept of the *tyranny of the majority* mean, and how does it relate to why Christians should not be utilitarians?
4. Why must the theological/normative domains be authoritative over the pastoral/contextual domains in an orthodox Christian ethic?
5. How do 1 Corinthians 8:4–13 and Romans 14:13–23 help a Christian understand how to obey the clear commands of Scripture while also knowing how to make appropriate application of ethical freedoms in a particular context?

For Further Reading

Buber, Martin. *I and Thou.* Translated by Ronald Gregor Smith. New York: Scribner Classics, 2000.

Budziszewski, J. *Written on the Heart: The Case for Natural Law.* Downers Grove, IL: InterVarsity Press, 1997.

Fletcher, Joseph. *Situation Ethics: The New Morality.* Philadelphia: Westminster Press, 1966.

Gilligan, Carol. *In a Different Voice.* Cambridge, MA: Harvard University Press, 1982.

Mill, John Stuart. *Utilitarianism.* London: Longmans, Green, 1897.

Noddings, Nel. "Caring." In *Justice and Care: Essential Readings in Feminist Ethics,* edited by Virginia Held, 7–30. Boulder, CO: Westview, 1995.

Rachels, James, and Stuart Rachels. *The Elements of Moral Philosophy.* 9th ed. New York: McGraw-Hill Education, 2019.

Rae, Scott B. *Moral Choices: An Introduction to Ethics.* 4th ed. Grand Rapids: Zondervan, 2018.

8

The Problem of Moral Dilemmas: Ethics as Worship in Morally Complex Contexts

"In a sinful world, believers may occasionally find themselves confronted with conflicting ethical obligations."[1]
—JOHN JEFFERSON DAVIS, Evangelical Ethics

"How should we act when two or more of our foundational moral principles seem to be at odds with each other? Ideally, of course, these rules never actually conflict. . . . Yet most of us would admit from personal experience that in actual situations of life we sometimes find ourselves unable to obey all the rules simultaneously."[2]
—STANLEY J. GRENZ, The Moral Quest

Introduction

In the previous chapter, it was our task to lay out a methodological bridge to help us move from the truths that God has revealed about his world to the application of those truths in daily living. That is, it has been our task to provide a means for understanding how to move from metaethics to applied ethics via the bridge of a normative ethical methodology that we describe as *ethics as worship*.

It is now our task in this chapter to build on that foundational methodology and explore how to live in a manner that most magnifies the Lord when we run into situations in which moral clarity is hard to attain. This is the problem of *moral dilemmas*. It refers to those complicated moral situations that occur in a

---

1. John Jefferson Davis, *Evangelical Ethics: Issues Facing the Church Today*, 4th ed. (Phillipsburg, NJ: P&R Publishing, 2015), 6.

2. Stanley J. Grenz, *The Moral Quest: Foundations of Christian Ethics* (Downers Grove, IL: InterVarsity Press, 1997), 32.

broken and fallen world where it appears that in order to obey the Lord, we must also simultaneously disobey one of his commandments.

The account of Rahab and her treatment of the Hebrew spies in Joshua 2 is perhaps one of the most perplexing moral events recorded in Scripture and also best illustrates the problem of moral dilemmas. The passage describes Rahab as sheltering the spies of known enemies, deceiving the men who are in pursuit of the spies, and sending the spies safely away by giving false information to the pursuers. The second chapter of Joshua describes the event as follows:

> Then Joshua the son of Nun sent two men as spies secretly from Shittim, saying, "Go, view the land, especially Jericho." So they went and came into the house of a harlot whose name was Rahab, and lodged there. It was told the king of Jericho, saying, "Behold, men from the sons of Israel have come here tonight to search out the land." And the king of Jericho sent word to Rahab, saying, "Bring out the men who have come to you, who have entered your house, for they have come to search out all the land." But the woman had taken the two men and hidden them, and she said, "Yes, the men came to me, but I did not know where they were from. It came about when it was time to shut the gate at dark, that the men went out; I do not know where the men went. Pursue them quickly, for you will overtake them." But she had brought them up to the roof and hidden them in the stalks of flax which she had laid in order on the roof. So the men pursued them on the road to the Jordan to the fords; and as soon as those who were pursuing them had gone out, they shut the gate. (Josh. 2:1–7)

What makes this event so perplexing is that while Scripture uniformly depicts lying as contrary to God's nature and will throughout Scripture,[3] the New Testament casts Rahab (and at least some of her choices in this passage) in a commendable light. The book of Hebrews states: "By faith Rahab the harlot did not perish along with those who were disobedient, after she had welcomed the spies in peace" (Heb. 11:31). Similarly, the book of James compares Rahab's faith with that of the patriarch Abraham, concluding, "In the same way, was not Rahab the harlot also *justified by works* when she received the messengers and sent them out by another way?" (James 2:25).

How should one understand this apparent incongruity? Is this an indication of a conflict in Scripture? Is an implicit, unspoken hierarchy of values involved that excuses Rahab from moral guilt for lying? Could this be an indication that what really matters in moral evaluation is one's heart intention and not the material

---

3. See, for example, Proverbs 6:16–19; 12:22; and 21:8, which describe God's hatred for lying. Also consider passages such as John 8:44 and Acts 5:3, which associate lying with satanic influence.

expression of the act itself? Or could it be that the New Testament texts are actually commending Rahab specifically for her faith in welcoming and sending out the spies while leaving silent any comment in regard to her lying?

These questions have led biblically driven Christian ethicists and theologians to varying conclusions about ethical methodology as well as the nature and function of moral absolutes when faced with what appear to be morally ambiguous situations or moral dilemmas. For those who consider Scripture to be inerrant, infallible, and the highest source of moral authority, the problem of moral dilemmas is far more than an academic puzzle. Indeed, one's conclusions have far-reaching theological and epistemological implications regarding the nature and function of Scripture as the rule of faith and practice before, during, and after morally difficult circumstances arise.

The purpose of this chapter is to consider the problem of morally complex contexts and these so-called moral dilemmas in order to provide a biblical path forward. In order to do so, we will first discuss the nature of moral dilemmas and offer clarity regarding the problem by defining our terms. Next, we seek to inform the reader of the larger discussion regarding the various influential positions that are commonly held by scholars in relation to the problem of moral dilemmas and illustrate the distinct nature of each by applying it to the context of Rahab. Third, we offer our own perspective on the problem that we call the *humble absolutist* approach. Before bringing the chapter to a conclusion, we give a final consideration to how our humble absolutist approach interprets Rahab's actions in Joshua 2 in light of apparent affirmations of her found in New Testament passages.

At the end of the day, real people facing difficult moral situations must make decisions and act. It is the calling of the gospel that believers are to seek first the kingdom of God and attempt to bring glory to God above all else (Matt. 6:33). It is the task of ethics as worship to help Christians learn to worship properly even in the most difficult of life's circumstances and choices. Therefore, knowing how to apply God's Word in light of these situations is anything but a mere academic exercise. It is central to the Christian faith. For this reason, and because wise and godly people have differed over this issue through time, such a discussion requires great care, careful reasoning, and, perhaps more than anything else, an attitude of humility in the face of human sin and the resultant darkening of our moral processing.

Understanding Moral Dilemmas

Moral Dilemmas: Forms and Distinctions

Sometimes described as *conflicts of duty* or *tragic moral choices, moral dilemmas* are said to occur in situations in which a moral agent finds himself or herself facing at least two absolute moral norms that demand allegiance, although not all the norms can be satisfied in that situation. Put another way, a so-called moral dilemma "is a situation in which there is a conflict between absolutes, that is, between several God-given moral norms that allow no exceptions. Whichever course of action a person follows in such cases, she will set aside or somehow violate at least one moral norm."[4]

For example, a moral agent may believe that, on moral grounds, he or she is obligated to behave in two distinct ways (to perform both *act x* and *act y*), yet is circumstantially prohibited in the situation from doing both.[5] Recalling our earlier discussion of the complex moral context in Victor Hugo's classic *Les Misérables*, the story presents a poignant example of this type of moral dilemma. The hero of the story, Jean Valjean, spends nineteen years in a hard-labor camp for stealing a loaf of bread in order to feed his starving niece. His dilemma was whether to obey a law not to steal (*act x*) or to honor a filial duty to preserve the life of a relative (*act y*). In this case, circumstances apparently prohibited him from doing both.

In the case of Rahab, we see that she was faced with the choice to tell the truth (*act x*) or protect the spies (*act y*). Her circumstances (at least apparently) forced her into a context in which she had to choose between breaking one moral requirement or another.

In each of these examples, the moral weight behind the possible alternatives is substantive and indicates a level of responsibility for the moral agents involved. The choice of one course of behavior appears to be both morally praiseworthy and yet morally unacceptable at the same time. Compliance with one moral obligation can happen only by an abrogation or omission of the other obligation.[6] Choosing not to act in order not to break either command appears to create a problem of neglecting responsibility, thus incurring guilt through omission.

Moral Dilemmas, Practical Dilemmas, and Apparent Dilemmas

Moral dilemmas can be described as "morally ambiguous situations that intrude inescapably into life in a fallen world," but not all morally ambiguous situations are actual moral dilemmas.[7] Some moral situations are ambiguous not so much because the course of action is unclear or one moral duty competes with another, but because of the practical implications or inconveniences that accompany proper moral behavior. For example, consider once again the case of our student Michelle in the previous chapter and her temptation to cheat in order to pass her exam. When

---

4. David K. Clark and Robert V. Rakestraw, "Moral Dilemmas," in *Theory and Method*, ed. David K. Clark and Robert V. Rakestraw, vol. 1 of *Readings in Christian Ethics* (Grand Rapids: Baker, 1994), 113.

5. Tom L. Beauchamp and James F. Childress, *Principles of Biomedical Ethics*, 6th ed. (New York: Oxford University Press, 2009), 11.

6. Beauchamp and Childress, *Principles of Biomedical Ethics*, 11.

7. Clark and Rakestraw, "Moral Dilemmas," 113.

we consider her case, we recognize that for her the choice may present an emotional difficulty, but that it certainly does not rise to the level of a moral dilemma. The moral obligation is to honor truthfulness and integrity and avoid stealing answers for personal gain. Thus, a *practical dilemma* occurs when moral obligations compete with strongly felt desires or needs that are not obligatory. Difficult questions of priority may still arise, but a moral dilemma is not really present.[8]

In addition to practical dilemmas, *apparent dilemmas* based on insufficient knowledge also do not constitute real moral dilemmas. For example, suppose that John works in a medical research lab whose primary area of research is exploring cures for Alzheimer's disease. John's concern arises from the fear that his company is conducting its stem-cell research using cells harvested from the remains of aborted fetuses. Being pro-life in his commitments, he fears that he will have to quit his job. As John explores the issue further, however, he discovers that the source of the cells in question is not aborted fetal tissue but cells taken from umbilical cords donated voluntarily by competent adults who are concerned that research continue without being at the expense of unborn children. In this situation, the apparent moral ambiguity of the situation was really only a *crisis of knowledge*. The apparent dilemma evaporated when John gained correct information.

Do Moral Dilemmas Actually Occur?

Distinguishing between moral dilemmas, practical dilemmas, and apparent dilemmas is important because it highlights a key theological and ethical issue at the center of the discussion in this chapter. That is, if so-called moral dilemmas are said to actually occur, how are we to understand and explain the possibility of God's Word's coming into conflict with itself? If these moral dilemmas actually occur, are we then admitting the possibility that the moral commands of Scripture at times contradict each other? If Scripture arises from—and is reflective of—God's own character, wouldn't an admission of an actual moral dilemma be an admission that there is a contradiction within God's own mind and nature? If, on the other hand, one holds to the belief that it is impossible for there to be any contradiction within the mind of God, then how would it be possible to say that Scripture (which is an expression of God's mind and nature) could actually conflict with itself? This latter question raises the possibility that there are in reality no such things as true moral dilemmas but only problematic and complex moral situations that at times either are very difficult for humans to rightly navigate or (given the fallen nature of human beings) are even beyond the ability of sinful humans to fully discern. Several approaches to solving the question whether moral dilemmas occur have been proposed, and we will explore some of them below.

---

8. Beauchamp and Childress, *Principles of Biomedical Ethics*, 12.

Various Methodological Approaches

In his book *Christian Ethics: Contemporary Issues and Options*, Norman Geisler addresses the problem of moral dilemmas by identifying and analyzing what he believes to be the six most prominent ethical attempts to address the question of moral dilemmas.[9] At least three of these systems avoid the problem of moral dilemmas in light of how they define moral obligations. *Morally complicated situations* may be a reality, but not *moral dilemmas* because there are no (or not enough) absolutes to conflict. For example, *antinomianism* asserts that because there are no objective, absolute moral principles by which an issue can be judged right or wrong, the decision must be made on subjective grounds. *Generalism* asserts that there are no universally binding absolute moral laws, only guidelines that govern moral behavior generally. *Situationalism* (a form of utilitarianism) claims that only one absolute moral law (either "do the most loving thing" or "greatest good to the greatest number of people") governs all behavior. All other moral considerations should be determined in light of this rule.[10]

For those who view Scripture as the primary source of authority and claim that it carries ultimate moral weight, there are arguably three other systems to consider. Each of these positions holds that at least two moral absolutes exist. Yet they differ on the question whether moral dilemmas actually occur, and, if so, how a moral agent ought to act in light of them. For example, hierarchicalism, or *graded absolutism* (GA), claims to hold that there are many moral absolutes that sometimes conflict, but that higher laws must be followed when there is a conflict. Unqualified absolutism, or *nonconflicting absolutism* (NCA), holds that many moral absolutes exist, none of which ever really conflict, and that they should therefore never be transgressed. Finally, conflicting absolutism, or *ideal absolutism* (IA), holds that there are many moral absolutes that sometimes conflict in a fallen world. In such situations, the moral agent must choose to break one law in order to keep the other. In so doing, he or she incurs moral guilt while at the same time attaining the highest moral accomplishment possible.[11] Table 8.1 highlights these various attempts to deal with the problem of moral dilemmas. For our purposes, because these latter three methodological systems are attempts to explain the problem of moral dilemmas by those who are committed to the inerrancy

9. Norman L. Geisler, *Christian Ethics: Contemporary Issues and Options*, 2nd ed. (Grand Rapids: Baker Academic, 2010), 18–19.

10. Geisler, 18. We will argue later that a version of this position is the actual default position of those who hold to a graded absolutism (GA) position. While distinct from the "situation ethics" of Joseph Fletcher in method, the GA position devolves into the same basic paradigm even though it attempts to remain faithful to a more biblically authoritative methodology than Fletcher's.

11. Geisler, *Christian Ethics*, 19–21.

and infallibility of Scripture, we now turn to a more nuanced explanation of each before arguing for our own position.

Table 8.1. Six Ethical Methods for Dealing with the Problem of Moral Dilemmas

Antinomianism	Because there are no objective, universally binding moral norms, moral dilemmas do not occur.
Generalism	Because moral norms are only *prima facie* binding, moral dilemmas do not actually occur.
Situationalism	Because there is only one objective, universally binding moral norm, moral dilemmas do not occur.
Graded Absolutism (Hierarchicalism)	There are multiple objective, universally binding moral norms. When they conflict as a moral dilemma, the lesser command can be broken without guilt.
Nonconflicting Absolutism	There are multiple objective, universally binding moral norms. God's commands never actually conflict. So-called moral dilemmas result from a crisis of knowledge.
Ideal Absolutism (Conflicting Absolutism)	There are multiple objective, universally binding moral norms. When they conflict as a moral dilemma, the lesser command should be disobeyed, but guilt does occur.

Graded Absolutism (GA) or Hierarchicalism Many moral absolutes

Graded absolutism (GA) is arguably the most well known and widely held position among evangelicals, primarily because Norman Geisler's helpful work on the topic not only provided the six categories for the discussion but also persuasively argued for this particular position. The GA position rests on three foundational assertions.

The first element of graded absolutism relies heavily on a reading of several narrative accounts in Scripture to support the idea that moral dilemmas are indeed real and unavoidable. For example, Geisler cites (among other biblical examples) the narrative account of the Hebrew midwives in Exodus 1 to make his case:

Then the king of Egypt spoke to the Hebrew midwives, one of whom was named Shiphrah and the other was named Puah; and he said, "When you are helping the Hebrew women to give birth and see them upon the birthstool, if it is a son, then you shall put him to death; but if it is a daughter, then she shall live." But the midwives feared God, and did not do as the king of Egypt had commanded them, but let the boys live. So the king of Egypt called for the midwives and said to them, "Why have you done this thing, and let the boys live?" The midwives said to them, "Why have you done this thing, and let the boys live?" The midwives said to Pharaoh, "Because the Hebrew women are not as the Egyptian women; for they are vigorous and give birth before the midwife can get to them." So God was good to the midwives, and the people multiplied, and became very mighty. Because the midwives feared God, He established households for them. (Ex. 1:15–21)

Graded absolutists commonly cite this text not merely as an account of what the midwives *did*, but also as a proof text to argue that the situation they faced put them in a position in which they were forced to decide between conflicting moral imperatives. That is, according to GA proponents, the midwives faced a context in which either they had to tell the truth about the birthing of children and find themselves guilty of not protecting the innocent children, or they showed mercy toward the children through the act of lying. According to Geisler, trying to find a third alternative of "silence" does not solve the issue because there is still the problem of omission regarding a responsibility to care for the needy and innocent (newborn male children). Similarly, the narrative account of Rahab cited in the introduction to this chapter involves the same type of scenario. Two irreconcilable moral obligations demand the attention of the moral agent, and yet both cannot be fulfilled. Geisler concludes that in certain moral situations, moral conflicts are simply unavoidable.[12]

The second assertion of the GA position holds that while there are many moral absolutes, these absolutes exist in a hierarchical ranking. Geisler argues that "all sins are not created equal, for there are clearly higher and lower moral laws." It is his belief, therefore, that because Jesus himself described some laws as "greatest," "first," or "weightier," some commands are more binding than others. From this point Geisler makes the ethical assumption that moral laws are and should be hierarchically graded in order to apply them in times of moral conflict.[13] Regarding the case of the Hebrew midwives, the GA proponent argues that because the text says that "God was good to the midwives" (Ex. 1:20), the assumption is made that God's favor rested on their decision to lie in order to save the lives of babies.

Of course, this assumption that an "absolute" command can be broken without incurring guilt has significant problems associated with it. The first is the problem of demonstrating a clear and unambiguous hierarchy that ranks the commands in a manner that provides action guidelines beyond something as ambiguous as "do the most loving thing." For example, where in Scripture is there a clear and unambiguous teaching that ranks truth-telling lower than protecting life? Is not

12. Geisler, *Christian Ethics*, 102.
13. Geisler, *Christian Ethics*, 101.

God's nature both truthful and life-affirming? Second, there is also the problem of suggesting that a command is a moral "absolute" while simultaneously suggesting that it does not bind absolutely. A normal understanding of the word *absolute* implies that breaking the command incurs guilt regardless of the circumstances. Suggesting otherwise places the burden of proof squarely on the advocates of GA not only to clearly rank the hierarchy of commands but also to show how breaking a so-called lower law does not incur guilt.

It would seem, then, that unless a clear and unambiguous exception is explicitly written in the text, the GA advocate cannot rightly claim the idea that there are multiple moral "absolute" commands in Scripture while also saying that some of those commands do not function as absolutes. Instead, the moral commands actually function as mere *prima facie* principles for the GA advocate. That is, the commands *appear* to be absolute, and can be said to *normally* apply, but in certain tough situations, they don't have to apply. The context of the situation provides a type of permission to break the so-called absolute command without incurring guilt. In reality, while the GA position claims to hold that Scripture contains multiple absolute commands, it actually functions as if there is really only one absolute command (love God) and the strength of all others is determined by context.

Finally, Geisler argues that given the reality that genuine moral conflicts are unavoidable, and given the reality of higher and lower moral laws in Scripture, it follows that God would not "hold the individual responsible for personally unavoidable moral conflicts, providing he keeps the higher law."[14] Geisler bases this claim to clemency largely on the reasoned argument that "a just God will not hold a person responsible for doing what is actually impossible."[15]

To summarize his argument, Geisler concludes:

> God exempts one from his duty to keep the lower law since he could not keep it without breaking a higher law. This exemption functions somewhat like an ethical "right of way" law. . . . When two cars simultaneously reach an intersection without signals or signs, the car on the right has the right of way. . . . Similarly, when a person enters an ethical intersection where two laws come into unavoidable conflict, it is evident that one law must yield to another.[16]

In this way, GA proponents ultimately argue that when facing a moral dilemma, a moral agent can be "personally guiltless" if he or she does the greatest good and chooses the lesser evil in a given situation.[17]

14. Geisler, *Christian Ethics*, 103.
15. Geisler, *Christian Ethics*, 103.
16. Geisler, *Christian Ethics*, 104.
17. Geisler, *Christian Ethics*, 83.

Table 8.2. Three Assertions of the Graded Absolutist Position

1. Moral dilemmas are real.

2. Scriptural commands are "absolute" but are ranked hierarchically.

3. When scriptural commands conflict, one can be disobeyed without incurring sin.

How does the GA position evaluate the scriptural account of Rahab? It concludes that Rahab did exactly as she should have done. She faced a moral dilemma and acted in a manner that showed mercy to the spies and spared their lives. Because James and Hebrews indicate that she was motivated by faith, those who hold to the GA position consequently argue that she fulfilled the higher law in the situation and was therefore not guilty of sin even though she lied. In addition, she presumably should have had no cause whatsoever for remorse or second thought at having lied, since the "lower law" simply did not apply in this case. Simply put, the prohibition on lying did not apply in this particular situation. In support of this conclusion, the GA position claims that it need only point to the two New Testament discussions of Rahab (Heb. 11:31; James 2:25), which speak of her only in a positive light. Neither passage condemns her or even mentions the possibility that what she did was wrong.

Nonconflicting Absolutism (NCA)

Nonconflicting absolutism (NCA) is a second option that many evangelicals claim as the proper approach to understanding moral dilemmas.[18] In his article "Ethical Choices: A Case for Non-Conflicting Absolutism," Robert V. Rakestraw describes the NCA position in the following way:

> NCA holds that there will never be a situation in which obedience to one absolute will entail disobedience to or the setting-aside of another absolute. If a friend's life will almost certainly be taken by a gun-waving maniac unless I lie concerning my friend's whereabouts, whatever else I do I must not lie. The command to speak truthfully (Eph. 4:15) is an absolute that must not be violated. Nothing else I may do or should do to protect my friend is any more clear than my obligation to be truthful. I am obligated to protect my friend, because of God's absolute to love my

---

18. Among NCA's most ardent supporters are John Murray, *Principles of Conduct: Aspects of Biblical Ethics* (Grand Rapids: Eerdmans, 1957); William F. Luck, "Moral Conflicts and Evangelical Ethics," *Grace Theological Journal* 8, no. 1 (Spring 1987): 19–34; and Robert V. Rakestraw, "Ethical Choices: A Case for Non-Conflicting Absolutism," in *Theory and Method*, ed. David K. Clark and Robert V. Rakestraw, vol. 1 of *Readings in Christian Ethics* (Grand Rapids: Baker, 1994), 118–24.

neighbor as myself, but I am not to do it with lying. NCA holds that all relevant absolutes can and must be followed in situations of apparent conflict.[19]

In order to understand how Rakestraw (and other NCA adherents) reaches such a conclusion, one must first understand four fundamental components of this view.

First, "non-conflicting absolutism builds its entire structure upon the foundational principle that there are numerous ethical absolutes given by God."[20] William Luck, for example, points out that there are *at least* thirteen absolutes, which include the Ten Commandments, the "first and greatest of the commandments and the second like unto it," and the obligation to love.[21] In claiming a multiplicity of absolutes, NCA does not attempt to redefine what the word *absolute* means to make the system work. According to Rakestraw, scriptural absolutes are commands of God that "should never be broken, they are without exception or exemption, and they are universal in nature—that is, they morally obligate all people, in all places, in all times."[22]

Second, not only are there a multitude of absolutes, these absolutes never actually conflict in reality. Moral dilemmas or "tragic moral choices" simply do not exist.[23] While it may be true that moral situations can be complicated and that a person may be uncertain of the proper or best course of action (or inaction), NCA argues that there will never be a situation or circumstance that obligates the breaking or setting aside of one command in order to obey another. "NCA, while admitting the very real sense of conflict . . . , contends that the two absolutes do not conflict in such a way that one of them must be disobeyed or transcended."[24]

This is not to say that NCA construes solving ethical issues in a simple manner. Certainly, moral situations can be very complicated. Figuring out which Scriptures apply to a given scenario, and how to apply them, requires much thoughtful consideration. But NCA advocates argue that complications and inconveniences do not change the nature of the commands. When Scripture is clearly understood, there are no dilemmas. There are only difficulties in adequately understanding Scripture or the situation. The difficulty stems from lack of information, improper interpretation, or, perhaps, lack of spiritual maturity.[25]

In support of this conclusion, NCA proponents point, first of all, to the nature

19. Rakestraw, "Ethical Choices," 119.

20. Rakestraw, "Ethical Choices," 119.

21. Luck, "Moral Conflicts and Evangelical Ethics," 32.

22. Clark and Rakestraw, "Moral Dilemmas," 118.

23. John M. Frame, *Medical Ethics: Principles, Persons, and Problems* (Phillipsburg, NJ: Presbyterian and Reformed, 1988), 9.

24. Robert V. Rakestraw, "Ethical Choices: A Case for Non-Conflicting Absolutism," *Criswell Theological Review* 2, no. 2 (1988): 258. See also Luck, "Moral Conflicts and Evangelical Ethics," 21.

25. Frame, *Medical Ethics*, 10.

and character of God. If God's commands reflect his character, then to suggest that an actual conflict exists in the commands similarly suggests that God's nature also has an internal conflict. John Frame argues that "it is the application of Scripture that constitutes its meaning. Therefore if the applications are contradictory, then Scripture itself is contradictory."[26] By extension, NCA advocates argue that any real conflict between scriptural commands actually impugns the character of the Divine Lawgiver:

> Because God is holy, He cannot ever tempt us to sin. "When tempted, no one should say, 'God is tempting me.' For God cannot be tempted by evil, nor does He tempt anyone" (James 1:13). Probably none of us ever imagines that God is actively soliciting us to do evil, but we may feel that God has put us in a situation where we have no choice. . . . Do we sometimes feel we have no choice but to shade the truth a little, or commit just a slightly dishonest act? When we feel this way, we are in effect saying that God is tempting us to sin, that He has put us in a position where we have no alternative.[27]

The third fundamental component of NCA is an emphasis on a deontological methodology in ethics over and above consequentialist ethics. While NCA does not simply dismiss consideration of results, it never determines action based on projected consequences. Instead, the goodness of the moral act is determined by obedience to the One issuing the command regardless of the cost or results. Therefore, because God issues biblical commands that are absolute, NCA proponents argue that the primary emphasis in moral action should be on obedience to absolute commands regardless of the consequences. Rakestraw comments, "We follow a given norm first of all because it is good in itself to do so, not primarily because it appears that it will produce good effects."[28] For the NCA advocate, the final tabulation of results lies in the hands of God himself. While one should not completely disregard the importance of consequences, the fact that human foresight and predictive ability is limited also makes it wrong (or at least morally inferior) to try to determine the rightness or wrongness of an action based exclusively (or even primarily) on a projected analysis of possible conclusions. Such an evaluation is better left in the hands of an omniscient God. What is clear for finite image-bearers is the fact that God gave, via the commands of Scripture, the rules of life and practice to guide moral action. The chief responsibility of the moral agent is to obey those commands at face value.

---

26. Frame, *Medical Ethics*, 9n3.
27. Jerry Bridges, *The Pursuit of Holiness* (Colorado Springs: NavPress, 2001), 26–27.
28. Clark and Rakestraw, "Moral Dilemmas," 121.

Fourth, if God issues commands and then holds people morally accountable for them, then it follows that obeying his commands is actually possible. Therefore, *ought* implies *can*. If one cannot see exactly how to follow the commands, the problem does not lie in the commands or the One who issued them, but in the moral agency of the one struggling to know what to do. Given enough time and maturity, the Spirit-filled believer can avoid or work out all morally ambiguous situations without sin.

Table 8.3. Four Assertions of the Nonconflicting Absolutist Position

1. Scripture contains numerous absolute commands.

2. Scriptural commands never actually conflict (*moral dilemmas* are in fact only *apparent dilemmas*).

3. Proper moral decision-making is to be based on obedience, not on projected consequences.

4. If God gives a command, then it is always possible to obey it.

When applying NCA to the case with Rahab, two versions of the NCA argument have emerged. The first form of the argument is that even though she had proper intentionality, Rahab was wrong to do what she did because she lied, and lying is an abomination before the Lord and is contrary to his character. Simply put, if she had it to do over again, she should tell the truth regardless of anticipated consequences or simply remain silent. Her faith, when properly informed by the commands of God, ought to compel her to simply tell the truth or seek a nonsinful third way out. What she did in the particular act of intentionally misleading the soldiers by her false words was contrary to the nature of the God who is truth, and thus it transgressed the will of God. If she had told the truth, then one can rest assured that God, in his omnipotent sovereignty, could have chosen to save the spies by some other means that we cannot now know and Rahab could not at the time foresee. Yes, she is exemplified later *for her faith*, even though certain aspects of how she put her faith into action was sinful and incurred moral guilt.[29]

29. J. Douma comments: "To us it seems impossible to claim (as many have claimed) that the midwives and Rahab were praised for their faith, but not for their lies. For their faith was expressed precisely in their works. It is an abstraction to disconnect the effect of their acts from the path they took to achieve that effect." J. Douma, *The Ten Commandments* (Phillipsburg, NJ: P&R Publishing, 1996), 327. While his critique may be correct that such an argument requires an abstraction in order to make the point, such an argument does not thereby disprove the point that NCA is trying to make. As the cases with Uzzah in 2 Samuel 6 and Jesus' words to the tomblike Pharisees (Matt. 23:4, 27) indicate, there is a very real distinction between act and motive. Discounting such a distinction by calling it an abstraction is not sufficient to deny the important point that NCA is trying to convey with this line of reasoning.

A second way that some nonconflicting absolutists try to resolve the Rahab argument is to suggest that Rahab did not actually lie, though she directly and intentionally gave false information to the soldiers to mislead them. This form of argumentation depends on the definition of *lying* and how best to interpret the ninth commandment to "not bear false witness." David W. Jones's argument is a good example of this: "As it is given in Scripture, the ninth commandment focuses on truth-telling in a legally binding format, such as in a court of law before a judge, where another's well-being is at stake."[30] While less persuasive, if this definition of *lying* holds, then an NCA proponent could argue that the command of truth-telling does not apply to the case of Rahab and that "Rahab's deception was not a violation of a moral absolute at all."[31]

Ideal Absolutism (IA)

Whereas GA affirms the real experience of moral dilemmas and attempts to solve them by creating a hierarchical view of scriptural norms, and NCA seeks to affirm the reality of multiple moral absolutes but denies the existence of real moral dilemmas, ideal absolutism (IA) attempts to affirm both the real experience of moral dilemmas and the existence of multiple moral absolutes. IA adopts a central point from both GA and NCA in order to arrive at a third alternative conclusion. How it does so and the conclusion it reaches require an understanding of the basic premises adopted by its adherents.

First, the ideal absolutist affirms that Scripture is simple to understand and straightforward. Absolute commands are absolute in the plain meaning of the word. If a clear exception is built into the text, only then does a command have an exception. Otherwise, it remains universally binding. To claim anything else is incoherent.

Systems of interpretation that allow exceptions or exemptions not explicit in Scripture run the risk of being simply human fabrications attempting to deal with the hard reality that fallen humans face in real life. IA holds that moral systems tampering with the absolute nature of God's commands are at best noble in their attempt to deal with difficult issues but misguided in the approach. At worst, they represent the extremes of pharisaical legalism or antinomian license. Either way, they wrongly attempt to mask the pervasive nature of sin that cripples fallen image-bearers. In contrast, the IA position argues that "it is simply always wrong

---

30. David W. Jones, *An Introduction to Biblical Ethics* (Nashville: B&H Academic, 2013), 190.

31. Jones, 104. Such a perspective, of course, raises significant questions related to both the ninth commandment and the definition of lying. For example, how does one justify the caveat regarding the ninth commandment only being applicable to a situation like a court of law? Why would truth-telling in a "legally binding format" be more important than any other setting? How would purposely giving untrue data for the purpose deception comport with the character of a God who identifies himself as "truth" (John 14:6)?

to break an absolute moral law of God. There are no exceptions, exemptions or divine immunity. Absolute moral laws are absolute, and that is that."[32]

Second, IA affirms that genuine moral conflicts do take place. Moral dilemmas are real. The fall and the resulting sin nature affect both human individuals and the context in which they live. This, in turn, leads to inevitable conflicts between exceptionless commands. Thus, fallen sinners live in an inherently evil setting in which absolute moral laws can come into inevitable conflict. "God has given many universal and absolute moral norms. Ideally—that is, apart from sin—these absolutes do not conflict. But because sin pervades this world and ourselves, God's absolutes will sometimes actually conflict."[33] In the words of Helmut Thielicke, "the most distinguishing feature of this state of injustice and illegality is to be found in the inescapable conflict of values for which there is no clear solution, so that whichever way I go I am guilty."[34]

It is important to note that most ideal absolutists reject the idea that the existence of moral dilemmas impugns the nature of God or his Word per se. Without sin, or before the fall, no moral dilemma would exist. There is no lack of integrity in God or his Word. Human application of God's Word, however, does lack integrity because fallen humans in a sinful world sometimes fail to apply the Scripture correctly. Thielicke comments that moral conflict results from "the complex of wrong decisions which lie behind us, which have their ultimate root in that primal decision recorded in the story of the Fall."[35] We are guilty of creating the very context that puts us in morally complex situations in the first place.

The key point that separates this view of sin from that of the NCA position is the emphasis on the enduring stain of the fall on human intent, character, act, and consequence. Whereas NCA suggests that sin leads to a crisis of knowledge, IA takes the issue a step further and argues that the problem of sin causes real conflict to occur between absolute commands—conflict in which there is no "third way" out. As a result, to try to deny the reality of dilemmas is to deny the reality of sin and the fall.

Third, when these situations of inevitable moral conflict occur, sin is unavoidable. All humans remain accountable at all times to exceptionless moral commands. When faced with a real moral dilemma, the moral agent must decide to follow one of the commands and thereby transgress the other. The best one can do in such a situation is to choose the option that results in the perceived greater good, with the recognition that he or she is simultaneously committing a lesser

32. Geisler, *Christian Ethics*, 89.

33. Clark and Rakestraw, "Moral Dilemmas," 115.

34. Helmut Thielicke, *Foundations*, vol. 1 of *Theological Ethics*, ed. William H. Lazareth (Philadelphia: Fortress Press, 1966), 583.

35. Thielicke, *Foundations*, 596.

evil. IA affirms that even though the person may have behaved in the best possible way, he or she has still sinned. Luck describes the situation well: "IA simply tells the person caught in conflict which moral obligation to follow and which to disobey, and leaves the morality and immorality up to the rules themselves."[36]

What about scriptural references that seem to negate the possibility of this third point in relation to believers? For example, doesn't Paul suggest that there will always be a "way of escape"? This question gets to the heart of how IA is most commonly misunderstood and therefore deserves a bit of attention. First Corinthians 10:13 reads, "No temptation has overtaken you but such as is common to man; and God is faithful, who will not allow you to be tempted beyond what you are able, but with the temptation will provide the way of escape also, so that you will be able to endure it." The apostle Paul wrote this passage in the context of encouraging the Corinthian believers to avoid the moral and spiritual mistakes made by the Israelites during their wilderness journey. The passage seems to address the temptation toward sinful pursuits and relates to both intent and behavior. Further, the particular language of a "way of escape" does seem to imply an ability to avoid particular sin in the particular context. So the relevant question for those supporting IA is: Does IA in effect support a form of moral fatalism that denies the "way of escape" that Paul discusses in 1 Corinthians 10:13?

IA holds that application of this passage describes most moral situations that Christians face. It does not deny, however, the possible reality of moral dilemmas. The reason for this is that the passage speaks of avoiding *temptation*, not avoiding *sin*. Indeed, IA agrees that it is never right to pursue or desire sin or foster temptation to commit sin. The IA position would also assert, however, that in rare situations, while pursuing God in holiness and proper motive, someone may be faced with a context in which he or she is not "tempted" to sin, but is nevertheless forced to sin by the nature of the moral dilemma that he or she is facing. The problem is not one's motivation or temptation to sin, but the reality that the situation does not allow the person to escape, having to choose a way that will leave him or her guilty. Thus, IA would argue that the "way of escape" referred to in 1 Corinthians 10:13 is to focus on that which one *can* do with *no desire* to break God's command. Since it is impossible to obey all the commands, the way of escape is to do that which is best and avoid temptation to choose the lesser good in any given scenario.

While some may suggest that this is just a battle of semantics, careful examination shows that this is not the case. The reason for this relates directly to the *telos* domain of moral evaluation and how it shapes one's *intentionality*. If the underlying motive of the moral agent is to please God and this motive is expressed in obedience to the command in the best way possible, then 1 Corinthians 10:13 has

---

36. Luck, "Moral Conflicts and Evangelical Ethics," 27.

been fulfilled. This is not to say that the person is exonerated from breaking the "lower command," as proponents of GA insist, but that the behavior should not be described as intending evil or "giving in to temptation." In this case, the moral agent does not want to sin and works hard to avoid it, but is limited by the effects of the fall on the moral circumstances and cannot escape sinning because of the context imposed on him or her. In the same moment, the moral agent is to act boldly to achieve the best result possible while simultaneously recognizing the need to cry for mercy in light of being a fallen person in a fallen world making a fallen choice.

Table 8.4. Three Assertions of the Ideal Absolutist Position

1. Scriptural commands are absolute and should be plainly understood.

2. Genuine moral conflicts do take place (moral dilemmas are real) *in a fallen world*.

3. When scriptural commands conflict, one must choose to obey the one that most highly honors God but is by default guilty of disobeying the other command.

When this evaluation is applied to Rahab's situation described in Joshua 2, the ideal absolutist would point out that Rahab was in a situation in which either she had to lie to protect the lives of the spies or she would have to allow the men to be caught and thus be responsible for being a part of harming the people of God. To remain silent would have been an omission of mercy to God's people. Thus, the best she could do, the act that entailed the least amount of evil, was to lie regarding the whereabouts of the spies.

If one looks closely at the biblical texts in both Hebrews and James related to Rahab's actions, one will discover that nowhere do these texts explicitly indicate that God blessed her for lying. Rather, they specifically indicate that God blessed Rahab's faith-filled intention to honor and bless the people of God. This blessing does not mean that it was somehow okay for her to lie. Rather, she remains guilty of that sin. In fact, nowhere does Scripture actually and explicitly exonerate her of it. In contrast, in every place in Scripture where lying is directly addressed, it is portrayed in a negative light. In fact, Scripture even directly states that God hates lying.[37] Using narrative texts such as Exodus 1 and Joshua 2 to affirm that lying is at times permissible is to beg the question. A better understanding, according to IA, is that God is gracious even toward the sinner. Even though Rahab's specific choice to lie was wrong, God honors her faith and attempt to bless his people.

---

37. See, for example, Proverbs 6:16–19; 12:22; and 21:8, which describe God's hatred for lying. Also consider passages such as John 8:44 and Acts 5:3, which associate lying with satanic influence.

Thus, her faith in welcoming the spies and sending them out makes her a person worthy to be mentioned in Hebrews 11. But having said this, there should also be no doubt that she needed to repent of her sin of lying.

Do Moral Dilemmas Exist? The Need for Reexamination

Given these three approaches, how should one think about the problem of so-called moral dilemmas? How does ethics as worship help us navigate through complex, difficult, and ambiguous moral situations and contexts so as to maximize the glory of God? We believe the key lies in a proper understanding of the devastating impact of the fall and the hope-filled doctrine of progressive sanctification.

For whatever reason, most discourses on the problem of moral dilemmas have consistently failed to address the issue in terms of one's epistemological ability before and after Christian conversion. As a result, there is a failure to emphasize the full impact of sin on human moral agency. Likewise, there is an apparent underestimation and lack of explanation of the struggle involved in the process of moral sanctification. Hope for the believer lies not in the simple statement that moral dilemmas do not actually exist, or the unlikely possibility that absolute commands are not absolutely binding when other weightier absolutes are encountered in a given context. Rather, hope for the believer is found in the progressive work of the Holy Spirit to finish the work begun at salvation (Phil. 1:6).

Particularly related to the issue of moral dilemmas, a Christian's hope stems from the positive effects of salvation and grace on the moral reasoning of Spirit-filled disciples of Christ. Put in simpler terms, while the contrast between a person's ability to see and understand reality before and after regeneration is often understressed, it is nonetheless dramatic and deserves our attention. Scripture clearly emphasizes a radical distinction between the epistemological ability of believers and unbelievers. That is, while there is no doubt that general revelation allows all humans to see moral absolutes, actually understanding the nature, purpose, and function of these absolutes requires the illumination of the Holy Spirit. Further, Scripture indicates that before regeneration takes place, a person is simply unable to see and interpret reality correctly. After conversion, however, regenerate sinners are given "the mind of Christ" (1 Cor. 2:16) and have the actual potential to grow in their understanding of reality, as well as in the application of moral absolutes to their lives in an increasingly accurate light (2 Peter 1:3–10).

In the remainder of the chapter, it is our hope to make the case that understanding the regenerative and transformative power of the gospel is the key to understanding and working out the problem of moral dilemmas. To make this case, we lay out six foundational premises that form the basis of a position that we describe as *humble absolutism* (HA) and then offer both a practical motivation and a practical methodology for working through morally complex situations.

Constructing the Humble Absolutist Position: Six Basic Premises

Table 8.5 summarizes the epistemological assumptions of the position we develop below. The six premises that follow lay the foundation for the position and provide the basis for constructing practical steps to determine action when facing morally complex scenarios.

Table 8.5. The Human Mind and Moral Dilemmas

Prefallen Humans	Postfallen Humans	Regenerate Believers	Believers in Eschaton
Innocent	Unregenerate	Regenerate (Positional & Progressive Sanctification)	Glorified (Perfect Sanctification)
Human minds unstained by sin and depravity	Darkened in understanding	Given the mind of Christ	Eternal reality revealed in full
No appearance of moral dilemmas	Moral dilemmas are real in agent's experience	Moral dilemmas are only apparent	No moral dilemmas
Genesis 1–2 Romans 1:19–20	Romans 1:21–23, 28 1 Corinthians 2:14	1 Corinthians 2:15–16 2 Peter 1:3–10	1 Corinthians 13:12 2 Corinthians 3:18

Premise 1: God's Character and Word Are Perfect

In order for an ethic to be truly Christian, it must begin with truths about God and evaluate all experiences in light of his self-revelation. This is so for at least three reasons. First, while the experience of a moral dilemma may *feel* real, evaluation whether a moral dilemma can actually occur or whether it is only an apparent dilemma must first be subjugated to what God reveals about himself and his Word. Among the many splendid attributes that God reveals about himself, he makes it clear that he is eternal, wise, good, and without fault or blemish. Scripture, as part of God's self-revelation, reflects these attributes. Indeed, because Jesus is God incarnate and the Word made flesh, to impugn the Scripture is to impugn the nature of God.

Because it reflects God's nature, Scripture is a source of true and enduring wisdom beyond that available from any earthly source. "Your commandments make me wiser than my enemies," the psalmist declares. "I have more insight than all my teachers" (Ps. 119:98–99). Adherence to God's laws provides direction like a lamp lighting a dark path (Ps. 119:105). Likewise, Scripture reflects God's goodness and love (Ps. 119:39).

As we pointed out more robustly in chapter 5, there is no contradiction in Scripture. Rather, like God, Scripture is perfect, and adherence to it provides benefits to the human soul (Ps. 19:7). Obeying God's law displays the truest form of love for God. Jesus himself stated, "He who has My commandments and keeps them is the one who loves Me" (John 14:21). He also comments, "Whoever then annuls one of the least of these commandments, and teaches others to do the same, shall be called least in the kingdom of heaven; but whoever keeps and teaches them, he shall be called great in the kingdom of heaven" (Matt. 5:19). Diligence in adherence to the Word of God is the proper expression of practical wisdom (Ps. 119:4).

Because God's words are fixed and immutable, like God himself, it is unwise to suggest, as do those who hold to both the graded absolutist (GA) and the ideal absolutist (IA) positions, that a real change somehow happens to God's perfect law as a result of sin, so that after the fall, God's perfect commands now somehow conflict in reality. John Frame rightly argues that "the character of God as a wise, compassionate, and powerful lawgiver is called into question by the notion of conflicting absolutes."[38] Therefore, the Word of God is wholly perfect as God himself is—there is no conflict in the Word.

Second, Jesus' rather clear statements about the enduring nature of the law in the Sermon on the Mount (Matt. 5:17–20) indicate not only that there are multiple moral absolutes in Scripture, but also that God's moral commands are unchanging and binding in nature:

> Do not think that I came to abolish the Law or the Prophets; I did not come to abolish but to fulfill. For truly I say to you, until heaven and earth pass away, not the smallest letter or stroke shall pass from the Law until all is accomplished. Whoever then annuls one of the least of these commandments, and teaches others to do the same, shall be called least in the kingdom of heaven; but whoever keeps and teaches them, he shall be called great in the kingdom of heaven.
>
> For I say to you that unless your righteousness surpasses that of the scribes and Pharisees, you will not enter the kingdom of heaven.

For this reason, unless a clear built-in exception to a given command is relevant to the situation at hand, strict adherence to the direct-action command in the face of an apparent moral dilemma is the proper indication and expression of love for God. For example, if the command requires that I do not lie, yet in a particular

---

38. Frame, *Medical Ethics*, 9.

context I predict that my lying will result in undesirable consequences, the clear command is not to be outweighed by the prediction of a possible (or even probable) outcome. As the text indicates, annulling *even the least* of God's commands is deplorable in the eyes of Jesus. Thus, critics of the graded absolutist position (GA) are right to point out that an appeal to any form of hierarchical ranking of commands that is not clearly built into the text, or clearly listed and explained, is dangerous and improperly asserts reasoned prediction above commandment and thus denigrates the nature of absolute commands.

Third, and directly following from the previous point, when doing ethics, the moral agent will by default appeal to one or many sources of authority in order to justify or support the position taken on any given issue. Generally speaking, an appeal will usually be made to one of four sources—Scripture, tradition, reason, or experience.[39] In order for an ethical system to be truly biblical, it must have at its core a commitment to Scripture as the primary source of authority from and by which all ethical decisions are made. This is not to deny that reasoning, tradition, and experience ought to play significant roles in the process of moral determination, but it is to affirm that Scripture is the ultimate authority in all ethical debates. Any suggestion that abrogating a moral absolute does not incur guilt is a subjugation of the biblical source of authority to one of the other three sources. Too often, it is the case that the experience of a dilemma drives the reasoning about Scripture instead of Scripture's driving the reasoning about experience. As we pointed out in the previous chapter, the theological/normative domains of ethics must have primacy over the pastoral/contextual domains.

A theocentric perspective on ethics resists the temptation to begin ethical inquiry with the particulars of a case and move inductively up to a general principle. Richard Weaver points out that "the denial of universals carries with it the denial of everything transcending experience. The denial of everything transcending experience means inevitably—though ways are found to hedge on this—the denial of truth. With the denial of objective truth there is no escape from relativism of 'man the measure of all things.'"[40] One must begin by emphasizing that the determination of truth in moral behavior must begin with what God has revealed about the nature of reality and move from those truths to particular action points—and not the other way around. This is the only way to enter morally confusing situations.

To put this in clearer theological terms, the believer must begin with the nature and character of God, and ask how scriptural absolutes are a reflection of his immutable nature. Moral behavior, even when human perspective might indicate

---

39. For an interesting discussion of this premise, see Thomas C. Oden, *The Living God*, vol. 1 of *Systematic Theology* (Peabody, MA: Hendriksen, 2008), 330–39. See also our discussion on this topic in chapters 1 and 5.

40. Richard M. Weaver, *Ideas Have Consequences* (Chicago: University of Chicago Press, 1948), 4.

otherwise, must be determined on the basis of the eternal and unchanging nature of God as he reveals himself through the commands of Scripture. When faced with difficult moral choices, Christ's disciples must choose to obey rather than sacrifice (1 Sam. 15:22; Ps. 40:4–6). Christians are to rely on the God who exhibits commands reflecting his character traits in times of moral uncertainty and not rely on their own understanding (Prov. 3:4–5).

Premise 2: Fallen Sinners Are Blinded by Sin

The problem of sin is real and pervasive. Scripture indicates that human beings not only experience guilt because of personal acts of sin, but also share in a sin nature. In addition to the problem of *sins*, humans face the reality of *sin* (i.e., all of us are *sinners*). Not only must a consideration of moral dilemmas include an attempt to avoid particular sins, it must also recognize the blinding and debilitating power of sin that can render even the best deeds as nothing more than "filthy rags" before the Lord (Isa. 64:6 NKJV). Left to our own devices, humans experience an existence marked by finiteness, fallenness, fallibility, and frustration.

When considering the problem of moral dilemmas, it is important not to underestimate the extent of the devastation that sin causes. Unfortunately, many of the discussions on moral dilemmas tend to address human experience as though the fall were a minor event. It is treated as though a person standing on the edge of a small stream loses her footing and gets a bit wet and dirty. With some effort and perhaps a little help, she will be able to extricate herself and go on her way. She may be a bit more uncomfortable, but she will still be able to function in relatively the same way as before she fell in.

If one mistakenly treats the fall as a stumble into a creek, then the effect on moral reasoning will appear minimal. The moral distinction between prefall humans (or unfallen Jesus) will also appear minimal. The plain truth is that a small estimation of the fall results in a small distinction in the moral ability between Christ and the fallen sinner. Further, a small estimation of the fallenness of humanity leads to a small estimation of humankind's need for a Savior or the ongoing need for reliance on God's grace.

In order to depict the effects of the sinful human condition more accurately, one must liken the fall to a plummet into the Grand Canyon or even a step off the edge of the universe. Such a depiction rightly emphasizes the severe tainting of human moral reasoning as well as the vast moral distinction between prefall humans (Adam and Eve) or unfallen Jesus from the rest of humanity after the fall. In regard to moral dilemmas, we must recognize that a moral situation that may have been easily understandable and navigable to an untarnished mind becomes confusing and blurred to the sin-stained mind. Moral action that was once possible is now perceived to be impossible unless, or until, it is aided by grace.

Too often, moral evaluations are made one-dimensionally with an isolated focus on a particular point of action. A perspective that takes into consideration both the proximate and ultimate picture, however, would see the action in light of the larger context of the human race and the fallen nature of the one who is acting. Consider once again the following diagram (see fig. 8.1) to help see the point.

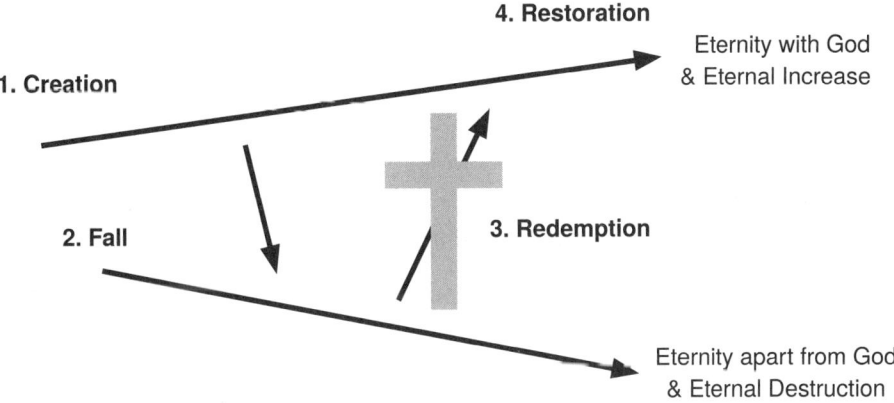

Fig. 8.1. Man's Trajectory Restored

When one makes the attempt to evaluate a moral act without considering it in the context of the larger scriptural metanarrative and a fallen human race, the ethical theory functions artificially as though the fallen stage of history were not only the prevailing one, but also the defining one. But to limit our view of the discussion only to this fallen stage of history is to wrongly divorce the discipline of ethics from God's revealed reality about the nature of his character and the full nature of the world he created. When this takes place, evaluation of moral behavior is wrongly separated from its larger metaphysical and theological context. A typical result of this limited perspective is the suggestion that one must have "freedom to choose" in order to be held accountable for an act or behavior. But such a conclusion unduly neglects the fact that we are guilty of creating the very environment that causes us to experience moral dilemmas in the first place. Again, Helmut Thielicke sheds an important light on this contextual reality: "This guilt consists in the fact that our origin and point of departure is always to be found in a complex of wrong decisions, those made by ourselves and others. . . . It is due rather to the complex of wrong decisions which lie behind us, which have their ultimate root in that primal decision recorded in the story of the fall."[41]

Far from being exonerated or deemed "personally guiltless" by this lack of

---

41. Thielicke, *Foundations*, 596.

freedom, we are all the more guilty because of it. To neglect this point is to create a moral methodology with an anemic view of sin, an underestimation of participation in the fall (Rom. 5:12–21), and our moment-by-moment need for the cross. Moral evaluation that takes into consideration a more holistic view of sin requires that in addition to the act, one must consider the theological status of the agent. The problem of moral dilemmas does not simply relate to the question of *sins*, but also involves evaluation in light of the fact that we are all *sinners* who also then create cultural and social contexts that are impacted by sinful ideas and darkened perspectives.

Recognizing this larger perspective on guilt and sin is foundational to the problem of moral dilemmas, for it is precisely the status as sinner that drastically affects the human ability to rightly perceive all the factors when facing apparent moral-dilemma situations. A focus that simply tries to avert particular *sins* without recognition of the broader category of *sin nature* (or the possible resulting embedded sin patterns in culture) will inevitably result in a misdiagnosis of the problem. It will also create a moral system that is the equivalent of putting a bandage over a lethal wound. For fallen, unregenerate humans, "personal guilt-lessness" is impossible.

Premise 3: Moral Dilemmas Are Existentially Real to Unbelievers

The apostle Paul indicates that fallen sinners experience the moral life "in the futility of their mind, being darkened in their understanding, excluded from the life of God because of the ignorance that is in them, because of the hardness of their heart" (Eph. 4:17–18). What, then, can a fallen image-bearer know about the situation he is facing, and how does that (lack of) knowledge affect the way he behaves in a morally complex situation? Before regeneration, one's sinful state leaves the moral agent in a condition in which moral dilemmas become *real in the experience* of the person, who, unaided by grace, finds himself without the ability to solve the problem.[42] Real, finite, fallen human persons are faced with moral dilemmas not because God's Word conflicts with itself, but because the fall leaves them unable to see the world correctly or understand the full nature of moral truth. Fallen humans are unable to see how Scripture could otherwise be perfectly applied in such a way that no dilemma occurs. As Paul indicates in 1 Corinthians 2:14, the non-Christian ("natural man") "does not accept the things of the Spirit of God, for they are foolishness to him; and he *cannot* understand them, because they are spiritually appraised."

---

42. While this point is vital for understanding the life situation of everyday moral persons, claiming that something is *real in experience* is very different from claiming that actual moral dilemmas exist. The distinction is that experience indicates the situation only from the existential perspective of the moral agent, but tells us nothing about actual reality seen from a completely objective point of view.

More than just a simple crisis of knowledge, this is the actual position of fallen image-bearers from which there is no escape in this world short of the miracle of regeneration and salvation. While it is true that the Word of God is without conflict and adequate for every situation, and while it is also true that the Holy Spirit leads believers into all truth, providing a way of escape, it is likewise true that unregenerate humans apart from grace are without these necessary resources.

In practical experience, unregenerate persons in this world do face morally complicated situations with no ability to solve them. Real people in a real fallen world have the real *experience* of moral dilemmas that as fallen, finite beings they cannot solve. In this sense, and this sense only, it is accurate to say that moral dilemmas are "real." Helmut Thielicke's comment, at least on this point, rightly indicates what nonbelievers experience: "the dilemma, the ambiguity is not due to any lack of clarity in the divine commandments themselves. It is due to the mist of the aeon, in which a clear beam of light becomes a diffused cloud of light."[43] This diffusion that Thielicke speaks of is not suggesting that there is a problem with the clear light of Scripture itself. Rather, nonbelievers' ability to rightly perceive and apply the clear teachings of Scripture is now darkened and depraved.

Premise 4: The Gospel Is Central to Ethical Evaluation

Needless to say, such an emphasis on sin and depravity places humans in a very needy position. No possibility of boasting remains. Working through moral dilemmas requires a humble pursuit of the cross. Scripture attests that all humans have sinned and that the compensation for sin is death (Rom. 3:23a; 6:23). Human moral ability is a shell of what it was intended to be. Even when actions seem to line up with scriptural demands, Scripture indicates that the motivations of the heart are often ignoble and self-seeking (Matt. 23:27).

Rightly understanding the blinding nature of sin shifts the central focus of ethics away from an individual's supposed ability to comply with the law, or to reason it away by the application of a hierarchical scheme, to an emphasis on one's need for the gospel. When rightly understood, the devastating reality of sin highlights both the human need for a Savior and the ongoing need of grace in the moral life. What becomes clear is that in order for a person to live an ethical life, he or she must abide in a continuously humble reliance on grace and the filling of the Holy Spirit to illuminate the moral life. One must live under forgiveness both for personal sin choices and for the whole theological context of the sin nature of which every human, save Christ, partakes. As Thielicke wisely puts it:

---

43. Helmut Thielicke, "The Borderline Situation of Extreme Conflict," in *Theology and Method*, ed. David K. Clark and Robert V. Rakestraw, vol. 1 of *Readings in Christian Ethics* (Grand Rapids: Baker, 1994), 129.

I stand under forgiveness not merely in respect of what is traditionally called "actual sin," but also in respect of the whole structural nexus of my situation. I bring to the reconciling sign of the cross not merely my own "individual sins"— indeed such an abstraction is impossible—but "the guilt of the world." For I am a participant in the guilt of the "one man" Adam (Rom. 5:12), and I cannot be "in Christ" until I have first seen myself to be "in Adam" (1 Cor. 15:22).[44]

In other words, the gospel must be placed in the central place of priority for ethics to be properly ordered as worship. For it is only through the gospel that the means become available for Christians to have access to a rightly ordered knowledge and understanding of the world. Further, it is through the gospel that a Christian receives the mind of Christ by which he or she can appraise all things rightly:

> But he who is spiritual appraises all things, yet he himself is appraised by no one. For who has known the mind of the Lord, that he will instruct Him? But we have the mind of Christ. (1 Cor. 2:15–16)

Properly understanding the devastation of the fall is the necessary precondition for a proper appreciation of the forgiveness made available through Christ's sacrificial death. The gospel becomes the foundation on which progressive sanctification occurs, by which our hearts and minds are renewed, and then serves as the pivot point for understanding and resolving the problem of moral dilemmas.

Premise 5: Moral Dilemmas Are Apparent Only for Believers

As has been shown, before salvation, moral dilemmas can be understood as being "real" in the experience of the unregenerate moral agent due to epistemological darkening. But because of God's gracious salvation, the Christian now has the capacity to see reality with new eyes, and with progressive sanctification taking place, he or she progressively understands that moral dilemmas are only apparent in nature. There is no conflict in the nature of God. And there is no conflict in his Word.

If this is true, then two important conclusions would seem to follow. First, one would expect that if a person remained unstained by sin, then he or she would be able to face all manner of temptations and situations and yet be able to rise above them. This is, in fact, the claim of Scripture in regard to Jesus—the only human being completely unstained by sin. Hebrews 4:15 states, "For we do not have a high priest who cannot sympathize with our weaknesses, but One who has been tempted in all things as we are, yet without sin."

44. Thielicke, *Foundations*, 597.

Jesus was able to negotiate, without error or sin, situations that fallen humans get lost in (apparent moral dilemmas). Thus, he faced all the situations *as we do*, but he did not face them as a sinner, *as we do*. While the sinful human condition may cause an apparent dilemma in which Scripture seems to conflict and demand opposing actions, one who is sinless—even in his humanity alone—would be able to see and understand how the law works perfectly all the time.

Second, if moral dilemmas are in reality only apparent, then Christians, who are now given the mind of Christ, should also be able to find a way of escape with practice and maturity as they become increasingly conformed to the image of Christ. This is consistent with scriptural affirmation: "No temptation has overtaken you but such as is common to man; and God is faithful, who will not allow you to be tempted beyond what you are able, but with the temptation will provide the way of escape also, so that you will be able to endure it" (1 Cor. 10:13).

Premise 6: Progressive Transformation

When seen through the perspective of the gospel and its transforming power, what once appeared as actual moral dilemmas (to the unregenerate) can now be rightly seen as morally complex situations that do not necessitate the transgression of absolute commands. This newly granted ability that comes with regeneration does not, however, guarantee that the Christian will no longer have difficult moral situations to work through. Nor does it guarantee that the Christian will always proceed successfully. It simply means that now he or she has the necessary means to negotiate a particular situation without having to sin or conjure up fanciful hierarchies to explain away moral absolutes.

Upon salvation, God declares that the believer is a new creation (2 Cor. 5:17), has access to the Holy Spirit's power to live the Christian life (Eph. 5:18), and therefore can have "the mind of Christ" to face all manner of situations (1 Cor. 2:16). Scripture also indicates that realizing these truths is a process that requires transformation, growth, and effort (Phil. 3:12–13). Progressive sanctification is the process of becoming in character and practice what God has declared a Christian to be in truth.

In regard to moral dilemmas, salvation marks the beginning of an epistemological revolution. The Christian's experience should be one of progressive transformation of the mind (Rom. 12:1–2). Through a continual renewal and transformation of the mind enabled by the power of the Holy Spirit, a Christian can attain "to all the wealth that comes from the full assurance of understanding, resulting in a true knowledge of God's mystery, that is, Christ Himself, in whom are hidden all the treasures of wisdom and knowledge" (Col. 2:2–3). While this scriptural truth brings great hope, one must keep in mind that because of the lingering effects of the fall, the perspective of the believer will often be clouded as if

Table 8.6. Six Assertions of the Humble Absolutist Position

1. Scripture contains numerous absolute commands, which never conflict.

2. Human sinners are blinded by sin.

3. Moral dilemmas are existentially/experientially "real" to nonbelievers.

4. Regeneration enables greater epistemological clarity.

5. Moral dilemmas are in actuality only apparent dilemmas for believers.

6. God brings about a progressive moral transformation such that believers improve in their ability to see and work out morally complex situations.

one gazes to see the true nature of things but it appears that he or she is looking "in a mirror dimly" (1 Cor. 13:12). The hope, however, is that progressively, as one seeks guidance from Christ, there will be a transformation (2 Cor. 3:18).

Ultimately, only Scripture and the illumination from the Holy Spirit (in agreement with Scripture) can truly augment the wisdom necessary to see through apparent moral dilemmas. Christians have an epistemological advantage over all other humans because the Word of God functions as a lamp to guide believers through the journey of life (Ps. 119:105). The role of Scripture, then, is crucial to solving moral dilemmas, for it functions not only to preserve society and convict of sinfulness, but also as a positive guide in the moral decision-making process.

The problem is that while Christians enjoy the passive righteousness of Christ, the positional sanctification given to them as a gift at salvation (2 Cor. 5:21), and freedom from condemnation (Rom. 8:1), the stain of sin enduringly taints earthly existence and prevents complete sinlessness in practice. Humble absolutism emphasizes that human depravity limits human moral understanding and ability throughout one's earthly existence.

Believers over time should become progressively better at seeing apparent moral dilemmas in a new light and be able to handle these apparent dilemmas in a manner that honors and upholds all the commands bearing on the situation. But this is not to suggest an eventual moral perfection before heaven. Progressive sanctification (as opposed to actual or *positional* sanctification) is a process, not an event. As such, it takes time, struggle, and effort. Also, it involves failure and forgiveness. It requires holy sweat. In fact, while a believer might become more able to work through apparent moral dilemmas, only in the eschaton is there hope for full transformation (1 Cor. 13:12). The experience in this life is like jumping into the ocean and swimming toward the horizon. Actual progress is made, but the reality of the distance makes actual completion impossible here. Only when the Christian sees Christ face to face will he or she be transformed into his likeness. The mirror will no longer be dim. Only then, presumably, will Christians have a clear understanding of how they could have avoided sin in each and every morally ambiguous situation faced.

Methodology: Applying the Humble Absolutist Position

Practical Motivation: Ethics as Worship

The solution presented by the graded absolutist position in the face of apparent moral dilemmas is to treat Scripture as *prima facie* norms and through a process of reasoned analysis determine which of the norms produces the greatest good. Such a position undermines the integrity and character of the absolute commands of Scripture and, by default, diminishes the moral ground of Scripture. The typical nonconflicting absolutist solution suggests that there are no such things as moral dilemmas and thereby discounts the everyday experience of moral persons. Ideal absolutists suggest that humans cannot escape sin and thus deny the power of the gospel to enable the believer to overcome sin in particular circumstances.

How, then, is one to act when faced with what appears to be an actual moral dilemma? In regard to the motive and direction of one's action, Scripture is clear. Jesus told his disciples that the greatest command is this:

> "Love the Lord your God with all your heart, and with all your soul, and with all your mind, and with all your strength." The second is this, "You shall love your neighbor as yourself." There is no other commandment greater than these. (Mark 12:30–31)

In keeping with this, humble absolutism recognizes that the proper motivation for all moral action is to first and foremost order one's actions to God in loving worship, become the kind of person who loves God reflexively in character when faced with all moral situations, and then behave in a manner that expresses obedience first and foremost as love for God. In other words, the greatest commandment should be understood primarily as a directional and motivational command, not as a rule determining hierarchy of action commands. That is, while there is no doubt that it is given as a command imperative, it is a command that directs the motive and intent of one's heart. It is meant not to pit certain laws against others in a graded ranking, but to guide one's motivations in acting.

How, then, does one know how to act in a manner that is directed in a heartfelt love for God? Jesus tells us! The material content of this command to love finds expression through obedience to the particular deontological commands given in Scripture. This is why Jesus proclaims in John 14:21, "He who has My commandments and *keeps* them, is the one who loves Me." For this reason, humble absolutism flows from a deontological virtue ethic in which the stress on rule-keeping is always cast in light of the highest motivation to love God with all that one is.

Breaking commands, regardless of the intent or some reasoned hierarchy, does not properly express love. Rather, the virtue of love is most clearly expressed through the deontological commands present in Scripture. In other words, one can know what true love is only by knowing and keeping the commands that Jesus taught. The behavioral commands (such as "speak the truth in love") give specific content to the primary, directional, and motivational command to love God. They show the believer how to put material content to the general command to love God. It is as if Jesus commands us to be a loving person and then goes on to indicate that the way to become that person is to practice obedience to the commands of Scripture through the power of the Holy Spirit. In light of our ethical methodology for ethics as worship, this is why the three moral domains in the theological/normative cluster must be kept together as a cluster and placed in priority over the pastoral/contextual domains.

In keeping with this, 1 Corinthians 10:31 indicates that no matter what actions or behaviors a person engages in, everything ought to be done for the glory of God. Above all else, moral determinations in the midst of apparent moral dilemmas must seek to demonstrate love for God and glorify his name. Moral decision-making must be an act of worship. Humble absolutism asserts that solving moral dilemmas will rightly occur only when it is engaged in as a positive activity in which moral persons act not to avoid sin, not to produce the least evil possible in a given situation, but in hopes of bringing the highest glory to the Godhead. Solving moral dilemmas is a loving pursuit of God in which the moral agent responds to him in a spirit of humble worship in light of the truth of human depravity and the grace of the gospel. While reason and method remain vital, the heart of ethics shifts away from a man-centered determination to avoid sin to a humble reliance on God's grace to inflame the heart, enlighten reason, motivate proper action, and offer the comfort of future grace in light of the reality that in our ongoing struggle with sin, we will fail more often than we care to realize or admit.

Practical Methodology: Criteria for Determining Behavior

Motivation and directional intent, important as they are, do not in themselves provide adequate criteria for making an actual decision. Even when a person's desire is to love and worship God, the reality still exists that a person must figure out what specific action to take in the contexts and circumstances that he or she faces day in and day out. While no system of ethics could adequately spell out particular action points to deal with each and every particular circumstance, Scripture does provide clear "moral markers" to guide a person toward worshipful behavior. It guides us normatively to both shape our character and give instruction regarding behavior. Indeed, the question arises that if the effects of sin remain a real problem that, even for believers, lingers and clouds one's view of reality, how is one to act with confidence when facing moral dilemmas?

Before the Situation Arises

Similar to our description in the previous chapter, some preliminary steps of preparation for moral decision-making are important to keep in mind and address before situations arise. These have to do with (1) how we ground ourselves in and on the grace of Christ, (2) our determination to obey, and (3) our practiced reliance on the Holy Spirit to engender wisdom. We will say a brief word about each before listing some steps for navigating morally complex situations.

First and foremost, the emphasis in humble absolutism is a recognition that confidence never derives from one's own moral ability or agility in the face of crisis. Rather, confidence is always reliant on Christ's work of redemption and the Holy Spirit's enabling grace. Practically, this means that while the Spirit-filled believer will ideally make a wise decision, regardless of outcome the gospel remains the central focus. If the action in fact avoids sin, then the credit belongs with God's gracious enabling made possible at Calvary and attained through the leading of the Holy Spirit. If in the situation the believer makes a wrong decision and sin occurs, then the place of hope is once again Calvary. Such an approach leaves no room for carelessness, nor does it impugn the high standard of God's infallible and inerrant Word. Rather, it properly addresses the radical nature of human sin and fallen status, while simultaneously casting such sinners onto the cross as the only worthy lifeboat in the sea of depravity. Either way, worship should be the emphasis regarding human responsibility.

Second, it is absolutely essential that the moral agent involved carefully assess the situation, consider possible third options, and explore whether clear built-in exceptions are present in Scripture. Humble absolutism affirms that when a regenerate believer faces what appears to be a moral dilemma, he or she must realize that the dilemma may *feel* very real but is in actuality only apparent. Hence, there is real hope for escape. With this truth in mind, the moral agent must call on the Holy Spirit to give wisdom and grace to guide his or her interpretation of the situation, seek counsel, and reason wisely. Then, he or she must decide in a manner that most clearly obeys the commands relevant to the situation, *regardless of perceived consequences*. All human desires for palatable consequences must be sublimated to the binding motivation to obey Jesus' commands and bring him the greatest glory in a given situation, *regardless of cost to self*. In such a case, the disciple must choose to trust in the sovereign hand of God and choose to believe that obedience is better than sacrifice.

Scripture promises that God, in his goodness, can and will work things out beyond hope or expectation. One must trust in the character of God and his Word over and above experience and reason. In other words (and this is a major point), *the situational elements of the so-called moral dilemma are to be treated as prima facie, not the commands of Scripture.* The apparent consequences are less binding than the scriptural commands that are to drive the decision-making. Otherwise, the moral authority of the Scripture is subjugated to the individual's sin-tainted reasoning.

Third, there must be a reliance on the power of the Holy Spirit to provide wisdom and enable a godly decision. For this reason, it is imperative that the believer make a life commitment to being filled (directed and empowered) by the Holy Spirit (Eph. 5:18). Only aided by grace can the believer hope to rise above perceived moral dilemmas. Only on this foundation can the believer confidently ask for wisdom (James 1:5–8) and avoid reliance solely on his or her own reasoning ability.

When Confronted by an Apparent Moral Dilemma

Following those first three steps does not guarantee that the right choice will become abundantly clear, nor does it guarantee that the person will avoid sin every time. It does, however, place the Christian in a position of humility and openness to the leading of God as the person engages his or her reason to determine a course of action.

Having affirmed these first three steps, humble absolutism recognizes that because of the continued influence of sin, even in the life of the believer, choosing the highest act of worship often requires a more extensive reasoning process. If an apparent dilemma remains unclear to the moral agent involved, the following steps can serve as moral markers outlining the process of determining proper behavior during morally complex times.

First, when making a decision, scriptural commands must always outweigh all other competing moral rules or principles. When Scripture is given top spot as the source of *moral authority* and when the apparent dilemma is carefully evaluated and defined in light of the Scriptures relevant to the situations, many apparent moral dilemmas will simply disappear. In those rare cases in which two or more commands of Scripture appear to irreconcilably bear on a single situation, the following guidelines help determine which biblical course to take.

Second, the person making the decision must have the *right intent.* The action that is chosen is most in keeping with the goal of bringing the maximum glory to the name of Christ.

Third, the decision to follow one course or another not only must be based on clear biblical command and the interpretation of that command as it applies to this scenario, but must also have sufficient and clear reason, or *just cause*, to support one course of action over the other. That is, better reasons can be offered to act in one direction than in the other.

Fourth, the decision to act in a manner that breaks a command must be a *last-resort* type of choice. That is, the situation has been thoroughly explored for other alternatives and "third options," and no morally preferable alternative actions can be substituted. Normally, most apparent moral dilemmas, if not settled by the first criterion, will find resolution here. It is often the case that the urgency of the situation will hinder the exploration of other options that are not at first apparent. It is for this reason that if at all possible, if the decision can be set aside until all options are explored (not always an available luxury), it is a good idea to do so.

If, after considering these four criteria, the direction of behavior is still unclear and the situation prevents the person involved from setting the issue aside in order to further contemplate right action, then one must move to the next step. One must recognize, however, that the following step is a much more subjective arena and is therefore far more prone to error.

Fifth, the decision or actions chosen should be considered *proportionally better* or the "lesser evil" choice. That is, at this stage of decision-making, when there is considerable uncertainty about how the scriptural commands can be applied without breaking one command or the other, the decision to act or behave in a particular manner will seek to bring the highest possible worship to the name of Christ while simultaneously avoiding all negative effects or cause the fewest negative effects possible in light of the information available to the moral agent at the time of action. Often this will involve a cost-benefit analysis of the possible positive and negative consequences that may result from the choices in any given context or situation.

Finally, if a proportional or "lesser evil" choice is made, then the moral agent in this situation should work to *minimize the negative effects* of his or her choice. If a command has been broken in order to seek the best form of obedience that one knows how to offer as worship in a confusing situation, then not only should a person adopt a position of sorrow over having broken the command, but he or she should also work to minimize any possible negative effects from the moral choice. It is not uncommon for the moral agent in such cases to simultaneously rejoice over the good end that is accomplished and yet also be sorrowful (or experience *moral traces*) over the reality that a command was broken in the process. Resting in the goodness of Christ's atoning work is crucial for a person to maintain a right balance at such a time.

A Final Consideration of Rahab

Should Rahab have lied? No. Lying is contrary to God's character and command. Yet in the sense that she followed her limited, unregenerate (or newly regenerate) conscience in a situation that demanded immediate response, she arguably did the best she could.[45] In this light, one could surmise that while her motive was properly ordered and she acted in faith, the material component of her decision was in reality antithetical to the nature of God. One might make the case that she simply did not or perhaps, if she was still an unregenerate person, could not see and understand this reality. She simply acted the best she could in light of her fallen (or newly regenerate) state. This does not excuse her, but it does account for how she can be both a sinner and yet blessed by God, as both Hebrews and James indicate.

This evaluation of Rahab's behavior points to the necessity of keeping the gospel as the pivot point of all Christian ethics. Rahab sinned. She was blessed not because she was excused from sin in light of her intent, or because the law didn't apply due to some unclear hierarchy. No, she was blessed because of the grace of God in spite of her wrong material expression of a rightly intended act. Jesus died for Rahab's sin; it was not excused or overlooked. Jesus absorbed the punishment in his nail-pierced hands.

Some in the graded absolutist position might argue that Scripture indicates no distinction between fearing God and the material act of lying, and would therefore conclude that *God blessed Rahab for lying*. But such a position denies the important distinction between the *telos* domain and the *act* domain and the difference between a right goal and the right form of achieving it. In this case, being clear on how they are distinguished is important. A person can do the right thing with a bad motive or—as was the case with Rahab—the wrong thing with a good motive. In either case, the sin is not excused by the positive dimension. All the theological domains of ethical assessment must align and be right for the act to be right. This is why the GA position runs the risk of robbing the cross of its central place in ethics. Rahab was blessed because God is gracious, not because she caused the right consequences to occur. Indeed, Genesis 12:3 indicates that those who honor or bless God's people will be blessed. Her intent to honor God's people was right, and she was blessed.[46] Her actions in how she attempted to honor God's people were wrong, and she needed a Savior.[47]

Could Rahab have behaved differently? The humble absolutist position would suggest that if she had a chance to do it over again, Rahab should not lie. The

---

45. This conclusion is made with the assumption that Rahab was either a nonbeliever (unregenerate) up to this point or perhaps (since Scripture indicates that she acted in faith) a very new believer whose only access to the law of God at this point was through general revelation.

46. As Hebrews 11:31 indicates, Rahab "welcomed the spies in peace."

47. From cover to cover, the didactic teaching of Scripture indicates that lying is counter to the nature of God as a God of truth. The only counterargument that can be made to this is based on narrative story interpreted in a particular direction.

authority of Scripture is clear regarding the commands of truthfulness. Therefore, even simply based on the first criterion of the HA methodology, the scenario is cleared up and the apparent moral dilemma disappears. She ought to have obeyed the command of truth-telling and trusted the sovereign God to take care of the results or looked for a third way out of the situation (e.g., remaining silent and allowing God to protect the spies).[48]

In partial agreement with ideal absolutism, however, humble absolutism might recognize that if Rahab was not a believer, or if she was very newly regenerate, she might not have the moral resources, access to information, maturity, or sophistication to navigate well in the situation. In spite of inability, however, God can recognize and even honor intent, while simultaneously holding a person accountable for his or her action. Indeed, loving parents do this very thing with their children all the time. Maturation and character development (virtue) come from recognition of wrong behavior coupled with forgiving grace and instructive correction.

Summary and Conclusion

In sum, the following diagram (see fig. 8.2) indicates where a humble absolutist position falls in relation to the other prevailing systems.

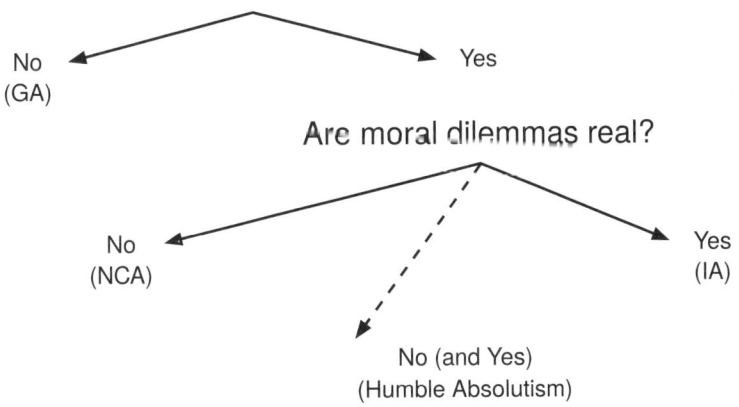

Is there more than one universal absolute in Scripture?

No (GA) ← → Yes

Are moral dilemmas real?

No (NCA) ← → Yes (IA)

No (and Yes) (Humble Absolutism)

Fig. 8.2. Humble Absolutist Position

48. First Samuel 13:1–3 is a fascinating scriptural text in which God instructs Samuel to tell the truth but not disclose the entirety of his mission. God gave permission to the prophet to remain silent about his anointing of David. This in turn allowed Saul to reach his own conclusions but did not require the purposeful giving of untrue data for the purpose of deception (i.e., "lying").

The graphic above helps put the idea of humble absolutism in the context of the prevailing views on the subject. It is distinct from graded absolutism in that it holds to a multiplicity of absolutes in Scripture that are norms without exceptions. It is distinct from ideal absolutism in its insistence that God's commands cannot actually conflict in reality without, by default, impugning the character and integrity of God. While most closely allied with nonconflicting absolutism, it is distinct from NCA in its emphasis on the depravity that occurs in humans because of sin and the very real state of moral inability for the nonregenerate moral agent.

Humble absolutism is similar to graded absolutism in its ultimate focus on the greatest commandment as the highest aim and possible hope of human existence. It is similar to ideal absolutism in its insistence that humans *experience* moral dilemmas and then sin when any command is broken in such a situation. It is most closely allied with nonconflicting absolutism because its starting point is the nature and character of God and his Word. It holds that in reality no conflict occurs between any commands of God and places emphasis and hope on the sovereign hand of God to bring all things to conclusion rightly even when human eyes cannot see rightly.

It is unique from all three in four ways: emphasis on humility in light of the reality of sin and its resulting impact on the experience of fallen image-bearers; its clarity of emphasis on the gospel as the center point of ethics and the nexus from which to understand the entire issue of moral dilemmas; its emphasis on the necessity of the filling of the Holy Spirit as the basis for hope for disciples of Christ to escape moral dilemmas; and its emphasis on biblically informed worship as the paradigm for action in the face of morally ambiguous situations.

What difference does this perspective make in relation to the understanding and handling of moral dilemmas? It provides three fundamental advantages. First, it provides the basis for one to unapologetically assert without hesitation that God is God and that the absolute moral commands present in his Word are perfect, without fault or blemish. One can have full hope and assurance that the Word of God is actually the one sufficient guide to life and practice.

Second, this perspective provides a basis to deal honestly and fairly with the real experience of the human moral agent. There is no need to deny the feeling of moral dilemma; there is no fear of recognizing the turmoil behind human existence. It provides a basis for understanding where these experiences come from, and points toward the only real hope in finding a solution.

Third, and most importantly, in keeping with the entire *Ethics as Worship* project, it keeps a Christocentric focus on worship as the central focus of the moral life. On the one hand, apart from regeneration and salvation, a human being cannot hope to live a moral life that rises above inevitable conflict and sin.

One must look to the gospel for hope. On the other hand, regeneration and salvation become the foundation on which to understand ultimate reality. Only in and through the gospel can one journey in progressive sanctification and begin to see reality as God sees it.

Whether or not we like to admit it, questions, speculations, and disagreements over the issue of so-called moral dilemmas are embedded in the reality and context of a sinful world. It is for this reason that humans are wise to approach questions on absolutes and moral dilemmas with a spirit of humility. We are not God, nor are we the arbiters of his absolutes. Rather, we are created beings given the opportunity to respond to the truths of God as he enables us in and through his Holy Spirit and in accord with his Word, that we might tackle these situations as disciples who worship in spirit and truth.

By way of conclusion, it is important to remember an earlier point about the nature of sanctification. That is, holiness is rightly understood as a separation *to God*, not just a separation *from sin*. This distinction is an important one in the pursuit of godliness and can distinguish Christian worship in moral practice from the "older brother" moralism of the Pharisees too often present in evangelical circles. When one is engaging in moral behavior and ethical determination, the motive should be a pursuit of the beauty of God that draws one into worship and not the false hope in moral perfectionism. The emphasis in ethics must fall on the gospel as the foundation for hope, the source of proper perspective, and the enabling power to behave in a manner that maximally glorifies Christ, not merely avoids sin.

Humble absolutism is at its core an attempt to explicitly place worship at the center of morally complicated situations and allow the gospel to shine light on the difficult moral circumstances that all humans face. Only in humility can humans properly acknowledge that all our best deeds fall far short of God's perfection. In this *now and not yet* between the cross and the beatific vision, we will struggle and toil. Yet in light of the work of the two Paracletes (Jesus and the Holy Spirit), there is real hope for us to avoid evil and worship well even in the most difficult of circumstances. This is the purpose of the cross, the meaning of sanctification, and the ultimate purpose of ethics.

In spite of all our very real human failings, toils, efforts, and struggles to find our way, one final truth helps cast perspective and gives us a final hope: "*Now we see in a mirror dimly, but then face to face; now I know in part, but then I will know fully just as I also have been fully known*" (1 Cor. 13:12). Between this day and that day, may we be found faithful in our practice of ethics as worship.

Key Terms and Concepts

antinomianism

built-in exception

conflicts of duty

debilitating effects of sin

depravity

freedom to choose

generalism

graded absolutism

greatest good

humble absolutism

ideal absolutism

lesser of two evils

mind of Christ

moral absolutes

moral dilemmas

moral traces

nonconflicting absolutism

principles, *prima facie*

progressive transformation

situationalism

tragic moral choices

Key Scriptures

Exodus 1:15–21

Joshua 2:1–7

1 Samuel 15:22

Proverbs 3:4–5

Isaiah 64:6

Micah 6:8

Matthew 5:17–20

John 14:21

Romans 1:19–28

Romans 5:12–21

1 Corinthians 2:16

1 Corinthians 10:13

1 Corinthians 13:12

2 Corinthians 3:18

2 Corinthians 5:17

Ephesians 4:17–18

Hebrews 4:15

Hebrews 11:31

James 2:10

James 2:25

2 Peter 1:3–10

1 John 4:4

Study Questions

1. What is the difference between a *moral dilemma* and a *practical dilemma*?
2. How does a robust understanding of the impact of sin and the fall (depravity) influence the humble absolutism perspective on the so-called problem of moral dilemmas?
3. How is the doctrine of progressive sanctification related to properly describing and then solving the problem of so-called moral dilemmas?
4. Imagine that you are a pastor or counselor meeting with Rahab for discipleship purposes. During the conversation, she asks you your opinion about whether she lied during the "spy encounter" (Josh. 2:1–7). Compare and contrast how you might answer her if you held to one of the four

following positions: *graded absolutism, ideal absolutism, nonconflicting absolutism, humble absolutism.*

5. Using the same situation from the previous question, now suppose that Rahab asked you your opinion about what she could have done differently. Compare and contrast how you might answer her if you held to one of the four following positions: *graded absolutism, ideal absolutism, nonconflicting absolutism, humble absolutism.*

For Further Reading

Douma, J. *The Ten Commandments.* Phillipsburg, NJ: P&R Publishing, 1996.

Geisler, Norman L. *Christian Ethics: Contemporary Issues and Options.* 2nd ed. Grand Rapids: Baker Academic, 2010.

Jones, David W. *An Introduction to Biblical Ethics.* Nashville: B&H Academic, 2013.

Luck, William F. "Moral Conflicts and Evangelical Ethics." *Grace Theological Journal* 8, no. 1 (Spring 1987): 19–34.

Murray, John. *Principles of Conduct: Aspects of Biblical Ethics.* Grand Rapids: Eerdmans, 1957.

Rakestraw, Robert V. "Ethical Choices: A Case for Non-Conflicting Absolutism." *Criswell Theological Review* 2, no. 2 (1988): 239–67.

Thielicke, Helmut. "The Borderline Situation of Extreme Conflict." In *Theology and Method,* edited by David K. Clark and Robert V. Rakestraw, 125–30. Vol. 1 of *Readings in Christian Ethics.* Grand Rapids: Baker, 1994.

PART 4

THE APPLICATION OF ETHICS AS WORSHIP

9

Justice and Social Engagement

*"If justice perished, the foundations of the whole cosmic order
would disintegrate, because justice is fundamental to the very nature
of the Lord, the creator of the universe and to the core of God's government
of history. . . . Justice on earth flows from justice in heaven."*[1]
—CHRISTOPHER J. H. WRIGHT, Old Testament Ethics for the People of God

*"Justice is any act of reconciliation that restores any part of God's creation
back to its original intent, purpose, or image. Justice is making right any of the
many things that have gone wrong in this very good world that God made—
and among the very good human beings he created to inhabit it."*[2]
—JOHN M. PERKINS, Dream with Me

Introduction

The single greatest injustice in human history– indeed, in the history of the
universe—is that God does not receive the worship he is due. This is true as it
relates to each and every living human being. It is true as it relates to all human
beings together. And given the special role that humans play in the created order,
it is also true of the entire cosmos. This is why we must address the topic of justice
in terms of both its personal implications and its social aspects. God's majesty
demands it, and the prospect of human flourishing desperately needs it.

As we have argued from the outset of this book, because God is the beginning
of all things and the center of reference for all things, and his glory is the final purpose of all things, ethics must be understood in terms of worship. Consequently,

1. Christopher J. H. Wright, *Old Testament Ethics for the People of God* (Downers Grove, IL: IVP Academic, 2004), 253–54.
2. John M. Perkins, *Dream with Me: Race, Love, and the Struggle We Must Win* (Grand Rapids: Baker, 2017), 207.

the pursuit of justice, so far as it pertains to ethics, must take place in reference to him. Understanding justice must begin with him, always center on him, and ultimately be concerned that he is magnified and maximally worshiped. From the theocentric perspective of ethics as worship, the pursuit of justice involves the alignment of all things to God in accord with his eternal plan.

Only from this theocentric perspective can we develop notions of justice that properly honor each and every one who bears God's image. Likewise, only from this perspective can we hope to address the places in our own hearts that bear the marks of sin and align them to God's holy standards. It is also only from this perspective that we can recognize and address the places in human culture where our social patterns bear the marks of sinfulness and foster (intentionally or unintentionally) various forms of injustice or what the Bible describes as "oppression" (Pss. 9:9; 72:4; Luke 4:17–21).

Tragically, the centrality and clarity of this point is lost on modern conversations about justice in general and social justice in particular. For many, the mere term *social justice* is problematic because it is linked (rightly or wrongly) to the ideology and liberal theological foundations of the "Social Gospel" movement initiated by Walter Rauschenbusch over a hundred years ago. For others, it is a problematic term because it is linked with Marxist economic policies and perhaps an overemphasis on a "preferential option for the poor" that have been imported into Christian thought through the liberation theology movement initiated by Gustavo Gutiérrez. In some quarters of evangelicalism, the mere mention of the term *social justice* raises fears of "cultural Marxism," "socialist agendas," "critical theories," and the legitimization of a "culture of victimization."

Whether such fear of the term *social justice* is warranted depends on several factors, including:

1. How the term is defined;
2. Whether that definition aligns with biblical standards and instructions; and
3. Whether the issue being described as a social-justice issue is being fairly assessed.

Too often, inadequate attention is given to properly defining terms and clearly stating the biblical doctrines that should shape our conceptions of justice. For example, consider commonly held notions about what is—or is not—a "social-justice teaching" or a "social-justice issue." Normally, we identify topics such as economic reform, immigration, racial reconciliation, and environmental ethics as social-justice issues, but not topics such as abortion, war, and capital punishment. Yet all the issues listed above are "social" issues because they impact society as a whole. Likewise, they are all "justice" issues because they require instruction from the Lord to guide how we (both individually and corporately as a society) ought to behave righteously (or "justly") in regard to them. Therefore, if any of them are going to be singled out as problematic either because of their "social" nature or because they require a rectification of "justice," then all of them are problematic in the same manner. Simply put, if the people of God can stand up for the unborn or go to war based on "just causes," then it logically follows that they ought to also stand up for the widow, the orphan, the poor, the sojourner, or any other person who is persecuted based solely on ethnicity or social status.

Recognizing this point is imperative. If God is the center of our universe and therefore is also the center point of ethics, then what God reveals about the nature of justice must be the standard of our definition (and practice) of justice. Sadly, however, it is too often the case that Christians err in their understanding of justice in one of two ways. On the one hand, more liberal Christians are prone to adopt uncareful notions of justice based in the suspect theological foundations of liberation theologies and the accompanying tendencies to affirm such things as socialist ideas of wealth redistribution and special rights based on notions of sexual fluidity. On the other hand, more conservatively minded Christians are prone to unwittingly adopt individualistic philosophical ideals of the Enlightenment freight-loaded with presuppositions about "personal rights" and assume that they are principles grounded in the Bible. Unfortunately, for many liberal Christians, their conceptions of justice are shaped more by Karl Marx and Walter Rauschenbusch than they are by King Jesus. Similarly, it is unfortunate that for many conservative Christians, their conceptions of justice are shaped more by Adam Smith and John Stuart Mill than they are by Christ the Lord. Regardless of which side of the liberal/conservative spectrum one falls on, we impoverish ourselves when we place individualism and a concern for our own "rights" at the center of the story of ethics and our understanding of social and civic responsibility. If we get the center of the story wrong, if we get the center of justice wrong . . . we get ethics wrong . . . we get life wrong . . . we get worship wrong.

A robust pursuit of justice and social engagement must have as a foundational element a strong commitment to evangelism and discipleship. Understanding justice requires that we see the world as God sees it and recognize that his standards are the only standards of justice that matter. Individuals who make up society must be rightly aligned with God and his design and mission for the world if there is to be any hope that the societies they create will also be rightly aligned with God's moral standards. Indeed, this is why Jesus made it clear that bringing the good news of the gospel to the poor and oppressed motivated him "to seek and to save that which was lost" (Luke 19:10). He makes this exact point unequivocally in Luke 4 when he quotes from Isaiah:

> The Spirit of the Lord is upon Me,
> Because He anointed Me to *preach* the gospel to the poor.
> He has sent Me to *proclaim* release to the captives,
> And recovery of sight to the blind,
> To set free those who are oppressed,
> To *proclaim* the favorable year of the Lord. (Luke 4:18–19)

It is through the preaching and proclamation of the gospel that restoration begins and hope is brought to fruition.

Paul also affirms the centrality of evangelism and discipleship to the pursuit of justice in Romans, where he, too, quotes Isaiah:

> How then will they call on Him in whom they have not believed? How will they believe in Him whom they have not heard? And how will they hear without a *preacher*? How will they *preach* unless they are sent? Just as it is written, "How beautiful are the feet of those who *bring good news* of good things!"
>
> However, they did not all heed the good news; for Isaiah says, "Lord, who has believed our report?" So faith comes from hearing, and *hearing* by the word of Christ. (Rom. 10:14–17)

Jesus commissioned his followers to "go . . . and make disciples of all the nations" (Matt. 28:19), and Paul understood that "faith comes from hearing, and hearing by the word of Christ" (Rom. 10:17). In a distinctly Christian ethic, the Great Commission is inextricably linked to any quest for justice on either a personal or a social level. Jesus is concerned that all persons and all societies might be reconciled to him through the proclamation of the "good news" of the gospel (i.e., *justification*). Only then would it be possible that the greatest (and most important) social-justice issue in history could be rectified. Only then could there be lasting hope that "the nations" could live in accord with all the implications that come from a right (or "just") relationship with God. In short, evangelism and discipleship are social-justice initiatives. When rightly understood, the Great Commission of Jesus Christ is the mission statement of any truly Christian social-justice movement.

This is not to say that a concern for justice at a societal level somehow reduces only to a concern for individual conversion and personal sanctification. As we pointed out in our earlier discussions of the biblical/theological foundations of ethics (chapters 2–5), *from the beginning* God has always been greatly concerned that all creation be rightly aligned to his eternal design and thereby flourish. It has always been God's design that the very structures of society and the culturally embedded patterns that we think and act from be rightly aligned or "justly ordered" to his eternal law. Rather, we are pointing out that genuine hope for solving culturally embedded patterns of sin and social-justice concerns *begins* with (and is made possible through) the proclamation of the gospel (we are saved by grace alone, through faith alone, by Christ alone) and the reality that Jesus alone is the saving King. It then *proceeds* from this truth to the prophetic truth that if Jesus is the saving King, then his lordship extends over—and has implications for—the entirety of creation and the fabric of human society. It is in Christ the Creator that we have the *foundation* of justice. It is in Christ the Redeemer that we have the *restoration* of justice. And it is under Christ the King that we have the imperative to *practice* justice.

The purpose of this chapter is to explore the concept of justice pertaining to the field of ethics, with particular focus on understanding how a biblically and theologically grounded notion of justice must result in social engagement. It is our hope that in doing so, we might also shed light on the meaning and proper use of the term *social justice* in order to expose immature ideas and ungodly accusations that are commonly leveled in ignorance against anyone whose work even touches on the topic or who utters the phrase.

In order to accomplish this task, we begin with a brief discussion of the classic understanding of justice that has shaped most of Western thought since the time of Plato and Aristotle. We then explore the scriptural use of the terms related to *justice* in order to arrive at a biblical understanding. Following this, we identify three categories of sin and discuss how the good news of the gospel enables us to pursue justice in relation to each. Finally, before bringing the chapter to conclusion, we will offer a brief apologetic interaction about the term *social justice* by identifying several ideas that are *not* necessarily connected to, or implied by, the use of the term and therefore should not be assumed as motivating those who use it.

Classical Justice

The classical Greeks, most notably Plato and Aristotle, believed that justice is concerned with both character (being a just person or a just society) and action (doing just deeds). Plato, in particular, considered justice to be one of the four "cardinal virtues." A person was said to be "just" when the three parts of his soul (reason, will, and appetite) were properly ordered and balanced through the cultivation of the other three cardinal virtues that relate to them respectively (prudence, fortitude, and temperance). Corresponding to these three parts of the personal soul, Plato argued, society also had three vital components: a ruling class (or philosopher class) that uses reason to order society, a warrior class that defends the country by acting as its will, and a class of artisans and farmers who are the working class and represent the appetitive part of society. Plato understood social justice to be a larger version or copy of personal justice. Each person is like a paper written in 10-point font and the society as a whole (the "republic") is an identical paper written in 1000-point font. He concluded that not only must a just republic consist of just persons, but its three vital components must also be properly balanced and aligned in society (as they must be in a just person) in order for that society to be a good or "just" society. According to Plato, justice was both a personal virtue to be worked toward in the development of virtuous persons and a social virtue to be attained by the proper development of a virtuous society (or "republic").[3]

Table 9.1. Plato on Justice

Person	Virtue	Society (Republic)
Reason Will Appetite	Prudence (Wisdom) Fortitude (Courage) Temperance (Self-Control)	Ruling Class Warrior Class Artisans & Farmers
Just persons and just societies result from a proper balance of the virtues in both persons and societies		

Aristotle used the term *universal justice* to describe the general justice that shapes the background of both persons and society.[4] There is an important connection between morality and justice—in order for a person to be moral, he or she must also be virtuous. But Aristotle argued that the virtuous person would also be a lawful person. While morality deals with the kind of person one is, a just person would be the kind of person who out of his or her virtuous character treats others appropriately and lawfully, i.e., justly. Similarly, a society is universally just if as a whole its members treat one another appropriately and lawfully, i.e., justly. Individuals and society are right to expect this kind of justice to be present in both persons and society.

While universal justice pertains largely to character and disposition of both persons and society, Aristotle also identified two categories of *particular justice* that relate to the proper distribution of goods within a society: distributive and remedial. The former deals primarily with the question of how to distribute wealth in a society (e.g., fair-trade laws), while the latter deals with correcting or rectifying

---

3. See book 4 of Plato, *Republic*, in *A Plato Reader: Eight Essential Dialogues*, ed. C. D. C. Reeve (Indianapolis: Hackett, 2012), 366–96.

4. Aristotle's discussion of justice is found in book 5 of his *Nicomachean Ethics*. Aristotle, *Nicomachean Ethics*, trans. Terence Irwin, 2nd ed. (Indianapolis: Hackett, 1999), 227–38.

unfair practices (e.g., theft, deceptive weights and measures). In contemporary culture, when we think of the term *social justice*, we are normally referring to one or both of these categories of particular justice: how do we justly distribute goods, and/or how do we justly deal with criminals and criminal behavior?

What should become clear at this point is that, historically speaking, the term *social justice* technically and simply referred to the moral formation and lawful ordering of society. Of course, we still need to answer the question of how best to go about doing so, and we still need to determine what value system we will use to shape the moral and lawful formation and ordering. At its simplest level, the idea of social justice is what any society does when it attempts to govern itself in a civilized manner. Technically, we could define the term as "proper ordering of civilized society." It is precisely here that the various questions of how we go about making these determinations and adopting values come into play. The underlying metaethical ideas will shape both the means of distribution and the laws we seek to affirm or correct that we must pay attention to.

Aristotle's Formal Principle of Justice

As for Aristotle, he argued that justice should be determined by giving to people what they are properly due. To ensure this, he argued, justice requires *equals to be treated equally and unequals to be treated unequally*. This principle has come to be known as the *formal principle of justice*. It is considered "formal" because as stated, it gives us a general criterion or *form* of justice—but herein lies the problem. As stated, it does not give us any substantive criteria by which to work justice out. Moreover, it does not tell us who are equals and why, nor does it tell us in what sense or in relation to what criteria equals need to be treated equally.

For example, as it relates to who is equal, we might ask questions related to abortion such as: "Is a newly conceived child, or an eight-day-old baby with Down syndrome, equal in value to a twenty-year-old college student? If so, how do we know this, and how should our laws about abortion reflect our conclusions? If not, on what basis can we make such an argument?" Or to address the same idea from the angle of race and ethnicity, we can ask: "Is a twelve-year-old girl who has white skin equal in value to a thirty-year-old male who has black skin? If so, how do we know this, and how should our laws, policies, and practices regarding criminal punishment reflect this? If not, on what basis can we make such an argument?" From yet another angle that relates to animal rights, we can ask, "Is a chimpanzee or gorilla that has learned how to pluck out a few notes on a piano equal in value to a human being who can play only the same notes?" In each case, we are highlighting this question: "Which differences between people or created beings do we consider relevant to determining when someone or something should be treated *equally*?"

To press the point a bit more, if we assume that persons are fundamentally equal in value because they are human, on what basis might we determine that it is appropriate to treat them unequally? For example, consider a scenario involving two college students who take the same exam in the same ethics class under the same conditions. If they both work equally hard, should they get the same grade even though one provided many more correct answers than the other? In what sense do we mean that they should be treated *equally*, and in what sense is it just to treat them *unequally*? On what criteria of justice can we say that one is "due" an "A" and the other a failing grade? If justice is equality, should not both be given exactly the same grade regardless of their level of achievement? In fact, should not every person be given exactly the same grade if the standard of justice is simply *equality*? Should not every child on every team get a trophy even when some are much better than others and only one team comes in first place?

Table 9.2. Aristotle on Justice

Formal Principle of Justice—Equals to be treated equally, and unequals to be treated unequally.

Material Principle of Justice—Provides more specific, guiding criteria for determining on what basis and how someone is to be treated equally or unequally.

Aristotle's Material Principle of Justice

This problem of specifying *how* we ought to judge what it means to be "equal" or "fair" in particular situations requires that in addition to a formal principle of justice, we must also have a *material principle of justice* that provides more specific, guiding criteria to inform how one determines what "just treatment" is in a specific context. Returning to the example about students taking the ethics exam, the *formal principle of justice* requires that a teacher treat all his or her students equally or fairly. The *material principle of justice* is what specifies how fairness is to be determined in the context of the class. In the classroom context, the material principle of justice used to determine that one student gets high marks while the other student gets low marks is the criterion of *merit*. Specifically, we would say that each student was judged equally in terms of what he or she "earned" or "merited" by the quality of his or her work.

Merit is only one of several options that could have been used to determine a final grade. For example, the teacher could decide that the grade would be based on the amount of work that a student put into the project and not the final quality. Thus, formal justice would be determined in light of the material criterion of *effort*. That is, as long as he or she worked as hard as anyone else, the student will get an "A." Yet another way to say that justice is served is to treat each student equally in light of his or her *need*. Thus, an "A" grade could be given to any student who needed an "A" to get financial aid even if his or her work is clearly subpar to that of everyone else in the class. The following list identifies other principles that have been proposed as ways to give material content to the formal principle of justice.[5]

- To each according to *merit*.
- To each according to *effort*.
- To each according to *need*.
- To each according to *free-market exchange*.
- To each according to *productive contribution to society*.
- To each the *same thing*.
- To each according to *equal share*.
- To each according to *participation*.

The popularly held idea that *justice* simply means "fairness" or "equal treatment" is not as simple as it first sounds.[6]

We can conclude, then, that the debates we have surrounding the term *social justice* are really not about seeking social justice per se; rather, the debate is about how best to achieve it. The concern is really about how one goes about determining the proper criteria for deciding what social justice should entail or on what standard it is going to be judged as "just" or "unjust." How one determines which or how many of these material principles apply—and in which context they apply—is shaped to a large degree by the underlying worldview and metaethical assumptions one holds about the nature of the world and the nature of morality. They are also heavily shaped by both our own personal experiences and desires and the perceived desires of a given sector of society or culture. Needless to say, our social, political, and ethical debates about public policies, economic theories, and public stances on moral issues are heated precisely because we do not agree on how best to go about choosing which *material principles of justice* should apply in the various contexts of our personal, public, and civil contexts.

For this reason, it is wise to turn to a consideration of how the Bible treats the issue of justice. While the question of how to enact justice in particular situations

---

5. For a helpful discussion of the formal and material principles of justice, see Gene Outka, *Agape: An Ethical Analysis* (New Haven, CT: Yale University Press, 1972), 88–92. See also Ronald H. Nash, *Life's Ultimate Questions: An Introduction to Philosophy* (Grand Rapids: Zondervan, 1999), 358–62.

6. The notion of *justice as fairness* has been popularized by the influential work of John Rawls in his books *A Theory of Justice* (Cambridge, MA: Harvard University Press, 1971) and *Justice as Fairness: A Restatement* (Cambridge, MA: Harvard University Press, 2001). Rawls's work affirms a form of distributive justice that focuses on equality of opportunity.

will still need to be worked out in light of particular contextual factors, it is from Scripture that we discover the character of a just person, the standard of just action, and—most importantly—the final goal toward which justice must be ordered.

The Biblical Language of Justice

Whereas classical Greek notions of justice focused on what people are "due" as equals and considered justice largely in terms of distribution of goods and the ordering of laws, the biblical notion has a different—though not contrary—root and form. The biblical notion of justice is thoroughly theological in nature. It begins with, and is grounded in, the nature and character of God. His holiness and righteousness are the standard of justice, and the expectations and practices of justice that he requires of us (both individually and corporately) are meant to be reflective of his desired outcomes.

We can see this borne out in the Hebrew words used for "righteousness" (*tsedāqāh*) and "justice" (*mishpāt*) in the Old Testament. The word *tsedāqāh* relates to God's standard for justice. Its root meaning implies something that is straight, fixed, or as full as it should be, and it carries the meaning of a "conformity to what is right or expected—not in some abstract or absolute generic way, but according to the demands of the relationship or the nature of the situation."[7] The root meaning of the word *mishpāt* relates to

> legal action over a wide range. . . . In the widest sense, it means to "put things right," to intervene in a situation that is wrong, oppressive or out of control and "fix" it. This may include confronting wrongdoers, on the one hand, and, on the other hand vindicating and delivering those who have been wronged. Such action is not confined to a court of law, but may take place in other ways; for example through battle.[8]

Because the two ideas of these words are closely related and because they are frequently linked directly with each other in the biblical text (e.g., Gen. 18:19; Pss. 33:5; 89:14; 97:2; 103:6; Prov. 21:3; Hos. 2:19), they function linguistically together, in a very distinctive manner known as a *hendiadys*. The idea is that by directly coupling these two words together, the biblical author is meaning to place a special emphasis and create one main idea. An example in English is saying something such as "I am sick and tired" of studying for this exam. Together the words provide emphasis as well as a richer meaning than if the words were used

7. Wright, *Old Testament Ethics for the People of God*, 255–56.
8. Wright, *Old Testament Ethics for the People of God*, 256.

separately.[9] When these two words are coupled in the Hebrew, possibly the nearest English expression available to capture the idea is "justice in social contexts" or the term *social justice*.[10]

In the New Testament, we see a similar idea emerge when we consider the Greek word *dikaiosunē* that is variously translated into English as "righteousness" or "justice." This word carries with it the idea of God's judicial approval or that which is deemed to be right by the Lord.[11] The New Testament frequently records Jesus as speaking of justice (*dikaiosunē*) in his moral instructions to his disciples (e.g., Matt. 5:6, 10; 20:1–16; 21:28–32). One particularly poignant passage occurs in Matthew 25:31–46, where Jesus separates the sheep and the goats at the end of the age and describes those who demonstrated love to the hungry, thirsty, stranger, or naked neighbor as the "just" or "righteous" who will enter eternal life.

In the Pauline literature, one prominent passage where we see the doctrinal import of *dikaiosunē* as it relates to the idea of justice is Romans 3:19–26. In this passage, we see the root word for "justice" (*dikaioō*) serve as the basis for translation into English of the concepts of both justification and righteousness:

> Now we know that whatever the Law says, it speaks to those who are under the Law, so that every mouth may be closed and all the world may become accountable to God; because by the works of the Law no flesh will be justified [*dikaioō*] in His sight; for through the Law comes the knowledge of sin.
>
> But now apart from the Law the righteousness [*dikaiosunē*] of God has been manifested, being witnessed by the Law and the Prophets, even the righteousness [*dikaiosunē*] of God through faith in Jesus Christ for all those who believe; for there is no distinction; for all have sinned and fall short of the glory of God, being justified [*dikaioō*] as a gift by His grace through the redemption which is in Christ Jesus; whom God displayed publicly as a propitiation in His blood through faith. This was to demonstrate His righteousness [*dikaiosunē*], because in the forbearance of God He passed over the sins previously committed; for the demonstration, I say, of His righteousness [*dikaiosunē*] at the present time, so that He would be just and the justifier of the one who has faith in Jesus.

This is particularly important for our discussion because Paul is linking the work that God does to make us righteous (by the grace of God through faith in Christ,

---

9. Bethany Hanke Hoang and Kristen Deede Johnson, *The Justice Calling: Where Passion Meets Perseverance* (Grand Rapids: Brazos, 2016), 19. See also Wright, *Old Testament Ethics for the People of God*, 255.

10. Wright, *Old Testament Ethics for the People of God*, 257.

11. Frederick William Danker et al., eds., *A Greek-English Lexicon of the New Testament and Other Early Christian Literature*, 3rd ed. (Chicago: University of Chicago Press, 2000) (BDAG), s.v. "δικαιοσύνη."

i.e., justification) with the reality that his saving work is itself a demonstration of his own righteous and just character.

Further, it is God's righteous and just work to save sinners that is meant, in turn, to serve as the basis by which Christians are then commissioned to "go" and bring the hope of the gospel to the nations as we teach them to obey the commandments to "love God *and* others rightly and justly."[12] Simply put, the biblical notion of justice is the idea of "putting things to right"[13]—right with God, and then right with each other, with society as a whole, and with the entire cosmos. In the words of John M. Perkins, justice is "any act of reconciliation that restores any part of God's creation back to its original intent, purpose, or image. Justice is making right any of the many things that have gone wrong in this very good world that God made—and among the very good human beings he created to inhabit it."[14]

In sum, Christopher J. H. Wright is correct when he writes, "Justice on earth flows from justice in heaven."[15] God's own just and righteous character is the foundation of the just and righteous design by which he created the world to function and also the means by which it will flourish. His own just and righteous character serves as the prototype and blueprint for understanding any and all systems of human justice. God is the source of just action, and just action is meant to be the embodiment of our love for both God and our neighbor. In fact, when rightly understood, there is an essential connection between the biblical concepts of love and justice. The standard of both love and justice is God's character. The commands of Scripture are meant to be obeyed precisely because our obedience demonstrates our love for God and because our obedience is the best path to bring a just alignment of all things to God's eternal plan. His standard of justice and love must be the standard by which we determine and evaluate what actions and behaviors we believe to be just and loving. "The entirety of Scripture shows that seeking the Lord and pursuing justice and righteousness belong together and were never meant to be separated. Justice and righteousness flow from the same source: God's steadfast love."[16]

Stated in the terms we have been using throughout the book, Scripture (*revealed morality*) is the standard of justice and the mark of true love for God precisely because it fully aligns with what God has revealed about himself and the nature of his kingdom (*revealed reality*). Or, to put it most succinctly, *loving worship requires just obedience both personally and in social contexts.*

---

12. Hoang and Johnson, *Justice Calling*, 18–19.

13. Wright, *Old Testament Ethics and the People of God*, 256. See also Hoang and Johnson, *Justice Calling*, 11n6.

14. Perkins, *Dream with Me*, 207.

15. Wright, *Old Testament Ethics for the People of God*, 254.

16. Hoang and Johnson, *Justice Calling*, 18.

Sin and the Need for Justice

In light of this biblically driven understanding of justice, we now turn to a discussion of the doctrine of sin so that we might in turn be better equipped to understand how the gospel ought to shape the way that we think about justice and motivate the way that we engage society in a biblically just manner.

As we unpacked with much greater detail in chapter 2, the book of Genesis teaches us that God created and designed the world such that all creation would flourish when those he created in his image to fill the earth, subdue it, and rule over it did so in complete accord with his loving and just character. Tragically, as we discussed in chapter 3, humans chose instead to sin and rebel against the Lord. By their doing so, not only did their own natures become sinful, so also did their choices and actions, as well as the very patterns they eventually wove into the structures of the societies they built through traditions, social mores, cultural norms, and civil laws. Therefore, when we speak of sin and our need for justice, it is helpful to think of three categories in which sinfulness has direct and profound impact and relevance, and three corresponding ways in which God demands justice.

Sinfulness and God's Demands for Justice

The first category of sinfulness that we must understand relates to the rebellion against God by each of us and all of us and our subsequent standing before him as *sinners*. As Romans 5 tells us, we inherit a sin nature from Adam and are in desperate need of salvation because of this fallen nature. Second, and directly related, we are also people (each of us and all of us) who commit *sins*. We make particular choices to daily rebel against God in our actions, behaviors, attitudes, and dispositions. These choices pertain to our morality, and they impact both ourselves and our neighbors as we love and pursue things contrary to the commands and design of God. These two categories, we believe that it is safe to presume, most Christians understand to some degree and have considered them both in terms of how the gospel satisfies God's demand for justice and the relevance of the gospel to these areas.

It is the third category of how sinfulness relates to justice, however, that many evangelicals have not been pressed to consider adequately. This is the category that is best described as *culturally embedded sin patterns*.[17] The idea here is that because sinful people create cultures and build societies, the foundational ideas, patterns, and structures they put in place to run these societies will also be tainted

---

17. This category is sometimes referred to in the field of ethics as *structural sin*. We have avoided this terminology here because the phrase can imply that structures themselves are moral agents that can sin. We believe our language better captures the prevailing idea without the pitfall of theological imprecision.

by sin. That is, sinful people create sin-tainted things. We cannot help it. It is our nature. Not only will our ideas about society reflect our depravity, but knowingly or unknowingly we will embed sinful ideas into the cultures we create and will weave bad ideas into the fabric of the societal norms and laws we put in place. Humans build golden calves. As John Calvin rightly noted, we are idol factories.[18]

As a result, the very building blocks and basic assumptions of our societies will reflect our sinfulness. At some level, all human societies will be out of alignment with God's perfect standard of righteousness and justice. As incredible as the United States Constitution is, it is still a flawed document. It was not handed down to Moses on Mount Sinai. But even if it had been, we *still* would have found ways to embed sin into the fabric of our culture. The Israelites certainly did.[19]

To cite a few biblical examples, first consider Mark 7:9–13:

> He was also saying to them, "You are experts at setting aside the commandment of God in order to keep your tradition. For Moses said, 'Honor your father and your mother'; and, 'He who speaks evil of father or mother, is to be put to death'; but you say, 'If a man says to his father or his mother, whatever I have that would help you is Corban (that is to say, given to God),' you no longer permit him to do anything for his father or his mother; thus invalidating the word of God by your tradition which you have handed down; and you do many things such as that."

In this passage we see that, contrary to God's standard of justice, the Jewish leadership had created a social pattern ("tradition") that actually moved contrary to God's design for love and justice. Over time, this sinful disregard for one's mother and father not only was morally justified by the religious leaders, but eventually became embedded as a cultural norm and governed the application of laws *in the name of God*. But as Jesus pointed out, these social patterns or structures ran contrary to God's design and instruction about how one ought to love his or her parents. True justice actually ran contrary to popularly accepted societal norms and socially ingrained practices. Note also that Jesus indicated that they "do *many* things such as that."

One can see a second example of this in John 4 and the commonly accepted Jewish practice of discrimination against the Samaritan people. In John 4:3–45, Jesus acts in a manner contrary to the social customs as well as the accepted religious practice of the day not only by crossing into and passing through the region of Samaria, but also by stopping and interacting with an adulterous Samaritan

---

18. John Calvin, *Institutes of the Christian Religion*, ed. John T. McNeill, trans. Ford Lewis Battles, 2 vols., Library of Christian Classics 20–21 (Philadelphia: Westminster Press, 1960), 1.11.8.

19. Divorce practices in ancient Israel are an excellent example of this. See Deut. 24:1–4.

woman. In his culture at the time, not only did Jews not interact with Samaritans, they socially distanced themselves from them and even shunned them. In addition, it was common practice for Jewish men to have very little interaction with women in public settings. Finally, it was certainly very uncommon—and against both cultural norms and even religious law—for a rabbi to interact alone with a woman of "ill repute." Yet in John 4 we see Jesus breaking through all these culturally embedded sin patterns in order to bring the hope of the gospel to a woman whose life overlapped at all these points. She was a Samaritan, a woman, and an adulteress—and yet Jesus, being fully aware of all these points at which she would normally be discriminated against, was willing to break through the embedded sinful social patterns and habits so that he might bring to her the saving words of life that would justify her before God the Father.

A third New Testament example of culturally embedded sin patterns is evident as the background for Paul's instruction to the church in Ephesians 2:11–22. In this passage, we see Paul helping believers in the new church overcome the prejudices that had become ingrained in the various cultural standards that separated Jews and Gentiles. In the ten verses before this passage, Paul described how the gospel is the means of justification for the problem of our sin nature (Eph. 2:1–9), and also indicated how we ought to justify (align) our works to God in light of God's intended moral order (v. 10). But in this passage (vv. 11–22), he builds on these two prior ideas to demonstrate how the gospel also provides the foundation for creating a just society of believers (i.e., the church) that breaks previously accepted sinful patterns of prejudice and instead models the multiethnic kingdom of God as "one new man." Whereas formerly the powerful traditions, norms, and religious laws that formed societal structures had separated Jews and Gentiles, now the gospel breaks down those unjust societal structures to build one united, glorious, multiethnic church.

Table 9.3. The Gospel and Justice

Ephesians 2:1–9	Sinners justified by grace through faith (justification)
Ephesians 2:10	Sinners learning to live justly (progressive sanctification)
Ephesians 2:11–22	Sinners learning to create a just society together (ecclesiology)

In addition to these biblical examples, one does not need to look far to discover socially embedded and habituated sin patterns in contemporary culture. Consider, for example, laws that legalize the killing of unborn children through abortion and the cultural momentum that normalizes such practices. Similarly, consider laws that make it possible for people of the same gender to "marry" (as though the joining of two men together or two women together could actually depict Christ's love for the church). While laws that legalize such things are relatively new, each to one degree or another has quickly become embedded in the very fabric of contemporary culture. Each has quickly become a matter of "justice" for many. Yet each of these new culturally embedded norms is contrary to what God has revealed about both reality and morality. They are sinful habits of thinking and acting that are embedded not just in individuals but in entire segments of society (including our legal *structures* and *systems*). And to those who are influenced by these types of culturally embedded sin patterns, the very idea that they could be wrong becomes as offensive as the sins are to those who see such practices as wrong.

With the passage of time, acceptance of unjust patterns can result not only in the inversion of a person's moral perspective, but also in moral blindness. That is, a sinful pattern (or patterns) can become so embedded into the social fabric of a society that it becomes virtually unrecognizable to those for whom these patterns have been normalized or are all they have ever known. Consider, as an example, the types of shows that many of us commonly watch on television. Most likely, your (and our) favorite shows will to some degree or another glorify a type of sexual behavior or physical violence that runs directly contrary to what we can expect to find in heaven. But because most of us have become so accustomed to these things in what we watch and find entertaining, we simply watch and enjoy them with little to no conviction. In this sense, we can say that the very fabric of our social structure as it pertains to what we believe is acceptable in visual media is tainted, is out of alignment with God's character, and is therefore "unjust" to some degree. It is often the case that one does not even become aware of how immoral some of this media intake is until one sits down to watch an episode with his or her own young children in the same room. Suddenly, the moral vertigo present in our own lives is revealed. What was easily tolerated is revealed in all its moral depravity.[20]

To be clear, the recognition of these patterns should not lead to the conclusion that all aspects of human society and entertainment media are completely bereft of moral justice. Rather, our point is to demonstrate that just as humans are impacted in every part of themselves because of our sin, so also are our societies impacted in every part because of our sinfulness. Just as depravity impacts each arena of the human person, so also it impacts every arena of human society. Furthermore, as we are sometimes blind to sin in our own personal lives, we can also

---

20. Other examples might be the increasing tolerance that Christians display toward divorce, birth control, or sexual activity outside the bonds of marriage. In each case, the attitudes and practices that Christians engaged in and tolerated about these things were very different a hundred years ago. But as each became more socially acceptable in one generation, the next generation's perspective on these same issues became more tolerant.

be blind to the ingrained sin patterns that are embedded in our own cultures and societies.

Culturally Embedded Sin Patterns and the Need for Justice

It is important to recognize this category of *culturally embedded sin patterns* because to some degree or another all of us are responsible for them simply because we live in them, take part in them, and have had a role in either accepting them or shaping them by our choices to tolerate or participate in them. The human race creates them, and corporately the human race is guilty of them. As Paul teaches us, we are all "in Adam," and thus we are all guilty together (1 Cor. 15:22; cf. Rom. 5:12–14).

Now, obviously, the degree to which each of us is *individually* guilty varies in regard to which culturally embedded sin pattern we are discussing and how long any particular embedded sin pattern has been in place. Who is individually responsible and how much they are individually responsible will vary from sin to sin. But at some level, because we are one human race impacted by Adam's sin, we are all guilty. Just as it is important to recognize that we all bear some responsibility for creating, perpetuating, or not overcoming sinful societal patterns of sin, we also all bear some responsibility for correcting them.

At this point, the discussion of culturally embedded sin patterns gets particularly difficult. On one hand, it would seem that those who are most well off in society and who likely benefit most from unjust social structures are also the ones who bear the greater responsibility to recognize injustice and then use their positions to eradicate any unjust embedded sin patterns that perpetuate it. Herein lies our first problem: often because those who are a part of the dominant or majority culture experience that culture as "normal," it takes hard work to see injustice and oppression because this group does not regularly feel its negative effects. In turn, this leads to the second problem: if someone is benefiting from unjust social structures, what incentive does he or she have to work to recognize the injustice? Even more so, what incentive does the person have to give those benefits up? This question is particularly important to consider if Christian values and sentiments about neighbor love wane in any given society.

Historically, this type of privilege has led to tragic results across time, around the globe, and among all people groups. Consider, for example, the evil ideologies ingrained into the nationalism of the Nazi Party in World War II Germany. Many of the "Christian" citizens of that country had such deeply ingrained sinful outlooks on Jewish people that when the Nazi Party took power, the immoral eradication of the Jews was overlooked or even embraced by those who enjoyed the social status of being a "non-Jew." Or consider two other poignant examples in relatively recent history in which other forms of ingrained racism systematized the discrimination of entire people groups: the apartheid government of South Africa, as well as the institutionalized slavery and later embedded racist practices that followed in the Jim Crow era of U.S. history. In all these cases, even after wars were fought and laws changed, the lingering effects of these culturally embedded sin patterns and societal engines of repression continued to reverberate for generations. Those who enjoyed the positions of power and influence in the culture were typically the slowest to seek change.

On the other hand, consider the point of view of those who experienced greater levels of hardship and prejudice in each of the given cultural contexts mentioned above. It is not hard to realize that in each case, it was the oppressed who could more easily see the culturally embedded sin patterns and repressive structures. After all, they experienced them daily. Hence, it is common that the people who experience various forms of injustice or oppression have a greater incentive to work for change. They do not, however, normatively have enough influence or persuasive positions within a given culture to help those who do have those positions to see and understand the need for change. Nor do they have the leverage to catalyze the change themselves. But they do have the motivation and the greater longing precisely because they have the greater need.

Historically, this type of vulnerability among groups experiencing oppression has also led to some unfortunate results. While the concept of "structural sin" is as old as St. Augustine's classic *City of God*, it was co-opted and popularized by liberation theology as a way to bring attention to the dehumanizing policies and laws impacting the poor in South America.[21] While bringing awareness to the plight of the poor is in itself a good thing, liberation theology went much further than bringing awareness. Unfortunately, it also embraced many elements of Marxist thought and ideology and subtly embedded them in its theological formulations. One of the negative results of this theological drift was a call to identifying structural sin and culturally embedded sin patterns, often to the exclusion of concern for personal sin and the need for personal redemption. The so-called gospel that liberation theology inevitably began to preach no longer emphasized the penal substitutionary death of Jesus Christ. Rather, Christ became the champion of the lower social classes, and salvation was often equated with a call for social changes and economic revolution.[22]

---

21. Harry J. Huebner, *An Introduction to Christian Ethics: History, Movements, People* (Waco, TX: Baylor University Press, 2012), 470.

22. For a very insightful analysis and correction of the failings of liberation theology, see Joseph Ratzinger, "Instruction on Certain Aspects of the 'Theology of Liberation,'" Congregation for the Doctrine of Faith, August 6, 1984, http://www.vatican.va/roman_curia/congregations/cfaith/documents/rc_con_cfaith_doc_19840806_theology-liberation_en.html. In terms of our moral methodology discussion (chapter 8) this is precisely why we argued that the pastoral domains must be subjugated to the normative theological domains of ethics.

Hand in hand with this doctrinal shift came a sense of *victimization* in which oppressed groups saw the primary problem as *others' having sinned against them*. With this combination of ideas, the recognition of, and preaching about, personal sin was largely lost. Sin was no longer understood as something "I did" for which the individual was responsible to repent. It was no longer a personal issue of a sinner's breaking God's perfect and just standard and thereby robbing him of the worship he is due. Instead, now sin was cast as unjust behaviors that "others committed against me" and for which the victims claimed a right to demand reparations as victims of sinful oppression. Therefore, while it seems that liberation theology may have actually provided some helpful ideas to *diagnose* a problem, it—and other liberation movements in the same tradition—offered a *cure* that stripped the gospel of its central point of emphasis.

These are significant problems. While liberation theology and similar movements can at times offer helpful observations of the possibility of sinful social patterns and culturally ingrained forms of repression, the underlying assumptions of their theological and ethical systems create more problems than they solve. We are right not only to be aware of these theological and ethical errors, but also to be responsible to diligently guard against them. Even more, when they undermine the historically orthodox notions of personal responsibility, sinfulness, and the need for Christ's penal substitutionary atonement, they must be aggressively rejected (2 Cor. 10:5).

Having identified these errors in recent theological movements and having noted the special concern we should have to avoid them, we must also be careful not to throw the baby out with the bathwater. It would be disingenuous to appeal to the wrong *solutions* provided by one heretical movement to deny that there is a problem in the first place. The wrong answer to a problem does not mean that the problem does not exist. If someone tells you that eating pizza is the cure for a disease, you do not deny that the disease exists merely because someone has suggested an absurd idea as the cure.

In addition, we must be careful not to assume a "guilt by association" posture when addressing ethical issues even though some who have spoken to those issues do so with false worldview assumptions. The fact that atheists believe that $2 + 2 = 4$ does not mean that I have to deny $2 + 2 = 4$ in order to avoid being an atheist. The New Testament Gospels are full of accounts in which demons proclaimed Jesus as the Son of God (e.g., Mark 5:6–7). Even demons can see truth in part. Agreeing with the demons on that one point does not mean that we agree with them in whole. Similarly, the fact that some theologians and ethicists influenced by liberation theology (e.g., critical race theorists) want to say that subtle forms of oppression and racism permeate our social structures does not mean that I have to deny that subtle forms of culturally embedded sin patterns that foster various types of oppression or racism permeate our social structures in order to avoid being a liberation theologian or a critical race theorist. Recognizing the possibility of a legitimate diagnosis does not mean that I have to affirm or accept either the cure or the worldview of the person making the diagnosis.

The question whether someone in the so-called majority culture should be vilified for benefiting from a culturally embedded sin pattern that may have been put in place decades or even centuries before is worthy of discussion and debate. It is our opinion that such a person *should not* be vilified or shamed but should be pressed to consider the responsibility that comes with such benefits (Luke 12:48b). It should be undebatable that it is at the very least a responsibility of our current generation to open our eyes and, through the power of the Holy Spirit and the quickening of the Word, become better at seeing these culturally embedded sin patterns for what they are and seek to eradicate them and their impact. In the same way that we rigorously defend orthodoxy, we must also rigorously seek to incarnate our orthodoxy by living lives of orthopraxy.

The gospel compels us to make it our responsibility to be a part of restoring justice for all three forms of sinfulness. Our concern for evangelism, discipleship, and teaching the nations to obey all that God commands must compel us to care about justice and social engagement.

Whether it be voting for the reversal of laws permitting the destruction of babies through abortion, campaigning for clear cultural policies pertaining to God-designed sexual order in public venues such as bathrooms, teaching our children the truth about the dehumanizing idea of same-sex marriage, or battling inherently discriminatory practices that may be present in various judicial processes, it matters that Christians bring a clear sense of biblical justice and the hope of the gospel to bear on the world they live in. While it is the church's primary task to "make disciples of all the nations" (Matt. 28:19), it is part of the responsibility of those disciples to seek justice in every quarter of life.

Three Ways That the Gospel Provides a Just Remedy for Sin and Sinfulness

How is the gospel relevant to all three of these areas of sinfulness? With regard to the first form of injustice against God, left to ourselves we have no way of making ourselves just. Because of our sin, the only "just" or "fair" solution would be for all sinful humans to be treated as equals in punishment. Since God is *infinitely holy*, our unjust offense against God is *infinitely wicked*. Indeed, justice demands that each of us be damned to hell eternally as just punishment for offending an infinitely holy God. This is what would be just.

Thankfully, God deals with our status as *sinners* in love, mercy, and grace. His justice is upheld and appeased through the working of the second person of the

Trinity, Jesus Christ, dying in the place of sinners and absorbing the just punishment that our sins deserved. In this sense, as James 2:13 puts it, God's mercy "triumphs over judgment." Jesus works as our High Priest to make intercession on our behalf before God the Father (Heb. 5:2–10). For those who place their faith in him, he then *justifies* them (Rom. 3:19–26). He legally/forensically declares them to be *made just* such that they can stand before God not as *sinners*, but as rescued *saints* who have the imputed righteousness of Christ. In short, sin is not overlooked, rather God's wrath is satisfied through Jesus' loving, merciful, and gracious work of justice (i.e., justification).

In regard to the second category of injustice and sin in which we choose sinful acts and adopt sinful dispositions, we like how Graeme Goldsworthy helps us properly understand the relationship of God's redeeming work and God's sanctifying work to properly align (or "justify") our behavior. He writes:

> Theologically the priority of justification to sanctification means that the action of God in Christ, the grace of God acting *for* us, is prior to, and is the source of, the action of God *in* us. . . . In simple terms, this means that God puts us into a right relationship with himself as the prerequisite for the ongoing change in our lives . . . as well as that of the society around us—be it the church or the world cultures in which we live.[23]

Based on this, we understand that once God justifies us into right relationship with him, he also desires to see us live in accord with his design for the world. Thus, as we pointed out in chapter 4, it is through the work of the third person of the Trinity, the Holy Spirit, that we are progressively sanctified. God is calling us to live justly and reflect his holiness in all that we are and all that we do. Because Jesus is our Lord and King, his dominion over every aspect of our lives needs to be progressively and increasingly accepted and honored.

It is helpful here to shift our metaphor so as to better understand the relationship of justice and *sins*. Whereas in the previous category of sin we understood justice through a legal metaphor of being "declared just" by a righteous Judge, now it is helpful to think of the work of a carpenter. Anyone who has ever tried to use 2x4 boards to construct a wall for a house knows that in order for the structure to be sound, the boards have to be put in proper alignment with one another, as well as in accord with the blueprints. In this sense, carpenters describe the process of aligning the wood properly as "justifying the boards." Similar to what takes place when a building is built properly, bringing our lives under the lordship of Christ

---

23. Graeme Goldsworthy, *Gospel-Centered Hermeneutics: Foundations and Principles of Evangelical Biblical Interpretation* (Downers Grove, IL: IVP Academic, 2006), 16 (emphasis added).

requires a proper alignment of the "boards of our lives." Thus, we can speak of our personal sanctification as a moral and ethical justification of these "boards of our lives" with God's particular moral standards and laws, which function as aspects of his eternally "just" design (blueprints).

This carpentry metaphor also works nicely to understand how God desires us to seek proper alignment (or justice) as it relates to the third category of sinfulness: *culturally embedded sin patterns*. Here we need to think of Jesus not only as our High Priest, but also as our Lord, our King, and the ultimate Prophet who is calling all aspects of creation back into alignment with God's eternal law. Every corner, every aspect, every square inch of the created order belongs to God. Therefore, the preaching of the gospel (we are saved by grace alone, through faith alone, by Christ alone) must result in making an impact on socially embedded sin patterns, whether they be economic, political, cultural, ecclesial, or moral. God's redemptive design for the world is that the gospel will change people (justification), those changed people will then obey God's commands and become conformed to the character of Christ (sanctification), and those people who are conformed to the character of Christ together bring hope, light, and life to the societies of the world (societal sanctification or "societal justice").

> *Jesus invaded the world through his incarnation.* The Word became flesh and dwelt among us! As his followers, his disciples, we have been tasked with being his incarnational witnesses until he returns. Christians need to be in the culture among the people, making an impact for the Gospel, and thus emulating the life of Jesus, who left his home in glory to come and live among us to give us the opportunity to be part of his kingdom. Missional worshipers understand that we must invade the world not to become like it, but so that it will become like our Lord.[24]

Table 9.4. Categories of Sin Related to Justice

Category of Sin	Impact of Sin	Remedy for Sin
Person as *sinner*	Our positional standing before God as fallen sinners	Jesus as High Priest
Personal *sins*	Our particular acts, behaviors, and daily moral choices that in turn shape our character	Jesus as King (Lord)
Culturally embedded patterns of *sinfulness*	The shape or fabric of culture	Jesus as Prophet

24. Mark D. Liederbach and Alvin L. Reid, *The Convergent Church: Missional Worshipers in an Emerging Culture* (Grand Rapids: Kregel, 2009), 278.

Conclusion

We believe it is imperative that Jesus' disciples process all their ideas about justice and its outworking through an explicitly theocentric lens. The people that God created to worship and enjoy him forever both individually and corporately have turned to lesser things. The greatest injustice in history has been committed against God. All other forms of injustice result from this fact and are best understood as deviations from his eternally good and just plan. This is true not only of the personally immoral acts of injustice that we commit against others and that are committed against us, but also of the culturally embedded sin patterns such as abortion laws, same-sex-marriage laws, and the subtler forms of oppression that pervade our cultures and societies. Failure to recognize this point will lead to confusion about the nature, purpose, and application of justice and social engagement.

When we get the theocentric starting point right, it is easy to see why Christians have a long history of seeking justice as it relates to all three categories of sins that we have identified and discussed. As R. E. O. White argues, the particular impulse to address social issues among American Protestants and evangelicals in particular stems from the very same "zeal and compassion" that leads them to do evangelism. The source is a genuine love for sinners in need of God's grace. This is as true for those who came from the Calvinist position as they strove to do good works in order to mitigate social evils as it was for those in the Wesleyan tradition who sought to transform sinners into "crusaders against social sin" long before the social-gospel movement became a point of concern.[25]

As we have attempted to show in this chapter, we ought to embrace the pursuit of justice at the level of culturally embedded sin patterns as a biblical imperative that arises from a right preaching of the gospel and as a fulfillment of the Great Commission's instruction for us to "teach them to observe" all that Jesus has commanded. When the idea of *social justice* is properly understood, it coincides with the way in which Christians have sought to bring hope for the world since the inception of the church. A quest for biblical justice requires social engagement.

Grounding the idea of justice and social engagement in a moral framework that emphasizes the necessity of verbal proclamation of the gospel and the Great Commission means that we can understand that striving for social justice does not necessitate either a neglect of evangelism or a compromise of the essential doctrines of the faith. In fact, it depends on these very things for its foundation and motivation. Grounding an understanding of social justice on historically

---

25. R. E. O. White, *Christian Ethics* (Macon, GA: Mercer University Press, 1994), 266–70. White's discussion in this chapter provides a helpful historical analysis of what he describes as the "social gospel in action."

orthodox doctrines does not necessitate the embracing of *victimization* as a legitimate category for demanding reparations. In fact, it necessitates an emphasis on personal sin and responsibility. Embracing the importance of justice at the level of culturally embedded sin patterns also does not necessitate the acceptance of either liberation theology or the Marxist socialist economic principles of redistribution that often accompany it. Further, it does not necessitate the rejection of capitalism as a viable economic structure. In fact, it recognizes that in spite of its various failings, capitalistic economic policies have arguably done far more to raise the overall wealth and well-being of humans globally than any other economic system in history.[26]

A concern for justice and social engagement does, however, press us to move with strength into the lives and contexts of people who suffer and are oppressed in order to tell them of the good news of the gospel (we are saved by grace alone, through faith alone, by Christ alone) and then seek to bring restoration to all aspects of their lives and all parts of society *as far as the curse is found*. In sum, while many questions pertaining to how best to apply justice remain (some of which we will address in subsequent chapters), at its most fundamental level, a biblical understanding of justice and social engagement is nothing more and nothing less than the total alignment of all creation with the eternal law of God. It is not based on a quest for human rights, but it seeks an expression of human responsibilities to love the Lord with all one's heart, soul, mind, and strength and to take the initiative to love one's neighbor as oneself. A biblical understanding of justice and social engagement seeks human flourishing at every level of existence such that all humans can grow into maturity. Justice is dependent on God's created design for the world. It must be worked for in light of the final *telos* toward which God ordered all things. It requires the alignment of character and behavior to the standards set forth for us through divine revelation (i.e., theological/normative domains), and it must be appropriately administered in context with reference to the circumstances, consequences, and persons that will feel the impact of our choices (i.e., pastoral/contextual domains). Indeed, when understood through a theocentric lens, the pursuit of justice *is* ethics as worship.

Key Terms and Concepts

cultural Marxism	material principle of justice
formal principle of justice	particular justice
justice	righteousness
liberation theology	sanctification, personal

26. See chapter 12 for further discussion.

social justice   universal justice

Key Scriptures

Luke 4:17–21   Ephesians 2:1–9
Luke 19:10   Ephesians 2:10
John 4:3–45   Ephesians 2:11–22
Romans 3:19–26   2 Timothy 2:14
Romans 10:14–17

Study Questions

1. How is the question of *justice* related to the *Godness* of God (the fact that God is God)? What is the source and standard of justice that a Christian should champion in the culture? How does this idea shape your understanding of *social justice*?   → *social justice*

2. Why must a concern for social justice be grounded in a concern for evangelism and discipleship? ←

3. Read Matthew 28:18–20, Luke 4:17–19, and Romans 10:14–17. What is the connection between the good news (gospel), proclamation, the mission of God, and justice?

4. What is the *formal principle of justice*? Why does the formal principle of justice need some type of *material principle of justice*?

5. How is a biblical understanding of justice related to the doctrines of justification, sanctification, and ecclesiology?

For Further Reading

DeYoung, Kevin, and Greg Gilbert. *What Is the Mission of the Church? Making Sense of Social Justice, Shalom, and the Great Commission*. Wheaton, IL: Crossway, 2011.

Hoang, Bethany Hanke, and Kristen Deede Johnson. *The Justice Calling: Where Passion Meets Perseverance*. Grand Rapids: Brazos, 2016.

Keller, Timothy. *Center Church: Doing Balanced, Gospel-Centered Ministry in Your Church*. Grand Rapids: Zondervan, 2012.

———. *Generous Justice: How God's Grace Makes Us Just*. New York: Riverhead Books, 2012.

Niebuhr, H. Richard. *Christ and Culture*. San Francisco: HarperCollins, 2001.

Perkins, John M. *Dream with Me: Race, Love, and the Struggle We Must Win*. Grand Rapids: Baker, 2017.

Ratzinger, Joseph. "Instruction on Certain Aspects of the 'Theology of Liberation.'" Congregation for the Doctrine of Faith, August 6, 1984. http://www.vatican .va/roman_curia/congregations/cfaith/documents/rc_con_cfaith_doc_198 40806_theology-liberation_en.html.

Wright, Christopher J. H. *Old Testament Ethics for the People of God*. Downers Grove, IL: IVP Academic, 2004.

10

Race, Ethnicity, and Kingdom Diversity

*"And He has made from one blood every nation of men to dwell on all the
face of the earth, and has determined their preappointed times and the
boundaries of their dwellings." —APOSTLE PAUL, ACTS 17:26 NKJV*

"No people are immune to the virus of racism."[1]
—ROBERTSON MCQUILKIN AND PAUL COPAN,
An Introduction to Biblical Ethics

Introduction

When Martin Luther King Jr. stood on the steps of the Lincoln Memorial and
delivered his "I Have a Dream" speech on August 28, 1963, he was trying to wake
us up to a dream that will someday come true. When he cited the truths that form
the heart of our country's founding documents, he not only pointed us backward
to the words that were meant to guide us as a nation, but also pointed us forward
to the day when those words would take shape around the throne of God. Looking backward at our Declaration of Independence, he pointed us to the words
"We hold these truths to be self-evident, that all men are created equal," so that we
could "cash this check" on the promise that all humans "would be guaranteed the
unalienable rights of life, liberty and the pursuit of happiness."[2]

Looking forward, he was pointing us to a dream—a dream of something far
more beautiful. He dreamed that we could move beyond the mere minimal thresh-
olds of societal justice to something more in keeping with biblical love. King had
a dream that one day little black boys and black girls would be able to join hands

---

1. Robertson McQuilkin and Paul Copan, *An Introduction to Biblical Ethics: Walking in the Way of
Wisdom*, 3rd ed. (Downers Grove, IL: IVP Academic, 2014), 356.

2. Martin Luther King Jr., "I Have a Dream," in *A Testament of Hope: The Essential Writings and Speeches
of Martin Luther King, Jr.*, ed. James M. Washington (New York: HarperOne, 1986), 217.

with little white boys and white girls as brothers and sisters. He dreamed that together we could speed up the journey and see a day when all of God's children—black and white alike—could not only enjoy a form of equal justice before the law in the here and now, but together truly be free in the eyes of God.[3]

In that remarkable speech, King pointed us to a dream that is already the reality of our future in heaven. It is a dream that coincides with Revelation 5:9 and 7:9 from which we learn that before the very throne of God, worship will rise equally from every people, tribe, tongue, and nation. Far from being color-blind, in heaven there is a beautiful celebration of both color and culture. Ultimately, it is a dream so tightly connected to the gospel that if we do not share it, we ought to reevaluate whether we are Christians.

Our purpose in this chapter is to address the issues of race and racism from the perspective of ethics as worship. It is our hope to offer clarity from the Bible regarding the term *race* and from that point of clarity understand why our expressions of racism are so wicked and grievous before the Lord. To paraphrase J. Deotis Roberts, what we are seeking is a Christian ethical approach to race relations that will lead us beyond a hypocritical tokenism to both a freedom and a genuine reconciliation between equals that can come only through the gospel.[4]

Because of the limitations of space as well as the breadth of the topic, we will limit ourselves here to a discussion that primarily addresses the topic of racism via the "black-white binary." In doing so, we recognize that we are in danger of overlooking the reality that many different ethnic groups (Chinese, Japanese, Native Americans, Hispanics, and so on) have experienced their own unique forms of discrimination at various points in U.S. history, as well as many other versions of discrimination in the global context.[5] Our reason for taking this approach is largely pragmatic: it will allow for a bit of simplification in order to attempt to make some sense of a very complicated social context and ethical issue. We hope that the ideas and principles we discuss will easily transfer to other ethnic contexts insofar as the historical context allows.

To accomplish our task, we first define several key terms and concepts to set a

3. King, "I Have a Dream," 217–20.

4. J. Deotis Roberts, *Liberation and Reconciliation: A Black Theology*, 2nd ed. (Louisville: Westminster John Knox, 2005), 9.

5. In this we fully recognize that we are tackling the discussion from a vantage point that supports an "exceptionalism" point of view as it relates to the black experience. We do not, however, wish to deny the validity of certain aspects of the "differential racialization thesis," which holds that different minority groups have been racialized in their own unique ways by majority groups. For an explanation of these terms and concepts, see Richard Delgado and Jean Stefancic, *Critical Race Theory: An Introduction*, 3rd ed. (New York: New York University Press, 2017), 77–84. While it should be obvious from our own conclusions and evaluation of race and racism in this chapter that we strongly reject both the worldview and the conclusions provided by Delgado and Stefancic, we found their clear writing style and their attempts to clarify terms to be very helpful.

baseline of understanding for the sections that follow. Next, we move to a consideration of Scripture and the relevant passages on theological doctrines that ought to shape a distinctively Christian view of race and ethnicity. Third, we explore how one's situatedness in society affects both how one perceives the problem of racism and what one emphasizes as the crucial steps toward reconciliation. Finally, by way of conclusion, we consider several implications from our discussion and offer several principles for guidance as together we seek to become mature and ministering worshipers of God.

Key Terms and Definitions

Race

When we use the word *race* in contemporary culture, we often assume it to be an accurate descriptor of various divisions within the human species. In actuality, this is not the case. There is quite a bit of disagreement among the scientific, social science, and theological communities about what the term means and how it is best applied.

In regard to the scientific community, in the past several centuries many attempts were made to define *race* as a biologically grounded category that could be used to identify various groups of people based on shared physical or genetic qualities. Until fairly recently, biologically based theories of race divided humankind into three racial groupings: Caucasoid, Negroid, Mongoloid (occasionally a fourth grouping of Australoid was also included as a possibility). Many have rightly pointed out that such a theory was not derived primarily from science, but rather was an attempt to co-opt scientific methods to justify bigotry and racial discrimination. One of the most influential (and infamous) early scientific arguments to make this claim was Arthur de Gobineau's *The Inequality of Human Races*, originally published in 1854.[6] He argued that there are multiple races and that the white race is superior. But while this biologically based idea of racial identity was widely popular a century ago and even persists to a large degree now in the general public, advances in genetic science have completely undermined its validity. In fact, when one considers the data, one discovers that there are

> no genetic characteristics possessed by all Blacks but not by non-Blacks; similarly, there is no gene or cluster of genes common to all Whites but not to non-Whites. . . . The data compiled by various scientists demonstrate, contrary to popular opinion,

---

6. Arthur de Gobineau, *The Inequality of Human Races*, trans. Adrian Collins (London: William Heinemann, 1915), accessed June 7, 2019, https://archive.org/details/inequalityofhuma00gobi. American anthropologist E. A. Hooton was one of many influential scientists to conceive of and argue for biologically based ideas of race.

that intra-group differences exceed inter-group differences. That is, greater genetic variation exists *within* the populations typically labeled Black and White than *between* these populations.[7]

Because genetic studies regarding race so clearly disrupt previously held ideas, most now believe that a biologically based account of race is largely an illusion. In his influential work on the topic, Ashley Montagu comments that

> the myth of race refers not to the fact that physically distinguishable populations of humans exist, but rather to the belief that races are populations of peoples whose physical differences are innately linked with significant differences in mental capacities, and that these innate hierarchical differences are measurable by the cultural achievements of such populations, as well as by standardized intelligence (IQ) tests. This belief is thoroughly and dangerously unsound. It is the belief of racists and racism.[8]

In comparison to the other extremely clear biological and genetic demarcations that distinguish humans from one another (sex: males and females), scientists find no similarly clear basis for distinguishing between human races. Simply put, from a scientific point of view, there is one race—the human race.[9]

Sociologists also deny biologically based categories of race and instead point to a social explanation. Eduardo Bonilla-Silva points out that contemporary sociologists almost unanimously agree that race is a *socially constructed category* with no ultimate grounding in either eternal or essential categories.[10] Instead, when

7. Ian F. Haney López, "The Social Construction of Race," in *Critical Race Theory: The Cutting Edge,* ed. Richard Delgado and Jean Stefancic, 3rd ed. (Philadelphia: Temple University Press, 2013), 242.

8. Ashley Montagu, *Man's Most Dangerous Myth: The Fallacy of Race*, 6th ed. (Walnut Creek, CA: AltaMira Press, 1997), 44.

9. For an interesting discussion of this reality, see Vivian Chou, "How Science and Genetics Are Reshaping the Race Debate of the 21st Century," Science in the News, Harvard University, Graduate School of Arts and Sciences, April 17, 2017, accessed June 4, 2020, http://sitn.hms.harvard.edu/flash/2017/science-genetics-reshaping-race-debate-21st-century/. Scientific conclusions such as these have led Ian Haney López to comment that the popularly held biologically based categories of race that were once considered objective (Caucasoid, Negroid, Mongoloid) "are now widely regarded as empty relics, persistent shadows of the social belief in races that permeated early scientific thought." Haney López, "Social Construction of Race," 246. Similarly, clarity on this point has led Barbara Fields to poignantly comment: "Anyone who continues to believe in race as a physical attribute of individuals, despite the now commonplace disclaimers of biologists and geneticists, might as well also believe that Santa Claus, the Easter Bunny, and the tooth fairy are real, and that the earth stands still while the sun moves." Karen E. Fields and Barbara J. Fields, *Racecraft: The Soul of Inequality in American Life* (Brooklyn, NY: Verso, 2012), 113.

10. Eduardo Bonilla-Silva, *Racism without Racists: Color Blind Racism and the Persistence of Racial Inequality in America*, 5th ed. (Lanham, MD: Rowman & Littlefield, 2018), 8. Bonilla-Silva notes that three competing ideas now replace the antiquated notion of biologically based racial distinctions. The first suggests

sociologists point to multiple "races," they are actually referring to "categories of difference that exist only in society: They are produced by myriad conflicting social forces; they overlap and inform other social categories; they are fluid rather than static and fixed; and they make sense only in relationship to other racial categories, having no meaningful independent existence."[11]

Important for our discussion moving forward, however, is that the *concept of race* remains sociologically important in spite of the reality that there is actually no biological foundation to the idea that there are multiple races. Once the socially constructed ideas of race are created and embedded within the cultural fabric of a society, they function *as though* they were real, they carry real power, and they have real social consequences.[12] The task that sociologists and ethicists must consider is how these non-biologically based, socially constructed ideas of race lead to the creation of social structures and institutions. From this viewpoint, many secular (and some Christian) sociologists and ethicists also seek to explain how these social structures of race may account for any real or perceived systemic patterns of oppression and privilege that continue to exist in society. One particularly helpful definition describes *race* as

> a socially constructed reality that attributes negative or positive meaning to biological characteristics and cultural manifestations that are used to categorize people. This categorization creates "in" and "out" groups. Inhabiting the "in" group is prerequisite for gaining social influence and requires diminishing distinctions within it (i.e., fabricating homogeneity) and simultaneously highlighting the distinctions among the "out" groups to ensure their perpetual marginalization.[13]

From the point of view of theological ethics—and specifically ethics as worship—we note, along with Walter Strickland and Dayton Hartman, that such an understanding of race "is unbiblical and will not appear in God's kingdom." It is imperative, therefore, to develop an understanding of race by placing primacy of authority not on scientific or sociological data, but first of all on the inerrant

---

that because race is a social construction that has no basis in objective reality, it is no longer a helpful category for understanding human social interaction. That is, the term *race* is ultimately no longer helpful. Other categories such as *class* or *ethnicity* may be better. A second view, he says, pays lip service to the idea that race is a social construction but then goes on to use the categories of biologically based race as its ground of evaluation. The third, and Bonilla-Silva's own, view is that race is a socially constructed idea with no metaphysical or essential foundation. But once it is created, it has a "social reality" or power that produces real effects on people and social structures.

11. Haney López, "Social Construction of Race," 245–46.

12. Bonilla-Silva, *Racism without Racists*, 8.

13. Walter R. Strickland II and Dayton Hartman, *For God So Loved the World* (Nashville: B&H Academic, 2020), xix–xx.

teachings of Scripture. From God's Word, we get not only clear teaching about the concept of *race* but also a clear understanding of how our conceptions of race have become so twisted and have resulted in the problem of racism. We will return to that discussion later in the chapter, but in anticipation of our study there, we believe Dave Unander is correct when he writes:

> There is only one human race . . . from every perspective: biological, historical, and in God's Word, the Bible. For the past five hundred years, Western society has been playing out a role in a drama written by the Enemy of our souls, the myth of the master race, and every act has been a tragedy. It's time to change the script.[14]

Ethnicity

The second term that we seek to clarify is *ethnicity*. Daniel Hays notes, "Defining and determining 'ethnicity' is complex and controversial, even among contemporary groups where mounds of sociological data exist and live interviews are possible."[15] The problem is determining which characteristics distinguish one ethnicity from another. Merriam-Webster defines *ethnic* as "of or relating to large groups of people classed according to common racial, national, tribal, religious, linguistic, or cultural origin or background."[16] Note that once the biological aspect is removed from the definition of *race*, the elements that remain by which sociologists seek to understand the nature of race are all categories that Webster lists as elements of *ethnicity*. Given this definition, it should be clear that at a functional level, once the term *race* is dislodged from a biological foundation, the concepts of *race* and *ethnicity* virtually overlap.

Based on this reality, and for reasons that will become clear in the next section, we believe the term *ethnicity* better fits the biblical paradigm of how best to understand the differences between human image-bearers than what we often describe in culture as differing *races*. The term *racism* would then be limited to a

14. Dave Unander, *Shattering the Myth of Race: Genetic Realities and Biblical Truths* (Valley Forge, PA: Judson, 2000), 2.

15. J. Daniel Hays, *From Every People and Nation: A Biblical Theology of Race* (Downers Grove, IL: InterVarsity Press, 2003), 28.

16. Merriam-Webster, s.v. "ethnic," accessed June 7, 2019, https://www.merriam-webster.com/dictionary/ethnic. This definition of *ethnicity* is very helpful for our purposes here, but in its own way it, too, is likely a bit simplistic. It may be helpful to further distinguish the category of *ethnicity* from the word *culture*—the former dealing primarily with physical differences within the one human race and the latter dealing with social elements such as language, food, and music that create affinities among various people groups. Walter R. Strickland II helpfully defines *culture* as "a nonbiological phenomenon that shapes common behaviors and thought patterns shared by a people group." This would better account for situations such as one in which someone with white skin feels more at home in "black culture," or vice versa. Strickland and Hartman, *For God So Loved the World*, xix.

description of how people adopt a wrong view of what it means to be human but that still functions to condition people to respond negatively to ethnic differences.

Prejudice, Discrimination, and Racism

Having provided clarity on these basic terms, we now move to an understanding of the words and ideas used to describe the moral problems associated with them. *Prejudice* commonly refers to the preconceived ideas, opinions, or biases we hold to and believe even though they are not based on reason and are certainly not present in Scripture. Merriam-Webster defines *prejudice* as "an adverse opinion or leaning formed without just grounds or before sufficient knowledge."[17] *Prejudice*, in this sense, has to do with our individual internal selves, the way we think about the world, and the values we assign to people regardless of whether they align with actual facts about either particular persons or groups of people. In fact, prejudice often manifests itself in an irrational attitude of varying degrees of hostility directed toward people or cultures that we do not like. These attitudes are based on stereotyped opinions that are often out of alignment with reality.

Discrimination, as the term relates to prejudice, involves the decision-making process and choices by which preferential treatment is given to one person or group. While a person can be said to use *discrimination* in a positive sense (e.g., "She has a discriminating taste for coffee"), normatively the term is used to describe unfair or evil choices based on prejudiced assumptions or racist perspectives and policies.

Racism moves from the reality of preferences and biases, the problem of prejudice, and the immorality of discrimination to a firmly held belief that the primary traits or tendencies of one particular people group are superior to that of another and can lead to social, political, economic, or even religious doctrines and practices that favor the group believed to be superior. Returning to the definition of *race* as given by Strickland and Hartman above, racism involves both attitudinal and behavioral choices and habits that perpetuate an emphasis on the socially constructed differences in such a way as to gain, maintain, or increase personal, communal, or systemic advantage.[18]

Over time, these initially constructed biases can become second nature and increasingly covert within the mental categories and communications patterns of individuals and communities as a whole. When this takes place, they can (and often do) ultimately become systemically embedded sin patterns within any given society. Eventually, these sin patterns can become so ingrained that "beneficiaries

17. Merriam-Webster, s.v. "prejudice," accessed June 6, 2019, https://www.merriam-webster.com/dictionary/prejudice.

18. Strickland and Hartman, *For God So Loved the World*, xx.

of systems rarely appreciate the value received and can unknowingly perpetuate such structures. By contrast, those disadvantaged by depressing systems consistently feel the negative effects of inequitable structures."[19]

When these biased patterns of thinking and communicating become rooted in either an individual or a society, the particular form of racist behavior may actually change, while the culturally embedded presence of racialized thinking and discriminatory biases does not. Michael Emerson and Christian Smith capture the idea well:

> A major problem in understanding race relations in the United States is that we tend to understand race, racism, and the form of racialization as constants rather than variables. . . . Racism, for instance, is often captured best in people's minds by the ideology and actions of the Ku Klux Klan: an overt doctrine of racial superiority—usually labeled prejudice—that leads to discrimination. Based on this unchanging standard, racism is viewed as an irrational psychological phenomenon that is the product of individuals, and is evidenced in overt, usually hostile behavior. . . . Based on this approach, [social scientists] conclude that racism is declining, since a smaller percentage of people over time respond in a prejudiced fashion.[20]

Thus, as we will discuss later, the ingrained mental categorizations that shape cultural expressions of which group is "in" and which is "out" become difficult to pin down or are even outright denied when particular expressions of racism disappear. Public schools, for example, may now be integrated, but this does not mean that the attitudes, biases, or behaviors that fueled the push for segregation are gone. The possibility of unrecognized and unintentional racism becomes a topic of extreme importance if true reconciliation is to occur. Later in the chapter, we will engage and analyze the importance of this topic with personal and practical examples. But first, we must look to Scripture to shape a proper vision of race and the problem of racism.

The Bible, Race, and Racism

What Does the Bible Teach about Race?

Christian discussions on the issue of race and the problem of racism too often adopt ideas and concepts from secular culture and literature rather than allowing

---

19. Strickland and Hartman, *For God So Loved the World*, xx.

20. Michael O. Emerson and Christian Smith, *Divided by Faith: Evangelical Religion and the Problem of Race in America* (Oxford: Oxford University Press, 2000), 8.

Scripture to drive one's understanding and solutions. As George Yancey points out in his *Beyond Racial Gridlock*: "When Christians write and speak about racial issues, they sound much like their secular counterparts. Instead of initiating our own solutions to the problems of racism, we merely copy the solutions offered by the rest of the world."[21] As a result, many treatments of the issue are incomplete and inadequate not only because they do not embrace the root issues that are at play (such as God's design and human sinfulness), but also because they offer inferior solutions based on false worldview assumptions. Many of the secular ideas about the problem of racism and the accompanying solutions offered to patterns of discrimination are deeply flawed precisely because they are derived from heretical ideas about God, human nature, and the means of salvation.

In contrast, Christians must look to Scripture and the theological tenets of our faith to shake ourselves loose from these inferior ideas and in turn look to Scripture to form in us a proper perspective about how God has structured both reality and morality.[22] Only then can we stand on God-honoring principles that inform our ideas about race and offer God-glorifying solutions to the problem of racism (see 2 Cor. 10:3–6; Col. 2:8).

As is the case with every other moral issue, the proper starting place for discussing race and racism is with the first four words of the Bible: "In the beginning God . . ." The reason for this is twofold. First, it is important to begin with the recognition that God is the Creator who designed the world for maximal flourishing and then powerfully spoke it into existence. Because of this, what we discover in the creation narratives about God's design as it relates to any moral issue provides a baseline of understanding against which all following discussions can be compared.

Second, it is not only God's existence and creative power that matter in this discussion, but also what God reveals about himself in terms of his moral attributes. For example, because God is a good God, we can know that his creation and his created design are inherently good. Likewise, the fact that he is all-powerful ensures that he is able to bring about a perfect fulfillment of his good intentions. Because he is upright and just in his very nature, we can know that in his goodness and power he will ultimately right all wrongs and bring to order all that sin has corrupted.

This is particularly helpful as it relates to race and the problem of racism because of what we see revealed about humans and human nature in Genesis 1:27–28. Note again how the passage unfolds:

21. George Yancey, *Beyond Racial Gridlock: Embracing Mutual Responsibility* (Downers Grove, IL: InterVarsity Press, 2006), 11.
22. Yancey, *Beyond Racial Gridlock*, 11.

God created man in His own image, in the image of God He created him; male and female He created them. God blessed them; and God said to them, "Be fruitful and multiply, and fill the earth, and subdue it; and rule over the fish of the sea and over the birds of the sky and over every living thing that moves on the earth."

Earlier in the book (chapter 2), we discussed at length both the nature of what it means to be created in the image of God and the purpose for human existence. We pointed out that because all human beings are image-bearers, all share an equal dignity regardless of factors such as gender, color, age on the spectrum of life, or one's ability to function in society. As image-bearers, not only do all humans share an infinite worth in the eyes of God (as demonstrated by God's willingness to pay an infinite price to redeem us), but all were created for the purpose of worshiping God and glorifying him maximally throughout all creation.

We can now build from these ideas to point out two other extremely important factors from this passage that relate to our discussion of race and ethnicity. First, science, as we learned from our earlier discussion, affirms what the Bible clearly teaches. Because all humans come from the one bloodline of Adam and Eve, all humans are united in their racial category. There is only one race among human beings—the human race. In Acts 17:26, Paul affirms this very point in his sermon on Mars Hill when he says before the Athenian philosophers that God "made from *one blood* every nation of men to dwell on all the face of the earth, and has determined their preappointed times and the boundaries of their dwellings" (NKJV).

Practically speaking, this means that the term *race* as it is most commonly used in contemporary conversations is neither an accurate nor a helpful term. Scripturally and theologically speaking, *race* is especially problematic when it is used to point out our differences. Instead, the term should be used to show our *united nature* as image-bearers that God created to corporately be on mission to fill the earth with worship. Sin, however, has twisted the very manner in which we understand who we are and what makes us one. Therefore, if our conversations about *race* are to make progress, it is wise to recognize that the fundamental concept and contemporary use of the terminology are in error.

While secular sociologists are right to struggle to understand and realign a meaning of the word *race* away from an erroneous biological grounding, they often seek to retain it as a helpful category demarcating our differences. Scripture, however, gives us clearer language and concepts. For example, we see in Acts 17:26 that Paul uses the Greek term *ethnos* (from which we get our English word *ethnicity*) to describe the "every nation" that each one of us represents. Thus, we are far better off to speak of our differences in terms of cultural *ethnicity* than racial differences. As Paul would have us understand it, we are *one race* with *multiple ethnicities*.

Having said this, we should also point out that Christians armed with these biblical and theological categories of *race* and *ethnicity* ought to be wise enough to recognize that in everyday language, people will often use the term *race* or *races* to highlight ethnic differences as well as the very real and distinct experiences that people have as they encounter the world in which they live. Thus, to be culturally sensitive and ethically wise, we need to avoid the extreme view on the one hand of denying that the problem of racism exists simply because we have rejected the idea of multiple races. No, racism is real, even if the idea of multiple races is not. On the other hand, when appropriate, we should seek to move away from using the word *race* or *races* to describe the differences between *black* and *white* culture because the continued use of these words as a dividing marker serves to perpetuate the very sinful structures that the language of *race* was created for: the purpose of oppressing people based on false and ungodly ideas. In sum, we believe David Platt is helpful when he points out that the language of *ethnicity* is superior because "instead of being strictly tied to biology, ethnicity is much more fluid, factoring in social, cultural, lingual, historical, and even religious characteristics."[23]

The second idea that we discover from Genesis 1:27–28 is the presumed goodness of the diversity that exists within our one human race. Note that the passage indicates that there is only one clear point of demarcation among human beings that God explicitly states: there are two sexes—male and female. Regarding all the other aspects of our physical appearance, because God himself is good and he declares all of his creation good, we can rightly conclude that all the other prefall physical differences are to be celebrated as part of God's wondrous design. This implies not *color-blindness* but *color celebration*. From the one blood of Adam, a world full of diversity would arise in terms of hair color, eye color and shape, body type, and skin tone. Each person bearing any of these physical characteristics would be a trophy of God's beautiful design. Physical diversity (including skin tone) is to be celebrated, not used as a point of division.

A third implication from Genesis 1:27–28 is well stated by John Stott: "Being equally created by him and like him, we are equal in his sight in worth and dignity, and, therefore, have an equal right to respect and justice."[24] As each point of physical diversity before the fall was meant to be celebrated, so also would a concordant expression of loving respect and ethical care for one another serve to celebrate the richness of God's kindness and the wonder of his multifaceted creation.

Tragically, it has been the experience of too many image-bearers that so-called racial differences have become the basis of discrimination and injustice. The

---

23. David Platt, *Counter Culture: A Compassionate Call to Counter Culture in a World of Poverty, Same-Sex Marriage, Racism, Sex Slavery, Immigration, Abortion, Persecution, Orphans, and Pornography* (Carol Stream, IL: Tyndale, 2015), 195–96.

24. John Stott, *Issues Facing Christians Today*, 4th ed. (Grand Rapids: Zondervan, 2006), 287.

reason is that "the problem of racism is the problem of sin."[25] Human depravity fundamentally perverts our understanding of what it means to be human. It leads to both personal sin choices and depraved thinking about society. As we discussed at greater length in chapter 9, this, in turn, creates culturally embedded patterns of sinfulness. It divides us in the places that we are meant to be one (race), and it confuses us in the aspects of our humanity that are meant to remain clearly demarcated (sex and gender).

How Should the Bible Shape Our Understanding of Racism?

What does the Bible teach us about the sin of racism? The entire category of racial division is contrary to God's design. It begins with our separation from God and directly leads to our alienation from one another. Following the creation narratives in Genesis 1–2, the Bible is quick to point out that all human relationships are marred from the moment Adam and Eve rebel against God. Not only are the first couple at odds with each other (Gen. 3:12–19), but shortly afterward murder happens among their children (Cain kills Abel, 4:1–15). Instead of God's image-bearers' going forth into the world to make it flourish as his champions, they limp out of the garden as broken sinners. Instead of ruling and subduing the world as a united race of stewards living to the glory of God, Scripture indicates that within a few generations they are diminished and divided into rival family groups (tribes) with various languages that will eventually become the peoples and nations that go to war with one another, competing for land, power, and status (Gen. 9–10).

Imagine what "going into the world" might have been like if Adam and Eve had never sinned and had subdued and ruled the world in accordance with God's eternal laws and character. Imagine how different our understanding of ethnic diversification might be. If sin had never happened, it is quite possible that as humans were fruitful and multiplied and filled the earth in accordance with God's design, groups of people living in various parts of the world would have developed differing foods, music, dances, arts, societal preferences, and cultural differences. Without sin, however, none of these would be deemed superior. Rather, they would be celebrated and used to enrich and expand human experience as God allowed them to creatively develop his world.

The problem is not diversity. God designed diversity. The problem is sin-marred diversity. Sin is never creative or expansive. It has power only to distort, pervert, and break that which was originally intended to be good, true, and beautiful. Racism is nothing more than a sin-induced twisting of something that was otherwise meant to display God's glory. Racism is the perversion of something

---

25. Yancey, *Beyond Racial Gridlock*, 9.

meant to bring delight into a horrific self-worshiping hate. It is the hideous dissection of a beautiful mosaic meant to be treasured as a grand masterpiece. Roberts rightly states that "brokenness between God and humanity is the basis of sin. This includes the sin of racism. Racism is self-glorification of skin color and all the rights and privileges associated with it. . . . Racism is the exaltation of the finite to the status of infinite."[26] In short, racism is a form of idolatry.

Thankfully, the biblical story and the problem of racism do not end with sin and destruction. While the peoples, tribes, tongues, and nations were separating and moving apart, God's plan of redemption and restoration was well underway. In Genesis 12:1–3, we find God calling out Abraham to make him into a "great nation" through whom all the families on earth would be blessed. It was through Abraham's faith in God that hope was made possible for the world. From Abraham's lineage, Jesus Christ was born into the world, that he might seek and save the lost from every people, tribe, tongue, and nation.

While in the Old Testament we see an accounting of the scattering of human beings into various people groups, in the New Testament we find both the means and the firstfruits of God's divine ingathering of all peoples and nations into one gloriously diverse community of faith. The ultimate source of this ingathering, of course, is the redemptive work of the Trinity instantiated through the incarnation of Jesus Christ. It was because "God so loved the *world*" that he sent Jesus Christ to be the hope of all nations and the rallying point for humanity to be reunited toward its final and ultimate end (John 3:16). As we learn from Galatians 3:28–29:

> There is neither Jew nor Greek, there is neither slave nor free man, there is neither male nor female; for you are all one in Christ Jesus. And if you belong to Christ, then you are Abraham's descendants, heirs according to promise.

Through the incarnation, life, death, and resurrection of Jesus Christ, humans once again have the possibility of life together—the life that God created us for. God does not erase the distinctions as though they were not there. On the contrary, they are identified, addressed, and brought under the lordship of Christ. Stott is correct: our oneness in salvation does not mean that our membership in Christ and his church "obliterates our nationality, any more than it does our masculinity or femininity. It means rather that, while our ethnic, national, social and sexual distinctions remain, they no longer divide us. They have been transcended in the unity of the family of God."[27] Given the context of Galatians 3:28–29 and the salvific emphasis, Paul is highlighting that all people—even in light of their

---

26. Roberts, *Liberation and Reconciliation*, 56.
27. Stott, *Issues Facing Christians Today*, 290.

differences—are welcomed into faith, that the gospel is powerful enough to redeem and unite all people together, and that God is worthy of each person's worship and all people's worship together. In sum, the gospel does not erase our differences; it realigns them with God's original purposes and eternal design and gives us the basis on which to celebrate them.

Race, Ethnicity, and World Evangelism

This realignment to God's eternal design, in turn, informs us why the Great Commission in Matthew 28:18–20 is such a powerful passage as it relates to the problem of racism. Jesus commanded his followers to "go" and make disciples of all "nations." Note here that again the word translated into English as "nations" in the original Greek is the plural form of *ethnos*—the root word for *ethnicity*. Through the preaching of the gospel (salvation by grace alone, through faith alone, in Christ alone) and disciple-making, the one human race is to be restored in all its beautiful ethnicities. The differences are not meant to remain *dividers*, but under the lordship of Christ they become *enrichers* as the beautiful mosaic of the human race is restored into the one body of Christ. Paul paints the picture beautifully in Ephesians 2:13–16, 18–19:

> But now in Christ Jesus you who formerly were far off have been brought near by the blood of Christ. For He Himself is our peace, who made both groups into one and broke down the barrier of the dividing wall, by abolishing in His flesh the enmity, which is the Law of commandments contained in ordinances, so that in Himself He might make the two into one new man, thus establishing peace, and might reconcile them both in one body to God through the cross, by it having put to death the enmity. . . . For through Him we both have our access in one Spirit to the Father. So then you are no longer strangers and aliens, but you are fellow citizens with the saints, and are of God's household.

David Platt's comments about this passage are helpful:

> These words beautifully describe the unique power of the gospel to reunite people from . . . different ethnic groups. And it makes sense, doesn't it? For *in the beginning*, sin separated man and woman from God and also from one another. This sin stood (and stands) at the root of ethnic pride and prejudice. When Christ went to the cross, he conquered sin, making the way for people to be free from its hold and restored to God. In so doing, he paved the way for all people to be reconciled to one another.[28]

28. Platt, *Counter Culture*, 200.

Hand in hand with the saving message of the gospel of Jesus Christ, Paul is emphasizing Jesus' teaching that the way in which we demonstrate to a watching world that we are his disciples is by loving one another and living together in unity as "one new man" (Eph. 2:15; see also John 13:35).

Building on this idea, we also need to recognize that God's instructions for Christians to love one another across the lines of ethnicity (what some might describe as "racial lines") as one people together (one race) are meant to be a powerful form of evangelism. Christian love that transcends ethnic barriers is meant to witness to the love of God by demonstrating to a watching world what true Christian love is, and it is meant to paint a stunning picture of the future kingdom where those from every tribe, tongue, people, and nation worship together the King of kings (Rev. 5:9; 7:9). To the degree that we do this well in the here and now, our presence together in a lost world will serve as a powerful invitation to the lost to taste and see that the Lord is good. If we do not love across the lines of ethnicity or live together as a beautifully diverse community of faith, we defame the name of Christ before a watching world.

In the end, Scripture tells us, the future kingdom and the new Jerusalem where Christ rules and reigns will be enriched by the diversity of various ethnicities as the kings of the earth bring the splendor of their nations into it (Rev. 21:24). What a beautiful bookend the Bible gives us to show the culmination in Christ's kingdom of what God designed to be the case *in the beginning*: one race—the human race—united in worship, bringing to Christ the best of all its vast diversity to lay at his feet in worship. Certainly, if the future eschatological kingdom is enriched by the diversity of ethnic cultures, then we ought to recognize and celebrate the wonder of diversity in the here and now. To the degree that we do not do so, we are impoverished, and so is our worship.

Summary of the Biblical Teaching: Five Key Ideas

When we look to the Scripture as our primary source of authority for understanding race and racism, we discover several principles that should shape both our character and our practice. First, with regard to the concept of *race*, the Bible teaches that God created one race—the human race. As image-bearers, humans are meant to be united in our worship and our work to fill the earth with worship. This does not dispel or downplay our differences; rather, it is meant to put them in proper context. We are not first of all black or white: we are image-bearers. But as image-bearers, we have been created with various physical realities as a part of who we are. When seen in light of God's order and the gospel's clarifying lens, we learn that our ethnic differences are meant to enrich one another and magnify our worship of God. This happens as we celebrate not only the beautiful differences that he builds into his people, but also the different aspects of God's own beauty that are discovered and celebrated by his diverse people. On the other hand, by assuming that the modern idea of *multiple races* is a correct concept, we enter the discussion of race at odds with God's Word. We begin and frame the entire discussion from a point of error. By maintaining the secular category of *multiple races*, we are in danger of unwittingly perpetuating an institutionalized and culturally embedded sin pattern in the form of language and the subtle linguistic affirmation of a false idea.

Second, with regard to racism, we learn that dividing over skin tones is not only senseless, but an embodiment of the pride of human sin and the fall, and is therefore a wicked display of false worship. As Waldo Beach puts it: "The problem of race is at its deepest level not a factual problem, nor a moral problem, but a theological problem. Its locus is not finally in man's cultural environment, nor in his inadequate knowledge of racial information, nor yet in his moral inertia. These are satellite powers to the final demonic iniquity, man's inner perversity of will, his worship of the finite."[29] Or, as Roberts simply puts it, "Racism is the purest form of self-glory; it exalts human beings over human beings."[30]

Thankfully, the third shaping idea is that the gospel is meant to both unite God's people and restore ethnic and cultural diversity to a place of wonder and hope. Through his birth, life, death, and resurrection, Jesus provides the means for the restoration of the one human race to himself and to one another.

Fourth, Scripture indicates that the future manifestation of God's kingdom will be one in which both our worship and our heavenly culture will be enriched by human diversity. Therefore, it follows that becoming the kind of people who love and appreciate the diversity of the body of Christ now not only pleases the Lord, but gives us a "jump start" on the joy we will experience in the future kingdom.

Finally, in our attempt to seek a just and loving expression of unity and diversity by abandoning the category of *race* as it is commonly used in secular discussion, we are by no means attempting to minimize the centuries of slavery, oppression, or various other forms of injustice as though they never happened. Arguing that the concept of multiple races is a social construct with no essential foundation does not deny the reality that this falsely created concept has had real and lasting impact. But by focusing our attention on "one race, many ethnicities," we accomplish at least two important ends: acknowledging the full folly of "racial oppression" while simultaneously highlighting the beauty of ethnic diversity. When biblically understood, an emphasis on kingdom diversity is an emphasis on properly displaying the kingdom of God to a watching world. It is by definition an

29. Waldo Beach, "A Theological Analysis of Race Relations," in *Faith and Ethics: The Theology of H. Richard Niebuhr*, ed. Paul Ramsey (New York: Harper & Brothers, 1957), 209.
30. Roberts, *Liberation and Reconciliation*, 52.

expression of evangelism because it displays something very beautiful about God and his creation. Far from being *color-blind*, God is *color-celebratory*.[31]

Contextual and Pastoral Considerations

Having recognized that, biblically speaking, there is only one human race with many ethnicities, we now turn to a consideration of how key contextual and pastoral factors ought to impact our understanding of, and ethical application to, the topic of racism. We begin with a recognition that one's interpretation of the problem depends to a large degree on where one is situated within culture. In keeping with this, we introduce two distinct ways in which people in the United States tend to approach the problem of racism and discuss how each contributes to the problem sometimes described as "racism without racists."[32]

Two Approaches to Understanding Racism

George Yancey is correct when he states that "the way we define a social problem will affect the way we conceive of its solution. If we have an incomplete definition of a problem, then we will envision a limited solution. If the real problem is larger than our restricted definition, then our solution will be insufficient."[33] Unfortunately, because the way that the problem of racism is addressed depends to a large degree on one's situational location in society, it is common that various groups attempting to define the problem and offer solutions end up talking past one another. For example, it is a normative pattern that when white Christians address the topic of racism, they do so with what Yancey describes as an "individualist definition of racism." Alternatively, it is a normative pattern that when black Christians address the topic, they do so through the lens of a "structuralist definition of racism."[34] The two would do well to listen to each other more carefully.

To understand these differences, recall our discussion of the three categories of sinfulness that we developed in chapter 9. Scripture teaches us that not only do we inherit original sin and thus are *sinners*, we also individually choose to act contrary to God's design and are guilty of particular *sins*. In addition to these two ways in which sin enters our lives, we must realize that as *sinners* who *sin*, when we build societies and create cultures, our sinful nature and our sinful choices end

---

31. See David Platt's helpful discussion along these lines in *Counter Culture*, 197.

32. *Racism without Racists* is the title of Eduardo Bonilla-Silva's influential book. We have found some of his cultural analysis to be helpful to our discussion, but as we discussed in our previous chapter on justice, we do not affirm either the worldview assumptions to which he holds or the solutions he offers for the problems he identifies.

33. Yancey, *Beyond Racial Gridlock*, 19.

34. Yancey, *Beyond Racial Gridlock*, 20–22.

up influencing the very institutions, cultural patterns, and societal structures we create to order society. That is, because we are fallen and live in a fallen world, we cannot help but create fallen institutions ingrained with culturally and socially embedded patterns of sin.

This is not to say that cultural institutions are bad, nor is it to suggest that all aspects of social tradition are evil. Further, we are also not implying that all elements of institutions or tradition are as bad as they could be. God's general grace prevents that. But just as each one of us individually is tainted by sin in all our parts, so also are all elements of society to some degree or another tainted by sin. Thus, just as there is *total depravity* among human persons, so also is there a sense of total depravity in postfall human institutions.[35]

We see examples of God's addressing various aspects of this societal and cultural depravity throughout Scripture. For example, in Genesis 18–19, we see the impact of patterns of sexual sin on both Sodom and Gomorrah. Nehemiah draws attention to socially embedded sin patterns by calling out the practice of unfair lending (usury) in his day (Neh. 5). Amos drew attention to socially embedded sin patterns when he rebuked unjust patterns of economics in his society (Amos 5). In the New Testament, James rebukes the pattern of favoritism given to the wealthy in church (James 2:1–13) as well as the pattern of paying unfair wages (5:1–6). One of the reasons Jesus drove out money-changers from the temple is that an entire sinful pattern of exploitation had become normative within the religious institution (Mark 11:15–17). Indeed, one could say that the entire code of law given by God to Israel in the book of Leviticus was put in place as an attempt to protect the people of Israel not only from individual sins but from developing and embedding sin patterns at the heart of their society like the nations that surrounded them. Yet even with the direct guidance from heaven, God's people still found ways to distort God's understanding of justice and just practices (e.g., see our discussion of Mark 7:9–13 in the previous chapter).

Returning to Yancey's point, if one approaches the problem with an *individualist definition of racism*, he or she will perceive the problem largely in terms of individual or personal choices and attitudes. From this perspective, the main sin of racism is located in the category of an individual person's sinful attitudes or actions. If, then, one can eliminate prejudiced attitudes and discriminatory choices in the individual, then one has eliminated the problem of racism.

In another way, if one approaches the problem from what Yancey describes as the *structuralist definition of racism*, he or she will look at society as a whole and consider whether patterns of racism are still at play even when individuals do not

---

35. Here we are using *total depravity* to mean that every part (*total*) is impacted by sin (*depravity*). We are not saying that every part is as bad as it could possibly be (*utter depravity*).

have racial intentions or act in racist ways. Solving the problem of racism requires the elimination of these structural and institutional patterns and ingrained practices. As Yancey puts it, "Structuralists may differ among themselves about how best to help people of color, but they agree that an alteration of social structures is a part of the solution."[36] Bonilla-Silva's comments summarize the points well: "One reason why, in general terms, whites and people of color cannot agree on racial matters is because they conceive terms such as 'racism' very differently. Whereas for most whites racism is [personal or individualized] prejudice, for most people of color racism is systematic or institutionalized."[37]

Racism without Racists?

In light of these two perspectives, it is not hard to see how each definition in its own way helps to foster socially embedded sin patterns and shape biases that perpetuate the problem of racism. This can happen even though individuals within the various groups do not intend to act in a prejudicial manner.

Consider, on the one hand, that from the *individualist* point of view many will honestly admit to having biases and will even recognize that attitudes of prejudice can creep into the soul. Further, many who see the problem from this perspective will also admit that these biases and prejudices should be dealt with because they are wrong. No one (with the exception of members of supremacist organizations) wants to be seen or labeled as a *racist*. Even more so, from a distinctly Christian point of view, serious disciples of Jesus in the "majority culture" will often admit that they have biases, prejudices, and even racial tendencies, and when made aware of them will often work hard to bring these under the lordship of Christ to change and become better people. As all this relates to white evangelicals more generally, there is a tendency to think that if one does not practice overt discrimination, if one has no problem with making African-American friends, and if one is delighted to worship together with African-American brothers and sisters in our churches, then certainly the label *racist* does not apply. All of this is excellent.

The problem, however, is that by limiting the understanding of racism to the personal level, the individualist runs the risk of living with a "blind spot" regarding the possibility that society itself is stained by culturally embedded sin patterns. The individualist may live unaware of the possibility that culturally embedded sin patterns even exist. Some will even become offended by the notion that embedded sin patterns allow them to have opportunities or experience certain advantages that others from minority contexts may not have or enjoy. "Certainly," someone in this camp might say, "the fact that we elected an African-American

---

36. Yancey, *Beyond Racial Gridlock*, 25.
37. Bonilla-Silva, *Racism without Racists*, 8.

president in 2008 demonstrates that racism is no longer a problem." While it is a good thing that Americans have progressed to the point of being willing to elect a black person to the office of president, this one reality does not negate the very real possibility that the fabric of society still bears the marks of socially embedded sin patterns that are highly racialized. Likewise, the fact that one man was able to navigate the contours of culture and ascend to that office in no way proves that we have somehow solved all our issues with racism or that all the barriers that accompany ethnicity are somehow gone. The exception to the rule does not mean that a pattern is no longer there. No doubt it is a good and hopeful sign of progress, but rarely does the elevation of one man mean that the problem has disappeared for all.

For example, the fact that Mark's son by birth (who is "white") has no fear when he is pulled over by a police officer while his son-in-law (who is African American) does may speak only to their personal perspectives. But it may also point to something bigger that is actually going on in society. The fact that Mark's son by birth has never been pulled over randomly when there are no driving infractions or auto violations while his son-in-law has been pulled over eleven times before the age of twenty-five when no violations were cited may indicate that something important—and likely very wrong—is taking place. This is not necessarily an indictment of any single police officer, nor is it necessarily an indictment of the police force as a whole. Rather, the fact that people on either side of the situation perceive it to be a reality, or actually act on it in reality, speaks to hundreds of years of social formation that still has an impact on our cultural practices. As Harold Baron describes it, the presence of discriminatory practices such as these types that may be woven into our social fabric are not necessarily "dependent upon specific discriminatory decision or acts." Rather,

> such behavior has become so well institutionalized that the individual generally does not have to exercise a choice to operate in a racist manner. The rules and procedures of the large organizations have already prestructured the choice. The individual only has to conform to the operating norms of the organization, and the institution will do the discrimination for him.[38]

Those who define *racism* merely from an individualist point of view have a hard time understanding this. There will be a tendency to give the benefit of the doubt to institutions such as a police force and dismiss the possibility that biases

---

38. Harold M. Baron, "The Web of Urban Racism," in *Institutional Racism in America*, ed. Louis L. Knowles and Kenneth Prewitt (Englewood Cliffs, NJ: Prentice-Hall, 1969), 142–43, quoted in Carl F. Ellis Jr., *Free at Last? The Gospel in the African-American Experience* (Downers Grove, IL: InterVarsity Press, 1996), 150.

leading to things such as racial profiling take place (by white or black police offi-cers). This, in turn, can result in the individualist's being color-blind in such a negative way that he or she does not even consider how the gospel might compel us to address sin or possible injustice taking place at a societal or systematic level.

On the other hand, those who think of racism as a structural problem will often place the blame for racism fully at the feet of white Americans who—as a whole—represent the majority culture. The tendency will be to see the police officer (white or black) as always racially profiling when a person of color is pulled over, when in actuality, any particular case may be one in which a law was actually broken, the stop was fully just, and no racism is involved in the particular traffic stop. Of course, in recent years there has been an increase in public awareness of the types of cases in which police stops have clearly been racially motivated and in which the unjust use of excessive force has rightly led to a public outcry. The 2020 case of George Floyd certainly exposed the painful wounds of societal patterns that have been systematically unjust. Thus, this perspective is founded on a legitimate desire to see the end of culturally embedded sin patterns and socially accepted patterns that motivate racist practices across societal levels, and it positively forces us to consider the reality of these culturally embedded patterns of sin.[39]

But even with the legitimate longing for change, two potential failings also may often accompany it. First, it may systematically (and unfairly) put all white people in the category of those who see only from the position of privilege and are unable to see the real problem. Second, it runs the risk of not taking seriously enough the enduring problem of human sin nature and individual responsibility. As Yancey states: "Of course this approach absolves people of color of account-ability for their own shortcomings. Thus we see a powerful tendency in some social and academic circles to deny the way that people of color victimize each other and even majority group members."[40]

In both cases, a truncated view of sin leads to a truncated view of the solution and leaves each perspective contributing in its own way to the persistent racializa-tion of culture. Yancey powerfully brings the point home:

> But cannot the two sides see how their perspectives affect each other? Cannot whites perceive that their unwillingness to take seriously the disadvantages of peo-ple of color only alienates them from racial minorities? Cannot people of color understand that contemporary whites should not forever bear the guilt of the sins

39. See Yancey, *Beyond Racial Gridlock*, 27–28. Yancey helpfully develops a taxonomy for describing proposed secular solutions to the problem of racism that are often adopted and adapted by Christians. In chapters 2–5, he addresses the models of *Colorblindness, Anglo-conformity, Multiculturalism*, and *White Responsibility*.

40. Yancey, *Beyond Racial Gridlock*, 23.

of their ancestors . . . ? Neither group will be able to recognize its own part in our racial problems until we acknowledge how our own sin nature contributes to those problems.[41]

Racial Situatedness

In light of the previous discussion, it is important to consider how a gospel-centered ethics-as-worship perspective should help us address the issue of racism. The first way that it should do so is to help us understand that sin has a darkening impact on the way that each of us sees the world (Rom. 1:21–22; 1 Cor. 2:14; Eph. 4:17–19; see chapters 3, 5). For this reason, it is likely that *all of us have biases* in how we see one another and how we view our life contexts. Becoming aware of these biases is an important first step toward recognizing the problem of racism and seeking to find Christ-honoring solutions. Next, it is important to look more closely at the societal patterns of sin that do exist and be willing to consider the possibility that these socially embedded sin patterns are woven into the fabric of culture even in ways that we do not currently recognize. Finally, if these patterns do exist, and if we can discern them with the help of the Word and the Spirit, then we do well to consider what role we as individual believers, and as one body of Christ together, can play in bringing them under the lordship of Christ in order to enact real change. We now consider each of these three ideas in turn.

Biases

Let's begin with a brief thought experiment. Imagine that you have been invited to attend the church of a new friend you met at school or work. When you enter the building for the first time, you notice a portrait of Jesus hanging on the wall. In this picture, Jesus is depicted as a black man with African features. What would your first unfiltered internal reaction be? Would this depiction appear normal for you? Would it surprise you? Startle you? Would it offend you? Now imagine the same context, except this time the picture depicts Jesus as a white man with European features. What would your first unfiltered internal reaction be? Is it the same? Is it different? Would the picture surprise you? Startle you? Would it offend you? Which one would be more "acceptable" to you? Why?

Experience tells us that when white evangelicals encounter a portrait of Jesus with African-American skin tone and features, they will immediately process the picture as "black Jesus" and perhaps even feel as though something is "wrong." When they encounter the picture of Jesus with white skin and European features, they immediately process the picture as "Jesus" (not "European Jesus"). They

---

41. Yancey, *Beyond Racial Gridlock*, 25–26.

simply accept it as normal and receive it as "correct." Similarly, some African Americans encountering a portrait of Jesus with African skin tone and features may process the picture as "my Jesus" and perhaps feel relief, comfort, or even a sense of safety. The interesting thing about this little exercise is to consider that neither a "white" nor a "black" portrait of Jesus is technically accurate. Jesus was a Middle Eastern Jewish man who likely had dark-olive-colored skin with Middle Eastern features. The point is that both the white Jesus and the black Jesus portraits—as well as the responses to them—are examples of ingrained cultural biases.[42]

Bryan Loritts provides us with a second example of how these biases can subtly shape our perspectives:

> When I teach preaching at a seminary level, one of the first exercises I have my students do is to define for me what "black preaching" and "black theology" are. Hands of all different colors go up. Then I ask students to define "white preaching" and "white theology." The pause is palpable. Moments of awkward silence ensue—a quiet admission that they have never entertained this question before.[43]

The fact that this question is not even entertained is the whole point. "White preaching" has particularities of style just as much as black preaching does. But because one is more "normative" in culture, it is simply accepted for what it is. Carl Ellis is right in pointing out that the simple fact of the matter is that "when people grow up in a particular cultural context, they fail to see the cultural biases they have inherited. They think of their own value system as neutral, the standard for all people."[44] Because of this, it takes hard work "to define what one has normalized and mainstreamed. It's like asking a fish to describe water."[45] All of us have biases—regardless of our skin color—simply because we are finite humans. Add to this the problem of sin and its impact on our ability to see the world correctly, and we begin to run into significant problems (see chapter 3).

Our biases can even influence how we interpret Scripture. Any hermeneutics (Bible interpretation) professor will tell you that when you come to the text, you bring much more than mere interpretation skill and technique. You also bring

42. Edward J. Blum and Paul Harvey offer an interesting survey of the different depictions of Jesus in the United States. See Edward J. Blum and Paul Harvey, *The Color of Christ: The Son of God and the Saga of Race in America* (Chapel Hill: University of North Carolina Press, 2012).

43. Bryan Loritts, *Insider Outsider: My Journey as a Stranger in White Evangelicalism and My Hope for Us All* (Grand Rapids: Zondervan, 2018), 22. There is a much larger discussion related to this point. For further discussion on this topic, see Anthony B. Bradley, *Liberating Black Theology: The Bible and the Black Experience in America* (Wheaton, IL: Crossway, 2010).

44. Ellis, *Free at Last?*, 19.

45. Loritts, *Insider Outsider*, 22.

your frame of reference. You bring your gender, ethnicity, cultural biases, and historical point of view. Proper interpretation skills and technique are vitally important so that we do not make the Bible say merely what *we want it to say*. Proper interpretation must account for and mitigate our own tendencies to shape the Bible to fit what we want, instead of *its* shaping *us* to become what God in his kindness demands of us.[46] This is precisely why sticking with a clear grammatical-historical interpretive rule is vital (see chapter 5). It keeps the text of Scripture tied to the real historical context in which it was given in light of the audience it was given to in order to limit the influence of our modern biases on the text.[47]

For example, as it relates to the discussion of race, when white Americans came to the biblical text in the antebellum South, their experience dramatically shaped the manner in which many in the South engaged the text. Most tragically, their biases warped their understanding of the Bible to the point that they justified the chattel slavery that propped up the entire economy of the southern United States based on arguments claiming that black skin was the mark of Cain (Gen. 4) or that black-skinned people should be enslaved because of the curse of Ham (Gen. 9).[48] Now this cultural bias is easily seen and rejected for the lie that it is. But at the time, these detestable forms of biblical interpretation shaped much of the way that Christians in those contexts saw their world. It is likely that some of the reverberations of these lies still echo in the prejudice that remains even today.

This example should both remind and warn us that when we read the Bible, we have to be aware that the text was originally written in a Jewish or Greco-Roman context whose readers might not have understood their world in the same way that we do. As the interpreter and perhaps even as a teacher of the text, we each have the responsibility to understand the meaning of the text as it was originally given for its audience in their context, and then apply that meaning to one's own context. On this point, refer back to our discussion on biblical interpretation in chapter 5.

---

46. This is most clearly where we would reject the deconstructive ideology and method of Critical Theory and so-called "standpoint epistemology" that suggests truth is relative to one's point of view. As we have argued throughout this text, truth is discovered, not invented. This is precisely why, however, great care must be taken in hermeneutics and text interpretation. No one is free from bias except the Lord.

47. For further discussion on this crucial point of hermeneutics, see Robert L. Plummer, *40 Questions about Interpreting the Bible* (Grand Rapids: Kregel, 2010), 103; Grant R. Osborne, *The Hermeneutical Spiral: A Comprehensive Introduction to Biblical Interpretation*, 2nd ed. (Downers Grove, IL: InterVarsity Press, 2006), 24–25, 89–90, 465–500. See also Graeme Goldsworthy, *Gospel-Centered Hermeneutics: Foundations and Principles of Evangelical Biblical Interpretation* (Downers Grove, IL: IVP Academic, 2006), 43–52, 190–93.

48. For an excellent discussion debunking both these ridiculous arguments, see Hays, *From Every People and Nation*, 51–53. See also John Piper, *Bloodlines: Race, Cross, and the Christian* (Wheaton, IL: Crossway, 2011), 263–67.

The point we are making here is that all of us have cultural biases that we must become aware of and evaluate. How each of us responds to examples such as the ones given above unveils for us how cultural biases and preferences may be shaping our views of life and faith at a deeper worldview level. The important question that each of us must wrestle with is not *whether* we have biases but *what* biases we have and *how* they shape our perspectives on the world. As the question of biases relates to the issue of race in particular, we may begin by asking whether we are aware of how our ingrained biases shape our understanding of the problem and whether we are willing to recognize and face them. Then, if need be, we must not only ask whether we are willing to repent of them on the personal level, but also explore whether we are willing to work to dislodge any forms of culturally embedded sin patterns that exist and thereby function as ungodly ideas or speculations raising themselves up against the knowledge of God (2 Cor. 10:3–5).

Unseen Culturally Embedded Sin Patterns of Injustice

Recognizing how my (Mark's) own upbringing and station in life unknowingly affect my perspective of the world, society, and justice has not been an easy process. Indeed, for individuals raised in the majority culture, it rarely is. My assumption for most of my life has been to approach the problem of racism from an individual sin perspective. I work hard (with many failings) to treat all as equal and move in love toward all. But I rarely gave much thought to how the situation into which I was born and the manner of upbringing I experienced (which I considered "normal") may have provided me with opportunities that others did not have. It was even rarer that I considered that some problematic causes or events may have given rise to those greater opportunities.

To illustrate this, consider the following comparison between two distinct families who came to the United States in the 1800s. The first family is introduced to us via a document by Richard Clagett. Entitled "Public Sale," it was posted in Charleston, South Carolina, on March 5, 1833:

> A valuable Negro woman accustomed to all kinds of house work. Is a good plain cook, and excellent dairy maid, washes and irons. She has four children, one a girl about 13 years of age. Another 7, a boy about 5, and an infant 11 months old. 2 of the children will be sold with mother, the others separately, if it best suits the purchaser.[49]

---

49. Roberts, *Liberation and Reconciliation*, 28–29. Roberts's footnote cites Richard Clagett, "Public Sale of Slaves," document dated Tuesday, March 5, 1833, at 1:00 **P.M.**, concerning sale at Potters Mart, Charleston, South Carolina.

Stop and think of the contextual factors connected to the situation of this family. Here is a nameless mother of four children being sold completely against her will. No word about the father, who was very possibly sold to another plantation or killed on that plantation, or perhaps the father was a previous slave owner who raped this woman to produce children to build his own wealth. Consider the idea of these image-bearers' being placed on an auction block and separated at the whim of the seller and buyer. What do you think happened to that seven-year-old girl or five-year-old boy who was sold off and separated from her or his mother? What kind of life would they experience as they grew to adults? What kind of legacy could they leave to their own children, who would likely also be born into a world of slavery, discrimination, and poverty? A hundred years later, what would be the impact on that family tree?

Now consider that this type of scenario was repeated through several *centuries* and among *millions* of families. Pause for a moment and contemplate the devastation that ripping millions and millions of families apart by the slave trade would have caused on the African continent even before this family was transported to the United States while chained to the hull of a slave ship. Consider the damage that both the individual sale of this family and the entire social system of slavery would cause for the entire family structure of the African-American people as a whole. Think about the generational wealth that was accumulated not just by slave owners but by all others who were allowed to benefit economically from the booming U.S. economy in which slave labor played a major role. This same wealth was simply inaccessible for people of African descent. Add to this the indignity of Jim Crow laws that segregated this same people group from the benefits of schools, transportation, jobs, and military benefits even after the institution of slavery was abolished.

By contrast, think of my (Mark's) family history. My ancestors came to the United States a few decades after this woman and her children were sold off for slave labor. My family made the free choice to emigrate to a country that they wanted to go to with high hopes of starting a new life. Through the next hundred years, the family structure remained intact. The men in the family not only were free to find work, but also were able to build wealth from their work (though modest) and return to their homes each day to see their kids and love them. My father was able to join the Navy and receive an ROTC scholarship that allowed him to train in nuclear engineering and hold a good job after World War II. Thus, after a hundred years, I was born into and benefited from both an intact family structure and accumulated wealth. I was able to live in an upper-middle-class neighborhood with a strong school system that prepared me well for college. My father modeled a strong work ethic that in turn enabled me to get jobs that paid for college, and I entered the workforce debt-free as a result. There is nothing wrong with any of this! But what I have rarely considered is how past culturally embedded sin patterns and practices may have allowed me to be born into a context that simply provided me with greater opportunities.

To put it plainly in terms of the family comparisons above, I wonder how many of the children of that mother put up for sale in Charleston, South Carolina, on March 5, 1833, were afforded that same level of access to opportunity and flourishing that I have had access to. How many, for no fault of their own, had anywhere close to the benefits I had merely because I had the good fortune to win the "social lottery" in which I was born with ancestors from Europe instead of Africa?

Not Guilt but Love

What's the point of this comparison? How does it help us move toward worshiping well in regard to the issue of racism? First let us state what the point is *not*. It certainly is *not* guilt. Clearly, this particular slave sale and the entire social system that resulted was not my fault. I did not put that mother or her children up for sale. I did not purchase those children for slave labor. Neither did you. Guilt at this point is both senseless and useless. As Roberts rightly puts it, "Guilt is personal only when free choice to sin or not to sin has been exercised by a particular person—not one's ancestors."[50]

Does this lack of personal guilt exonerate us from responsibility as individuals or *as a people* to lend a helping hand to those whom our ancestors knocked over? Is it even possible to think that somehow we *as a nation* do not have *some* responsibility to right this systemic wrong? Especially for us who claim the name of Christ, does not love compel us to at least think about ways that we might help realign our culturally embedded pattern and structures to aid those who had no prospect or even possible access to the same type of opportunities my family did for the past 150 years?

Guilt of this type does not serve us here. But what about lament? What about compassion? What about love? Certainly, love serves us here!

What *is* the point? Perhaps it is that until I take the time to drill down into the deeper contextual factors that have led to some of the deeply embedded cultural patterns that cause the problem that we call *racism*, my biases may lead me to believe two lies. The first is that I got to my position in society completely on my own while others are likewise fully and solely responsible for their societal position. The truth is that I did not earn all the opportunities I received—where I was born, who my parents were, and how I was raised; these are the result of God's sovereign providence (what some might describe as a "social lottery"). In the same way, others did not earn all the disadvantages they experienced—many of these also are the result of where they were born, who their parents were, and how

---

50. Roberts, *Liberation and Reconciliation*, 57.

they were raised. This biblical truth should humble us, make us less judgmental, and drive us to worship. Further, it is true that many (if not all) of the situations that someone is born into are heavily shaped by the sins of previous generations. This fact in no way reduces a person's responsibility for how he or she moves forward in life, but it likewise cannot be denied as a factor that impacts *how* he or she moves forward. To deny this fact is to be asleep to reality.

The second lie is closely related, but it is even more problematic because it reflects not only ignorance, but a stunning lack of understanding of what it means to be a Christ-follower. This lie is the idea that simply *because I did not personally cause the problem, I don't have responsibility to fix it*. To this form of foolishness Jesus has much to say. In the parable of the Good Samaritan (Luke 10:25–37), Jesus clearly taught his listeners that when confronted with the result of someone else's sin, a disciple must not move to the other side of the road and walk around. Love opens its eyes, lends a hand, and seeks to right wrongs. Love does not move to the other side of the road and walk around. The socially constructed religious pattern of behavior that played a role in both the scribe's and the Pharisee's moving to the other side of the road instead of being a good neighbor demonstrated a complete misunderstanding of divine love and the kind of ethic that Jesus would demand from his disciples. For this reason, it received the severest of rebukes. May God protect us from being so concerned about people's playing the "victimization card" that we fail to care for people who actually are victims. May God have mercy on us that in claiming, "I didn't cause the problem," we do not end up on the wrong side of the road and on the wrong side of the parable.

We must all face a simple but important idea: we are not *personally* guilty of the sins that someone else did 300 years ago, 150 years ago, or even 3 years ago. But we as a human race are together guilty of creating a society that includes injustice of any kind (Rom. 5). Further, each one of us *is* individually accountable to God for how we each respond to the consequences of sins that we encounter each and every day throughout our society. God holds his people responsible for all forms of sin, sinfulness, and the culturally embedded sin patterns that result from them. This means for some of us that we need to wake up to a bigger vision of the problem. For others, we need to stop shifting blame. For all, we need to own responsibility and love as Jesus teaches us to love. "In preaching the cross, one must communicate not only what the gospel is, but also what the gospel does. If we say what it is but don't proclaim what it does, then we communicate God's power abstractly."[51]

It is important as Christ's disciples not only to seek alignment of our own personal lives to the things of God, but also to consider whether patterns of bias,

---

51. Eric Mason, *Woke Church: An Urgent Call for Christians in America to Confront Racism and Injustice* (Chicago: Moody, 2018), 119.

prejudice, discrimination, or racism have become so ingrained in the fabric of our culture that we *as a people* (one race, many ethnicities) may think, act (perhaps unwittingly), and benefit from racialized ideas, biases, and patterns still at work in our culture.

To be clear, at this point in the discussion, we are making no comments or judgments about political affiliations, economic policies, or voting patterns. We are pressing into our theological understanding of what it means to be human, what it means to be a sinner, and what it means to be a person who is saved by grace through faith and called to worship God in spirit and truth both as individuals and as a new people—God's people. The Christian flag flies higher than the flag of any political party, and the cross calls each of them to account.

In addition, at this point in the discussion, we are also not placing the reality and problem of culturally embedded sin patterns only at the feet of people with white skin. All humans have biases and prejudices. All of us must repent of them. The point of particular concern here, however, is with how these culturally embedded sin patterns play out in everyday life and what we can do about them. We are concerned with the very real likelihood that people in majority cultures anywhere in the world (regardless of who makes up that majority culture) normatively have access to a greater position of influence by which to bring about change, but also simultaneously have less clarity on the problem and less motivation to do so.

At the very least, awareness of these possibilities and ideas must lead us to a greater understanding and compassion to care, act, and love in fresh and God-honoring ways. We must remember that because we all bear the image of God as one race of people created by God and commissioned to build a holy society that displays God's glory, there is truth to the statement that "an injustice done to one human being is an injustice done to us all."[52] Love never moves to the other side of the road!

Summary and Conclusion

The So-Called Problem of Race

As we pointed out in the previous chapter, the greatest social-justice issue in history is the fact that the society of human beings that God created to worship and enjoy him forever has turned away from him to false ideas and gods. As a result, we have become alienated not only from him but also from one another. The people—the society—that God created to worship him supremely does not do so. This is the greatest injustice in history.

At the end of the day, the "problem of race" is merely a subcategory of this

---

52. Mason, *Woke Church*, 150.

great injustice. This is why the problem of race or any other ethics or social-justice issue is ultimately a Great Commission issue. Jesus died so that through his death and resurrection he might call to himself a people from every tribe, tongue, and nation and form them into "one new man" (Eph. 2:11–22) as he intended for us to be *in the beginning* (Gen. 1). In reconciling us to himself and to one another, Jesus also commissions his followers to go forth to every people, tribe, tongue, and nation—to all ethnicities—and make disciples of all nations (Matt. 28:18–20, *ta ethnē*). The reason we seek kingdom diversity through evangelism and discipleship on earth is that the eternal kingdom of God in heaven is made up of humans from every tribe, tongue, people, and nation (Rev. 5:9, *ethnē*). In sum, we are to be agents of kingdom diversity precisely because:

1. God *created* us to display his beauty and glory in and through our different colors, ethnicities, and cultural expressions;
2. God *redeemed* us so that we could once again display his beauty and glory in and through our different colors, ethnicities, and cultural expressions; and
3. God is progressively *restoring* us to forever display his beauty and glory through our different colors, ethnicities, and cultural expressions.

God created all humans in his image, and this singular defining mark is what unites all of us as the one human race. The so-called problem of race can be boiled down to the tragic reality that we think and act as though there were more than one race. It is sin that divides us, not God or his design. The gospel is our only hope for restoration. Therefore, the sooner we get back to the business of reintroducing human beings to their Creator and his grand design for the world, the more likely we are to see an end to the problem of race.

Waking Up to the Dream That Will Someday Be True

When Martin Luther King Jr. stood on the steps of the Lincoln Memorial and delivered his "I Have a Dream" speech in 1963, he was trying to wake us up to a dream that will someday come true. The dream that King called us to is the future reality of heaven. His dream was that we would be the kind of Christians on earth that we will one day be in heaven: one race of people who together will perfectly embody the worship of God.

How, then, ought we to live in light of these great truths? What are the implications for ethics as worship in the here and now? The long march to unity and oneness in Christ begins and rests on the saving work of Christ for our salvation, but it then involves the hard work of faith, effort, and perseverance to work out the gospel in all its amazing beauty. John Perkins writes:

Justice is any act of reconciliation that restores any part of God's creation back to its original intent, purpose, or image. Justice is making right any of the many things that have gone wrong in this very good world that God made—and among the very good human beings he created to inhabit it.[53]

Is this not the Christian story that has been told throughout the ages? Have we not always been a people on a pilgrimage that involves repenting and seeking to align ourselves and others individually with God through the preaching of the Word and then seeking the outworking of that good news in every aspect of society *as far as the curse is found*? By way of conclusion, then, we offer the following five admonitions to God's people as principles of guidance that are meant to build on our evangelistic efforts and shape our discipleship and worship in the here and now such that we begin to embody, celebrate, and ultimately display God's eternal design of kingdom diversity.

See: "Open my eyes, that I may behold wonderful things from Your law" (Ps. 119:18). The first step of growth and discipleship as it pertains to kingdom diversity is seeing or becoming aware of the beautiful and rich teachings of Scripture related to the human race and ethnic diversity. This involves not only studying God's Word but learning from it to see a larger vision of reality than the habits and biases of our upbringing and experience alone would reveal to us. Paul teaches us that living in the Spirit gives us the ability to appraise our world in new and Christ-honoring ways (1 Cor. 2:15). We should pray with the psalmist that God would open our eyes to behold from his Word the beauty of his design for the one human race. We should also pray that he would reveal to us our own sin and the sins that mar our culture so that we may properly repent of anything that hinders us from reconciliation with God or others.

Listen: "Everyone must be quick to hear, slow to speak and slow to anger" (James 1:19). A wise second step involves the lost art of listening. In a day and age in which social media platforms give us plenty of opportunity to air our grievances and meanly shout our accusations at others, Scripture is clear that God would have us learn instead to be slow to speak and quick to listen. This is particularly important on the topic of race because of our long and painful history not only as Americans but as the one human race. Norman Peart's words from his insightful book *Separate No More* are a helpful guide here:

A major challenge to racial reconciliation being realized is that most white Americans do not consider that the history of oppression and discrimination in America

---

53. John M. Perkins, *Dream with Me: Race, Love, and the Struggle We Must Win* (Grand Rapids: Baker, 2017), 207.

is relevant for race relations today. "The past is behind us," is the outlook many whites have toward America's race history. But the past is very relevant for most African Americans. For this reason it is very insensitive for someone who is white to brush aside the wrongs of the past as irrelevant and insignificant. . . . One of the first things a black person will seek to know when coming into any meaningful interaction with a white person . . . is whether that person understands and can empathize with the struggles African Americans have endured in America.[54]

Listening with an open heart and mind is an important step in reconciliation. Bryan Loritts likens the process to a husband who learns of a past hurt in his wife's background. A wise husband will not take a "just move on" approach but will instead take the time to listen and learn so that he can best understand and love his bride. Listening of this type involves a willingness to move beyond a discussion of mere facts about race-related topics to a deeper willingness to hear someone else's story.[55] While the burden to listen likely falls heavier on a person who represents the majority culture in the context of this issue, the principle goes for both whites and blacks (or persons of any other ethnicity) seeking to make progress together. All of us have stories that shape our journey, and love will take the time to empathetically listen.

Mourn and Lament: "Blessed are those who mourn, for they shall be comforted" (Matt. 5:4). Scripture teaches us that mourning and lamenting over injustice is a good and wise part of growing as a disciple. The Old Testament prophets mourned injustice, mourned the wandering hearts of the people of God, and mourned what felt to them to be the long delay of God's justice in restoring his people (e.g., Hab. 1:2–4). Jesus mourned the sin and injustice that separated Israel from proper worship of God (Matt. 23:37–39). He grieved over the consequences of sin that resulted in the death of his friend Lazarus (John 11:35). He also taught his disciples that God will comfort and give hope to those who mourn over the brokenness of this world (Matt. 5:4).

It is likely that as God opens our eyes to see, and teaches us to be a people who empathetically listen, we will also need to be a people who learn how to properly mourn and lament over those things that grieve the heart of God (Eph. 4:30). As proper theology regarding the human race commingles with the Christian virtue of neighbor love, we must learn to move into the pain, suffering, and disappointments of our brothers and sisters who feel the weight of our broken world (Gal. 6:2). Perkins is again correct in saying that

54. Norman Anthony Peart, *Separate No More: Understanding and Developing Racial Reconciliation in Your Church* (Grand Rapids: Baker, 2000), 167–68.

55. Loritts, *Insider Outsider*, 29.

the church in America has much to lament: our separation because of race, our misuse of Scriptures to justify the ugly system of slavery, the multitude of missed opportunities for the kingdom, our shortsighted vision concerning social justice and the gospel, our misdirected mission effort, and finally our lack of contrition for our collective sin.[56]

Biblically speaking, however, mourning and lamenting are not the same things as complaining or grumbling. Nor are they meant to be a cul-de-sac of despair. Rather, while mourning does involve feeling the weight of brokenness, it also includes prayerfully looking to God in hope with an expectation of a future healing and lasting change. It involves praising God in a faith that rests on the good character of God in spite of circumstances. Lament is a sorrowful yet hopeful cry to God to bring about a just solution to the long march through a broken world. Bethany Hanke Hoang and Kristen Deede Johnson state that "lament is a gift. In the midst of everything going wrong around us—whether in the world at large or in the lives of people whose names and faces we know and hold dear—lament is a gift given to us to help us hold fast to God."[57]

Act: "You have faith and I have works; show me your faith without the works, and I will show you my faith by my works" (James 2:18). When Jesus was asked by some Pharisees who were trying to test him which commandment was the greatest in the law, Jesus replied:

> "You shall love the Lord your God with all your heart, and with all your soul, and with all your mind." This is the great and foremost commandment. The second is like it, "You shall love your neighbor as yourself." On these two commandments depend the whole Law and the Prophets. (Matt. 22:37–40)

The gospel depends on God's grace toward us and rightly ordering our faith and love to God. It is embodied by how we demonstrate our love for our neighbor. The vertical dimension of reconciliation to God must always be first in priority, but it must also lead to the horizontal dimension of reconciliation with our neighbor. While the gospel *is* the saving grace of God to rescue sinners and the preaching of this good news to the lost (Rom. 5:8), the gospel *does* then lead to bringing real and tangible hope to the poor, captive, blind, and oppressed (Luke 4:18). Simply put, the Bible does not allow for an either/or understanding. While we are saved by grace alone, through faith alone, in Christ alone, that saving grace is never sup-

---

56. John M. Perkins, *One Blood: Parting Words to the Church on Race and Love* (Chicago: Moody, 2018), 21.

57. Bethany Hanke Hoang and Kristen Deede Johnson, *The Justice Calling: Where Passion Meets Perseverance* (Grand Rapids: Brazos, 2016), 104–5.

posed to remain alone. If we love God, we will love our neighbor. Being saved by grace through faith restores us to the joy of performing the good works that God created for us to do *in the beginning* (Eph. 2:8–10).

While there may be a tendency for some of us to measure our orthodoxy on the ground of conceptual ideas (i.e., the confession of proper doctrines and creeds), Scripture is constantly reminding us that our faith is best proved by our deeds. That is, our orthodoxy is best demonstrated by our orthopraxy. In Jesus' words, "you will know them by their fruits" (Matt. 7:13–20; see also Luke 6:43–45). Therefore, as Christians seek proper reconciliation across ethnic boundaries, we must act intentionally to preach the message of salvation across ethnic boundaries and national borders and raise up disciples who can minister among every people, tribe, tongue, and nation. In addition, we must also act decisively to stand up to racism in any form and at any time.

In my (Mark's) own experience, I have realized through time that I have missed many opportunities to stand with my African-American brothers and sisters—sometimes through ignorance and sometimes through fear. In repentance and faith, that response must be put to death. Christ's lordship over my life demands it of me. And it also demands it of you. This is why we must also cultivate relationships of depth with men and women from differing backgrounds and ethnicities so that we can better learn and love actively as we develop kingdom diversity in our communities and spheres of influence. We must seek to empower efforts to end injustice *as far as the curse is found.*

Table 10.1. Five Admonitions for the People of God

> 1. See (Ps. 119:18)
> 2. Listen (James 1:19)
> 3. Lament (Matt. 5:4)
> 4. Act (James 2:18)
> 5. Love (1 John 4:7–8)

Love: "Beloved, let us love one another, for love is from God; and everyone who loves is born of God and knows God. The one who does not love does not know God, for God is love" (1 John 4:7–8). Sometimes love is hard. Sometimes we do not want to love the people that Jesus asks us to love. In fact, in the face of prejudice, racial bigotry, discrimination, and injustice, loving our God by loving our neighbor can be the hardest thing in the world to do. This is as true for the person who is a bigot and a racist as it is for those who are the target of bigotry and racism. As John teaches us, "If someone says, 'I love God,' and hates his brother, he is a liar; for the one who does not love his brother whom he has seen, cannot love God whom he has not seen" (1 John 4:20). Therefore, no matter which side of racism one stands on, God's instruction for loving one's neighbor requires both a dying to self and a death to any and all patterns of prejudice, discrimination, bigotry, or race-based injustice, seen or unseen. The hard but very good reality is that the Bible leaves no room for racism. "The Bible knows nothing of a vertical reconciliation that is not evident in horizontal reconciliation with others. An unforgiving Christian is an oxymoron. So is a racist one."[58]

Because all of us are stained by sin and the fall, we all have hard work to do. Moving past all our sinful prejudice and bigotry requires the work of the Holy Spirit in each of us to help us become in practice what God originally designed us to be and then reconciled us to be in truth through the gospel. The work of progressive sanctification in this area will require of each of us the holy sweat of working out our salvation with fear and trembling (Phil. 2:12). It will be only by the *work of God* pressing the *Word of God* into our minds, hearts, and wills that we, as *the people of God*, will be able to rightly display *the kingdom of God*. But thanks be to God, what may seem impossible for us in the here and now is not only *possible* for God, but also *promised* by God as our future reality.

Someday, those of us who call on the name of Jesus Christ for salvation will have the unimaginable privilege to join together in what seems like only a dream to us now. Someday, we will stand with other humans who lived across the span of human history from every people, tribe, tongue, and nation before the throne of God. There, in that place, with those people, together we will joyfully worship the King of kings and Lord of lords. On that day, we will glory in the beautiful diversity of God's kingdom as we see God face to face and know the joy that we were created for. And that joy will be enriched because we stand in the company of all the people with whom we were created to enjoy that moment. That is a dream worth waking up for! In fact, it is a dream worth working hard to make a reality now so that as many as possible from all those peoples, tribes, tongues, and nations can taste and see that the Lord is good and long to be a part of it.

Between *that* day and this day, we have a lot of work to do. God has commanded us both to be a good neighbor and to love our neighbors. He desires us to live together as "one new man" in order to display to a watching world the beauty of his diverse kingdom. To obey this command, we must act in great *faith* that giving up our biases and preferences is the right thing to do. To repent of our sin and forgive others for their sins will require of us an even greater *hope* in a day of final reckoning that will bring a perfect justice. For us to truly worship God in spirit and truth, our obedience will require most of all a self-sacrificial love. It will require a love willing to die to self—indeed, the kind of love that saved our very

---

58. Loritts, *Insider Outsider*, 98.

souls. On that day, we will be able to look back at this day and know that it was all *worth it*. For on *that* day, we will finally understand that the love of God that created us, rescued us, and is now restoring us will have brought us home together in heaven. And there, in the great harmony of God's love, the people of God will represent every tribe, tongue, and nation and will forever worship our God in a beautifully diverse kingdom. God have mercy on us so that we may do better here to embody what we will forever enjoy there (Rev. 5:9; 7:9).

Key Terms and Concepts

bias	prejudice
culturally embedded sin patterns	race
discrimination	racism
ethnicity	structuralist definition of *racism*
individualist definition of *racism*	

Key Scriptures

Genesis 1:26–28	Galatians 3:28–29
Genesis 9–10	Ephesians 2:11–22
Matthew 5:4	Revelation 5:9
Matthew 28:18–20	Revelation 7:9
Luke 10:25–37	Revelation 21:24
Acts 17:26	

Study Questions

1. What is the difference between a biological attempt to define many races and a biblical definition of *race*?
2. How should Genesis 1:1, Genesis 1:27–28, Acts 17:26, and Revelation 7:9 influence our understanding of *race*?
3. The authors suggest that instead of Christians' adopting a "color-blind" perspective, we should rather adopt a "color-celebratory" perspective. Explain this idea, and then discuss whether (and why) you agree or disagree.
4. Why and how is a rejection of racism and an embracing of a biblical understanding of kingdom diversity linked to evangelism and the Great Commission?
5. How should the parable of the Good Samaritan help us understand the difference between love and guilt as a motive to face the problem of racism?

For Further Reading

Ellis, Carl F., Jr. *Free at Last? The Gospel in the African-American Experience.* Downers Grove, IL: InterVarsity Press, 1996.

Emerson, Michael O., and Christian Smith. *Divided by Faith: Evangelical Religion and the Problem of Race in America.* Oxford: Oxford University Press, 2000.

Hays, J. Daniel. *From Every People and Nation: A Biblical Theology of Race.* Downers Grove, IL: InterVarsity Press, 2003.

King, Martin Luther, Jr. "Letter from Birmingham City Jail." In *A Testament of Hope: The Essential Writings and Speeches of Martin Luther King, Jr.*, edited by James M. Washington, 289–302. New York: HarperOne, 1986.

Mason, Eric. *Woke Church: An Urgent Call for Christians in America to Confront Racism and Injustice.* Chicago: Moody, 2018.

Peart, Norman Anthony. *Separate No More: Understanding and Developing Racial Reconciliation in Your Church.* Grand Rapids: Baker, 2000.

Perkins, John M. *Dream with Me: Race, Love, and the Struggle We Must Win.* Grand Rapids: Baker, 2017.

Piper, John. *Bloodlines: Race, Cross, and the Christian.* Wheaton, IL: Crossway, 2011.

Strickland, Walter R., II, and Dayton Hartman. *For God So Loved the World.* Nashville: B&H Academic, 2020.

Williams, Jarvis J. *One New Man: The Cross and Racial Reconciliation in Pauline Theology.* Nashville: B&H Academic, 2010.

Yancey, George. *Beyond Racial Gridlock: Embracing Mutual Responsibility.* Downers Grove, IL: InterVarsity Press, 2006.

11

Wealth and Poverty

---

*"Two things I asked of You, do not refuse me before I die: keep deception and lies
far from me, give me neither poverty nor riches; feed me with the food that is my
portion, that I not be full and deny You and say, 'Who is the Lord?' Or that I not
be in want and steal, and profane the name of my God." —*Proverbs 30:7–9

*"As human beings, we obsess over our possessions. The very poorest of us
strive desperately to acquire at least enough to survive. Those with only their basic
needs met naturally want more, in order to provide a cushion should times get worse.
The middle class remains discontent because they see people with so much more.
The affluent compete with their peers in countless contests of material one-
upmanship. The truly wealthy worry about how to invest their resources,
because mere savings may not keep pace with cost of living increases."*[1]
—Craig L. Blomberg, Christians in an Age of Wealth

Introduction

Several years ago, while walking the streets of San Francisco, I (Evan) encountered a large encampment on the edge of the city's financial district where individuals were protesting against what they called the "1 percent." These individuals
claimed to be part of the 99 percent who did not have vast amounts of accumulated wealth, and they wanted the 1 percent who did to share it with the rest of the
population. The whole idea behind these protests was that the wealthiest 1 percent of the world's population control an inordinate amount of the world's wealth
while the remaining 99 percent are left to scrape by on what is left—and to the
protesters, something about this was unfair and immoral.

---

1. Craig L. Blomberg, *Christians in an Age of Wealth: A Biblical Theology of Stewardship* (Grand Rapids:
Zondervan, 2013), 21.

It is safe to say that a wealth gap has existed among the rich and poor for much of human history. As individuals managed their resources, some stockpiled assets and learned how to increase wealth, while others lived on a subsistence basis. To be sure, some have increased wealth by immoral means, but others have simply been justly enterprising. Likewise, some who have remained poor have done so because of injustices committed against them, while others have been less able or gifted in producing wealth, while still others have been unproductive by choice. Thus, inequality has been a consistent feature of the human experience.

It is true that in recent years the wealth gap between the wealthiest and the rest of society is growing. For example, the Federal Reserve notes: "In 2018, the top 10% of U.S. households controlled 70 percent of total household wealth, up from 60 percent in 1989. The share of the top 1% of the wealth distribution increased from 23 percent to nearly 32 percent from 1989 to 2018."[2] At the same time, total wealth across all U.S. households has quadrupled over the last thirty years.[3] On a global scale, the median wealth of all adults doubled from 2000 to 2008 and has risen less rapidly since then.[4] But do the facts that a wealth gap exists and that it is growing necessarily mean that a moral problem resides in the fact that the richest among us are richer than the rest of us by a larger margin?

Consider the above-stated fact that the total wealth of *all* U.S. households quadrupled over the past thirty years. When one figures in the benefits of modern conveniences such as cars, televisions, radios, cell phones, entertainment, and healthcare, the fact is that the average American now lives at the same level as some of the richest Americans who lived just a hundred years ago. How does this remarkable rise in standard of living for the vast majority lead to the conclusion that the 99 percent are merely "scraping by"? What is the standard of measurement being used for such a conclusion? How is *justice* being measured in light of such realities?

To the degree that this wealth gap exists as a result of either unjust causes or idleness, one could say that it has an immoral component. Is the disparity of wealth *itself* the issue, or does the problem reside elsewhere? Should our concern focus on how much richer some are than the rest, or should it focus on how well off the least well off are? How much wealth is too much, and how do we know it? What obligations do the wealthy have toward the poor? Whose responsibility is it

2. Michael Batty et al., "Introducing the Distributional Financial Accounts of the United States," Finance and Economic Discussion Series 2019–017, Board of Governors of the Federal Reserve System, 2019, 26, https://www.federalreserve.gov/econres/feds/files/2019017pap.pdf.

3. Batty et al., "Introducing the Distributional Financial Accounts of the United States."

4. Credit Suisse, *Global Wealth Report 2018* (Zurich: Credit Suisse Research Institute, 2018), 17, https://www.credit-suisse.com/corporate/en/research/research-institute/global-wealth-report.html.

if a person is poor? What role should individuals, the church, and the government play in alleviating poverty?

There has been a tendency within the Christian community to adopt extreme positions in attempting to answer these questions. On the one hand, some have equated personal righteousness (or the lack thereof) with one's level of wealth or poverty. Some claim that the wealthy are inherently unrighteous by citing Jesus' words to the rich young ruler that it is "easier for a camel to go through the eye of a needle than for a rich man to enter the kingdom of God" (Luke 18:25). Corresponding to this, the poor are then depicted as being inherently righteous based on proof texts such as James 2:5, which reads, "Listen, my beloved brethren: did not God choose the poor of this world to be rich in faith and heirs of the kingdom which He promised to those who love Him?"

On the other hand, some have based an evaluation of personal righteousness on exactly the opposite foundations. The wealthy are considered to be righteous based on Solomon's words in Proverbs 8:18: "Riches and honor are with me, enduring wealth and righteousness." The poor, conversely, are depicted as the unwise and lazy who have necessarily caused their own plight: "How long will you lie down, O sluggard? When will you arise from your sleep? 'A little sleep, a little slumber, a little folding of the hands to rest'—your poverty will come in like a vagabond and your need like an armed man" (Prov. 6:9–11).

Are such all-or-nothing perspectives really an accurate depiction of Scripture and its teachings regarding wealth and poverty? Is an assessment of wealth or poverty really the best means to determine a person's just or righteous character? Or is it possible to find a more mediating position in which wealth is understood to be a tool in the hands of mankind that can be used for all sorts of good or evil?

The purpose of this chapter is to explore the topic of wealth and poverty, with the goal of understanding how we can *use* our wealth—no matter how much or little we have—as a means of worshiping God. In order to accomplish this goal, we begin with a discussion of several key terms that help to frame the discussion of wealth and poverty. Next, we address three biblical principles related to the shaping of a proper understanding of wealth and poverty. Finally, we explore several specific ethical issues related to questions of the accumulation of wealth, the alleviation of poverty, and the government's role in matters of wealth and poverty. It is crucial that in all this discussion we keep our focus on how we live out ethics as worship through our possessions. Keeping worship of God front and center in this discussion is important because Jesus warned us, "No servant can serve two masters; for either he will hate the one and love the other, or else he will be devoted to one and despise the other. You cannot serve God and wealth" (Luke 16:13).

Key Terms and Definitions

Before we address the questions of wealth and poverty, we need to define some terms used throughout this chapter and in contemporary discussions on these matters. While none of these terms are particularly complex in themselves, they represent complex ideas that are not always thoroughly understood. Three basic terms will set the stage for further discussion on these issues—*wealth, poverty*, and *stewardship*.

Wealth

When we hear the word *wealth*, we generally associate it with being wealthy. Yet wealth is more than just the accumulation of large amounts of material goods. A standard definition of *wealth* connects the ideas of an "abundance of valuable material possessions or resources" and "all property that has a money value or an exchangeable value."[5] For our purposes, we want to focus on the second idea: that is, *wealth* is the accumulation of property and possessions that have value. This is important for our discussion because everyone has a level of wealth. Even the most poverty-stricken individual likely has something that can be exchanged for value. It may not be wise for the poor to exchange their few possessions for money or something else of value, but they have a level of wealth that could be measured.

Wealth also includes more than material possessions. It is a representation of our choices related to time, money, and knowledge. Victor Claar and Robin Klay note, "One of the fundamental assumptions economists make about human activity is that we are limited in our choices by scarce time, resources and knowledge."[6] How we make use of scarce time, resources, and knowledge impacts the way in which we accumulate wealth. Since all of us share the same scarcity of time, resources, and knowledge, they are often the determining factors in creating wealth for oneself. Sometimes those resources come as the result of hard work, but they can also be the product of good fortune. The converse is true for those who have less access to resources. Lack of resources may be due to laziness, or it could be the result of factors beyond one's control. Knowledge also plays a role in wealth creation. Knowing how to create a product of value, market it, and exchange it for something else of value is not equal across the board. Those with greater access to resources and knowledge typically accumulate more wealth.

---

5. Merriam-Webster, s.v. "wealth," accessed May 13, 2020, https://www.merriam-webster.com/dictionary/wealth.

6. Victor V. Claar and Robin J. Klay, *Economics in Christian Perspective: Theory, Policy and Life Choices* (Downers Grove, IL: IVP Academic, 2007), 15.

Income

Breaking down the matter of wealth even further, we need to consider two additional concepts that are commonly associated with wealth: *income* and *net worth*. *Income* represents the wages (paid in money or another valuable form of exchange) that one earns for work performed. This is the primary way that most individuals accumulate wealth. The U.S. Census Bureau reports that the median household income in 2019 was $68,703.[7] Such income is used to pay for food, shelter, clothing, and other basic necessities. Those who are able to generate more income than necessary to meet their basic needs may also save and invest to prepare for the future.

Income inequality is a related matter that highlights the variation between those at the top of the income spectrum and those at various points all the way to the bottom. Complete income inequality occurs when one household controls all income while the rest have none. Perfect income equality exists when all households control an equal amount of income. The Census Bureau reports that income inequality currently sits at approximately a middle ground between perfect inequality and perfect equality.[8] Since income represents the most significant way for an individual (or family) to accumulate wealth, income inequality demonstrates the difficulty for those at the bottom of the income spectrum to achieve the same financial independence of those at the top.

Scripture testifies to the significance of income by requiring the payment of proper wages for work that is done. In the Old Testament, the Israelites were commanded to pay wages promptly and not to withhold fair wages from their countrymen or foreigners. In Deuteronomy 24:14–15, Moses instructed the Israelites: "You shall not oppress a hired servant who is poor and needy, whether he is one of your countrymen or one of your aliens who is in your land in your towns. You shall give him his wages on his day before the sun sets, for he is poor and sets his heart on it; so that he will not cry against you to the LORD and it become sin in you." Moses was particularly concerned that those who lacked sufficient income not have their daily wages withheld from them. Even animals were worthy of a proper reward for hard work: Moses commanded that the ox was not to be muzzled while it was working in the threshing floor (Deut. 25:4). Paul appeals to this

7. Jessica Semega et al., *Income and Poverty in the United States: 2019* (Washington, D.C.: U.S. Census Bureau, 2020), 1, accessed November 6, 2020, https://www.census.gov/content/dam/Census/library/publications/2020/demo/p60-270.pdf.

8. The Gini index is a good measure of income inequality and helps highlight the statistical distribution of income. This index is "a statistical measure of income inequality ranging from 0 to 1, with a measure of 1 indicating perfect inequality (one household having all the income and the rest having none) and a measure of 0 indicating perfect equality (all households having an equal share of income)." In 2019, the Gini index measured income inequality at 0.484. Semega, *Income and Poverty in the United States: 2019*, 6–7.

same concept to advocate for paying elders in the church: "The elders who rule well are to be considered worthy of double honor, especially those who work hard at preaching and teaching. For the Scripture says, 'You shall not muzzle the ox while he is threshing,' and 'The laborer is worthy of his wages'" (1 Tim. 5:17–18).

Earning wages comes back to the divine command in the garden of Eden to work. God instructed Adam to cultivate and keep the garden, working hard in God's good creation (Gen. 2:15). As we discussed earlier in chapter 2, this work is also an act of obedience to God. The income we receive from our work today is a reward for doing what God has commanded us. Claar and Klay summarize this point well:

> Human beings have an obligation to work, and their societies must afford them many opportunities to do so, since work is the principle [*sic*] means for exercising stewardship. . . . Work is more than a job or profession, however. It is a calling in which men and women apply and expand their God-given talents, thereby reflecting the image of God (who was at "work" in creation). Through work, people have an opportunity to meet their personal and family needs as well as those of the community.[9]

When work produces income, it leads to the creation of wealth for the individual and the opportunity for that person to express the image of God.

Net Worth

The second concept commonly associated with wealth is net worth. *Net worth* is the value of all of one's assets minus the value of one's liabilities. Assets are all items of value that are owned by an individual, including cash, investments, and property. Liabilities are all the obligations and debts that an individual owes. When the value of the liabilities is subtracted from the assets, we can determine net worth. For example, if Elizabeth has $10,000 in the bank, has $25,000 in a retirement account, and owns a house and car valued at a total of $115,000, her total assets are $150,000. But she owes $80,000 on her mortgage, $5,000 on her car, and $10,000 in student loans, bringing her total liabilities to $95,000. When she subtracts her liabilities from her assets, she finds that her net worth is $55,000. We see that income does not specifically factor into the equation of net worth except that income is the primary means by which one pays down obligations and purchases assets of value. Whether or not they are thinking specifically about this calculation, many people would consider net worth to be the most exact measure of wealth.

---

9. Claar and Klay, *Economics in Christian Perspective*, 22–23.

Taken together, income and net worth contribute significantly to our understanding of wealth. As we continue to discuss the topic of wealth throughout this chapter, we need to keep both these concepts in mind. In fact, the absence of wealth is the basis for our next key term—*poverty*.

Poverty

Poverty is the absence of sufficient wealth to meet the basic necessities of life. Hundreds of millions of people live in poverty around the world, but it can be difficult to determine exactly who the poor are. The U.S. federal government publishes annual poverty guidelines that determine eligibility for certain government-assistance programs. In 2020, the poverty threshold for a family of four was $26,200 in the contiguous forty-eight states.[10] The U.S. Census Bureau reported that the official poverty rate in 2019 was 10.5 percent, representing 34 million people living in poverty.[11] In contrast to poverty rates in the United States, poverty around the globe is defined at a much lower level. The World Bank defines *extreme poverty* as living on less than $1.90 per day. In 2017, 9.2 percent of the world's population, or 689 million people, lived below that level.[12]

The lack of sufficient income is often cited as a major cause of poverty. Scarcity of jobs that pay sufficiently to provide for a family has been a topic of Catholic moral thought for more than a century. In 1891, Pope Leo XIII issued an encyclical addressing the conditions of labor at the end of the nineteenth century and called on employers to provide a wage suitable for supporting a family as a matter of justice.[13] This could be considered the beginning of the call for a "living wage" based on a theological foundation of justice. At the same time, we must recognize that contemporary calls for a living wage often incorporate socialistic ideas that present a new set of problems to be addressed.[14]

Despite the hard numbers provided by the Census Bureau and the World Bank, lack of sufficient income is still not a complete indicator of poverty levels. Poverty is probably better understood as something that is contextually measured. The reason for this is that individuals living above the poverty line in one

10. Department of Health and Human Services, "Annual Update of the HHS Poverty Guidelines," *Federal Register* 85 (January 17, 2020), 3060, https://www.govinfo.gov/content/pkg/FR-2020-01-17/pdf/2020-00858.pdf.

11. Semega, *Income and Poverty in the United States: 2019*, 12.

12. World Bank, "Poverty Overview," accessed November 12, 2020, http://www.worldbank.org/en/topic/poverty/overview.

13. Leo XIII, *Rerum Novarum*, 45–46, accessed November 11, 2020, http://www.vatican.va/content/leo-xiii/en/encyclicals/documents/hf_l-xiii_enc_15051891_rerum-novarum.html.

14. Pope Leo XIII actually warned against these socialist tendencies in his encyclical. See *Rerum Novarum*, 4. See also William P. Quigley, "The Living Wage and Catholic Social Teaching," *America: The Jesuit Review of Faith & Culture*, August 28, 2006, accessed November 11, 2020, https://www.americamagazine.org/issue/581/article/living-wage-and-catholic-social-teaching.

country or region may be well below the poverty line in another. That is why we cannot simply look at income or net worth to determine poverty. Cost of living and employment opportunities are significant factors for determining whether one will live in poverty. At the same time, other social indicators correlate to greater likelihood of living in poverty. Divorce and bearing a child out of wedlock are often connected to higher rates of poverty.[15] While they may not be the direct cause of poverty, the correlation between poverty and these social indicators is intriguing.

From a biblical perspective, poverty can be a curse or a blessing. For the most part, poverty is not a desirable state as described in Scripture. Those who were poor in ancient times suffered the same problems that the poor experience today—food instability, inadequate shelter, lack of education, no social mobility, and disease. Different Hebrew terms are used to describe the poor in the Old Testament, and they cover a range of meanings, including "lacking material possessions," "destitute," "oppressed," and "needy."[16] The New Testament continues the theme of poverty and regularly addresses the matter. David Kotter highlights four causes of poverty from a New Testament perspective—oppression, sinful laziness, sudden calamities, and living in a fallen world.[17] The biblical witness seems fairly clear that poverty is not desirable and should be avoided.

At the same time, however, God regularly singled out the poor in Scripture for his special protection.[18] In the Old Testament, poor individuals were allowed to offer less expensive sacrifices (Lev. 5:7–13) and were given a regular opportunity to be relieved of their debts and to reclaim family land that had been sold (sabbath years and the Year of Jubilee, Leviticus 25 and Deuteronomy 15).[19] God describes himself as One who helps the poor and provides justice for the oppressed. In Psalm 9, David describes God's protection of the poor and oppressed: "The LORD also will be a stronghold for the oppressed, a stronghold in times of trouble; and

---

15. W. Bradford Wilcox, "The Marriage Divide: How and Why Working-Class Families Are More Fragile Today," Institute for Family Studies, September 25, 2017, accessed May 15, 2020, https://ifstudies.org/blog/the-marriage-divide-how-and-why-working-class-families-are-more-fragile-today; W. Bradford Wilcox, "Married Parents: One Way to Reduce Child Poverty," Institute for Family Studies, June 21, 2017, accessed May 15, 2020, https://ifstudies.org/blog/married-parents-one-way-to-reduce-child-poverty.

16. Walter C. Kaiser Jr., "Poverty and the Poor in the Old Testament," in *For the Least of These: A Biblical Answer to Poverty*, ed. Anne R. Bradley and Art Lindsley (Grand Rapids: Zondervan, 2014), 41–42.

17. David Kotter, "Remember the Poor: A New Testament Perspective on the Problems of Poverty, Riches, and Redistribution," in *For the Least of These: A Biblical Answer to Poverty*, ed. Anne R. Bradley and Art Lindsley (Grand Rapids: Zondervan, 2014), 63–67.

18. One could make the case that God is giving a preferential option for the poor in these passages. On the positive side, God is offering special protection and provision for the poor, so such a preferential option may be deemed as biblical. On the negative side, such preferential options have been linked to liberation theology and its attempts to redistribute wealth by force if necessary. See chapter 9 for a brief discussion.

19. Blomberg, *Christians in an Age of Wealth*, 61.

those who know Your name will put their trust in You, for You, O LORD, have not forsaken those who seek You. . . . For the needy will not always be forgotten, nor the hope of the afflicted perish forever" (Ps. 9:9–10, 18). Psalm 113:7–8 also describes the Lord's concern for the poor: "He raises the poor from the dust and lifts the needy from the ash heap, to make them sit with princes, with the princes of His people."

In the New Testament, Jesus expressed special concern for the poor and described his own ministry as one of helping the poor and oppressed. Calling on the words of Isaiah, Jesus said:

"The Spirit of the Lord is upon Me,
Because He anointed Me to preach the gospel to the poor.
He has sent Me to proclaim release to the captives,
And recovery of sight to the blind,
To set free those who are oppressed,
To proclaim the favorable year of the Lord."

. . . And He began to say to them, "Today this Scripture has been fulfilled in your hearing." (Luke 4:18–19, 21)

In 2 Corinthians 8–9, we see Paul calling the church in Corinth to join the church in Macedonia to assist the poverty-stricken believers in Jerusalem. James also warned his readers against showing favoritism to the wealthy and to show neighbor love to the poor:

My brethren, do not hold your faith in our glorious Lord Jesus Christ with an attitude of personal favoritism. For if a man comes into your assembly with a gold ring and dressed in fine clothes, and there also comes in a poor man in dirty clothes, and you pay special attention to the one who is wearing the fine clothes, and say, "You sit here in a good place," and you say to the poor man, "You stand over there, or sit down by my footstool," have you not made distinctions among yourselves, and become judges with evil motives? Listen, my beloved brethren: *did not God choose the poor of this world to be rich in faith and heirs of the kingdom* which He promised to those who love Him? But you have dishonored the poor man. Is it not the rich who oppress you and personally drag you into court? Do they not blaspheme the fair name by which you have been called? (James 2:1–7)

While it is safe to say that from a biblical perspective poverty is not the most desirable financial state, we should also recognize that God provides special protections for the poor. Above all else, Scripture makes it clear that the poor bear the image of God in the same way as the rich; therefore, the poor have inherent dignity and worth before God.

Stewardship

Stewardship is the management of resources by one individual on behalf of the owner whereby both the owner and the manager benefit. The key point to note is that a steward is a manager rather than the owner. A steward is in a position of trust because such a manager functions on behalf of the owner in financial dealings that directly affect the owner's well-being. While we may not use the language of stewardship regularly in contemporary settings, the concept of stewardship exists anywhere that financial dealings take place on the individual and corporate level.

One of the most famous biblical passages on stewardship is the parable of the talents found in Matthew 25:14–30 (cf. Luke 19:12–27). In this parable, Jesus relates stewardship of the kingdom of God to financial stewardship. The parable begins with a man who is about to go on a journey of an unspecified length and calls three of his servants. He entrusts each servant with a specific amount of money according to his abilities. Two of the servants immediately use the money in financial dealings and reap rewards for the owner. The third servant buries the money in the ground and awaits his master's return. When the master returns from his journey, he calls the servants together to find out what they have done with the resources he entrusted to them. After hearing the report of the first two, the master responds: "Well done, good and faithful slave. You were faithful with a few things, I will put you in charge of many things; enter into the joy of your master" (Matt. 25:21, 23). The third servant returns the one talent that he had been given and says: "Master, I knew you to be a hard man, reaping where you did not sow and gathering where you scattered no seed. And I was afraid, and went away and hid your talent in the ground. See, you have what is yours" (vv. 24–25). Upon hearing this report, the master condemns the third servant for his failure of stewardship and gives the one talent to the first servant, who had ten. Then he throws the third servant out of his presence.

As we think about this parable, we need to remember that it is about the kingdom of God. Jesus' words are meant to point our attention to how we are stewarding the eternal resources that God has given us for the kingdom. The principle of wise financial stewardship still applies in this passage, however, because it is the means by which Jesus draws our attention to the spiritual side. Effective, faithful stewardship involves the management of all resources for the benefit of both the owner and the manager. The Greek term for *steward* is *oikonomos*, and it is used ten times in the New Testament. The most common usage of the term is of a house manager, but we see a specific reference to the management of "the mysteries of

God" in 1 Corinthians 4:1. All these occurrences should remind us that God is the Owner of all things (Ps. 24:1) and that we are his stewards. Ultimately, this should point us back to the initial calling of stewardship given by God to humankind in Genesis 1. Ruling over and subduing the earth is an act of stewardship whereby we champion God's plan by stewarding his creation.

Now that we have defined some key terms, we will explore three biblical principles related to wealth and poverty. These principles should set the tone for our own lives and how we relate to the poor around us. They will also guide us as we explore the ethical questions related to wealth and poverty in the final section of the chapter.

Three Guiding Biblical Principles Related to Wealth and Poverty

The Bible contains more than two thousand verses that address money and wealth; thus, we can safely surmise that the Bible has plenty to say about money, wealth, and poverty.[20] In fact, approximately 40 percent of Jesus' parables address matters of money.[21] We do not have the space to explore the entire corpus of biblical literature on money, but we can glean three key principles that will help us apply biblical teaching on the various ethical issues related to wealth and poverty.

God Is the Owner of All Wealth

All biblical teaching on matters of wealth and poverty must begin with the fact that God is the Owner of all wealth. In Psalm 24:1, David articulates the idea that God owns everything: "The earth is the LORD's, and all it contains, the world, and those who dwell in it." At the very least, this verse highlights God's sovereignty over every aspect of creation. More specifically, it affirms God's possession of the whole of creation. Interestingly, David appeals to the creation narrative to justify God's ownership in the very next verse: "For He has founded it upon the seas and established it upon the rivers" (v. 2). Because God created the universe and everything that is part of it—including us—he has divine ownership over all things. Randy Alcorn states: "It's hard to imagine a more comprehensive declaration of absolute divine ownership of everything. Furthermore, search carefully, and you won't find a single verse of Scripture that suggests God has ever surrendered his

---

20. Howard Dayton, the founder of Crown Ministries, set out to categorize all the verses in Scripture that address money and wealth. He identified over 2,350 verses, far more than the total number of verses on prayer, faith, and heaven. John Cortines and Gregory Baumer, *God and Money: How We Discovered True Riches at Harvard Business School* (Carson, CA: Rose Publishing, 2016), 13. For Dayton's entire list with categories, see https://compass1.org/the-bible-on-money/.

21. Cortines and Baumer, *God and Money*, 13.

ownership to us!"[22] In keeping with what we have already said throughout the book, the creation narrative sets the tone for our worship of the Creator. God formed the world and placed us in it along with everything else in creation. Our worship is a response to God's gracious kindness in creation and continued sovereignty over his creation.

Since God owns everything, we serve as stewards of the parts of creation that he has placed under our authority. As we noted in chapter 2, God gave humans dominion over the rest of creation. Part of that dominion certainly includes the ability to produce wealth and manage that wealth on his behalf. This is merely a temporary stewardship of God's resources during our lifetimes, and we find ourselves accountable to God for managing what permanently belongs only to him.[23] Every subsequent generation receives the same mandate to steward what God owns, and our obedience to this mandate is an act of worship. Greg Forster goes so far as to say: "The purpose of human life is worship and service, and we are designed such that we flourish best when we carry out our purpose. In practice, this means we should be *cultivating blessings out of the creation order*."[24]

As part of our stewarding what God already owns, he has entrusted to us certain portions of his property to function as our own personal property. The eighth commandment (Ex. 20:15) assumes the claim of personal property as an aspect of stewardship because it forbids stealing. The scope of the Old Testament application of the commandment extends to all types of possessions and personal property, including money, land, and livestock.[25] The most significant Old Testament support for personal property comes from the gift of the promised land that God gave the Israelites. Beginning with the promise to Abraham that God would give him the land that he would show him (Gen. 12:1–7), the land has served as a source for the idea of private property in ancient Israel.[26] Continued possession and use of the land in the Old Testament were dependent on proper worship of and obedience to the Lord by the people of Israel. When they followed after other gods, they ultimately found themselves in exile as punishment for their wayward worship.

The New Testament continues an affirmation of private property as a means of stewardship of God's resources. In Ephesians 4:28, Paul repeats the sentiment of

---

22. Randy Alcorn, *Managing God's Money: A Biblical Guide* (Carol Stream, IL: Tyndale, 2011), 16.

23. Ronald H. Nash, *Poverty and Wealth: Why Socialism Doesn't Work* (Richardson, TX: Probe, 1986), 60.

24. Greg Forster, *Joy for the World: How Christianity Lost Its Cultural Influence and Can Begin Rebuilding It* (Wheaton, IL: Crossway, 2014), 161.

25. David W. Jones, *An Introduction to Biblical Ethics* (Nashville: B&H Academic, 2013), 185.

26. Christopher J. H. Wright states that "it was the historical land-gift tradition that generated property rights in Israel." Christopher J. H. Wright, *Old Testament Ethics for the People of God* (Downers Grove, IL: IVP Academic, 2004), 89.

the eighth commandment and redirects his readers to fruitful labor so that they may give what they have to those in need: "He who steals must steal no longer; but rather he must labor, performing with his own hands what is good, so that he will have something to share with one who has need." In a similar fashion, 1 John 3:17 warns against hoarding one's possessions when they could be used to help someone in need: "But whoever has the world's goods, and sees his brother in need and closes his heart against him, how does the love of God abide in him?" In both these instances, the focus is on aiding someone in need, but the resources to do so come from one's personal possessions. Private property is the mechanism by which we express generosity to others; therefore, we can see how stewardship over God's resources in the form of private property functions to facilitate worship through neighbor love (see Rom. 13:8–10).

By keeping the idea that God owns everything at the forefront of our discussion of wealth and poverty, we shift our focus away from the accumulation of wealth to the need for worshipful stewardship. God owns everything, and we act as stewards of his resources. Although we may possess private property as part of God's gift of creation, our claims on this property are not absolute. Private property is merely an extension of the mandate that God has given humanity to rule over and subdue creation as image-bearers. The idea that God owns everything is the key principle for all other aspects of the discussion about money. If we do not comprehend and apply this point, then we will misdirect our worship. The *telos* of money is God.

Neither Wealth nor Poverty Is Necessarily an Indicator of Personal Righteousness

As we noted earlier in this chapter, there is a temptation to find ourselves at one extreme or another related to a connection between wealth and poverty as a sign of righteousness and unrighteousness. Ultimately, the question of righteousness comes down to the focus of our worship. We have been very clear that our *telos* is to worship God maximally. Does wealth—or a lack thereof—demonstrate a proper *telos*? Not necessarily. As Glenn Sunshine writes, "Just as poverty doesn't guarantee virtue, wealth does not guarantee vice."[27]

Wealth and Personal Righteousness

First, Scripture affirms that God is the giver of wealth and that he often does it as a sign of his blessing. But the accumulation of wealth can also be a sign of greed. God reminded the people of Israel as they waited to enter the promised

---

27. Glenn Sunshine, "Who Are the Poor?," in *For the Least of These: A Biblical Answer to Poverty*, ed. Anne R. Bradley and Art Lindsley (Grand Rapids: Zondervan, 2014), 19.

land that he had given them their wealth. Deuteronomy 8:18 reads, "But you shall remember the LORD your God, for it is He who is giving you power to make wealth, that He may confirm His covenant which He swore to your fathers, as it is this day." David even tells us that the Lord delights in the prosperity of his servants: "Let them shout for joy and rejoice, who favor my vindication; and let them say continually, 'The LORD be magnified, Who delights in the prosperity of His servant'" (Ps. 35:27).

Even though wealth can be evidence of the proper direction of our worship, we must be aware of the warnings about money in order to prevent any misdirected worship. The most poignant verses warning against the vice of greed come from Paul's first letter to Timothy: "But those who want to get rich fall into temptation and a snare and many foolish and harmful desires which plunge men into ruin and destruction. For the love of money is a root of all sorts of evil, and some by longing for it have wandered away from the faith and pierced themselves with many griefs" (1 Tim. 6:9–10). There is a close connection between what we love and what we worship. When money becomes the object of our worship, we are no longer characterized by the virtues of godliness and Christlikeness; instead, we are characterized by greed. The result that Paul warns against in this verse is the possibility of wandering from the faith in a pursuit of material gain.[28] Those who live in relative comfort and wealth must be especially careful to avoid the temptation of greed that leads to foolishness and destruction.

A slide into greed is likely similar to what was happening with the rich young ruler in Luke 18. The young man came to Jesus with a sincere question of what he must do to be saved. After talking to him about obedience to the commandments, Jesus instructed him to "sell all that you possess and distribute it to the poor" (Luke 18:22). The man walked away sad because he had great wealth. In response, Jesus said: "How hard it is for those who are wealthy to enter the kingdom of God! For it is easier for a camel to go through the eye of a needle than for a rich man to enter the kingdom of God" (vv. 24–25). The rich young ruler probably had his heart focused more on his wealth than on his worship of God. Greed corrupts our worship and causes us to lose sight of what is truly valuable. Scripture has numerous warnings against greed that we must take to heart if our worship is to be rightly directed.

Another influential passage warning against greed is Matthew 6:19–21, where Jesus declares: "Do not store up for yourselves treasures on earth, where moth and rust destroy, and where thieves break in and steal. But store up for yourselves treasures in heaven, where neither moth nor rust destroys, and where thieves do not break in or steal; for where your treasure is, there your heart will be also."

---

28. Thomas D. Lea and Hayne P. Griffin Jr., *1, 2 Timothy, Titus*, NAC 34 (Nashville: B&H, 1992), 170.

We have a tendency to stockpile our wealth as an insurance policy against poverty; this can also demonstrate, however, that our hearts trust more greatly in earthly possessions than in the providence of God. Greed demonstrates that our hearts are not fully devoted to the Lord. Michael Rhodes and Robby Holt offer a frightening vision of greed: "Because our material possessions so often seduce us into worshiping them like gods, they pose possibly the preeminent threat to worshiping Jesus. When we worship money, it mauls us. Money becomes a spiritual power that too often uses us rather than the other way around."[29] Greed is not exclusively the domain of the wealthy, but it seems to be more prominent in those who have wealth.

Even though wealth can be a sign of God's blessing, why does Scripture contain so many condemnations of the wealthy? Sunshine suggests that the condemnations against the wealthy are predominantly based on two matters: (1) how the wealthy make their money, and (2) how the wealthy use their money.[30] Specifically, he highlights that the wealthy sometimes make their money at the expense of the poor and do not use their wealth to help the poor. He notes: "To put it differently, the rich are not always oppressors, but oppressors are almost always rich. And that is why they incur condemnation in Scripture."[31] The idea of oppression here ties back to our discussion of justice in chapter 9. Oppression of the poor does not always equate with individual action of the rich against the poor. There can also be structural systems of oppression that reverberate for generations (e.g., Jim Crow laws, apartheid government in South Africa).

Poverty and Personal Righteousness

Second, poverty can be the product of laziness, but God also gives special protection to the poor and defenseless. Many people living in poverty suffer from circumstances beyond their control. The same is true of the poor in Scripture.[32] Since poverty is often beyond the control of those trapped in it, we can understand why God describes them as the object of his concern. Solomon notes the special concern of the Lord for the poor in a few proverbs, including Proverbs 14:31 and 19:17. He declares, "He who oppresses the poor taunts his Maker, but he who is gracious to the needy honors Him" (14:31). And he notes, "One who is gracious to a poor man lends to the LORD, and He will repay him for his good deed" (19:17).

29. Michael Rhodes and Robby Holt with Brian Fikkert, *Practicing the King's Economy: Honoring Jesus in How We Work, Earn, Spend, Save, and Give* (Grand Rapids: Baker, 2018), 57.

30. Sunshine, "Who Are the Poor?," 19–20.

31. Sunshine, "Who Are the Poor?," 20.

32. Ronald Sider states, "Thus the primary connotation of 'the poor' in Scripture has to do with low economic status usually due to calamity or some form of oppression." Ronald J. Sider, *Rich Christians in an Age of Hunger*, rev. ed. (Dallas: Word, 1997), 41.

In these verses, we see that God has a special concern for how the poor are treated. In other Old Testament passages, God identifies the poor, fatherless, widows, and foreigners as those of special concern (e.g., Ex. 22:21–22; Deut. 24:17; Lev. 23:22; Isa. 1:17; 10:1–2; Amos 8:4–6; Zech. 7:9–10).

In the New Testament, this theme continues beginning with the ministry of Jesus. David Kotter notes, "Jesus Christ incarnated the love of God toward the poor throughout his personal ministry, and he impressed this concern on his disciples and the leaders of the early church."[33] Paul encouraged the believers in wealthier churches to contribute toward the needs of those churches living in poverty and oppression (e.g., 2 Cor. 8–9). And James warns against faith without action, especially as it relates to helping the poor, by telling his readers not to send their fellow believers away simply with a word of encouragement when food and clothing is what they really need (James 2:15–16).

Despite the difficulties and hardships of poverty, Scripture generally suggests that poverty with godliness is preferred to mere material wealth. Proverbs 28:6 tells us, "Better is the poor who walks in his integrity than he who is crooked though he be rich." Thus, the overarching theme related to poverty in Scripture is that the poor receive the protection of the Lord and that poverty with virtue is better than riches with vice.

By contrast, poverty may be the result of sin and not be an example of God's special protection. Laziness, drunkenness, and gluttony can lead to a life of poverty (Prov. 6:6–11; 23:20–21; 24:30–34). Poverty can also result in envy of the wealthy (Ps. 73:1–14). Paul warns those who long for riches that they will meet a bitter end: "But those who want to get rich fall into temptation and a snare and many foolish and harmful desires which plunge men into ruin and destruction" (1 Tim. 6:9). Pursuit of wealth often results in unrighteous behavior and may even end in spiritual and financial disaster.[34]

As we can see from these passages, the relationship between wealth and righteousness is complex, and concluding that one is righteous or unrighteous based solely on economic status is problematic. Jesus, on the other hand, puts the entire discussion in perspective when he focuses our attention on a theocentric, worship-oriented perspective:

> Do not store up for yourselves treasures on earth, where moth and rust destroy, and where thieves break in and steal. But store up for yourselves treasures in heaven, where neither moth nor rust destroys, and where thieves do not break in or steal; *for where your treasure is, there your heart will be also.* . . .

33. Kotter, "Remember the Poor," 58.
34. Sider, *Rich Christians in an Age of Hunger*, 96.

No one can serve two masters; for either he will hate the one and love the other, or he will be devoted to one and despise the other. You cannot serve God and wealth.

. . . But seek first [the] kingdom [of God] and His righteousness, and all these things will be added to you. (Matt. 6:19–21, 24, 33)

When our worship is rightly directed to our Lord, then we can be content in either poverty or riches (Phil. 4:11–12). When our worship is misdirected, we can become consumed by either poverty or greed. Thus, the *telos* is key here. We must understand that the end and purpose of our worship is to respond appropriately in situations of wealth or poverty.

The Wealthy Have a Moral Duty to Assist the Poor

Assistance to the poor is a third key principle of God's teaching about wealth and poverty. It is a command found in both the Old Testament and the New Testament and forms the basis for a long tradition of serving those in need throughout Christian history.[35] Wayne Grudem sets the tone best for this idea: "The fact that not all inequality is wrong does not nullify another frequent theme in Scripture, that *poverty* is not pleasing to God but is a condition that Scripture commands us to seek to eradicate."[36] Why would God command that we eradicate poverty? The simple idea is that eliminating poverty will help our fellow image-bearers flourish as stewards in God's economy.

Individual Assistance to the Poor

Beginning with the Old Testament, God gave specific instructions to the people of Israel to take note of their brothers in poverty and aid them. While discussing the implications of the sabbatic year, God reminds the Israelites not to withhold from those in need simply because they will be forgiven of their debts in that year. Deuteronomy 15:7–11 reads:

If there is a poor man with you, one of your brothers, in any of your towns in your land which the LORD your God is giving you, you shall not harden your heart, nor close your hand from your poor brother; but you shall freely open your hand to him, and shall generously lend him sufficient for his need in whatever he lacks. Beware that there is no base thought in your heart, saying, "The seventh year, the

---

35. Justo González has provided an interesting survey of attitudes regarding wealth and poverty from the early days of the church through the patristic period. See Justo L. González, *Faith and Wealth: A History of Early Christian Ideas on the Origin, Significance, and Use of Money* (San Francisco: Harper & Row, 1990).

36. Wayne Grudem, *Christian Ethics: An Introduction to Biblical Moral Reasoning* (Wheaton, IL: Crossway, 2018), 961.

year of remission, is near," and your eye is hostile toward your poor brother, and you give him nothing; then he may cry to the LORD against you, and it will be a sin in you. You shall generously give to him, and your heart shall not be grieved when you give to him, because for this thing the LORD your God will bless you in all your work and in all your undertakings. For the poor will never cease to be in the land; therefore I command you, saying, "You shall freely open your hand to your brother, to your needy and poor in your land."

In this passage, God warns his people against ignoring the poor—even if their poverty is going to be only short-lived. Instead, believers are to open their hands freely to those in need. In Proverbs 14:31, the admonition is even stronger: "He who oppresses the poor taunts his Maker, but he who is gracious to the needy honors Him." God takes personal offense when someone oppresses a poor man but is honored when someone is generous. Generosity is an expression of neighbor love that also demonstrates a heart of worship for the One who ultimately owns everything.

These types of instructions continue into the New Testament as Jesus focuses on the needs of the poor in his teaching. As already noted, Jesus' ministry began with a proclamation that he had come "to preach the gospel to the poor" (Luke 4:18). By invoking the words of Isaiah 61, he connected the mission of the Messiah to helping those in need. Kotter notes, "Proclaiming good news to the poor was at the forefront of Jesus' announcement, and this attentiveness to the poor continued throughout his earthly ministry."[37] Jesus healed the sick, restored sight to the blind, and made the lame to walk. In most of these cases, the people suffering from these physical hardships would also be suffering economic difficulties. Therefore, by restoring them to full health, Jesus gave these individuals economic opportunities that had previously been unavailable to them.

Beyond Jesus' ministry, the instructions regarding the poor continue into the early church. Whether it is the Jerusalem church's sharing possessions to ensure that no one was in need (Acts 4:32–35) or Paul's collecting an offering for the impoverished church in Jerusalem (2 Cor. 8–9), the theme of aiding those in need is evident. One interesting point about these other New Testament instructions is that the focus appears first on the poor among the body of believers. The first priority of the instructions is to provide assistance to the church community. This concern and care for the poor would then certainly extend beyond those who were part of the church, as a means of caring for all people in the name of Christ. This reflects how the instructions in the Old Testament were first focused on people in the nation of Israel but then also extended to the sojourner, widow, and

37. Kotter, "Remember the Poor," 58.

orphan. As Jesus taught, "to the extent that you did it to one of these brothers of Mine, even the least of them, you did it to Me" (Matt. 25:40).

Societal Assistance to the Poor

In addition to speaking of individual responsibilities to alleviate poverty, Scripture addresses some societal actions designed to aid those at the bottom of the economic spectrum within the greater context of society. One good example in ancient Israel was the practice of gleaning. Mosaic law required that landowners not harvest the outer edges of their fields in order to allow the poor to glean from their lands (Lev. 19:9–10; 23:22; Deut. 24:19–22). Leviticus 19:9–10 states:

> Now when you reap the harvest of your land, you shall not reap to the very corners of your field, nor shall you gather the gleanings of your harvest. Nor shall you glean your vineyard, nor shall you gather the fallen fruit of your vineyard; you shall leave them for the needy and for the stranger. I am the LORD your God.

By incorporating these instructions into the legal code for the Israelites, God demonstrates his concern that society itself have built-in structures to help alleviate poverty. Note that these instructions do not specifically address the problem of greed or wealth. Rather, their objective is to ensure that those who had the least were able to survive. Even more interesting is the idea that these instructions were not to be viewed by the Israelites as a handout but rather as a demonstration of the virtue of holiness. That is, caring for the poor in this way was to be a means of demonstrating one's love for God and love for one's neighbor as an act of worship. As the Theology of Work Project puts it: "We might classify gleaning as an expression of compassion or justice, but according to Leviticus, allowing others to glean on our property is the fruit of holiness. We do it because God says, 'I am the LORD your God' (Lev. 19:10)."[38]

The laws of Israel required one to leave part of the harvest in the field or vineyard, but the motivation is obedience to and love for God. It is a question of living under God's lordship. What this implies rather directly is that the proper response of worship to "the LORD your God" in regard to the fruit of one's own labor results in a society that assists those in greatest need. This example and others (e.g., the Year of Jubilee) provide systematic societal structures that were meant to ensure that God's people assist the poor as an act of worship. Not only would the poor be taken care of, but these practices were also meant to help the people of Israel to become the kind of people who properly represented the Lord in and through

---

38. Theology of Work Project, "Gleaning (Leviticus 19:9–10)," *Leviticus and Work*, 2014, https://www.theologyofwork.org/old-testament/leviticus-and-work/holiness-leviticus-1727/gleaning-leviticus-19910.

both their character and their actions. Obedience to these commands would work to defeat the vices of greed and covetousness and also work to create virtues reflective of God's own loving character.

Ethical Implications of Assisting the Poor

In sum, as we consider the implications for ethics as worship, we first note that God places the final ordering of our attitudes and actions—the *telos*—in the position of primary importance. As mentioned earlier in this chapter, the *telos* for our use of money must always be worship of God alone. Some of the strongest warnings about money in Scripture relate directly to misdirected worship. The love of money is the root of all sorts of evil. When we treasure money above all else, we find that our hearts are no longer directed to God. We cannot serve two masters. We either serve God or serve money.

Second, our character is an important factor in living out the biblical vision of wealth and poverty. One of the key virtues is contentment. Paul offers his personal testimony in Philippians 4:11–13 as an example of contentment. In verses 11–12, he writes: "Not that I speak from want, for I have learned to be content in whatever circumstances I am. I know how to get along with humble means, and I also know how to live in prosperity; in any and every circumstance I have learned the secret of being filled and going hungry, both of having abundance and suffering need." Paul had been in prison and free. He had lived in abundance and in poverty. Through all of this, he had learned the secret to contentment. That secret is the focus of his worship—"I can do all things through Him who strengthens me" (Phil. 4:13). With a proper *telos*, his character is shaped toward contentment.

Another key virtue is generosity. The duty of the wealthy to serve the poor with their financial resources must be observed out of a heart of generosity. As Paul called the church members at Corinth to use their financial resources to serve the impoverished church at Jerusalem, he reminded them that God's desire was for their gift to be made out of cheerfulness and generosity: "Each one must do just as he has purposed in his heart, not grudgingly or under compulsion, for God loves a cheerful giver. And God is able to make all grace abound to you, so that always having all sufficiency in everything, you may have an abundance for every good deed" (2 Cor. 9:7–8). Those who are wealthy worship God when they cheerfully aid those with fewer resources. In doing so, they will find that God's grace abounds.

A final key virtue in assisting the poor is neighbor love. The motivation for assisting the poor is love of neighbor that flows from a heart of worship to the One who owns everything. Jesus made this point clear in his discussion of the final judgment:

Then the King will say to those on His right, "Come, you who are blessed of My Father, inherit the kingdom prepared for you from the foundation of the world. For I was hungry, and you gave Me something to eat; I was thirsty, and you gave Me something to drink; I was a stranger, and you invited Me in; naked, and you clothed Me; I was sick, and you visited Me; I was in prison, and you came to Me." Then the righteous will answer Him, "Lord, when did we see You hungry, and feed You, or thirsty, and give You something to drink? And when did we see You a stranger, and invite You in, or naked, and clothe You? When did we see You sick, or in prison, and come to You?" The King will answer and say to them, "Truly I say to you, to the extent that you did it to one of these brothers of Mine, even the least of them, you did it to Me." (Matt. 25:34–40)

Out of our worship of Jesus, we express neighbor love to those who are in need. Service to the poor, hungry, naked, and sick is simultaneously an act of love for neighbor and worship of our Savior. When we combine these three virtues of contentment, generosity, and neighbor love, we find the most worshipful motivation for assisting the poor.

Our conduct related to wealth and poverty is derived from the instructions found in Scripture. We have already addressed many of the themes of these instructions in the biblical vision for wealth and poverty. We must recognize that God owns it all. Those with financial resources have a duty to aid the poor, especially among the community of faith. And we must not attach personal righteousness to either wealth or poverty. Yet we will explore a number of other specific applications of conduct later in this chapter that do not have explicit instructions in Scripture. As God enables us to place worship at the center of our attitudes and actions and shapes our character and deeds in keeping with his Word, we then consider how best to address issues of wealth and poverty in light of the contextual or pastoral contexts we face in daily life. Here the questions of how to live out ethics as worship become harder to discern.

Ethical Questions Related to Wealth and Poverty

The issues of wealth and poverty are vast enough to fill multiple volumes. Rather than exploring individual issues, we have chosen to address three overarching questions that apply to a number of broader ethical concerns. In doing so, we will address these questions and provide guidance for applying the domains of ethical assessment to other wealth and poverty topics. Using the biblical principles we highlighted above, we will answer these questions and suggest guidance for further application.

How Much Wealth Is Too Much?

There is no easy way to answer the question of how much wealth is too much. In large part, it is dependent on how much wealth one can handle while not succumbing to the temptations that often accompany the possession of great wealth.[39] Simply put, there are too many situational factors related to each specific person, community scenario, and geographical context to make a "one size fits all" type of argument for an ideal living standard. What is great wealth in the Mississippi Delta may be average in New York City. But both appear excessive compared to Indonesia. In this light, Ronald Sider is insightful when he asks, "Can overfed, comfortably clothed, and luxuriously housed persons understand poverty?"[40] When comparing the type of poverty experienced by Americans to that which exists in many other places in the world, the answer to his question is probably "no."

So what should we do? Should we abandon all wealth and luxury and live in abject poverty like many other people around the world? Even if we minimized our lifestyles to the lowest conceivable standard in American culture, we would still find ourselves wealthier than most other people in the world. Therefore, our focus should not be on a specific value for net worth or income, but instead our focus must be on character. We discussed three key virtues above—contentment, generosity, and neighbor love—and contentment is the operative virtue for this question. It is best summarized biblically in the words of Proverbs 30:8–9:

> Keep deception and lies far from me,
> Give me neither poverty nor riches;
> Feed me with the food that is my portion,
> That I not be full and deny You and say, "Who is the LORD?"
> Or that I not be in want and steal,
> And profane the name of my God.

This proverb paints a clear picture of the extremes on either side of contentment. On one hand, it depicts abundance as a vice because it may cause a person to deny the Lord. In the self-sufficiency of abundance, we are often tempted to forget our reliance on our Creator. He made us. He sustains us. But we forget him when we become satisfied in our relative wealth. On the other hand, the proverb points to the opposite extreme of poverty. The author asks the Lord not to leave him in want because he might steal to meet his needs and defame the name of

---

39. John Cortines and Gregory Baumer propose a spending limit of $100,000 per year needed to live comfortably in the United States, but their number is likely too high for some and too low for others. Cortines and Baumer, *God and Money*, 137–44.

40. Sider, *Rich Christians in an Age of Hunger*, 1.

God. This is why poverty alleviation is a necessary step. Those who experience extreme poverty may be tempted to do something that would profane the name of God. This passage helps us see that neither of these options is desirable. Instead, it instructs us to ask God to give us just enough to be content. It also secondarily helps those of us who have an abundance to be free with our wealth—because all we need is enough to be content.

Again, this leaves us with the question "how much is enough?" The question is simply unanswerable on a universal scale. On the individual level, we must be able to identify our own weaknesses and understand how wealth exacerbates them. Then in our use of wealth, we must limit accumulation of wealth accordingly. The goal, however, is not simply to abide by a certain standard of living; instead, we place these limits on ourselves for the sake of worshiping God well. This conclusion demonstrates why the question of wealth inequality is so difficult to answer. What is too much wealth for one person may be quite manageable for someone else. Therefore, a natural gap will occur even as people seek to worship God fully with their wealth. A flourishing life is one that expresses contentment no matter the economic circumstances, that knows one's own limits, and that seeks to love and serve others through the wealth that God gives one to steward.

How Can We Alleviate Poverty?

John M. Perkins defines *justice* as "any act of reconciliation that restores any part of God's creation back to its original intent, purpose, or image. Justice is making right any of the many things that have gone wrong in this very good world that God made—and among the very good human beings he created to inhabit it."[41] If Perkins's idea of justice is correct (and we believe this is a good depiction of biblical justice), then the goal of poverty alleviation is to see a restoration back to God's original intent for the world and the development of contexts in which human beings can flourish as they were created to do as image-bearers. Thus, if wealth can be used for good, then certainly one of those good and just ends is the alleviation of poverty.

The problem for most of us is determining *how* we go about participating in such activity. As part of Moses' instructions to the people of Israel before entering the land of Canaan, he admonished them, "For the poor will never cease to be in the land; therefore I command you, saying, 'You shall freely open your hand to your brother, to your needy and poor in your land'" (Deut. 15:11). Jesus made a similar statement about the poor's always being with us when he was challenged

---

41. John M. Perkins, *Dream with Me: Race, Love, and the Struggle We Must Win* (Grand Rapids: Baker, 2017), 207. Perkins offers his own vision for economic recovery for impoverished areas that includes relationships, relocation, and reconciliation. John M. Perkins, *Beyond Charity: The Call to Christian Community Development* (Grand Rapids: Baker, 1993).

regarding the woman who anointed him with an alabaster vial of expensive perfume. When the disciples remarked that the perfume could have been sold and the money given to the poor, Jesus said, "For you always have the poor with you; but you do not always have Me" (Matt. 26:11). What should we make of such instructions? It seems clear that we should aid the poor, but we must do it in such a way that glorifies God and points others to him.

The easy response to poverty alleviation is to let the government or someone else do it. But how does that make us better worshipers? We need to begin by recognizing that we will encounter poverty everywhere we go. We also need to recognize that those in poverty are made in the image of God just like everyone else. They are not lesser people. Treating other image-bearers with the inherent value that God gives them will help us to become better worshipers.

We also need to work on poverty alleviation in ways that do not harm others. Steve Corbett and Brian Fikkert's *When Helping Hurts* is one of the best discussions of Christian attempts to help the poor. They present a three-part methodology for assisting the poor—relief, rehabilitation, and development.[42] Here is how they define these three steps:

> "Relief" can be defined as the urgent and temporary provision of emergency aid to reduce immediate suffering from a natural or man-made crisis.

> "Rehabilitation" begins as soon as the bleeding stops; it seeks to restore people and their communities to the positive elements of their precrisis conditions.

> "Development" is a process of ongoing change that moves all the people involved—both the "helpers" and the "helped"—closer to being in right relationship with God, self, others, and the rest of creation. In particular, as the materially poor develop, they are better able to fulfill their calling of glorifying God by working and supporting themselves and their families with the fruits of that work.[43]

The problem with much of our efforts at poverty alleviation is that we either stop at relief or provide relief when rehabilitation or development is more appropriate. For many of us, relief takes the form of a charitable donation or handing a few coins to someone in need. It gives a temporary feeling of altruism and generosity, but it may actually hurt the individual who needs rehabilitation and development.[44]

---

42. Steve Corbett and Brian Fikkert, *When Helping Hurts: How to Alleviate Poverty without Hurting the Poor . . . and Yourself* (Chicago: Moody, 2012), 99–116.

43. Corbett and Fikkert, *When Helping Hurts*, 99–100.

44. Corbett and Fikkert also critique common practices of short-term mission trips that generate the same

Following Corbett and Fikkert's model, much of what is done as poverty alleviation falls only into the category of relief. While relief is necessary in the immediate aftermath of a crisis, that cannot be all that we do. The problem is that continued relief actually undermines the value of the person whom we are trying to assist. Worshiping God maximally requires that we see his people the way he does. In so doing, we need to treat the poor as image-bearers and assist them in ways that dignify them and allow them to flourish. Therefore, any type of assistance that leads to continued dependence on relief undermines the inherent dignity of the recipient. The flourishing life is one built on the dignity of being made in God's image and relating to other image-bearers as equals. Assisting the poor in order to help them flourish reflects maximal worship of God.

What Is the Government's Role in Wealth Creation and Poverty Alleviation?

On questions of poverty and economic development, government is often at the center of the controversy. Scholars from different ends of the evangelical spectrum agree that government is an important component of the discussion, but they differ on how government should be involved. Our goal is not to settle the debate, but to acknowledge that government has a role in both these areas.[45] At the same time, we believe that government should not take an ever-expanding role in wealth creation and poverty alleviation.

In Scripture, government has a specific function. Romans 13:4 tells us that government is "a minister of God to you for good." It is safe to assume that part of the ministry of good that a government performs is to protect its citizens from dire circumstances of poverty. Grudem notes, "From a biblical perspective on government, it seems to me that if a government official is 'God's servant *for your good*' (Rom. 13:4), then surely we could agree that a government aid program is doing 'good' for people when it prevents them from starving or from dying because of a lack of clothing or shelter—and it would certainly not be 'good' for a society to allow such tragedies to happen."[46] Thus, government should make an effort—at least on the policy level—of working toward the alleviation of poverty. As we learned from our earlier discussion on gleaning, it seems that at the very least, the creation of a societal "safety net" that helps the least well off with basic needs is a good and right thing for a government to provide. Historically, this has been the

---

problems. Corbett and Fikkert, *When Helping Hurts*, 151–67.

45. On one hand, Ronald Sider addresses government problems and solutions in *Rich Christians in an Age of Hunger*. Wayne Grudem and Barry Asmus offer alternative explanations for the role of government in economic development and poverty alleviation in *The Poverty of Nations*. See Sider, *Rich Christians in an Age of Hunger*, esp. chaps. 7–8, 11; Wayne Grudem and Barry Asmus, *The Poverty of Nations: A Sustainable Solution* (Wheaton, IL: Crossway, 2013).

46. Grudem, *Christian Ethics*, 966.

purpose of the welfare system, Medicare, and a host of other government-funded projects, including unemployment assistance such as that which was needed on a massive level during the 2020 COVID-19 pandemic.

The main problem with this government role, however, is that government is often not fully prepared to make adequate policies because those making the policies are not close enough to the problem to know the best solution. That is where the *principle of subsidiarity* comes into play. Subsidiarity "holds that nothing should be done by a larger and more complex organization which can be done as well by a smaller and simpler organization."[47] From a government standpoint, this means that local and state governments are better placed to help citizens than the federal government. We can also extend the principle of subsidiarity down to the individual and community level to say that sometimes the government can actually interfere with the poverty-alleviation efforts of individuals and groups within the community. Government's role, especially on the federal level, is to come alongside and assist the community when the job is more than the community can handle. Poverty alleviation should not be left to the federal government as the primary actor.

On the other side of the equation, part of government's role in helping its citizens is to stimulate economic conditions that can help those citizens flourish. How the government should be involved in stimulating the right economic conditions, however, is also a point of great controversy. In the United States, various political factions find some of their greatest disagreements over this exact point. On the one hand, some argue that free-market systems are best suited to human flourishing because the generation of new wealth lifts all people out of poverty.[48] On the other hand, others argue that free markets tend to generate a greater inequality of wealth and often result in systemic abuse of the poor. Therefore, a better plan is to create an aggressive system of federally funded programs that requires massive redistribution of wealth to ensure that the least well off are as well off as possible.[49]

As we discussed in chapter 9, it is our belief that no current economic system is without its faults, but it is our conviction that within certain qualifiers, the free-market system tends to lead to great wealth production and the opportunity to alleviate poverty through the work of individuals, communities, and the government. As the statistics noted at the beginning of the chapter highlight, the creation of new wealth in the United States through the processes of a predominantly free-market economy has led to a rather dramatic overall increase of the standard of living of

47. David A. Bosnich, "The Principle of Subsidiarity," *Religion & Liberty* 6, no. 4 (1996): 9.

48. See Grudem and Ausmus, *Poverty of Nations*; Grudem, *Christian Ethics*, 966–89; Nash, *Poverty and Wealth*, chaps. 1–7.

49. See Sider, *Rich Christians in an Age of Hunger*, 137–86.

all Americans. While inequality may result as part of the free-market system and that inequality may normatively foster injustice in various forms, ultimately economic inequality is not in itself inherently immoral. The fact of the matter is that God owns all things and we do not. That reality is the epitome of inequality. But certainly this is not inherently "unfair" or "unjust."

Scripture seems to indicate that the problem is not primarily the unequal distribution of wealth but the sinfulness that often accompanies wealth disparities. As we discussed in chapter 9, sinfulness affects our motives and actions, and culturally embedded sin patterns can even impact our economic ideas and structures. Personally and corporately, it is vitally important that we grow in and embody the virtues of contentment, generosity, and neighbor love as God desires. Only then could the issue of a wealth gap actually be used beneficially by the most well off to care for the least well off by not only sacrificially giving but also innovatively creating new wealth for all through God-honoring business and entrepreneurial endeavors.

The question remains, however, what role the government should play and how we should hold government accountable for its role in economic issues. When possible, we should be part of the government process. First, Scripture makes it clear that Christian citizens have a duty to pay taxes to the government. Jesus made this very point in Matthew 22:21 when he said, "Then render to Caesar the things that are Caesar's; and to God the things that are God's." Paul reiterates this point in Romans 13:7 as he tells his readers to pay taxes to whom taxes are due. Implied in these verses—especially Romans 13—is that the government will then use these taxes for the benefit and protection of its citizens. Thus, we have a duty to pay taxes that will fund economic enterprises of government.

Second, we should participate in the selection of government officials whenever possible. It is not enough for us to pay our taxes and expect the government to do what is good and just. We need to be part of the governing process through voting and potentially even running for office. We like to think of the voting process as government-sanctioned, regularly scheduled civil disobedience. If the government is causing harm to the poor or implementing economic policies that create more hardships, then we should vote to change elected officials. In addition, Christians who are capable of governing should make themselves available for the public to elect them.[50]

Government, therefore, has a specific role to play in creating wealth and alleviating poverty, but it is not the final answer to economic problems. As believers,

---

50. There is a historic debate over whether a Christian should participate in an otherwise secular government. Tertullian was the most ardent detractor from this position in the early church. But we believe that Christians can apply their beliefs and worship of God to serve their fellow citizens in certain governing roles.

we should take note of the principle of subsidiarity and recognize that poverty alleviation begins at the individual level of loving the poor well and extends to ever-widening constituencies that are better able to address the problem of poverty. Government assists along the way, but it must not be viewed as the first solution.

Conclusion

The encampment of the 99 percent in San Francisco that we referred to at the beginning of the chapter wanted to see change in how the world's wealth was distributed. While they noted correctly that the wealthiest 1 percent control vast amounts of wealth, their proposed solution of redistributing that wealth did not take into account the complex nature of the questions of wealth and poverty. Rather than an overdependence on redistribution of wealth, we have advocated a biblical vision of wealth and poverty that calls on those who have access to wealth to aid the poor in various ways that will help them establish themselves on more stable economic footing with a recognition that government has an important but comparatively minimal role in providing a basic "safety net" to assist the least well off to rise above poverty.

One of the most difficult parts of the discussion relates to the alleviation of poverty because it seems to be an ever-present problem. On this point, Corbett and Fikkert offer fresh insight on how many evangelicals have created more problems than they have solved. We should instead implement their threefold model for poverty alleviation—relief, rehabilitation, and development—as the standard in the United States and in our work around the world. When we love our neighbors well, we will not simply give them a handout and hope they get back on their feet. We should use the wealth that God has entrusted to us as his stewards to aid those who are in need and work to correct systems that may prevent them from being able to care for themselves.

Scripture offers numerous instructions for how we are to treat matters of wealth and poverty, but the most striking is the call to exhibit the virtues of contentment, generosity, and neighbor love no matter our circumstances. This is the point of Paul's description of himself in Philippians 4:11–12: "Not that I speak from want, for I have learned to be content in whatever circumstances I am. I know how to get along with humble means, and I also know how to live in prosperity; in any and every circumstance I have learned the secret of being filled and going hungry, both of having abundance and suffering need." It is on this basis of contentment that Paul declares, "I can do all things through Him who strengthens me" (Phil. 4:13). When we are content, this character trait frees us up to focus on loving our neighbor in a manner that maximizes generosity, much like that of our Lord, who so loved the world that he gave his richest possession for the lost, broken, and spiritually impoverished—his own Son (John 3:16). May it be said of us that we are content and generous no matter our financial circumstances so that we will love our neighbors well and trust in the power of Christ to live a flourishing life.

Key Terms and Concepts

development

poverty

poverty alleviation

principle of subsidiarity

rehabilitation

relief

stewardship

wealth

wealth creation

wealth gap

Year of Jubilee

Key Scriptures

Exodus 20:15

Psalm 24:1–2

Proverbs 14:31

Proverbs 19:17

Matthew 6:19–33

Matthew 22:21

Matthew 25:34–40

Luke 4:18–19

Luke 18:22–25

Romans 13:7

Philippians 4:11–13

James 2:15–16

1 John 3:17

Study Questions

1. What are the key components of a biblical vision of wealth and poverty?
2. What is the *wealth gap*, and how should we evaluate it in light of scriptural teachings?
3. How much wealth is too much?
4. What problems might we create with poverty-alleviation programs?
5. What are some practical ways in which we can worship God through our wealth?

For Further Reading

Blomberg, Craig L. *Christians in an Age of Wealth: A Biblical Theology of Stewardship*. Grand Rapids: Zondervan, 2013.

Bradley, Anne R., and Art Lindsley, eds. *For the Least of These: A Biblical Answer to Poverty*. Grand Rapids: Zondervan, 2014.

Corbett, Steve, and Brian Fikkert. *When Helping Hurts: How to Alleviate Poverty without Hurting the Poor . . . and Yourself.* Chicago: Moody, 2012.

Cortines, John, and Gregory Baumer. *God and Money: How We Discovered True Riches at Harvard Business School.* Carson, CA: Rose Publishing, 2016.

González, Justo L. *Faith and Wealth: A History of Early Christian Ideas on the Origin, Significance, and Use of Money.* San Francisco: Harper & Row, 1990.

Grudem, Wayne, and Barry Ausmus. *The Poverty of Nations: A Sustainable Solution.* Wheaton, IL: Crossway, 2013.

Nyquist, J. Paul. *Is Justice Possible? The Elusive Pursuit of What Is Right.* Chicago: Moody, 2017.

Platt, David. *Radical: Taking Back Your Faith from the American Dream.* Colorado Springs: Multnomah, 2010.

Sider, Ronald J. *Rich Christians in an Age of Hunger.* Rev. ed. Dallas: Word, 1997.

12

Creation Care and Environmental Stewardship

"Christians have in the biblical story line and worldview unique resources to explain, respond to, and keep in right perspective the 'environmental crisis.'"[1]
—DOUGLAS J. MOO AND JONATHAN A. MOO, Creation Care

"Creation care opens new doors for sharing Christ's love. . . . We can and should be concerned with telling others about Christ while also caring for his creation."[2]
—NANCY SLEETH, "Isn't It All Going to Burn Anyway?"

Introduction: A Two-Level Discussion

Perhaps the single most important verse in the Bible about creation care and environmental stewardship is Psalm 24:1, which tells us that "the earth is the LORD's, and all it contains." Simply put, the world belongs to God, not us. It is for his glory, not ours.

Given the clarity of this point, we can then say that on one level, the creation-care discussion is extremely simple. Humans pollute what God has created, and we shouldn't. Misuse of God's creation is a sinful act of self-centeredness on the part of humankind, and it reflects a disposition of disrespect and rebellion against the One who is both Creator and Owner of all things. This is especially true in light of the fact that he gave humans explicit instructions to steward the earth on his behalf by subduing the earth and ruling over it in such a way that it would be filled with his glory. In the same way that it would not be right to go into your parents' house, throw your trash around, graffiti the walls, burn their house

1. Douglas J. Moo and Jonathan A. Moo, *Creation Care: A Biblical Theology for the World* (Grand Rapids: Zondervan, 2018), 30.
2. Nancy Sleeth, "Isn't It All Going to Burn Anyway? Finding Common Ground with Creation Care Skeptics," in *A Faith Encompassing All Creation*, ed. Tripp York and Andy Alexis-Baker (Eugene, OR: Cascade, 2014), 118.

plants, mistreat their pets, drain their bank account, and then claim that you did nothing wrong, why would we think it would be acceptable to do exactly this kind of thing to God's world?

Sadly, however, this is exactly what his image-bearers have done. The evidence is everywhere. Next time you drive home from work or school, just look out the window at the side of the road. Almost anywhere in the world, you will discover that if people live nearby, you will see trash. Someone's litter is fouling up the scenery that God created to sing his praise. On a larger scale, whether it is the clouds of smog that hover over Los Angeles or Beijing, the lingering oil that remains from the *Exxon Valdez* and *Deepwater Horizon* oil spills, or the tons of plastic and trash items washing up on the shores of the world's remotest islands, it is pretty obvious that we humans are trashing God's world.

On another level, however, the discussion of creation care is extremely complex. After all, God did instruct humans to go into all the world and subdue it and rule over it (Gen. 1:27–28). Implied by this command is that human interaction with, and manipulation of, the created order is a good thing. Due to our sinful nature, however, the manner in which we interact with and manipulate God's world has far-reaching and negative implications, many of which are beyond our current ability to comprehend. The discussion of creation care and environmental stewardship is complex precisely because of the amount of intelligence, science, and wisdom needed to comprehensively and definitively understand the vast network of all the systems God created to function in harmony—not to mention understanding all the different ways that we are impacting it.

How much does our pollution impact the planet's ecosystems? How resilient is God's world? Scripture tells us that God will not destroy the world a second time *as he did in the days of Noah* (Gen. 8:21), but does this mean that humans can't destroy it? Does his promise that "while the earth remains, seedtime and harvest, and cold and heat, and summer and winter, and day and night shall not cease" (v. 22) mean that the earth's biofeedback mechanisms are so resilient that there is nothing we can do to dangerously alter those systems or even make them crash? Human activity has a significant impact on the planet. Will human activity lead to crisis-level problems and increase the likelihood of human suffering? Could the solutions to such problems create a new set of complications that are unforeseen or ignored? Research suggests that there may be a causal connection between human activity and environmental degradation. For those who doubt that there really is a causal connection between human actions and areas of potential environmental crisis, is it reasonable to think that *all* the studies are linked to bad scientific models or even twisted motives? Even if only a fraction of these studies turn out to be accurate predictors of possible future calamity, what should we do about it now? What economic and political strategy to combat the negative environmental effects of human activity is wise or comprehensive enough to teach us how to both "serve God and save the planet"?[3]

The complexity of this debate leads to significant disagreements about how we as individuals and all of us as the human race together ought to respond and act. Should we shift into crisis mode? Should we wait and see? Should we do whatever we want because "it's all going to burn anyway"? How should an ethical response seeking to maximize the worship and praise of God compel us to think and act?

Our purpose in this chapter is *not* to address the particulars of the scientific, economic, or political debates that clutter news headlines and social media. While such discussions are needed, speaking conclusively about the particulars of these fields lies outside our area of expertise. Rather, it *is* our task here to lay the biblical, theological, and moral foundations for a robust ethic of creation care. It is our task to help our readers move into discussions about the scientific, economic, and political particulars with an eye clearly fixed on God and his glory and the good of his creation. Our hope is to guide our readers into understanding why creation care and environmental ethics are vitally important elements of Christian discipleship. Ultimately, it is our goal that as the Christian doctrines and ethical imperatives discussed in this chapter become clear, our readers will then develop sound moral convictions and theocentric motivations that stimulate them to develop creation-care convictions and practices that are both evangelistically oriented and ecologically sound.

In order to accomplish this goal, we begin by offering a few basic definitions of terms and concepts, identifying the main lines of concern that are up for debate, and giving a very brief overview of various perspectives on environmental ethics in order to help provide context for the larger discussion. Next, we develop scriptural and theological foundations that ought to drive our understanding of the ethics of creation care. Finally, before bringing the chapter to conclusion, we discuss how an *ethics of worship* ought to shape the way in which we engage the discussion in the public square as well as the central role that evangelism plays in a Christ-centered ethic of creation care.

Key Terms and Concepts in the Discussion on Creation Care and Environmental Ethics

Defining terms and understanding the basic concepts used in any moral or ethical conversation is always important. It is especially so when either the topic under discussion is controversial or there is a lack of general understanding about

---

3. J. Matthew Sleeth, *Serve God, Save the Planet: A Christian Call to Action* (Grand Rapids: Zondervan, 2006).

the nature of the topic. Precision of language helps to clarify the moral debate and also protects participants from unnecessary misunderstandings.

Ecology and Environmental Ethics

When we speak of *ecology*, we are speaking of the branch of biological studies that has to do with the relationship between living organisms and their physical surroundings, or *environment*. The focus is on an observation of how organisms interact with their environment. It is a discipline of study that is based on observation of facts. A distinctly *Christian view of ecology* adds to this observation of facts the underlying presupposition that God created the living organisms and embedded them in their physical surroundings. Whether the approach to ecology is Christian or secular, both depend on accurate scientific data collection and interpretation of that data to be successful.

An important element in any discussion related to the environment has to do with the gathering of accurate and comprehensive scientific data as it relates to the proper caretaking of God's world. But it is precisely at this point that we run into the first point of controversy. While there is a general consensus regarding which aspects of the environment we should be concerned about, there is significant disagreement about whether we have enough data to reach a settled conclusion as well as how that data should best be interpreted. That is, most scientists recognize that we need to keep an eye on such things as population numbers, biodiversity, deforestation, water systems, air systems, waste management, land use, energy consumption, and climate change. Not all agree, however, that the data show that we have reached *crisis* levels in terms of any of these categories. Further, even though the majority of scientists agree that there is cause for great concern, there is significant disagreement on how bad the problem is in each area. Simply put, the vast size and complexity of each of these various systems make gathering enough data to reach a single agreed-upon and certain conclusion about any one of them extremely difficult. This, in turn, makes the arrival at a certain and conclusive prediction about the future of the entire ecosphere even that much more difficult.

Further, not only does significant disagreement exist on the nature of the problem, there is also significant difference of opinion regarding what solutions would best address the problem even if we can be convinced that we have come to a moment requiring crisis intervention. This is where the conversation turns from ecology to the discussion of environmental ethics.

Environmental ethics involves a shift in the focus of the conversation from mere observation of what *is* the case to how organisms *ought* to interact with the physical surroundings that they are embedded within. The discussion shifts from matters of *fact* to matters of *value*. "In general, environmental ethics is a systematic account of the moral relations between human beings and their natural environment. Environmental ethics assumes that ethical norms can and do govern human behavior toward the natural world. A theory of environmental ethics, then, must go on to explain what these norms are, to whom or to what humans have responsibilities, and how these responsibilities are justified."[4]

A distinctly *Christian view of environmental ethics* would then involve discovering how living organisms that God created ought to interact with the physical surroundings or environment he created and then embedded them within. In particular, it involves ecology in that it includes an observation of how humans *do* interact with their environment, but the primary focus is on giving a systematic account of what the moral relationship between human beings and the environment that they are embedded within *ought* to be like. A distinctly Christian view of environmental ethics will delve into Scripture to discover what ethical norms should inform us of our responsibilities to God's world and guide our behaviors toward it. If the manner in which we *do* behave does not match how we *ought* to behave, then it also includes recommendations for altering our behavior as a part of our discipleship and as an act of worshipful repentance before God.

Worldviews and Various Environmental Perspectives

As it is in all ethical discussions, one's underlying worldview perspective and metaethical assumptions about the *nature of reality* (i.e., *revealed reality*) and the *nature of morality* (i.e., *revealed morality*) provide the foundational justifications that shape how moral and ethical convictions are developed and what moral decisions are ultimately recommended (see table 6.3 in chapter 6). In the field of environmental ethics, this is certainly no different. In fact, it is common to describe the various ethical perspectives and recommended moral methodologies in terms of what aspect of the natural world one believes the discussion ought to be centered on. Consider, for example, the differences between anthropocentric, biocentric, ecocentric, and theocentric approaches to the discussion of environmental ethics.

First, *anthropocentric*, or human-centered, ethical theories assume that humans are the measure of all things and therefore should enjoy the place of moral superiority over and above their environment. Anthropocentrism typically arises from a materialistic view of the universe that is most consistent with a Darwinist evolutionary understanding of the cosmos. If the universe is a product of chance and change through time without a personal creator, then it follows that any sense of moral value or status must be derived or assigned to an object or being and not inherent to it. That is, morality is invented and not discovered. Because there

---

4. Joseph R. DesJardins, *Environmental Ethics: An Introduction to Environmental Philosophy*, 5th ed. (Boston: Wadsworth, 2013), 17.

is no inherent moral order to be discovered, the right to rule and reign goes to the strongest or most able. The unique and elevated position that human beings hold in the environment becomes the determinative factor in developing an environmental ethic. One could arrive at a similar conclusion without Darwinism by arguing that humans have been given a divine right with autonomy to use the created order however they wish. This, in fact, is a charge that has been leveled against Christians and something that we will address later in the chapter.

Regardless of the ultimate justification, anthropocentric views hold that humans have a *superior moral value* over the rest of nature due in large part to their ability to reason and manipulate their environment. Nature and the rest of the environment, however, are perceived to have only an *instrumental value*. That is, the environment has value only insofar as it is useful to serve human ends. As one might imagine, this rather utilitarian perspective can result in an exploitive relationship between humans and their environment. The use and depletion of natural resources, the dumping of waste into either air or water, the abuse of animals as a food source or test subjects, and any number of issues related to the environmental-ethics discussion would be limited only through a consideration of how that limitation would positively or negatively impact human want and consumption. In the later discussion, we will argue from Scripture that Christians must reject this perspective in light of the ultimate supremacy of God over all things and his instructions to us on how to govern our relationship with the created order as his *image-bearers*.

Second, *biocentric*, or life-centered, ethical theories are predicated on the notion that all living organisms (human and nonhuman) have an *inherent*, non-instrumental value. More specifically, biocentrism is "any theory that views all life as possessing intrinsic value."[5] According to Paul Taylor, four basic premises drive a biocentric view of nature:

1. The belief that humans are members of the Earth's Community of Life in the same sense and on the same terms in which other living things are members of that Community.
2. The belief that the human species, along with all other species, are integral elements in a system of interdependence such that the survival of each living thing, as well as its chances of faring well or poorly, is determined not only by the physical conditions of its environment but also by its relations to other living things.

5. DesJardins, *Environmental Ethics*, 131. See also Thomas Sieger Derr with James A. Nash and Richard John Neuhaus, *Environmental Ethics and Christian Humanism* (Nashville: Abingdon, 1996), 36–62. Derr suggests that animal-rights activists, ecofeminists, and those adhering to James Lovelock's "Gaia Hypothesis" practice forms of biocentrism.

3. The belief that all organisms are teleological centers of life [i.e., "ends in themselves"] in the sense that each is a unique individual pursuing its own good in its own way.
4. The belief that humans are not inherently superior to other living things.[6]

Like anthropocentrism, this perspective can arise from a Darwinist evolutionary understanding of the cosmos, or from some type of appeal to God as the author of all life. The key idea is that all beings that possess life are considered to have inherent moral value. The claim is further made that no single being or species has moral superiority or value over another. From this perspective, humans may be recognized as being *unique* among other created beings but are not inherently superior or of any greater value. In fact, some will even argue that giving humans a privileged position of higher value is nothing more than a form of *speciesism* (which is akin to *racism*).[7]

The positive side of this perspective is that the moral status of animals, plants, and all other living things is elevated such that their existence should be protected and their thriving should be encouraged. On the other hand, however, the net effect is that human life is by default devalued to the level of all other animals. Ethical principles related to killing, for example, would then need to be given equal application between those of the human species and those of any other species at similar stages of development.[8]

Table 12.1. Worldviews and Environmental Perspectives

System of Thought	Moral Status	Role of Humans
Anthropocentrism	Only *humans* have inherent moral standing; creation's value is instrumental.	Dominators
Biocentrism	All *living things* have moral status.	Participants
Ecocentrism	The entire biosphere and its *ecosystems as a whole* have moral status.	Participants/virus
Theocentrism	All creation has inherent value, but humans have highest value as *image-bearers*.	Stewards, servants, vice-regents, God's champions of worship

6. Paul Taylor, *Respect for Nature: A Theory of Environmental Ethics* (Princeton, NJ: Princeton University Press, 1986), 99–100.

7. See Peter Singer, *Animal Liberation* (New York: Harper Collins, 2009), 6.

8. See Peter Singer, *Practical Ethics*, 3rd ed. (Cambridge: Cambridge University Press, 2011). See esp. chaps. 3, 5, 10.

Third, *ecocentric* views of environmental ethics are similar to biocentric ones in the sense that they focus on the inherent value of nonhuman entities. Yet ecocentrism expands on this notion to be logically consistent with its premises and not only seeks to recognize the inherent moral value of all living organisms (biocentrism) but also extends moral valuation to that which is considered life-less, such as rocks, dirt, and land. Further, ecocentric views also place an emphasis on a consideration of the inherent value not just of individual parts of the environment, but of the ecosystems as a whole. That is, in addition to recognizing the value of each element of nature, ecocentrism also places emphasis and value on the interconnectedness of nature in all its parts.

This position was originally (and most often) identified with the *land ethic* espoused by Aldo Leopold and is sometimes referred to as *ethical holism*.[9] Leopold's work placed emphasis on the scientific *fact* that ecosystems are interconnected and must be viewed as a whole in order for them to function healthily. As the environmental movement grew and developed, however, Leopold's scientific work was later adopted and adapted to be compatible with various religious worldview perspectives—most notably, the pantheistic influences of Hinduism giving rise to a *deep ecology* and progressive liberation theologies that fuel many of the underlying assumptions present in *ecofeminism*. As a result, while an *ecocentric* perspective about the manner in which nature functions does not necessitate a buy-in to these non-Christian worldviews, many who champion this perspective hold these worldview assumptions, and thus this perspective is often equated with an anti-Christian pantheism. Some of the more extreme non-Christian versions of ecocentrism view human involvement in the ecosphere like a virus that causes a sickness that is impacting the health of the entire system.

Finally, while it is possible to suggest that any religious perspective on environmental ethics places its own view of God at the center of the discussion, most commonly when an environmental ethics is described as *theocentric*, the reference is to a Christian ethic that places emphasis on the fact that the triune God of the Bible created the world and imbued each part—and all of it together—with inherent value. That is, each part of the created order has inherent value because God created it, gave it its own being, and loves it for itself. Further, in his wisdom,

9. Aldo Leopold, *A Sand County Almanac and Sketches Here and There* (Oxford: Oxford University Press, 1949). DesJardins' work is helpful in understanding this position, especially as it is distinguished from the biocentric position. DesJardins argues that there are three different types of ecocentrism (ecocentric holism). First, there is a metaphysical holism, which claims that wholes are real, perhaps more real than their constituent parts. This is generally the position of Aldo Leopold, J. Baird Callicott, and Holmes Rolston III. Second, there is a methodological or epistemological holism, which focuses on how best to understand various phenomena concerning the ecosystem. The third category is labeled *ethical holism* and suggests that moral considerability should be extended to wholes. See DesJardins, *Environmental Ethics*, 170–71.

God created an entire world as an interdependent whole. Thus, God also cares for the entire creation order, cosmos, or "world" as a singular whole (John 3:16). By extension, his image-bearers should do so as well. This is why Christians will often refer to the discipline of environmental ethics as *creation care.*

Table 12.2. Versions of Ecocentrism

Version of Ecocentrism	Moral Status	Role of Humans
Land Ethic	Ecological processes are valued for themselves.	Preservers of the land
Deep Ecology	The interconnected *Web of Life* is deified.	Participants/ parasites
Ecofeminism	Relationships between elements of nature are valued. Some also place emphasis on a deification of "Mother Nature."	Caregivers

Evangelical Approaches to Environmental Ethics and Creation Care

Within a theocentric point of view, most Christian versions of environmental ethics and creation care hold that while each part has an inherent value, God values humans above all other aspects of the created order and gives to them a special role as his image-bearers (Gen. 1:26–28; Matt. 6:26). As such, they are tasked to properly order and rule over God's creation.

Beginning with Francis Schaeffer's influential work *Pollution and the Death of Man* published in 1970 (the year of the first Earth Day), a growing number of evangelical Christians have attempted to motivate the larger Christian community toward a greater concern for God's world and the development of a robust theology of creation care. As a result, there is an increasing awareness among evangelicals of the importance of the discussion as well as a growing amount of scholarship concerning how to go about caring for God's world as an important aspect of Christian worship and discipleship. This, in turn, has led to several distinct ethical approaches among evangelicals regarding how best to envision the role that God's image-bearers ought to play in caring for God's world: the *dominionist* model, the *dependence* model, and the *stewardship* model.[10] Table 12.3 highlights key aspects of these distinct models.

---

10. The identification and discussion of these three categories rely heavily on the work of Donald R. McDaniel Jr., "Becoming Good Shepherds: A New Model of Creation Care for Evangelical Christians" (PhD diss., Southeastern Baptist Theological Seminary, 2011), 2. For a more in-depth discussion of these nuanced positions, see Mark Liederbach and Seth Bible, *True North: Christ, the Gospel, and Creation Care* (Nashville: B&H Academic, 2012), 15–17.

Table 12.3. Christian Versions of Theocentric Environmental Ethics

Christian Version of Theocentric Environmental Ethics	Moral Status	Role of Humans
Dominionist	Humans have supreme value. Creation has instrumental value.	Kings/rulers
Dependence	Creation has inherent value. Humans serve and protect the garden.	Servants
Stewardship	Creation has inherent value. Humans are to rule in God's name.	Ambassadors/ caretakers
Ethics as Worship (a version of the *stewardship* model)	Creation has inherent value. Humans are to rule in God's name.	Worship leaders (embedded headship/champions)

With these various approaches to creation care among evangelicals in mind, based on our greater discussion of the creation narrative in chapter 2, we are persuaded that a form of the *stewardship* model ought to serve as the basis from which to develop an ethic of creation care. We further believe, however, that such a model must also place the idea of stewardship directly in a theological ethic that emphasizes the centrality of worship to all that we say, think, do, and act (1 Cor. 10:31) in order to remain true to both the fundamental story line of Scripture and the mission of God presented therein. It is to this discussion that we now turn.

Scriptural and Theological Foundations for Creation Care

Having provided a basic framework by which to understand the contemporary discussion of environmental ethics, we are now faced with the task of developing the scriptural, theological, and moral foundations that ought to drive a Christian ethic of creation care, as well as motivate God-honoring actions that embody such an ethic. To do so, we believe it will prove helpful to develop our ethic in contrast to what is arguably the single most influential critique leveled against Christians regarding the treatment of the environment.

Lynn White Jr.'s Infamous Critique of Christianity

In 1967, medieval historian Lynn White Jr. published a now widely disseminated article asserting that Christianity was to blame for the current and ongoing ecological crisis. He stated:

What we do about ecology depends on our ideas of the man-nature relationship. More science and more technology are not going to get us out of the present ecologic crisis until we find a new religion, or rethink our old one. . . . The present increasing disruption of the global environment is the product of a dynamic technology and science which were originated in the Western medieval world. . . . *Their growth cannot be understood historically apart from distinctive attitudes toward nature which are deeply grounded in Christian dogma.* The fact that most people do not think of these attitudes as Christian is irrelevant. No new set of basic values has been accepted in our society to displace those of Christianity. *Hence we shall continue to have a worsening ecologic crisis until we reject the Christian axiom that nature has no reason for existence save to serve man.* . . . Both our present science and our present technology are so tinctured with *orthodox Christian arrogance toward nature* that no solution for our ecologic crisis can be expected from them alone. Since the roots of our trouble are so largely religious, the remedy must also be essentially religious.[11]

Shortly after its publication, White's article seemed to take on a life of its own. In the 1970s, the idea that Christianity was the source of our ecological problems resonated with those who were already exploring Eastern religions in order to ground their environmental ethics in pantheistic ideas and concepts. Alister McGrath notes that even though "the intellectual roots of [White's argument] turned out to be surprisingly shallow," his article "became a sacred text, passed on with an almost uncritical reverence. Many ecologists would no more criticize White's article than fundamentalist Christians would criticize the Bible."[12]

Much of White's critique rested on the assumption that the Bible's instruction to Adam and Eve to "subdue" and "rule" over creation in Genesis 1 was in essence a license for humankind to exploit the created realm with an unlimited dominion. White interpreted Genesis 1:26–28 to mean that God gave unlimited authority and autonomy to Adam and Eve to do with the rest of creation whatever they pleased. While certainly there are places and times within human history when those who claimed to be Christians acted exactly as White claimed, such a reality by no means implies that the basic teachings of Christianity actually support such a position.[13] Indeed, we suggest that to the degree that any blame falls on Christianity, it should not be on the Christian teachings per se but on persons who

11. Lynn White Jr., "The Historical Roots of Our Ecological Crisis," *Science* 155 (March 10, 1967): 1206–7, accessed May 26, 2020, http://inters.org/files/white1967.pdf (emphasis added).

12. Alister McGrath, *The Reenchantment of Nature: The Denial of Religion and the Ecological Crisis* (New York: Doubleday, 2002), xv–xvi.

13. Steven Bouma-Prediger, *For the Beauty of the Earth: A Christian Vision for Creation Care*, 2nd ed. (Grand Rapids: Baker, 2010), 74.

are wrongly acting in the name of Christianity or wrongly interpreting Christian doctrine. In fact, a close and careful reading of Scripture leads us to a conclusion quite the opposite of White's claims.

Genesis 1:1

In order to counter White's claims that Christianity is at fault for any ecological crisis, we must return to the key passages of Scripture that shape our understanding of the stewardship of creation. While we discussed these passages at greater length in chapter 2, we highlight them again here because they form the basis for our understanding of humankind's relationship to the rest of our environment. To begin, consider several important truths that Christianity affirms based on the first verse of the Bible: "In the beginning God created the heavens and the earth" (Gen. 1:1).

A Dependent Creation

First, this passage indicates that God is the ontological ground of all things that exist. That is, everything that exists in the created realm does so because he gives it life or being. Nothing other than God existed before his creating all things and giving them their existence. Thus, it has been the historical teaching of the church that God created *ex nihilo* ("out of nothing"), that passages such as Psalm 33:6–9; John 1:3; Acts 4:24; Romans 4:17; Colossians 1:16; and Revelation 4:11 all support the reality that God is an eternal Being who created all things, and that all things have their beginning in God's creative activity.[14] Hebrews 11:3 affirms this historically orthodox notion by unequivocally stating that "the worlds were prepared by the word of God, so that what is seen was not made out of things which are visible." This means, then, not only that God eternally existed before the creation, but also that all creation is dependent on him for its existence. Our existence—and the existence of the entire universe—is impossible without the prior existence of the One who created it. In more philosophical terms, we can describe God as the one *noncontingent* Being, whereas all creation is *contingent* on him for its existence.

A Creation That Is Good but Not Divine

A second important element builds on the previous idea. Not only is the created realm utterly dependent on God for its existence and ordering, it is also

---

14. John S. Feinberg, *No One like Him: The Doctrine of God* (Wheaton, IL: Crossway, 2001), 552–57. In his extensive work on the doctrine of God, Feinberg helpfully points out that the phrase "in the beginning" provides the reference point for understanding how God created the heavens and the earth. This phrase in the Hebrew sentence structure sets forth an absolute sense of beginning in which nothing existed before creation but God alone.

clearly distinct in nature from God. That is, when God created the world, he gave the created order its own being. As the rest of Genesis 1 unfolds, the Lord declares that the creation itself is "good" in its own right, and he does so before the existence of human beings (Gen. 1:4, 10, 12, 18, 21, 25). Then in Genesis 1:31, after God creates humans, he declares his creation to be "very good." Thus, creation without humans has its own inherent value because God created it, values it, and loves it. This simple fact helps us understand that while humans play an important role as part of the created order, their presence in it was not necessary for the rest of creation to be considered good in its own right. The value of nonhuman creation, then, is not merely *instrumental*; it is not merely good because humans can use it for their own ends.

A related point that emerges from this reading of Scripture also helps us to understand that the recognition of the inherent goodness and beauty of the non-human creation in no way implies that the creation itself is somehow divine in nature. In no way should a high valuation of nature imply that God and nature are somehow one in essence or that "nature is God" or "God is nature." Attributing qualities of divinity to any part of creation is totally inappropriate from a Christian point of view. Only the second person of the Trinity, in and through his incarnation as Jesus Christ, could be considered divine while also being a part of the creation order (John 1).

This is an important point to consider because within some branches of Christianity, there has been a tendency to suggest that those who are greatly concerned about the environment are somehow in danger of slipping into a pantheistic view of the universe. This certainly need not be the case. As John Frame rightly puts it, the doctrine of creation as we see it here revealed in Genesis 1:1 "denies pantheism or monism, the view that creation is made of God's own being, a kind of emanation from him, as light from the sun, so that the creation itself is divine."[15] Simply put, Scripture is clear on this point, and in a carefully developed Christian ethic, any suggestion of pantheism or monism must be utterly rejected.[16] The fact that some forms of environmental ethics espouse wrong views of God and nature does not mean that all do.

In showing a loving care for creation, the Christian is to steer his or her appreciation and love for that which is created toward a higher and more perfect

---

15. John M. Frame, *The Doctrine of God* (Phillipsburg, NJ: P&R Publishing, 2002), 299.

16. *Pantheism* is the idea that God and the universe are the same. From the perspective of environmental issues, *pantheism* refers to the concept that God is the universe and the universe is God. As a result, there is no room for a transcendent view of God. Monism is a similar concept in the sense that there is only one substance. God and the universe must then be the same because there can be no distinctive substances. For a further discussion of why pantheism must be rejected from a Christian point of view, see Francis Schaeffer and Udo W. Middelmann, *Pollution and the Death of Man* (Wheaton, IL: Crossway, 2011), 15–35.

wonder over and love for the Creator. Likewise, he or she should always seek to point all others who love and esteem elements of the creation to the God who created beauty and made it manifest in the created order. In this sense, then, a Christian view of creation care is inherently evangelistic in nature. We will return to this point in our conclusion.

A Creation That Belongs to the Lord

A third point to draw from Genesis 1:1 pertains to God's ownership of the world. As the God who is "in the beginning," and the God who created "the heavens and the earth," he is also the ultimate Owner of all things and the One who both designed the world and gave to it an ultimate purpose. The psalmist teaches us, "The earth is the Lord's, and all it contains, the world, and those who dwell in it" (Ps. 24:1). From a distinctly Christian point of view, this mere fact of God's ownership over the entirety of creation is enough to tell us that human beings do not have—and should not act as though they had—total freedom to do with God's property whatever they would like. This is God's world, and thus it should be respected and cared for simply on that basis alone.

A Purposeful Creation (Teleological Ordering)

Further, it follows from these preceding points that not only is our being or existence contingent on God and his decision to create us, so also is the purpose of our existence dependent on him. As Colossians 1:16 tells us, "For by Him all things were created, both in the heavens and on earth, visible and invisible, whether thrones or dominions or rulers or authorities—all things have been created through Him and *for Him*." Contrary to the popular philosophical myths of Enlightenment modernity and now postmodernity, human beings are not autonomous beings. We did not create ourselves; we do not determine reality; and human purpose and meaning is not merely the product of social invention or culturally constructed ideas. Rather, not only do each of us individually, all of us together, and all of nature as a whole belong to God as his creations, but each of us also has an inherent purpose given to us by our Creator. In other words, if it is true that we (and all creation) are not here of our own accord, if Someone put us here, then it is only logical to assume that he put us here for a purpose—a purpose that is bigger than ourselves. Ethically, then, we can describe the creation as being *teleologically ordered* (ordered toward a final purpose, end, or *telos*).

A Theocentric Universe

Finally, all these points clearly indicate that God, not humans or the creation, is the center of the story, and that all creation exists not only by his commands but for his purposes. While it may be tempting to focus one's reading of Genesis 1 on that which is created, it is crucial instead to recognize that the subject of the biblical creation narrative is God himself. Properly understood, the opening words of the Bible are meant to rivet our attention not on the created order, but on the Creator and his stunning power and grace displayed in his creating activity that follows.

As the Scripture elsewhere affirms, the heavens themselves "are telling of the glory of God" and in their massive expanse are "declaring the work of His hands" (Ps. 19:1). All creation is designed to be a megaphone broadcasting the fact that God exists and that he is worthy of all glory, honor, and praise. Creation exists to awaken in us a longing to rightly align our lives to his purposes, live for him in all possible ways, and join with the rest of creation to declare his worthiness. Ultimately, the purpose of the universe as a whole—and every single element or person in it—is to magnify the glory of God. Therefore, it follows that God's stewards should care for every single element of creation and every person who is embedded in it. It also follows that each element will attain to its highest end and purpose if, and only if, it does what it was created to do and is rightly ordered toward its final purpose or *telos*.

Lynn White Jr.'s critique of Christianity most significantly misses the mark at this point. In light of the previous truths, we see that loving and caring for God's creation is not a mere matter of personal preference for the Christian; it is a matter of *lordship*. Because God is who God is, we as his image-bearers must care for his world in a manner that glorifies him. If we currently are not, then this, too, is not a mere matter of preference; it is a matter of repentance. If Christians have missed the mark on this in the past, it is not because the underlying doctrine of God is wrong; it is due to a failure of God's appointed stewards to live under God's right rule as Creator and King. This becomes even more clear in light of the contextual understanding of God's instructions to Adam to "subdue" the earth and "rule" over it. As will become clear below, these instructions were not meant to delegate to humans an unbridled autonomy or facilitate an idolatry of material things. Rather, God's instructions to humans regarding their role in creation are connected to the much higher purpose of maximizing the manifest glory of God.

Genesis 1:26–28

The next passage of Scripture that shapes our understanding of what it means to be a steward of creation is found in Genesis 1:26–28. Following the preceding discussion of Genesis 1:1 and its implications on creation as a whole, we now move to a discussion of the creation of humankind and God's instructions to subdue and rule over the rest of creation. This passage will take us from an overall perspective of creation to the specific role of humankind in God's creation.

The Chiastic Ordering of Genesis 1:26–28

Earlier in the book (chapter 2), we discussed the meaning of these verses at length. There we pointed out that this passage has a chiastic structure indicating that because humans are made in the image and likeness of God (A), they are tasked with the function to subdue and rule (A'). Similarly, because humans are created male and female (B), the corresponding function is to be fruitful and multiply and fill the earth (B'). We used the chart below (see table 12.4) to illustrate the idea.

Table 12.4. The Chiastic Ordering of Genesis 1:27–28

A—God creates humans in his image and likeness → A'—subdue the earth and rule over the earth
B—God creates human beings as male and female → B'—be fruitful and multiply, fill the earth

We then pointed out that it is precisely because human beings are *uniquely created* in the image and likeness of God that they have a *unique role* of leadership within the created order. As God's image-bearers, they are embedded within the creation to stand as God's representatives who point all creation up to God, and as those made in his likeness, they represent God and his authority down to the creation order. To make the point another way, God has both embedded his image-bearers in the creation order to have solidarity with it and also made them in his likeness to lead the creation into the proper worship of God. In chapter 2, we illustrated this point in the following way:

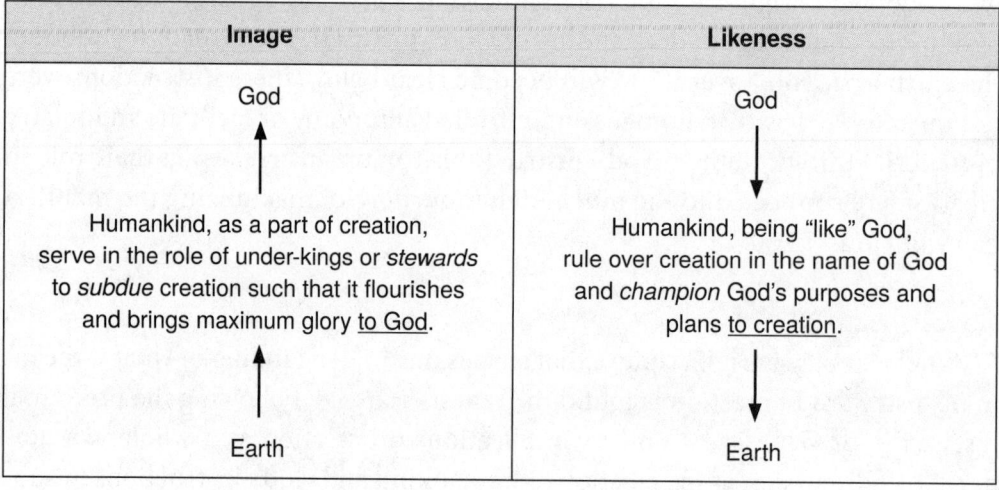

Image	Likeness
God	God
↑	↓
Humankind, as a part of creation, serve in the role of under-kings or *stewards* to *subdue* creation such that it flourishes and brings maximum glory <u>to God</u>.	Humankind, being "like" God, rule over creation in the name of God and *champion* God's purposes and plans <u>to creation</u>.
↑	↓
Earth	Earth

Fig. 12.1. Image and Likeness of God

Understanding this unique positioning of human beings gives us the context to properly appreciate the nature of the instructions that God gave to Adam and Eve when he commanded them to "subdue" and "rule" over the earth.

"Subdue" and "Rule" in the Context of Genesis 1:26–28

An exploration of the meaning of these words and their context in Genesis 1 proves helpful to further understand the unique role that God has given to humans within the created order. First, the word "subdue" in the Hebrew is *kabash*. Its root meaning relates to the use of strength to exercise control over something or even to tread something down.[17] The other word, "rule," in the Hebrew is *radah*. In this passage, *radah* relates to the expression of a ruler or king exercising his authority or "having dominion" over his kingdom.[18] In the context of Genesis 1:26–28, Adam and Eve had not yet sinned and the fall had not yet stained the creation order. Crucial to understanding God's instructions for Adam and Eve to "subdue" and "rule" over the earth is the idea that they were to do so *as God's representatives*, not as independent or sinful agents looking out for their own agendas. God both designed them and situated them in such a way that the only proper way to execute their subduing and ruling authority would be to do so in complete accord with God's loving, good, and just moral character. That is, they would properly "subdue" and "rule" only when they did so *as God himself would have done it.*

Genesis 2:15

Given the theocentric nature of the universe (Gen. 1:1) and the role that God gave to humans when he charged them to be fruitful and multiply and fill the earth with people who would subdue it and rule it *as he desired* (1:26–28), we are now in a position to consider what Genesis 2:15 teaches us about the final purpose of human existence in the created order. That is, Genesis 2:15 helps us understand the *why* behind God's giving humans instructions to subdue and rule the world. Crucial to this discussion is an evaluation of the meaning of the phrase often translated into English as "cultivate it and keep it."

> Then the LORD God took the man and put him into the garden of Eden to *cultivate it and keep it.* (Gen. 2:15)

---

17. Strong's, 3533, accessed April 20, 2020, https://biblehub.com/hebrew/3533.htm. See, e.g., Num. 32:22, 29; Josh. 10:24; 18:1; 2 Chron. 28:10; Neh. 5:5; Mic. 7:19. For further discussion, see Richard A. Young, *Healing the Earth: A Theocentric Perspective on Environmental Problems and Their Solutions* (Nashville: B&H, 1994), 161–62.

18. Strong's, 7287, accessed April 20, 2020, https://biblehub.com/hebrew/7287.htm. See, e.g., Lev. 26:17; 2 Chron. 8:10; Ps. 72:8; Isa. 41:2. For further discussion, see Young, *Healing the Earth*, 162.

As we pointed out in chapter 2, the Hebrew words translated in this verse as "cultivate" and "keep" are *'abad* and *shamar*. While technically these Hebrew words can refer to the task of "cultivating" and "keeping" the garden (or even "serving" and "protecting" the garden), there are many reasons to believe that the better way to translate these words into English is "worship" and "obey." In order to avoid a redundant statement of this argument, we refer our readers back to the larger discussion in chapter 2. Here we will simply remind our readers that key elements in reaching this conclusion include the following:

1. The God-centered context of the creation narratives in which this passage falls;
2. The recognition that the Genesis narrative depicts the creation order as a type of "temple of worship" in which Adam was to serve as a type of "priest" unto God in the garden;
3. The possible interpretive range and meaning that each of the words *'abad* and *shamar* can carry; and
4. The grammatical structure of the two words (*'abad* and *shamar*) as they are used together in this and other passages in the Old Testament (i.e., collocation).

In light of this, we believe that it is best to understand that Genesis 2:15 is telling us that God placed Adam into the garden so that Adam might *worship and obey God*. That is, given the theocentric nature of the universe and the fact that God is the main focus of the Genesis 1 and 2 narratives, it makes most sense to see that Genesis 2:15 indicates that Adam's ultimate purpose and primary calling was not to be a *gardener* but a *worshiper*. In fact, it would be an appropriate understanding of Genesis 2:15 to read it as saying that *God placed Adam into the garden of Eden to worship and obey God as he cultivated it and kept it.*

Ultimately, it was Adam and Eve's job to function as stewards, ambassadors, mediators, or those who use their delegated authority to champion the cause of God to the rest of creation. Simultaneously, they were also to represent the creation order as its champion by using their strength to gather from the creation all the glory, praise, honor, wealth, and flourishing that is possible and then offer it unto God in a beautiful act of worship. As those made uniquely in the image and likeness of God, Adam and Eve were to function as worship leaders in the great symphony hall of worship that we call the created realm.

Understanding this ultimate purpose given to humans to worship God and obey him also helps to shed light back onto the Genesis 1:26–28 passage and God's instructions to Adam and Eve to "subdue" and "rule" the earth. Combining the ideas of Genesis 1:26–28 with Genesis 2:15, we should understand that God tells Adam and Eve *to worship and obey him by using all their strength and wisdom as image-bearers to subdue the earth and rule it in such a way that as they cultivate and keep it, the creation order will maximally flourish and thereby give unto God all the glory he is due.*

With this idea in mind, then, we can now identify why the critique of Christianity offered by Lynn White Jr. is so off base. Contrary to White's claim, the biblical text does not give humans unlimited dominion or absolute authority to do with creation whatever they please. Rather, the prefall Adam and Eve were given the task of subduing and ruling in complete concert with God's loving nature and inherently good purposes. Their authority was a derived and *delegated authority* that was to be neither oppressive nor unlimited. Any expression of their subduing or ruling that usurped God's authority or ran contrary to his loving character and intent for the world would be sinful and wrong.[19] Far from giving humans license to use and oppress the rest of creation as tyrants, Christian teaching is clear: their dominion over creation was meant to allow them to use their freedom to rule in complete harmony with God's divine intent, heart, and will. Theirs was to be a leadership not of exploitive domination but of joy-filled, delightful, servant-hearted, worshipful stewardship that resulted in the flourishing of all creation.[20]

The Fall and Its Impact on Creation

The impact of the fall cannot be overstated when it comes to our relationship to the rest of creation. Not only did mankind suffer from the disobedience of Adam and Eve in the garden, but all creation now groans and longs for a return to the pattern of God's creation. Two passages help us better account for how the fall impacts our stewardship of creation. Genesis 3 and the epistle of Romans will shed light on how the fall impacts the creation.

Genesis 3

Tragically, humans usurped God's authority in the garden. They rebelled against his ethical standards. They sinned. Not only was this sinful rebellion wrong, but it resulted in tragic consequences for Adam, Eve, their future offspring, and the rest of creation as well. As the ever-present signs of pollution daily remind us, things are not the way they are supposed to be.

The Genesis 3 account of the fall of humanity highlights the incredible tragedy of sin as it allures and deceives the first couple. Adam and Eve initially experienced life in the fullness of God's bounty. Not only were they given freedom to eat from

19. James A. Nash, *Loving Nature: Ecological Integrity and Christian Responsibility* (Nashville: Abingdon, 1991), 104.

20. Vern S. Poythress, *Redeeming Science* (Wheaton, IL: Crossway, 2006), 150.

any tree except one, but, much more fulfilling, they also had uninhibited access to God *himself*. As the text will go on to imply, they had the unimaginable freedom to walk with God and talk with God and enjoy his very presence (Gen. 3:8–13). In spite of all this, they somehow found themselves lured into rebellion and sin.

In the presence of untold wonders, they rejected the inherent purpose and orientation of their being in outright defiance of God himself. Adam and Eve exchanged the infinite riches of the glory of God for a piece of fruit. In so doing, our first parents squandered paradise and plunged all creation into the fall. As Al Wolters points out: "Adam and Eve's fall into sin was not just an isolated act of disobedience but an event of catastrophic significance for creation as a whole. The effects of sin touch all of creation; no created thing is in principle untouched by the corrosive effects of the fall."[21]

With this contextual background in place, two significant points emerge from Genesis 3:17–19 that relate directly to our larger discussion of environmental ethics:

> Then to Adam He said, "Because you have listened to the voice of your wife, and have eaten from the tree about which I commanded you, saying, 'You shall not eat from it';
>
> Cursed is the ground because of you;
> In toil you will eat of it
> All the days of your life.
> Both thorns and thistles it shall grow for you;
> And you will eat the plants of the field;
> By the sweat of your face
> You will eat bread,
> Till you return to the ground,
> Because from it you were taken;
> For you are dust,
> And to dust you shall return."

Note first that the text indicates that an immediate consequence of the fall was that the nonhuman elements of the created order were affected. The ground that God declared to be "good" in Genesis 1:9–10 became "cursed" because of Adam's sin. Only through laborious hardship would it now yield its fruits. Note that the text does not say that the ground sinned, but that rather, as a consequence of

---

21. Albert M. Wolters, *Creation Regained: Biblical Basics for a Reformational Worldview*, 2nd ed. (Grand Rapids: Eerdmans, 2005), 53.

human rebellion, the created order itself was now affected. This point is important because it demonstrates the reality that God did not create humans separate and distinct from the rest of creation, but embedded them in it. They are a part of nature. They have solidarity with the rest of nature. Therefore, the entire created order was bound up with the moral nature of the one created from the dust of the earth as God's image-bearer tasked to lead it and lovingly care for it.

Second, the promised result of death from sin (Gen. 2:17) now also began to take effect in Adam's body. In verse 17 we see that God, who had used the good ground he created to form Adam, now informs Adam that he will die and his body will return to the ground. From that point on, Adam (and all his race) would experience in his own body a slow degradation until finally someday physical death would take him (5:5).

Not only did physical death result from sin on the day that Adam and Eve ate the fruit, but they were also banished from the loving presence of God—a spiritual death that is fundamentally related to their disordering from God and his purposes. This death, as Scripture will later confirm, is an exclusion from the loving presence of God for eternity future. This became the new destiny of the entire human race (Rom. 5).

Hell is the price of rebellion. And hellish effects of that rebellion impact the created order. Wolters argues:

> Wherever anything wrong exists in the world, anything we experience as anti-normative, evil, distorted, or sick, there we meet the perversion of God's good creation. It is one of the unique and distinct features of the Bible's teaching on the human situation that all evil and perversity in the world is ultimately the result of humanity's fall, of its refusal to live according to the good ordinances of God's creation.[22]

Corrupted by sin and separated from a loving and whole relationship with God, Genesis 3:23 then tells us that God sends Adam and Eve out of the garden. Instead of "subduing" and "ruling" over the earth in an ever-expansive God-glorifying manner, humans are now forced to leave it as distorted and broken sinners. As such, all of Adam's race will now wrongfully use the power and authority that was delegated to them to subdue and rule in corrupt and dishonorable ways.

Romans

In relation to consequences that come from the fall, the New Testament affirms the same two effects of sin on creation that we discovered from Genesis

---

22. Wolters, *Creation Regained*, 55.

3:17–19. First, Paul addresses how human sin impacts the nonhuman portion of the created order:

> For the *anxious longing of the creation* waits eagerly for the revealing of the sons of God. For the creation was subjected to futility, not willingly, but because of Him who subjected it, in hope that the creation itself also will be set free from its slavery to corruption into the freedom of the glory of the children of God. For we know that *the whole creation groans and suffers* the pains of childbirth together until now. (Rom. 8:19–22)

This passage is a reference back to Genesis 3:17 and affirms that "the predicament of the whole of creation is tied to the fate of humankind. . . . The whole created order suffers as a result of human rebellion."[23] Instead of a stewardship that leads to joyous worship, humans now "lead" creation into futile groaning with a stewardship driven by selfish desire and disordered greed. David Dockery's comments capture the idea well:

> Our task of living in the image of God as stewards . . . has become deformed. In human attempts to become autonomous, the man's and woman's sin resulted in the perversion of the whole order of nature in heaven and earth. The whole of creation was disrupted. The peace that existed in the garden between God, humanity, and nature was greatly disturbed. [It is right to conclude that] in the Fall lie the roots of our ecological crisis.[24]

Second, the New Testament affirms that sin impacts the human portion of the created order as well. Romans 5:12 indicates that "through one man sin entered into the world, and death through sin, and so death spread to all men, because all sinned." Paul then goes on to assert in Romans 5:18 that "through one transgression there resulted condemnation to all men" so that through Adam all human beings in his lineage would inherit a sin nature. In other words, "God counted Adam's guilt as belonging to us, and since God is the ultimate judge of all things in the universe, and since His thoughts are always true, Adam's guilt does in fact belong to us."[25]

Not only have we inherited a sin nature, Romans 3:23 indicates that "all" of us have sinned in our own right and have thus "fallen short of the glory of God."

23. Steve Jeffery, Michael Ovey, and Andrew Sach, *Pierced for Our Transgressions: Rediscovering the Glory of Penal Substitution* (Wheaton, IL: Crossway, 2007), 311–12.

24. David S. Dockery, "The Environment, Ethics, and Exposition," in *The Earth Is the Lord's: Christians and the Environment*, ed. Richard D. Land and Louis A. Moore (Nashville: Broadman Press, 1992), 120.

25. Wayne Grudem, *Systematic Theology: An Introduction to Biblical Doctrine* (Grand Rapids: Zondervan, 1994), 495.

Romans 6:23 further indicates that the consequence for our sin nature and personal choices of sin is "death." Thus, like Adam, all of us have inherited a body that will degrade unto physical death, but also like Adam, all of us through sin have been separated from a right relationship with God and are thus destined to an eternity apart from his favor and loving presence unless a right relationship is restored by some other means. Those whom God tasked to lead the creation in a grand chorus of worship instead are themselves broken and lost. Theirs is a song of desperate rebellion. It is no wonder that God's great symphony hall of worship is full of groaning.

The Gospel and Its Import for All of Creation

Our concern for stewarding all of God's creation does not end with the mandate to subdue and rule over creation for the purpose of worshiping the Creator. The implications of Christ-centered creation care extend to our understanding of the gospel. Redemption is a theme in Scripture that applies both to humankind and to the created order. Our attempt to steward the creation well has specific implications for the gospel message of redemption.

God's Redemption of Sinners and the Revealing of the Sons of God

Thankfully, God's work of redemption has tremendous implications for both the horrific consequences of human sin and the resulting environmental degradations that accompany sin. To understand this, consider again the above-quoted passage of Romans in which Paul tells us that "the anxious longing of the creation waits eagerly for the revealing of the sons of God" (Rom. 8:19). In our discussion above, we learned that Adam's sin caused the ground to be cursed and that creation itself groans because of human rebellion. Here, however, we see Paul indicating that creation longs to be restored and that the restoration is connected to the "revealing of the sons of God." To understand what he means and the import of this passage for the discussion of creation care, we must consider this verse in the larger context of the book of Romans.

We saw earlier from Romans 3:23 and 6:23 that all humans have sinned and that all humans have earned death as a consequence. But the good news of the gospel is that while the wages of sin leads to death, "the free gift of God is eternal life in Christ Jesus our Lord" (Rom. 6:23b). That is, as Romans 5:8 says it, "God demonstrates His own love toward us, in that while we were yet sinners, Christ died for us." Romans 8:1 then indicates that once a person places his or her faith in Jesus Christ as Savior and by God's grace receives forgiveness, there is "no condemnation for those who are in Christ Jesus."

Not only are these basic truths "good news" for individual sinners who need to be restored by God's mercy to a right relationship with him, they also have immense importance for our discussion of creation care. They establish the baseline by which human image-bearers can be restored to the purpose for which they were created. As John 1:12 notes, "But as many as received Him, to them He gave the right to become children of God, even to those who believe in His name." It is by faith in Christ and through the grace of Christ that sinners who were originally tasked with subduing and ruling the earth can once again be considered (in the words of John) "children of God." Or as Paul puts it in Romans 8:19, they are by faith in Christ revealed as the "sons of God." By means of the gospel as it transforms individual sinners, the rest of creation then has a basis to hope that it may once again receive the kind of leadership that it was meant to receive from Adam and that it currently longs for. As new believers grow in their discipleship, they learn how to "subdue" and "rule" the earth as God intended for them *in the beginning*.

God's Redemption of Sinners and the Whole of Creation

Recalling the fact that the nonhuman part of creation did not sin is important as we consider the role that Christians should play in the creation order. According to Genesis 3:17, the ground became cursed because of Adam's sin. And as Romans 8:18–23 indicates, the nonhuman visible creation was then "subjected" passively to the effects of sin under which it now "groans." While the creation experiences the effects of the fall, it is not a person with the capacity for moral choice; therefore, the nonhuman creation does not have a need of "redemption" in the same sense that human beings do. Yet human beings are a part of the created order and are indeed embedded in it. Thus, there is a very real sense in which we must say that Christ's atoning work does indeed bring redemption to the created realm.

How should we understand the work of redemption as it applies to the entire created realm? As we have seen, human sin and sinful patterns follow in the legacy of the first Adam and thereby negatively affect the rest of the visible created order. On the other hand, through the redemption of Christ, humans have the opportunity to be reconciled to God, adopted as his sons, and thus placed in the legacy of Christ—the second Adam. In a similar manner to how Adam's followers affected the environment negatively, so also should Christ's followers begin to positively reverse the effects of the fall on the created order and impact the environment in a positive manner *as far as the curse is found*.

By implication, those redeemed in Christ who live under his lordship would seem to have a renewed obligation and task to reassume their role of "embedded headship" and loving dominion over the rest of creation. In this way, redeemed human beings become God's agents of "re-creation" in light of the original worship mandate that God gave to Adam in Genesis 1:28.

Human redemption provides the basis for restorative work for the whole of creation. Image-bearers restored by the gospel are reestablished in the role of leadership as "stewards" or "ambassadors" of God (2 Cor. 5:20). This role first entails instructions to "go" and make disciples of all nations (Matt. 28:18–20). As this happens, the disciple-making process necessarily includes teaching a life of worship and mission in keeping with how God designed the world. As stewards now redeemed back into right relationship with God by grace through faith in Christ, they are to lovingly shepherd the rest of creation into a posture of maximizing the glory of God throughout the created realm. In sum, a properly grounded understanding of creation care must include an emphasis on evangelism, and a properly grounded understanding of evangelism must result in a discipleship that cares for creation.

It would seem, then, that perhaps a more precise way to discuss Christ's redeeming work in creation would be to understand that Christ's atoning work provides the basis for redemption of the unique part of creation that bears his image and that has been given the role of leadership among the created order. In and through these redeemed image-bearers, the rest of creation can be called back to its created purpose and be rightly ordered or "reconciled" to God (Col. 1:20).[26]

In this sense, we can understand not only that God is the One who originally created all things, but also that through his life, death, and resurrection in the person of Jesus Christ, God is the One who makes *re-creation* possible. Christ's death enables the mitigation of creation's groaning and replaces it with the harmonizing of all things in the created order back into the music of rightly ordered worship.[27] The gospel gives Christians a renewed calling to present the rest of the created order to God in such a way that he might be maximally worshiped and praised. Redeemed image-bearers, above all others, ought to be leading the way as "revealed sons of God" in this great, God-glorifying work of "re-creation" that we know as the ethics of creation care.

The Future Hope for Creation

Not only is it important to consider God's created design and purpose for humans and how the gospel is meant to rescue sinners back into that calling, it is also important to consider our future destiny and hope in Christ and how it also plays an important role in shaping a Christian ethic of creation care. Scripture indicates that in the future, when Christ returns and finally sets in place the fullness of his kingdom, he will do so by transforming the world we now live in into a

---

26. We do not mean to imply here that all elements of the curse will be reversed, but to argue that human contribution toward it can lessen (at least) and that humans can also begin to reverse the effects that their sinful actions have inflicted on creation. A very simple example would be to stop slash-and-burn farming techniques in certain portions of the rainforest as well as to effectively engage in restorative reforestation projects.

27. Wolters, *Creation Regained*, 24.

"new earth" full of both beauty and joy (2 Peter 3:10).[28] At that time, the creation order will be revealed as it was meant to be from the beginning; the people of God will inhabit this new earth in totally renewed and transformed bodies. Sickness and sorrow will be eradicated, tears will be wiped away, darkness will be replaced by everlasting light, streets will be made of gold, sparkling clean waters will melodiously flow from the throne of God, and God's people will finally be able to eat from the once-forbidden Tree of Life. Most importantly, however, on *that day* the greatest joy will come in knowing that God will forever dwell with his people (Rev. 21–22).

Ultimately, God will bring full, complete, and permanent restoration of the entire cosmos by restoring it to its original created ordering and trajectory. As it was created to be in the beginning, so it shall be in the end—the entire cosmos will be rightly aligned and under the leadership of God's image-bearers. It will forever joyfully render worship unto the One who is worthy of all glory, honor, and praise. God cares for his world: past, present, and future.

Answering Lynn White Jr.: Why Christians Should Care about Creation Care

In sum, we can conclude this section of the chapter by returning to our interaction with Lynn White Jr.'s critique of Christianity as the source of the ecological crisis. Recall that at the end of the quote we set out above, White argued that because "the roots of our trouble are so largely religious, the remedy must also be essentially religious."[29] On this point we agree: the environmental problems we face do indeed require a profoundly "religious" solution—just not the one that White suggests. The fact of the matter is that we don't need to reject Christian doctrine; we need to actually understand it and embrace it as the only adequate source of religious values to guide us through the maze of the environmental-ethics debate.

To the degree that Christians are guilty of not properly embodying our theology and doctrines about God's world, we should be rebuked. But this is very different from blaming Christianity itself. Contrary to White's distorted understanding of Christian doctrine, our study makes it clear that when the Christian worldview is rightly understood and its doctrines are rightly taught, it provides all the motivation necessary to care both *about* creation and *for* creation.

- We care because God made it (Gen. 1:1).
- We care because he asked us to (Gen. 1:28).

28. There is considerable debate concerning whether this passage teaches that the heavens and the earth will "burn up" or be "dissolved" at the day of the Lord or whether the elements of the earth will be "revealed" or "found" after passing through a refining fire. We take the latter view. For a fuller discussion of this passage and the implications for the "new earth," see Liederbach and Bible, *True North*, 123–28.

29. White, "Historical Roots of Our Ecological Crisis," 1207 (emphasis added).

- We care because he cares (Gen. 1:31).
- We care because he put us on mission (Gen. 1:28).
- We care because when we care, he is most glorified (Gen. 1:28; 2:15; Hab. 2:14; Matt. 28:18–20).
- We care because he redeemed creation (Rom. 8).
- We care because he is coming again to transform creation (2 Peter 3:10).
- We care because he will live and reign with us in the newly transformed creation (Rev. 21–22).[30]

Implications for the Public Square

In light of these biblical, theological, and ethical principles, we now turn to the question "how ought these foundational ideas to shape the way that Christians engage the discussion of environmental ethics in the public square?" The answer to this question depends to a large degree on all the *whys* that we just discovered in the previous section. Clarity on the doctrinal foundations makes it possible both to discern the inferior extreme positions that dominate the modern debate and to enable the Christian to find the "more excellent way" of worshipful love as it relates to the topic of caring for God's creation (1 Cor. 12:31).

Avoiding the Extremes

Regarding the extreme positions, it is unfortunate that among evangelicals there tend to be two polarized perspectives that shape how Christians respond to the call for environmental action. On the one hand, there are those who are convinced that we are in the midst of (or at least on the verge of) a massive worldwide environmental crisis. Thus, like "Chicken Little" in the classic children's fable, their conviction is that, environmentally speaking, "the sky is falling." Because this group believes that there is a very real ecological cataclysm threatening on the horizon, they argue that environmental concern and creation-care initiatives must become the number-one social issue into which Christians ought to pour their energies.

On the other hand, there is a large contingency of skeptics who tend to deny (or some would say "live in denial of") the urgency of the entire matter. Like the proverbial ostrich that sticks its head in the sand when danger approaches, this group denies the possibility that an environmental crisis is at hand. According to these "ostriches," while there may be some acknowledgment that humans do indeed pollute the earth, there is significant doubt that the problem is as bad as many claim.[31] They either are skeptical of evidence presented or are so convinced

---

30. Adapted from Liederbach and Bible, *True North*, 140.
31. For example, recent statistics show that Protestant pastors are divided on the topic. See Aaron Earls,

that a technological solution will be found that they refuse to support or adopt political initiatives or personal practices that promote creation care.

So how does clarity of doctrine help the believer react to these extreme positions? Doctrine helps us discern the underlying motivations that drive the extreme positions and then enables us to evaluate these positions in the light of Scripture so as to correct them to the glory of God.

Chicken Little and the Problems with Crisis Motivation

One of the main reasons that these differing perspectives (and the resulting animosities) exist has to do with a similar level of conviction for moral issues but a disagreement on which issues deserve primary attention. The Chicken Little types are convinced that *human-caused environmental degradations* pose an immediate threat. Therefore, for them it is a matter of survival that we mobilize immediate action to protect and restore God's creation. Because the perceived urgency of this task is so intense, these folks often become immensely frustrated with those "ostriches" who do not share their level of conviction.

For this reason, there is a temptation for the Chicken Little types to find allies and cobelligerents in the battle to save the planet either with those who are non-Christian or with "Christians" who may hold to a variety of liberal ideas about the nature of God as well as suspect understandings on the nature of Scripture and the person and work of Christ. The danger, of course, is that such allegiances (even if motivated by very orthodox reasoning) tend to invite criticisms related to "watering down the gospel." Guilt by association is a real danger here. Often, they are then lumped into a category of those who are "liberal" and therefore must be drifting away both from orthodox beliefs and from a singular focus on evangelism—all for the sake of rescuing endangered species or preserving melting glaciers.

Of even greater importance (assuming that this group of believers stays true to orthodox teaching—as many do) is the problem of crisis-motivated ethics. Much of the disagreement that takes place regarding the importance of creation-care initiatives stems from the varying perspectives on how to interpret the scientific data available related to the actual state of the planet and debated levels of environmental degradation.[32] Right or wrong, the lack of consensus within the reli-

---

"Most Protestant Pastors See Human Activity behind Global Warming," *Baptist Press*, April 21, 2020, accessed May 27, 2020, http://www.bpnews.net/54678/most-protestant-pastors-see-human-activity-behind-global-warming.

32. Consider, as an example, the very different conclusions reached by Steven Bouma-Prediger and Wayne Grudem while each considers similar topics and areas of concern regarding the environment. See Bouma-Prediger, *For the Beauty of the Earth*, 23–55; Wayne Grudem, *Christian Ethics: An Introduction to Biblical Moral Reasoning* (Wheaton, IL: Crossway, 2018), 1095–1169.

gious, scientific, economic, and political realms understandably leaves many who are less trained in the nuances of these debates wondering whether the incessant cry that "the sky is falling" is simply "hype." This is why, in part, we suggest that a crisis mentality and utilitarian form of moral argument is ultimately not the best way to address the issue of creation care. Nor should it serve as the *primary motivation* for believers to act. While concern for the environment can certainly play a role in *catalyzing* response, acting from a crisis modality is problematic. See table 12.5 for a summary of reasons why crisis motivation is problematic.[33]

Table 12.5. Problems with Crisis Motivation

Seven Reasons Why Crisis Motivation as the Basis for Creation Care Is Problematic
1. There is disagreement about the level of "crisis" that exists.
2. Fear is the basis of crisis motivation.
3. If the crisis is solved, motivation for continued creation care evaporates.
4. Crisis motivation fosters a human-centered motivation for creation care.
5. If crisis and impending doom is the motivating factor, a "by any means necessary" approach may lead to the adoption of ungodly solutions to solve the crisis. Example: abortion to lower population growth rates.
6. Character formation takes a back seat to behavior modification to get through the crisis.
7. Focus on the crisis distracts from ultimate *telos*: glorifying God through worship-based creation care.

In sum, we do not suggest that Christians should be unconcerned about potential environmental consequences; rather, we are trying to emphasize that engaging the issue of creation care (or any other moral issue) based on crisis modality will ultimately prove to be an inferior form of motivation. The richer biblical ethic will seek to motivate action and behavior based on principles of conduct that in turn shape a character in both individuals and the church. Crisis motivations rely on fear, whereas properly formed Christian ethics relies on a pursuit of fullness of joy in Christlike character founded in, and shaped by, worshipful obedience to God.

"Ostriches" and the Danger of Disembodied Doctrine

Having considered some of the concerns regarding the thinking of "Chicken Littles," it is now appropriate for us to analyze the motivational elements of "ostriches." Those who deny the existence of such a crisis (or who are simply not

---

33. For a more robust development of these ideas, see Liederbach and Bible, *True North*, 22–26.

yet convinced that it is as bad as some claim) do not want to be distracted from what they perceive to be the more pressing mission for the church—primarily evangelism. As Christopher Wright describes it:

> Christians sometimes feel anxious that "the world is setting the agenda," that is, that we simply respond to the flavor of the month in the changing fads of secular concerns. And it is certainly true that environmental concern is very high on the list of anxieties of the world today. Surveys of young people in the West often find that the very survival of planet Earth comes out top of the list of the things they worry about.[34]

Christians may reject the "Chicken Little" agenda for a number of reasons. Some argue that the mission of the church is to focus on evangelism and not ethics. For this reason, they do not stand opposed to those who would put effort into creation care, but at the same time they do not want this or any other ethical issue distracting the church from its primary mission of evangelism. For others, there is an understanding that moral and social ethics issues are an important part of discipleship and moral witness, but it is their conviction that the more clear and present dangers are associated with moral issues of life and death (abortion, cloning, stem-cell research, euthanasia) and the foundational moral fabric of society (marriage, sex and gender issues, political concerns related to the church and the state). Because, they argue, these issues are already at crisis level and are clear forms of *moral, societal, and spiritual degradations*, we cannot afford to shift our focus and efforts away from the first-order priorities of saving souls, saving lives, and saving society.

The temptation that faces members of this group is the tendency to unfairly stereotype anyone who has great concern and is motivated to care for the environment as being out of step with orthodoxy. They are tempted to label anyone who does not prioritize their convictions in the same manner as a "tree-hugger" who is on the verge of embracing pantheism or perhaps as someone who is backsliding into a "social gospel" understanding of Christianity. Further, because many theologically and morally liberal Christians place great concern on environmentalism, there is a temptation for the more theologically conservative to oversimplify the issue, generalize the concepts, and lump together any and all who call for a prioritization of environmental concern into the category of *liberal*, and judge any form of environmental concern merely by a standard of guilt by association. Table 12.6 highlights four reasons why ostrich-like denial is problematic.[35]

---

34. Christopher J. H. Wright, *The Mission of God* (Downers Grove, IL: IVP Academic, 2006), 417.
35. See Liederbach and Bible, *True North*, 22–26.

Table 12.6. Problems with Denial of an Environmental Crisis

Four Problems for Those Who Deny the Need for Urgency Related to Creation Care
1. If God commands us to care for his world, then it is an urgent concern of worship even if there is no crisis.
2. If God commands us to care for his world, then by definition concern for his world cannot be counter to gospel witness.
3. It is possible that an environmental crisis actually is at hand and that denial is thus unwise.
4. Denying a role in creation care fosters a "Gnostic" view of Christianity suggesting that the gospel is only spiritual and has no implications for the physical world.

In the end, regardless of which of the perspectives above one may have a tendency to embody, Christians earnestly seeking to honor Christ and live a life of worship must learn to see through the inadequate or misplaced values that drive extreme positions of crisis and denial. Even when Christians find themselves unsure about all the particulars relating to the scientific, economic, or political aspects of the debate, they should work hard to bring to bear on those discussions the profound hope of the gospel that shapes the very essence of ethics as worship. At the very least, they should be able to discern when attitudes of either fear or disregard for God's world are in play as motivating factors driving behaviors and attitudes that dishonor the Lord. When we keep the deeply and profoundly Christian *whys* in place as our primary motivation, we are able to steer a course through the labyrinth of conflicting ideas and chart a path by using ethics as worship as our map and compass.

Creation Care and the Great Commission

The primary point that we hope to have communicated is that creation care is part of our worship of the Creator. As we have noted elsewhere in the book, fully worshiping God is an act of discipleship in which we mature and grow in our walk with Christ. In addition, our personal discipleship should help us embrace a living out of the Great Commission because Jesus told us, "Let your light shine before men in such a way that they may see your good works, and glorify your Father who is in heaven" (Matt. 5:16). It is this integration of living out the Great Commission through our care for creation with which we want to conclude.

Creation Care Ought to Foster the Great Commission

It is our hope that by this point in the chapter, the link between a God-honoring ethic of creation care and the urgent need and responsibility for

personal evangelism has become readily apparent for the Christian environmentalist. For as God told Adam and Eve to "be fruitful and multiply, and fill the
earth" in Genesis 1:28 (the first "great commission") so that they might fill the
earth with image-bearers who would subdue and rule the earth and maximally
glorify God, so also does he give a Great Commission to all the revealed sons of
God to "go" and "make disciples of all the nations, baptizing them in the name
of the Father and the Son and the Holy Spirit" (Matt. 28:18–19). The task is the
same: fill the earth with worshipers who will maximize the glory of God in their
environment—all the earth!

Simply put, those who are most concerned about creation care must also *by
definition* be those who are most highly motivated to share the gospel message of
Jesus Christ as committed evangelists. This is so for two very specific reasons.

First, human beings are a fundamental part of the created order—creation
care includes them. Not only does this mean a commitment to the protection
of innocent human life (at the beginning and end of life as well as by living as
peacemakers), but in light of the argument here, it means that caring for this part
of creation in its highest form will seek to bring all human beings into a rightly
ordered relationship with Jesus Christ, that they might truly bring glory to God
and in that vocation truly flourish. This form of creation care, then, requires verbal, not just demonstrative, forms of evangelical witness.

The second reason why those most concerned with creation care must be
motivated evangelists is more pragmatic in nature. The only hope to stop further
pollution of God's earth from taking place in the created order is for humans
to be rightly ordered to God's creation purposes. Only then will they be able to
take up the mantle of God-honoring leadership over the created order in their
own lives and spheres of influence. Otherwise, environmentalism will remain
a slave to externally imposed forms of laws and civil legislations or fear-based
responses to perceived environmental crises. For the true environmentalist who
understands the purposes of creation and the hope of redemption in and through
Christ's atoning work, evangelism becomes the number-one priority in his or her
efforts to stop human-imposed degradations on the environment and in seeking
the rightly ordered use and flourishing of all things created.

This is not to say that we are not to work hard in more traditional forms of
environmental care. To the contrary, this is not an either/or paradigm.[36] Rather,

36. To this end, it is important for any Christ-follower to remember that Christians have always felt a tension between the call to verbal proclamation of the gospel and the moral imperative to do good works. The
debate between faith and works (which is ultimately a false dichotomy) has raged since Paul (Eph. 2:8–9) and
James (James 2:18) wrote their epistles. Part of the struggle toward maturity for believers in any age and context
is to learn how to integrate these elements of evangelism and discipleship into a unified whole. In truth, a worshiper should grow to understand as he or she matures in the faith that every opportunity to speak or preach

we believe that evangelism and more traditional forms of creation care are mutually reinforcing and synergizing in nature. The principal and long-term hope of seeing humans behave more responsibly toward the entire created realm is this: those who are created as image-bearers and who have, by definition, been given headship over the created realm will have proper motivation and proper ordering in their efforts to guide and lovingly shepherd the creation only when they are rightly related to the Creator: Jesus Christ.

Let us be clear that in asserting this point, we are in no way offering some naive pretense suggesting that if "we get 'em all saved, we'll save the planet." We recognize that much debate and hard work must be done in ecological, economic, and political reform. But this reality does not change or lessen the immensity of the point we are making. If God has placed image-bearers in a position of leadership over creation, then if those leaders are not rightly related to God and rightly ordered to his ethic, then neither will our environmental, economic, or political efforts be rightly ordered to the end of maximizing God-honoring worship throughout all the earth. John Frame is right when he observes: "Only a regenerate society will find agreement on the worldview questions sufficient to save the earth. So the chief need of the environment is evangelism."[37]

The Great Commission Ought to Foster Creation Care

Keeping this in mind, we must also be careful not to miss the reality that because much of the world is increasingly interested in the topic of creation care and environmental ethics, a wise missional strategy is to recognize that "creation care opens new doors for sharing Christ's love." And because this is true, we wholeheartedly agree with Nancy Sleeth when she points out that a wise evangelistic strategy will recognize that "we can and should be concerned with telling others about Christ while also caring for his creation."[38] The link between Genesis 1:26–28 and Matthew 28:18–20 also has implications for the way that we care for the planet. Those who are most concerned about evangelism should also be those who are most highly motivated to live in God's world in a manner that embodies the gospel message for a watching world.

One of the ways that Francis Schaeffer encouraged believers to embody their

---

the message of the gospel is also an invitation to establish a God-honoring ethic in the life of an image-bearer. Likewise, every opportunity to live ethically and honorably before the Lord is an opportunity to embody and speak boldly about the saving work of Jesus Christ. These two elements of following Christ *should never be seen as substitutes for each other*. Rather, as believers grow in their faith and understanding of what it means to submit our lives to the supremacy of Christ in all things, we need to understand that evangelism and ethics are *two sides of the same coin*. In the history of the church, this understanding has sometimes been known as *incarnational theology*. It is the living out of the truth we believe in and through both our words and our deeds.

37. John M. Frame, *The Doctrine of the Christian Life* (Phillipsburg, NJ: P&R Publishing, 2008), 745.

38. Sleeth, "Isn't It All Going to Burn Anyway?," 118.

faith in his pioneering and influential work *Pollution and the Death of Man* was by encouraging Christians in their local contexts to function as a sort of "pilot plant."[39] He meant that just as some large businesses or manufacturers will build a small manufacturing plant to test out or "pilot" a new product in hopes of building a future full-scale plant, so also individual Christians and the church as a whole should model in the here and now the kind of environmental values that will some-day be true of the new heaven and the new earth. His concern was that if Christians did not learn to think differently about the world from their atheist friends, who simply exploited the earth as though it had no meaning or inherent value, their witness would prove powerless. Even worse, he was afraid that if unbelievers who followed false views of God actually embodied a stronger love for God's world than a Christian, many would reject Christianity because the watching world would perceive it to be a creation-denying, self-centered religion—just as Lynn White Jr. accused it of being. Schaeffer rightly argued that if our life practices look more like a materialistic consumerism than Christian discipleship, then there is a great and urgent need for us to repent *for the sake of the gospel*.

Conclusion: Creation Care as Worship

In conclusion, when we look a bit below the surface, there is a sense in which the public debate about creation care should be very simple for all of us. God created the world, God loves the world, God owns the world. Therefore, no one should trash God's world—especially not his followers. But there is also a sense in which the public debate about creation care and environmental ethics is very complicated. How much development and the accompanying pollution God's world can sustain is hard to know for certain. Likewise, it is also very difficult to determine the best way to remedy the problems that this development and accompanying pollution bring.

Even at these more complicated layers of discussion, it is imperative that the Christian stay focused on the main point. Bottom line, the center point of the discussion needs to be the simple reality that "the earth is the LORD's, and all it contains" (Ps. 24:1; 1 Cor. 10:26). It is therefore a matter of orthodoxy that we must care for it in a manner that pleases the Father. There is room to debate *how* we best care for God's world, but there can be no doubt that we *must* care for it. This is our Father's world. Al Wolters is correct when he reminds us:

God does not make junk, and we dishonor the Creator if we take a negative view of the work of his hands when he himself takes such a positive view. In fact, so positive

39. Schaeffer and Middelmann, *Pollution and the Death of Man*, 79ff.

a view did he take of what he had created that he refused to scrap it when mankind spoiled it, but determined instead, at the cost of his Son's life, to make it new and good again. God does not make junk and he does not junk what he has made.[40]

This is why from an ethic of worship a discussion of creation care does not begin with a concern for possible dire consequences or in fear of possible crises. Christians are not utilitarians. We are Christ-lovers. We are not pragmatists. We are Christ-followers. We seek above all to serve and obey our Lord. This means that we should love that which God loves and that we should care for the things that belong to God. Whether or not we may differ on how best to care for God's world, it is imperative *that we do care for it*.

While this certainly does not answer the particulars of the scientific, economic, or political debates, it should at least make us ask new questions about how we live in God's world. It should press us to limit the pollution we create and pour into his world. It should encourage us to pick up what others have left as litter. It should encourage us to preserve ecosystems and to clean up the ones that are breaking or are broken. It should help us remember that humans are a part of the created order, and thus it should press each of us to remember that creation-care issues are human-life issues.

This means that we should be concerned about the amount of toxins we dump into our water and air systems. We should care whether species are going extinct. We should study to determine whether drilling for oil or fracking is having a proportionally negative impact on an ecosystem. We should care whether people groups are being discriminated against by our choosing to place toxic-waste dumps in poor population areas. We should care and have rigorous debate about whether it is wise to divert trillions of dollars to lower carbon emissions globally in hopes of preventing climate change when the diversion of those dollars may debilitate entire economies and quite possibly even hurt the poor by doing so. We should also care whether humans are being aborted or trafficked. All of these are creation-care questions that deserve our attention.

We certainly should be concerned with the verbal proclamation of the gospel to our neighbor, who very well may be the same guy who is throwing the cigarette butt out the car window. To be sure, if one is pressed to determine a level of priority of one over the other, then by all means, preach the Word! But the either/or dichotomy is almost never a reality. Pick up the cigarette butt on the way over to his house to tell him about Jesus in the full realization that both acts please the Father and can work toward maximizing the manifest glory of God in all the earth. In the end, there is really one central point. Why should we care *about* and

40. Wolters, *Creation Regained*, 49.

for creation? Because the Creator, Redeemer, and future coming King of the universe is worthy of it. Indeed, his very nature as God demands it of us. After all, he is our Father, and this is our Father's world.

Key Terms and Concepts

anthropocentrism
biocentrism
creation care
crisis mentality
deep ecology
ecocentrism
ecofeminism
ecology
environmental ethics
human-caused environmental
    degradations

intrinsic value versus instrumental
    value
Lynn White Jr.
revealed morality
revealed reality
stewardship
subdue and rule
theocentrism

Key Scriptures

Genesis 1:1
Genesis 1:26–28
Genesis 1:31
Genesis 2:15
Genesis 3
Genesis 8:21–22
Psalm 24:1

Matthew 28:18–20
John 1:12
Romans 5
Romans 8:18–23
Colossians 1:16
2 Peter 3:10
Revelation 21–22

Study Questions

1. How does understanding God's "ownership" of the world impact your view of pollution and creation care?

2. How does the reality that the creation itself is meant to declare "the glory of God" (Ps. 19:1) impact your view (and practice) of caring for creation (see 24:1)?

3. Lynn White Jr.'s influential essay "The Historical Roots of Our Ecological Crisis" places much of the blame for human-caused pollution and climate change at the feet of Christianity. After reading this chapter, how would you summarize White's argument, and how would you answer it from a biblical perspective?

4. The authors make a distinction between those who have a "Chicken Little" approach to the question of climate change and others who take an "ostrich" approach. Where do you fall in terms of these categories? What is the most important weakness of your own perspective that you need to consider? What is the strongest point from the other perspective that you need to consider?

5. The authors suggest that the issue of creation care is closely related to the Great Commission and God's concern for global evangelism. How did they make that argument, and what do you think about it?

For Further Reading

Bauckham, Richard. *The Bible and Ecology: Rediscovering the Community of Creation*. Waco, TX: Baylor University Press, 2010.

Beisner, E. Calvin. *Where Garden Meets Wilderness: Evangelical Entry into the Environmental Debate*. Grand Rapids: Acton Institute/Eerdmans, 1997.

Bouma-Prediger, Steven. *For the Beauty of the Earth: A Christian Vision for Creation Care*. 2nd ed. Grand Rapids: Baker, 2010.

Liederbach, Mark, and Seth Bible. *True North: Christ, the Gospel, and Creation Care*. Nashville: B&H Academic, 2012.

Moo, Douglas J., and Jonathan A. Moo. *Creation Care: A Biblical Theology for the World*. Grand Rapids: Zondervan, 2018.

Schaeffer, Francis A., and Udo W. Middelmann. *Pollution and the Death of Man*. Wheaton, IL: Crossway, 2011.

Torrance, Andrew B., and Thomas H. McCall, eds. *Christ and the Created Order: Perspectives from Theology, Philosophy, and Science*. Grand Rapids: Zondervan, 2018.

White, Lynn, Jr. "The Historical Roots of Our Ecological Crisis." *Science* 155 (March 10, 1967): 1203–7.

Wirzba, Norman. *From Nature to Creation: A Christian Vision for Understanding and Loving Our World*. Grand Rapids: Baker, 2015.

Wolters, Albert M. *Creation Regained: Biblical Basics for a Reformational Worldview*. 2nd ed. Grand Rapids: Eerdmans, 2005.

13

Capital Punishment

"Whoever sheds man's blood, by man his blood shall be shed,
for in the image of God He made man."
—GENESIS 9:6

"Excessive bail shall not be required, nor excessive fines imposed,
nor cruel and unusual punishments inflicted."[1]
—EIGHTH AMENDMENT, Constitution of the United States of America

Introduction

History and Statistics

On January 17, 1977, Gary Gilmore was executed by firing squad in the state of Utah. At that time, he was the first person executed in the United States in ten years. His execution was particularly notable because less than five years before, the United States Supreme Court had ruled the death penalty unconstitutional in the landmark case *Furman v. Georgia* (1972).[2] That ruling, however, did not suggest that capital punishment either amounted to "cruel and unusual punishment" or was somehow wrong in *principle*. Rather, the Court reached its decision over concerns related to unequal and unfair sentencing *practices*. Up to that point, administration and application of the death penalty had been inconsistent from state to state and appeared to many to be both arbitrary and capricious.

Following the *Furman v. Georgia* ruling, thirty-five states (led by Florida, Georgia, and Texas) rewrote their laws concerning the death penalty. Their intent

---

1. "Eighth Amendment," Constitution of the United States of America, accessed June 10, 2020, https://constitution.congress.gov/constitution/amendment-8/.

2. 408 U.S. 238 (1972).

was to address the concerns identified by the Supreme Court with the hope of reinstating capital punishment as a constitutional state right.[3] It was not long before the Supreme Court handed down the *Gregg v. Georgia* decision (1976)[4] that recognized the constitutional grounding of the death penalty under the guidance of the Eighth Amendment and thereby enabled the reinstatement of the death penalty.[5]

Since the *Gregg* ruling, over fifteen hundred people have been legally executed in the United States. As of October 2020, capital punishment was legal in twenty-eight states, with nearly twenty-six hundred inmates on death row.[6] Globally, over fifty countries retain the death penalty as an option for criminal punishment in both law and practice. The United States was seventh on the list of active countries in terms of number of executions in 2018.[7] China leads all nations in the implementation of the death penalty.

These Supreme Court rulings leading to Gilmore's execution in 1977 highlight the two central questions at the heart of the capital-punishment debate. First, is capital punishment ever morally justified? In other words, is it ever good and right for a government to take the life of a criminal? Second, if capital punishment can be morally justified in principle, what guidelines should be put in place to ensure that the manner in which it is implemented is both moral and just?

In order to address these questions from the perspective of ethics as worship, we begin by first offering some basic definitions and highlighting various ideas about which goals and intended outcomes should shape a criminal justice system. We then turn specifically to the question whether capital punishment is biblically justifiable and how a worshiper of Christ ought to think about the issue in *principle*. Next, we turn to a discussion related to the just application of capital punishment while also addressing some of the problems that have been related to its implementation (*practice*). Finally, and by way of conclusion, we summarize our position by identifying how the principles of the sanctity of human life and neighbor love must guide the shaping of Christian character and thought regarding this issue.

3. Death Penalty Information Center, "Constitutionality of the Death Penalty in America," accessed January 3, 2020, https://deathpenaltyinfo.org/facts-and-research/history-of-the-death-penalty/constitutionality-of-the-death-penalty-in-america.

4. 428 U.S. 153 (1976).

5. The Eighth Amendment reads: "Excessive bail shall not be required, nor excessive fines imposed, nor cruel and unusual punishments inflicted."

6. Death Penalty Information Center, "Facts about the Death Penalty," accessed November 13, 2020, https://files.deathpenaltyinfo.org/documents/pdf/FactSheet.f1601652961.pdf.

7. Amnesty International, "Death Sentences and Executions 2018," accessed March 30, 2020, https://www.amnesty.org/download/Documents/ACT5098702019ENGLISH.PDF. China, Iran, Saudi Arabia, Vietnam, Iraq, and Egypt all exceeded the United States in number of executions in 2018.

Definitions and Motivations

Definitions

Before jumping into the specific debate about capital punishment, it will prove helpful to frame the discussion by offering a few basic definitions. First, we understand a *crime* to be any behavior or activity that violates a society's legal code. This can include actions of commission as well as omission. Note that we are making a distinction between that which is a crime according to the law and that which may be a *moral offense* but may not be considered illegal in a given context or culture. For example, in many societies it is not illegal to take the Lord's name in vain, but that does not mean that using the Lord's name inappropriately is not immoral. It simply means that a culture may find it hard to enforce such laws or that a culture may have lost any respect for God and the names that represent his existence and presence. On the other hand, societies sometimes enforce laws as legal rights that may be considered immoral (e.g., laws legalizing abortion) or unjust (e.g., Jim Crow laws). This does not mean that simply because something is legal, it should be considered moral. While there is an important overlap between the concepts of morality and legality, the two are not necessarily the same. Ideally, all laws would be reflective of proper morality and would align with God's moral order.

This raises the questions of what makes a law just and how we ensure that our laws are just so that we have proper grounds by which to justify punishing crime. Earlier in the book, we addressed the nature of law at some length (chapter 5). In summary, all laws are based on some understanding of what is good, right, or moral. How goodness, rightness, and morality are determined is a fundamental question that every society must answer. The Christian understands that goodness, rightness, and morality are properly grounded in the character of God, and that they must be understood in the light of God's creation order and divine revelation. Questions of utility and whether a given law "works" as a prevention or deterrent are important but ultimately secondary considerations when evaluating the moral foundation of any given law.

Second, we define legal or criminal *punishment* as a penalty or disutility (pain, loss, suffering, and the like) imposed on a person as a consequence for his or her criminal actions in order to achieve a desired outcome. Punishments for crimes committed in the United States, for example, include a range of penalties, such as monetary fines, forced community service, forfeiture of property, loss of liberties or civic privileges, jail, prison, and death.

Given these two definitions, it should be clear that any citizen of any society should care greatly not only which laws are enforced, but how punishment of crimes should be determined and then assessed. Not only should the laws be just, so also should the manner in which they are enforced be just. If a law is unjust in itself, a good citizen (and a good society) should seek to revise or replace it. Likewise, if a law (even a just one) is wrongly applied, resulting in unjust punishment, then citizens of that society should seek to correct the miscarriage of justice that occurs through poor administration or application.

Motivations

Earlier, we stated that criminal punishment is imposed on a person as a consequence of his or her actions in order *to achieve a desired outcome*. This brings us to the question of what goals or desired ends a society should seek when it inflicts punishment. In other words, what motivations ought to guide a society in assessing punishment for crimes? Historically, one of four ideals (or some combination) has served as the motive for punishing criminal behavior: rehabilitation, restitution, retarding future crime (prevention or deterrence), and retribution.[8]

Rehabilitation

One of the greatest problems facing any criminal justice system is that of *recidivism*: the tendency of a person who has been convicted of a crime to repeat a similar criminal behavior after having been arrested and serving a sentence of punishment. National statistics on the rate of recidivism in the United States indicate that an estimated 68 percent of released prisoners are rearrested within three years, 79 percent within six years, and 83 percent within nine years.[9] Not only do these rearrest patterns place heavy strains on local, state, and federal budgets, they also place heavy strain on the moral fabric of a society. These alarming statistics suggest that our criminal justice system needs to improve on preparing convicted criminals to reenter society as productive members. With this in mind, many proponents of social change suggest that the primary emphasis of the criminal justice system should shift from a punitive emphasis toward a focus on rehabilitation. Indeed, we see some biblical warrant for this approach when we consider both Jesus' and Paul's teaching about church discipline (Matt. 18:15–17; 1 Cor. 5:5). In both instances, a major motivation for confronting sin is restoration.

When rehabilitation is the primary motive of a penal justice system, energy and resources focus on attempts to "repair" or "restore" an individual in some way such that he or she can make a successful reentry into society and the workforce

---

8. Here we are indebted to the work of John and Paul Feinberg for their identification of these categories and their excellent discussion of this topic. John S. Feinberg and Paul D. Feinberg, *Ethics for a Brave New World*, 2nd ed. (Wheaton, IL: Crossway, 2010), 233–42.

9. Mariel Alper, Matthew R. Durose, and Joshua Markman, "2018 Update on Prisoner Recidivism: A 9-Year Follow-Up Period (2005–2014)," Bureau of Justice Statistics, May 2018, accessed January 7, 2020, https://www.bjs.gov/index.cfm?ty=pbdetail&iid=6266.

at the end of a prison sentence. Usually these attempts at rehabilitation emphasize programs that address issues of mental health, drug abuse, or the delivery
of education programs inside the correctional facilities. Studies suggest a high
correlation between each of these rehabilitation programs and the reduction of
recidivism rates among released prisoners.[10]

From both a general social point of view and a distinctly Christian point of
view, we agree with John and Paul Feinberg when they comment that "in non-
capital cases, in which the criminal will likely be released from prison someday
either on parole or after they serve the required time of their sentence, rehabilitat-
ing or restoring a person from a life of crime to a productive life should be a major
goal of the penal system."[11] If rehabilitation is the *exclusive* goal of a penal justice
system, then it would seem to follow that the death penalty should be abolished.
Simply put, dead people cannot be reformed.

But if rehabilitation is considered a *major* goal not exclusive of other goals,
then perhaps prison programs could be available to those convicted of capital
crimes by which they could have access to opportunities that might facilitate
repentance and flourishing even as they await the final consequences of their
actions. Of course, any rehabilitation for death-row inmates would not be pre-
paratory for reentry into society, and thus programs for such inmates may be
considered pointless from the perspective of a secular state. A distinctly Christian
perspective, however, would seek opportunities for repentance and growth even
for the "least of these" on death row because they are image-bearers even as they
prepare to face the consequences of their actions.

Restitution

A second motivation for punishment is the idea of *restitution*. Scripturally,
we see an example of this type of motivation in Exodus 22:4–12, where the Bible
gives instructions to criminals to "make restitution" by paying back what they
have stolen. In the context of the criminal justice system, *restitution* refers to the
idea of the criminal's returning to the victim that which was stolen or taken away.
If that which was stolen or taken away is no longer available, then the criminal
must make some sort of payment to the victim (or the victim's family) in order to
cover the cost of that which was lost or stolen. The idea is to "make good" for that
which was lost, stolen, or damaged. To some degree, restitution does play a part in
our current justice system. Convicted offenders can be required to cover medical
expenses, court costs, counseling costs, legal fees, lost wages, and so on.

10. Council of Economic Advisors, "Returns on Investment in Recidivism Reducing Programs," May
2018, accessed January 7, 2020, https://www.whitehouse.gov/wp-content/uploads/2018/05/Returns-on
-Investments-in-Recidivism-Reducing-Programs.pdf.

11. Feinberg and Feinberg, *Ethics for a Brave New World*, 234.

Restitution plays an important role in a criminal justice system, but it has serious limitations as the sole or primary goal. Certain crimes and costs simply cannot be replaced by offering financial compensation. For example, how would one ever be able to repay a *crime against culture* for destroying a priceless work of art, as the Nazis did in World War II? How does one repay *crimes against a state*, such as treason and espionage? Once a state secret is released, there is no means by which it can be unlearned by an enemy state. Similarly, when we think about *crimes against nature*, how would one call someone such as Saddam Hussein to repay the world for his decision to detonate oil wells and pour millions of gallons of crude oil into the soil and untold metric tons of pollutants into the atmosphere when retreating from Kuwait in the Persian Gulf War? How does one ever repay a family or a society for crimes against human life that take place when a son, daughter, father, mother, brother, or sister is murdered either individually or in mass genocide? In such cases, restitution does not begin to repay the damage done by the crime.

If the primary goal of a criminal justice system is restitution, then it seems logical that the criminal would be kept alive in hopes of repaying the debt owed from the crime committed. The death penalty, at least at first glance, undermines the goals of such a system. On the other hand, when one considers those crimes that seem "beyond the ability to repay," perhaps the only form of restitution that could be approximated would be the giving of one's life. Indeed, some suggest that even if restitution were the final goal of a criminal justice system, it would be possible to argue in favor of the death penalty on the basis of suggesting that the only thing that can approximate the value of the loss of life is another life. But such an argument actually has more in common with the concept of retribution, which we will discuss below.

Retarding Future Crime (Prevention and Deterrence)

A third motivation for punishing crime is that of *retarding future crime*. Scripturally, we can see a clear example of this motive for punishing crime in Deuteronomy 13 regarding the sin of idolatry. When someone is found to have committed idolatry, Moses commands that capital punishment be enacted: "So you shall stone him to death because he has sought to seduce you from the LORD your God who brought you out from the land of Egypt, out of the house of slavery. *Then all Israel will hear and be afraid, and will never again do such a wicked thing among you*" (Deut. 13:10–11). In this passage, we see a combination of motivations at work. First, a penalty is assessed in light of the offense against God (retribution; see discussion below), which leads to the secondary impact of having a deterring effect on the people as they take part in the act of punishment and hear of its severity.

Table 13.1. Four Motives for Punishing Criminal Behavior

1. Rehabilitation
2. Restitution
3. Retarding Future Crime
4. Retribution

When we speak of prevention and deterrence in relation to criminal punishment, it is important to distinguish between the two terms. Regarding the *prevention* of future crime, the focus is placed on ensuring that a particular criminal does not repeat his or her crime or injure others or society again. Sometimes this is also referred to with the term *incapacitation*. The referent point is the criminal who has already committed a crime, and the goal is retarding future crime by keeping him or her from doing it again. This serves as the justification for removing a criminal offender from society by confining the person to a jail cell, or possibly even putting him or her to death. In this regard, if one were to inflict the death penalty on a criminal, there would be absolute certainty that he or she would be prevented from committing future crimes. The same could not be said about incarceration because a criminal could potentially be released back into society at the end of a sentence and commit a crime again, or could commit crimes against other inmates.

The more controversial question related to retarding future crime is whether the punishment of one person works effectually to *deter* other potential criminals from committing crimes. Generally speaking, most would recognize that punishment *does* have a deterrent effect to some degree. For example, when I am tempted to speed while driving to work, the fact that my boss recently related to me the trouble of going to court over his speeding ticket and the size of the fine he incurred impacts my thinking and behavior about how fast I drive. The threat of punishment and the severity of the ticket work to slow me down. The point is, however, that even in my hypocrisy, the threat of punishment for a crime and the reality that a severe punishment was inflicted on my boss works effectually to help me slow down and obey the law.

Even though experience and common sense tell us that the nature of criminal punishment functions as a deterrent (especially when it specifically comes to the question of capital punishment), there is great debate regarding its effectiveness. One of the reasons for this debate arises from the fact that many of the murder cases that may deserve capital punishment are described as *crimes of passion*. These are crimes that are committed in the heat of the moment without premeditation and occur as emotive responses to events. For example, if a husband walks in on his wife, who is having an affair with another man, and he shoots them both while they lie in bed, the argument against capital punishment in such cases stems from the idea that rarely does someone in such a situation slow down to rationally consider whether he will be put to death if he pulls the trigger. Such an argument does not necessarily suggest that capital punishment would be wrong in principle, but rather suggests that when it comes to crimes of passion, it is uncertain that it works as an effective deterrent.

A second argument against the deterrent value of capital punishment relates to what many cite as inconclusive evidence from sociological studies about its effectiveness. Critics of laws allowing capital punishment often cite statistical analysis showing that murder rates in non-death-penalty states have remained consistently lower than murder rates in states allowing the death penalty.[12] The reasons suggested for this fact by those seeking to abolish the death penalty are numerous. Perhaps most common is the claim that the practice of capital punishment actually "brutalizes society" by lowering the value of life and introducing violent and vengeful practices into the criminal justice system. In essence, the government increases murderous acts in society when it sets the example of "murdering" criminals. Of course, such an argument presumes that the death penalty is an act of murder. We will discuss this idea in relationship to the sixth commandment later in this chapter.

On the other hand, proponents of the death penalty suggest that such statistics cannot be cited as evidence against capital punishment because there is no way to demonstrate either that the higher crime rates directly result from the presence of the death penalty or that the number of crimes would not have been even greater if the death penalty were not in effect. In fact, death-penalty proponents often counter that if the death penalty were not a legal option in those states, the murder rates could be significantly higher. Thus, it has been argued that if the death penalty is not effectual in lowering crime, it is not because people are being sentenced to death, but rather it is because we are not catching and killing enough criminals to increase its effectiveness. Specifically, the death penalty would clearly be a deterrent if it were quickly and justly applied in more cases.[13]

Regardless of how the data are spun in such pro and con arguments, it is interesting to note that a recent study by the National Research Council of the National Academies reviewing and evaluating the research done by both sides on this debate over the course of three decades concluded that

---

12. Death Penalty Information Center, "Murder Rate of Death Penalty States Compared to Non-Death Penalty States," accessed January 7, 2020, https://deathpenaltyinfo.org/facts-and-research/murder-rates/murder-rate-of-death-penalty-states-compared-to-non-death-penalty-states.

13. For a helpful source for understanding the pro and con arguments related to capital punishment, we recommend Hugo Adam Bedau, ed., *The Death Penalty in America: Current Controversies* (New York: Oxford University Press, 1997).

research to date on the effect of capital punishment on homicide is not informative about whether capital punishment decreases, increases, or has no effect on homicide rates. Therefore, *the committee recommends that these studies not be used to inform deliberations requiring judgments about the effect of the death penalty on homicide.* Consequently, claims that research demonstrates that capital punishment decreases or increases the homicide rate by a specified amount or has no effect on the homicide rate should not influence policy judgments about capital punishment.[14]

In short, whether capital punishment can be definitively shown to be an effective deterrent to future crime is likely impossible. From the point of view of Christian ethics, however, a consequentialist argument about whether it is effective should not serve as the primary ground for one's conviction about the issue anyway. The value of God's instructions cannot be measured by human-centered cost-benefit analysis. They can be evaluated only in light of his moral character and will from which they are given.

Retribution

Finally, the fourth motivation is *retribution*. In its most basic form, the idea of retributive justice requires that when a person breaks the law and commits a crime, he or she should suffer in return. The principle of *just deserts* comes into play here—not in the sense of "having only cheesecake for dinner" (i.e., desserts), but rather as in giving something to someone that he or she *deserves* in light of what he or she has done (i.e., deserts). Scripturally, we see this most clearly in Exodus 21:24–25 when Scripture prescribes that a punishment should be proportional:

> Eye for eye, tooth for tooth, hand for hand, foot for foot, burn for burn, wound for wound, bruise for bruise.

In this case, the focus is on repaying someone the equivalent harm that he or she inflicted on someone else.

Positively, the concept of just deserts can mean being fairly or *justly* paid for a job well done. Negatively, and in the case of crime, it means being fairly or *justly* punished in accord with what laws one has broken. As it relates to the topic of capital punishment, the question has to do with the rightness and wrongness of the act in question and being repaid in proportional kind for the act.

14. Daniel S. Nagin and John V. Pepper, eds., *Deterrence and the Death Penalty* (Washington, DC: National Academies Press, 2012), 2, accessed March 30, 2020, https://www.nap.edu/read/13363/chapter/2#2 (emphasis added).

It is important to understand that various moral perspectives can dramatically shape how one thinks about retributive justice for either good or evil. For example, one might approach the concept of retribution from the viewpoint of revenge. Here, the motive of the heart is to repay evil for evil and take into one's own hands a desire to inflict harm. Biblically speaking, Scripture very specifically warns against this type of retribution. Jesus tells us that one can break the sixth commandment not only by the wrongful taking of human life, but also by the murderous attitude and vile longings that drive a heart toward hating and moving with ruinous intentions toward others:

> You have heard that the ancients were told, "You shall not commit murder" and "Whoever commits murder shall be liable to the court." But I say to you that everyone who is angry with his brother shall be guilty before the court; and whoever says to his brother, "You good-for-nothing," shall be guilty before the supreme court; and whoever says, "You fool," shall be guilty enough to go into the fiery hell. (Matt. 5:21–22)

The thrust of Jesus' teachings in these verses comes from a context in which he instructs his disciples to love their enemies and pray for those who persecute them (Matt. 5:44). This is why the apostles Paul and Peter, following the teaching of Christ, instruct us not to "pay back evil for evil" (Rom. 12:17), but to give "a blessing instead" (1 Peter 3:9).

Disciples of Jesus Christ are instructed to leave retribution and vengeance in the hands of God and the means by which he has delegated his authority to humans to bring about justice in his name (Rom. 12:19; 13:1–7). Their job is to pray for others and implore God to forgive others for their sins (Matt. 5:44).

Unfortunately, it is often assumed by those who oppose the death penalty that a revenge-filled view of retributive justice is the only form of retributive justice that a person can hold, but historically this has not been the foundation of the idea. While on the one hand retribution can be sinful, on the other hand it is entirely possible to approach the concept of retributive justice without the assumption of personal revenge, hatred of persons, or murderous intent toward others. The focus is to properly deal with evil, to protect the integrity of society while seeking for it to flourish, and to show respect both for the victim and for the perpetrator of a crime. When properly understood, a Christian view of retributive justice takes no pleasure in the harmful consequences that result from the enforcement of justice. Yet it does delight in the satisfaction of justice in its own right and the positive standards it upholds that will in turn positively shape the moral formation of both individuals and society.

To highlight the distinctive approaches of these two perspectives on retributive justice, consider, for example, two starkly contrasting responses to the execution of domestic terrorist Timothy McVeigh, who was responsible for the bombing of the Alfred P. Murrah Federal Building in Oklahoma City on April 19, 1995. McVeigh's actions resulted in 168 deaths, with at least 680 others injured. On the day of his execution, it was reported that as the time for his death approached, death-penalty supporters at the scene chanted the words "Rot in Hell, McVeigh."[15] On the same day, President George W. Bush spoke these words to the American people:

> This morning, the United States of America carried out the severest sentence for the gravest of crimes. The victims of the Oklahoma City bombing have been given *not vengeance, but justice.* And one young man met the fate he chose for himself six years ago.
>
> For the survivors of the crime and for the families of the dead, the pain goes on. Final punishment of the guilty cannot alone bring peace to the innocent. It cannot recover the loss or balance the scales, and it is not meant to do so. Today, every living person who was hurt by the evil done in Oklahoma City can rest in the knowledge that *there has been a reckoning. . . .*
>
> Under the laws of our country, the matter is concluded. Life and history bring tragedies, and often they cannot be explained. But they can be redeemed. They are redeemed by dispensing justice, though eternal justice is not ours to deliver. By remembering those who grieve, including Timothy McVeigh's mother, father and sisters, and by trusting in purposes greater than our own, may God in his mercy grant peace to all; to the lives that were taken six years ago, to the lives that go on, and to the life that ended today.[16]

The contrast between a perspective of retributive justice driven by a heart of murderous revenge and another driven by a desire to achieve righteous justice could not be clearer. One desires harm and the other a reckoning.

From a secular viewpoint, one can arrive at an approximation of this higher view of retributive justice by asserting that there are self-evident rules and moral principles (such as doing no harm, treating people as ends in themselves and never as means to an end, and so on) that either are right in themselves or function to maximize the good of society. As we discussed in earlier chapters, however, such

---

15. Nolan Clay, Penny Owen, and Ed Godfrey, "McVEIGH EXECUTED: Bomber Silenced Forever; Handwritten Final Statement Quotes Poem," *Oklahoman*, June 12, 2001, accessed January 7, 2020, https://oklahoman.com/article/2744588/mcveigh-executed-bomber-silenced-forever-handwritten-final-statement-quotes-poem.

16. George W. Bush, "Remarks by President Bush on McVeigh Execution," June 11, 2001, accessed January 7, 2020, https://georgewbush-whitehouse.archives.gov/news/releases/2001/06/20010611.html (emphasis added).

concepts are ultimately anemic in themselves and inevitably are parasitic on theistic conceptions of right and wrong, justice and injustice. In order for morality to be considered good and right in and of itself, it must ultimately have a source that is true, eternal, and unchangeable for it to serve as a fixed standard. It must come from God's own character and be evident in his design of creation. Ultimately, we argue that in order for one to hold a higher view of retributive justice that is more concerned with a proper "reckoning" of justice than personal revenge, it is best to ground such a view in a Christian worldview. It is to the development of such a view that we now turn.

The Question of Capital Punishment: Is It Just in Principle?

Romans 13 and the Question of Government Authority

As we mentioned in the introduction to this chapter, it is of primary importance that the laws governing a country be just in *principle*. From a secular perspective, this would at a minimum mean that the laws of the land comport with cultural norms and standards that have been agreed on by a given society. From a distinctly Christian point of view, laws that are just in principle must align with God's moral order as it is revealed through general revelation evident in the created order and much more clearly through the special revelation given to us in Scripture. More specifically, what God reveals about moral law should serve as the foundation for the laws that govern our society.

Within the Christian tradition, Romans 13:1–7 serves as the pivotal scriptural passage from which we gain an understanding not only of the role of government but also the government's authority to enforce laws and punish crimes in a fallen world:

> Every person is to be in subjection to the governing authorities. For there is no authority except from God, and those which exist are established by God. Therefore whoever resists authority has opposed the ordinance of God; and they who have opposed will receive condemnation upon themselves. For rulers are not a cause of fear for good behavior, but for evil. Do you want to have no fear of authority? Do what is good and you will have praise from the same; for it is a *minister* of God to you for good. But if you do what is evil, be afraid; for it does not bear the sword for nothing; for it is a *minister* of God, an avenger who brings wrath on the one who practices evil. Therefore it is necessary to be in subjection, not only because of wrath, but also for conscience' sake. For because of this you also pay taxes, for rulers are *servants* of God, devoting themselves to this very thing. Render to all what is due them: tax to whom tax is due; custom to whom custom; fear to whom fear; honor to whom honor.

There is little disagreement among Christians that in this passage God delegates his authority to human governments for the purposes of ordering society. Of course, this does not mean that every government will always function in a manner that honors God and perfectly reflects his moral character. But it does mean that the authority to govern comes from God and that when it is rightly ordered and applied, it *should* reflect, honor, protect, and propagate only those things that are demonstrative of God's good, righteous, and just character.

Romans 13:4 and 6 are of critical importance; there, the government is described as being a "minister" or "servant" of God. The Greek word used in this text is *diakonos*, from which we get our English word *deacon*. This implies that governments need both accountability and direction regarding how they use their delegated authority. As a deacon or servant of God, much like a deacon in a local church, government should champion the things of God and be held accountable to do so. In verse 4, the passage indicates that the direction of that service is "to you for good." Therefore, government is meant to serve its citizens. Much like the role that God imparts to Adam toward the rest of creation in Genesis 1–2, God desires that human governments function as his stewards to bring about the well-being of the people being governed. Government is meant to do so by causing citizens to flourish through the service it offers as it represents and champions God's causes.

One of the clear distinctions between the world in which Adam was created and given delegated authority to rule and the world as it is now is the presence of sin. Whereas Adam was meant to rule and subdue the earth without sinful and selfish intentions, we now live in a world in which the governments that rule over us with delegated authority are made up of human sinners. Furthermore, they govern sinful people. Because of this, the lofty goal of filling the earth with the glory of the Lord as the waters cover the sea (as human government was originally meant to accomplish) is now by necessity replaced by the important but much less lofty goals of protection from harm and the deterrence of crime. To use a sports metaphor, we have moved from playing offense to playing defense.

Human government should seek to provide services toward human flourishing. But in a fallen world, much of its energies and resources are now shifted toward the protection and correction of its citizens. This means that in a fallen world, government must now use its delegated authority largely to defend against injustice and protect a right ordering of society. Both these goals will often require the use of force to both impede and punish crime. The question is, as it relates to the discussion of capital punishment, how much force is it allowed to use?

While there may be general agreement among Christians regarding the fact that God has delegated authority to human governments, there is a considerable amount of debate about what Romans 13:4 means when it says that the state "does not bear the sword for nothing." What does Paul mean by using this language of "the sword"? Does he mean to use that phrase as a metaphor that merely recognizes that human governments have delegated authority from God to govern and order society but not that a government can literally take up the sword to accomplish justice through the taking of life? Or does it also mean that the divinely delegated authority includes the use of the sword to take human life as a form of governance and a means of punishing crime? *Abolitionists* (those who want to abolish the death penalty) will argue for the former interpretation, while *retentionists* (those who want to retain the death penalty as a viable option for governments) will argue for the latter.

To properly understand this passage and its instruction regarding the rights of the state to take human life, we must first consider key teachings about God's commands related to the taking of human life in the larger context of the grand story line of Scripture. Once we have done so, we can gain a better understanding of Paul's instruction about the sword in light of the specific context of this passage from the immediate setting in the book of Romans.

Understanding the Biblical Context regarding Capital Punishment

Genesis 1:26–27

Any conversation relating to questions of the life and death of human beings must begin by recognizing the special nature and role that God gives to human life. In the Genesis account of creation, we see that while God created all things and all creatures, only the human beings are made "in the image of God" (Gen. 1:26–27). This special standing that all human beings hold as image-bearers serves as the basis for the principle of the *sanctity* or *sacredness* of human life. From the beginning of creation, human beings have been "set apart" (sanctity) and are meant to uniquely display and represent things about God and his nature (sacredness). Therefore, while all of God's creation should be honored and protected, the lives of image-bearers are uniquely and preeminently valuable.

Genesis 3–9

While God created human beings with a unique value and role within the created order, the early chapters of Genesis indicate that it was not long after sin entered the picture through Adam and Eve's rebellion that murderous events took place. In Genesis 2, God told Adam that he should avoid the sinful choice of eating from the Tree of Knowledge of Good and Evil. In fact, God warned Adam that eating of this fruit would bring about death as the just consequence of rebellion (Gen. 2:17). But Adam and Eve rebelled against God and sinned by plucking the fruit and eating it (3:1–7). While the spiritual consequences of their rebellion led to an immediate "death" in the sense of relational and eternal separation from

God (Rom. 6:23; Eph. 2:1–3), their physical lives were spared. God mercifully allowed them to live while removing them from the garden.

In Genesis 4, we read that Adam and Eve's first child, Cain, murders his younger brother, Abel (Gen. 4:3–8). Here we learn that God is displeased with Cain for killing his brother and also that this murderous act results in consequences that include both a life of wandering and the desire for retribution from his fellow humans (vv. 9–14). Interestingly, God again shows his grace in the face of rebellion that deserves death. We see in this passage that not only does God show amazing grace in sparing Cain, but who God also places a sign of protection on him so that others will not kill him either (v. 15). Additionally, in other passages of the Old Testament we see instances of other figures whose actions warranted the death penalty according to the law of Moses but who were spared by God's grace (e.g., David in 2 Samuel 12). Abolitionists will often point to these instances of mercy and ask, "If God does not impose the death penalty on Cain for killing his brother (as well as the other instances), then on what basis could we claim that the death penalty is a viable punitive option?"—the supposed answer being "We can't." But perhaps a continued reading of the whole counsel of Scripture leads to a different conclusion.

As one continues to read through the Genesis narrative, it becomes clear that as human beings began to multiply on the face of the earth, their corruption became more and more obvious for all to see and increasingly odious in the sight of God (Gen. 6:11–12). As a result, the entire human race had earned the death penalty. God chose to enforce it when he destroyed the earth through the flood. Indeed, it was again only by God's mercy and grace that Noah and his family were spared (Gen. 6–9).

Genesis 9:5–7

After the flood ended and Noah and his family were back on dry land, God once again reiterated the original creation mandate given to Adam in Genesis 1:28 as he instructed Noah to "be fruitful and multiply, and fill the earth" (Gen. 9:1). But this time, the instructions he gave them included provisions for how to govern now that they were to live within a fallen and sinful context:

> Surely I will require your lifeblood; from every beast I will require it. And from every man, from every man's brother I will require the life of man.

> "Whoever sheds man's blood,
> By man his blood shall be shed,
> For in the image of God
> He made man.

> As for you, be fruitful and multiply;
> Populate the earth abundantly and multiply in it." (Gen. 9:5–7)

Verses 5–6 of Genesis 9 are of particular interest. In verse 5, God reiterates the principle of the sanctity of human life by indicating that there will be a reckoning for the taking of human life. God will hold accountable any being responsible for the taking of human life—whether that death results from the behavior of an animal or by the hand of another human being. In this context, verse 6 states the matter plainly: whoever sheds the blood of a human being will be held accountable. Once again, the reason given is that humans are made in the image of God and their lives have a special and unique value among all living things in the created order. Based on the principle of retributive justice discussed above, the reckoning for taking a life requires that the "just deserts" for murder is one's own life. As it will be stated later in the law of Moses, "life for life" (Ex. 21:22–24).

It is common at this point for abolitionists to argue that instead of seeing this passage as an action command on how to protect human life by holding others accountable for murder, it is preferable to understand Genesis 9:6 as merely a predictive proverb offering prophetic guidance about the likelihood of a person's being killed if he or she takes someone else's life. As Glen Stassen and David Gushee argue, "As it stands in Genesis, it does not command the death penalty but gives wise advice based on the likely consequence of your action: if you kill someone, you will end up being killed."[17] Indeed, Stassen and Gushee further argue that Jesus' instruction to his disciple in the garden of Gethsemane to "put away his sword" in Matthew 26:52 is further indication that Genesis 9:6 is merely predictive in nature because Jesus goes on to tell him that "all who draw the sword will die by the sword."[18]

The abolitionist interpretation of the text is both problematic and improbable given the context of the preceding verse (Gen. 9:5) that establishes the setting of accountability, the present verse (v. 6) indicating the special status of human beings, and even the following verse that reiterates the special role that humans are to play in the created order (v. 7). As Wayne Grudem rightly puts it: "The murder of another human being is therefore a kind of attack against God himself, for it is an attack against his representative on the earth, an attack against the 'image' of himself that he has left on the earth."[19] Regarding Jesus' words to his disciple in Matthew 26:52, Jesus could very well have been warning the disciple that authority had not been delegated to the disciple in that context to take a life. Even if the

17. Glen H. Stassen and David P. Gushee, *Kingdom Ethics: Following Jesus in Contemporary Context* (Downers Grove, IL: InterVarsity Press, 2003), 202.

18. Stassen and Gushee, *Kingdom Ethics*, 202.

19. Wayne Grudem, *Christian Ethics: An Introduction to Biblical Moral Reasoning* (Wheaton, IL: Crossway, 2018), 507.

intent were to protect his Lord, the disciple would be taking justice into his own hands, contrary to God's design, and would be acting in the manner of a vigilante. Killing the Roman guard in this manner would earn him the death penalty.

Not only does the Genesis 9 passage reestablish the principle of the sanctity of human life, it also sets an important foundation for understanding that God is delegating authority for humans to govern themselves justly and hold accountable those who act unjustly in the taking of human life. The moral instruction given in this context to Noah as the new "father of humanity" is therefore instructive for the whole human race who follow from his lineage. It is not bound by the constraints of time as a civil law applicable only to the people of Israel, nor is it merely a ceremonial law. Rather, it is reflective of the very nature of God as he seeks to place protection around those who bear his image.[20]

Exodus 20:13

Understanding Genesis 9:1–7 in this way proves helpful in setting a biblical context for understanding God's instructions about capital punishment. Even if one does not agree with the interpretation above, what becomes exceptionally clear as one continues to read the Old Testament is that God authorizes and prescribes capital punishment for a large number of crimes. For example, God prescribes the death penalty for such things as murder (Lev. 24:17), kidnapping (Ex. 21:16; Deut. 24:7), bearing false witness in a trial (Deut. 19:16–21), adultery (Lev. 20:10; Deut. 22:21–24), rape (Deut. 22:25), homosexual behavior (Lev. 20:13), witchcraft (Lev. 20:27), Sabbath-breaking (Ex. 31:14; 35:2; Num. 15:32–36), and blasphemy (Lev. 24:11–16, 23).

Table 13.2. Examples of Capital Punishment in the Old Testament

Adultery	Leviticus 20:10; Deuteronomy 22:21–24
Bearing False Witness in a Trial	Deuteronomy 19:16–21
Blasphemy	Leviticus 24:11–16, 23
Homosexual Behavior	Leviticus 20:13
Kidnapping	Exodus 21:16; Deuteronomy 24:7
Rape	Deuteronomy 22:25
Sabbath-Breaking	Exodus 31:14; 35:2; Numbers 15:32–36
Witchcraft	Leviticus 20:27

20. Grudem, *Christian Ethics*, 508.

This reality becomes extremely important for understanding the meaning of the sixth commandment: "You shall not murder" (Ex. 20:13). If God gives instruction for his people to employ the death penalty as a just means of punishment, then the sixth commandment cannot be understood to forbid all manner of taking human life. Indeed, this is why the best translation of this commandment from the original Hebrew is with "murder" rather than "kill." In Hebrew, the word used in Exodus 20:13 is *ratsakh*. As John Frame explains: "Most often, *ratsakh* refers to killing that is unlawful or forbidden. It is not used for the killing of animals or for killing in war. That should suggest that the best translation here is 'murder,' not the more general 'kill.'"[21] Hence, God's instruction is not that the taking of human life is prohibited at all times; rather, it is the unjust homicide of human beings that is the focus of this command. Further, as it relates to the question of capital punishment, in all the instructions above in which God commands his people to take a human life, the Hebrew word used is not *ratsakh* but *muth*. The use of this distinct word indicates that God considers some forms of the taking of human life to be morally distinct from others and not subject to the prohibition given in the sixth commandment.[22]

While the sixth commandment clearly teaches that it is always wrong to *unjustly* take a human life, it does not preclude the taking of a human life when the cause is *just*. In other words, it is always wrong to *murder* (unjustly kill a human being), but it is not always wrong to *kill*. Those who would insist on categorically describing capital punishment as murder misunderstand both the nature of the sixth commandment and the nature of God. If God commands capital punishment and delegates authority to his people to employ it, then it cannot be wrong in principle.

Capital Punishment and the Context of Romans 13

Having considered key passages related to the taking of human life in the larger context of Scripture, we now turn our attention back to understanding Paul's instruction about the government's "bearing the sword" by looking at the specific context of this passage in Romans 13. We have already seen in the earlier discussion that government is described as a "minister," "servant," or "deacon" of God toward the people. There is little to no disagreement that God has delegated

---

21. John M. Frame, *The Doctrine of the Christian Life* (Phillipsburg, NJ: P&R Publishing, 2008), 686–87. Frame goes on to point out that the term *ratsakh* also differs from our English word *murder* in that it applies to both manslaughter and "negligent homicide," which he defines as the "failure to take adequate precautions" to guard human life.

22. For example, consider instances in which the death is inflicted by God himself, such as in the case of the sons of Aaron in Leviticus 10:2, an ox in Exodus 21:29, idolaters in Deuteronomy 17:2–7, and Sabbath-breakers in Exodus 35:2.

his authority to governments to rule, protect, and seek the prosperity of its citizens. We have also seen from the context of the Old Testament not only that God holds the right to take human life, but also that it is not contrary to his nature to do so, nor is it contrary to his nature to delegate to governmental authorities the authority to take human life.

One particularly influential scholar who disagrees with this point of view, however, is John Howard Yoder. In his book *The Politics of Jesus*, Yoder argues that this normative interpretation of Romans 13:1–7 is mistaken because it refuses to take seriously the larger context of Romans 12–14. In particular, he argues that because Romans 12:14–21 and 13:8–10 urge the individual believer to respond to persecution with love and avoid vengeful responses, then Romans 13:1–7 cannot be understood as an affirmation for Christians to support a state-sponsored death penalty. Instead, he argues, Christians should oppose the death penalty and merely recognize that the state may have authority to rule, but that in a fallen world such rule is not ultimately rightly ordered or legitimate.[23]

We argue that this interpretation is ultimately not persuasive given the particular language and syntax of Romans 13:1–7 (as we will discuss further below). In addition, it does not consider the common distinction made in Scripture between (1) the proper disposition and role of individual believers and their personal virtues and (2) the delegated role of the state as a servant of God. As we pointed out in our discussion above, one must make an important distinction between an understanding of retribution driven by hatred and a desire for appropriate justice. In Romans 12–14, Paul's argument highlights this very thing. Individuals are not permitted to seek vengeance. Vengeance is the Lord's, and the Lord has delegated his authority to the state. These ideas of shaping one's personal motives toward love and justice and against hatred and revenge are not mutually exclusive or ultimately in conflict with a longing for justice to prevail on the societal level.

As we turn directly to Romans 13, we find that there is complete consistency with these ideas as Paul describes the government as an "avenger" that brings wrath or punishment on the one who practices evil and indicates that it is to bring this wrath by the use of the "sword":

> for it is a minister of God to you for good. But if you do what is evil, be afraid; for it does not bear the *sword* for nothing; for it is a minister of God, an *avenger* who brings wrath on the one who practices evil. (Rom. 13:4)

In the text, the word translated from the original Greek to describe government as an "avenger" is *ekdikos*. This word signifies one who acts as an "agent of

---

23. John Howard Yoder, *The Politics of Jesus: Victi Agnus Noster* (Grand Rapids: Eerdmans, 1972), 195–200.

punishment" to rectify a wrong done to someone else.[24] In the specific context, we see that the government, as a minister of God, is to function as an agent of retribution who carries out punishment on the "one who practices evil." Paul's teaching here is consistent with Peter's teaching that the government has the authority to administer "punishment" (*ekdikēsis*) on those who do evil (1 Peter 2:13–14).

Paul indicates that it is as this "agent of retribution" or "avenger" that the state has the right to wield the "sword." This use of "sword" is significant for two reasons. First, the sword is symbolic of something very specific. It is not merely a sign of authority; it is the application of justice in a particular manner. In the historical context of the Roman world, the emperor himself held the *sceptrum Augusti*, or the "emperor's scepter," as a symbol of his general authority to rule. Those under the emperor similarly held the *sceptrum eburneum*, or the "ivory scepter," to symbolize their right to rule in general. Thus, it was the scepter, not the sword, that represented delegated authority to legislate on behalf of, or in the name of, the emperor. The sword, however, was commonly understood to be a more specific symbol that represented the authority to execute retributive justice.

Second, the Greek word for "sword" as it is used in this passage is *machaira*. This indicates a short sword or dagger that is used for killing as well as the power "to punish evildoers."[25] This word is used in many other passages to speak of the instrument by which people are put to death (e.g., Acts 16:27; Heb. 11:37).[26] Grudem correctly concludes:

> The idea, suggested by some, that the sword here is simply a symbol of governmental authority is hardly persuasive. When Paul says the civil government in general is authorized to "bear the sword," he means that it has been given authority from God to use the sword for the purpose for which people used it in the first century, and this is to put people to death.[27]

Objections

Doesn't This Interpretation in Essence "Fence Jesus Out" from Speaking to This Issue?

Having reached this conclusion by focusing on Paul's teaching in Romans 13, is it possible that we may be "fencing out" Jesus' teachings and thereby reaching a conclusion that contradicts Jesus' own instructions to his disciples? This is in essence the claim made by some abolitionists who argue that Jesus' teachings

---

24. Frederick William Danker et al., eds., *A Greek-English Lexicon of the New Testament and Other Early Christian Literature*, 3rd ed. (Chicago: University of Chicago Press, 2000) (BDAG), s.v. "ἔκδικος."

25. BDAG, s.v. "μάχαιρα."

26. See Grudem, *Christian Ethics*, 509; Feinberg and Feinberg, *Ethics for a Brave New World*, 259.

27. Grudem, *Christian Ethics*, 509–10.

leave no room for allowing or supporting capital punishment within a Christian ethic because disciples of Jesus are called to "practice forgiveness" and "deeds of deliverance" that reflect a heart to give enemies love and prayer, not hate and vengeance. Rather than seeking revengeful retaliation, so the argument goes, Christian disciples are instead called on by Jesus to "look for transforming initiatives that can begin to deliver us from the cycles of violence" that affirming capital punishment represents.[28]

This objection, which is very similar to Yoder's position addressed above, has much that we can agree with and appreciate in regard to its sentiment. There can be no disagreement that Jesus emphasizes love and forgiveness. Both the Old and New Testaments urge individuals to love their enemies, and both rebuke a disposition of hatred and vengeance. Likewise, there can be no disagreement in principle that Christians should seek (as Pope John Paul II famously urged in his encyclical *Evangelium Vitae*) to bring about a transformative influence that champions a "culture of life" rather than a "culture of death."[29]

Yet while we can agree with much of the sentiment, we ultimately believe that a conclusion that takes an emphasis on love, forgiveness, and deliverance and makes it necessarily opposed to affirming capital punishment as a viable form of justice is misplaced. First, this objection presumes an unfortunate split between the principles of love and justice, mercy and discipline, humility and accountability. *Appropriately ordered retribution is meant to show love through the application of justice.* It recognizes that discipline is at times the very best type of merciful action, and that holding someone accountable need not be based in arrogance or a sense of superiority but in a humble desire for an appropriate reckoning. In fact, it is from the very same scriptural context (the Pentateuch) from which we have seen God command his people to employ the death penalty as a means of justice that he also gives his people his commands of neighbor love.

> You shall not hate your fellow countryman in your heart; you may surely reprove your neighbor, but shall not incur sin because of him. You shall not take vengeance, nor bear any grudge against the sons of your people, but you shall love your neighbor as yourself; I am the LORD. (Lev. 19:17–18)

In short, this type of objection misunderstands the nature of retributive justice and the proper place of *just deserts* as discussed above by erroneously placing all arguments for capital punishment within the category of wrongful vengeance.

---

28. Stassen and Gushee, *Kingdom Ethics*, 195, 198, 213.

29. John Paul II, *Evangelium Vitae*, accessed March 30, 2020, http://www.vatican.va/content/john-paul-ii /en/encyclicals/documents/hf_jp-ii_enc_25031995_evangelium-vitae.html.

Second, we argue that far from "fencing Jesus out" of the discussion, the application of capital punishment actually allows his teachings to take the place of preeminence. Since Jesus is the second person of the Trinity, the teachings from the whole counsel of Scripture *are* his teachings. The words spoken in the Old Testament are *his* words. The authority given by God to human government in both the Old and New Testaments is *his* to delegate. The high view of the sanctity and sacredness of human life that was taught from the beginning of Genesis—and that capital punishment seeks to uphold—is *his* view of the sanctity of life. It would be a terrible mistake to artificially separate Old Testament teachings from Jesus' as though there were two different sources of Scripture. Truth is a person, not a set of distinct concepts. The source and ground of Scripture is the nature and character of God in three persons. Thus, if it is not contrary to the character of God to command his people to employ capital punishment in the Old Testament, it cannot be contrary to the character of Jesus in the New Testament.

Therefore, far from fencing Jesus out, the argument that retributive justice must not be motivated by hatred and vengeance *requires* the teachings of Jesus to be central. Whether or not God delegates authority to take life is not the only important element of the discussion. Jesus is greatly concerned with the heart of his disciples and the culture they shape in the world in which he has placed them. That being said, Jesus' teachings on love, forgiveness, and deliverance must play a central role in shaping the hearts of persons at all times. Importantly, they must also play a central role in all matters of justice. Whether the criminal is fined, jailed, or put to death—but especially in cases in which the death penalty is an option—Jesus' teachings about Christian virtues are essential. Again, we point out that God gives his commands regarding capital punishment in the same context in which he tells his people to embody neighbor love. Only through the work and teachings of Christ can one truly find the grace to genuinely offer personal forgiveness while also recognizing the need for proper justice to be done.

Didn't Jesus Do Away with the Death Penalty When He Told Us to Turn the Other Cheek (Matt. 5:38–42)?

Jesus' instruction to "turn the other cheek" in Matthew 5:38–39 is a perfect example of the point we made in the previous section. In the Sermon on the Mount, much of the focus of Jesus' teaching is on the importance of Christian virtue and the shaping of the personal character of those who are part of the kingdom of God. In the particular context of these verses, Jesus promotes grace and patience in the face of personal offense. His concern is that we avoid retaliation and act generously toward those who insult us. The nature of the offense in these verses has more to do with personal insults than with crimes against human life.

There is still a lesson to be learned from these verses, and it applies to capital punishment. Leon Morris notes: "'Do not resist the evil person' does not mean that we should let evil triumph throughout our communities. Jesus is referring to private retaliation, not to public order, and he is instructing his followers not to be intent on getting their own back when someone wrongs them. To be the victim of some form of evil does not give us the right to hit back."[30] The key here is that Jesus limits *personal* retaliation against the one who strikes us on the cheek, sues for our shirt, or demands that we go a mile with his pack. Even though personal retaliation is forbidden for the sake of building character, the state is not forbidden from acting when an unjust action is perpetrated against one of its citizens.

In the case of a murder, the individual no longer has the ability to defend himself against the perpetrator. The state, however, needs to protect its citizens and establish justice for society. If the state allowed murder to go unchecked, then anarchy would result. A capital crime is the perfect example of a scenario in which justice is to be pursued by the state as a proxy for the citizen who can no longer defend himself. Such capital crimes are not what Jesus had in mind—he was warning against taking vengeance for personal offense or insult. Feinberg and Feinberg state: "If one demands that these passages [Matt. 5:38ff.] be applied to criminal justice, then the logical result would be to rule out all punishment for all crimes. Obviously, that would mean the collapse of orderly society and would negate biblical teaching that governments are instituted by God to reward the just and to punish evildoers (Rom 13:1–4)."[31] Government receives its power from God and reserves the right to enact vengeance on behalf of a citizen, therefore allowing the citizen to fall in line with Jesus' teaching not to pursue personal vengeance.

Jesus' teaching in this section of Scripture is not oriented toward instructing believers about how the government should be shaped. Thus, as we pointed out above, this passage is not meant to negate the proper place of retributive justice. Rather, it is meant to shape the hearts of disciples such that they do not become the kind of people who merely keep the letter of the law about retribution, while also desiring revenge from a hate-filled heart.

Doesn't Support for the Death Penalty in Principle Conflict with a Pro-Life Ethic?

The ethical principle of the sanctity of human life is evident in Scripture from the first chapter of the Bible to the last. The Bible makes it clear that God made human beings unique among all creation when he created them in his image. Scripture is also clear that for this reason, human life is to be honored and protected by each of us individually and all of us corporately.

---

30. Leon Morris, *The Gospel according to Matthew*, PNTC (Grand Rapids: Eerdmans, 1992), 126–27.
31. Feinberg and Feinberg, *Ethics for a Brave New World*, 255.

This biblical reality has led some to question whether a pro-capital-punishment stance conflicts with the principle of the sanctity of human life. But as John Frame points out, some objections to capital punishment "spring from a generalized view of the sanctity of life, without the biblical distinction between murderers and victims. The Bible teaches that human life is sacred, but it does not teach that murderers and nonmurderers have the same right to life."[32] The categories of guilt and innocence become important for how one makes the distinction between just killing and murder. The unjust taking of an innocent human life conflicts with a pro-life ethic.

On the other hand, when a murderer's life is taken in accord with the laws of retribution ("life for life"), the principle of the sanctity of human life is actually affirmed in two ways. First, it honors the life of the victim, who was unjustly murdered, by recognizing that the highest of prices must be paid to properly value the life that was lost. Second, it shows value for the life of the murderer by recognizing that even though his or her life is now forfeit, its inherent value is the fitting price to render a reckoning for the taking of another's life.

The Question of Capital Punishment: Is It Just in Practice?

Is It Justly Applied?

Just because capital punishment is right in *principle* does not necessarily mean that one can support the manner in which a government actually employs the death penalty. The disciple of Jesus Christ must also be concerned with the manner in which capital punishment is practiced. It is interesting to note that while there is disagreement among Christian retentionists and abolitionists about whether capital punishment is right in principle, there is a shared concern regarding how it is practiced in the United States.

At the beginning of this chapter, we noted that this very concern led the United States Supreme Court to suspend the practice of capital punishment in 1972. Of primary concern at the time was that sentences being handed down for capital cases appeared to be arbitrary and capricious. Even now, after laws have been passed and capital punishment has been reinstated, concern still exists about the practice of capital punishment specifically in regard to the possibility of innocent parties' being executed in light of the relatively recent emergence of DNA evidence (*miscarriage of justice*) as well as the possibility of racial and gender bias in the sentencing process (*maldistribution*). Not only is it important that a society's laws be just in principle, they must also be just in the manner in which they are enforced. If a law (even a just one) is wrongly applied, then the punishment will

32. Frame, *Doctrine of the Christian Life*, 702–3.

be unjust. With this in mind, we suggest the following guiding principles to assist in the proper application of the death penalty.

Principles for Just Application
Discrimination
   As we noted in chapter 10, the term *discrimination* can have several meanings related to ethics. Here the principle of discrimination, as it is used in a discussion of capital punishment (and also of war), has to do with the attempt to separate the innocent from the guilty in the process of making a judgment. The goal is to avoid miscarriages of justice that occur from the killing of innocent people. Specifically, the goal is to punish only those who are guilty by being careful and discriminating in the process of discerning who deserves punishment. The Bible seeks to provide a basis for certainty of judgment by requiring a high burden of proof. Consider the following two verses:

> If anyone kills a person, the murderer shall be put to death at the evidence of witnesses, but no person shall be put to death on the testimony of one witness. (Num. 35:30)

> On the evidence of two witnesses or three witnesses, he who is to die shall be put to death; he shall not be put to death on the evidence of one witness. (Deut. 17:6)

   In recent years, the emergence of DNA testing has shown that not all those who sit on death row awaiting execution deserve to be there. In fact, several state governors, beginning with Illinois Governor George Ryan in January 2000, have imposed a statewide moratorium on executions. The reason why Ryan called for the moratorium was that in the years just before his decision, DNA evidence had shown that several convicted inmates could not have committed the crimes for which they were incarcerated. At the time of their trials, DNA evidence had not yet become available. In calling for the moratorium, the governor commented:

> We reinstated the death penalty in 1977 in Illinois and since that time we have executed twelve death row inmates. But, thirteen times, innocent men were convicted of capital crimes by judges and juries based on evidence they thought was beyond a reasonable doubt. On thirteen occasions, innocent men were condemned to die. And thirteen times, innocent men were exonerated after rotting for years on death row. For that to happen even once is unjust. For that to happen thirteen times is shameful and beyond belief.[33]

33. Governor George Ryan, "An Address on the Death Penalty," University of Chicago Divinity School,

Before his departure from office, Governor Ryan granted clemency to the remaining 167 inmates on Illinois' death row, citing what he argued was the flawed process of sentencing.[34] The wrongful sentencing that triggered Ryan's action is precisely what the principle of discrimination is trying to avoid.

Of course, one could respond that innocent people are punished all the time and in every form of punishment. This is a complaint not merely against capital punishment, but against all other forms of punishment as well. If one were to argue that we must abolish capital punishment based on this principle of discrimination, then one could logically make the argument that we would have to abolish all forms of punishment. Therefore, it does not necessarily follow that capital punishment must be abolished per se. This principle does suggest, however, that we must work harder in all areas of state-sponsored criminal punishment to reasonably ensure that only the guilty are convicted. When it comes to contexts in which the ultimate penalty of taking a person's life lies in the balance, the burden of proof seems all that much higher.

Impartiality

The principle of impartiality has to do with the fair distribution of punishment. The concern is with maldistribution, meaning that a particular punishment may be applied in an unfair way. The goal is to ensure equal consequences in equal situations that are not skewed in light of color, gender, or some other factor. Scripture speaks to this issue of impartiality rather pointedly. Consider the following passages:

> He appointed judges in the land in all the fortified cities of Judah, city by city. He said to the judges, "Consider what you are doing, for you do not judge for man but for the LORD who is with you when you render judgment. Now then let the fear of the LORD be upon you; be very careful what you do, for the LORD our God will have no part in unrighteousness or partiality or the taking of a bribe." (2 Chron. 19:5–7)

> For there is no partiality with God. (Rom. 2:11)

> If, however, you are fulfilling the royal law according to the Scripture, "You shall love your neighbor as yourself," you are doing well. But if you show partiality, you are committing sin and are convicted by the law as transgressors. (James 2:8–9)

June 3, 2002, accessed January 10, 2020, https://www.pewforum.org/2002/06/03/governor-george-ryan-an-address-on-the-death-penalty/.

34. Jodi Wilgoren, "Citing Issue of Fairness, Governor Clears Out Death Row in Illinois," *New York Times*, January 12, 2003, accessed March 31, 2020, https://www.nytimes.com/2003/01/12/us/citing-issue-of-fairness-governor-clears-out-death-row-in-illinois.html.

In Acts 10:34, Peter speaks to the impartiality of God when he states that God is not one to show favoritism, or, as the King James Version puts it, he is not a "respecter of persons." The Greek word that is translated "partiality" or "favoritism" is *prosōpolēmptēs*, which refers to lifting someone's face as an act of honor or preference over someone else. When done by a judge, this is an act of partiality.[35] God, being a perfect Judge, neither judges with partiality nor partakes in the unrighteousness that injustice exhibits (2 Chron. 19:5–7).

Proportionality

A third guiding principle for ensuring that capital punishment is justly applied and practiced is proportionality. This principle seeks to ensure that the punishment assessed actually matches the crime. When we say "matches the crime," we do not necessarily mean "the same type" of crime, for in such an understanding a rape would require a rape or a theft would require a theft. Rather, the focus in seeking proportional forms of punishment is that an equal or appropriate amount of severity is assessed related to the severity of the crime.

This is what the *lex talionis* ("law of retaliation") depicts in Exodus 21:23–25 (see also Lev. 24:17–22):

> You shall appoint as a penalty life for life, eye for eye, tooth for tooth, hand for hand, foot for foot, burn for burn, wound for wound, bruise for bruise.

This passage not only seeks to guard proportionality by requiring equal justice for the crime committed, but also limits the amount of retribution allowed. This limiting aspect of the *lex talionis* is important because it recognizes that the human heart will often want to go further in handing out retribution than what would be just in the eyes of God. So by exacting a "life for life," "foot for foot," or "tooth for tooth," the passage works to ensure proportional justice—not too much, not too little.

Table 13.3. Biblical Principles to Shape Just Application of Capital Punishment

Discrimination (certainty of guilt)	Numbers 35:30; Deuteronomy 17:6
Impartiality	2 Chronicles 19:5–7; Romans 2:11
Proportionality	Exodus 21:23–25
Timeliness	Ecclesiastes 8:11
Public	Deuteronomy 13:6–11

35. Gerhard Kittel and Gerhard Friedrich, eds., *Theological Dictionary of the New Testament*, trans. Geoffrey W. Bromiley (Grand Rapids: Eerdmans, 1968), s.v. "προσωπολημψία."

The focus on proportionality might lead some to suggest that life in prison is equally severe and could serve as a replacement for capital punishment. Two responses seem appropriate. First, making the case that life in prison is equal to death is very difficult because the two cannot be easily measured. It seems that because life in prison and death are such different kinds of things, they defy any clear standard of comparison on a spectrum of severity. Second, Scripture seems to clarify this debate by indicating that while a ransom may be paid for some types of crime, when it comes to the crime of murder, paying a ransom is not an option. Consider Numbers 35:31, for example: "Moreover, you shall not take ransom for the life of a murderer who is guilty of death, but he shall surely be put to death."

Other Considerations

Scripture also seems to indicate two other principles related to the just and wise practice of capital punishment. The first relates to *timeliness*—namely, that if the death penalty is an appropriate form of punishment and the criminal in question is justly tried and sentenced, then it should be carried out expediently. In the United States, however, prisoners sentenced to death typically spend more than a decade on death row, and some live in that context for over twenty years.[36] This seems radically opposed to the wisdom of Scripture that says:

> Because the sentence against an evil deed is not executed quickly, therefore the hearts of the sons of men among them are given fully to do evil. (Eccl. 8:11)

The other principle worthy of consideration based on scriptural teaching is the *public nature of execution*. In ancient Israel, not only was the trial and sentencing process a public event, so also was the execution. Consider the following passage:

> If your brother, your mother's son, or your son or daughter, or the wife you cherish, or your friend who is as your own soul, entice you secretly, saying, "Let us go and serve other gods" (whom neither you nor your fathers have known, of the gods of the peoples who are around you, near you or far from you, from one end of the earth to the other end), you shall not yield to him or listen to him; and your eye shall not pity him, nor shall you spare or conceal him. *But you shall surely kill him; your hand shall be first against him to put him to death, and afterwards the hand of all the people.* So you shall stone him to death because he has sought to seduce you from the LORD your God who brought you out from the land of Egypt, out of the

36. For helpful statistics and discussion, see the following webpage and the accompanying links: https://deathpenaltyinfo.org/death-row/death-row-time-on-death-row.

house of slavery. *Then all Israel will hear and be afraid, and will never again do such a wicked thing among you.* (Deut. 13:6–11; see also 17:7)

Far from brutalizing the culture, Scripture indicates that public executions are meant to instill character and devotion to God.

Scripture ties both the emphasis on timeliness and the public nature of execution to the impact that the practice of capital punishment is meant to have on shaping the virtues of society. Not only are they meant to encourage the people to remain close to their God and abide by his moral statutes, but both passages indicate that these practices would have a deterring effect on future wickedness. There can be no doubt that both these ideas would require a radical shift in the manner in which capital punishment is currently practiced in most countries. But given the tenor of these passages, one does wonder what the impact would be if these principles were employed.

Conclusion

In the final analysis, it is important to keep in mind that the principles of the sanctity of human life and neighbor love must always shape our Christian ethic as it relates to capital punishment. Indeed, as Christians debate the issue, this is precisely why retentionists and abolitionists need each other. For as the pro and con arguments are developed, each side in the debate will address these two principles in distinct manners that can help the other side remain humble before the Lord. It is the tendency of retentionists to focus on the principle of the sanctity of human life from a point of view that emphasizes the value of the victim's life. Abolitionists tend to place emphasis on the value of the life of the criminal as one who still retains the image of God no matter what crime he or she has committed.

Likewise, with the principle of neighbor love, retentionists will often express their convictions with a focus on loving the victim and the victim's family as well as any potential future victims who could be harmed if the death penalty does not prevent or deter future crimes. They believe that love also requires discipline and justice in order to be properly ordered to God's standards of holiness. On the other hand, abolitionists will often express their conviction about neighbor love in a manner that seeks to express the love of Christ to the criminal in hopes of restoration and rehabilitation. Jesus instructs his disciples to love even "the least of these" (Matt. 25:45), which includes even those guilty of a capital crime.

Each side can help the other recognize that there are *moral traces* left behind regardless of what position one holds. The abolitionist can help the retentionist remember to seek a heart of forgiveness toward the criminal, to fight against the hound of revenge that lurks in the human heart, to grieve over the possibility of a lost soul's going to hell, and to pray for the ultimate salvation of the criminal's soul. The abolitionist can also help the retentionist to be reluctant to take a life even if the criminal is deserving.

On the other hand, the retentionist can help the abolitionist remember that love holds human beings accountable. The retentionist helps the abolitionist recognize that a desire for a *just reckoning* is not opposed to love. The retentionist can help the abolitionist understand that a just and loving society must find a tangible way to honor the life of the victim in order for that society to be good. The retentionist can also help the abolitionist be reluctant about sparing the life of the criminal in light of the fact that the victim's life is also of immense value and that society must protect such a valuation of the victim's life if it is going to remain just and good.

It is imperative that believers work hard to simultaneously be shaped by the virtues of love, mercy, forgiveness, and concern for evangelism while also recognizing the need to preserve in society the sacred view of life for God's image-bearers—which includes both victims and criminals. Both sets of virtues are crucial to understanding ethics as worship. When these principles are held in appropriate tension within the Christian worldview, they provide the grounding on which one can understand and support the legal use of capital punishment that both seeks a right and good form of retribution that maximally guards and seeks human flourishing at the societal level while longing for forgiveness, redemption, and restoration of all parties at the individual level.

With these admonitions in mind, we conclude that God delegates authority to human government to wield the sword as a means of punishing criminals and that in *principle* it is a completely legitimate ethical stance to support the state's right to employ the death penalty from within a Christian worldview. In light of the principles related to the just implementation of capital punishment, however, it seems that in many instances our current system and practice leave much to be desired. It may be wise, then, to consider whether our governing bodies ought to once again place a moratorium on the practice of capital punishment in order to refine the administration to further ensure just *practice*.

Key Terms and Concepts

abolitionist	incapacitation
crime of commission	just deserts
crimes of passion	justice
deterrence	*lex talionis*
discrimination	maldistribution
impartiality	miscarriage of justice

moral offense versus crime
moral traces
murder versus killing
prevention
punishment
recidivism
rehabilitation

restitution
retentionist
retribution
sacredness of human life
sanctity of human life
vengeance

Key Scriptures

Genesis 1:26–28
Genesis 9:5–7
Exodus 20:13
Exodus 21:24–25
Exodus 22:4–14
Matthew 5:9
Matthew 5:21–22
Matthew 5:38–42

Matthew 5:44
Matthew 26:52
Romans 12:17–19
Romans 13:1–7
1 Corinthians 5:5
James 2:8–9
1 Peter 2:13–14
1 Peter 3:9

Study Questions

1. The sixth commandment (Ex. 20:13) is often translated into English as "You shall not kill." What is the meaning of the Hebrew word for "kill," and how does that shape the proper understanding and application of the commandment to the issue of capital punishment?

2. If your current position on capital punishment is that the practice should be abolished, state the main reason why, and then see whether that same reason undermines all forms of civil punishment (e.g., putting someone in jail). Compare your view to the issue of abortion. Does your view against capital punishment suggest that you should be against abortion as well?

3. If your current position on capital punishment is that it is morally permissible and that the practice should be retained, state the main reason why, and then see whether that same reasoning should press you toward being "pro-abortion." Explain why or why not.

4. In this chapter, the authors list four different goals of state-sponsored criminal punishment. What are the strengths and weaknesses of each? Which view do you believe should serve as the proper goal for our criminal justice system? How do you think your answer to this question ought to shape our country's stance on the practice of capital punishment?

5. What is the significance of Jesus' statement to "turn the other cheek" (Matt. 5:38–42) for the issue of capital punishment?

For Further Reading

Bedau, Hugo Adam, and Paul G. Cassell. *Debating the Death Penalty: Should America Have Capital Punishment? The Experts on Both Sides Make Their Best Case*. New York: Oxford University Press, 2004.

Bernardin, Joseph Cardinal. *Consistent Ethic of Life*. Kansas City, MO: Sheed & Ward, 1988.

House, H. Wayne, and John Howard Yoder, eds. *The Death Penalty Debate: Two Opposing Views of Capital Punishment*. Waco, TX: Word, 1991.

John Paul II. *Evangelium Vitae* ("The Gospel of Life"), March 25, 1996.

Lewis, C. S. "The Humanitarian Theory of Punishment." In *God in the Dock: Essays on Theology and Ethics*, edited by Walter Hooper, 224–30. Grand Rapids: Eerdmans, 1970.

Moreland, J. P., and Norman L. Geisler. *The Life and Death Debate: Moral Issues of Our Time*. New York: Greenwood, 1990.

Owens, Erik C., John D. Carlson, and Eric P. Elshtain, eds. *Religion and the Death Penalty: A Call for Reckoning*. Grand Rapids: Eerdmans, 2004.

Sider, Ronald J., ed. *The Early Church on Killing: A Comprehensive Sourcebook on War, Abortion, and Capital Punishment*. Grand Rapids: Baker Academic, 2012.

Wright, Christopher J. H. *Old Testament Ethics for the People of God*. Downers Grove, IL: IVP Academic, 2004.

14

War

"If the just-war theory did not already exist,
Christians would have to invent it."[1]
—PAUL RAMSEY, The Just War

"When wars are waged, ordinary citizens are turned into killers.
In war, men, women, and children are violently killed. . . . Christians should
be uncomfortable with violence in general and especially with war."[2]
—MARK J. ALLMAN, Who Would Jesus Kill?

Introduction: War and Worship?

Human history is filled with contexts and situations in which deadly force has been unjustly used to oppress the innocent. It is also filled with contexts in which deadly force has been used in order to prevent or put an end to these injustices. As the author of Ecclesiastes laments: "There is an appointed time for everything. And there is a time for every event under heaven—. . . a time for war and a time for peace" (Eccl. 3:1, 8b). The question for the Christian is whether it is ever justifiable to use deadly force in order to prevent or put an end to injustice.

Of course, this question not only applies to the topic of capital punishment, as we explored in the previous chapter, but is also the central question related to the topic of war. Indeed, as will become clear in our discussion, there is quite a bit of overlap between these two topics. In fact, in many ways they are merely an extension of one another. Whereas in the previous chapter we asked whether it is ever justifiable to use deadly force in the context of criminal punishment as an act

---

1. Paul Ramsey, *The Just War: Force and Political Responsibility* (Lanham, MD: Rowman & Littlefield, 1983), 145.

2. Mark J. Allman, *Who Would Jesus Kill? War, Peace, and the Christian Tradition* (Winona, MN: St. Mary's, 2008), 11.

of worship, here our central question is this: Is it ever possible to consider the use of deadly force *in the context of war* as an act of God-honoring worship?

In the four Gospels, we have no record of Jesus' ever directly addressing the morality of war. While he recognized the inevitability of wars and various strategies of war, nowhere in the Gospels can one find him speaking directly to whether waging war was just or unjust. This relative silence in his teaching should not lead to the conclusion that somehow Jesus had nothing instructive to say to the topic. Rather, it requires that we investigate the whole counsel of Scripture (of which he is the ultimate author) to understand how his teachings should apply. How should a disciple of Jesus Christ, who is seeking to maximize the worship of God, behave in a fallen and broken world? More specifically to our topic in this chapter, is it ever justifiable for Christians to support a war effort? Is it ever appropriate for a Christian to go to war? To use force? To kill?

Thankfully, we are not the first to engage these questions. Throughout the history of the church, Christians have pondered these ideas and have come to various conclusions.[3] Some have argued that when Jesus told Peter to put away his sword, he disarmed the church forever (Tertullian). Others have argued that Jesus' teaching about love actually compels Christians to engage in war if war is necessary to save lives from unjust attacks (Augustine). One of the more intriguing and influential arguments about the ethics of war put forth in recent years engaged the issue through a thought experiment involving the parable of the Good Samaritan in Luke 10:30–37:

> Jesus replied and said, "A man was going down from Jerusalem to Jericho, and fell among robbers, and they stripped him and beat him, and went away leaving him half dead. And by chance a priest was going down on that road, and when he saw him, he passed by on the other side. Likewise a Levite also, when he came to the place and saw him, passed by on the other side. But a Samaritan, who was on a journey, came upon him; and when he saw him, he felt compassion, and came to him and bandaged up his wounds, pouring oil and wine on them; and he put him on his own beast, and brought him to an inn and took care of him. On the next day he took out two denarii and gave them to the innkeeper and said, 'Take care of him; and whatever more you spend, when I return I will repay you.' Which of these three do you think proved to be a neighbor to the man who fell into the robbers' hands?" And he said, "The one who showed mercy toward him." Then Jesus said to him, "Go and do the same."

3. J. Daryl Charles is right when he comments that "Christian reflection on the ethics of war is rooted squarely within the mainstream of the Christian moral tradition; it is by no means a peripheral issue." J. Daryl Charles, *Between Pacifism and Jihad: Just War and the Christian Tradition* (Downers Grove, IL: InterVarsity Press, 2005), 10.

The late Princeton University ethicist Paul Ramsey (1913–88) used this parable to cut to the heart of the debate by asking the following questions:

> What do you imagine Jesus would have had the Samaritan do if in the story he had come upon the scene when the robbers had just begun their attack and while they were still at their nefarious work? Would it not then be a work of charity to resort to the only available and effective means of preventing or punishing the attack and resisting the injustice? Is not anyone obliged to do this if he can?[4]

As Ramsey admits, this thought experiment moves us off Jesus' central point when he first told this parable. But in asking these questions, Ramsey sought to highlight the central issue: What does neighbor love require when the life of a fellow image-bearer hangs in the balance?

What do *you* think? What if while the Good Samaritan happened down the road to Jericho he turned a bend and actually came upon the robbery and beating while it was taking place? What ethical convictions should drive him? What moral obligations should bind him? Should neighbor love cause him to use force to stop the attack? Would neighbor love justify his even taking the life of an attacker to protect the life of the innocent traveler?

What if you were in the position of the Good Samaritan and it was your mother, father, sister, brother, husband, wife, or child who was being beaten? Would you be compelled to act? Do you think that you would be justified to use force to protect a loved one being unjustly and brutally attacked? Could the use of force actually be the highest form of worship in such a context?

While Ramsey could have just as easily jumped from this discussion into the question of capital punishment, he used this thought experiment to get people thinking deeply about the problem of war. His goal was to press his reader to explore not only whether it is ever justifiable to go to war, but also whether there are limits to one's behavior once one does decide to go to war. These two considerations shape the foundational contours of what is known as the *just-war tradition*.

It is the purpose of this chapter to explore this tradition. In order to do so, we first offer a few basic definitions and concepts to help frame the larger discussion. Next, we develop scriptural and theological foundations that drive our understanding of the ethics of war. Third, we develop a just-war criterion that entails both how one determines if and when it is right to go to war (*jus ad bellum*) and proper conduct in war (*jus in bello*). Finally, before bringing our discussion

---

4. Paul Ramsey, "Military Service as a Moral System," *MCR* 2, no. 1 (January 1973): 15. See also Ramsey, *Just War*, 142.

to a conclusion, we address the question whether pacifism is a viable Christian response by highlighting three various types.

Framing Definitions and Concepts

Three Commonly Identified Perspectives on War

Various perspectives exist regarding how Christians believe that the principles of the sanctity of life and neighbor love ought to be applied in situations in which injustice prevails. Generally speaking, there are three main traditions regarding the moral evaluation of war: pacifism, just war, and crusade.

On one end of the spectrum is the *pacifist* perspective. This tradition contends that the use of forceful violence, including violence in war, is never justifiable under any circumstance and that conflicts should always be solved through non-violent means. Within this perspective, however, there are nuances as to how one should respond to contexts of injustice. Some pacifists who hold to the position of *nonresistance* would argue that Christians are called to be distinct from this world and resist using the means of a fallen world to solve a fallen world's problems. Under no circumstances should physical force or resistance be used. In the case of our thought experiment regarding the Good Samaritan story, if a person with these convictions came upon the beating, he or she may call for help, may yell at the attackers to stop, and may certainly pray for God to intervene and bring about justice. But otherwise, there would be no form of physical intervention. Historically, Quaker, Amish, and Mennonite communities are examples of those who have held such positions.

Others within the pacifist tradition may, however, hold to a *nonviolent resistance* perspective. Those who do would argue that while Christians should not use physical violence or force to resolve injustice, there is a place for physical resistance. The threshold of bodily involvement is crossed with this position in the sense that in addition to praying and perhaps calling for help, a Christian could also try to physically intervene by placing his or her body in between the attackers and the victim. In the case of the Good Samaritan story, this would mean an attempt to pull the victim out of the trouble or perhaps use the Christian's own body as a "human shield" against the injustice.

On the other end of the spectrum lies the militaristic position sometimes known as the *crusade* perspective. Those who hold this position would suggest that there are no moral limits in war. Because this perspective approaches war as an unconditional effort of good versus evil, there is little concern for restricting the type of weapons used, the amount of force used, the people or structures targeted, or the strategies of warfare. Victory in the name of the driving ideology is all that matters. From this point of view, the use of force is not something to avoid, but that which is justifiable in any circumstance with no moral constraints.[5] Once it is decided to engage in war, then there are no boundaries or limits. The goal is simply to get the job done by whatever means possible. Slogans that might accompany such a position would be "all is fair in love and war" and "war is hell, so fight like a hellion."

In the case of Paul Ramsey's thought experiment regarding the Good Samaritan, for someone who approaches war with this perspective, there would be no concerns about "overkill." Any type or amount of force would be allowed even if it included finding the families of the bandits and torturing and killing their children in order to stop their thieving. As the following discussion will point out, such a position is nearly impossible to include as a viable option for a Christian. It has, however, been the perspective of many in religious wars (including many in the name of Christ) in which the entirety of the enemy community and culture is depicted as inferior, subhuman, or in league with the devil, therefore warranting no restraint, mercy, or pardon.

Between these two is the *just-war* tradition, which focuses not on force (its avoidance or use) but on the injustice that must be addressed. It shares with pacifism a reluctance to use force and violence over concern for the sanctity of human life, and it has in common with the crusade mentality a willingness to use force. It is distinct from the crusade perspective, however, in that it considers limiting force according to various criteria. In short, the just warrior does not want to go to war, but is resolved to do so if necessary. The primary question for the just warrior, then, is not "is war okay?" but "is war sometimes necessary to prevent injustice, preserve human flourishing, or foster the conditions for a *just peace*?"

As was the case with the pacifistic perspective, there are nuances within the just-war tradition regarding how one ought to respond to injustice. For example, some in the just-war tradition hold to a *violence within deontological limits* perspective. This position supports the use of force and violence in order to stop the injustice from taking place. The use of force or violence, however, must be limited in regard to the means or type of force that is used. While certain types of violence are acceptable, there are types of violence that should never be used to stop injustice even if they would be effective. Thus, in the Good Samaritan parable, not only would praying and getting in the way be good ideas, so also might throwing punches or even picking up a stick to beat the attackers into retreat. In a modern context, the Good Samaritan could never utilize certain types of violence (e.g.,

---

5. Interestingly enough, Ramsey points out that when one penetrates to the heart of the moral discussion, it turns out that "the absolute pacifist and the total devastation warrior are brothers under the skin. One says that warring is such wickedness it should never be done. The other may agree that war is such a total immorality that once you're in it there are no distinctions to be made and no limits upon the conduct of war." Ramsey, "Military Service as a Moral System," 12.

torture, biological weapons, nuclear weapons). These would always be off limits because they are *evil in themselves* (*mala in se*), and thus the very use of them would break the principle of the sanctity of human life because of the nature of the type of force itself.

Others in the just-war tradition, however, limit violence not due to *type* but rather by *amount*. This *violence within proportional limits* perspective stresses the need to use only the amount of force necessary for—or proportional to—the stopping of the unjust attack on the victim. In the Good Samaritan story, this would mean that the Good Samaritan not only could pray or use his body as a shield, but could also throw punches, pick up sticks, or (in a modern context) use torture or any type of biological and nuclear weapons to stop the injustice from taking place. The key to this perspective, however, is to avoid the problem of "overkill." The only legitimate force is the minimal amount necessary to stop the attack and accomplish the goal of restoring peace.

In early-church tradition, it was the position of both St. Ambrose and St. Augustine that the use of force to defend one's neighbor was a moral duty.[6] In more recent times, Paul Ramsey said:

> While Jesus taught that a disciple in his own case should turn the other cheek, he did not enjoin that his disciples should lift up the face of another oppressed man for *him* to be struck again on *his* other cheek. It is no part of the work of charity to allow this to continue to happen. Instead, it is the work of love and mercy to deliver as many as possible of God's children from tyranny, and to protect from oppression, if one can, as many of those for whom Christ died as it may be possible to save. When choice must be made between the perpetrator of injustice and the many victims of it, the latter may and should be preferred—even if effectively to do so would require the use of armed force against some evil power.[7]

Sometimes, he concluded, resorting to armed conflict "originates in the interior of the ethics of Christian love" and is therefore entirely just.[8]

Theologians and ethicists have debated for centuries over which of these views is correct. Each tradition has proponents within church history. So how do we determine which perspective is correct? We must begin by defining what we mean when we speak of *peace* and *war* and the relationship of each to a biblical concept of justice.

---

6. See Charles, *Between Pacifism and Jihad*, 37–45.
7. Ramsey, *Just War*, 143.
8. Ramsey, "Military Service as a Moral System," 15. See also Ramsey, *Just War*, 143.

Table 14.1. Three Perspectives on War

Pacifism	Just-War Tradition	Crusade
Violence and war are never justified.	War and violence are justified only in specific and limited contexts for the purpose of ending injustice, protecting the innocent, and fostering conditions for a just peace. Behavior in war is also limited.	Total war is justified to achieve ideological purity.

Defining *Justified Peace*

At the simplest level, *peace* can be defined as "the absence of conflict." To be sure, this is an important element. Understanding the nature of peace should certainly mean at the very least that we are not taking up arms against one another. The mere fact that people or nations are not fighting with one another, however, somehow seems to fall short of an ideal. In our everyday experience, the language of *peace* often invokes not merely the absence of something undesired, but also the presence of something desired. For example, when we say, "That family has a peaceful home," we typically mean far more than "that family doesn't fight." A more robust understanding conjures up ideas of harmony, agreement, or walking in one accord.

This should not be surprising to the Christian in light of the biblical notion of *peace* that comes from both the Old and New Testaments. As we mentioned earlier in the book (see chapter 4), the Hebrew concept of *peace* or *shalom* relates to an inner harmony, wholeness, or sense of completeness that results from living a life rightly ordered to God in the manner that he designed. This idea has both an individual application as an image-bearer living rightly with God and a corporate application as the people of God flourish together, living under the guidelines of God's covenantal instruction.

In the New Testament, the Greek noun commonly translated as "peace" is *eirēnē*. It is used in the Scripture not only to mean an absence of conflict or war, but also (depending on context) to convey the idea of being rightly related to oneself (internal harmony), one's community (communal harmony), and God (oneness with God—atonement).[9] This richer notion of *peace* comports completely with what we learned from Genesis 1–2 regarding the state in which God created

9. Daniel C. Arichea Jr., "Peace in the New Testament," *Practical Papers for the Bible Translator* 38, no. 2 (April 1987): 201, accessed January 17, 2020, http://www.ubs-translations.org/tbt/1987/02/TBT198702.html?seq=3.

humans to exist as well as the eternal context for which he created them (see chapters 2–5). Simply put, the will of God for humankind is to live and flourish in a state of peace. God's peace is the original context of the creation order, it is a goal of history, and it is the practical demand that God has placed on his image-bearers.[10] It is the context of existence that enables worshipers to be fully human and fully alive (flourishing), and it is the context that is symbiotically created when we live in a fully human and fully flourishing manner.

Because this notion of *peace* is grounded in the very nature of God and the manner in which he created the world, we also understand that a biblical notion of *peace* is rightly understood as a *justified peace*. Recalling our earlier discussion in chapter 9, a biblical notion of justice and justification begins and rests on Christ's work of penal substitutionary atonement. Through Christ's death and resurrection, God has made it possible for individuals to be positionally reconciled to God and thereby be counted "justified" by grace through faith in Jesus. Once a person has become a Christ-follower, the process of progressive and ongoing sanctification also involves justification in the sense of bringing one's life into alignment with God's character, design, plan, and mission. The same can also be said to be true of society as God's people once again seek to maximize his glory throughout all the earth by bringing the hope of the gospel to bear on every square inch of creation—*as far as the curse is found*.

Justified peace involves the seeking of *shalom*. It involves not only the preaching of the gospel, that individuals may be rescued and restored to a right relationship with God, but also that each of them individually and all of them corporately might experience the flourishing that God designed for them individually and as a society.

Defining *Just War*

In the previous chapter on capital punishment, we defined *crime* to be "any behavior or activity that violates a society's legal code." When we discuss war, we can describe the choices and activities leading up to and causing war as a type of crime committed against the civic peace (*tranquillitas ordinis*) or, more fully, the "peace on earth" that God intended for his creation.[11] This does not necessarily mean that *an armed response* to massive injustice through the waging of war is immoral, inherently wrong, or "criminal," nor does it mean that *participation* in war is evil by default. The *causes* of war are what is criminal. Injustice is the evil, not the response and not necessarily the use of force. If a response to evil is properly ordered in accord with God's moral character, and then engaged for the right

---

10. Oliver O'Donovan, *The Just War Revisited* (Cambridge: Cambridge University Press, 2003), 1–2.

11. For a discussion of war as a type of crime, see Michael Walzer, *Just and Unjust Wars: A Moral Argument with Historical Illustrations*, 5th ed. (New York: Basic, 2015), 21–33.

purposes, it can then be described as a *just response* to wickedness and evil in an attempt to restore or make peace. War can be a form of retributive punishment with the ultimate goal of appropriately addressing evil and restoring the moral order that makes a peaceful society possible.

With these distinctions in mind, then, we find the following definition to be a helpful and clear description of war:

> the freely chosen use of physical and usually deadly force by one political community against another political community to compel the latter to submit to a social, political, economic, or ideological objective.[12]

This description, however, is merely factual. What it lacks is the ability to tell us whether the war itself is moral or not. It lacks clarity on evaluating whether the war itself is right or wrong, good or evil, just or unjust.

A *just war* would need just reasons to freely engage the use of force to compel an opposing political community to submit. In the absence of a just cause, the war would be considered an *unjust war*. Minimally, the goal of a just war would be to bring cessation to conflict. Ideally, it would restore a context in which humans could flourish both as individuals and as a society. Maximally, it would culminate in an eternal state of peace, as it will in the eschaton (Rev. 19). With these ideas in mind, then, we can say that a just war involves *the justified use of physical force by one political community against another political community to compel the latter to submit to a social, political, economic, or ideological objective in keeping with the minimal goal of ending injustice, the ideal goal of establishing a context for human flourishing, and ultimately to foster the conditions for a complete and lasting just peace.*

Having provided a definition for these basic terms and concepts, we now move to a discussion of the scriptural and theological foundations that must drive our understanding of the ethics of war. Once we have done so, we can then address what criteria are necessary to justify the use of war in the pursuit of a just peace.

Biblical and Theological Foundations

The Nature of God Is the Center of the Discussion
The Holiness of God, the Sin of Humans, and the Hope of the Gospel
From a distinctly Christian point of view, it is important that we place the quest for peace and the possibility of using war as a means of achieving it within the context of the paradigm of creation, fall, redemption, and restoration that we have been appealing to throughout the book. The discussion about war ultimately

---

12. Allman, *Who Would Jesus Kill?*, 15.

relates to one's view of God, his nature, the problem of sin, and the role that Christ's disciples should play in the *now and not yet* context of history in which the people of God currently exist. We are Jesus' disciples born again into his kingdom, and yet he has left us here to be in the world as salt and light (Matt. 5; John 15). We are citizens of the City of God while sojourning in the City of Man.

God is holy. He is opposed to evil. He is free from sin, and he will not tolerate sin in his presence. God hates the injustice that arises from sin. He will hold it accountable, judge it, and punish it. This, in fact, is the very reason why Christ's penal substitutionary atonement was necessary. The death of Christ was the necessary means of atonement precisely because retributive justice was the appropriate means of settling the debt that humans had incurred. As the apostle Paul reminds us, Jesus took on our sin (it was imputed to him):

> [God] made [Jesus] who knew no sin to be sin on our behalf, so that we might become the righteousness of God in Him. (2 Cor. 5:21)

And in full agreement, the Divine Trinity deemed Jesus' death to be the proper cost of atonement as he died in our place:

> But God demonstrates His own love toward us, in that while we were yet sinners, Christ died for us. (Rom. 5:8)

Love and Justice

In a biblical worldview, there is no ultimate conflict between love and justice because both are rooted in the nature and character of God, and both are central in the gospel. Because this is true and because the Divine Trinity in full and willing agreement ordained that the second person of the Trinity (Jesus) be killed on our behalf, there is also no necessary conflict between the determination to kill and the expression of love, justice, or both. God chose the killing of Jesus as the basis of the gospel (see Isa. 53:4–5, 10: Jesus was "smitten of God" and "crushed" by God for our iniquities). To deny that killing is in line with God's moral character is to deny the gospel.

In regard to the question of war, whether any particular Christian stands for or against military engagement usually depends on how he or she reconciles two core Christian *virtues* and then negotiates two Christian *principles* to arrive at a conclusion related to the use of force. In regard to the *virtues*, there is a question about how to reconcile God's love with his holy and just character. From a historically orthodox point of view, God has revealed himself to be the perfect embodiment of *both* love and justice. It is therefore unwise to pit these attributes of God against each other. Those who want to reduce God's character merely to love without consideration of all the other characteristics that God reveals about himself (that he is holy, just, kind, good, and so on) are in danger of creating a caricature of God. It reduces God to a type of sentimentalism that is in denial of the hard demands of love. Yes, Scripture tells us that "God is love" (1 John 4:8), but it does not say that he is "only love" or that "love is God." Rather, as the Gospel of John tells us, it is precisely because God so loved the world that Christ died (John 3:16). Or as Paul teaches us, love is demonstrated by God's sending Christ to die (Rom. 5:8). Because of the demands of God's justice, God's love is invoked to act. Similarly, because God is loving, he cannot overlook injustice. To do so would be to say that people such as Adolf Hitler need not be held accountable for heinous crimes, that God can overlook them, and that no final reckoning need be made for such atrocities. To confuse or deny this point is to make impotent the effectual work of Christ on the cross for salvation. It was God's love that compelled him to live and die on our behalf, but it was God's justice and wrath toward sin that was appeased through the violent yet loving act of Christ's atoning death.

The views of those who want to deny the possibility of Christian involvement in war based on a sentimentalized understanding of love or a similarly romanti-cized vision of a "loving Jesus" are rather easily dismissed. As we will point out in our final section of this chapter, any argument for a pacifistic position *from such perspectives* would not be truly Christian. Historically, orthodox versions of both the pacifist and just-war traditions recognize that God's love and his justice are equally important considerations when deliberating the question of how (or whether) a Christian should engage in flesh-and-blood wars.

The question then shifts to how best to honor both the loving and just nature of God by negotiating between the *principles* of neighbor love and honoring the sanctity of human life. As Paul Christopher rightly points out, "these two moral inclinations or precepts seem to be at the center of debate concerning when to wage war and how to wage it."[13] From the *pacifistic* point of view, it can be argued that love requires one to honor every human being as a neighbor—including one's enemy. Similarly, justice demands that one uphold the value of life of every image-bearer—even one's enemy. The principle of the sanctity of human life is inter-preted to mean that no one should ever be killed. Intentionally taking human life in war, even the life of an enemy, would be contrary to the principles of neighbor love and the sanctity of human life.

On the other hand, from the *just-war* point of view, it can be argued that while every neighbor must be loved, that same love requires that one come to the aid of the oppressed and unjustly treated. Likewise, it is precisely because all lives are sacred that the lives of the innocent must be defended—even if it sometimes requires the

---

13. Paul Christopher, *The Ethics of War and Peace* (Upper Saddle River, NJ: Prentice Hall, 1999), 1.

taking of the guilty party's life to do so. In this case, the principle of the sanctity of life is understood with a nuance pertaining to a person's guilt or innocence. In certain contexts, intentionally taking the life of those who have relinquished the right to live because of their moral guilt would be the proper expression of neighbor love.

Thus, the Christian must determine whether the use of force is ever an appropriate means to honor the sanctity of life and express neighbor love as a proper means to acquiring peace. If, based on the interpretation of scriptural passages such as Matthew 5:38–39, 43–44 (in which Jesus admonishes his followers to "turn the other cheek" when wronged and to "pray for those who persecute you"), the believer arrives at pacifistic convictions, then any consideration of the use of violence as a means to moral justice must be jettisoned from the start. For such a person, war is never the right choice of action regardless of what justifying cause there might be. On the other hand, if Scripture teaches that the use of force and even the taking of life can be a legitimate means of protection and a proper expression of neighbor love, then the question shifts from whether it is permissible to use force to how one justifies the use of force and what expression of force is appropriate in any given circumstance.

The Bible and Killing

What does the Bible teach about the use of coercive force and the possibility of using enough force to intentionally take a human life? As we discussed at length in the previous chapter, Scripture plainly teaches that all human life is sacred. The principle of the sanctity of human life rests on the creation narrative of Genesis 1–2, is reiterated in the account of God's instructions to Noah after the flood (Gen. 9:6), is affirmed by the sixth commandment (Ex. 20:13), and is generally affirmed throughout the text of Scripture. We also recognize, however, that the sanctity-of-life principle does not prohibit all taking of human life. A clear distinction is made throughout the Bible between the protections put in place to guard the life of the innocent and, when appropriate, punishing the guilty through the taking of life. The language of the sixth commandment helps us understand this distinction:

You shall not *murder*. (Ex. 20:13)

As we pointed out in the previous chapter, the word translated "murder" in this passage is the Hebrew verb *ratsakh*. Throughout the Old Testament, this word is used to indicate specifically the wrongful taking of human life.[14] In fact, nowhere

14. Old Testament scholar Mark Rooker provides a brief but informative discussion of the Hebrew root in Mark F. Rooker, *The Ten Commandments: Ethics for the Twenty-First Century* (Nashville: B&H Academic, 2010), 123–29.

in the Bible is the word *ratsakh* used to describe the killing of plants, the killing of animals, or the taking of human life in war or capital punishment. Indeed, in the vast majority of places where God commands his people to take a human life, the Hebrew word used is not *ratsakh* but *muth*.[15] The use of this distinct word indicates that God considers some forms of the taking of human life to be morally distinct from others and therefore not subject to the prohibition given in the sixth commandment.[16] One can conclude, at the very least, that while God expressly prohibits the wrongful taking of innocent life (i.e., murder, *ratsakh*), there is no absolute prohibition against the taking of human life (i.e., killing, *muth*).

The Bible and War

God Commands War

We are now left with this question: "When is it appropriate to take a human life?" In our chapter on capital punishment, we pointed out that God gave specific instructions to his people to put to death those who are guilty of various crimes (Lev. 24:17; Deut. 22:25). Not only did certain behaviors warrant death, but in certain contexts God mandated it and delegated the authority to the government to employ the death penalty. When it comes to the topic of war, we discover many places in the Bible where God does exactly the same thing. Scripture indicates that God not only permits his people to go to war, but many times commands it (e.g., Num. 31:1–3; 1 Sam. 15:1–3). In fact, as the Israelites are preparing to go to war to conquer the promised land (Num. 32), the tribes of Reuben and Gad are told that not going to war would be sinful (Num. 32:6–7, 20–23). Even more, in many places Scripture indicates that God is fighting *for* Israel (Ex. 14:13–14; Deut. 7:1–6; 20:4; Josh. 1:9).

While there is little direct discussion about the ethics of war in the New Testament, God clearly presents himself as a warrior whose perfect justice includes the waging of war to bring final consummation to the age (Rev. 19:11–21). Despite disagreement about the nature of the apocalyptic language in the book of Revelation and the degree to which it should be understood literally, one could certainly make the argument that if God were morally opposed to war, then he would not use immoral imagery to describe the culminating moment of his final triumph.

We can learn three very specific things from passages such as these where God

---

15. Strong's, 4191, accessed April 8, 2020, https://biblehub.com/hebrew/4191.htm. Wayne Grudem points out that of the forty-nine instances of *ratsakh* in the Old Testament, it is used only once in reference to capital punishment and never used in reference to killing in war. Wayne Grudem, *Christian Ethics: An Introduction to Biblical Moral Reasoning* (Wheaton, IL: Crossway, 2018), 505, 527.

16. For example, consider instances in which death is inflicted by God himself, such as in the case of the sons of Aaron in Leviticus 10:2, an ox in Exodus 21:29, idolaters in Deuteronomy 17:2–7, and Sabbath-breakers in Exodus 35:2.

commands his people to take life specifically through engaging in warfare. First, God is not opposed to the taking of human life in certain circumstances. Second, he is not categorically opposed to human beings' taking the life of other human beings. Third, God is not opposed to warfare in principle. If he commands it and at times wages it, it cannot be contrary to his nature, nor can it always be wrong.

Did Jesus Restrict Christians?

While Scripture indicates that God gave direct commands to his people regarding the taking of life in war, this does not necessarily mean that Christians should support or participate in war. One could make the case that Jesus restricts Christian participation in war in order to highlight a movement away from violence and killing as a sign of the coming kingdom of God in which there will be an end to all wars. To be sure, the biblical language lends some credence to this position. Jesus' instructions in the Gospels certainly have some pacifistic strains as they relate to his personal disciples and moral behavior. As we have noted, those who hold a pacifistic perspective often cite Matthew 5:38–39 to make this very point. Romans 12:19–21 is also often cited in support of this perspective:

> Never take your own revenge, beloved, but leave room for the wrath of God, for it is written, "Vengeance is Mine, I will repay," says the Lord. "But if your enemy is hungry, feed him, and if he is thirsty, give him a drink; for in so doing you will heap burning coals on his head." Do not be overcome by evil, but overcome evil with good.

This is why some argue that when Jesus told his disciple to put away his sword in Matthew 26:52, he, in effect, disarmed the church forever.[17]

While there can be no doubt that Jesus' instructions seek to limit a hate-filled use of violence and highlight sacrificial service as the default disposition of his disciples, we are hardly warranted to presume from these texts that his instructions forbid the use of force to protect the innocent. Rather, each of these passages should be understood as Jesus' instructing his disciples about the tendency in the human heart to allow hatred and revenge to be the motivation for using force against others. Earlier in Matthew 5, Jesus indicated that the sixth commandment prohibits not only wrongful killing, but even hatred in the heart (Matt. 5:21–26). In Romans 12:19, the passage specifically indicates that it is wrong to "take your own revenge," but it does not say that punishing crime is wrong or that a Christian

---

17. Tertullian famously wrote, "But how will a Christian man war, nay, how will he serve even in peace, without a sword, which the Lord has taken away?" Tertullian, *On Idolatry*, ed. Alexander Roberts, James Donaldson, and A. Cleveland Coxe, trans. S. Thelwall, Ante-Nicene Fathers 3 (Buffalo: Christian Literature, 1885), accessed April 3, 2020, http://www.newadvent.org/fathers/0302.htm.

cannot participate in a legal system that punishes crime. The clear context is that God instructs his followers not to be dominated by hateful or evil intentions.

Are such intentions descriptive of the just-war perspective? May it never be! As we will see later in the discussion, a faithful disciple who holds the convictions of a just warrior is not eager to go to war. He does not want to kill; instead, his longing is for social peace and the personal salvation of even his enemy. What the just warrior desires is the right application of love and justice for both the innocent and guilty such that we can attain peace. He longs to be a peacemaker. For this reason, he would never go to war if God did not give permission to do so and the context of his neighbor did not demand it.

We have seen, however, that God has certainly given permission to his people to go to war in the past. Again, as we have seen in the previous chapter, Paul's teachings in Romans 13:1–7 seem to indicate rather clearly that God has delegated his authority to civil governments to act as "servants" or "ministers" (*diakonos*)[18] of his cause and to use the "sword" as a means of ensuring justice for all our neighbors who make up society (see our fuller discussion in the previous chapter on capital punishment). As J. Daryl Charles puts it, "God has ordained 'the sword' in the hand of governing authorities for the express purpose of limiting as well as punishing evildoers, thereby safeguarding society."[19]

For the believer who is willing to turn the other cheek and not repay evil for evil with a heart of hatred or vile revenge, this is a great comfort. Even in the midst of this fallen and broken world, God has provided a means for lives to be protected, justice to be served, and peace to be pursued so that humans might flourish in an ordered society. Even in the *now and not yet*, there can be an approximation of the just peace that will one day be fully realized in heaven.

Table 14.2. Was Jesus a Pacifist?

Yes	No
One of God's names is Prince of Peace.	One of God's names is Mighty Warrior (*El Shaddai*).
Sermon on the Mount—blessed are the peacemakers; turn the other cheek.	Sermon on the Mount—primarily a personal ethic encouraging believers to avoid hatred and murderous motives.
Disarmed the disciple in Gethsemane (Matt. 26:52).	Uses force to drive out money-changers.
Refused to call angels to war for him at his arrest (Matt. 26:53).	Is depicted as a righteous warrior in Revelation 19.

18. From which we get the English word *deacon*. BibleHub, accessed April 7, 2020, https://biblehub.com/greek/1249.htm.

19. Charles, *Between Pacifism and Jihad*, 15.

Can Christians Participate in War?

One could protest that while God may have ordained civil governments to use the sword, that does not necessarily mean that Christians can be a part of those civil governments. More specifically, it does not necessarily free a believer to be a part of the military arm of the government if killing would likely need to take place at some point in time. Interestingly enough, however, nowhere does the New Testament explicitly forbid a Christian's participation in government, the military, or war. While one might infer that God disarmed the church when he disarmed the disciple in Gethsemane (Matt. 26:52), such an interpretation is speculative and not ultimately persuasive. In fact, in several examples in the New Testament, military personnel are addressed in the context of their conversion to faith, and in neither situation are they instructed to leave their military profession. Not only is this the case with the soldiers who come to John the Baptist and ask for instructions on proper repentance (Luke 3:14), it is also the case with the Roman centurion Cornelius as he comes to faith and is then baptized by Peter in Caesarea (Acts 10:1, 44–48).[20]

Regarding Matthew 26:52 and Jesus' instructions to the disciple to put away his sword, one could ask why after three years of teaching he was carrying a sword in the first place. Possibly Jesus told him to put it away in Gethsemane not because wielding it was inherently wrong, but because the disciple in question personally did not have the authority to do so and perhaps his heart was full of the kind of vile hatred that Jesus warned against in Matthew 5:21–26.

An important distinction present throughout the Bible identifies both a personal ethic and a public responsibility. While there is sometimes a tension between the two, there need not be a fundamental conflict between them. Otherwise, God would not have, and indeed *could* not have, commanded his image-bearers to go to war in any era. An individual can act in the name of God as a government representative serving the community under its authority to do things that if the individual did under his or her own authority would be morally reprehensible. This conclusion, in fact, has been the majority position throughout most of the long history of the church.[21]

In order for one to faithfully honor both the principle of the sanctity of human life and the impulse of neighbor love to protect the innocent through the means of war, one must always resist hatred and revenge as motives for action. Likewise, there

---

20. James Turner Johnson notes that there is evidence for early Christian participation in the military. He states, "In fact, . . . there is clear documentary evidence of a sizable presence of Christians in the Roman army from the year 174, and from this may be inferred an earlier acceptance of the possibility of military service for Christians, dating perhaps to the beginning of the second century." James Turner Johnson, *The Quest for Peace: Three Moral Traditions in Western Cultural History* (Princeton, NJ: Princeton University Press, 1987), 15–16.

21. Johnson has a helpful discussion on the views of war in church history. His first chapter, dealing with the early church, is especially helpful. See Johnson, 3–66.

must be clarity on the reasons for going to war as well as great restraint, discipline, and clear guidelines in regard to how one engages in warfare once war is waged.

The Just-War Criteria

We turn now to a discussion of what has come to be known as the *just-war criteria*. Various versions of just-war theory can be traced back both to the Old Testament and to classical Greek philosophy. In the fourth century, the concept was brought directly into Christian thought by both Ambrose and Augustine.[22] It was later affirmed by Thomas Aquinas in the thirteenth century and sanctioned by both Martin Luther and John Calvin in the Reformation. In contemporary thought, just-war theory represents the majority position (albeit to varying degrees) in both the Catholic and Protestant traditions.[23] The principles of just war can be divided into two closely related categories, both of which make up the just-war criteria. *Jus ad bellum* is the category of principles used to determine when it is appropriate (or not) to go to war, and *jus in bello* is the category that regulates the appropriateness of conduct in war. Two questions, then, will guide the following discussion: How do we determine when it is permissible to go to war? What are the proper means of war?[24]

Jus ad Bellum—How Do We Determine When It Is Permissible to Go to War?
Legitimate Authority
The criterion of *legitimate authority* is the foundational stone on which lie all the principles of just war.[25] This principle entails that decisions to go to war

22. St. Augustine argued that war itself is not evil but that the motive and intentions of governing authorities and soldiers may be evil because of their "love of violence, revengeful cruelty, fierce and implacable hatred of the enemy, wild resistance, the lust of power, and such like." For the just warrior, however, he argued that "it is generally to punish these things, when force is required to inflict the punishment, that, in obedience to God or some lawful authority, good men undertake wars, when they find themselves in such a position as regards the conduct of human affairs that right conduct requires them to act, or to make others act in this way." Augustine, *Contra Faustum*, 22.74, accessed January 19, 2020, http://www.newadvent.org /fathers/140622.htm.

23. For a fuller discussion of the history of both pacifism and just-war theory within Christendom, see Allman, *Who Would Jesus Kill?*, chaps. 2, 4. See also J. Daryl Charles and Timothy J. Demy, *War, Peace, and Christianity: Questions and Answers from a Just-War Perspective* (Wheaton, IL: Crossway, 2010), pt. 2.

24. There is a growing discussion about a third category of just-war theory—*jus post bellum*—that asks questions about postwar justice. While this discussion is not part of the classic just-war theory, it is a legitimate topic of discussion. Our chapter will not delve into this category, but we acknowledge that postwar justice is worthy of future discussion. See Gary J. Bass, "Jus Post Bellum," *Philosophy & Public Affairs* 32, no. 4 (October 2004): 384–412.

25. A. J. Coates argues that not only is it foundational but it is perhaps also the most neglected of the principles, as evidenced by what he describes as "the popular assessment of contemporary terrorism." A. J. Coates, *The Ethics of War* (Manchester, UK: Manchester University Press, 1997), 123. He argues that modern

466 The Application of Ethics as Worship

can be made only by an authority with the legal right to do so.[26] The remaining principles of just war become operative only after the question "by what standard is justice being judged?" has been asked. It has become common in the modern renditions of just-war theories to seek the establishment of this criterion through an appeal either to the governing documents of a nation-state (such as the U.S. Constitution and the War Powers Act) or, as was the case with the 1991 Gulf War, to a world body such as the United Nations Security Council to issue a resolution in favor of the use of force. While such sources of authority may be the highest level that a secular world is willing to acknowledge, Christian ethics recognizes a superior source. From a Christian perspective, legitimate authority rests on a normative morality revealed in and through the creation (general revelation and natural law) and specified in and through scriptural revelation. All other just-war considerations, then, depend on whether the moral claim to go to war stems from the legitimizing source of God's revelation.

This interpretation of legitimate authority becomes problematic when neither general revelation nor special revelation specifically addresses the particular circumstances of a given war. For example, whether the United Nations should have supported the use of force by the U.S. military in Iraq in 2003 or whether the United States should go to war with North Korea today is not a question specifically addressed by the biblical text. This is not to say, however, that Scripture is unhelpful in making such decisions. Rather, Scripture is clear that legal authority for the enforcement of moral justice resides with the systems of human government that "bear the sword" (John 19:11; Rom. 13:1–7). All authority is from God, and nation-states are ideally to be an accurate representation of that authority. For this reason, they are to serve in this world as the legitimizing authority behind the enforcement of justice. Thomas Aquinas makes this point by arguing that righteous use of war must come from

> the authority of the sovereign by whose command war is waged. For it is not the business of a private individual to declare war, because he can seek for redress of his rights from the tribunal of his superior. . . . And just as it is lawful for them to have recourse to the sword in defending that common weal against internal disturbances, when they punish evil-doers, . . . so too, it is their business to have

---

evaluation of terrorism wrongly relies on a critique more of the category of just cause than of legitimate authority. No doubt his conclusion is right and reflects a postmodern epistemology wherein no legitimate authority can arbitrate over all different traditions and perspectives. But on such reasoning, one would have to admit that there is likewise no real foundation for arguing a just cause or even proportionality or discrimination.

26. Richard J. Regan, *Just War: Principles and Cases* (Washington, DC: Catholic University of America Press, 1996), 20.

recourse to the sword of war in defending the common weal against external enemies.[27]

The legitimate authority of the state, however, is not without limits, nor is it de facto correct. The stark reality in a fallen world is that nation-states that wield God-given authority all comprise sinful men and women. It is vital, therefore, that the moral authority of any government (and governmental leaders) flow out of a higher moral law. A state need not be a "Christian state" or a theocracy to align itself with the general moral order present in creation. All human government, however, must ultimately bend the knee to the moral authority of God evident in the creation through general revelation or natural law and specified in the revealed Word of God. The degree to which it does so in any given situation is the degree to which any particular government will use its moral authority righteously. Francis Schaeffer comments toward this end that "it is time we consciously realize that when any office commands what is contrary to God's Law it abrogates its authority. And our loyalty to the God who gave this law then requires that we make the appropriate response."[28]

For this reason, simply because a country claims that it has the moral authority to declare a war just does not mean that the war actually *is* just.[29] Christians must prayerfully seek illumination from the Holy Spirit when considering whether to support governmental use of force. Militaristic claims that a Christian (or anyone else) is duty-bound to participate in or support *every* war in which his or her government engages are misplaced. Clearly, Scripture teaches that Pharaoh was unjust to condemn the Hebrew children (Ex. 1), and Jesus' parents were right to flee the country when Herod attempted to unjustly slaughter the children of Bethlehem (Matt. 2). Compliance with the use of military force by these two governing authorities would clearly have been wrong and unjust. Christians must remember that while allegiance to one's country is noble, no flag should fly higher than the Christian flag. Properly determining whether a country should go to war requires that the justifying reasons to go to war rise above simplistic forms of nationalism.

27. Thomas Aquinas, *Summa Theologica*, trans. Fathers of the English Dominican Province (Notre Dame, IN: Christian Classics, 1981), 2–2.40.1 reply.

28. Francis Schaeffer, *A Christian Manifesto* (Westchester, IL: Crossway, 1981), 131–32.

29. This discussion obviously engages the larger question raised by the title of Alasdair MacIntyre's book *Whose Justice? Which Rationality?* (Notre Dame, IN: University of Notre Dame Press, 1988). That is, when two nations both claim that opposing reasons justifying war are correct, the question of legitimate authority boils down to one of worldview superiority. For example, if tensions arise in the Middle East due to claims of opposing moral beliefs based on differing commitments to religious orthodoxies, then who is to say which side holds a greater moral authority? From a clearly Christian point of view, this problem demonstrates why Christians must first and foremost be concerned with the task of evangelism (spiritual warfare) as the ultimate battleground and place where true hope for peace rests.

Just-war criteria demand that the legitimate authority not rest merely on the conventions of men, mere loyalty to a nation-state, or the tempting slogan of "might makes right." Rather, legitimate authority for any nation is tightly linked to its alliance with divinely revealed morality that indicates that a clear injustice needs reckoning with.

For this reason, once a governing authority declares that a particular war is just, it is then the responsibility of each individual citizen to decide whether he or she can conscientiously obey the state's order. One would hope that the state's determination aligns with objective moral principles and that the decision to engage in warfare is correct. Likewise, one would hope that a potential soldier would carefully consider this reality before enlisting (if that is an option). If, however, the individual soldier believes that the determination of the state is wrong or unjust, he or she has the "moral right" to obey the majesty of his or her own conscience and the "moral duty" to resist the governing authority on that point.[30] "Conscientious objection may well be necessary and legitimate in a situation in which one or more persons cannot fail to see that the cause for which the state is arming or waging war is concretely an evil one."[31] Obviously, a "moral right" may not equate with a "legal right" in a given country; nevertheless, both the social and personal appeals to legitimate authority are foundational to evaluating whether a state or a person (respectively) can go to war.[32]

Just Cause

Just cause follows on the heels of legitimate authority as the second most important principle of *jus ad bellum*. *Just cause* refers to the reason for going to war.

---

30. If a Christian confronts a situation in which he or she is uncertain whether to support a country's decision to go to war, or if a particular action in war that the Christian is being required to participate in appears to be contrary to God's moral authority, then he or she must consider the costs of conscientious objection. In such a case, he or she should first pray for wisdom and discernment (James 1:5–6). Second, this person will have to decide whether he or she is willing to defy an order. Such a decision is not without biblical warrant, as we see in Acts 5:29. Third, if one does choose to defy the governing authority, then that individual must be prepared to suffer the consequences of his or her choice. The consequences could range in a given country from jail time to a death sentence. In such a scenario, there is biblical warrant to flee the country (1 Sam. 19:10–12; Matt. 2; 2 Cor. 11:33). Finally, in this regard it may also be important for the Christian to consider whether there are alternative methods to serve in a context in which, even though he or she may disagree with the overall intent of the war, he or she can find a place within the war context to provide a Christian influence for good. Examples could be those who are serving in the chaplaincy and the medical rescue units. Great care would need to be taken, however, so as not to be tacitly implying an overall support for the war or the particular strategy in question.

31. Karl Barth, *The Doctrine of Creation*, ed. G. W. Bromiley and T. F. Torrance, trans. A. T. Mackay et al., vol. 3.4 of *Church Dogmatics* (London: T. & T. Clark, 2004), 468.

32. James F. Childress, "Just-War Theories: The Bases, Interrelations, Priorities, and Functions of Their Criteria," *MCR* (Fall 1982): 28.

A legitimate authority can wage war only if justice is the underlying cause. Richard Regan notes: "The justice of the cause of waging war involves two elements. First, the aim of a nation waging war should be to prevent or rectify wrongful, that is, unjust action by another nation against itself or a third nation. Second, there should be a due, that is, just, proportion between the wrong to be prevented or rectified and the human and material destruction that the war can be reasonably expected to entail."[33] In order for a cause to be just, it must be right and good as judged by its evaluation in light of clear biblical commands or principles (*revealed morality*), such as unjust oppression. Simply put, having a just cause means that a serious enough moral issue has emerged to justify the use of force in order to satisfy the requirements of neighbor love. Note that this criterion recognizes not simply that there is an abrogation of justice, but that the injustice is a sufficiently serious reason to warrant the use of war.

The importance of clarifying the just cause is captured nicely by A. J. Coates: "a one-sided and exaggerated emphasis on just cause may generate moral triumphalism and moral enthusiasm for war that transforms a 'just war' into a 'holy' or crusading war. . . . The absolute conviction that their cause is just . . . may encourage combatants to override the moral limits of war or to neglect other equally weighty moral considerations."[34] The truth of this point provides sufficient reason for attempting to identify what actually qualifies as a just cause. Secular notions of just war will often appeal to the notion of whether "a group of reasonable, unbiased persons" would concur with the state's determination. Indeed, such a perspective is not without warrant. Given the sheer number of differing ideologies represented in a pluralist state, however, total agreement may be elusive regardless of what may appear to some as a simple or obvious just cause. Therefore, public affirmation is desired but not necessary to satisfy this criterion unless it is so constitutionally ordered by a nation's own laws. The crucial point is that the evaluation of a just cause must fall under the jurisdiction of a legitimate authority and also be shaped by the remaining principles of just war.

Right Intent

The third criterion for just war is *right intent*. This principle derives from the motivation to satisfy the just cause as a demonstration of neighbor love for both the victim and the attacker. As we have argued throughout this chapter and the previous one, the chosen intention and behavior must not be shaped by a desire for revenge or motivated by an abiding hatred or jingoistic mentality. Scripture is clear that the role of vengeance belongs to God alone (Rom. 12:19). It is the place

33. Regan, *Just War*, 48.
34. Coates, *Ethics of War*, 146.

of the governing body not to seek revenge, but to amend the injustice that has occurred and perhaps seek to prevent future like occurrences. "The right intention of those waging war is required, that is, they must intend to promote the good and to avoid evil. Hence Augustine writes, 'among true worshipers of God those wars are looked on as peacemaking which are waged neither from aggrandizement nor cruelty, but with the object of securing peace, of repressing the evil and supporting the good.'"[35] Augustine amplifies the foundation of this criterion when he comments that the greatest form of evil in war is the possible motives of "love of violence, revengeful cruelty, fierce and implacable enmity, wild resistance and the lust of power."[36]

It is also wise to recognize that intentionality should not be solely geared toward the restoration of peace if *peace* is defined as "the absence of conflict." Such an end can be achieved through the eradication of the enemy. This approach, however, would result in a greater moral travesty than the one that gave initial just cause for war. For this reason, the intention must be to satisfy the just cause with an eye toward at least the moral compliance on the part of the renegade state and ideally a congruently repentant spirit. Clarity on this issue is vital, since it will influence much of the way in which the battle is engaged once it begins.

Last Resort

Romans 12:18 teaches, "If possible, so far as it depends on you, be at peace with all men." Thus, as the fourth criterion of just war, *last resort* demands that every reasonable effort should be made to resolve the conflict in a peaceful manner before waging war. Karl Barth writes, "Christian ethics cannot insist too loudly that such mass slaughter [from warfare] might well be mass murder, and therefore that this final possibility should not be seized like any other, but only at the very last hour in the darkest of days."[37] If, after careful evaluation and painstaking efforts to avoid the use of force through diplomacy or other types of sanction, no morally preferable alternatives remain, then the use of force is justified. As Schaeffer puts it: "there does come a time when force, even physical force, is appropriate. The Christian is not to take the law into his own hands and become a law unto himself. But when all avenues to flight and protest have closed, force . . . is appropriate."[38]

With this stipulation in mind, however, it is also important to consider that "the requirement that war be the last resort does not mean that all possible measures

---

35. Aquinas, *Summa Theologica*, 2–2.40.1 reply.

36. Augustine, *Reply to Faustus the Manichean*, 22, quoted in *War and Christian Ethics: Classic and Contemporary Readings on the Morality of War*, ed. Arthur F. Holmes, 2nd ed. (Grand Rapids: Baker, 2005), 64.

37. Barth, *Church Dogmatics*, 3.4:456.

38. Schaeffer, *Christian Manifesto*, 117.

have to be attempted and exhausted if there is no reasonable expectation that they will be successful."[39] There comes a point at which one must evaluate whether more options or lack of action become more harmful than good. In order for the just-war criteria to have any real potency, some actual point of accountability must be set and *acted on*. Otherwise, the offending nation will have no incentive to desist in its hostilities, change its practices, or comply with stated objectives set by the legitimate authority.

Proportionality

The fifth criterion, *proportionality*, is founded on the virtue of practical wisdom. *Proportionality* means that in regard to the war as a whole, the type of military force selected is the least possible commensurate with achieving the action's primary goal. War is never right, no matter how just the cause, unless proportionality can be established between military/political objectives and their price. In the end, one must have reason to believe that more good will be done than undone, or a greater measure of evil prevented. But of all the tests for judging whether to resort to or participate in war, this one balancing an evil or good effect against another is open to the greatest uncertainty.[40] Because of the inexact nature of any proportional evaluation in a distinctively Christian ethic, this principle must rank behind the four clearer biblical principles listed above. The danger in placing it any higher is the tendency to adopt a utilitarian "ends justifies the means" mentality that enables pragmatism to override biblical principles of proper conduct and motives.

Reasonable Prospect of Achievement

Finally, once a legitimate authority has established a just cause, finds that its motivation is rightly intended, seeks every other avenue of conflict resolution available, and maps out a proportional scheme of attack, practical wisdom also requires an evaluation of whether the moral objective necessitating the infringement has a *reasonable prospect of achievement*. In the words of Jesus:

> Or what king, when he sets out to meet another king in battle, will not first sit down and consider whether he is strong enough with ten thousand men to encounter the one coming against him with twenty thousand? Or else, while the other is still far away, he sends a delegation and asks for terms of peace. (Luke 14:31–32)

It is the responsibility of the legitimate authority to weigh the prospects of success in war and determine whether the war can be won. In most circumstances,

---

39. Childress, "Just-War Theories," 28.
40. Ramsey, *Just War*, 195.

a government should not wage war unless the prospect of achievement is in its favor. Granted, this is a very subjective principle because no one can perfectly predict the future. But a legitimate authority that has been diligent to walk through the steps of just war will likely have a reasonable understanding of its prospect for success.

As with the previous criterion, this one is at the end of the list because it may lead to a utilitarian approach to waging war. In addition, there may be times when a reasonable prospect of achievement does not exist, yet war must still be waged. Even though practical wisdom suggests that a government should look after the survival of its people, it is foreseeable that a context could arise in which the type of evil being perpetrated is so great that even though there is no likely successful outcome, it is better to fight than not. In such a case, the virtue of love may compel the attempt to wage war even in the face of what appears to be the overwhelming likelihood that the attempt will fail. Sometimes it is better to try and die than not try at all. "Greater love has no one than this, that one lay down his life for his friends" (John 15:13).

Jus in Bello—What Are the Proper Means of War?

Having satisfied the criteria for going to war, the conduct of just warriors in battle (*jus in bello*) must also be tempered by limiting criteria in order to preserve Christian neighbor love. Just behavior in war depends much on the preceding principles justifying going to war. For example, if peaceful resolution is the intended goal and *peace* is defined simply as "the absence of conflict," then total annihilation of the enemy via weapons of mass destruction would be not only a justifiable means to the end, but arguably the best choice, for it could be accomplished the quickest.[41] The intended goal would have been met, but at the cost of genocide and mass murder.

If, however, the correct aim of war is a *just peace*, then John Rawls is helpful when he points out that "the means employed must not destroy the possibility of peace or encourage a contempt for human life that puts the safety of ourselves and of mankind in jeopardy."[42] For Christians, utilitarian ideas such as "all is fair in love and war" and "war is hell, so fight like a hellion" are not acceptable. The motivating virtue of neighbor love takes on a definite shape when it is informed by scriptural principles such as the sanctity of human life, which then guides and limits behavior regardless of situation or circumstance. Therefore, while neighbor love provides the impetus for engaging in a just war, this proper motive does not legitimize any kind of behavior. That which justifies war must also rein it in.

---

41. Childress, "Just-War Theories," 48.

42. John Rawls, *A Theory of Justice* (Cambridge, MA: Harvard University Press, 1971), 113–14.

For a Christian just-war theory, the behavior of warriors in combat must be subject to the *deontological limits established by God and his Word.* These limits form the logical foundation on which the following criteria rest. Norman Geisler argues that "no individual member of the armed forces of any country should be excused for engaging in a war crime simply because they have been ordered to commit the act by a superior officer. Evil is evil whether a government commands it or not."[43] Just behavior in war requires acting in light of the limits that rest on scriptural principles to guide such questions as "who may be attacked?" and "how may they be attacked?"

Discrimination

The first criterion, *discrimination* (or *noncombatant immunity*), seeks to answer the question "who may be attacked?" Because war is engaged to prevent injustice to the innocent, oppressed, and downtrodden, it would be self-defeating and wrong to intentionally target and kill innocent people as a means of winning a war. From this thinking arises the distinction between combatant and noncombatant as well as legitimate and illegitimate targets in war.[44] Scriptural passages prohibiting murder (Ex. 20:13) as well as those encouraging virtuous behavior (Mic. 6:8—justice, mercy, and humility) demand that discriminating care be taken in the determination of targets. Intentional targeting of innocent civilians is simply wrong. Noncombatant immunity extends to any individual who is not directly involved in the war effort. This is why, as Louis Pojman points out, "civilian bombing is outlawed by international law."[45]

Because gray areas exist regarding who is and who is not a legitimate target of war, practical reasoning must guide in situations to which Scripture does not speak directly. For example, some may argue that milk-pasteurizing facilities that provide food for military personnel are legitimate targets because they help support the overall war machinery of the state. Such an evaluation seems faulty, however, for the simple reason that if one were to remove the state from the context of war, the milk factory and its workers would still provide a vital service connected to the basic needs of the citizenry. Any connection to the war effort is only a secondary one. Therefore, because the pasteurization of milk is not a war-dependent industry, but serves a basic life necessity, it would be inappropriate to treat it or its workers as legitimate war targets. On the other hand, a missile-production factory has a direct tie with the military and would therefore be an obvious target. Even though the

---

43. Norman L. Geisler, *Christian Ethics: Contemporary Issues and Options*, 2nd ed. (Grand Rapids: Baker Academic, 2010), 230.

44. Ramsey, *Just War*, 143.

45. Louis P. Pojman, *Life and Death: Grappling with the Moral Dilemmas of Our Time* (Belmont, CA: Wadsworth, 2000), 194.

factory may be a legitimate target, the principle of the sanctity of human life would further shape this criterion of discrimination. That is, the moral presumption to honor life and love all neighbors motivates the just warrior to consider attacking the military complex at night when the fewest human casualties would occur.

The application of this noncombatant category will also be relative in many cases to the context of the given war and the nations or factions fighting. In more traditional warfare, such as that of World War II, there was greater clarity about who was and who was not a combatant. In modern warfare against terrorist factions, however, the problem of distinguishing combatants and noncombatants becomes harder when women and children are armed for combat and used in nefarious ways to kill and destroy. While normatively they would fall into categories not typically considered combatant, the contexts and specifics of the situation may move them into the category of legitimate targets.

The determination of a target and the force of the weapon used may also be subject to this principle of discrimination. If the weapon is so large that the death of many noncombatants is foreseen, then it may be that the noncombatants themselves become an actual part of what is targeted. The larger the weapon is, the more likely that it will be indiscriminate. Targeting a 10-million-person city, for example, in order to take out an airport that serves the military on the corner edge of that city would be an example of indiscriminate targeting and, if used, an indiscriminate (and immoral) action. In such a context, the intent alone does not legitimize any means. To be clear, it is not the targeting of the airport or even the buildings that is the problem. In this case, the size of the destructive power of the chosen weapon alters the moral evaluation because of the people indiscriminately included in the weapon's known blast range. Unintended collateral damage is one thing, but targeting areas where large groups of noncombatants live with a weapon whose blast range or impact far exceeds the particular point of interest does not legitimize the killing as merely a case of "collateral damage." It would fail the criterion of discrimination and likely fail the next two criteria of *jus in bello* as well.

Avoidance of Evil Means (Mala in Se)

This leads us to the second criterion of *jus in bello*: the *avoidance of evil means*. This criterion seeks to evaluate whether the tactics or weapons used are, by their nature or design, evil in themselves (*mala in se*). For example, the use of torture to extract information or force surrender is evil by nature.[46] Other examples are

---

46. See Mark Liederbach, "Evaluating the 'Caiaphas Ethic' of Charles Krauthammer." This article is part of a Christian-ethics symposium on "The Truth about Torture," hosted by The Gospel Coalition. Articles are now hosted by First Things. See https://www.firstthings.com/blogs/firstthoughts/2010/01/mark-liederbach-on-torture. For a helpful discussion about the nature of torture, see Christopher Tollefson's article "Torture: What It Is, and Why It Is Wrong," *Real Clear Politics*, April 28, 2009, https://www.realclearpolitics

strategies such as genocide or mass-rape campaigns to subdue a people group. As for weapons, this criterion would be concerned with certain types of weapons used against human beings often known as weapons of mass destruction (WMDs), such as biological, chemical, or nuclear weapons. In each case, the concern is with the inherent nature of the weapon. Does the damage it causes to the human body by its very nature amount to a form of torture or "cruel and unusual punishment"? In addition, as pointed out above, could it be that by the very size of the weapon, it becomes inherently evil because of its destructive power? As Mark Allman puts it, "While not all just war theorists reject the use of WMDs . . . , they tend to harbor deep suspicions regarding the legitimate or justified use of WMDs precisely because such weapons fail to distinguish between soldiers and civilians."[47]

Table 14.3. Just-War Criteria

Justification to Go to War (*Jus ad Bellum*)	Just Behavior in War (*Jus in Bello*)
1. Legitimate Authority 2. Just Cause 3. Right Intent 4. Last Resort 5. Proportionality 6. Reasonable Prospect of Achievement	1. Discrimination 2. Avoidance of Evil Means 3. Proportionality

Proportionality

Proportionality serves as the third criterion for determining proper conduct in war. The determination of a proportional relationship between the projected gain from any particular act of war and its projected cost is vital in planning war maneuvers that satisfy just-war criteria. Obviously, it is very difficult to predict with a great degree of accuracy the actual net effect of any military maneuver. Therefore, while *jus in bello* requires a reasonable attempt to determine ahead of time the least amount of force necessary in a military action in order to accomplish stated objectives, reliance on this as a tool of justification must first be subject to the principle of *discrimination*.

While the just warrior may be tempted to engage in an ethic of utility in which "the ends justify the means," a biblical ethic does not allow such reasoning to rule the day. Weighing the potential positive effect against the probable negative effect must be done *only after* one has first determined whether a particular form of

.com/articles/2009/04/28/torture_what_it_is_and_why_it_is_wrong_96216.html.
47. Allman, *Who Would Jesus Kill?*, 202.

engagement falls within predetermined deontological limits such as the protection of innocent life. For this reason, efforts by the U.S. government and military to spend huge sums of money on "smart weapons" that hit targets with precision and seek to lower the possibility of the death of innocents as collateral damage are well placed. No monetary value can be placed on innocent life.

Likewise, while a massive nuclear explosion may force an enemy to surrender and perhaps save a projected 1 million lives, the destruction of fifty thousand *noncombatants* under the guise of "collateral damage" is an unacceptable price because it transgresses principles of wrongful death and the practice of noncombatant immunity.[48] The justifying claim that "it works; therefore, it is right" is based on mere pragmatism, not on the biblical morality of neighbor love. For this reason, proportionality must be rejected as the chief determining mechanism for *jus in bello* and employed only once the deontological limits of discrimination and avoidance of evil means are firmly in place. The following quote from Paul Ramsey is instructive:

> This means that nuclear war against the civil center of an enemy population, the A-bomb on Hiroshima, or obliteration bombing perpetrated by both sides in World War II were all alike immoral acts of war; and that Christians can support such actions only by dismissing the entire western tradition of civilized warfare that was originally born in the interior of that supreme compassion which always seeks if possible to wound none whom by His wounds Christ died to save. This theory of just and severely limited conflict has guided action and served as the regulative norm for military conduct for [millennia].[49]

A Few More Thoughts on Nuclear Weapons

Before concluding this discussion on *jus in bello* and particularly on the use of nuclear weapons, a few more clarifying thoughts are in order. First, we want to

---

48. One might argue that the principle of discrimination does not apply in such a case because the fifty thousand deaths were not targeted directly. We must be skeptical of such an argument, however, because of such weapons' destructive nature. For example, targeting an airport that lies a few miles from a populated city with a one-megaton nuclear weapon does not exempt one from the principle of discrimination because of the clearly foreseen and intended effect of the weapon's power. Such a weapon has a hundred times the destructive force of the bomb dropped on Hiroshima in 1945. The blast wave of such a bomb would flatten most buildings within a 4.5-mile radius of the target. That equals a sixty-three-square-mile area of destruction. While technically the airport was the only target, the known destructive force de facto expands the target area to include the entire area of the destructive force. The principle of proportionality would require a lower-yielding bomb that would limit collateral damage. Recognition of this point should not be confused with an accusation that U.S. efforts to win the war with Japan were immoral, but suggests that certain actions chosen may well have been.

49. Ramsey, *Just War*, 145.

make it clear that in our discussion of the use of nuclear weapons, we are not also suggesting that the development and use of nuclear power is somehow wrong. On the contrary: with proper care and continued technological advancement, nuclear power will likely be an increasing and very welcome source of energy for the inhabitants of planet Earth for the foreseeable future.

Second, much of the discussion regarding the use of nuclear weapons in warfare has been heavily influenced by the dropping of the two atomic bombs on Japan in World War II and the subsequent development and proliferation of nuclear weaponry far exceeding those initial two bombs in power and blast impact. This, coupled with the political strategy of deterrence commonly described as *mutually assured destruction*, has shaped the discussion about the use of nuclear weapons as an all-or-nothing proposal. That is, nuclear weaponry and war is a Pandora's box that, once opened in a battle scenario, would likely lead to this mutually assured destruction. It is important to recognize, however, that with the development of advanced targeting technologies and with the greater ability to determine a blast yield with more precision in nuclear weaponry, modern discussions of the possible use of nuclear weapons in war must be more nuanced.

For example, it is now possible to create a low-yield nuclear weapon that can be delivered to a target area with precision guidance. This would make it possible for a country with precision nuclear bombing capabilities to use a low-yield nuclear weapon to destroy an underground missile complex of an enemy that exists in a remote area such as the arctic tundra of Alaska or Siberia. While we are certainly not advocating for this or suggesting that it is a wise move in war, the advancement of technologies makes the discussion of the use of nuclear weapons in the modern era a bit different from what it was when the technologies were first developed and deterrent policies aimed high-yield weapons at population centers.

A third consideration that is very important for a Christian to process in thinking through the just-war criteria has to do with the connection of past military behaviors of a particular country and one's deep and abiding loyalty to, and patriotism for, that country. As we said above, for the Christian, one's loyalty to God far exceeds one's loyalty to a nation-state. Therefore, if in evaluating Christian just-war criteria we conclude that a particular military action by a country was immoral, that in no way necessarily suggests that one has a lack of patriotism. Indeed, it normatively suggests exactly the opposite. Our sense of patriotism should make us long for our country to do what is right in the eyes of God. Sometimes this includes well-placed and well-intended critique.

Finally, related to the topic of nuclear deterrence, we think that three penetrating questions must be asked as one evaluates the appropriateness of stockpiling nuclear weapons and aiming them at population centers. First, does such a policy meet the requirements of discrimination as noted above? Second, does such a policy meet the requirements of proportionality as noted above? Third, if the answer was no to either or both of those questions, does the policy of aiming nuclear weapons at population centers, even if the intent is to keep the enemy from firing its own missiles, amount to a form of terrorism? That is, even though such a policy may "work" to limit the enemy, does the threat to kill millions of people as a deterrent rest on a principle of terror? We believe that such a practice is in stark contrast to the Christian principles of both neighbor love and justice.

Table 14.4. Three Crucial Questions about Using Nuclear Weapons

1. Does it meet the requirements of discrimination?
2. Does it meet the requirements of proportionality?
3. Is nuclear deterrence in which civilian populations are targeted a form of terrorism?

Is Pacifism a Christian Option?

While it has been our argument in this chapter that the just-war position most faithfully represents the Bible's moral instruction regarding the use of force to honor life, embody love, and thereby restore justice, we do not want to imply that all forms of pacifism should then be considered immoral. Indeed, while we would disagree in principle with many who hold such positions, there are some versions of pacifism that we would simultaneously honor and respect because of how the conclusions are reached. It is helpful, then, to distinguish between three different types of pacifism to clarify this point: *deontological pacifism, utilitarian pacifism,* and *redemptive-witness pacifism.*[50]

Deontological pacifism argues that taking a position of nonviolence or nonviolent resistance is the right thing to do because Jesus commands it. The argument here is based on the words of Christ and the interpretation of his commands to "turn the other cheek" or Paul's instruction "not to resist evil with evil." This perspective argues that some actions are intrinsically right and that some are intrinsically wrong regardless of the consequences. Therefore, even if pacifism results in death or annihilation, participation in warfare would be wrong regardless of the consequences. This view rests on a high view of God's ultimate sovereign control. Often this position holds that God will pick up the pieces and make history come out right in the end. Psalm 20:7 serves as a summary: "Some boast in chariots and

50. James F. Childress, "Pacifism," in *Encyclopedia of Political Theory,* ed. Mark Bevir (Thousand Oaks, CA: SAGE, 2010), 1003–5.

some in horses, but we will boast in the name of the LORD, our God." A Christian's vocation is to imitate Christ and be willing to go to the cross and even die for what is true and right. While we do not agree with how these passages are interpreted, this position should be respected as a faithful attempt to honor the commands of Christ and principles of Christian discipleship.

A second form, *utilitarian pacifism*, is one that is based on consequentialist reasoning. This form of pacifism argues that the consequences for going to war are always going to be more negative than positive. Positively, it will argue that if a nation-state adopts a policy of pacifism, its actions will "on the whole produce a net balance of good over bad effects." Wars, it is argued, "do not always achieve their intended end goal, are always unsuccessful for one side and often unsuccessful for both sides."[51]

In addition, such a view is normatively connected to a high view of human nature that suggests that humans can and likely will respond ultimately to reason and the better angels of their nature to limit violence. Thus, this form of pacifism will argue that it is through pacifistic means that we will always reach the best conclusions. In pop culture, the lyrics from John Lennon capture the idea perfectly: "All we are saying is give peace a chance."[52] We believe that this form of pacifism is incompatible with a Christian worldview, and that if ever adopted by a Christian it is theologically problematic because it rests on a wrong view of the problem of sin and its impact on human nature.

A third perspective on pacifism that finds its way into Christian circles is *redemptive-witness pacifism*. This perspective attempts to combine ideas from the previous two perspectives. First, it argues that pacifism is right because Jesus commands it, and that a Christian should therefore bear witness to the commands of Christ by refusing to be a part of a war effort. But it also argues along with the utilitarian form that pacifism will also always work out more positively than negatively. In short, pacifism is both right and effective.[53] Once again we make the argument that this position does not rightly understand the impact of our fallen nature on our ability to bring about a peaceful end. It is influenced by utopian ideals that shaped much of liberal humanism precisely because it underestimates the potency and power of sin to degrade not only individual human hearts but society as a whole.

In sum, while we do not see how, either biblically or pragmatically, one can sustain an argument that pacifism is always the right answer, there are some types of arguments that we can respect and honor as a godly attempt to obey

51. Childress, "Pacifism," 1004.
52. John Lennon, "Give Peace a Chance" (1969).
53. Childress, "Pacifism," 1005.

the commands of Christ. Given the theological facts about the depraved status of human nature, there are others that we cannot.

Conclusion

We began this chapter by engaging a thought experiment introduced by the late Princeton University ethics professor Paul Ramsey: What should a neighbor like the Good Samaritan do if he or she were to come across a scenario in which an image-bearer were actively being beaten and killed? This, in turn, led us to engage important questions such as these: How should neighbor love compel a believer to act in the face of injustice? What impact should a desire to honor the sanctity of human life have on a Christ-follower? How should the principles of neighbor love and the sanctity of human life shape a Christian's understanding of what justice requires? Would the use of lethal force ever be justifiable in the name of love and life? How do these questions help us think about the ethics of war?

In order to answer these questions, we first framed our discussion by defining *just peace* and war and by identifying various perspectives on how Christians have thought about war in history. Next, we explored scriptural and theological themes to shape our understanding of the ethics of war and peacemaking. Following that, we then developed just-war criteria addressing both when it is right to go to war (*jus ad bellum*) and how one should behave in war (*jus in bello*). Finally, we addressed whether pacifism is a viable Christian response to the problem of injustice by briefly highlighting three distinct forms of pacifism.

In conclusion, we recognize that there have obviously been many unjust wars throughout human history. Despite this reality, Charles Hodge was correct when he wrote that "the vast majority of wars which have desolated the world have been unjustifiable in the sight of God and man. Nevertheless, it does not follow from this that war in all cases is to be condemned."[54] Indeed, we have argued that the very types of injustices that *lead to war* at times make the *waging of war* a moral duty for those who seek justice, love mercy, and walk humbly with their God.

Jesus instructed his disciples that the greatest commandments include both loving God *and* loving one's neighbor. These two commandments go hand in hand. Neighbor love flows from one's primary love for God and demonstrates one's love for God. Jesus also taught that if we neglect the needs of the downtrodden, we are in effect neglecting him (Matt. 25:31–45).

War is a consequence of sin. It results from human choice, malformation, and depravity. As long as sin is in the world, humans will mistreat one another. Until Christ returns and makes all things new, humans will abuse one another. If the

---

54. Charles Hodge, *Systematic Theology*, vol. 3 (Grand Rapids: Hendrickson, 2003), 365.

Bible's teachings about human sin are correct, then we can say unequivocally that until sin is gone from the world, neighbor love requires that we seek to restrain the impact of our sinfulness in society by protecting the sanctity of human life. And this will require the use of force. Regarding the question of war, then, if we define *force* as "the amount of power that must be exerted to restrain sin, crime, and injustice," then until the return of Christ and the removal of sin from the world, there will be a need to use force to restrain evil. Further, if it is justifiable to use force to arrest a criminal for a crime or to make a bully step down—as even most pacifists would agree—then the issue is ultimately not about the use of force. Rather, it must be about either the type or amount of force used. And from the earliest pages of the Bible until the last, God has not only given instruction to his people on how to restrain evil both in themselves and in society as a whole, but at times even commanded the means of taking human life by human hands and the waging of war.

Because of this, we can know that killing is not opposed to the nature of God because the Divine Trinity ordained that Christ should be killed as the just penalty for human sin. We can know that humans killing humans is not necessarily opposed to the nature of God because God at times commanded it as a legitimate response to human sin and crime. We can know that war is not opposed to the nature of God because not only did he at times command it of his people, but the Scripture also tells us that he wages it himself. What God opposes, then, is neither the use of force nor the waging of war. God opposes the hate-filled and evil intentions of the heart that often result in injustice and wrongful death. When the principle of neighbor love is rightly balanced with the principle of the sanctity of human life, it is possible for human beings to seek a just peace and wage peacemaking even though it may at times require the appropriate use of force to do so. This is the foundation of the Christian just-war perspective. For the Christian, there must always be great reluctance to use force, and there must be an extremely serious threat to a neighbor in order for that reluctance to be overcome.

This is precisely why just warriors and pacifists need each other. Just warriors remind pacifists of the high costs of love and justice when it comes to protecting the sanctity of life for the "least of these" who are sometimes beaten and left for dead on the side of the road. Pacifists remind just warriors that even the life of the guilty is sacred and that we should be reluctant to ever use force to take it. Neighbor love must guard us from hate-filled desires for revenge. Sometimes, however, honoring the sanctity of life for my neighbor and loving him well means a willingness and resolve to take up arms and protect the downtrodden against others who have relinquished their right to life because of their evil choices and behaviors.

The pursuit of justice based on the standard of God's holiness, righteousness, and love requires us to face a hard truth—sometimes the waging of just war is the means of acquiring a just peace. This was the choice of the Divine Trinity when God decided that the death of Christ was the necessary means of retributive justice for the problem of human sin. Placing love and justice in opposition to each other signals a malformed understanding of theology proper and results in a fundamental denial of the very foundations of the gospel. Sometimes love must kill; sometimes life requires life; and sometimes worship requires war.

Key Terms and Concepts

crusade

deontological pacifism

discrimination

jus ad bellum

jus in bello

just cause

just peace

just-war criteria

last resort

legitimate authority

mala in se

nonresistance

nonviolent resistance

pacifism

proportionality

ratsakh

reasonable prospect of achievement

redemptive-witness pacifism

right intent

shalom

utilitarian pacifism

Key Scriptures

Numbers 31:1–3

Numbers 32

Exodus 14:13–14

Exodus 20:13

Deuteronomy 7:1–6

Joshua 1:9

1 Samuel 15:1–3

Isaiah 53:10

Matthew 5:9

Matthew 5:21–26

Matthew 5:38–39

Matthew 26:52

Luke 3:14

Luke 14:31–32

John 19:11

Romans 5:8

Romans 12:19

Romans 13:1–7

Revelation 19:11–21

Study Questions

1. The authors open the chapter with a discussion placing the "Good Samaritan" in a context of having to choose whether it is our duty to use force to protect the innocent. What would you do if you happened upon

a situation in which a close loved one of yours was being beaten by a criminal? Would you use force to defend him or her? Would you think it permissible to do so?

2. How are the doctrine of the Trinity and the doctrine of penal substitutionary atonement (Christ's death as payment for sin) related to the discussion of whether God is willing to put someone to death? How is this discussion related to the question of the morality of war?

3. Can Christians participate in war? What are the pros and cons of this argument? Does Scripture allow it? Does Scripture forbid it? What does the Old Testament indicate? What does the New Testament indicate?

4. In regard to the *jus in bello* ("just actions in war") discussion, the authors argue that the principles of discrimination and the avoidance of evil means must be given higher priority than an evaluation of proportionality. What are the implications of this regarding how Christians must evaluate modern warfare? What are the implications for the use of such things as weapons of mass destruction versus "smart bombs"?

5. If a person takes a pacifist position on war, what are the implications from this same person's stance regarding the state's ability to punish any crime? That is, does the way in which a pacifist argument is made cause any problems regarding the use of any type of force to restrain crime or injustice? Discuss.

For Further Reading

Allman, Mark J. *Who Would Jesus Kill? War, Peace, and the Christian Tradition.* Winona, MN: St. Mary's, 2008.

Bainton, Roland H. *Christian Attitudes toward War and Peace: A Historical Survey and Critical Re-evaluation.* New York: Abingdon, 1960.

Bell, Daniel M., Jr. *Just War as Christian Discipleship: Recentering the Tradition in the Church Rather than the State.* Grand Rapids: Brazos, 2009.

Charles, J. Daryl, and Timothy J. Demy. *War, Peace, and Christianity: Questions and Answers from a Just-War Perspective.* Wheaton, IL: Crossway, 2010.

Copan, Paul. *Is God a Moral Monster? Making Sense of the Old Testament God.* Grand Rapids: Baker, 2011.

Johnson, James Turner. *The Quest for Peace: Three Moral Traditions in Western Cultural History.* Princeton, NJ: Princeton University Press, 1987.

Longman, Tremper, III, and Daniel G. Reid. *God Is a Warrior.* Grand Rapids: Zondervan, 2010.

O'Donovan, Oliver. *The Just War Revisited.* Cambridge: Cambridge University Press, 2003.

Ramsey, Paul. *The Just War: Force and Political Responsibility*. Lanham, MD: Rowman & Littlefield, 1983.

———. *War and the Christian Conscience: How Shall Modern War Be Conducted Justly?* Durham, NC: Duke University Press, 1961.

Walzer, Michael. *Just and Unjust Wars: A Moral Argument with Historical Illustrations*. 5th ed. New York: Basic, 2015.

15

Abortion

"For You formed my inward parts; You wove me in my mother's womb.
I will give thanks to You, for I am fearfully and wonderfully made."
—Psalm 139:13–14

"The texts of Sacred Scripture never address the question of deliberate abortion and
so do not directly and specifically condemn it. But they show such great respect for the
human being in the mother's womb that they require as a logical consequence that
God's commandment 'You shall not kill' be extended to the unborn child as well."[1]
—Pope John Paul II, Evangelium Vitae

Introduction

Roe v. Wade **and** *Doe v. Bolton*

On January 22, 1973, the Supreme Court of the United States issued two opinions that altered the face of the abortion debate in America. The joint decisions of *Roe v. Wade*[2] and *Doe v. Bolton*[3] declared that women had a Fourteenth Amendment right to have an abortion as part of their right to privacy. The decisions specifically allowed women to choose abortion in situations in which their health was at stake; the Court decisions, however, defined *health of the mother* so broadly that virtually any physical, emotional, psychological, or familial issue could qualify as a legitimate reason for having an abortion. Tens of millions of abortions have been performed in the United States since 1973.

The first ruling, *Roe v. Wade*, struck down all state laws banning abortion, divided pregnancy into three trimesters (roughly twelve-week periods), and

---

1. John Paul II, *Evangelium Vitae*, 61, accessed April 6, 2020, http://www.vatican.va/content/john-paul-ii
/en/encyclicals/documents/hf_jp-ii_enc_25031995_evangelium-vitae.html.

2. 410 U.S. 113 (1973).

3. 410 U.S. 179 (1973).

imposed various regulations related to the development of the child and the health of the mother. *Roe* ruled that while abortion on demand was allowed without restriction in the first trimester, the state could limit abortion in the second trimester to ensure the safety of the mother. The Court allowed for states to ban abortion during the third trimester based on the obvious development of the child, but allowed abortion if the mother's health was threatened.

The companion case, *Doe v. Bolton*, ruled that the factors considered to be a threat to the woman's health included anything "physical, emotional, psychological, familial, [or related to] the woman's age."[4] These two rulings, handed down together, made abortion on demand from conception to full term the law of the land.

The key element of the Supreme Court's rulings had to do with the question of the life of the baby. The majority opinion reads: "We need not resolve the difficult question of when life begins. When those trained in the respective disciplines of medicine, philosophy, and theology are unable to arrive at any consensus, the judiciary, at this point in the development of man's knowledge, is not in a position to speculate as to the answer."[5] By sidestepping the question of when life begins, the Court ruled that the Due Process Clause of the Fourteenth Amendment guaranteed a fundamental right to privacy, giving a woman the right to abort. Practically reversing the basic standards of justice commonly used to protect human life in all other circumstances, the Court placed the burden of proof on those who wanted to protect life. That is, the benefit of the doubt was given not to the innocent and unprotected child who "might" be alive, but to those who wanted to have the "choice" whether to terminate the baby.

The years since *Roe v. Wade* and *Doe v. Bolton* have seen remarkable advances in the fields of science and medicine that have effectively removed all doubt related to the question of when life begins. It is a scientific reality that the baby is a living, growing entity with the following characteristics:

1. The full human genetic code is present at the moment of conception; this information guides the growth of the person who will become an adult.
2. The nervous system begins by day 20.
3. The child's brain is fully proportioned by day 30.
4. The child will exhibit spontaneous movement by day 45.
5. His or her lips react to touch by 7 weeks.
6. The eyelids and palms of hands react to touch by 8½ weeks.
7. By the 9th or 10th week, the baby can turn somersaults, frown, and swallow.

4. *Doe*, 410 U.S. at 192.
5. *Roe*, 410 U.S. at 159.

8. By the 11th week, the baby normatively responds to touch, light, heat, and noise. The baby will recoil if pricked by a needle and will even learn and try to avoid the needle if a beep is sounded before subsequent needle pricks.

Based on these and other scientific facts, all parties are forced to agree that what is growing in a mother's womb is:

- Undeniably human (it is not a pig, horse, monkey, and so on);
- Undeniably alive (contrary to the *Roe v. Wade* language);
- Undeniably distinct from the mother (it is not merely tissue that is part of the mother's body);
- Undeniably unique (it has its own unique DNA); and
- Undeniably innocent (it has not broken the law in some way to warrant a death penalty).

Scientifically speaking, there is no longer a serious debate. When a woman is pregnant, she is pregnant with a human being—a human child. Moreover, this leads to the inescapable conclusion that abortion is without question the killing of an innocent, unique, distinct, living human being.

Statistics: U.S. and Global

In the United States alone, it is estimated that over 60 million babies have been killed through various forms of abortion since the *Roe* and *Doe* rulings. That number equates to nearly one-fifth of the current U.S. population. While some politicians may want to suggest that U.S. policies on abortion are restrictive of women's rights, the fact of the matter is that only nine countries report a higher abortion rate: Bulgaria, Cuba, Estonia, Georgia, Kazakhstan, Romania, Russia, Sweden, and Ukraine.[6] In the words of C. Ben Mitchell and D. Joy Riley, these two Supreme Court rulings "secured a place for the United States as the most permissive society in the world with respect to abortion laws and policy."[7] Tragically, these U.S. figures are only a fraction of the total number of abortions that take place worldwide.

---

6. Abort 73, "U.S. Abortion Statistics," accessed January 23, 2020, https://abort73.com/abortion_facts/us_abortion_statistics/. This site comments regarding China: "Though the UN lists China's official abortion rate at 19.2, China's actual abortion rate is likely much higher. According to China's 2010 census, there were approximately 310 million women of reproductive age in the country. An estimated 13–23 million abortions happen annually in China, resulting in an adjusted abortion rate of 41.9–74.2. The abortion rate is the number of abortions per 1,000 women aged 15–44."

7. C. Ben Mitchell and D. Joy Riley, *Christian Bioethics: A Guide for Pastors, Health Care Professionals, and Families* (Nashville: B&H Academic, 2014), 47.

Globally, it is estimated that approximately 56 million babies are aborted *each year*, which equates to roughly 150,000 babies *per day*.[8] The United Nations periodically reviews abortion laws around the world, taking note of changes to the availability of abortion. In its 2020 report (citing statistics through 2017), the UN noted that "legal grounds for abortion have become less restrictive. Between 1996 and 2017, the percentage of countries permitting abortion increased gradually for all legal grounds, while the percentage of countries not permitting abortion on any grounds declined. As of 2017, four countries did not permit abortion on any grounds."[9] Abortion for reasons of fetal development has grown significantly around the world. The UN reports: "At the global level, there has been a marked increase in the proportion of countries permitting abortion in cases of foetal impairment. Sixty-one per cent of countries allowed abortion in cases of foetal impairment in 2017, up from 41 per cent in 1996." Recent news has focused on the virtual elimination of Down syndrome in some countries, such as Iceland, by means of abortion. With prenatal screening, a pregnant woman can identify whether her unborn child is at high risk for a disorder such as Down syndrome and then terminate the pregnancy through abortion.[10]

According to studies done by the Guttmacher Institute, about one in four women in the United States will have an abortion by age forty-five. Most of the women who have abortions in the United States are in their twenties (roughly 60 percent). Some 39 percent identified as white, 28 percent as black, and 25 percent as Hispanic. About 75 percent of women who have abortions are considered "poor" in that they live near or below the federal poverty level. In regard to faith, 38 percent reported no religious affiliation, 24 percent of women identified themselves as Catholic, 17 percent as mainline Protestants, 13 percent as evangelical, and the remaining 8 percent as some other affiliation.[11]

In the United States and around the world, the number of abortions is staggering. Interestingly, abortion rates have dropped in the United States from their highest levels in the early 1980s.[12] Globally, the total number of abortions has

---

8. Abort 73, "Worldwide Abortion Statistics," accessed January 23, 2020, https://abort73.com/abortion_facts/worldwide_abortion_statistics/.

9. United Nations, *World Population Policies 2017: Abortion Laws and Policies* (2020), v, accessed April 7, 2020, https://www.un.org/en/development/desa/population/publications/pdf/policy/WPP2017/WPP2017_Report.pdf.

10. Julian Quinones and Arijeta Lajka, "What Kind of Society Do You Want to Live In? Inside the Country Where Down Syndrome Is Disappearing," CBS News, August 14, 2017, accessed April 7, 2020, https://www.cbsnews.com/news/down-syndrome-iceland/.

11. Guttmacher Institute, "Induced Abortion in the United States," accessed April 7, 2020, https://www.guttmacher.org/fact-sheet/induced-abortion-united-states. These statistics reflect the most recent data available as of September 2019.

12. Guttmacher Institute, "Induced Abortion in the United States."

increased in recent years, but the overall abortion rate has declined slightly. This can be explained by an increase in population accounting for more total abortions despite fewer abortions per woman.[13] Even with overall abortion rates declining, the total number of abortions should remind us of the significance of this issue for our faith and society.

Core Issue: Life versus Choice

Why is abortion still a debate in our culture? There are many factors at play, but one of the key elements has to do with how the Supreme Court set up its rulings. By sidestepping the question of life and ruling based on a woman's right to choose, the Court set two lines of argument in opposition to each other. One side makes "pro-life" arguments revolving around the life of the baby in question, while the other side makes "pro-choice" arguments about a woman's right to control what happens to, and in, her own body. The former focuses on the principle of the *sanctity of human life*, while the latter centers on the principle of *autonomy*. This is, in fact, why those who argue opposing sides of the debate so often talk past each other and the discussions generate more heat than light.

Both these moral arguments have their rightful place in ethical and civil discourse. The problem comes not in a desire to honor these moral claims, but in trying to decide two things: (1) the extent to which each should hold sway over our moral choices, and (2) which one should be more binding when the life of a baby weighs in the balance. We must ask whether there are any limits to one's personal autonomy. Should a woman's autonomy and choice ("right to privacy") about her body trump the baby's right to survival? Or, on the other hand, we must ask: Is the sanctity of life absolute? Does the value of an innocent human life place limitations on one's freedoms such that we cannot kill an innocent person even when that innocent person's survival restricts our own autonomy?

Another closely related reason why this is still a debate in our country is that the way in which one answers the questions above has massive ramifications for many other applied ethical issues relating to the beginning and end of life. Issues such as euthanasia, physician-assisted suicide, cloning, stem-cell research, genetic engineering, and even contraception and assisted reproductive technologies are closely related because the underlying ethical principles in question here are important factors in those issues as well. Keep in mind that (as we discussed in the first chapter) this is not a question whether we should legislate morality. All legislation related to these issues—regardless of one's position—is a form of

13. Gilda Sedgh et al., "Abortion Incidence between 1990 and 2014: Global, Regional, and Subregional Levels and Trends," *Lancet* 388, no. 10041 (July 16, 2016): 258–67, accessed April 7, 2020, https://www.thelancet.com/journals/lancet/article/PIIS0140-6736(16)30380-4/fulltext.

legislating morality. The question, then, is not *whether* we should legislate morality but *whose* morality will be legislated. The abortion debate functions as a watershed debate because the arguments that hold sway in this debate will greatly influence the moral, legal, and social implications on many other issues as well.

We will need to address these issues and seek biblical wisdom to know how best to worship God maximally. In order to do so, we begin by defining key terms and highlighting key concepts to orient and frame the discussion. Next, we explore central biblical and theological concepts to ground a particular Christian understanding of the problem of abortion. Third, we will then address the most common lines of objection to a distinctly pro-life point of view. Finally, before bringing the chapter to a conclusion, we will address hard cases that frequently come up for debate about the application of a pro-life ethic.

Key Terms and Concepts

Definition of *Abortion*

The term *abort* means to "stop" or "cease" something in a premature stage. When we speak of aborting a pregnancy, we mean the termination of a pregnancy both before the time of fetal viability (the ability of the child to live independently outside the mother's womb) and after fetal viability and before live birth. Generally speaking, four categories of abortion reflect the reasons why an abortion takes place. The first is *spontaneous abortion*, which is most commonly known as a *miscarriage*. It is the abrupt and unplanned (spontaneous) early end of a pregnancy that takes place before the fetus is viable.

Table 15.1. Four Categories of Abortion

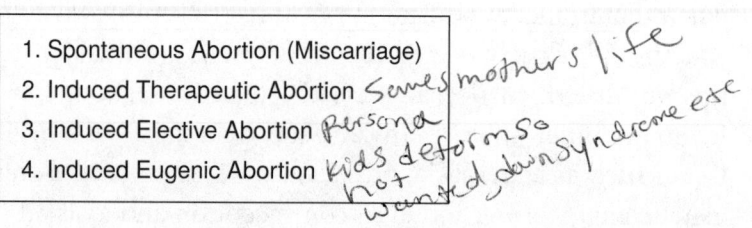

1. Spontaneous Abortion (Miscarriage)
2. Induced Therapeutic Abortion *Saves mothers life*
3. Induced Elective Abortion *Personal*
4. Induced Eugenic Abortion *Kids deforms so not wanted downSyndrome etc.*

Much more commonly, however, the term *abortion* is used to refer to what is technically better described as *induced abortion*. An induced abortion is distinct from a miscarriage in that it involves the intentional interruption of a pregnancy. This category can be further differentiated between *therapeutic abortion*, *elective abortion*, and *eugenic abortion*. *Therapeutic abortions* are induced or caused for purposes directly related to either terminal fetal disease or the *health of the mother* (broadly defined by the *Doe v. Bolton* case), and most often they refer to those rare situations when a pregnancy is purposely terminated in order to save the mother's life.

An *elective* (or voluntary) *abortion* is not medically necessary but instead reflects a response to some other social or personal factor(s). For example, a 2005 study listed such reasons as the woman's feeling that she was too young to be a mother, the absence of a partner, pressure from the genetic father, and the lack of financial means as some of the more common reasons why women elect to have abortions.[14] The vast majority of induced abortions are elective abortions.

Eugenic abortion (sometimes referred to as *selective termination*) differs from both therapeutic abortion and elective abortion in that the primary motive is not merely about the mother's or baby's survival, nor is it focused primarily on a woman's right to "reproductive choice." Instead, eugenic abortion involves the decision to abort a child who may have unwanted characteristics that can range anywhere from having debilitating diseases such as Down syndrome, to being a particular gender (e.g., aborting female babies in China), to having undesirable eye color. It involves the selective termination of life based on factors discovered in prenatal genetic screening that are related not to the viability of a child, but to whether the genetics are either "normal" or "preferred." The term *eugenics* literally means "good genes." As a "science," eugenics involves the attempt to improve the human race through a manipulation of the gene pool via methods such as selective breeding, elimination of those with defective genes, and the sterilization of individuals who may be carriers of undesirable traits. Eugenics raises questions pertaining to the morality of terminating the life of the handicapped, the creation of "designer babies," and a desire for a "pure," or "master," race.

Methods of Abortion

The methods of abortion fall into two broad categories. The first category is medical abortion. "'Medical' refers to the administration of medications or drugs that, by differing mechanisms, cause the uterus to contract and expel its contents early."[15] Medically induced abortions normally involve the use of two drugs. Mifepristone is taken orally and functions to decrease the hormones that help maintain a viable pregnancy, which results in a depletion of the uterine lining necessary for a pregnancy to continue. Subsequently, it causes the embryo to detach from the uterus. The other drug, misoprostol, is taken in order to cause the uterus

---

14. Lawrence B. Finer et al., "Reasons U.S. Women Have Abortions: Quantitative and Qualitative Perspectives," *Perspectives on Sexual and Reproductive Health* 37, no. 3 (2005): 112–14, accessed April 6, 2020, https://www.guttmacher.org/sites/default/files/pdfs/journals/3711005.pdf. See also Maggie Kirkman et al., "Reasons Women Give for Abortion: A Review of the Literature," *Archives of Women's Mental Health* 12, no. 6 (December 2009): 365–78.

15. Mitchell and Riley, *Christian Bioethics*, 47.

to contract and thereby discharge the embryo. Medical abortions are performed within the first sixty-three days (nine weeks) of the first trimester. According to the Guttmacher Institute, this form of abortion accounted for 39 percent of all U.S. abortions in 2017.[16]

Surgical abortion, the second method, is performed either by opening the mother's cervix and passing surgical instruments into the uterus to remove the developing baby and placenta or through abdominal surgery.[17] The exact method depends to a large degree on the level of development of the baby that is going to be aborted. *Vacuum (suction) aspiration* is the most common method of surgical abortion in the first trimester. This method involves the dilation of the cervix and the insertion of a hollow vacuum tube with a sharp knife-edged tip known as a vacuum curette. The tube is connected to a powerful vacuum. The baby and the placenta are torn into small pieces and suctioned out into a jar and discarded. *Dilation and curettage (D&C)* is often used in conjunction with vacuum aspiration in first-trimester abortions. In this method, the cervix is dilated, and the uterine wall is scraped to release the fetus and placenta before using suction to remove them from the mother's body.

Other methods of surgical abortion are commonly used in the second trimester and beyond. The most common is *dilation and evacuation (D&E)*. This method involves the use of a pair of forceps inserted into the uterus to grasp the fetus and break and twist off the bones of the child. The spine is then snapped and the baby's skull is crushed. Once the baby is completely dismembered, the body parts are removed with a vacuum (suction) curette. Another method of abortion that has also been used in later-term abortions is known as *dilation and extraction (D&X)*. This procedure, which is also known as *partial-birth abortion*, involves the use of forceps to turn the baby into a breech position (birthing feet-first) in order to deliver the entire lower part of the baby with the exception of the head. While the baby's head is still in the womb, the physician then punctures the base of the baby's skull and suctions out the brain in order to collapse the skull. The rest of the body is removed from the mother. This particular procedure was banned in the United States in 2003 (with the possible exception of an emergency situation to save a mother's life).[18]

The Moral Principles at Play in the Abortion Debate

In contemporary healthcare settings, the decision whether to terminate a pregnancy is almost exclusively determined through an emphasis on the autonomy of

16. Guttmacher Institute, "Induced Abortion in the United States."

17. Maureen Paul et al., *Management of Unintended and Abnormal Pregnancy: Comprehensive Abortion Care* (West Sussex, UK: Wiley-Blackwell, 2009), 135–56.

18. John and Paul Feinberg have a helpful discussion of these and other methods of abortion. See John S. Feinberg and Paul D. Feinberg, *Ethics for a Brave New World*, 2nd ed. (Wheaton, IL: Crossway, 2010), 74–75.

the woman making the decision. As we alluded to in the introduction above, the core of the moral debate about abortion is a battle over the principle of moral autonomy and the principle of the sanctity of human life.

The word *autonomy* most literally means "self-rule" or "a law unto oneself" (Greek, *autos* "self," *nomos* "law"). In the field of ethics, the principle of autonomy can be traced back to the Enlightenment philosopher Immanuel Kant and his emphasis on respect for persons as a foundational moral category. Per his view, even without an appeal to God, universal moral principles can still be determined based on the idea that humans should be treated as "ends in themselves" and never merely as a "means to an end."[19] This ethical move by Kant ultimately paved the way for what has become known as a "rights-based" understanding of ethics in Western society. That is, the idea that I am an "end in myself" and should not be treated merely as a means to an end leads to the conclusion that I must also have some *inalienable rights* that govern how I should (or should not) be treated. This emphasis on rights has in time led to an emphasis on personal liberty and the autonomy of a person to be his or her own decision-maker about his or her life and body.[20] As Tom Beauchamp and James Childress summarize:

> Personal autonomy encompasses, at a minimum, self-rule that is free from both controlling interference by others and from certain limitations.... The autonomous individual acts freely in accordance with a self-chosen plan.... Virtually all theories of autonomy view two conditions as essential for autonomy: liberty (independence from controlling influences) and agency (capacity for intentional action).[21]

In the abortion debate, the application of the principle of autonomy happens most commonly when a woman expresses her right to govern her own body as she chooses (liberty) as long as she has the capacity to make an informed choice (agency). It is common, for example, to see a bumper sticker or a placard at a rally that says something to the effect of "Keep your laws off my body" or "My body, my choice." These signs are indicative of this principle of autonomy.

The same principle could be appealed to with regard to the baby who is going to be aborted. Should not the baby also be given the same dignity regarding its

---

19. Kant formulates this version of his categorical imperative by stating that a person should always "act in such a way that you treat humanity, whether in your own person or in the person of another, always at the same time as an end and never simply as a means." This is the second formulation of his categorical imperative. Immanuel Kant, *Grounding for the Metaphysics of Morals*, in *Ethical Philosophy*, ed. Warner A. Wick, trans. James W. Ellington, 2nd ed. (Indianapolis: Hackett, 1994), 36.

20. Particularly in the field of medical ethics, the principle of autonomy has risen to a position of priority largely due to the influence of Tom L. Beauchamp and James F. Childress's influential work *Principles of Biomedical Ethics*, 8th ed. (New York: Oxford University Press, 2019).

21. Beauchamp and Childress, *Principles of Biomedical Ethics*, 99–100.

own body? Would it not be wrong to take the life of the child? If the baby is considered to have the same *moral status* (or *moral standing*) as the mother, then he or she is also "an end in himself or herself."[22] And if so, then the baby should also not be treated as merely a means to an end. The baby, too, would have a right not to be killed. This is exactly what those who focus on the right to life argue in opposition to abortion. From the Kantian perspective, life is set apart as a fundamental value of existence. While there is no appeal to God for justification of this value, the rational argument that supports the child's "right to life" flows from the basic premise that in order to have a choice, one has to be alive. Thus, the right to not be killed is both logically prior to, and more fundamental than, the right to choose. This is especially the case if my autonomous choice would result in the death of another person with equal moral status.

From a distinctly Christian point of view, the principle of autonomy is likewise not fundamentally denied, but understood in a more limited form. Liberty and freedom are best understood as living in accord with one's own design and the design God wove into the fabric of the universe. When we make our decisions freely *in accord with God's design and moral order*, we will find ourselves most fully human and most fully alive. Likewise, from a distinctively Christian point of view, this is why an unlimited view of autonomy is understood to be so dangerous. As we saw in our earlier discussion (chapter 3) of Genesis 3, when Adam and Eve asserted their own autonomy from God's benevolent leadership and moral direction, they earned striving, toil, alienation, and ultimately death. Thus, Christians do not deny the importance of the principle of autonomy, but rather recognize that it must be brought into the context of what God has revealed about the nature of reality and the nature of morality. We can claim autonomy from the law of gravity, but when we step off a cliff, we will realize that we are still subject to the reality of the way that things actually are. Similarly with the principle of autonomy, God has given us free moral agency, but moral agency is truly free only when the choices made are in accord with the way in which God made the world. From a Christian point of view, the Kantian-based rational appeal to respect the life of another person who is an "end in himself or herself" is not necessarily rejected but is further grounded on the biblical passages to affirm the special moral status of human beings, who are made in God's image (*imago Dei*). As God's image-bearers, human beings have inherent value in themselves (because God gave it to them), but also find their final *end in God*.

Given this line of reasoning, it seems clear that much of the debate then comes down to the question of the moral status of the child. Should the child be granted

---

22. For a fuller discussion of the concept of moral status, see Beauchamp and Childress, *Principles of Biomedical Ethics*, 64–81.

the same status as the mother? Should the baby be granted the same right to not be killed as the mother? Could we make bumper stickers or hold placards on behalf of the baby that read "Keep your laws off my body" or "My body, my choice" as well? Or is there a sense in which the child is somehow "less than" the mother in terms of his or her moral standing? David Platt is correct when he writes:

> The key question that we all must answer—and the question that determines how we view abortion—is this: What is contained in the womb? Is it a person? Or is it merely an embryo, a fetus? Virtually every other question and every single argument in the abortion controversy comes back to this question: What, or who, is in the womb? And once this question is answered, everything else comes into perspective.[23]

A Biblical Understanding of Moral Status and the Question of Abortion

Moral Status

The Christian is duty-bound to seek Scripture for clarity regarding the moral standing of the child who inhabits the womb of a mother. What does the Bible teach about the value of human beings? Does the Bible give clarity on whether a child in the womb should be considered a human being in the same sense as a human being who has been born?

In regard to the value of human beings, as we have argued elsewhere (see our discussion on the sanctity of human life in chapter 13 on capital punishment), biblical passages such as Genesis 1:26–27; 9:6; Psalm 8:3–8; and James 3:9 all indicate that God places a high and unique value on human life because human beings carry the special status of *image-bearers*. For this reason, Scripture also clearly prohibits the taking of innocent human life. The commandment "You shall not murder" (Ex. 20:13) applies to all human beings who have not relinquished their right to life through ungodly or immoral behavior as specified in Scripture.

Scott Rae is helpful here when he points out that simply because we know it is wrong to unjustly take an innocent human life, that does not necessarily mean that we have gained clarity on the issue of abortion. As Rae suggests, applying Exodus 20:13 "directly to the unborn involves begging the question about the moral and ontological status of the unborn. That is, to apply this to the unborn involves a further argument that the embryo/fetus in the womb constitutes a person who possesses the right to life. . . . The important part of the argument is to

---

23. David Platt, *Counter Culture: A Compassionate Call to Counter Culture in a World of Poverty, Same-Sex Marriage, Racism, Sex Slavery, Immigration, Abortion, Persecution, Orphans, and Pornography* (Carol Stream, IL: Tyndale, 2015), 63.

show that God attributes the same characteristics to the unborn in the womb as to a person out of the womb."[24]

Theologically, one can make the strongest argument regarding the full moral status of an unborn child by considering the incarnation of Jesus Christ. Regarding the incarnation, both the Bible and church tradition recognize that the person Jesus Christ is both fully God and fully human (i.e., the doctrine of *hypostatic union*, Heb. 1:3) from the moment of conception. In the Gospel of Luke, we learn that Jesus was born of a woman (Luke 1:31) and that although his conception was miraculous, his gestation would proceed normally as Mary carried him in pregnancy for nine months. Not only did his life begin at the moment of conception, it was also at that point that the angel Gabriel told Mary to name him Jesus, thereby recognizing his personal nature. The text further indicates that soon after learning that she was pregnant,

> Mary arose and went in a hurry to the hill country, to a city of Judah, and entered the house of Zacharias and greeted Elizabeth. When Elizabeth heard Mary's greeting, the baby leaped in her womb; and Elizabeth was filled with the Holy Spirit. And she cried out with a loud voice and said, "Blessed are you among women, and blessed is the fruit of your womb! And how has it happened to me, that the mother of my Lord would come to me? For behold, when the sound of your greeting reached my ears, the baby leaped in my womb for joy." (Luke 1:39–44)

Note that in this passage not only does Elizabeth recognize that Mary is already the mother of the "Lord" and not merely the incubator of a fetus, but she also indicates that her own child (John) "leaped in my womb for joy." The passage leads us to a conclusion that from the earliest stages of pregnancy, not only was Jesus an embodied human, but he was clearly accorded the moral standing of personhood as well.

Lest one think that Jesus could be a special case since his incarnation was miraculous in nature, it is good to consider other passages of Scripture that affirm a similar moral status for preborn children. Biblically speaking, several passages affirm this conclusion and give clarity regarding the continuity of a human being's moral status from the earliest moments of human life into eternity.[25] For example, in Jeremiah 1:5, the Lord says, "Before I formed you in the womb I knew you, and before you were born I consecrated you; I have appointed you a prophet to the nations." This passage clearly indicates a type of personal knowledge that God has

---

24. Scott B. Rae, *Moral Choices: An Introduction to Ethics*, 4th ed. (Grand Rapids: Zondervan, 2018), 133.

25. We are indebted here to Mitchell and Riley's discussion of the importance of the doctrine of Christology in the abortion debate. See Mitchell and Riley, *Christian Bioethics*, 54–55.

of Jeremiah before birth. It indicates that God "knew" Jeremiah in the same way as an embryo as he does as an adult. Similarly, with the poetic language of Job 3:3, "Let the day perish on which I was to be born, and the night which said, 'A boy is conceived,'" the child in question at the day of birth is considered to be the same person as he was on the day of conception.

In Psalm 51:5, David writes, "Behold, I was brought forth in iniquity, and in sin my mother conceived me." As David writes a poem of contrition and lament, he not only expresses sorrow over his sinful actions, but also recognizes that his proclivity to sin (a trait of personhood) began at his conception and has carried forth into his adulthood. He uses a similar line of reasoning in Psalm 139:13–16. Here David acknowledges God's intimate and careful process in forming an unborn child throughout the process of a pregnancy:

> For You formed my inward parts;
> You wove me in my mother's womb.
> I will give thanks to You, for I am fearfully and wonderfully made;
> Wonderful are Your works,
> And my soul knows it very well.
> My frame was not hidden from You,
> When I was made in secret,
> And skillfully wrought in the depths of the earth;
> Your eyes have seen my unformed substance;
> And in Your book were all written
> The days that were ordained for me,
> When as yet there was not one of them.

In the Hebrew language, the imagery of "inward parts" was used to refer to the seat of a person's affections and passions. Such language is used elsewhere in Scripture to refer to the inner part of a person where emotions are felt, where the conscience dwells, and where spiritual distress is experienced (e.g., Job 16:13; Pss. 51:7; 73:21).[26] It is evident that the general tenor of Scripture supports for all pre-born children the conclusion we reached by considering the incarnation of Jesus. In particular, "the unborn is considered a person by God, being described with many of the same characteristics that apply to children and adults."[27]

The "law of retribution" (*lex talionis*) in Exodus 21:22–25 also highlights the idea that the unborn is considered a person from God's perspective. This passage emphasizes the sanctity of human life both by its demand for appropriate

---

26. Mitchell and Riley, *Christian Bioethics*, 57.

27. Rae, *Moral Choices*, 138.

measures of retribution in the face of evil and by the limitation of its extent in view of the nature of the evil committed. The passage reads:

> If men struggle with each other and strike a woman with child so that she *gives birth prematurely*, yet there is no injury, he shall surely be fined as the woman's husband may demand of him, and he shall pay as the judges decide. But if there is any further injury, then you shall appoint as a penalty life for life, eye for eye, tooth for tooth, hand for hand, foot for foot, burn for burn, wound for wound, bruise for bruise. (Ex. 21:22–25)

In context, this passage falls within a section of the law of Moses that is concerned with giving instruction on how the Israelites were to compensate or penalize people for loss of property or personal injury (Ex. 21:12–36). These particular verses describe a case in which two men are fighting and in the midst of their scuffle they accidentally hit a pregnant woman.

The phrase "gives birth prematurely" in the passage is an English interpretation of the Hebrew verb *yātzā*, which literally means "to go or come out." In Scripture, when this word is used in relation to pregnancy, it describes the birth of a living child.[28] In contrast, the word normally used for a miscarriage—which is not present in this verse—is *shākōl* (e.g., Gen. 42:36; 43:14; Ex. 23:26; Lev. 26:22). In fact, the term *shākōl* is used only two chapters later in Exodus 23:26 as God describes what he will do for the people of Israel once they enter the promised land ("There shall be no one miscarrying or barren in your land; I will fulfill the number of your days."). In light of this evidence, Exodus 21:22–25 should be understood to mean that while fighting, the men bump into a pregnant woman and cause her to go into premature labor. The law indicates that if there is "no injury" to either the mother or the child, the guilty party should still be penalized for endangering either the mother or the baby. If, however, the men bump the pregnant woman and cause harm to either the baby or the mother, then the normative standards of the law apply: life for life, eye for eye, and the like.[29]

---

28. Walter Kaiser states, "Moreover, the verb 'to come out' is used in every case except one (Num. 12:12, [where] it is used for a stillborn child) for the birth of an ordinary child." Walter C. Kaiser Jr., *Toward Old Testament Ethics* (Grand Rapids: Zondervan, 1983), 171.

29. Some have interpreted this passage alternatively to mean "she has a miscarriage," implying that the miscarriage of a child would result in only a fine's being assessed and thus it could be concluded that the preborn child carried less moral standing than an already-born child or adult human person. These arguments are not persuasive given either the context of the passage or the language used. In addition, even if the incident resulted in the accidental death of the child (miscarriage), this would not necessarily lead to the conclusion that somehow the unborn child carried less moral status. The discussion would then shift to whether different penalties should be incurred for an accidental death versus a premeditated murder—much like the laws for manslaughter versus first-degree murder in modern legal contexts. For a fuller discussion, see

In light of the incarnation of Christ, the general tenor of biblical passages that address contexts of preborn life, and the law of Moses regarding appropriate retribution for behavior that threatens the life of the innocent, we can conclude that the Bible indicates that from the earliest stages of development, every living human being is granted the same moral status. In sum, *there is no such thing as a living human being who is not also granted the full moral status of a human person.*

A Biblical Perspective on Abortion

Having arrived at this conclusion, we can now directly address the morality of abortion. It is important that those who take a *pro-life position* realize that the Bible never specifically says either that an unborn child is a person or that abortion is morally wrong. One cannot look in a concordance for the word *abortion* and find a direct statement about it in the Bible. As the previous discussion indicates, however, this should not be taken to mean that the Bible is silent about the issue. Recalling our discussion earlier in the book about biblical hermeneutics, this is a specific situation in which the moral question is best answered by using Scriptures to derive an ethical principle and then driving that ethical principle into the topic in question (see chapter 5 on the role of the Bible in ethics as worship). Here, the principle of the sanctity of human life moves to the central position in the debate. Since unborn children are given equal status as adult humans, the sixth commandment directly applies to the discussion: "You shall not murder" (Ex. 20:13).

Recalling what we have highlighted in previous chapters about this commandment, the Hebrew word translated into English as "murder" is *ratsakh*. In the Bible, *ratsakh* is never used to describe the killing that takes place in contexts in which God has commanded humans to take other human life (such as in the just application of capital punishment or divinely permitted involvement in war). Also, this word is never used in the Bible to refer to the killing of animals or plants. Thus, not all killing is forbidden by Scripture, but *the unjust taking of innocent life* is forbidden, which is what this command addresses. This includes not just intended homicide, but also negligent homicide in which a death takes place because of a failure to take adequate precautions. Therefore, in relation to the discussion of abortion, we can conclude that the sixth commandment does indeed speak directly to this topic. Any intentional and direct killing of a child (born or preborn) would fall into the category of *murder.*

Even though Scripture does not directly address the topic of abortion, this does not mean that the Bible is silent about the issue, nor were the early-church fathers. Some of the earliest church documents, which were heavily influenced

Jack W. Cottrell, "Abortion and the Mosaic Law," in *Issues and Applications*, ed. David K. Clark and Robert V. Rakestraw, vol. 2 of *Readings in Christian Ethics* (Grand Rapids: Baker, 1996), 32–35.

by Jesus' teaching in the Sermon on the Mount, specifically forbid the practice of both abortion and infanticide and set the standard for an overwhelmingly pro-life ethical stance throughout the history of the church. For example, as early as 120 A.D., the *Didache* (an early guide on Christian teaching) specifically teaches that "you shall not murder a child by abortion nor kill that which is begotten."[30] In like manner, the *Epistle of Barnabas* (125 A.D.) gives this instruction: "You shall not slay the child by procuring abortion; nor, again, shall you destroy it after it is born."[31] The second-century theologian and apologist Athenagoras offered one of the most reasoned cases against abortion in the early church. In his defense of the Christian faith, written to the Roman emperor, he drew on the issue of abortion to defend the nonviolence of Christians:

> And when we say that those women who use drugs to bring on abortion commit murder, and will have to give an account to God for the abortion, on what principle should we commit murder? For it does not belong to the same person to regard the very fetus in the womb as a created being, and therefore an object of God's care, and when it has passed into life, to kill it; and not to expose an infant, because those who expose them are chargeable with child-murder, and on the other hand, when it has been reared to destroy it. But we are in all things always alike and the same, submitting ourselves to reason, and not ruling over it.[32]

These and a host of other documents from the church fathers uniformly speak against the morality of abortion.[33]

It seems that as we consider a Christian perspective on abortion and the morality of the practice, practical wisdom should dictate what has generally been true of any civilized society. When there is any doubt, the benefit of the doubt should go toward the protection of human life. Therefore, not only is abortion wrong, this would also call into question the use of some forms of birth control as well as embryonic research conducted for either therapeutic reasons or reproductive purposes. We will address these topics in greater detail in subsequent chapters.

---

30. *Didache*, 2, ed. Alexander Roberts, James Donaldson, and A. Cleveland Coxe, trans. M. B. Riddle, Ante-Nicene Fathers 7 (Buffalo: Christian Literature, 1886), accessed January 25, 2020, http://www.newadvent.org/fathers/0714.htm.

31. *Epistle of Barnabas*, 19, ed. Alexander Roberts, James Donaldson, and A. Cleveland Coxe, trans. Alexander Roberts and James Donaldson, Ante-Nicene Fathers 1 (Buffalo: Christian Literature, 1885), accessed January 25, 2020, http://www.newadvent.org/fathers/0124.htm.

32. Athenagoras, "A Plea for the Christians," in *Fathers of the Second Century: Hermas, Tatian, Athenagoras, Theophilus, and Clement of Alexandria (Entire)*, ed. Alexander Roberts, James Donaldson, and A. Cleveland Coxe, trans. B. P. Pratten, Ante-Nicene Fathers 2 (Buffalo: Christian Literature, 1885), 147.

33. For a focused list of early-church writings about abortion, see "The Fathers on Abortion," accessed April 8, 2020, https://catholicism.org/fathers-abortion.html.

In sum, Scripture and church history attest that the child in the womb has moral status as an image-bearer and deserves protection against the travesty of abortion. Pope John Paul II was correct when he wrote that "the texts of Sacred Scripture never address the question of deliberate abortion and so do not directly and specifically condemn it. But they show such great respect for the human being in the mother's womb that they require as a logical consequence that God's commandment 'You shall not kill' be extended to the unborn child as well."[34] And this, then, is precisely why the Supreme Court's *Roe v. Wade* decision was so immensely tragic.

Objections

Even though we have made the case from Scripture and church history that abortion is a violation of God's design for human life, we still need to engage in the abortion debate with a society that may not accept biblical and theological arguments. Therefore, we need to be prepared to answer objections that we find in the public square. Francis Beckwith is on point when he writes:

> Most supporters of abortion choice agree with pro-life advocates that the question of abortion's permissibility rests on the moral status of the unborn: abortion is prima facie unjustified homicide if and only if the unborn entity is a full-fledged member of the human community (i.e., a person or subject of moral rights).[35]

Philosophically, the right to life is both logically prior to and more fundamental than the right to choose. Biblically, the taking of innocent human life is considered murder. The only way to justify that a right to choose trumps a right to life is either by attempting to make the case that the preborn baby does not have full moral status (denial of personhood) or by arguing that autonomy is the more binding moral norm even when an innocent life weighs in the balance. Most of the objections that are made to the biblical case against abortion fall along these two lines. In this section, we address examples of each in turn.

Personhood Objections

Two prominent forms of argument bring into question the moral status or personhood of the preborn child. Both forms suggest that moral status is not attained until some decisive point in the baby's development. The first is related to

---

34. John Paul II, *Evangelium Vitae*, 61.

35. Francis J. Beckwith, *Defending Life: A Moral and Legal Case against Abortion Choice* (Cambridge: Cambridge University Press, 2007), 130.

the question of biological development and the point of *ensoulment*. The second type of personhood objection focuses on the functional development of the child and can thus apply to unborn children as well as to children who are already born (thus raising the possibility of infanticide).

Developmental and Ensoulment Objections

Ensoulment has to do with an attempt to identify the point at which a soul inhabits a human body. The basic idea behind this objection is recognition of the living status of the unborn child but a denial of the status of personhood until the soul is present. This type of argument rests on the idea that at some decisive point in the process of biological development, God imparts a soul to the child and that it thus moves from the category of human being to human person.

Philosophically, this is a difficult argument to make because the soul is commonly understood as the animating principle of life in any living organism. As Aristotle argued, if something is alive, it has a soul.[36] Theologically, this is problematic because Christian doctrines related to anthropology have always held that human beings are "embodied selves" that are best understood as a body-soul duality integrated into one united self. Hence, the soul and the body are united at the point at which a unique life begins. Biblically, we have already seen this in our discussion of Jesus' incarnation in the Gospel of Luke.

Nonetheless, there are some who will appeal to a passage such as Genesis 2:7 to suggest that a human being does not receive a soul until the person receives the "breath of life." This passage reads, "Then the LORD God formed man of dust from the ground, and breathed into his nostrils the breath of life; and man became a living being." Before a child is born, it receives oxygen through the mother's body. The mother delivers oxygen to the baby through the blood that circulates through the placenta by means of the umbilical cord. This "breath of life" argument suggests that personhood does not begin until a baby draws its first breath at birth and only then becomes a living soul with full moral status. In addition to the philosophical, theological, and biblical reasons mentioned above, such an argument lacks substance for two additional reasons. First, the biblical text of Genesis 2:7 is speaking to "life" of the being in question, not personhood. To make a personhood argument is to demand from the text an argument that is not present in it. The better understanding is to recognize that Adam was a full person when he came to life, and that therefore the same would be true of a child at the moment of conception. Second, this type of argument does not take into account the unique nature of Adam's (and Eve's) creation. The first humans were uniquely created as adults. All other humans are conceived and grow through a normal

---

36. Aristotle, *De Anima*, 2.1 (412a20, 415b8).

process of gestation. Therefore, to appeal to this unique example as the normative understanding of when a human "becomes alive" or receives a soul is to compare apples to oranges.

A second version of this ensoulment objection identifies the point of quickening as the decisive point when the soul transforms the living being to a living person. *Quickening* is an old-fashioned word used to describe the point in a pregnancy when a mother becomes aware of the baby's movement. As it relates to this discussion, the argument is sometimes made that it is at the point of quickening that a rational soul enters the child and that thus, before this point, the baby is not a person, just living tissue. Those who want to make this type of argument often appeal to the Catholic theologian Thomas Aquinas (1224–74). Based on the scientific data available to him at the time, Aquinas concluded that God placed a rational soul within the body after conception: in males at the forty-day point and in females roughly at the eighty-day point.[37] This appeal to Aquinas was even present in the *Roe v. Wade* decision, noting the historical and legal significance of quickening as the point of ensoulment.

The problem with this form of reasoning, however, is twofold. First, it relies on an antiquated understanding of biology, which is all that Aquinas had available at the time, and second, it assumes that he would have retained the same perspective even if he did have a better sense of fetal development. Even though Aquinas never directly discussed the issue of abortion, there are two places in the *Summa Theologica* where he clearly indicates that taking the life of a preborn child would be a form of murder.[38] Thus, given his overall perspective on the sanctity of life, it is certainly possible to suggest that had he had a better understanding of modern biology, he very likely would have taken a much different view on the issue.

A third version would point to an even earlier stage in development by appealing to Leviticus 17:11 (see also Deut. 12:23), which states, "For the life of the flesh is in the blood." Here the argument is made that it is at the biological point when a fetus develops its own blood supply (around three weeks after conception) that the baby attains moral status. Biologically speaking, it is true that blood actively maintains life by providing oxygen and other vital nutrients to cells, tissues, and organs. But it would be wrong to suggest that a baby is not actually alive before having its own blood supply. Technically speaking, in the early stages of development before a child acquires its own blood supply, it is both alive and dependent

---

37. Thomas Aquinas, *Commentary on the Sentences*, trans. Ralph McInerny, bk. 3, d.2, q.5, a.2, resp., accessed June 23, 2020, https://isidore.co/aquinas/english/Sentences.htm.

38. Thomas Aquinas, *Summa Theologica*, 2–2.64.8; 3.68.11. We are indebted to Douglas Beaumont's helpful discussion on this topic. See his blog post "Aquinas on Abortion," March 1, 2012, accessed January 25, 2020, https://douglasbeaumont.com/2012/03/01/aquinas-on-abortion/.

on blood for its survival. In this case, its life is dependent on the mother's blood. It follows that the fact that the early-stage fetus does not yet have its own blood supply does not limit its "life."

Further, for the animals alluded to in Leviticus 17:11, given their stage of development, blood is necessary for them to be alive. It is the necessary precondition for their moral existence. Without blood, an animal will indeed die, as would also an early-stage embryo. But with a pre-twenty-day-old human embryo, the presence of its own blood supply is not a necessary precondition for life. Logically, it does not follow that the lack of an independent blood supply indicates that the child in question either is not alive or is not a person.

Finally, as we saw with Genesis 2:7, this text is speaking to the "life" of an animal, not the soul or personhood. Using this text as grounds for arguing a later stage of ensoulment both takes the text out of context and forces on it a discussion that is not inherent in it. Again, it is not a direct comparison and therefore results in the problem of eisegesis.

In sum, any appeal to a decisive moment of biological development other than conception is going to run into the problem of explaining the existence of "life" without the presence of the animating soul. As we have seen from these three examples, such arguments often appeal to sketchy attempts to force an idea into the text of Scripture that it does not speak to and to shift the argument being made about life to an artificial discussion about the soul. While biological development does indeed raise important and sometimes troubling questions about the human soul (e.g., the possibility of twinning and recombination), none of these necessarily lead to the conclusion that the soul is not present from the moment of conception. As we have argued above, the most compelling case both biblically and theologically is the one that places the point of ensoulment at the moment of conception.[39]

Functionalism Objections

The second type of personhood objection, *functionalism*, suggests that not all humans have equal moral status because some do not currently possess (or have not developed) the ability to function at a level deemed necessary to qualify for the full moral status of *person*. Influential ethicists such as Michael Tooley, Peter Singer, Tristram Engelhardt, and Jeffrey Reiman all suggest that personhood requires the presence of some combination of specific human functions such as self-consciousness, rationality, the ability to freely choose, moral agency,

---

39. For a helpful discussion regarding the nature of human personhood in light of early stages of human development (a "substance view of personhood"), see Beckwith, *Defending Life*, 132–34. See also J. P. Moreland and Scott Rae, *Body and Soul: Human Nature and the Crisis in Ethics* (Downers Grove, IL: InterVarsity Press, 2000), 206.

the ability to interact with others, and the ability to feel pain.[40] Singer, for example, comments: "My suggestion, then, is that we accord the fetus no higher moral status than we give to a nonhuman animal at a similar level of rationality, self-consciousness, awareness, capacity to feel and so on. Because no fetus is a person, no fetus has the same claim to life as a person."[41] From this point of view, unborn children do not have the status of fully human persons and therefore should be granted fewer moral and legal rights than someone who qualifies as a person.

The following diagram (see fig. 15.1) helps illustrate the idea.

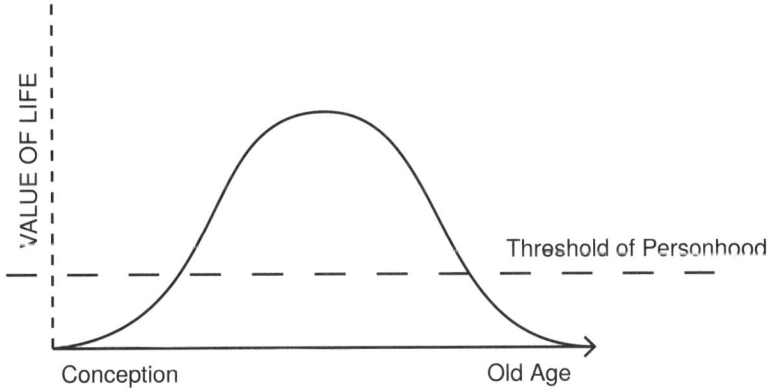

Fig. 15.1. Functionalism Perspective on Personhood

Note that this view of *functionalism* leads to several very troubling logical conclusions. First, not only does this view of personhood lead to the possible conclusion that abortion would be permissible from conception to birth, it actually rejects birth as a clear line of demarcation altogether. Following the logic of his own reasoning, for example, Singer comments: "A week-old baby is not a rational and self-aware being, and there are many nonhuman animals whose rationality, self-awareness, capacity to feel and so on, exceed that of a human baby a week or a month old. If, for the reasons I have given, the fetus does not have the same claim to life as a person, it appears that the newborn baby does not either."[42] Thus, not

---

40. See, e.g., Michael Tooley, "Abortion and Infanticide," in *Rights and Wrongs of Abortion*, ed. Marshall Cohen, Thomas Nagel, and Thomas Scanlon (Princeton, NJ: Princeton University Press, 1974), 57; Peter Singer, *Practical Ethics*, 3rd ed. (Cambridge: Cambridge University Press, 2011), 136; H. Tristram Engelhardt Jr., *The Foundations of Bioethics*, 2nd ed. (New York: Oxford University Press, 1996), 136; Jeffrey Reiman, *Critical Moral Liberalism* (Lanham, MD: Rowman & Littlefield, 1997), 121.

41. Peter Singer, *Practical Ethics*, 136. Singer goes on to claim that the status of nonperson extends to a child after birth as well. He acknowledges that abortion-rights proponents are uncomfortable with his logical consistency, but he believes that he is the one being consistent. Therefore, he argues for infanticide as well. See Singer, *Practical Ethics*, 151–54.

42. Singer, *Practical Ethics*, 151.

only is his argument "pro-choice" in regard to abortion, it is pro-choice in regard to infanticide.

Second, functionalism also has massive implications related to end-of-life scenarios in which, through age, injury, or illness, someone who may have once had the abilities that would qualify an individual for full moral status as a person may lose them. Logical consistency would suggest that in such cases, these humans no longer qualify as persons and also have fewer rights to life. In certain circumstances, it would then be morally permissible to terminate these lives as well. If this is the case with the aged, infirm, or ill, it logically follows that in certain contexts this must also be true of those who have disabilities that limit their ability to function.

As troubling as these types of arguments are, they can actually play a helpful role for pro-life advocates. There are two reasons that this is so. First, Singer's brutal honesty about the logical conclusions that follow from his (and all functionalist) arguments demonstrates the arbitrary nature of any form of pro-choice or pro-abortion positions that suggest a clear and obvious dividing line between those who have the lesser moral status of a human being and those granted the full moral status of a human person. Regardless of whether the standard is judged in terms of biological or rational development, certain questions emerge: Who gets to determine where that dividing line falls? Who is qualified to set the minimal standards required for someone to cross the threshold from human being into human person? It seems that the logical answer to those questions would be either "God" or "those who hold positions of power or influence." If the decision-maker is God, then what is said in the Bible pushes our understanding of personhood back toward the moment of conception, and abortion becomes immoral. If the decision-makers are persons of influence and power, the moral conclusion is not only much more liberal regarding abortion, but also much more frightening. History suggests that a dystopian reality with eugenics as the principal moral goal will be the result.

This leads to the second reason that this kind of argument can actually be helpful to the pro-life cause. The endgame of *functionalism* is horrifying. Therefore, although Singer's ultimate conclusion leads him to support legalized abortion, his critique of the classic pro-choice argument is, in a rather twisted way, very helpful. As this debate continues in the public square, it might be useful for pro-lifers to take note of Singer's critiques and the logical conclusions that follow from a functionalist type of argument about personhood and employ them by appealing to whatever sense of human dignity remains in our social and cultural bloodstream.

Autonomy Objection

In addition to the preceding personhood objections, a second category of pro-choice objections to pro-life arguments is best described as the *autonomy argument*. The autonomy argument emphasizes the right of a person to do with his or her own body whatever he or she deems favorable. In the abortion debate, the emphasis is the mother's body. The autonomy argument attempts to make the case that even if we grant the full moral status of personhood to a preborn baby all the way from the moment of conception, this fact does not necessarily require the moral conclusion that aborting the child is wrong. In the public square, this type of objection is often expressed by statements such as these: "Keep your laws off my body" and "My body, my choice." This argument is also often coupled with sentiments such as "I would never have an abortion myself, but I support a woman's right to choose." The foundational idea of the argument, in essence, is that *a woman should have the right to do with her own body whatever she chooses.*[43]

The Sovereign-Zone Argument

In his book *Persuasive Pro-Life*, Trent Horn helpfully distinguishes between two versions of this type of argument.[44] The first he calls the "sovereign zone" argument. Simply put, this argument rests on the claim that a woman has the absolute right to do whatever she wants with anything that is *inside* her body. While a woman would not be permitted to kill an infant or toddler because that child is outside her body, it is different with an unborn child. Since an unborn baby is inside the "sovereign zone" of her body, she can do whatever she wants with it.

This is a remarkably extreme argument. First, it is extreme because it flies in the face of how we generally think about the limits of sovereignty over property in general. Nowhere in society do we use the idea of personal ownership to do on our property whatever we choose. If a stranger wanders onto my land, I am not permitted to torture him because he has wandered into the sovereign zone of my private land. Likewise, I am not permitted to kill him on sight. Certainly, I cannot lure someone onto my land and kill him with impunity simply because he is in the "sovereign zone." Private-property rights are not absolute—especially when someone else's life is at stake.

Further, this type of absolute personal-sovereignty argument violates many laws that seek to protect both the mother and the child from behaviors that might endanger either. For example, we have laws that prohibit drug abuse and prostitution for a reason. But if we stick specifically to the type of "sovereign zone" that this argument is claiming, it leads to an extreme understanding of sovereignty. Consider the following two scenarios. First, if a woman were to cut open her own body and mutilate parts of her intestines or kidneys, we would question her claim to sovereignty based on concern for her sanity. "Who would do such a

---

43. Rae, *Moral Choices*, 139.

44. Trent Horn, *Persuasive Pro-Life: How to Talk about Our Culture's Toughest Issue* (El Cajon, CA: Catholic Answers, 2014), 155–73.

thing?" we would rightly ask. "Certainly no one in her right mind!" would be our answer. Common decency would move us to call authorities to get her help, and a civilized society would use the coercive force of the law to limit her own choices regarding her own body for her own good. Second, in the same flow of argument, if a mother chose to open her abdomen for the purpose not of aborting her unborn child, but of purposely maiming or torturing it, society not only would question her sanity, but would use the force of the law to protect the child for *its* own sake precisely because the sovereign claim over the mother's own body finds its limits at the boundary of causing harm to another person.[45] How much more so with killing her child? While bodily autonomy is important, there are limits. Both reasonable people and civilized societies recognize this.

Judith Jarvis Thomson's "Right to Refuse" Argument: "Unplugging the Violinist"
The second type of autonomy argument that Horn describes is the "right to refuse" argument. Instead of arguing that a woman can do whatever she wants within her body, this more subtle approach argues that she has the right to refuse to do something in her body. That is, she has the right to not be forced to care for a child that is living inside her.

Without question, Judith Jarvis Thomson introduced the most influential version of this argument in her article "A Defense of Abortion." Her argument has come to be known as "the violinist" argument. In the first part of her argument, she fully grants the status of personhood to the unborn from the point of conception. Then, having granted this, she goes on to make her case for autonomous choice by proposing the following (and now very famous) thought experiment:

> Let me ask you to imagine this. You wake up in the morning and find yourself back to back in bed with an unconscious violinist. A famous unconscious violinist. He has been found to have a fatal kidney ailment, and the Society of Music Lovers has canvassed all the available medical records and found that you alone have the right blood type to help. They have therefore kidnapped you, and last night the violinist's circulatory system was plugged into yours, so that your kidneys can be used to extract poisons from his blood as well as your own. The director of the hospital now tells you, "Look, we're sorry the Society of Music Lovers did this to you—we

---

45. This has been a long-standing limit to even utilitarian arguments such as those of John Stuart Mill, who asserted the "simple principle" or "harm principle," which states that a person can do whatever he wants as long as his actions do not harm others. Further, if they do harm others, then society is justified to use coercive force to prevent those actions that cause harm to others. In Mill's words, "the only purpose for which power can be rightfully exercised over any member of a civilized community, against his will, is to prevent harm to others. His own good, either physical or moral, is not a sufficient warrant." John Stuart Mill, *On Liberty* (New York: Penguin, 1974), 68–69.

would never have permitted it if we had known. But still, they did it, and the violinist is now plugged into you. To unplug you would be to kill him. But never mind, it's only for nine months. By then he will have recovered from his ailment, and can safely be unplugged from you." Is it morally incumbent on you to accede to this situation? No doubt it would be very nice of you if you did, a great kindness. But do you have to accede to it? What if it were not nine months, but nine years? Or longer still? What if the director of the hospital says, "Tough luck, I agree, but now you've got to stay in bed, with the violinist plugged into you, for the rest of your life. Because remember this. All persons have a right to life, and violinists are persons. Granted you have a right to decide what happens in and to your body, but a person's right to life outweighs your right to decide what happens in and to your body. So you cannot ever be unplugged from him."[46]

At first blush, this case typically elicits strong sympathy from any reader. The reason is that Thomson invites readers to put themselves in the shoes of someone who has unjustly and involuntarily been forced into a position of carrying a heavy and unwanted burden. She uses an emotional appeal to personal freedom in an attempt to place the principle of autonomy above the principle of the sanctity of human life. In doing so, she concludes that while it would be very nice for someone (like you) to provide the means for the other person's survival, certainly (she reasons) remaining connected to the violinist *cannot* be morally *obligatory*. Her move at this point is to suggest that it must be reasonable to see that in the same way, one could not require a mother to continue to sustain the life of an unwanted child. Abortion, she concludes, is therefore morally permissible because a mother is simply "unplugging" herself from a burden. If the mother wants to withdraw her uterus from the child, says Thomson, it is her right to do so.

Nevertheless, is such an argument logical? It is not, for several very important reasons. First, recognize that the scenario that Thomson sets up is not a direct comparison. Recalling our earlier discussion of the methods of abortion, actual abortions are nothing like this rather gentle description of "unplugging." To make the scenarios equal, we would have to be willing to say that it would be morally permissible to detach ourselves from the violinist through an act of violence in order to "unplug" him. It is not merely about allowing the violinist to die; he would need to be attacked and directly and purposely killed in a remarkably brutal manner.

Second, the violinist case is very different from that of abortion because in the vast majority of cases, the father and mother voluntarily entered into a sexual relationship. It is the natural order of the biology God created for sexual

46. Judith Jarvis Thomson, "A Defense of Abortion," *Philosophy & Public Affairs* 1, no. 1 (Fall 1971): 47–48.

intercourse to result in conception and pregnancy. Therefore, the parents do indeed bear a responsibility for the child. Remember, the autonomy argument (my body, my choice) grants that the baby is a full human person. Therefore, if it is wrong to kill the child to be free from it *after birth*, it is also wrong to kill the child *before birth*.

Third, it should be pointed out that if radical choice like this is allowable even in the face of the full moral status of another person, then why would such an argument be limited to the context of abortion? Why would such an argument be limited to the location of the baby in the woman's body? Wouldn't the same logic work in other situations and contexts in which someone else's existence places what I consider to be undue hardship on me? I can think of a few graduate students who might be willing to "unplug" me because of the heavy burden I place on them! On a serious note, would not this kind of argument lead to conclusions in which care for the invalid, comatose, or severely handicapped would become grounds for "unplugging" that person because his or her continued existence demands much of me?

Finally, Thomson's argument also seems to lead to the conclusion that if she saw an infant drowning in a puddle, she would have no moral obligation to seek to offer life-saving aid if it meant that doing so was burdensome. Granted, she is making the case that a nine-month pregnancy requires a much longer and more sustained effort to save a life. But if the argument is that one is not required to do so because of the principle of autonomy, then the length of inconvenience is ultimately not a determining factor. If I have the right to do with my body what I want, then there is no moral requirement to spend nine months or nine seconds to save the baby. The length of time just serves as a smoke screen regarding the fundamental nature of the argument she is making.[47]

Based on this reasoning, one can see why even these autonomy-based arguments ultimately fall back to questions of the moral status of human beings and personhood. Returning to the previous question that David Platt raised, what is in the womb is the central question:

> The key question that we all must answer—and the question that determines how we view abortion—is this: What is contained in the womb? Is it a person? Or is it merely an embryo, a fetus?[48]

47. For a more in-depth response to Thomson's argument, we refer our readers to two very helpful sources. See Mathew Lu, "Defusing the Violinist Analogy," *Human Life Review* 39, no. 1 (Winter 2013): 46–62, https://www.humanlifereview.com/wp-content/uploads/2015/11/2013-winter.pdf. See also Beckwith, *Defending Life*, 172–99. On a more popular level, we refer our readers to the excellent work of Randy Alcorn in *ProLife Answers to ProChoice Arguments*, expanded and updated ed. (Colorado Springs: Multnomah, 2000), 103–38.
48. Platt, *Counter Culture*, 63.

We cannot pretend to be a just and good society if we allow the killing of innocent persons either because they are in the wrong place (in the uterus of a mother who does not want the child) or because the person in question is burdensome.

Some well-meaning people may make a statement to this effect: "*while I would never have an abortion, I don't think it is right to limit the right of a woman to do with her own body whatever she chooses.*" Such a statement, however, espouses a level of autonomy that no society can tolerate. The logical extension of such absolute autonomy means that all manner of activities should be legal, including drug use and prostitution. This absolute autonomy may also allow for the direct, intentional killing of *anyone* simply based on location or the burdensome nature of the person's existence. This is not the mark of a just and good society.

On the other hand, perhaps the more consistent (and morally upright) understanding would be a recognition that a baby has full personhood from the moment of conception, and that if a mother has a right to bodily integrity, so also does a baby. Therefore, from the moment of conception, the baby has a right to not have his or her bodily integrity literally dismembered, poisoned, or crushed through abortion.[49]

Worship in the Hard Cases

Rape and Incest

We mentioned in the previous section that the vast majority of pregnancies that end in abortion are the result of consensual sexual encounters. Yet some are not. In a broken world, the tragic reality is that some pregnancies result from the wickedness of rape or incest. In the midst of debate and rational discussion, the Christian must not lose sight of the personal empathy, care, and love that must shape the way that we care for victims of such crimes. Likewise, Christians must not lose sight of the importance of seeing justice applied on behalf of both

---

49. Interestingly enough, Thomson in essence makes this point herself when she clarifies in her conclusion that while she is arguing for the permissibility of abortion if the child could simply be unplugged, she is not arguing for the right to secure the death of the unborn child. She writes: "I have argued that you are not morally required to spend nine months in bed, sustaining the life of that violinist, but to say this is by no means to say that if, when you unplug yourself, there is a miracle and he survives, you then have a right to turn round and slit his throat. You may detach yourself even if this costs him his life; you have no right to be guaranteed his death, by some other means, if unplugging yourself does not kill him." But here is precisely where this bodily-right argument fails. If Thomson is correct in making this distinction, then she has undercut her own argument for abortion because the process of abortion by definition intentionally and purposely secures the death of a child by the means of its procedure. Thus, her violinist case would actually apply only in scenarios in which the entire uterus is removed without directly harming the child. The indirect result may be the child's death, but not because of direct action to the child. Thomson, "Defense of Abortion," 66.

the woman and the society that are violated. No human being should ever have to experience rape or incest, and no society should be stained by such crimes. For this reason, those who commit these acts should be prosecuted to the full extent of the law. But given the horrible reality that such crimes do take place and the fact that these types of acts could lead to unwanted pregnancy, how should a Christian think about abortion when the child conceived results from either rape or incest?

First, it is important to keep in mind that the number of abortions that are sought out for reasons of rape or incest is very low in comparison to the overall number. The Guttmacher Institute conducted a survey in 2004 that reported that the number of abortions sought for the reason of rape is roughly 1 percent. Incest accounts for an even smaller percentage, at less than 0.5 percent.[50] The state of Florida records a reason for every abortion performed in the state, and rape was the reason reported for less than 0.2 percent of abortions and incest accounted for just over 0.01 percent of abortions in 2019.[51] While behind each of those requests for an abortion is a real person with a real story, it is important to keep in mind that these types of cases are much rarer than one might think—less than 1.5 percent of the total number of abortions annually.

In those cases in which pregnancy does occur, some argue, it would be better to allow the victim to terminate the pregnancy. Scott Klusendorf points out in response to this type of argument that we must remain clear about who is actually guilty of the crimes of rape and incest. It may be our desire and tendency to displace our grief and even anger toward the child, but the child is not the person who committed the crime. Thus, in a civilized society, we must be careful to not wrongly punish the innocent in order to be rid of a problem or to limit our experience of the aftermath of wickedness. Even if the presence of a child would bring to mind the painful memories of the rape or incest, this does not justify the killing of another person who had nothing to do with the crime itself. If we ask, "How should we treat innocent human beings who remind us of painful events?," surely the best answer is not "Kill them."[52]

Further, it is far from certain that encouraging a pregnant victim of rape or incest to abort is actually helpful to the woman in question. In fact, adding the trauma of abortion may actually exacerbate the problem. In the words of Planned Parenthood member Fred E. Mecklenburg, professor of obstetrics and gynecology

---

50. Finer et al., "Reasons U.S. Women Have Abortions," 113.

51. Agency for Health Care Administration, "Reported Induced Terminations of Pregnancy (ITOP) by Reason, by Trimester: 2019," accessed April 7, 2020, https://ahca.myflorida.com/MCHQ/Central_Services/Training_Support/docs/TrimesterByReason_2019.pdf.

52. Scott Klusendorf, *The Case for Life: Equipping Christians to Engage the Culture* (Wheaton, IL: Crossway, 2009), 173–74.

at the University of Minnesota Medical School: "There are no known psychiatric diseases which can be cured by abortion. . . . It may leave unresolved conflicts coupled with guilt and added depression which may be more harmful than the continuation of the pregnancy."[53]

Life of Mother

As pregnancies due to rape and incest are very rare, so also are contexts in which an unborn child's life needs to be taken in order to save the *life* of the mother. While there are many situations in which the mother's *health* may be compromised, this is not the same as concluding that her *life* may be in danger. Clarity on this point is important given the wording of *Roe v. Wade*, which conflated the language of *health* to be virtually all-inclusive. Concerns for the mother's general health are always important, but not all health issues are life-and-death concerns.

In those rare situations in which both the life of the mother and the life of the child are in question, doctors should do all they can to make sure that both patients survive. In some cases, normally in the later stages of a pregnancy, complications arise in which the mother cannot be saved but the baby can. In one example that we are familiar with, the mother was diagnosed with an aggressive form of cancer and chose to forgo treatments for fear that those treatments would harm her unborn baby.

Most often, however, the concern is raised in relation to the rare situations in which the mother's life can be saved only by the removal and subsequent death of the child. In these cases, a consistently pro-life stance will recognize the important distinction between providing a medical treatment for the particular attending problem or disease and the practice of abortion. For example, in the case of a "tubal pregnancy" (ectopic pregnancy), since the fertilized egg attaches outside the uterus (normally in the fallopian tube), it is particularly dangerous for the mother because the continued growth of the child can cause the tube to rupture, resulting in both the child's death and internal bleeding, infection, and possibly the mother's death. Often ectopic pregnancies resolve naturally in the form of miscarriages, but when they do not, medical intervention is needed.

When medical intervention is necessary, a consideration of both the *intent* and the *manner* of treatment is important to the overall moral evaluation. What distinguishes these cases from abortion is that the death of the baby is not desired, and the means chosen to treat the problem must not involve a direct and intentional killing of the child. No matter how the scenario is resolved, it is virtually a foregone conclusion that the child will perish. This foreseen fact, however, does

---

53. Quoted in Francis J. Beckwith, *Politically Correct Death: Answering the Arguments for Abortion Rights* (Grand Rapids: Baker, 1993), 71.

not legitimize wanting to kill the child or choosing to commit an act that directly targets the child and causes his or her death.

The *principle of double effect* proves to be a helpful guide in determining how best to proceed in such a situation. This principle helps determine when it is morally permissible to choose a course of action that will result in both good and bad effects. In order to invoke the principle of double effect, all four of the following criteria must be met:

1. The act being contemplated must be good in itself or at least morally neutral.
2. The evil result/effect must not be desired in itself but only permitted.
3. The good result/effect must not come about as a result of the evil effect. It must come directly from the good action.
4. There must be a sufficiently grave reason for permitting the evil effect to occur.

In using medical intervention to save the life of a mother in the case of an ectopic pregnancy, the principle guides in the following way:

1. The goal of the surgery is to save the life of the mother.
2. The removal of an ectopic pregnancy is not intended to kill the child; the baby's death is unwanted and not sought after.
3. Because directly targeting the baby to kill it is not an acceptable act, the doctors choose to remove the fallopian tube that would be the source of the bleeding and rupture. The death of the baby is foreseen but not directly chosen.
4. The reason that this drastic step has been chosen is that all other options have been exhausted and the life of the mother hangs in the balance.

In conclusion, while it is a foreseen consequence that the baby will die, the death is not intended and there was no direct attack on the baby in the procedure. The baby's death was a secondary result of removing the fallopian tube. For this reason, there is a critical difference between this form of medical treatment and abortion. Both the intent of the procedure and the cause of the baby's death are different.

For this reason, such a procedure would technically not be an abortion. In fact, given the pro-life ethic driving the decision-making process, it would be inappropriate to say that the procedure is a justification for "abortion in the case of saving the life of the mother." Rather, it is more accurate to say that sometimes medical intervention to save the life of the mother is permissible—even when there is a foreseen secondary effect of the baby's death—when, in an emergency situation, her life hangs in the balance. If ever in the course of treatment it is determined that the lives of the mother and the child can both be saved, the principle of double effect is no longer relevant to the context.[54]

Conclusion: Abortion Is a Watershed Issue

We began this chapter by considering the Supreme Court decision to legalize abortion in 1973. We have argued that by sidestepping the question of "when life begins" and by granting women legal permission to terminate a pregnancy based on a "right to privacy," the Court pitted the principles of the sanctity of human life and the principle of moral autonomy against each other. The resulting culture war has raged ever since.

As we conclude our discussion, it is important to remember what we argued in the opening chapter of this book. All human laws reflect and arise from underlying worldview assumptions. All laws are based on some perspective of morality. Therefore, whether someone claims to be pro-life or pro-choice, the arguments made in support of either position will reflect some underlying moral commitments. There is no such thing as a neutral position. The essential question, then, is not *whether* morality will be legislated, but *whose*.

When it comes to the issue of abortion, this reality plays out in very specific ways. Those who argue from a pro-life position will elevate the principle of the sanctity of human life, and suggest that from the moment of conception not only is a baby a human life, but because he or she bears the image of God, that child is also a human person. For this reason, our morality and our laws related to the issue of abortion should prioritize the protection and valuation of human life from the moment of conception. On the other hand, those who argue from a pro-choice perspective will elevate the principle of personal autonomy and suggest that one qualifies for the category of personhood only when one demonstrates the functional ability to qualify as a person. At such a point, not only does the person

---

54. Understanding this principle is why we (as otherwise very highly loyal and proud Southern Baptists) found the 2018 resolution by Southern Baptists at the 2018 SBC Annual Meeting in Dallas Texas, June 2018, to be so very disappointing. The resolution read as follows: "RESOLVED, That we affirm the full dignity of every unborn child and denounce every act of abortion *except to save the mother's physical life*." The exception included in the resolution represented muddled ethical thinking for at least one of the following three possible reasons: First, it suggests directly and intentionally targeting the life of an innocent human being to bring about a favorable result (i.e., murder to save a life); second, it fails to recognize the distinction between abortion and secondary effects of medical treatments; third (as a melded form of the previous two reasons), it presumes a form of "hierarchicalism" in the ethical process that suggests that it is sometimes permissible to break a command and commit an evil to bring about good without recognition that the evil is still evil. "On Reaffirming the Full Dignity of Every Human Being," accessed January 29, 2020, http://sbcannualmeeting.net/sbc18/resolutions/.

have the right to govern the person's own body as he or she will, but the person also has the moral right to kill those humans who do not qualify as persons. Both perspectives reflect a moral system. The question is, which one is correct?

We have argued in this chapter that while both these moral principles are important and have their place in ethical and civil discourse, Scripture and logic have led us to the conclusion not only that the principle of the sanctity of human life is the more fundamental and binding principle of the two, but that it should rightly shape how we understand who qualifies as a "person," as well as how we place restrictions on our own personal autonomy. From the moment of conception, a human child is an innocent, unique, distinct, living human being, who also bears the image of God. Directly and intentionally taking the life of a human child at any stage of its development is the same thing as killing an innocent human person. It breaks the sixth commandment and is therefore a form of murder.

In the end, this conclusion once again casts us back on the foundations of ethics as worship. God creates us to worship him maximally in all aspects of our lives. Human beings, however, not only have sinned but have thereby defiled themselves and broken the world in which we live. Each of us is a sinner; each of us needs a Savior. Thanks be to God that Jesus was willing to die on the cross for our sins, and praise be to God that he rose again to conquer sin and death. With all our brokenness, but especially with regard to this topic of abortion, God is good and his kindness draws us to repentance. While his grace, goodness, and kindness do not excuse our sin or provide a basis for justifying abortion, these qualities of God do invite us to be cleansed and made free. May it be that this kind of unmerited favor becomes the basis not only of why we "go our way and sin no more" in relationship to this issue, but also for the way in which we invite any and all who may have been involved in the abortive process in any way to find their way to forgiveness, hope, and life.

Key Terms and Concepts

abortion, elective

abortion, eugenic

abortion, induced

abortion, spontaneous

abortion, therapeutic

autonomy

Doe v. Bolton

ectopic pregnancy ("tubal pregnancy")

ensoulment

functionalism

image-bearer (*imago Dei*)

moral status

personhood

principle of double effect

ratsakh

right to life

right to privacy

Roe v. Wade   *shākōl*
sanctity of human life   *yātzā*

Key Scriptures

Genesis 1:26–28   Psalm 139:13–16
Exodus 20:13   Jeremiah 1:5
Exodus 21:12–36 (22–25)   Luke 1:39–44
Job 3:3   Luke 2:6–7
Psalm 8:3–8   Romans 13:9
Psalm 51:5   1 Peter 4:15

Study Questions

1. What does the Bible teach about the sanctity of human life, and how should that shape a person's view of abortion? How does understanding the Hebrew word *ratsakh* in the sixth commandment ("You shall not murder," Ex. 20:13) shape your view?

2. What is the significance of Exodus 21:22–25 for the abortion debate?

3. What is the pro-choice *functionalism* argument? Why is this problematic from a Christian worldview? What are the logical consequences of such an argument for people with disabilities or infirmities, or whose "social value" may be considered low?

4. If one is a retentionist regarding capital punishment and in support of a "just-war" perspective, does consistency demand that he or she should also adopt a pro-abortion stance? Identify the key issues and discuss. How is the question of "guilt" related to the discussion?

5. If one is an abolitionist regarding capital punishment or a pacifist regarding war, does consistency demand that the person also be pro-life regarding the debate on abortion? Identify the key issues and discuss. How is the question of personhood related to the discussion?

For Further Reading

Alcorn, Randy. *ProLife Answers to ProChoice Arguments*. Expanded and updated ed. Colorado Springs: Multnomah, 2000.

———. *Why Pro-Life? Caring for the Unborn and Their Mothers*. Rev. and updated ed. Peabody, MA: Hendrickson, 2012.

Beckwith, Francis J. *Defending Life: A Moral and Legal Case against Abortion Choice*. Cambridge: Cambridge University Press, 2007.

_____. *Politically Correct Death: Answering the Arguments for Abortion Rights.* Grand Rapids: Baker, 1993.

George, Robert P., and Christopher Tollefsen. *Embryo: A Defense of Human Life.* 2nd ed. Princeton, NJ: Witherspoon Institute, 2011.

Klusendorf, Scott. *The Case for Life: Equipping Christians to Engage the Culture.* Wheaton, IL: Crossway, 2009.

Mitchell, C. Ben, and D. Joy Riley. *Christian Bioethics: A Guide for Pastors, Health Care Professionals, and Families.* Nashville: B&H Academic, 2014.

Moreland, J. P., and Scott Rae. *Body and Soul: Human Nature and the Crisis in Ethics.* Downers Grove, IL: InterVarsity Press, 2000.

16

Euthanasia, Physician-Assisted Suicide, and End-of-Life Decision-Making

---

"Authority is not given to you, Steward of Gondor, to order the hour of your death."[1]
—GANDALF, The Return of the King

"There is nobility and dignity in caring for the dying, but not in dying itself."[2]
—PAUL RAMSEY, *"The Indignity of 'Death with Dignity'"*

Introduction

Death. For most of us, the mention of the topic conjures up some combination of uncertainty, fear, and, depending on one's situation in life, a poignant sorrow over remembered or impending loss. It is a difficult topic to discuss. It is a hard reality to face. And it is a subject that most of us are uncomfortable contemplating—especially when it concerns our own end. At the same time, short of some form of divine intervention, it is a reality that all of us will experience. As the old saying goes, only two things are certain in life: death and taxes. Despite our best medical efforts, the mortality rate remains 100 percent.

No matter what form death comes in, it is fair to say that all of us desire a *good death*. By saying that we want a good death, we normally mean one of two things. The first relates to the *purpose* of our death. If death is inevitable, most of us would desire that in some way our death served a good or noble purpose. Much like a firefighter or police officer who runs into a burning building to save a child or a soldier who throws his body over a grenade to save his brother-in-arms, we long

---

1. J. R. R. Tolkien, *The Return of the King: Being the Third Part of the Lord of the Rings* (New York: Ballantine, 2012), 129.
2. Paul Ramsey, "The Indignity of 'Death with Dignity,'" *Hastings Center Studies* 2, no. 2 (May 1974): 48.

for death to have some good meaning or *purpose* attached to it. After all, Jesus himself told us that great love is demonstrated when one lays down his or her life for another (John 15:13).

Most of us, however, will slip into eternity without such a noble form of death. The hard reality is that most of us will die not from martyrdom but from age, disease, or accident. In a wealthy society such as the United States, the availability of world-class healthcare services and advanced medical technology presents us with a double-edged sword. The desired benefit of increased life expectancy is coupled with the burden of an extended dying process that often happens in strange places. While the average life expectancy in 1920 was about fifty-four years, in 2020 that number hovered around seventy-seven years. It was common a hundred years ago for a person to die comparatively quickly and at home, but now our modern medicine and technology extend our dying process and result in a shift in the location of our death. In contemporary society, roughly 60 percent of Americans die in acute-care hospitals, 20 percent in nursing homes, and only 20 percent at home.[3]

This leads us to the second sense of how we often use the term *good death*. If death is inevitable, we want the *manner* of the death and dying process to be as quick and free from pain and suffering as possible. Indeed, it is not uncommon for most of us to feel relief, comfort, and even an anticipatory longing regarding our own death when we learn of a loved one who has "died peacefully in her sleep." This vicarious longing brings us directly into the discussion of ethics as worship as it relates to the end of a person's life. The word *euthanasia* literally means "good death" (Greek, *eu* "good," *thanatos* "death"), and it most often relates to the *manner* of a person's death and his or her end-of-life determinations in medically related contexts. It is concerned with the question whether it is morally permissible to cause death or allow a person to die in such a way as to minimize pain and suffering. More specifically, it pertains to the morality of choosing to hasten death as a means of preventing a person from experiencing further suffering or to use death as the means to end suffering.[4]

The point at which we desire a good death is also the place at which we encounter problems. While we desire the *cause* and *manner* of our death to be good, biblically and theologically speaking, the *nature* of death is evil. According to Scripture, death is an enemy (1 Cor. 15:25–26). It is a result of human rebellion

---

3. Joan M. Teno et al., "Change in End-of-Life Care for Medicare Beneficiaries," *JAMA* 309, no. 5 (2013): 470–77, accessed February 4, 2020, https://jamanetwork.com/journals/jama/fullarticle/1568250. See also Stanford School of Medicine, "Where Do Americans Die?," accessed February 4, 2020, https://palliative .stanford.edu/home-hospice-home-care-of-the-dying-patient/where-do-americans-die/.

4. Paul Ramsey, "'Euthanasia' and Dying Well Enough," *Linacre Quarterly* 44, no. 1 (February 1977): 38, accessed February 5, 2020, https://epublications.marquette.edu/lnq/vol44/iss1/7/.

and is a consequence of sin. It is what humans earned for turning away from the sovereign Creator, who is the God of life and goodness (Gen. 2:16–3:7). Paul connects sin and death as he writes that "all have sinned and fall short of the glory of God" (Rom. 3:23) and that "the wages of sin is death" (6:23a). As the late Princeton theologian and ethicist Paul Ramsey pointed out, it is problematic to put the words *good* and *death* together because the concept of *good death* is ultimately a contradiction in terms.[5]

Not only is death an evil consequence of sin, Scripture forbids us to seek it except in the exceptional cases of grave civil injustice (i.e., capital punishment, war) or the laying down of our life for others in an act of martyrdom or sacrificial service. The Christian, then, has to ask a different question before discussing the manner of death: is it ever permissible to desire or even pursue death (our own or another's) as a means of ending suffering? Only when one clearly answers this question can one properly turn to engage questions pertaining to the manner of one's death. In other words, how one answers this question will in turn have great impact on what one thinks about the moral and legal permissibility of such things as allowing a person to refuse medical treatment, allowing doctors to assist a patient in taking his or her own life, and allowing medical professionals to directly take the life of a person who asks them to do so.

In light of this, we begin the chapter by first identifying several landmark legal cases and cultural trends related to the topic of euthanasia. Our purpose is to help demonstrate the importance of the topic. Second, because *death* and *euthanasia* are heavily disputed concepts, we offer discussion on and definition of these terms in order to properly shape the contours of the ethical discussion. Third, we develop the scriptural ideas and theological principles that ought to drive a proper understanding of the issue. Fourth, we contrast a biblical perspective of death and dying with alternative perspectives and prevailing ideas present in the contemporary debate. Finally, before bringing the chapter to a conclusion, we offer some guidelines for how a Christian ought to apply an ethic of worship when facing end-of-life decision-making.

Cases and Trends

We mentioned in the previous chapter that there is a close connection between the topic of abortion and the topic of euthanasia. In many ways, the moral questions are almost identical because the cultural debates about these issues are ultimately concerned with how to prioritize and balance the same moral principles: the sanctity of human life and personal autonomy. The differences lie primarily

---

5. Ramsey, "Indignity of 'Death with Dignity,'" 48.

in the application of these principles. For the abortion question, the application is at the beginning of life, whereas the topic of euthanasia focuses attention on how these principles should be applied to end-of-life contexts.

It should come as no surprise that once the United States Supreme Court decided to treat questions about the beginning of life primarily in terms of the principle of autonomy ("right to privacy"), questions related to the end of life would eventually be treated in a similar fashion. Indeed, this is exactly the trend that has emerged. Not only are "right to die" laws and initiatives based on the moral principle of personal autonomy and the "right to privacy" gaining momentum, so also are requests granting legal access to help from medical professionals for the purpose of bringing about one's own death and even the death of others.

Terminating Life-Sustaining Treatments

Three legal cases highlight the moral and legal trends related to terminating end-of-life treatments. The first case involved Karen Ann Quinlan. On April 15, 1975, after arriving home from a party, the twenty-one-year-old woman collapsed from a drug overdose and stopped breathing for two fifteen-minute periods. Afterward, she lapsed into a persistent vegetative state (PVS). For the next several months, she was kept alive on a respirator but showed no signs of improvement despite efforts to wean her off dependency on the machine. Her doctors ultimately concluded that she would never emerge from her coma. Eventually, her parents requested that she be removed from the respirator. Initially the hospital, doctors, and a lower court refused their request based on concerns related to sanctity of life and the fear that allowing the termination of treatment in this case would weaken protections for others in similar conditions. This decision, however, was ultimately reversed when her father appealed to the New Jersey Supreme Court.

In 1976, that court ruled in favor of Joseph Quinlan's request based on a constitutional "right to privacy." In doing so, not only did the court set a precedent regarding the legality of terminating end-of-life treatment, it also recognized the right of a family member to provide a *substituted judgment* on behalf of the patient who could not herself give *consent*. Such a ruling was unprecedented in both regards before 1976.

It is important to note the connection that the New Jersey Supreme Court made between this case and the earlier U.S. Supreme Court ruling on abortion. It reached its ruling by concluding that the unwritten constitutional "right to privacy" is "broad enough to encompass a patient's decision to decline medical treatment under certain circumstances *in much the same way as it is broad enough to encompass a woman's decision to terminate pregnancy under certain conditions*."[6] As the

---

6. *In re Quinlan*, 355 A.2d 647, 663 (N.J. 1976) (emphasis added).

U.S. Supreme Court prioritized the principle of autonomy such that a woman was given the legal right to make a "private" decision about her own body in regard to pregnancy, so also the New Jersey Supreme Court prioritized the principle of autonomy such that a person could exercise the right to refuse medical treatment and thereby terminate life-sustaining treatment. The particular application of the underlying moral principles differed, but the ethical assumptions and processing were the same. A right to "choose" took the place of primacy over the "sanctity of life" principle.

Other landmark rulings followed that further cemented the principle of autonomy and the notion of a "right to privacy" as the ruling ethic for end-of-life decision-making. The second landmark case was similar to the Quinlan situation in its request to terminate life-sustaining care. This time, however, the focus was not on the removal of treatment directly related to the underlying disease, but on the removal of nutrition and hydration. In 1990, the parents of Nancy Beth Cruzan asked the courts to authorize the removal of feeding tubes that provided life-sustaining nutrition and hydration based on the argument that Nancy herself would not want to continue in a permanently vegetative state.[7] On December 14, 1990, her feeding tube was removed. She died just twelve days later.

The third case is that of Terri Schiavo. On March 31, 2005, Terri Schiavo's long and highly publicized case concluded with her death fourteen days after the Florida Supreme Court upheld her husband's request to have her feeding tube removed. This case is significant because while Terri's husband believed it was contrary to her wishes to continue in a permanent vegetative state, Terri's parents argued in the opposite direction: that even though she was severely disabled, she was responsive to interaction with others and displayed elements of *higher brain function*. Further, they argued that there was not enough court-required "clear and convincing evidence" that Terri would want to die, that the husband was not a fit guardian, and that they themselves would be willing to take over care for Terri. It was their contention that removing food and water would be a form of murder. Like the cases before it, because Terri could not express her own wishes, and because she had made no advance directive to guide her caretakers, the court sided with the husband as the legal guardian. Citing a right to privacy about Terri's own life, the court accepted the notion that the husband was speaking on her behalf with substituted judgment.

Landmark Assisted-Suicide Events and Cases

Following hard on the heels of these legal cases allowing for the withdrawal or removal of life-sustaining treatments, there have been a number of initiatives

7. *Cruzan v. Director*, 497 U.S. 261 (1990).

pressing not only to make physician assistance in hastening death a legal right, but also to positively frame *physician-assisted suicide* (PAS) as merely the next proper step on the "continuum of medical care."[8]

Perhaps the most infamous example is the case of Dr. Jack Kevorkian. On June 4, 1990, Kevorkian was thrust into the national spotlight when he helped a forty-five-year-old Oregon woman named Janet Adkins commit suicide. Adkins, who had recently been diagnosed with Alzheimer's disease, contacted Kevorkian after reading about his homemade "suicide machine." Adkins then flew to Michigan to meet with Kevorkian. After some brief discussions, he agreed to drive her to a public park in his old Volkswagen van and assist her in dying. At the park, Kevorkian first inserted an IV tube into her arm and began a saline drip. He then instructed her to push a button, which would first release a painkiller followed by a lethal dose of poison (potassium chloride). Within a few minutes, Janet Adkins was dead.

Initially, Kevorkian was charged with murder, but in December of that same year a Michigan judge ruled that the prosecutors had failed to make their case and that the lack of laws against physician-assisted suicide prohibited the state from pursuing the charges. Throughout the remainder of the decade, Kevorkian would assist an estimated 130 people in taking their own lives. In November 1999, however, Kevorkian filmed himself personally administering a lethal dose of poison to a man named Thomas Youk, who suffered from amyotrophic lateral sclerosis (ALS, or Lou Gehrig's disease). This time, a jury found him guilty of second-degree murder.

While Kevorkian's extreme methods were widely condemned by doctors, lawyers, and ethicists of all stripes, many in each of those professions shared similar convictions about the right of a patient to seek assistance in dying. In fact, not long after Kevorkian helped Janet Adkins commit suicide, the prestigious *New England Journal of Medicine* published an article by Dr. Timothy Quill that sparked a parallel debate within the medical profession. In that article, Quill recounted his experience with a woman named Diane, who had been a patient of his for more than eight years. Over the course of his interaction with her, Diane repeatedly refused treatment for leukemia and also requested Quill's assistance in helping her die. In the article, Quill describes how he agonized with the patient over the decision, but eventually not only prescribed her an overdose of barbiturates, but also clarified for her how to overdose on the pills in order to commit suicide.[9]

Quill's article was particularly important for at least two reasons. First, his

---

8. Tom L. Beauchamp and James F. Childress, *Principles of Biomedical Ethics*, 6th ed. (New York: Oxford University Press, 2009), 184.

9. Timothy E. Quill, "Death and Dignity: A Case of Individualized Decision-making," *NEJM* 324 (March 7, 1991): 691–94.

methodology for decision-making was distinct from Kevorkian's because his moral reasoning fit much more carefully into a medical model that honored personal autonomy and privacy of choice. Second, and closely related, his methodology also attempted to stay within a system of guidelines and accepted patient-care protocols. In this way, he sought to cast his decision to help Diane commit suicide as merely the next form of compassionate end-of-life care.

The problem is that while Quill's patient-care and ethical decision-making process followed many of the acceptable guidelines of a medical tradition that maximizes patient autonomy, in the end his decision and actions radically departed from the time-honored moral standards most associated with the medical profession. While Western medicine has been largely framed within the long-standing Judeo-Christian ethic that honors and protects life, Quill argued that assisting in suicide under certain conditions was actually the most compassionate form of patient care.[10] Once again, the principle of autonomy that fuels the recognized "right to privacy" was given priority in the moral evaluation over a concern for protecting life.

These and other events eventually led to the U.S. Supreme Court's landmark decision in a joint ruling on the *Vacco v. Quill* and *Washington v. Glucksberg* cases.[11] The Court was asked to rule on the legality of two different state laws that prohibited physician-assisted suicide. On June 26, 1997, the Court rendered a 9–0 ruling upholding a New York ban on physician-assisted suicide, thereby preventing doctors from assisting their patients in taking their own lives.

This case is significant because the complainants (who notably included Timothy Quill) argued that there is no significant moral difference between a patient's being able to refuse end-of-life treatment and asking for assistance in ending life.[12] Thus, they were demanding the right to assist in dying under the Equal Protection Clause of the Fourteenth Amendment. The Court, however, disagreed and rightly ruled that there is an important difference between *letting someone die* by removing treatment and *causing someone to die* with an intentional prescription of life-ending medication. In the former situation, the ultimate cause of death is the underlying disease, and in the latter, the ultimate cause of death is the

10. The classic version of the Hippocratic Oath states: "I will neither give a deadly drug to anybody who asked for it, nor will I make a suggestion to this effect." Ludwig Edelstein, *The Hippocratic Oath: Text, Translation, and Interpretation* (Baltimore: Johns Hopkins University Press, 1943).

11. *Vacco v. Quill*, 521 U.S. 793 (1997); *Washington v. Glucksberg*, 521 U.S. 702 (1997).

12. The respondents in the *Vacco v. Quill* case were three physicians who practiced medicine in the state of New York: Timothy E. Quill, Samuel C. Klagsbrun, and Howard A. Grossman. They argued that it would be consistent with the standards of medical practice to assist a patient in dying by prescribing lethal medication if the patient was mentally competent, terminally ill, and suffering from unbearable pain and who made an informed decision to ask for a doctor's help in taking his or her own life within the context of an ongoing patient-physician relationship.

introduction of life-ending drugs. The Court was also interested in upholding the state's duty to preserve the lives of its citizens, to keep physicians as healers, and to protect future vulnerable people who might become victims of intentional killing in the name of euthanasia.[13]

While the Court upheld the New York ban, it did not rule that assisted suicide was wrong per se, only that the New York and Washington laws prohibiting assisted suicide did not violate the Equal Protection Clause of the Fourteenth Amendment. In simpler terms, the Court effectively ruled that there is no constitutional guarantee of a "right to die." Based on earlier rulings regarding a "right to privacy," a patient can refuse treatment, but nowhere in the Constitution is there a basis to claim a right to have someone else assist a person in committing suicide.

Unfortunately, the Court left open the possibility for a state to introduce laws to make physician-assisted suicide legal. Simply put, a state cannot say that a physician must help a person commit suicide when asked, but a state can make it legal for a physician to assist if he or she is willing to do so. States that allow for physician-assisted suicide use either the language of "death with dignity" or "right to die" to describe their laws. Most of these laws require a patient to be of a certain age, to have been diagnosed with an underlying disease that would cause the patient to die within a certain period, and to conform to rigorous informed-consent guidelines. As of 2019, all fifty states allow patients to refuse treatment, but only seven states allow doctors to assist a patient in suicide: California (2015), Colorado (2016), Hawaii (2018), Montana (2009), Oregon (1994), Vermont (2013), and Washington (2008). The District of Columbia (Washington, DC) also has an assisted-dying statute (2017).

One of the better-known cases of physician-assisted suicide in the United States involved a twenty-nine-year-old woman named Brittany Maynard. In January 2014, Maynard was diagnosed with brain cancer and by the early spring was told that her condition was terminal (stage 4 glioblastoma multiforme) and that she had only six months to live. Shortly after the diagnosis, she and her husband moved from California to Oregon to take advantage of Oregon's Death with Dignity Act. During her last months, Maynard became a prominent spokeswoman for the death-with-dignity movement and gained national attention when she wrote an opinion column for CNN and released a widely viewed video expressing her plans to end her own life. She is quoted as saying: "I'm not killing myself. Cancer is killing me."[14] On November 1, 2014, however, Maynard chose to take a

---

13. The majority of state legislatures make a clear distinction between assisted suicide and withdrawing or permitting the refusal of unwanted end-of-life medical treatment. The former is understood to be a form of *killing*, the latter a form of *letting die*.

14. "Death with Dignity Advocate Brittany Maynard Dies in Oregon," NBC News, November 3, 2014, accessed February 7, 2020, https://www.nbcnews.com/health/health-news/death-dignity-advocate-brittany

lethal dose of barbiturates provided by her doctor. Those doctor-prescribed drugs killed her, not the cancer.

Despite the significant ethical problems that are associated with these trends, Gallup polls indicate that there is a high level of support (72 percent) for the idea that "doctors should be legally allowed, at a patient's and a family's request, to end a terminally ill patient's life using painless means." Importantly, support drops significantly among those who identify themselves as weekly churchgoers of any denomination (37 percent).[15] While it is better that these numbers are lower among regular church attenders, the fact that more than one in three regular churchgoers are willing to approve of such practices means that Christian instruction on the sanctity of life and the proper care of the dying is severely lacking.

Euthanasia

The active killing of a person by the hands of medical professionals is still illegal in the United States. Given the trends and trajectory of moral argumentation in the cases above, however, it should come as no surprise that the pressure is mounting to legalize this practice as the next step down on the slippery slope of what is often called the "death with dignity" movement. In fact, this is exactly what has already taken place in several European countries. For example, in the Netherlands and Belgium, the so-called right-to-die or death-with-dignity arguments have led to very liberal and aggressive laws allowing for direct *voluntary euthanasia* (defined below). Not only do both countries allow for physician assistance in suicide, they also allow for the direct act of killing by doctors (via injection of poison) for people who are "suffering unbearably" with no hope of relief but who may not even be terminally ill. Even more remarkable, and frightening, the minimum age for euthanasia is only twelve years old in the Netherlands, while Belgium has no minimum age limit at all.[16]

At the core of these culture trends lie several very important ethical questions. First, is there any real moral difference between an act of *commission* and *omission* or between the *active killing of someone* and the *choice to remove treatment to allow someone to die*? Second, is it ever permissible to take one's own life (commit suicide) in order to end suffering? Third, is it morally justifiable to assist someone in committing suicide? Fourth, is it ever morally justified to directly and intentionally put another person to death even if he or she persistently asks you to do so? How one believes these questions ought to be answered depends almost

---

-maynard-dies-oregon-n235091.

15. Megan Brenan, "Americans' Strong Support for Euthanasia Persists," Gallup, May 31, 2018, accessed February 7, 2020, https://news.gallup.com/poll/235145/americans-strong-support-euthanasia-persists.aspx.

16. At the time of writing (2020), euthanasia is legal in the Netherlands, Belgium, Colombia, Luxembourg, Canada, India, and South Korea. Assisted suicide is lawful in Switzerland, Germany, South Korea, and Japan.

entirely on how one seeks to balance the two moral principles of *respect for personal autonomy* and *the duty to protect innocent human life* (the sanctity of human life). We will return to this discussion once we have defined several key concepts and discussed the biblical and theological principles that must shape one's ethical perspective.

Key Terms and Definitions

Death

Three Prominent Definitions of Death

In the previous chapter, we pointed out that much of the debate about abortion revolved around when human *life begins*. In a similar fashion, the debate about euthanasia revolves around how we should determine when *death begins*. While it may be tempting to take for granted what we mean when we speak of *death*, as John Jefferson Davis rightly states, "the very definition of death has been a matter of moral and medical dispute."[17] As we discovered in the abortion discussion, if a baby is alive from the moment of conception, then it would logically follow that the principle of the sanctity of human life should give the benefit of the doubt to the person in the womb and create laws to protect the child at the beginning of life. In the same way, when we consider end-of-life issues, the principle of the sanctity of life should give the benefit of the doubt to protecting life for those who are nearing the end of their lives even up to the very point of death.

As one might imagine, if there is confusion or disagreement about the nature of death itself, then one would expect there also to be significant disagreement about end-of-life care and when it is proper (or not) to discontinue treatment. The moral status of the individual changes drastically at the point of death. That is, once an individual is declared to be dead, the individual no longer has the same moral or legal status as when he or she was living. Society no longer has the same moral duties toward the individual. Treatment can cease, organs can be harvested, the body can be cremated or buried—all things that may not be proper to do to a living person (certainly not the last two!). How *death* is defined and how it is determined has massive implications for the ethics of end-of-life decision-making. C. Ben Mitchell is correct: "the importance of a correct definition of death cannot be overstated, especially from the perspective of the Christian faith."[18]

How should we define *death*? Medically speaking, when we discuss physical death, there are three major perspectives on what it means to be dead. The first

---

17. John Jefferson Davis, *Evangelical Ethics: Issues Facing the Church Today*, 4th ed. (Phillipsburg, NJ: P&R Publishing, 2015), 178.

18. C. Ben Mitchell and D. Joy Riley, *Christian Bioethics: A Guide for Pastors, Health Care Professionals, and Families* (Nashville: B&H Academic, 2014), 135.

one is known as the *cardiopulmonary* definition. This one is the most traditional definition and was the dominant definition before the advent of modern medical technologies in the 1960s. Under this definition, a person is considered dead when there is an irreversible stoppage of the circulatory and respiratory functions (heart and lungs).

Table 16.1. Three Prominent Definitions of *Death*

Cardiopulmonary	Irreversible loss of circulatory and respiratory functions (heart and lungs).	Traditional
Whole Brain	Irreversible loss of all functions of the entire brain: cerebrum, cerebellum, brain stem ("total brain failure," "flatline EEG").	Currently Accepted
Higher Brain	Irreversible loss of higher brain functions (governed by the neocortex, or only those areas responsible for consciousness and motor control).	Proposed (highly controversial)

With the advent of more advanced lifesaving technologies, the ability to determine whether and when an *irreversible* stoppage of respiratory function occurs became harder to determine. This reality, coupled with the advances in organ-transplant technologies, spurred initiatives to develop a new "brain death" criterion. In 1968, the Harvard Medical School's Ad Hoc Committee on Brain Death first coined the term, and then in 1981, the President's Commission for the Study of Ethical Problems in Medicine and Biomedical and Behavioral Research advanced the Uniform Determination of Death Act (UDDA). The UDDA defined someone as *dead* if the person "has sustained either (1) irreversible cessation of circulatory and respiratory functions, or (2) irreversible cessation of all function of the entire brain, including the brain stem."[19] Importantly, because the three major life systems governed by the heart, lungs, and brain are mutually dependent, if one of these criteria is met, the others will eventually follow.[20] While it would be possible to introduce artificial means (respirator, artificial heart) to keep the body functioning in such a scenario, this would not therefore mean that the person was still alive. If the artificial means were removed, the body would cease to function and thereby confirm that death had taken place. This *whole brain death* definition is currently the most widely accepted definition of *death* used in both legal and medical contexts.

19. "Guidelines for the Determination of Death," *JAMA* 246, no. 19 (1981): 2184–86.
20. John M. Frame, *The Doctrine of the Christian Life* (Phillipsburg, NJ: P&R Publishing, 2008), 733.

The third—most recent and most controversial—proposal is often described as the *higher brain death* definition. While generally not accepted legally, recent years have seen a strong push for this definition among various physicians, lawyers, and ethicists who advocate for many of the right-to-die and death-with-dignity initiatives we identified above. In this view, a person would be considered dead if there were an irreversible loss of just the higher brain functions. The human brain consists of three parts: (1) the cerebrum or cortex, which controls areas related to conscious awareness, emotions, and most of our communication skills, (2) the cerebellum, which is largely responsible for control of voluntary muscle movements and motor skills, and (3) the brain stem, which is the lower part of the brain, connected to the spinal cord. The brain stem controls the spontaneous aspects of our body and life functions, such as breathing, heart rate, and digestion.

This view introduces the idea that a human being can have a body that is living and functioning apart from artificial means and yet the person would be considered dead. Even though the heart beats on its own, the lungs breathe without aid, and the digestive tract functions to process nutrition without medical intervention, the person is considered dead. Organs could be harvested, medical treatments ceased, food and water no longer provided, and the death of the body even hastened by direct actions (such as injection of lethal drugs) that would otherwise be considered murderous.

A Christian Definition of Death

From a distinctly Christian perspective, the Bible speaks of death in three ways: spiritual, eternal, and physical. Spiritual death relates to our loss of right standing before God due to our trespasses and sins and results in our loss of personal fellowship with God (Eph. 2:1–5). Eternal death is directly related to our spiritual death as the permanent state of separation from God's blessing and loving, benevolent fellowship (i.e., hell, 2 Thess. 1:9).[21] Physical death is also a result of sin and rebellion, but in God's mercy he allows us to have bodily life as a part of his general grace. Scripturally, physical death is most often described in terms of a person's "breathing his last" (e.g., Gen. 25:8, 17; 35:29; 49:33; Mark 15:39; Acts 5:5, 10; 12:23). Jesus commented on his own death by saying, "Father, into your hands I commit my spirit." The text then goes on to say that at this point, Jesus "breathed His last" (Luke 23:46).

As we discussed in chapter 2, a living human being consists of an integration of both body and soul, with the soul as the animating principle of the body (Gen. 2:7). In light of Jesus' comments, the Christian best defines *physical death* as that point at which the soul departs from the earthly body (2 Cor. 5:6–8), which is then

---

21. Frame, *Doctrine of the Christian Life*, 685, 733.

marked by an irreversible cessation of breathing. Making a clear determination of when the soul departs the body is difficult, as is the determination of irreversible cessation of breathing. Thus, the Christian also relies heavily on the first two medical criteria for determining death mentioned above (heart and lung cessation and whole brain death) to help discern when death has occurred. Further, because the departure of the soul marks the time when a person's body can no longer live on its own, the Christian must reject the "higher brain" definition of *death*. If the body can function on its own, then the soul is present, and because that living person still bears the image of God, the principles relating to the sanctity of life still apply.

Euthanasia

How we understand and use the word *euthanasia* is also of great importance. The term *euthanasia* literally means "good death." Broadly speaking, it has to do with the intentional hastening of death for the purpose of ending suffering. Nevertheless, as the cases above illustrate, this "hastening of death" can take place in various ways, each of which needs care and specification in order to arrive at a proper moral evaluation.

In an attempt to bring proper nuance and moral evaluation to the discussion, ethicists have identified distinct categories of euthanasia that reflect two distinct elements of the end-of-life decision-making process. The first relates directly to the principle of autonomy and is normally described as *consent* or *voluntariness*. Consent has to do with one's awareness of what one is deciding and whether one gives permission or agrees with the decision made. A patient who is deemed to be competent and adequately informed can give voluntary consent by stating his or her wishes directly or by deputizing another person to do so through a living will or a durable power of attorney for healthcare. This element of end-of-life decision-making seeks to determine whether a person's choice about end-of-life treatment is voluntary, nonvoluntary, or involuntary. When a patient gives consent or has left prior instructions, the treatment is considered voluntary. When a patient is unable to give consent and has not left prior instructions, the decision for treatment is considered nonvoluntary. When a patient has given consent or left instructions but those instructions are not followed, the decision on treatment is considered involuntary.

Causality (or *agency*) is concerned with how a person's death comes about. The focus is on how the death is carried out. Is death *actively* caused by introducing a new cause of death separate from the underlying disease? Or does death occur *passively* by allowing the underlying disease to run its course? Historically, ethicists have used the distinction between *active* and *passive* to help identify the final or ultimate cause of death. *Active euthanasia*, then, is typically understood to involve the act of killing someone (including the self) through a definite action intending to end a person's life (an act of *commission*). By contrast, *passive euthanasia* has been generally understood to mean refusing or forgoing life-sustaining treatments (an act of *omission*).

The following table (see table 16.2) helps to illustrate these six categories.

Table 16.2. Six Categories of Euthanasia

Consent/Causality	Voluntary	Nonvoluntary	Involuntary
Active	Voluntary/Active	Nonvoluntary/Active	Involuntary/Active
Passive	Voluntary/Passive	Nonvoluntary/Passive	Involuntary/Passive

As we will see below, while these terms have been helpful to some degree to make academic distinction, they are not without problems.

Three Types of Active Euthanasia

Voluntary active euthanasia involves the patient's not only giving informed consent to dying but also requesting and receiving help in doing so. An example of this would involve a physician's hastening death by actively administering a lethal drug to a patient upon the patient's request. *Nonvoluntary active euthanasia* involves a patient whose final wishes about the manner of death are not known with certainty. The reason for lack of knowledge, for example, could be that the person is too young to understand or consent, is mentally incompetent, or has slipped into a coma without having provided an advance directive. In this case, a physician would take it upon himself or herself to hasten death by administering a lethal dose of a drug without being certain of the patient's wishes. *Involuntary active euthanasia* involves a person's acting directly to kill a patient not only without informed consent but also contrary to the patient's wishes. The key element in these active-euthanasia categories is that death is the intention of the action. For this reason, all three of these categories are morally problematic.

It is important to note that when the word *euthanasia* is used in the regular, contemporary culture, its assumed meaning is one of these three categories of *active euthanasia*. It is generally taken to convey a context in which a second party actively and directly causes the death of the patient. This may take place through a lethal injection, smothering with a pillow, gunshot, and so on. When this takes place, the means of death is no longer the underlying disease or medical condition but something new that is introduced into the situation in order to cause death. For this reason, serious questions related to the breaking of the sixth commandment—"You shall not murder" (Ex. 20:13)—come directly into play.

Active Euthanasia and Physician-Assisted Suicide

Physician-assisted suicide (PAS) also raises serious questions related to the sixth commandment because it involves the voluntary choice to take one's own life (self-killing/self-murder) with the assistance of a medical professional. Technically speaking, the World Medical Association defines *assistance in suicide* as "knowingly and intentionally providing a person with the knowledge or means or both required to commit suicide, including counseling about lethal doses of drugs, prescribing such lethal doses, or supplying the drugs."[22] The moral evaluation of PAS involves a consideration of three key elements. First, a person intends his or her own death. Second, the person voluntarily takes direct action to bring about his or her own death. Third, the person asks and enlists someone else to assist by providing the means for inflicting his or her own death. Therefore, physician-assisted suicide is a form of voluntary active euthanasia. The only significant difference between euthanasia and physician-assisted suicide is who performs the final act of killing. The only real difference is that the physician does not "pull the trigger." He or she just "sets the gun in the hand."

Morally, both voluntary active euthanasia and physician-assisted suicide are versions of what was described above as an active voluntary decision to hasten death by the intentional introduction of a new cause of death. Both are intentional killing. Returning to the Brittany Maynard case, contrary to her argument that she was not killing herself, the fact is that she willfully ingested the drugs that a physician gave her expressly for the purpose of taking her own life. The lethal drug prescription killed her, not the cancer.

Three Types of Passive Euthanasia

Traditionally, the language of *passive euthanasia* has been employed in an attempt to make a distinction between the introduction of a new agency of death through a physician's active means and the withholding or withdrawing of treatment to allow the underlying disease to run its course. In this sense, the word *passive* has to do with omitting an action that might otherwise prolong life. *Voluntary passive euthanasia* involves the patient's giving full informed consent to the withholding or withdrawing of treatments to allow the underlying disease to run its course. Typically, this is the least morally problematic of the six categories. *Nonvoluntary passive euthanasia* involves a patient whose final wishes are not known but for whom the decision is nonetheless made to remove life-sustaining or prolonging treatments. *Involuntary passive euthanasia* is the removal of

22. John R. Williams, *Medical Ethics Manual*, 3rd ed. (Ferncy-Voltaire Cedex, France: World Medical Association, 2015), 58, accessed February 14, 2020, https://www.wma.net/wp-content/uploads/2016/11/Ethics_manual_3rd_Nov2015_en_1x1.pdf#page=38.

life-sustaining or prolonging treatments against a patient's wishes. And for this reason, the third form is morally problematic.

Consider once again the Terri Schiavo case to highlight how these distinct categories could help us better understand the moral situation faced by the family members and courts. In that situation, Terri did not leave any type of clear advance instructions or directives—hers was a *nonvoluntary* situation. Her husband, however, argued before the courts that it would have been Terri's wish to remove *life-sustaining* treatments. Thus, he sued to allow Terri to die. Her parents, on the other hand, viewed the situation differently. They argued that it would be against Terri's wishes to remove *life-sustaining* treatments. To do so, they believed, would be a case of involuntary passive euthanasia. Moreover, because the decision to remove feeding tubes was involuntary (*against* her wishes), the husband's request to have them removed should be refused by the courts to protect Terri from being murdered.

In more recent ethical discussions, the term *passive euthanasia* has come upon hard times. The reason for this is that the word *passive* can be a bit misleading. In an end-of-life decision-making context, when a patient, family, or doctor chooses to withhold or withdraw treatment, that decision-making process is very much an *active* choice that requires careful reasoning and willful decision-making. It is not something that merely happens *passively* as though no agency or process of choosing were involved. So if the word *passive* is going to be used, it has to be particularly nuanced and further defined to mean the *allowance of the underlying sickness to run its course.* For this reason, it is no longer commonly used in end-of-life decision-making discussions.

Instead, it is now much more common in contemporary contexts to hear the language of *forgoing end-of-life medical treatment* or *terminating life-sustaining treatments* instead of referencing some form of *passive euthanasia.* These terms help clarify what is actually taking place medically with end-of-life decisions that involve *withholding* treatments. Yet while these terms help clarify what is happening medically, they do not necessarily clarify what is happening morally. The moral discussion, as we saw in the Supreme Court's ruling on the *Vacco v. Quill* case earlier in the chapter, now most normatively revolves around the language of *killing* versus *letting die.* We will return to a discussion of *killing* versus *letting die* after making one other point of practical wisdom relating to the common usage of the word *euthanasia.*

Care Needed When Using the Term Euthanasia

While historically distinguishing these six categories of euthanasia may have proved helpful to introduce the various elements of the end-of-life-treatment debate in academic settings, using the word *euthanasia* as the umbrella term to capture all these ideas is itself also problematic.[23] The reason is that the generally understood meaning of the word *euthanasia* is typically equated with the idea of hastening death by *actively* putting someone to death. Therefore, while in academic settings it may be helpful to use the six categories above to identify specific moral nuances, these nuances are often lost in common usage.

To illustrate this, imagine the following scenario. A pastor of a small rural church, after taking an ethics class, encounters a situation in which Mrs. Jones, an eighty-year-old grandmother and forty-year member of his congregation, is diagnosed with an aggressive form of stage 4 pancreatic cancer. She is given four weeks to live and has therefore chosen to forgo chemotherapy treatments because such treatments would be futile and she does not want to reduce the quality of her life that remains. Imagine further that, having taken the ethics class, the pastor recognizes that this grandmother's decision could be classified as *voluntary passive euthanasia* according to the table above (see table 16.2). Finally, imagine that on Sunday morning he then announces to his congregation that he is in favor of Mrs. Jones's decision to *euthanize* herself. According to the academic language, he may be saying something that is technically accurate. Given his context and the commonly accepted meaning of *euthanasia* as a form of active killing, however, his announcement would be taken to mean something very different from Mrs. Jones's values. Not only would he send his congregation into an uproar, he would probably be looking for a new job.

Killing versus Letting Die

Because the term *euthanasia* has become so generally understood to mean the act of putting someone else to death and because nuancing it with terms such as *active/passive* or *voluntary/involuntary/nonvoluntary* is so cumbersome, most ethicists believe that the better language to use for the moral debate is the important distinction between *killing* and *letting die*.

Killing is the commission of an act that directly causes death. It can be done by the agent himself or herself or by a second person. In this context, however, it not only involves a direct action that takes a life, but also involves the intentionality to do so *as a means to ending the suffering* of the patient. The relevant moral factors include an evaluation of the consequences (the fact that the patient dies), the means of death, and the intention of the act that causes the death. Killing, then, not only involves the introduction of a new cause of death, but also identifies that the primary intention of the chosen path of treatment is to purposefully bring about the patient's death.

Letting die, on the other hand, also results in death, but the means of death

---

23. One of the earliest was Paul Ramsey. See Ramsey, "'Euthanasia' and Dying Well Enough," 37–46.

and the intentionality involved in the process are very different. In terms of the means of death, letting die involves forgoing medical treatment (withholding or withdrawing) such that the cause of death remains the underlying disease that was already at work. While there is a recognition that death will come as a result and that death may even be a relief in light of the patient's ongoing suffering, the intent is never to kill or use death as the strategy to end suffering.

By way of example, refer once again to eighty-year-old Mrs. Jones, who is diagnosed with an aggressive form of pancreatic cancer and who is given just four weeks to live. On the one hand, she could choose a strategy of killing to deal with her situation by asking a doctor either for an overdose of pills or for a lethal injection. There is no question that she would die, but the means of death would now be something new. The pills or injection would be the means of death, not the underlying disease. In addition, the purpose of taking the pills or giving the injection would expressly be for the purpose of ending her life. There may be mixed and confused desires to attempt to show "mercy" or "compassion," but ultimately the intent would be to use death as the means to end Mrs. Jones's suffering.

On the other hand, she could choose to forgo treatments in light of the fact that the aggressive nature of the cancer will make such treatments futile and that they will also greatly increase her discomfort at the end of her life. By forgoing the treatments, the underlying disease (pancreatic cancer) will ultimately kill her. Also, if she chooses this route, she can do so with no intention of causing her own death and without any intention to use death as a strategy to end suffering. In this course of action, it is likely that as the end of her life approaches, she will be glad that death ends her suffering. She can choose to use appropriate painkilling medications to help her endure and relieve her pain. Nevertheless, neither the glad anticipation that her suffering will soon come to conclusion nor the use of painkillers necessarily means that she is intending death. The recognition that death will be a relief is very different from intending it. Foreseeing is morally distinct from intending.

As we pointed out in the previous chapter on abortion, the *principle of double effect* is a helpful guide to making these types of morally nuanced distinctions. Because we developed that idea more fully in the previous chapter, here we simply refer our readers to the chart below (see table 16.3).

Table 16.3. The Principle of Double Effect

1. The act being contemplated must be good in itself or at least morally neutral.
2. The evil result/effect must not be desired in itself but only permitted.
3. The good result/effect must not come about as a result of the evil effect. It must come directly from the good action.
4. There must be a sufficiently grave reason for permitting the evil effect to occur.

To be fair, if a person believed that the only relevant factor (or the dominant factor) in ethics were the final consequence, then this distinction between killing and letting die would appear rather silly. Indeed, this is the position that some scholars and ethicists take.[24] Yet if ethics involves a respect for God's moral commands related to the sanctity of life as well as an ordering of our worship to God and the shaping of our virtues in accordance with these things, then this distinction proves very useful in guiding and evaluating our choices.

Likewise, it is important to state that it is not merely the act of forgoing treatment that makes the concept of letting die morally superior. It is possible for someone to mask his or her intentions of seeking death merely through a passive means of suicide. For example, returning to our case with Mrs. Jones, it is conceivable that a person in her situation could decide to forgo treatment because she wants to die and is seeking death as the means to end suffering. Yet perhaps she is scared of killing herself through an overdose, or perhaps she does not want her long reputation as a faithful church member to be tainted by a suicidal act. In this situation, even the passive forgoing of end-of-life treatment could have a suicidal intent and would also be morally suspect.

Therefore, it is important to recognize that intentionality, while very hard to judge from an external source, is a key factor and must also be guided by both the principle of the sanctity of life and practical action guides on how to make wise and God-honoring decisions at the end of life. Because the *killing* versus *letting die* language seeks to bring intentionality into the moral discussion, it is a morally relevant and helpful distinction.

In sum, we affirm that while it is not perfect, we believe the *killing* versus *letting die* distinction is superior to the categories of both *active* and *passive euthanasia* because it is concerned not only with *consent* and *causality*, but also with *intentionality*. It likely does not answer all the questions because in each particular case there will be a need for evaluation of a person's intentions in particular situations. Using the *killing* versus *letting die* language, however, can serve to give guidance and provide moral clarity by accounting for some evaluation of intentionality as a third major factor in decision-making.

Guiding Biblical and Theological Principles

As is the case with many of the other ethical issues we are discussing, the Bible does not name and address euthanasia or physician-assisted suicide directly. This fact, however, should not be taken to mean that the Bible does not speak

---

24. See James Rachels's article from his perspective as a utilitarian. James Rachels, "Active and Passive Euthanasia," *NEJM* 292, no. 2 (January 9, 1975): 78–80.

to the issue of euthanasia and assisted suicide. As God's fully sufficient guide-book for life and practice, the Bible not only records narrative stories of humans who struggled with end-of-life decision-making (e.g., Judg. 9:50–57; 1 Sam. 31; 2 Sam. 1), but also records poetry and wisdom related to the human struggle with death (e.g., Pss. 23; 116:15; Eccl. 9:5) and in many places gives instructions that directly apply to the topic of euthanasia and physician-assisted suicide (e.g., Ex. 20:13; 1 Cor. 15). Moral discernment regarding euthanasia and physician-assisted suicide must be grounded in Scripture and the biblical and theological principles found there.

Humans as Image-Bearers (Gen. 1:27–28)

Genesis 1:27 teaches us that all human beings are *image-bearers* of God: "God created man in His own image, in the image of God He created him; male and female He created them."

This image-bearing status makes human beings unique among all creation. For this reason, human beings' moral status is not dependent on their actions or their ability to function. Rather, it is dependent on the inherent value that God gives them simply by the fact that he has created them, and that he has created them uniquely in his image.

Humans as Embodied Selves (Gen. 2:7)

Genesis 2:7 references that God also created human beings as embodied selves: "The LORD God formed man of dust from the ground, and breathed into his nostrils the breath of life; and man became a living being." Not only did God create all things physical and so our physical bodies should be received as a good thing, God also integrated into the human being a living soul. That is, when God breathed into Adam's nostrils the breath of life, he imparted to the body a soul and integrated this together into a unified whole, sometimes described by theologians as a *psychosomatic whole* or, more popularly, as an *embodied self.* Humans have both a material and an immaterial element, and the impartation of the soul "animates" the body or causes it to live. Contrary to ancient Greek ideas or philosophical dualism, this passage teaches us that human beings are both body and soul together. In philosophical language, we would say that humans are *dualistic,* but their makeup is not one that we would describe as *dualism.*

Viewing persons as embodied selves is an important point concerning the topic of euthanasia because a body living on its own entails that the soul is present. It also means that if a person chooses an action to bring about the death of the body, that action also brings about the death of the person. This would be the case if someone were in a permanently vegetative state, in an unresponsive coma, asleep, or walking around with a full sense of self-awareness. Personhood exists in a human being because a human being has a soul, and that soul is what animates the body. Conversely, if a body is being maintained by medical equipment that performs all the basic functions of respiration, heart-pumping, and digestion but would not be able to continue if these machines were removed, and if the whole brain is unresponsive, then that is not a living person in the same sense that we have been discussing here.

Life as Stewardship (Gen. 1:28)

Not only are human beings image-bearers who are embodied selves, but Genesis 1:28 describes humans as having a special role as God's stewards over creation:

> God blessed them; and God said to them, "Be fruitful and multiply, and fill the earth, and subdue it; and rule over the fish of the sea and over the birds of the sky and over every living thing that moves on the earth."

God gave human beings as his image-bearers a high level of responsibility to champion his cause and purposes among the rest of creation. That is, God created humans to be his *stewards* who would "subdue" the earth and "rule over" it in his name and in accord with his character. As we discussed more fully in chapter 2, this leadership and ruling function was not meant to give complete, unrestricted freedom to humans to "subdue" the earth in any way they desired, but in accordance with God's design and instruction. While God did give them a certain amount of autonomy to rule the earth, this "self-rule" would lead to flourishing and fulfillment only when it was aligned with God's design, morally ordered to his character, and oriented toward his ultimate goal and purposes. Human beings do not exist for themselves. Their own happiness and flourishing will find maximal fulfillment only when they live for the glory of God in accord with his design and instruction.

Death as an Alien Enemy (Rom. 6:23)

We learn from Scripture that it is precisely because humans attempted to express their autonomy in a manner contrary to God's design and instruction that death entered the picture. In Genesis 3, we learn that Adam and Eve chose to sin, and as Romans 6:23a indicates, "the wages of sin is death." Death is a consequence of sin and rebellion. It is not "natural" in the sense of being something that God desired for us to experience, but it is inevitable now as a consequence of sin. Death is alien to the way in which he designed the world and us. As humans, we face the "last enemy" of death because of our misdirected autonomy (1 Cor. 15:26).

As we pointed out earlier in the chapter, when the Bible speaks of death, it refers to spiritual death, eternal death, and physical death. Each of these should be resisted. Spiritual and eternal death can be resisted only through the saving work and sacrifice of Jesus Christ. Salvation comes by faith alone, through grace alone, in Jesus Christ alone. But as God's image-bearers and stewards, it is good and right for humans to resist physical death and not embrace it as a good in itself.

Resisting Death by Protecting Life (Ex. 20:13)

God's instructions indicate that in a fallen world tainted by sin, we should both protect physical life and seek human flourishing in our physical life, and yet not place our ultimate hope in the life we live in the here and now. God's clearest and simplest instruction regarding how to resist death properly is found in Exodus 20:13, "You shall not murder." The Hebrew word translated into English in this verse is *ratsakh*. The closest word that we have in English is *murder*. But the meaning of *ratsakh* not only encompasses the intentional killing of the innocent, but also implies that we should be careful to avoid any type of manslaughter or negligent homicide that results from failing to take adequate precautions to guard human life.[25]

This verse helps us understand how we should resist death in at least two senses. In the narrowest sense, it means that we should not intentionally kill innocent persons. The immediate application to the topic of euthanasia should be clear. Intentionally seeking the death of a patient runs directly contrary to God's loving instruction found in this command. The same is true with the question of suicide or seeking the assistance of a physician in suicide. Whether the person killed is the self or another, the action is a form of *ratsakh* ("murder"). Choosing this path is as much a rebellion against God as was Adam and Eve's rebellion in Genesis 3.

In a broader sense, the verse also instructs us to create a context among individuals and in society as a whole in which life is championed by the way that we seek to guard human life. Not only would it be wrong for a society to enable the killing of innocent people upon their request, it would also be wrong to empower others to grant such requests. Human life is to be protected unless a clear exception is granted (e.g., see our discussion of the sixth commandment and taking the life of the unjust or those guilty of capital crimes in contexts of capital punishment and war in chapters 13 and 14). As we learned in our discussions of capital punishment and war, even when taking the life of the unjust is biblically warranted, the motive is for the very purpose of protecting the life of the innocent.

Authority has not been granted to God's stewards to break this command even in the name of compassion. Contrary to the idea that human dignity can be found or preserved through killing or assisting in suicide, this command recognizes that humans have an inherent dignity as image-bearers. Thus, the intentional killing of a patient or assisting one to kill oneself can never be, by definition, a dignified act. True compassion never kills the innocent. When this verse is properly

---

25. Frame, *Doctrine of the Christian Life*, 686–87. See esp. 687n2.

understood, it teaches us that euthanasia, suicide, and assisting in suicide are all versions of *ratsakh* ("murder"), and that legalizing them based on the idea that someone has a right to request them amounts to nothing more than legalizing "murder by request."

Beyond these two senses of protecting life, this command should also be understood as a key element of God's design to promote human flourishing throughout all of life. This command falls within the context of the Decalogue, which plays an important role in spelling out how image-bearers are to obey the two greatest commandments that Jesus identifies in loving God preeminently and loving one's neighbor as oneself (Mark 12:29–31). It teaches us that *the principle of the sanctity of human life* not only seeks to avoid unjust killing, but also seeks to protect human life. Furthermore, it seeks to demonstrate our love for God and neighbor by creating a pro-life ethic that reaches from conception to natural death and includes the promotion of human flourishing in all stages of life in between.

The Redemptive Nature of Suffering (Rom. 5:1–5)

Another biblical principle that needs to be kept in mind does not speak directly to the protection of life and why it would be wrong to put someone to death or to assist in suicide, but does have relevance to the discussion of flourishing even in the face of suffering. Scripture often indicates that there is a redemptive nature to our suffering, which does not make suffering in itself a good thing, but places it in a larger context by which we understand it and recognize the good that could ultimately come from it.

To be clear, when we use the word *redemptive* in this discussion, we do not mean that suffering earns our salvation. Rather, we mean that God can use our suffering in a valuable manner. Specifically, God can use it to help us become conformed to his image. In many places in Scripture, suffering is described as a tool God uses to shape us into the kind of people that he wants us to be. For example, Romans 5:1–5 tells us to rejoice in our sufferings because our sufferings produce positive fruits of character that make us more like Christ. Therefore, from a Christian worldview, it is wrong to think of suffering as valueless or something that must be escaped at all costs. As C. S. Lewis eloquently put it, "God whispers to us in our pleasures, speaks in our conscience, but shouts in our pain: it is His megaphone to rouse a deaf world."[26]

While a positive redemptive value can be found in suffering, nowhere does the Christian faith attempt to sugarcoat the hardship of suffering. For as Lewis went on to rightly add, pain can serve as God's megaphone to humble us and draw us into reliance on him, and it can also lead a person to final and unrepented

---

26. C. S. Lewis, *The Problem of Pain* (New York: HarperCollins, 1996), 91.

rebellion. It is important that one always keep in mind the greater story line of Scripture in which God gives to us not only *revealed morality*, but also *revealed reality*. While he instructs us to not take innocent human life or intentionally cause death in times of suffering, he also gives us a higher vista from which to understand why suffering is present in the world (a natural consequence of rebellious expressions of human autonomy), how it can be used by God to shape our character (conforming us to the image of Christ), and toward whom our hope must ultimately be oriented (Jesus, who is the way, the truth, and the life).

Hope (1 Cor. 15:51–58)

Finally, as we think through the scriptural teachings that are related to the topic of euthanasia and physician-assisted suicide, it is important for a Christian to have a proper perspective on death itself. As we have alluded to earlier in the chapter, death is an alien experience. We were not created for it. While it is inevitable, it should not be embraced, nor should it be downplayed. It should not be feared, and it should not be avoided at all costs. Philippians 1:21 helps us gain a proper perspective. The apostle Paul understood that if he was going to live his life even in difficult circumstances, he needed to live them to the glory of God. But because of the work of Christ, if he were to die, there would be an even greater gain. In a similar line of teaching in 1 Corinthians 15, we see these beautiful words:

> Behold, I tell you a mystery; we will not all sleep, but we will all be changed, in a moment, in the twinkling of an eye, at the last trumpet; for the trumpet will sound, and the dead will be raised imperishable, and we will be changed. For this perishable must put on the imperishable, and this mortal must put on immortality. But when this perishable will have put on the imperishable, and this mortal will have put on immortality, then will come about the saying that is written, "Death is swallowed up in victory. O death, where is your victory? O death, where is your sting?" The sting of death is sin, and the power of sin is the law; but thanks be to God, who gives us the victory through our Lord Jesus Christ.
>
> Therefore, my beloved brethren, be steadfast, immovable, always abounding in the work of the Lord, knowing that your toil is not in vain in the Lord. (1 Cor. 15:51–58)

For the Christian, the sting of death has been removed. While it is important for the Christian to resist death and protect life by not killing a patient, ultimately we do not cling to our physical life at all costs as though this life were our final hope. For the Christian, this life is not the last chapter of the story. Death is an enemy to be conquered, but God has already conquered it. While the dying process is likely to be hard and perhaps frightening, a greater hope overwhelms it.

This is why Scripture likens the death of a Christian to falling asleep (Acts 7:60; 1 Cor. 15:51). The waking on the other side is the waking into the joy that we were created and rescued for in Christ to enjoy forever. For the person who is in Christ, death is not the end of life; it is the beginning. Death is merely the passage into an ever-increasingly joy-filled life of eternal fellowship with our infinite God. The weightiness of this truth fuels the potency of the Christian's hope.

Objections to the Biblical View and Arguments for Euthanasia—Personhood and Autonomy

Given the previous discussion, it should be clear that any person wrestling with the ethics of euthanasia and physician-assisted suicide must deal with whether it is morally permissible to kill innocent human beings. In a civilized society, the burden of proof lies on those in favor of legalizing these forms of killing to demonstrate how the act of killing oneself or killing someone else is not murder.

In a manner that is strikingly similar to the abortion debate, two types of arguments are commonly used in an attempt to justify the morality of euthanasia and physician-assisted suicide. The first is a personhood-based argument suggesting that it is permissible to kill the patient because he or she has somehow lost the full moral status necessary to qualify for personhood. The other is an autonomy-based line of reasoning suggesting that a right to personal choice and privacy not only provides the basis to refuse treatment, but also legitimizes a right to request—or even demand—assistance in causing one's own death. That is, the right to personal self-governance and choice about one's own manner of death is a weightier moral principle than the principle of the sanctity of human life.

Personhood Objections

Two prominent forms of argument bring into question personhood at the end of life. Both forms suggest that moral status is no longer attained after some decisive point in that individual's dying process. The first is related to the question of when the soul departs the body. The second type of personhood argument focuses on the functional ability of the person in question.

Departure-of-the Soul Arguments

Earlier in the chapter, we introduced the case of a young woman named Nancy Beth Cruzan who, as a result of an automobile accident, was considered to be in a permanently vegetative state. After eight years of litigation, the family won the right to terminate all life-sustaining treatments, including nutrition and hydration, which resulted in her death twelve days later. An interesting aspect of this case relates to the tombstone that her parents put on her grave. It reads:

Nancy Beth Cruzan, Most Loved Daughter—Sister—Aunt
Born July 20, 1957
Departed Jan. 11, 1983
At Peace Dec. 26, 1990

This headstone is a poignant example of the type of philosophical and moral reasoning that seeks to distinguish the categories of a human being and a human person. From the parents' point of view, even though Nancy's heart and lungs were able to function without assistance and her body could process food, the tombstone indicates that they concluded that Nancy herself was somehow *no longer there.*

As a mirror image of the ensoulment argument regarding abortion that we discussed in the previous chapter, this line of reasoning suggests that while there is no question that Nancy was a living *human being,* she was no longer a living *human person.* Thus, terminating treatments as well as food and water was not morally problematic and did not amount to a form of unjust killing.

The problem, however, is in how one can conclusively demonstrate that a person is no longer present even though his or her body is able to function completely on its own. This is a morally problematic form of reasoning because, as Aristotle famously argued, the soul is commonly understood as the animating principle of life in any living organism. More importantly for the Christian, this is a problematic argument because Scripture teaches us that human beings are best understood as "embodied selves" or a body-soul duality integrated into one united self (Gen. 2:7). Hence, the soul and the body are united at the point when a unique life begins all the way up to the point when the body can no longer live on its own. From a Christian perspective, Nancy departed not on January 11, 1983, but on December 26, 1990.

Functionalism Arguments

The second type of personhood argument often used to justify purposeful killing of patients is labeled as *functionalism.* This line of reasoning suggests that not all humans have equal moral status because they no longer possess the ability to function at a level deemed necessary to qualify for the full moral status of a *person.* This argument is similar to the previous one in its denial of personhood, but it seeks a less arbitrary means of measurement for determining when the person is "no longer there." The most common form will appeal to the "higher brain death" definition discussed earlier in the chapter to justify intentional killing.

Recalling our earlier discussion, the human brain consists of three parts: (1) the cerebrum or cortex, which controls areas related to conscious awareness, emotions, and most of our communication skills, (2) the cerebellum, which is largely responsible for control of voluntary muscle movements and motor skills, and (3) the brain stem, which is the lower part of the brain connected to the spinal cord. The brain stem controls the spontaneous aspects of our body and life functions such as breathing, heart rate, and digestion. Using these categories, a functionalism argument suggests that because the higher brain regions govern such things as self-consciousness, rationality, the ability to interact with others, and moral agency and are key to personhood, if they no longer function to enable these key elements, then this lack of ability to function indicates a change of moral status. Personhood, so the argument goes, has been lost. The individual can no longer function at a level that demonstrates personhood. Thus, the individual may qualify as a living being, but not a living person who has full moral status. Consider the words of Peter Singer as a case in point:

> The fact that a being is a human being, in the sense of a member of the species Homo sapiens, is not relevant to the wrongness of killing it; it is, rather, characteristics like rationality, autonomy, and self-awareness that make a difference. . . . Killing them, therefore, cannot be equated with killing normal human beings, or any other self-aware beings.[27]

The following diagram (see fig. 16.1), as it did in the previous chapter on abortion, helps to illustrate the idea.

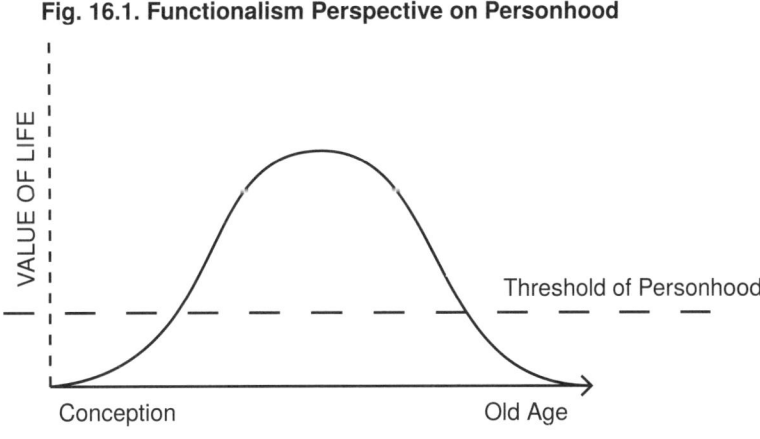

Fig. 16.1. Functionalism Perspective on Personhood

VALUE OF LIFE

Threshold of Personhood

Conception   Old Age

27. Peter Singer, *Practical Ethics*, 3rd ed. (Cambridge: Cambridge University Press, 2011), 160. The context of Singer's comments is in a discussion directly related to the killing of infants. The ethical principle he is citing, however, directly relates. In his influential *Morals and Medicine*, Joseph Fletcher comments in a similar fashion relating to end-of-life contexts: "Personality is supreme over mere life. To prolong life uselessly, while the personal qualities of freedom, knowledge, self-possession and control, and responsibility are sacrificed is to attack the moral status of a person." Joseph Fletcher, *Morals and Medicine: The Moral Problems of the Patient's Right to Know the Truth, Contraception, Artificial Insemination, Sterilization, Euthanasia* (Princeton, NJ: Princeton University Press, 1979), 191.

Note that this view of functionalism leads to some very troubling conclusions. First, it suggests that even if an individual has a healthy, functioning heart, is able to breathe independently, and has a digestive system that is able to process food and water normally, the individual's body parts could be harvested for organ transplantation or other medical uses without concern that harvesting these organs might cause the body to die.

Second, note that though this version of functionalism is relying on a definition of *death* that seeks to locate death in the loss of function of the higher brain, it does not adequately clarify *why* the loss of these functions distinguishes a living being from a living person. What if someone slips into a long-term coma and has higher brain functioning to some degree? Why would it be wrong to limit personhood discussions to the lack of higher brain function? Who gets to be the moral arbiter of how an individual qualifies for the high moral status of personhood? The functionalism argument suggests a degradation of moral status over time such that the aging may not qualify for healthcare, social security, or disability services because of degrading function even though they may not yet qualify for euthanasia.

Lest one think that such a conclusion is beyond the realm of possibility in the world of modern ethics, consider the following words of Joseph Fletcher:

> It is ridiculous to give ethical approval to the positive ending of subhuman life in utero, as we do in therapeutic abortions for reasons of mercy and compassion, but refuse to approve of positively ending a subhuman life in extremis [i.e., when they are near death]. If we are morally obliged to put an end to a pregnancy when an amniocentesis reveals a terribly defective fetus, we are equally obliged to put an end to a patient's hopeless misery when a brain scan reveals that a patient with cancer has advanced brain metastases.[28]

Fletcher's comments make it clear. Not only is the argument between abortion and euthanasia virtually identical if the logic of such personhood arguments holds, but actively killing patients for a number of reasons becomes permissible and even "obligatory." While our society is not at this point, the logical conclusion of this form of moral argument sets these kinds of discussions in motion. Who is ultimately qualified to determine these new standards of personhood? Who gets to decide when a person becomes "subhuman"? Who gets to decide when the person's death becomes "obligatory"?

Thus, as we pointed out in our similar discussion regarding the abortion debate

---

28. Joseph Fletcher, "Ethics and Euthanasia," in *To Live and to Die: When, Why, and How*, ed. Robert H. Williams (New York: Springer-Verlag, 1973), 116.

in the previous chapter, the logical answer to these questions would be either "God" or "those who hold positions of power or influence." If the decision-maker is God, then what is said in the Bible pushes our understanding of personhood back toward the moment of conception and forward to the point of heart and lung cessation coupled with whole brain death.[29] If the decision-makers are persons of influence and power, the potential moral conclusions become much more frightening.

Autonomy Objections (Personal Freedom and Rights, Quality of Life)

The second category of pro-euthanasia and physician-assisted-suicide argumentation is best described as the *autonomy argument*. In this category, the emphasis is placed squarely on the right of a person to do with his or her own body whatever he or she deems favorable. These arguments seek to justify the morality of killing not based on the lower moral status of an individual in question but by elevating the person's right to choose how and when to die. This right to private choice is then said to outweigh arguments suggesting that human life is sacred and must be protected. In the public square, this type of pro-euthanasia argumentation is often expressed with "right to die" or "death with dignity" language. The underlying assumption is that the ability to choose, not one's status as an image-bearer, is the key element to dignity.

When we speak of the principle of *autonomy*, we are referring to the idea of self-rule or self-governance (Greek, *autos* "self," *nomos* "rule, governance"). In modern thought, the principles find their roots in the work and thought of such Enlightenment philosophers as Immanuel Kant and John Stuart Mill. The moral principle of respecting a person's autonomy flows from two foundational ideas. The first is the assumption that each and every individual has inherent and unconditional worth and therefore should always be treated as an end in himself or herself and never merely (or only) as a means to an end. The second is closely related and dependent on the first. It is the idea that because individuals are ends in themselves, each person *should* be given the freedom to make his or her own decisions in accord with his or her own goals.[30] And this *should* implies an obligation that is normally expressed with the language of *rights*.

Rights of autonomy are usually stated or claimed in terms of either a *negative right* or a *positive right*. A *negative right* is a claim to be left alone. It implies an obligation on the part of others to let an individual determine his or her own

---

29. An important note of clarity regarding this point; personhood does extend into eternity. Our discussion here is in reference to how to think about the nature of personhood on earth in our current state as embodied selves and in reference to how best to think about physical death.

30. See Immanuel Kant, *Grounding for the Metaphysics of Morals*, in *Ethical Philosophy*, ed. Warner A. Wick, trans. James W. Ellington, 2nd ed. (Indianapolis: Hackett, 1994). See also John Stuart Mill, *On Liberty* (New York: Penguin, 1974).

course of action without interference. Often the language used in regard to negative rights of autonomy is that of *liberty* or *freedom*. A purely autonomous choice would be one that is not subject to limitations imposed by others and is therefore free from external constraints. A *positive right* of autonomy is one that not only presupposes freedom to act without interference in accord with one's own choices and goals, but also suggests that a person has a right to the means necessary to achieve his or her goals or enable his or her choices. Sometimes the language used in regard to positive rights of autonomy is that of *entitlement*.

Claims to such positive rights or entitlements are much more controversial and are often at the center of many moral, legal, and civil debates. The reason for this is that the extent to which one believes society has an obligation to fulfill such positive rights or entitlements relates directly to the extent to which a government will be required to create laws to establish such entitlements and then tax all members of society in order to redistribute wealth to ensure that these entitlement rights are fulfilled. For example, as we pointed out in the previous chapter on abortion, a pro-choice form of argument will claim that a woman should have the *negative right* of liberty or freedom to be left alone when choosing how to control her own body. In this sense, her choice of self-governance could be described as a *right to privacy* regarding her personal autonomous choices. Further, she could go on to claim that because it is her right to do with her body whatever she wants, society has the obligation to provide her with the means of abortion (*positive right* or *entitlement right*).

As this discussion relates to end-of-life situations, we have already seen in our earlier discussion of the *Vacco v. Quill* case an example of how those who are in favor of legalizing such things as physician-assisted suicide and the practice of active euthanasia want to suggest not only that a person should have autonomous choice (*negative right to privacy*) regarding when he or she can choose to forgo treatments, but further that society has an obligation to provide the means to end life. That is, not only should a person be free to decide when he or she can refuse treatments, society should also afford the person the means to carry out the death of his or her own choice (*positive right* or *entitlement right*) as simply the next step on a "continuum of medical care." Here, the problem comes specifically in regard to the value of human life as the fundamental idea on which the principle of autonomy rests. Human beings must be treated as ends in themselves with inherent and unconditional worth in order for the principle of choice to be considered obligatory. It follows that because individuals have inherent value and worth, it is in the vested interest of society to protect human life. After all, one must be alive in order to have choice.

For this reason, society is warranted in putting guardrails in place to protect life and should resist practices or policies that undermine the protection of life even if that limits certain aspects of personal autonomy and choice. Even apart from a Christian understanding of personal worth, society has a vested interest in protecting the life of its citizens by limiting access to lethal choices and practices in order to safeguard and honor the inherent and unconditional value of life. Similarly, it should also vigorously resist and outright prohibit any legislation of a morality that seeks to legitimize a lower valuation of life through either enabling assistance in self-killing (suicide) or direct killing of another.

From a distinctly Christian point of view, these arguments get even stronger. Not only do human beings have inherent and unconditional value as image-bearers, God specifically forbids the unjust taking of human life either by one's own hand or by another's. Even if someone continually requests assistance in dying or direct killing, that person's reasons for demanding a right to be killed based on the notion of autonomous choice would need to be biblically justified—something impossible to do. When an individual's requests run contrary to the direct commands of God, they must never be honored.

True *compassion*—as God would define it—can never run contrary to God's commands. The so-called mercy killing of euthanasia in such instances is still murder and thus is never really a form of mercy. Moreover, given the full meaning of the sixth commandment's instruction regarding the protection of human life, the same conclusion would be true of so-called physician-assisted death.

Table 16.4. How Differing Ethics Principles Result in Distinct Conclusions regarding End-of-Life Decision-Making

Principle of Sanctity of Life	Principle of Autonomy
Self as image-bearer (Gen. 1:26–27)	Self as "god in itself"/"Inventor of self"
Self as steward of life; self belongs to God	Owner of self (self-determination)
Right to life	Right to privacy/right to die
Psychosomatic whole with duality (Gen. 2:7)	Platonic/Gnostic dualism or existential self
Honor and protect life (Ex. 20:13)	Quality of life
"Do no harm" (Hippocratic Oath)	Pro-choice
Culture of life (Pope John Paul II)	Culture of death
Example: Joni Eareckson Tada	Example: Brittany Maynard

Guidelines for End-of-Life Care

The Patient Is a Person

Having discussed the ethics of euthanasia and physician-assisted suicide, we now turn to a discussion of properly caring for those in end-of-life circumstances.

Here, we define *end-of-life contexts* as those situations that involve the care of persons who have been diagnosed with terminal illness, those who are actively dying and near death, and those who have, in light of a terminal diagnosis, made a conscious choice to shift the goals of their care from a curative to a comfort orientation.[31] When addressing such situations, it is important to keep in mind that every individual at the end of life is a human being who is an image-bearer and therefore a person whom God created and for whom Christ died. The personhood discussion is far more than academic. It means that someone whom God created in his image and for whom Christ died is now experiencing the ultimate consequences of human sin in the form of death. Therefore, we should seek to address the situation properly so that the image-bearer who is dying is loved well, cared for, and treated properly in a manner that honors the Lord at the end of the person's life.

Four Goals for End-of-Life Treatment and Care

In order to do so, it is important to think through the appropriate goals of end-of-life treatment and care as it pertains to each particular person who has begun the dying process. Generally speaking, there are four possible goals.[32] The first is an attempt to achieve a *cure* for the underlying condition that is leading to a terminal diagnosis (e.g., the removal of a cancerous tumor through surgical means or perhaps chemotherapy). The second goal, similarly, is to consider how to *control* the condition that would otherwise be terminal. For example, a disease such as diabetes can often be controlled through proper diet, weight loss, and exercise in addition to any needed medication. The effects of such a disease can often be controlled through specified care and treatment. But given a terminal diagnosis, such a goal is no longer viable. A third goal of treatment is often implemented through what is referred to as *palliative care.* Palliative care or treatment focuses on providing relief from symptoms to improve the patient's quality of life. Palliative care can be provided alongside potentially curative or controlling treatments, such as chemotherapy. The fourth goal of medical treatment comes into play when the patient's disease process has been deemed terminal by his or her medical provider and curative treatment has ceased. At that point, medical treatment is given neither to cause or hasten death nor to cure or control the terminal illness, but instead to achieve and maintain the comfort of the person who is suffering at the end of life.

Each of these four goals is founded on the principle of the sanctity of human

---

31. Michael R. Panicola et al., *Health Care Ethics: Theological Foundations, Contemporary Issues, and Controversial Cases* (Winona, MN: Anselm Academic, 2011), 326.

32. In this section, we rely heavily on the work and wisdom of Robert D. Orr and Susan Salladay, "Wisdom from Health Care," in *Why the Church Needs Bioethics: A Guide to Wise Engagement with Life's Challenges*, ed. John F. Kilner (Grand Rapids: Zondervan, 2011), 206–22.

life. Each is seeking to honor the person who bears the image of God while also using reasonable evaluation given the best information available related to the particular circumstances of the person who is experiencing the illness. The goals chosen not only seek to preserve life, but also seek to honor the person when death is not only inevitable but also imminent. Which goals are chosen will depend to a great degree on the medical diagnosis, but will also take into consideration the particular desires of the patient and the family. While decision-making at the end stages of life can be emotionally very difficult for some, when curing or controlling the disease (without a miracle) becomes virtually impossible, there is a sense in which some patients and families may experience something akin to a "sorrow-filled form of relief," knowing that the medical goal no longer involves the "fight" to survive. At such points, decisions often become more straightfor-ward as the medical goals shift from curing toward proper palliative care and providing comfort at the end of life. The specific means of doing so at that point become very case-specific and require a massive amount of wisdom.

In order to see how these goals might affect how one goes about determin-ing a course of treatment, consider again the fictional case of our eighty-year-old Mrs. Jones, who is diagnosed with stage 4 pancreatic cancer. In the vast major-ity of such cases, surgical attempts to effect a cure are impossible. Radiation and chemotherapy are also not curative and, in most cases, do not have a significant controlling impact on the disease. Further, given that Mrs. Jones is eighty years old, the negative side effects of pursuing radiation or chemotherapy treatments may make the last few months of her life extremely difficult because the burdens of her treatment might outweigh the possible benefits. When the chance of curing or controlling a disease is very low, many patients choose to forgo chemotherapy or radiation so that they might have a better quality of life for the time they have remaining.

Christians must avoid two opposite extreme approaches to facing the end of life. One extreme, as we have been discussing throughout this chapter, is to purpose-fully hasten death. We have already discussed the problems with such an approach. In the case of Mrs. Jones, forgoing treatment in order to protect the quality of life at the end of life is not wrong *if the treatment is either futile or unlikely to achieve any significant benefit*. In such a situation, forgoing medical treatment is not a case of "giving up." It may simply be recognition that end-of-life treatment will likely have no positive benefit and may actually take away from the ability to die well.

The other extreme that Christians must avoid is a form of clinging to life as though our physical life itself were our highest value. At such a point, clinging to life can actually become a form of idolatry. Sometimes in practice, this can take the shape of a person's believing that he or she must exhaust all possible means of treatment in order to fight to the bitter end even when a medical diagnosis is that death is inevitable and curative treatments are ineffective and futile. This kind of thinking is sometimes referred to as *vitalism*, which is characterized by placing a premium valuation on the continuation of biological life "regardless of quality or cost, and . . . [being] unwilling to accept the inevitability of death."[33] It is important for the Christian to realize that it is "not unbelief to recognize that miracles are distinctly uncommon, accept the limitations of the human condition, and rejoice in the life God has already given us, looking forward to the eternal life with him. Trusting oneself to God should not be construed as giving up but as trusting in whatever God wishes to do."[34]

When a terminal diagnosis is given, it is often the best approach to pursue end-of-life care and seek to comfort a person as he or she passes. As D. Joy Riley notes, at such a point the five basic needs of a dying patient are these:

1. Being cherished
2. Being clean
3. Being comfortable
4. Being nourished
5. Being able and allowed to do the work of dying well[35]

The remainder of the chapter will speak to the final three of these needs.

Guidelines for Palliative Care

Comfort involves a consideration of how best to manage pain in the dying patient. Pain is not a good in itself and is a result of the fall. As humans seek to express their stewardship over the creation order, it is completely legitimate to seek to limit and relieve pain as long as it is done within the boundaries of God's instructions regarding the protection of human life. Thus, the goal of limited pain should never include using death as the means to do so. Under no circumstances should one introduce a new cause of death in order to end life, and under no circumstances should one aid a patient in seeking death as the means to ending pain or suffering.

Having said that, it is important to note that given the strides in medicine particularly as they relate to pain management, as physician and ethicist Edmund Pellegrino points out, when the optimum and wise use of pain-management treatment is used, "there are virtually no patients whose pain cannot be relieved."[36]

---

33. Orr and Salladay, "Wisdom from Health Care," 210–11.
34. Orr and Salladay, "Wisdom from Health Care," 210.
35. Mitchell and Riley, *Christian Bioethics*, 72.
36. Edmund D. Pellegrino, "The False Promise of Beneficent Killing," in *Regulating How We Die: The Ethical, Medical, and Legal Issues Surrounding Physician-Assisted Suicide*, ed. Linda L. Emanuel (Cambridge, MA: Harvard University Press, 1998), 73.

Thus, the argument that euthanasia or assisting in suicide is a necessary means of compassion actually holds no real moral weight in the question of how to show compassion in end-of-life care. Pain can be managed in virtually every situation.

It is important to recognize, however, that in the process of managing pain, there is often a secondary effect that may weaken the body and unintentionally hasten death. For example, in some instances, increasing pain medications to compensate for increased pain may also lower the body's ability to fight the underlying disease. This foreseeable double effect should not be confused with an intentional hastening of death as is the case with euthanasia or assisted suicide. In keeping with the ethics of the principle of double effect discussed earlier, as long as the negative effect of hastening death is not intended and not the means of controlling pain, it is a morally acceptable side effect.

Terminating Life Support
As the final stages of life draw near, family members will commonly have to face the difficult decision of when either to forgo any additional attempts to prolong life by withholding new treatment or to withdraw treatments currently being administered. At such a point, it is important to realize that neither withholding nor withdrawing treatments is necessarily evil. Sometimes the only way to know whether a treatment could be effective is to try it. If it is not effective, then discontinuing that treatment is morally permissible. But some family members at this point may struggle with the idea of "pulling the plug" or "turning off the machine" because they feel that by doing so they may actually be causing death. If the treatment is medically ineffectual, then this is not the case. It is simply the discontinuation of ineffective treatment. In a similar vein, there may be cases in which family members are reluctant to even try a new treatment for fear that they may have to decide to discontinue that treatment or "pull the plug" at some point in the future. Again, such a fear is unwarranted when these ethical principles are understood in context. In fact, it would be far worse to never turn on a machine that might help and then decide to turn it off once it is determined to be ineffectual than to never turn it on and not know whether it could have been helpful. Turning off a machine when there is no indication of medicinal benefit does not make one the agent of death in such a situation. Turning off the machine or pulling the plug in these instances may simply be the discontinuance of ineffective treatment. It would be no different in moral evaluation from stopping the administration of antibiotics that are no longer helping to fight a disease.

Further, if a patient's life is being artificially and indefinitely sustained by machine and there is no longer any medically diagnosable hope of recovery, then disconnecting the patient from the machine to allow the natural death process to occur is a morally acceptable option. Crucial to this evaluation is the intent of the agent. Again, the principle of double effect comes into play. It should never be the intent to use death as a means to end suffering. This should never be the motivation for turning off the machine. This is very different from ceasing medical treatments that cause unnecessary burdens on the body and that are futile in regard to their effectiveness. The key evaluation point is that the treatment must be medically effective in that it does what it is supposed to do and it should provide a foreseeable benefit or aid in recovery. If these conditions are not met, it is morally acceptable to either withhold or withdraw the treatments in question. As Scott Rae suggests:

> Termination of life support is generally acceptable, but only under the right conditions: (1) if a competent adult patient requests it, either in writing in an advance directive or orally; (2) if the treatment is futile or clearly of no benefit to the patient; (3) if the burden to the patient outweighs the benefit.[37]

Nutrition and Hydration

Finally, in regard to the need to provide nourishment to a dying patient, it is important to keep in mind Jesus' description about separating the sheep and the goats at the last judgment:

> Then the King will say to those on His right, "Come, you who are blessed of My Father, inherit the kingdom prepared for you from the foundation of the world. For I was hungry, and you gave Me something to eat; I was thirsty, and you gave Me something to drink; I was a stranger, and you invited Me in; naked, and you clothed Me; I was sick, and you visited Me; I was in prison, and you came to Me." Then the righteous will answer Him, "Lord, when did we see You hungry, and feed You, or thirsty, and give You something to drink? And when did we see You a stranger, and invite You in, or naked, and clothe You? When did we see You sick, or in prison, and come to You?" The King will answer and say to them, "Truly I say to you, *to the extent that you did it to one of these brothers of Mine, even the least of them, you did it to Me.*" (Matt. 25:34–40)

Basic care for the dying should include the provision of food and water. At the end of life, however, how food and water is provided can complicate this question of giving the best care. For example, in some situations when kidney failure is present, a dying patient's body cannot process food and water even if it is given through a feeding tube. Thus, the removal of food and water would be warranted temporarily and purposefully in order to make any possible adjustments to how it

---

37. Scott B. Rae, *Moral Choices: An Introduction to Ethics*, 4th ed. (Grand Rapids: Zondervan, 2018), 241.

is administered and processed. Only when it is clear that the patient's body can no longer process the nutrition and hydration input (e.g., the kidneys shut down and the body is too weak to handle dialysis) is it proper to permanently discontinue nutrition and hydration. In other situations, if food and water can be processed normally, there should be no question that nutrition and hydration are provided. Much in the same way as we care for and feed an infant at the beginning of life, so also should we be willing to feed those at the end of life even if they need our assistance to eat.

The question gets more problematic when a patient's body can process the food, but a feeding tube is required to deliver the food and water. In such cases (both Terri Schiavo and Nancy Cruzan, for example), there is significant disagreement among ethicists about whether medically provided nutrition and hydration should be categorized as *medical treatments* or *basic care*.

In the midst of such situations, it is important that our decision-making remain obedient to the commands of Scripture while also keeping the patient the focus of our moral debate. If one is not careful, the need to feed a dying patient can shift in the direction of what the caregiver desires over and above what is best for the patient. It is often the case in end-of-life situations that patients do not have a felt need for food and water. Caregivers must be careful not to impose their own felt need to "feed the hungry" to force onto the context a need not *felt* by the patient if the provision of food is not actually beneficial to the patient. Having said this, in many cases the patient's lack of a felt need does not mean that there is not a real need to feed him or her. Thus, if death is not imminent and the body can process the nutrition and hydration, the giving of food and water is far more than symbolic—it is life-sustaining.

At this point, the discussion whether the provision of nutrition and hydration is *medical treatment* or *basic care* becomes extremely important. Some would suggest that there is a strong parallel between the use of a breathing machine (ventilator) and that of medically provided nutrition and hydration. In both cases, medical intervention is needed to assist with an essential bodily function. The difference between these two types of intervention, however, is significant. The function of the ventilator is to force the body to *process* the air. Without it, the body cannot process air that is readily available. In most cases regarding the provision of nutrition and hydration, the body does not need help with *processing* the food. It only needs the food to be available. These are not, therefore, parallel situations. When the ventilator is removed, the patient dies from the underlying disease that caused the respiratory system not to function. When medically provided nutrition and hydration is removed, it opens the possibility of the patient's dying from a new cause—starvation and dehydration.

Because medically provided nutrition and hydration is considered *medical treatment*, like other treatments at the end of life, the courts have recognized the right to terminate life-sustaining treatments if clear and convincing evidence can be provided that it is the wish of the dying patient to do so. Keep in mind that something's being made "legal" does not necessarily mean that the decision is morally acceptable. Morally, a good rule of thumb that is consistent with what we have argued throughout the chapter is that the removal of nutrition and hydration should never be done in such a way so as to introduce starvation as the actual cause of death. Likewise, removing food and water should never be done to purposely bring about death. Compassion will feed and nourish the sick and dying unless there are clear medical reasons not to do so.[38]

Conclusion

In this chapter, we have explored moral and ethical questions related to euthanasia, physician-assisted suicide, and decision-making at the end of life. In order to demonstrate the pressing need for clarity on these topics, we began our chapter by highlighting prominent cases and trends that shape how our culture understands these issues. After clarifying the meaning of the key concepts, we discussed biblical and theological principles that ought to shape a particularly Christian point of view that enables us to apply an ethic of worship to these topics. Having done so, we then contrasted our Christian view with two prominent alternative perspectives commonly used in contemporary culture in an attempt to justify a moral and legal stance in favor of physician-assisted suicide and euthanasia. In the final section of the chapter, we sought to give some practical guidelines for how a Christian ought to apply an ethic of worship when facing actual contexts of end-of-life decision-making.

Our hope in pursuing this line of reasoning has been to answer this question: is it ever permissible to desire or even pursue death (our own or the death of another) as a means to ending suffering? Scripture makes it clear that the answer is "no." Even when the particulars of each case, context, and moral scenario relating to sick, suffering, and dying people become complex, God's moral instructions remain the sufficient guide to help us navigate a path to proper worship.

We hope it has also become clear that at the most basic level, the ethical discussion surrounding issues related to the end of life are almost identical to those that are taking place at the beginning of life. At their core, both the abortion discussion and the euthanasia discussion revolve around a debate regarding how

38. For further information and discussion that pursues the question of nutrition and hydration from a Christian perspective, see the following article: Christian Medical and Dental Associations, "Artificially-Administered Nutrition and Hydration," https://cmda.org/wp-content/uploads/2018/04/Artificial-Hydration-and-Nutrition.pdf.

to prioritize the two moral principles of the *sanctity of human life* and *personal autonomy*. We have argued that while both must be honored, the sanctity of life is both logically prior to and morally more binding than a person's right to autonomous decision-making. As image-bearers that God has placed on the earth as his stewards, humans have the responsibility to make self-directing choices. But in order for these choices to be truly free and morally responsible, they must be made in light of the manner in which God made the world and in accord with his moral instruction. The sixth commandment instructs us to protect life not only by not taking innocent life, but also through our laws and our cultural ethical norms.

Ultimately, the academic discussions that happen at the worldview level must appear in the real-life cases and contexts that real people face every day. The concepts that we have discussed matter precisely because they serve to guide real people who are living and dying and facing life's joyful moments as well as life's most troubling and difficult seasons. Unless the Lord returns first, death is something that we will all face.

Given the complexity of the discussion, it is right to recognize that often the application of ethics as worship in end-of-life situations will feel more like a work of art than the simple application of formulas and principles. Prayerful meditation on how the Word applies in light of the details from each case must be coupled with wise counsel and humility. In light of this and given all that we have discussed about the problems related to *euthanasia* and seeking a "good death," perhaps it is wise for us to shift our focus instead to learning more about how to worship God even at the hour of our death.[39]

In the end, it is good to remember what 1 Corinthians 10:31 teaches about ethics as worship. Whatever we do, we are to do it to the glory of God. This includes dying. The goal of both the dying patient and the caregiver must be to maximize the glory of God at the very edge of life in this world. No doubt this will require much of us as we seek to do the work (or assist others in doing the work) of dying well. An ethic of worship should not only help us live well to the glory of God, but guide us through the valley of the shadow of death so that we may also die well for the glory of God.

Key Terms and Concepts

active euthanasia	commission versus omission
causality	consent

---

39. The language of "the art of dying" (*ars moriendi*) in a Christian context refers to the art of learning how to honor God through joyful and worshipful obedience that honors the sanctity of life even when pain and suffering may increase at the hour of our death. Toward this end, we recommend Bill Bright, *The Journey Home: Finishing with Joy* (Nashville: Thomas Nelson, 2003).

death, cardiopulmonary

death, Christian understanding of

death, higher brain

death, whole brain

euthanasia

involuntary euthanasia

killing versus letting die

life-sustaining treatment

nonvoluntary euthanasia

nutrition and hydration

palliative care

passive euthanasia

personal autonomy

physician-assisted suicide

positive rights versus negative rights

ratsakh

redemptive suffering

rights of entitlement

sanctity of human life

voluntariness

voluntary euthanasia

Key Scriptures

Genesis 1:26–28

Genesis 2:7

Exodus 20:13

Psalm 8:3–8

Romans 5:1–5

Romans 6:23

Romans 13:9

1 Corinthians 15:26

1 Corinthians 15:51–58

1 Peter 4:15

Study Questions

1. What is the difference between physician-assisted suicide and euthanasia?
2. What is the difference between passive and active euthanasia?
3. The authors make the argument that at the core of both the abortion and euthanasia discussions is a debate regarding how to prioritize the two moral principles of the *sanctity of human life* and *personal autonomy*. Clarify the meaning of each of these principles and discuss which one should be given priority and why.
4. What is the functionalism argument regarding end-of-life issues? How is it mirrored in beginning-of-life questions? What are the logical consequences of such an argument in favor of euthanasia and physician-assisted suicide?
5. If the Scripture tells us that intentionally putting an innocent person to death is murder (Ex. 20:13), then what are the implications for how we should understand the nature of biblical compassion at the end of life when someone is suffering? What does biblical compassion provide for those who are suffering?

For Further Reading

Beauchamp, Tom L., and James F. Childress. *Principles of Biomedical Ethics*. 8th ed. New York: Oxford University Press, 2019.

Beville, Kieran. *Dying to Kill: A Christian Perspective on Euthanasia and Assisted Suicide*. Cambridge, OH: Christian Publishing House, 2014.

Foley, Kathleen, and Herbert Hendin. *The Case against Assisted Suicide*. Baltimore: Johns Hopkins University Press, 2002.

Kilner, John F. *Why the Church Needs Bioethics: A Guide to Wise Engagement with Life's Challenges*. Grand Rapids: Zondervan, 2011.

Kilner, John F., and C. Ben Mitchell. *Does God Need Our Help? Cloning, Assisted Suicide, and Other Challenges in Bioethics*. Edited by Daniel Taylor. Wheaton, IL: Tyndale, 2003.

Mitchell, C. Ben, and D. Joy Riley. *Christian Bioethics: A Guide for Pastors, Health Care Professionals, and Families*. Nashville: B&H Academic, 2014.

Quill, Timothy E., and Margaret E. Battin. *Physician-Assisted Dying: The Case for Palliative Care and Patient Choice*. Baltimore: Johns Hopkins University Press, 2004.

Verhey, Allen. *The Christian Art of Dying: Learning from Jesus*. Grand Rapids: Eerdmans, 2011.

Biblical Sexuality and Disordered Sexuality

*"For this reason God gave them over to degrading passions; for their women
exchanged the natural function for that which is unnatural, and in the same
way also the men abandoned the natural function of the woman and burned in
their desire toward one another, men with men committing indecent acts and
receiving in their own persons the due penalty of their error."*
—ROMANS 1:26–27

"Human life and sexuality have become the watershed moral issues of our age."[1]
—NANCY R. PEARCEY, Love Thy Body

Introduction

June 26, 2015, is a day that changed the landscape of discussion regarding
marriage and sexuality within the United States. On that day, the Supreme Court
of the United States issued its landmark decision in *Obergefell v. Hodges*,[2] which
legalized so-called same-sex marriage nationwide. The lead-up to the decision was
fraught with legal maneuvering and hand-wringing on both sides of the debate.
Proponents of same-sex marriage considered this case to be the most important
decision related to equal rights since the Civil Rights Act of 1964. Opponents
of same-sex marriage viewed this case with suspicion and foretold the ultimate
demise of a culture if same-sex marriage were legalized. Regardless of where
one stands on the issue, there is no question that the *Obergefell* ruling signaled a
state-sanctioned overturn of traditional views of sex and sexuality.

On the backside of the *Obergefell* decision, the jury is still out on the long-term

1. Nancy R. Pearcey, *Love Thy Body: Answering Hard Questions about Life and Sexuality* (Grand Rapids:
Baker, 2018), 9.
2. 576 U.S. 644 (2015).

ramifications of the historic case. In the short term, however, the culture wars related to it have been far from dull. Since the legalization of same-sex marriage, bakers and florists have been sued for refusing to use their artistic talents to celebrate these unions. Many churches and wedding chapels have rewritten their bylaws and facility usage guidelines to either celebrate or prohibit this newfound right for marriage. Other related issues pertaining to such things as whether the state should support single-gendered bathrooms or whether biological sex ought to be the basis for who can compete in athletic events have also moved to the center of the cultural debate.

Transgenderism has also risen to a place of prominence among discussions about alternatives to traditional sexuality. The transgender debate involves the idea that an individual can change or choose his or her own gender if there is a perceived incongruence between one's *biological sex* and *gender identity*. In essence, if one feels that the body, mind, or desires are not aligned regarding one's biological sex and one's sense of sexual or gender preference, then various actions, from cross-dressing to gender-reassignment surgery, are now considered positive means to finding congruence. Perhaps the most famous and most influential transgender moment came when former Olympic gold medalist Bruce Jenner announced that he no longer identified as a male and was now the female Caitlyn Jenner in a 2015 interview with Diane Sawyer on ABC's *20/20*. Jenner's transition brought the transgender conversation into the mainstream.

Beyond these controversies related to sexuality, other issues are also gaining traction even though they may not dominate the headlines as the other issues have. Polygamy, polyamory, and open marriage have growing support in the media and society at large. They represent another alternative to traditional marriage, and it will not be long before these expressions of sexuality become more mainstream.

What we cannot ignore is that these and other alternative expressions of sexuality violate the biblical vision for marriage that we will address in the next chapter and the underlying biblical understanding of sexuality that we will address in more detail in the pages that follow. For this reason, we identify each of these expressions of sexuality as *disordered sexuality*.

Disordered sexuality is any form of sexual perception, desire, or expression that deviates from God's intended creation order and design. In the words of the apostle Paul, disordered sexuality is anything that is "unnatural" precisely because it is discordant with the way in which God designed and gifted sex and sexual expression to his image-bearers before the fall (Rom. 1:18–27). God designed sexual desire to be heterosexual, and he reserved sexual expression for a husband and wife within the confines of a comprehensive, covenantal union between one man and one woman that would endure for a lifetime and be proximally directed toward the rearing of the next generation, while ultimately being directed toward

God as an act of worship.[3] Yet the reality of the fall entails that all aspects of life have been distorted to a certain degree for all people.[4] This includes the area of human sexuality. All humans experience the distortion and disordering of the fall in some way that pertains to their own sexuality. Whether it be through lustful desire, the lack of desire, the desire for things God never intended, or even the physical malfunctioning of sexual organs, all of us are touched by the impact of sin and its effects in some way. The result is that sexuality is no longer rightly ordered toward God's plan. Instead, we see various degrees of disorder that all lead to a departure from the creation order.

Tragically, we live in a day and age when a person's desire for fulfillment has replaced God's vastly superior design and desire for his image-bearers. Rosaria Butterfield is right when she observes:

> With the onset of the theological negligence . . . , we have created a generation of Christians who blame the Holy Spirit for their sinful desires ("God made me this way, and it's a proof of good fruit when I act in accordance with my heart's desires"). . . . The idol of our historical epoch is this: your sexual desires define you, determine you, and should always delight you.[5]

But God desires for us to experience so much more. Quite opposite from the tired story often told about Christianity, God is not anti-pleasure or anti-joy. As we have argued throughout *Ethics as Worship*, God wants us to know what it means to be fully human and fully alive. This is true even as it relates to the area of sex and sexuality. As C. S. Lewis so beautifully stated:

> It would seem that Our Lord finds our desires not too strong, but too weak. We are half-hearted creatures, fooling about with drink and sex and ambition when infinite joy is offered us, like an ignorant child who wants to go on making mud pies in a slum because he cannot imagine what is meant by the offer of a holiday at the sea. We are far too easily pleased.[6]

---

3. We will discuss this definition of *marriage* in the next chapter.

4. To this end, John Piper helpfully argues that "same-sex desires and same-sex orientation are in that category of groaning [see Rom. 8:20–21]—waiting for the redemption of our bodies. Which means they are in the same broad category with all kinds of disordered bodies and minds and emotions. If we tried to make a list of all the kinds of emotional and mental and physical brokenness of the human family, the list would be unending. All of us are bent to desire things in different degrees that we should not want. We are all disordered in our emotions, minds, and our bodies." John Piper, "What Does the Gospel Say?," in *The Gospel and Same-Sex Marriage*, ed. Russell D. Moore and Andrew T. Walker (Nashville: B&H Academic, 2016), 32–33.

5. Rosaria Butterfield, foreword to *Holy Sexuality and the Gospel: Sex, Desire, and Relationships Shaped by God's Grand Story*, by Christopher Yuan (New York: Multnomah, 2018), xiv.

6. C. S. Lewis, *The Weight of Glory and Other Addresses* (New York: HarperOne, 2001), 26.

This is why a look into God's design for sex and sexual expression is of utmost importance. Only a proper understanding of Scripture and doctrine can rightly order and enflame our desires for what is true, good, and beautiful in the arena of human sexuality. "A robust theology cannot be built on what we're not allowed to do, for the Christian life is much more than the avoidance of sinful behavior. If scriptural prohibitions are the only lens through which we see things, then we may well miss the gospel."[7]

It is therefore our intention in this chapter to explore the beautiful scriptural and theological foundations for an understanding of sex and sexuality within the context of ethics as worship. In order to do so, we will first consider some key terms and definitions that are necessary for engaging in fruitful discussions about sexuality. After defining these terms, we will consider the biblical and theological principles that guide our understanding of sexuality so that we can adequately evaluate when sexuality is rightly ordered to worshiping God and when it has become disordered. Third, we will address some of the most common challenges to God's design for sexuality and offer biblical critique so that we will be able to answer these challenges.

Key Terms and Definitions

Much of the debate over sexuality revolves around the use of terms whose definitions were at one time universally agreed on, but are so no longer. In fact, most of the terms we will highlight below are familiar to the average reader, but they have often taken on nuanced meanings in our sexually charged society. If we neglect to address and clarify these terms, we run the risk of talking past one another rather than with one another.

Sex

Defining *sex* takes two distinct paths that are both important and necessary in our task of identifying important elements of this term. First, we need to think about sex biologically in reference to the body. *Biological sex* is the identification of maleness or femaleness on the basis of distinct biological markers that are unique to one or the other.[8] Mark Yarhouse explains, "When we refer to a person's sex, we are commonly making reference to the physical, biological and

---

7. Christopher Yuan, *Holy Sexuality and the Gospel: Sex, Desire, and Relationships Shaped by God's Grand Story* (New York: Multnomah, 2018), 4.

8. Susannah Cornwall offers a similar definition that focuses on the biology of the body: "SEX: biological maleness or femaleness (or, occasionally, a biological sex which can't easily be classified as male or female). Sex, in this initial definition, is to do with the biology of someone's body, rather than their sense of being a man or woman." Susannah Cornwall, *Theology and Sexuality* (London: SCM, 2013), 1.

anatomic dimensions of being male or female."[9] The easiest way to make such an identification is by the presence of male genitalia or female genitalia. This is the simple approach used by individuals from midwives to doctors who have assisted in the process of giving birth. When a doctor announces to the new mother, "It's a girl!" or "It's a boy!," the doctor does so on the basis of visually inspecting the genitalia as presented in the human body. For millennia, this was the primary (if not exclusive) means for defining biological sex.

As science progressed through the twentieth century, we became aware that certain chromosomes controlled the various components of biological sex so that we could perform a genetic test and determine whether an individual had the chromosomal markers of a female (XX) or a male (XY). Generally speaking, such genetic analysis was not necessary because the presence of female genitalia or male genitalia aligned with the chromosomal markers as well. In addition to the presence of external genitalia and chromosomal markers, biological sex also includes "gonads, sex hormones, and internal reproductive anatomy."[10]

Biological and genetic evidence gives us the binary categories of male and female by which individuals have been classified since the creation of mankind. In fact, we are first introduced to these binary categories in Genesis 1:27 as we read, "God created man in His own image, in the image of God He created him; male and female He created them." From the very first description of the creation of mankind, God made it clear that there are two sexes—male and female. In the verse that immediately follows, we read that God tells them to be "fruitful and multiply," filling the earth with their offspring to rule over and subdue the rest of creation. We can safely assume that God intended for this multiplication to take place through the sexual relationship between the man and the woman. When we move ahead in the creation narrative to Genesis 2, we see the binary nature of biological sex affirmed as God first creates Adam from the dust of the ground, breathing life into him (Gen. 2:7), and then later creates a complementary woman from one of the man's ribs and presents her to the man (vv. 21–22). Even as we read further into the chapter, we see the affirmation of the binary sexes when the man leaves his father and mother and joins with his wife (v. 24). This double affirmation of male and female—father and mother, husband and wife—confirms the creation-order design for the binary biological sexes of male and female.

The exception to this rule is the case of *intersex* individuals, who do not present clear biological markers to determine male or female. Intersex individuals "may have any one of numerous diagnoses, but their common feature is gender-atypical

---

9. Mark A. Yarhouse, *Understanding Gender Dysphoria: Navigating Transgender Issues in a Changing Culture* (Downers Grove, IL: IVP Academic, 2015), 16.

10. Yarhouse, *Understanding Gender Dysphoria*, 17.

anatomy—a combination of what are typically considered male and female chromosomal, gonadal, and genital characteristics—which is often signaled by the presence of what clinicians call ambiguous genitalia."[11] Intersex represents a category of individuals with a range of developmental disorders primarily affecting the reproductive system.[12] Yarhouse further explains that *intersex* is a "term to describe conditions (e.g., congenital renal hyperplasia) in which a person is born with sex characteristics or anatomy that does not allow clear identification as male or female. The causes of an intersex condition can be chromosomal, gonadal or genital."[13] The prevalence of intersex conditions is difficult to determine because of the variety of diagnoses and the uncertainty about how to classify them. Katrina Karkazis notes: "Even with these questions settled it would remain extraordinarily difficult to determine population-based statistics for intersex diagnoses. In the United States, there is no national census or method for keeping track of intersex conditions."[14]

From a theological standpoint, we recognize that intersex conditions are the product of the fall just like all other diseases and developmental disorders. Those born with intersex conditions fully bear the image of God and have full dignity and inherent value like all other humans. In addition, the existence of intersex conditions does not negate the general rule that the creation-order design reflects the existence of two sexes.

The second distinct path for the definition of *sex* relates to sex as an action rather than a human characteristic. Sex as an action refers to the act of sexual intercourse that takes place between a man and a woman. Once again, we see that God's design for sexual intercourse is that it is to take place between a man and a woman within the context of the covenant of marriage. In fact, sex serves as a coordinating sign of the covenant of marriage by giving physical representation of the metaphysical union between a husband and wife ("they shall become one

11. Katrina Karkazis, *Fixing Sex: Intersex, Medical Authority, and Lived Experience* (Durham, NC: Duke University Press, 2008), 6–7.

12. Denny Burk, *What Is the Meaning of Sex?* (Wheaton, IL: Crossway, 2013), 173.

13. Yarhouse, *Understanding Gender Dysphoria*, 21. Yarhouse offers further clarification on what sex characteristics are. He identifies primary sex characteristics as "features that are directly part of the reproductive system, such as testes, penis and scrotum in males, and ovaries, uterus and vagina in females." Secondary sex characteristics "have no direct reproductive function, for example, facial hair in males and enlarged breasts in females." Yarhouse, 17.

14. Karkazis, *Fixing Sex*, 23. Ryan Anderson notes that disorders of sexual development (DSDs) "occur in approximately one out of every 5,000 live births, but specific types vary in frequency and in severity." Ryan T. Anderson, *When Harry Became Sally: Responding to the Transgender Moment* (New York: Encounter, 2018), 90. The Intersex Society of North America reports that the rates of intersex are much more frequent. It states that one in 100 births result in bodies that differ from standard male and female and that one or two in 1,000 births result in "people receiving surgery to 'normalize' genital appearance." Intersex Society of North America, "How Common Is Intersex?," accessed April 30, 2020, https://isna.org/faq/frequency/.

flesh," Gen. 2:24). When God inaugurated the first marriage in the garden, he intended for the action of sex to bring the man and woman together and that it would bring about the results of his command to be fruitful and multiply (1:28).

God created sex—both biological sex and sexual intercourse—as part of his good creation. The biological markers of sex and the context through which intercourse is to take place reflect his plan for human flourishing. God desires that we experience human sexuality as part of his creation-order design. Even though the fall has impacted sex in numerous ways, God's gracious providence over creation (Col. 1:16–17) ensures that the creation-order design is still embedded in us. Intersex conditions are a tragic consequence of the fall, but they do not undermine the original design.

Both these definitions are subject to direct challenges in our culture. The idea of binary sexes runs afoul of many who view sex as a spectrum with choices far beyond male and female. One of the easiest ways to see this challenge is through the popular social media site Facebook, where users have more than seventy preloaded options to select when choosing a custom field for sex. Sometimes this relates more directly to gender identity (which will be discussed below), but the idea of binary categories for sex is viewed as antiquated by many in contemporary culture. The second definition of *sex* is challenged by many of the distortions of biblical sexuality that we will see below. From intercourse between unmarried individuals to sexual activity between members of the same sex, we see God's design for sex under attack. We will discuss these challenges in more detail in the pages to come.

Sexual Orientation

Sexual orientation generally refers to the psychosexual attraction of one person toward someone else. The American Psychological Association (APA) defines *sexual orientation* as follows:

> Sexual orientation refers to an enduring pattern of emotional, romantic and/or sexual attractions to men, women or both sexes. Sexual orientation also refers to a person's sense of identity based on those attractions, related behaviors and membership in a community of others who share those attractions.[15]

The conversation regarding sexual orientation often focuses on the direction of such attractions and the subsequent actions taken. This direction is typically identified in terms of sex so that a person who is attracted to the opposite sex is considered to have a *heterosexual orientation*, but someone attracted to a member

---

15. American Psychological Association, "Answers to Your Questions for a Better Understanding of Sexual Orientation and Homosexuality," 2008, accessed April 30, 2020, http://www.apa.org/topics/lgbt/orientation.

of the same sex is considered to have a *homosexual orientation*. An individual attracted to members of both sexes is considered to be *bisexual*.

Sexual orientation does not necessarily equate with sexual behavior. John and Paul Feinberg suggest that sexual behavior can include "celibacy, monogamy, promiscuity, etc., and homosexuals, heterosexuals, and bisexuals can engage in any and all of those behaviors."[16] Although sexual behavior is typically linked to sexual orientation, an individual who claims a certain sexual orientation may act outside the norm for that orientation. For example, someone who identifies as a heterosexual may participate in homosexual behavior (and vice versa). Participating in a single act, or series of acts, does not necessarily determine orientation, nor does one's perceived orientation always determine one's action.

Sexual orientation is a complex topic that goes beyond simply the direction of our sexual attractions and consequent actions. The APA even denotes a component of identity or membership within a group based on orientation, but such components create problems from a theological perspective. Christopher Yuan warns:

> It's nearly impossible to disassociate sexual orientation from personal identity. This definition from the American Psychological Association clearly links the two. . . . From the definition above, we also see that orientation has a sociological aspect. That is, identifying oneself as a "gay Christian" implies that one identifies as much with the gay community as with the Christian community, if not more. Should Christ's body be placed at the same level with any demographic?[17]

When we think of sexual orientation simply in terms of enduring patterns of attraction and sociological identification, we lose sight of God's design for sexuality. Yuan is especially helpful here as he describes the concept of sexual orientation in terms of biblical desires. He argues: "Instead of differentiating between opposite-sex desires and same-sex desires, let's use the biblical categories of good desires and sinful desires. Good sexual desires are those whose end is biblical marriage. Sinful sexual desires are those whose end is outside the context of biblical marriage."[18] When spoken of in these terms, we can identify sexual orientation biblically as desires that accord with God's design for marriage and sexuality and those that do not. Yuan further suggests that "enduring, unchosen sinful desires" should be identified as the sin nature.[19]

We believe that God's design for sexual orientation is for men to be sexually

16. John S. Feinberg and Paul D. Feinberg, *Ethics for a Brave New World*, 2nd ed. (Wheaton, IL: Crossway, 2010), 310.

17. Yuan, *Holy Sexuality and the Gospel*, 68–69.

18. Yuan, *Holy Sexuality and the Gospel*, 69–70.

19. Yuan, *Holy Sexuality and the Gospel*, 70.

attracted to women and women to men. But this is not the ultimate end. God's design for human flourishing is much richer than heterosexual attraction or orientation. Yuan is correct; God desires a "holy sexuality" in which we are oriented to God's desires and we fight against desires that do not align with his creation-order design for sexuality. Thankfully, he has given believers the Holy Spirit to fight against sinful desires on our behalf. It is an ongoing battle between the flesh and the Spirit, but it is one that results in flourishing when we follow godly desires (Gal. 5:16–17).

Gender and Gender Identity

Gender and gender identity are closely related concepts that tie in to our previous two categories as well. In fact, some may confuse these two ideas or at least pair them together in such a way that they are considered a unified whole. According to Yarhouse, *gender* concerns "the psychological, social and cultural aspects of being male or female."[20] Typically, gender has been connected with biological sex, but the two are not identical. *Biological sex* refers to the physical, anatomical, and genetic markers of maleness and femaleness. Gender is not so much concerned with biology as it is with psychology. Most would agree, however, that the traditional understanding of gender is that one's biological sex and gender align and that the descriptor of *male* or *female* refers to both biological sex and gender.

Gender identity is the way in which a person self-identifies as male or female. Yarhouse explains: "When we refer to someone's gender identity, we are thinking of how a person experiences him- or herself (or thinks of him- or herself) as male or female, including how masculine or feminine a person feels. Gender identity is often associated with gender role. Gender role, then, refers to ways in which people adopt cultural expectations for maleness and femaleness."[21] Just like gender, gender identity has traditionally been understood to be directly linked to one's biological sex; therefore, an individual whose biological sex was female would identify as a "woman" or a "girl." Yarhouse notes:

> For most people, these various facets or dimensions of sex and gender align in ways that are essentially taken-for-granted realities. Most people you have met have a relatively unremarkable experience (or remarkable in the sense of all these facets coming into alignment) of being born male or female (with the alignment of the various biological/physical/anatomical features noted above), identifying as a man or a woman, and feeling masculine or feminine within the cultural context in which they are raised.[22]

---

20. Yarhouse, *Understanding Gender Dysphoria*, 16.
21. Yarhouse, *Understanding Gender Dysphoria*, 16–17.
22. Yarhouse, *Understanding Gender Dysphoria*, 17.

Yet such an unremarkable experience is no longer understood to be the only option or even the accepted norm. Susannah Cornwall writes, "Gender identity may not always 'match' biological sex: some people whose biological sex is male, for example, have a feminine gender identity and want to live as women."[23] When the physical traits of biological sex and its concomitant gender do not align with the psychological identification, this is called *gender dysphoria.* Such gender dysphoria has spawned the transgender (T) component of the LGBTQ movement. By contrast, when biological sex and gender identity align, such individuals are sometimes identified as *cisgender.*[24]

According to God's creation-order design, gender and gender identity should align seamlessly with biological sex. This alignment should be the accepted norm for all people, but especially Christians, as we live out the design for which God created us. In a perfect world, we would not see any discrepancies, but we also recognize the realities of the fall. Gender dysphoria is a product of the fall and evidence of how pervasive the effects of the fall are. Those who struggle with gender dysphoria experience a real conflict in their minds. And the existence of such a conflict does not lessen their value as image-bearers. But we also see cultural trends pushing to normalize a separation between the physical characteristics of biological sex and the psychological components of gender and gender identity. Nancy Pearcey labels this separation as a form of Gnosticism:

> Christianity is often accused of being anti-sex and anti-body. But in reality it is the secular ethic that is anti-body. Gay activists downplay the body—our biological identity as male or female—and define our true selves by our feelings and desires. They assume that the body gives no reference points for our gender identity or our moral choices. In essence, the secular worldview has revived the ancient Gnostic disdain for the body. It is Christianity that honors the body as male and female, instead of subordinating biological sex to psychological feelings.[25]

We will explore this distinction between the mind and body at more length in our discussion on transgenderism, but note that such a distinction does not line up with how Scripture speaks of sex and gender. Scripture views an alignment of these two concepts as normative in which male sex is normatively aligned with a masculine gender and female sex likewise is normatively aligned with a

23. Cornwall, *Theology and Sexuality*, 1.

24. The Latin prefix *cis-* carries the meaning of "on this side" and is contrasted with *trans-*, which connotes "on the other side." Thus, a cisgendered person is one whose gender aligns with, or is "on the same side with," one's biological sex.

25. Pearcey, *Love Thy Body*, 161–62. Ryan Anderson also offers a helpful discussion along the same lines. See Anderson, *When Harry Became Sally*, 45–48.

feminine gender. Indeed, God's design for human flourishing in sexuality is built on this idea.

Sexuality

Sexuality is the broadest term among our key terms in this section because it encompasses all that we have already discussed. It is the comprehensive nature of an embodied self as a sexual being, including one's attractions, desires, and gender. Dennis Hollinger suggests that "our sexuality is the form of our bodily or physical being within the world. It certainly encompasses our emotional, social, and spiritual selves, but it is related to the very way in which we as embodied beings exist in relationship to others."[26] Ultimately, this points to our maleness and femaleness.[27] The definition of *sexuality* encompasses sex as both a biological feature and an action in which individuals participate. Sexuality connects to orientation because it includes the idea of joining with someone. Stanley Grenz further states: "At its core this embodied existence includes a fundamental incompleteness, one which is symbolized by biological sex and is based in our sexuality. Through sexuality, we give expression both to our existence as embodied creatures and to our basic incompleteness as embodied persons in our relationships to each other and to the world. Our sexuality, then, calls us to move toward completeness."[28] This is not to say that sexuality demands that a person be united with another in order to find completeness. Instead, Grenz means that we relate to one another in the world as sexual beings and that this often—perhaps even typically—results in the union of marriage.

This holistic approach to sexuality means that we are embodied selves who relate to our world as sexual beings. Sexuality is not the sum total of our existence, but it is a core feature of who we are. As we have so often done, we appeal to the creation narrative once again to drive this point home. God created mankind as male and female (Gen. 1:27). We cannot escape the fact that God created us as sexual beings and designed us so that we would relate to one another through our sexuality as a component to relationships. We do not mean that every relationship has sexual overtones in the sense of attraction. Instead, we mean that how we relate to one another in all relationships involves an expression of sexuality.

26. Dennis P. Hollinger, *The Meaning of Sex: Christian Ethics and the Moral Life* (Grand Rapids: Baker, 2009), 16.

27. Stanley Grenz notes: "Being a human means being an embodied creature, and embodiment entails being male or female. Sexuality, therefore, includes the various dimensions of being in the world and relating to it as persons embodied as male or female, together with the various internalized understandings of the meaning of maleness and femaleness." Stanley J. Grenz, *The Social God and the Relational Self: A Trinitarian Theology of the Imago Dei* (Louisville: Westminster John Knox, 2001), 277.

28. Stanley J. Grenz, *Sexual Ethics: An Evangelical Perspective* (Louisville: Westminster John Knox, 1990), 20.

Two men do not relate to each other in the same way as two women or a man and a woman. These differences are part of our sexuality and the way in which we express ourselves as sexual beings in society. This is nothing to downplay or be ashamed of. It is how God created us.

Table 17.1. Components of Sexuality

Sexuality			
The comprehensive nature of an embodied self as a sexual being			
Sex Biological sex Sexual intercourse	**Sexual Orientation** Holy desires Sinful desires	**Gender** Psychological, social, and cultural aspects of being male or female	**Gender Identity** Self-identification as male or female

Biblical and Theological Principles for Sexuality[29]

Since *sexuality* is a broad concept encompassing so many aspects of our being and how we relate to one another, we want to present several biblical and theological principles that guide the conversation on human sexuality. These principles are the theological application of Scripture to a field that is often lacking in theological and biblical precision. So much of our world desires sexual expression without adherence to the guidelines of Scripture, but we know that following these guidelines makes us better worshipers of the One who created us as sexual beings.

God Created Male and Female

We noted earlier in our discussion of biological sex that God's creation of humankind involved two distinct sexes—male and female. In the first two verses regarding the creation of man (Gen. 1:26–27), we see affirmation of this distinction:

> Then God said, "Let Us make man in Our image, according to Our likeness; and let them rule over the fish of the sea and over the birds of the sky and over the cattle and over all the earth, and over every creeping thing that creeps on the earth." God created man in His own image, in the image of God He created him; male and female He created them.

---

29. Many of these principles are derived from an earlier article by Mark. See Mark D. Liederbach, "'What Is Sexy?' Exploring the Question of How a Biblical Ethic of Worship Shapes One's View of Sex and Sexuality," *Southeastern Theological Review* 7, no. 1 (Summer 2016): 43–62. Used by permission.

We could close the book on binary biological sex at Genesis 1:27 because the text tells us that "male and female He created them." Such a pronouncement limits the scope of biological sex to only two. Despite arguments by those who argue for more options, Scripture does not allow us to go beyond the two biological sexes that God created. Connected to this idea is that the psychological and social component of sexuality—gender—is designed to align with biological sex. Therefore, God's creation of humankind as male and female speaks to both biological sex and gender. As we live out what God intends for our full humanity, his design points to alignment between the body and mind.

The text also indicates that the *imago Dei* is foundational to humanness and that each human being—by God's design—was created to bear the image of God according to an assigned sex and gender. Maleness or femaleness is written into our very nature.[30] This suggests not that the *imago Dei* is defined by maleness and femaleness, but rather that one can bear the *imago Dei* only as either a male or a female and that being male or female expresses the *imago Dei*.[31] Because human sexuality is a gift from God closely linked to the *imago Dei*, we can unabashedly state that sexuality is an inherent quality of humanness and not a social construct. A man is male not only because his body has male parts and his society then constructs a pattern for how he is to behave. Rather, he is male and has male parts and ought to behave a certain way because God made him a male and desired for him to reflect his image in a masculine manner that accords not only with his biology but with the instructions God gives regarding how he ought to function as a man in order to fully flourish as he has been designed. The same is true for women. God created them female with female parts and made them so that they ought to behave as women in accordance with the instructions he gave regarding womanhood. Our sexuality, then, finds its ultimate grounding in God's creation order and is an inherent part of our makeup as image-bearers. Particular expressions of masculinity or femininity may be influenced by varying cultural norms, but neither is merely a social construct.

The fact that God created male and female is significant in the conversation about disordered sexuality. Several of the issues that we will address in the coming pages make the case for gender fluidity or the absence of defined gender. Scripture, however, upholds the notion that God created two—and only two—genders that are clearly identified through biological traits. Without such a limitation, current

---

30. Gilbert Meilaender, "The First Institutions," *Pro Ecclesia* 6, no. 4 (1997): 444–55.

31. For a fuller discussion of this point, see Jack W. Cottrell, *Gender Roles and the Bible: Creation, the Fall, and Redemption: A Critique of Feminist Biblical Interpretation* (Joplin, MO: College Press, 1994), 70–76. Maleness and femaleness do not constitute the image of God—but male humans and female humans express the image of God by God's design. Thus, ontologically, they are equal in value, but ontologically, they are also distinct in nature.

cultural pressure would have us support one of a few different options. First, a denial of the biblical principle of two genders may lead to an acceptance of a multiplicity of genders. If there is no limit at male and female, then we have no way to place a limit at any larger number. Second, a denial of God's creation of male and female may lead to the acceptance of no gender at all. In fact, this is probably the most common outcome. If male and female do not exist, then the lines between them will be so blurred that no distinction can be made. Third, a denial of God's creation of male and female may lead to a rejection of any biological connection to gender. This third option is not mutually exclusive of the other two and often serves as the driving force to adopt either of the previous alternatives. All these options represent a distortion of God's design for sexuality.

Table 17.2. Possible Consequences of the Denial of Binary Gender

Acceptance of a multiplicity of genders
Acceptance of no gender at all
Rejection of any biological connection to gender

Males and Females Are Complementary in Nature

Closely related to the previous principle, God created males and females to be complementary in nature. This principle connects biology to function. After God had created Adam, he set him in the garden of Eden to cultivate and keep it. Since Adam was the only human being in existence, God pointed out Adam's solitary existence. He declared, "It is not good for the man to be alone; I will make him a helper suitable for him" (Gen. 2:18). Adam's solitary existence was the only thing in all creation that was labeled as "not good." But God most likely intended for Adam to recognize his aloneness while naming the animals so that he could better understand the significance of the suitable helper that God was about to create for him. The suitable helper that God created was the woman he fashioned from Adam's rib (vv. 21–22). God did not create someone identical to Adam, but he created a complement.

Sexual Complementarity

The man and woman are complementary to each other in two ways. First, they are *sexual* complements. The mandate of Genesis 1:28 declared that the man and woman are to be fruitful and multiply. The only mechanism for such multiplication was (and is) the sexual relationship between a man and a woman.[32] Had God

32. Even with modern artificial reproductive technologies, the process of reproduction is based on manipulation of male and female gametes and chromosomal markers.

created another man to be Adam's suitable partner, or had he identified one of the animals as Adam's partner, this mandate to be fruitful and multiply could not have been accomplished; therefore, God's creation of the woman as a complementary sexual partner was necessary for the fulfillment of his command to fill the earth with worshipers. Any departure from this complementary design of sexuality is sinful. Daniel Heimbach argues: "Sex unites beings made for each other. Men and women are human and neither is more or less human than the other. But our equal humanity does not mean we are perfectly identical. As sexual creatures, men and women are different in ways that complement each other, and the value of complementary relationship in sex is so positive that any denial or attempt to erase it is immoral."[33]

Sexual complementarity draws out the importance of understanding the purposes of sex—procreation, sexual purity, and unity—which are drawn from God's design for marriage.[34] These purposes are adopted from Augustine's three goods of marriage in *On the Good of Marriage*. Augustine argued that marriage had three ends—offspring, fidelity, and sacrament—that relate directly to our three purposes of sex.[35] Procreation is the first purpose mentioned in Scripture in Genesis 1:28. We recognize the biological differences between men and women, and these biological differences facilitate procreation. God takes this purpose of sex so seriously that any departure from it is called an "abomination" (*tō'ēbāh*—see Lev. 18:6–23). Sexual purity is a purpose of sex that can be fulfilled only within the context of a monogamous marriage. In 1 Corinthians 7:8–9, Paul tells his readers: "But I say to the unmarried and to widows that it is good for them if they remain even as I. But if they do not have self-control, let them marry; for it

33. Daniel R. Heimbach, *True Sexual Morality: Recovering Biblical Standards for a Culture in Crisis* (Wheaton, IL: Crossway, 2004), 169–70.

34. There is healthy discussion on what the purposes of sex are. Dennis Hollinger has proposed four purposes of sex—consummation of marriage, procreation, love, and pleasure. John and Paul Feinberg suggest six purposes of sex—procreation, companionship, unity, pleasure, to raise up a godly seed, and curbing fornication and adultery. J. Budziszewski proposes only two purposes of sex—procreation and union. While we consider all three contributions to be useful, we lean on the goods of marriage developed by Augustine to form the foundation for the purposes we propose. See Hollinger, *The Meaning of Sex*, 93–115; Feinberg and Feinberg, *Ethics for a Brave New World*, 300–302; J. Budziszewski, *On the Meaning of Sex* (Wilmington, DE: ISI, 2012), 24–33.

35. In his work *De Bono Coniugali* ("On the Good of Marriage"), Augustine notes three goods of marriage—offspring, fidelity (or faith in chastity), and sacrament. The three purposes of sex as developed from Augustine include procreation (offspring), sexual purity (fidelity), and unity (sacrament). Although we do not take the sacramental language of Augustine's formulation to have any soteriological significance in our discussion of the purposes of sex and marriage, it should be noted that a sacramental understanding of marriage developed from Augustine's formulation as the Roman Catholic Church developed its sacramental theology. Yet most believe that Augustine was not using the Latin term *sacramentum* in the technical sense of a sacrament in this specific work. See Augustine, *De Bono Coniugali*, in *The Fathers of the Church: A New Translation*, trans. Charles T. Wilcox, vol. 27 (New York: Fathers of the Church, 1955), 24–32.

is better to marry than to burn with passion." As a husband and wife engage in a sexual relationship, they satisfy their own and each other's sexual desires within the covenant of their marriage. This outlet of sexual fulfillment then serves as a mechanism for purity. The third purpose of sex is unity. Genesis 2:24 tells us, "For this reason a man shall leave his father and mother, and be joined to his wife; and they shall become one flesh." One of the key aspects of Genesis 2:24 is the unique one-flesh union that is both physical and metaphysical. The unity of sexual intercourse reveals the physical component as two bodies are joined together in the complementary fashion to which their unique biological features testify. The metaphysical side of unity comes from the perspective that sexual intercourse is a coordinating sign of the covenant of marriage—depicting the intimate union between a man and a woman.

Human flourishing from the standpoint of sexual complementarity reflects the creation-order design of a man and a woman engaged in a sexual relationship within the context of marriage. While procreation can be accomplished outside marriage, the unity that God desires and sexual purity are experienced only within marriage. Since all three of these purposes are connected to God's design for sexuality, the most human approach is to express this sexual complementarity through God's plan of marriage.

Role Complementarity

Second, the man and woman are complementary in their roles. Man and woman are not identical in the way that they are designed to function. We see the first hint of role complementarity in Genesis 2:18–25 as God declares that he will make a suitable helper for Adam and creates the woman. John Hammett states: "Male and female have differing roles within the home and in male and female relationships. This difference is hinted at in Genesis 2:18–25, an important text for understanding God's intention for male and female, because it and Genesis 1 are the only prefall references to the male and female roles. Adam is specifically said to be in need of 'a helper suitable for him'; Eve is created to meet that need."[36] These different roles do not undermine the inherent value that both man and woman have. The two can have different roles while still having equal dignity and worth as image-bearers.

These different roles are further confirmed in New Testament passages on marriage. Within the context of marriage, we understand that husbands are to love their wives as Christ loved the church—sacrificing, cherishing, nourishing (Eph. 5:25–29). Wives, on their part, submit themselves to the leadership of their

---

36. John S. Hammett, "Human Nature," in *A Theology for the Church*, ed. Daniel L. Akin, rev. ed. (Nashville: B&H Academic, 2014), 296.

husbands just as the church submits to Christ. The wife respects her husband and seeks his counsel (1 Cor. 11:3; 14:35; Eph. 5:22–24, 33). The language of roles is often misunderstood today. It is fairly simple to see from Ephesians 5:25–29 that husbands are to love their wives as Christ loved the church and to love their wives as they love their own bodies. This is a sacrificial love on the part of the husband as he seeks to serve his wife and lead her as they walk together in godliness. The language of submission, however, is not so simple. When Scripture says that a wife should submit to her husband, it is not saying that she has less dignity or worth than her husband. Instead, it means that she comes under his leadership as the God-ordained head of the family while still functioning as an image-bearer with inherent value and worth. The language of submission does not make her a servant. She makes great contributions to the family. It simply means that she submits to her husband's spiritual authority in the same way that the church submits to Christ. Such a view is often labeled *complementarianism.*[37]

As complementarians, we believe these gender roles were instituted at creation (Gen. 2:18, 20) and are reaffirmed after the fall (3:16–19). By identifying the various roles that men and women have, particularly in the home, we see that God's design for men and women includes role complementarity. Budziszewski notes: "Men and women aren't just different, but different in corresponding ways. They are complementary opposites—alike in their humanity, but different in ways that make them natural partners. Each sex completes what the other lacks, and helps bring the other into balance."[38] Balancing these roles is accomplished only through God's plan for marriage between a man and a woman.

Sexual complementarity and role complementarity are essential to our understanding of the nature of mankind. God created man and woman as distinct, complementary partners who live out such distinctions within the contexts that God designed for them—namely, marriage. Those who are not married live out the physical side of sexuality in chastity. This is not merely refraining from sexual intercourse, but also bringing one's sexual desires in line with God's purposes. In addition, married individuals do the same by channeling their sexual desires through the God-ordained institution of marriage. From the perspective of roles, married couples can express role complementarity through their marriage. This is more difficult for those who are not married; singles, however, can exhibit an attitude of service and sacrifice for those around them and watch good models of role complementarity in preparation for marriage if that is their desire.

37. For a more detailed description of complementarianism, see the 1987 Danvers Statement adopted by the Council on Biblical Manhood and Womanhood at https://cbmw.org/about/danvers-statement/. See also Wayne Grudem, "Equality and Leadership in Marriage," in *Christian Ethics: An Introduction to Biblical Moral Reasoning* (Wheaton, IL: Crossway, 2018), 389–425.

38. Budziszewski, *On the Meaning of Sex*, 41.

Physical Sexuality Is Part of God's Good Creation

The third theological principle that guides our understanding of sexuality is the idea that physical sexuality is part of God's good creation. When thinking about sexuality, we often find an overemphasis on the internal or spiritual component of sexuality. Testing to see whether the college and seminary students we teach might have some insight into the question of how we should understand sexuality, over the past several years we have tasked them with writing papers giving a biblical answer to the question "what is sexy?" Fascinatingly, the vast majority of the papers betrayed Gnostic understandings of human anthropology that predictably emphasized internal/spiritual qualities and almost completely neglected all substantive discussions of external/bodily elements. No doubt many felt such thinking governed what they were "supposed to write" for a seminary class, when in fact many of these same students admitted in private conversation that they really defined *sexiness* mostly in physical terms.

We must not forget that God created human beings as part of a physical world that he declared to be "good." Genesis 2:7 declares, "Then the LORD God formed man of dust from the ground, and breathed into his nostrils the breath of life; and man became a living being." This text reveals that human anthropology involves both a material/physical element and an immaterial/spiritual or soul element. Not only are we bodies, but we are bodies made alive by the breath of God. What sets humans apart from other living creatures is not that we have physical life, but that our life is "God-breathed" in a way that gives us a unique "soul" that bears the image of God. But we must not become inordinately focused on the soul. The body is a central element of human life as well. As we discussed at greater length in chapter 2, a human is best understood as a *psychosomatic unity* or an *embodied self*. From this we can infer that if God made bodies with a sexual nature, and if God declared these sexual bodies to be "good," then God must intend for there to be a bodily element to sexuality. By God's declaration, the body is good, and it is right for us to appreciate it as good.

Thus, when we (in appropriate ways) appreciate the physical qualities of the other gender and (in appropriate contexts) enjoy the physical pleasure that God built to accompany the proper expressions of our sexuality, we can rejoice in the goodness of our Maker's design. The question, then, is not whether we can appreciate the body and bodily elements of our sexuality, but how and when it is right to do so.

Sexuality Has a Spiritual Component

In addition to the physical side, we must see that sexuality has a nonphysical, or spiritual, component that it is also good and right to appreciate. That is, contrary to what sexually infused advertisements indicate, issues of spirituality and holiness, character and virtue, personality and disposition are also very important elements of sexuality. As Paul describes in 1 Timothy 4:8: "bodily discipline is only of little profit, but godliness is profitable for all things, since it holds promise for the present life and also for the life to come." Thus, because godliness is of such great value, then we ought to find the expression of godliness in and through gender-appropriate behavior to be a good component of biblical sexuality.

Thinking back to Augustine's goods of marriage and the related purposes of sex, one of these purposes stands out as significant for the spiritual component of sexuality. The union that God designed to grow through the relationship of marriage and the shared sexual experience goes far beyond the physical components of sexuality. Yes, two individuals who participate in sexual intercourse will form a bond emotionally and spiritually. The strongest and only appropriate bond, however, will be built by those who engage in the comprehensive relationship of marriage. The joining together of all aspects of life will bring a couple together in ways that mere intercourse cannot. We may joke about the idea of longtime spouses' being able to finish each other's sentences, but the fact of the matter is that they have entered a spiritual bond so that their thoughts and desires grow in unity with each other. That is why some couples are able to know how each other will react in certain circumstances without ever having to communicate.

Because our sexuality includes how we relate to one another, our personal and corporate spiritual development is also important to sexuality. As a man and woman grow in intimacy through their relationship, they also function to spur each other along to godliness. In fact, we believe that before a couple enters an exclusive relationship, spiritual maturity is a characteristic that ought to attract unmarried individuals to each other. For example, when Evan first started dating his wife, an older mentor pulled him aside and purposefully identified a number of key spiritual characteristics that his then-girlfriend exhibited and why those characteristics would be important for a future of flourishing together. That mentor was wise enough to see what a twenty-year-old was not quite mature enough to recognize, and he was right. This is an example of how sexuality moves beyond the physical to encompass the spiritual as well.

God Designed Marriage as the Context for Sexual Activity

We have already discussed at length the idea that God's design for marriage requires a monogamous union of a man and a woman. Throughout Scripture, the only positive discussions of sex and sexuality take place in the context of a heterosexual, monogamous marital union. In no place is any other form of sexual expression viewed or discussed positively. Thus, Genesis 1–2 is the *norma normans* for the entire paradigm. To put it another way, we read the Bible from left to right. God set the standard in Genesis 1–2 at the beginning of the Pentateuch.

Thus, all Jewish readers would have understood that any other picture of sexuality or marriage differing from Genesis 1–2 would be wrong by default. God does not need to say that it is wrong every time it occurs because that idea was implicit. This union is exclusive and is the only biblically sanctioned context for sexual activity.

We see the seriousness of this aspect of sexuality throughout all of Scripture. The most direct prohibition against sexual activity outside marriage comes in the seventh commandment. God declares, "You shall not commit adultery" (Ex. 20:14). In addition to this commandment, we find prohibitions on adultery, fornication, prostitution, and same-sex intercourse throughout the Old and New Testaments (e.g., Lev. 18:22; 20:10, 13; Deut. 22:22; 23:17–18; Prov. 5:1–6; 6:23–35; Matt. 5:27–28; Rom. 1:26–27; 1 Cor. 6:9–10, 18; Gal. 5:19–21; Heb. 13:4). In addition, Christian history teaches that marriage remains the exclusive context for sexual activity throughout church history. Only in recent years have some attempted to make a Christian case for sex outside the biblical definition of *marriage*. Despite the legality of a particular disordered sexual expression, only sexual intercourse in the context of biblical marriage (between one man and one woman) is moral.

God Intended Childbearing and Rearing to Take Place in the Context of Biblically Defined *Marriage*

If procreation is one of the purposes of sex and sex is designed by God to take place within the context of biblical marriage, then the logical conclusion is that God intended childbearing and rearing to take place within the context of marriage. This guiding principle for sexuality takes us back to the mandate in Genesis 1:28, where God instructed the man and woman to be fruitful and multiply and fill the earth. When we include the inauguration of the first marriage in Genesis 2, we see that God's design for fruitfulness and multiplication is in the context of marriage. We will address this in more detail in the next chapter, but for now it will suffice to say that Scripture is full of admonitions about married couples' bearing and rearing their children.

Before we conclude this section, it is interesting to note that numerous studies confirm this theological principle by concluding that the best environment for children is the married home of their biological mother and father.[39] Children

---

39. Wendy Wang notes: "Finally, despite the legalization of same-sex marriage in 2015, the number of children being raised by *married* same-sex parents is quite small. In 2018, an estimated 233,000 children (or 0.3% of all children) lived in a home with two married same-sex parents, while another 86,000 children (0.1% of all children) lived with cohabiting same-sex parents. In total, 319,000 children, or 0.4% of the overall population of children in the U.S., lived with same-sex parents in 2018." Wendy Wang, "A Portrait of Contemporary Family Living Arrangements for U.S. Children," Institute for Family Studies, April 14, 2020,

reared in intact, married families typically perform better in school and are less likely to be reported for misconduct in the classroom or on school grounds.[40] In addition, those children who are reared by their married biological parents are less likely to be abused in their household. Sara McLanahan and Gary Sandefur write:

> If we were asked to design a system for making sure that children's basic needs were met, we would probably come up with something quite similar to the two-parent family ideal. Such a design, in theory, would not only ensure that children had access to the time and money of two adults, it also would provide a system of checks and balances that promoted quality parenting. The fact that both adults have a biological connection to the child would increase the likelihood that the parents would identify with the child and be willing to sacrifice for that child, and it would reduce the likelihood that either parent would abuse the child. Last but not least, the fact that two parents had connections to the community would increase the child's access to information about opportunities outside the household and would, at the same time, strengthen social control.[41]

These studies, and others like them, confirm that God's design for childbearing and rearing is the best model even to this day. As a result, we should affirm this principle as a key element of our understanding of biblical sexuality.

These six guiding principles help us understand more fully God's design for biblical sexuality so that we can fully worship him in this aspect of our lives. It is important for us to have this positive perspective on sexuality before we discuss the challenges that the culture presents us for two reasons. First, knowing God's design for sexuality will promote a heart of worship for believers to live out a biblical sexual ethic. No matter what the world presents to us, we will know how best to worship our God, who created us as sexual beings. Second, a positive perspective on sexuality will answer the critics who say that Christians are merely obsessed with condemning the sexual ethic of those they oppose. We do not merely condemn disordered sexuality; we offer a biblical perspective that promotes human flourishing in the context of our sexuality.

---

accessed April 16, 2020, https://ifstudies.org/blog/a-portrait-of-contemporary-family-living-arrangements -for-us-children.

40. Nicholas Zill, "Family Still Matters for Key Indicators of Student Performance," Institute for Family Studies, April 6, 2020, accessed April 16, 2020, https://ifstudies.org/blog/family-still-matters-for-key -indicators-of-student-performance.

41. Sara McLanahan and Gary Sandefur, *Growing Up with a Single Parent: What Hurts, What Helps* (Cambridge, MA: Harvard University Press, 1994), 38.

Challenges to Biblical Sexuality

Numerous challenges to biblical sexuality have been present for most of human history. Immediately following the fall of the human race in Genesis 3, we see that sin-caused disordered sexuality begins to impact individuals, families, and cultures in rather dramatic ways. As the Scriptures unfold, the counter ideas and practices that present a challenge to God's instructions in the creation passages are met with corrective and protective commands throughout the Old and New Testaments. In his kindness, God's moral instruction in the Bible always derives from his goodness and wisdom as he seeks to protect humans from errant ideas and choices as well as to provide a better alternative. This is true even when the commands appear as negative prohibitions (i.e., "thou shalt not . . .") or even appear to have a condemning tone. As Proverbs 3:12 tells us, "For whom the LORD loves He reproves, even as a father corrects the son in whom he delights" (see also Heb. 12:6).

In light of this kind desire of God to protect his image-bearers and provide for them the proper path for worship in the area of sex and sexuality, we now turn to a discussion that identifies key ideas and sexual issues that stand in contrast to God's design. Our hope in the pages that follow is to help believers understand how and why these contrasting views of sex and sexuality pose a challenge to God's design for human flourishing and God-honoring worship. In the pages ahead, we address the issues of adultery and fornication, homosexuality, transgenderism, polygamy, polyamory, and open marriage by highlighting the nature of the problem, exploring the scriptural passages relevant to each, and offering a biblical response.

Adultery and Fornication

Even though we could address adultery and fornication as two separate challenges, we view them in similar terms and as a similar violation of God's design for sexuality. Both adultery and fornication are distortions of God's design for fidelity in sexuality through the marital union. We typically think of adultery as a sexual relationship consummated outside the bounds of marriage by someone who is married. Fornication is a sexual relationship consummated outside the bounds of marriage by individuals who are not married.

Biblical Instructions

From a biblical standpoint, the distinction between adultery and fornication rests primarily on the marital status of the woman in the illicit relationship. The Hebrew verb that means "to commit adultery" (*n'p*) refers to an illicit sexual relationship between a man and a married woman who is not his wife. The Hebrew term for "fornication" is a much broader term. Mark Rooker notes, "This verb refers to all forms of illicit sexual behavior including prostitution (Gen 38:15) and sexual relations outside marriage (Num 25:1), as well as the figurative use of following after other gods (Exod 34:15–16; Lev 20:5–6; Deut 31:16)."[42] A similar distinction exists between the Greek terms for "adultery" and "fornication." *Moicheia* is the Greek term for "adultery," and *porneia* is the term for "sexual immorality," including fornication. Johannes Louw and Eugene Nida describe the difference in this way: "From the standpoint of the NT, adultery was normally defined in terms of the married status of the woman involved in any such act. In other words, sexual intercourse of a married man with an unmarried woman would usually be regarded as πορνεία 'fornication,' but sexual intercourse of either an unmarried or a married man with someone else's wife was regarded as adultery, both on the part of the man as well as the woman."[43] Thus, from a technical standpoint fornication and adultery are not identical—fornication is a broader term that encompasses all forms of sexual immorality. Therefore, all adultery is fornication, but not all fornication is adultery.

Despite the technical distinctions, both fornication and adultery are condemned throughout Scripture.[44] We can begin with the seventh commandment as the clearest denunciation of adultery: "You shall not commit adultery" (Ex. 20:14). There is virtually no controversy over the meaning of the seventh commandment because it so explicitly outlaws adultery. Douglas Stuart goes so far as to say that this commandment is the most important of the prohibitions against sexual immorality.[45] Without this prohibition, marriage could no longer function as the foundation of society. Stuart goes on to say: "Adultery was known in the ancient world as 'the great sin.' Marriage is foundational to the creation order and to human society; husbands and wives can hardly function fully as one flesh if they do not trust each other. Sexual relations are the virtual seal of a marriage covenant, and adultery betrays the emotional-psychological intimacy that specially connects adult men and women within marriage."[46] While this specific commandment does not explicitly condemn fornication and other forms of sexual sin, the basic idea of the seventh commandment applies to these other sins. In addition, other Old Testament passages cover the majority of sins that would be

---

42. Mark F. Rooker, *The Ten Commandments: Ethics for the Twenty-First Century* (Nashville: B&H Academic, 2010), 136n11.

43. Johannes P. Louw and Eugene A. Nida, *Greek-English Lexicon of the New Testament Based on Semantic Domains*, vol. 1 (New York: United Bible Societies, 1989), 772.

44. Rooker makes the case that consensual sex between two unmarried, consenting adults is not condemned as strongly as adultery. See Rooker, *Ten Commandments*, 135.

45. Douglas K. Stuart, *Exodus*, NAC 2 (Nashville: B&H, 2006), 463.

46. Stuart, *Exodus*, 463–64.

considered fornication—for example, Exodus 22:16–17 and Deuteronomy 22:13–22 prohibit premarital sex; Leviticus 18:6–18 and 20:17–20 prohibit incest. The Old Testament consequence for adultery and other sexual immoralities typically was the death penalty (e.g., Lev. 20:10–14).

When we move to the New Testament, Jesus sets the tone for the biblical prohibition against adultery. In the Sermon on the Mount, Jesus references the seventh commandment and then expands its application beyond the technical application of adultery to include lust:

> You have heard that it was said, "You shall not commit adultery"; but I say to you that everyone who looks at a woman with lust for her has already committed adultery with her in his heart. (Matt. 5:27–28)

Jesus draws on the narrow application of the commandment against adultery and then informs his hearers that the commandment expands well beyond literal adultery to address the heart. He makes the case that a man who looks upon a woman with lust has already broken the commandment. David Jones suggests: "What the seventh commandment prohibits, then, is not just (or even primarily) illicit sexual intercourse. Rather, this moral precept is aimed at one's inner being— that is, one's thoughts, motives, and emotions that bear upon relational intimacy."[47] Therefore, Jesus makes broad application to both external behavior and internal motivations connected to the sexual relationship. His interpretation of the commandment, then, seeks proper alignment of the whole self with God's created and good design for sex. So a proper view of holy and good sexual expression forbids adultery, fornication, cohabitation, incest, pornography, and numerous other immoralities in addition to the internal desires and lusts that could lead to them even if one never acts on them. The strength of Jesus' instruction on these matters indicates the importance of the topic and his desire to see humans flourish by following God's instructions and living in light of how he designed them sexually.

The Current Challenge

Without much controversy on the meaning of Scripture's prohibitions against adultery and fornication, why is it a challenge to biblical sexuality? From a secular standpoint, adultery and fornication are becoming more mainstream. Several years ago, the online dating platform Ashley Madison catered services for married individuals seeking to find a partner for a sexual encounter without ending their marriages. The company's motto was "Life is short. Have an affair." The company's founder, Noel Biderman, argued that adultery could actually "save the institution

---

47. David W. Jones, *An Introduction to Biblical Ethics* (Nashville: B&H Academic, 2013), 182.

of marriage."[48] In addition, cohabitation has increased dramatically in recent decades. For women who married from 1980 to 1984, approximately 40 percent cohabited with their husbands before marriage. Three decades later, 70 percent of women who married from 2010 to 2014 cohabited with their husbands before marriage.[49] The growth of cohabitation and the prevalence of adultery in society mean that these trends are also slipping into the church. Therefore, Christians must be on the alert to answer the challenges of adultery and cohabitation to aid our fellow image-bearers in being faithful worshipers of our Creator. Otherwise, we may find ourselves violating the good guidelines and clear instructions that God put in place to maximize worship through our sexuality.

Homosexuality

The second challenge to biblical sexuality is not as prevalent as adultery and fornication, but it receives much more support in the media and culture. Homosexuality is a distortion of God's design for sexuality to be expressed between a man and a woman. As we mentioned at the beginning of the chapter, same-sex marriage was legalized in the United States as a result of the 2015 Supreme Court decision *Obergefell v. Hodges*. Debates over the impact of same-sex marriage on culture continue to this day. Beyond the public debates, internal debates within denominations have increased over whether Scripture condones homosexual activity. Different denominations have staked their claim on one side of the issue or the other (e.g., the United Church of Christ, the Episcopal Church in the U.S., the Presbyterian Church [U.S.A.], and segments of other denominations have affirmed same-sex marriage). Scripture contains a limited amount of information regarding homosexuality (Gen. 19:1–11; Lev. 18:22; 20:13; Rom. 1:26–27; 1 Cor. 6:9–11; 1 Tim. 1:8–11), but the overall message is clear—homosexuality violates God's design for sexuality and marriage. By contrast, God depicts true human flourishing in sexuality in such a way that commends marriage between one man and one woman.

Genesis 19:1–11

We first encounter same-sex sexual behavior in the story of Sodom in Genesis 19. In this passage, we see God executing his judgment against the people of Sodom for their grotesque wickedness. Included in their detestable acts is an

---

48. Eric Johnson, "Born to Cheat? Tempers Meet Testimony at Debate on Adultery," ABC News, September 24, 2009, accessed April 17, 2020, https://abcnews.go.com/Nightline/10Commandments/affairs-cheating-nightline-face-off-debate-adultery-infidelity/story?id=8645026.

49. P. Hemez and W. D. Manning, "Thirty years of change in women's premarital cohabitation experience," Family Profiles, FP-17-05, National Center for Family & Marriage Research, accessed April 17, 2020, https://www.bgsu.edu/ncfmr/resources/data/family-profiles/hemez-manning-30-yrs-change-women-premarital-cohab-fp-17-05.html.

interaction with Lot and the angelic visitors. Upon arriving in Sodom, Lot invites the angelic visitors to spend the night at his home. During their visit, the men of Sodom arrive and demand that Lot hand the visitors over to them so that they "may have relations with them" (v. 5). Lot responds by offering his two daughters, "who have not had relations with man" (v. 8). Ultimately, the angelic visitors strike the men of Sodom with blindness and lead Lot and his family out of the city before God destroys it.

Two questions generally arise from Genesis 19. While the NASB translates the Hebrew word *yāda'* as "have relations," other translations use "know." The question then comes whether the text is talking about sexual relations or simply knowledge. While *yāda'* often means "to know" or "to get acquainted with," the context of this verb in Genesis points to its sexual meaning in this passage. The verb clearly carries a sexual connotation in Genesis 4:1, 17, 25; 24:16; 38:26. And the use of the term for Lot's daughters makes the sexual nature of the term evident in chapter 19. It would be foolish to think that Lot's daughters had never become acquainted with a man in the sense of knowledge because they knew their own father.[50]

The other question that arises from this passage is whether the homosexuality of the men of Sodom was the cause of their destruction. A number of passages list the sins of Sodom (Deut. 29:23; 32:32; Isa. 3:9; 13:19; Jer. 23:14; 49:18; 50:40; Lam. 4:6; Ezek. 16:46–48; Amos 4:11; Zeph. 2:9; Matt. 10:15; Luke 17:29; Rom. 9:29; 2 Peter 2:6; Jude 7). Among these lists, there are a host of sins. In Jude 7, we see a specific reference to the sexual sin of Sodom:

> Just as Sodom and Gomorrah and the cities around them, since they in the same way as these indulged in gross immorality and went after strange flesh, are exhibited as an example in undergoing the punishment of eternal fire.

Some proponents of homosexuality make the case that the sin of Sodom has nothing to do with homosexual behavior. Instead, they argue, Sodom was condemned for its inhospitality. Rather than homosexual sex being what the men of Sodom desired, Simon Parker argues, we should see their sin as gang rape that violated the ancient Near Eastern hospitality code. Parker writes: "In short,

---

50. Andreas Köstenberger and David Jones write: "Concerning the Hebrew word *yāda'* it must be noted that while this term usually does mean 'to get acquainted with,' it can also refer to sexual relations, as it clearly does in Gen 4:1, 17, 25; 24:16; 38:26. The decisive factor in determining the definition of this word (or any term with multiple possible meanings) necessarily must be the context. Following this principle, in the context of the Sodom and Gomorrah passage *yāda'* must have a sexual connotation when it occurs in Genesis 19:5, for when the term recurs three verses later the sexual meaning is the only one that makes sense." Andreas J. Köstenberger with David W. Jones, *God, Marriage, and Family: Rebuilding the Biblical Foundation*, 2nd ed. (Wheaton, IL: Crossway, 2010), 204.

this mob is no more homosexual than any other street gang. On this occasion it sees an opportunity for violence and humiliation. But the enormity of the mob's offence is not just that they attempt rape, which is heinous enough, but that they attempt to rape guests in their own town and under Lot's roof. In other words, the ultimate offense here is the violation of hospitality."[51] Other interpreters do not even go so far as Parker. They hold that the term *yāda'* should be understood as "to get acquainted with" and that therefore the sin of Sodom is merely pushing the envelope of hospitality beyond social norms, since Lot had already received the visitors into his home.[52] Robert Gagnon refutes this interpretation by noting that the immediate context of the passage and other Old Testament parallels "leave[s] little room for doubting the sexual connotation."[53]

As we can see, the sins of Sodom were many. Homosexuality was not the only one, but it was certainly among the vices that led to the city's destruction. Therefore, the purpose of Genesis 19 is probably not to give us an unequivocal condemnation of homosexuality as the cause of Sodom's judgment; it is safe to say, however, that homosexuality had something to do with the judgment from God.

Leviticus 18:22 and 20:13

The next time we see homosexuality explicitly mentioned in Scripture is the Holiness Code in Leviticus 18:22 and 20:13. These two verses provide similar condemnations of homosexuality in no uncertain terms:

> You shall not lie with a male as one lies with a female; it is an abomination. (Lev. 18:22)

> If there is a man who lies with a male as those who lie with a woman, both of them have committed a detestable act; they shall surely be put to death. Their blood-guiltiness is upon them. (Lev. 20:13)[54]

These commands are significant because they unequivocally forbid the people of Israel from participating in the same-sex intercourse that was being practiced by their neighbors. The entirety of the Holiness Code (Lev. 17–26) was designed

---

51. Simon B. Parker, "The Hebrew Bible and Homosexuality," *Quarterly Review* 11, no. 3 (Fall 1991): 6.

52. See Derrick Sherwin Bailey, *Homosexuality and the Western Christian Tradition* (London: Longmans, Green and Co., 1955), 3–4; John Boswell, *Christianity, Social Tolerance, and Homosexuality* (Chicago: University of Chicago Press, 1980), 93–94; John J. McNeill, *The Church and the Homosexual* (Kansas City, MO: Sheed, Andrews, and McMeel, 1976), 54–55.

53. Robert A. J. Gagnon, *The Bible and Homosexual Practice: Texts and Hermeneutics* (Nashville: Abingdon, 2001), 73–74.

54. See the earlier discussions of Leviticus 20:13 on pages 149-50 ("The Threefold Division of the Law"). Also see pages 156-62 ("Six Basic Rules of Hermeneutics for Ethics as Worship").

to separate the Israelites from the pagan practices of people in neighboring countries. Therefore, these prohibitions against homosexual behavior represent the desire for God's people to be holy.

There are two significant aspects regarding these verses and their significance for the Old Testament discussion of homosexuality. First, the death penalty is prescribed for those who participate in homosexual intercourse. Leviticus 20:13 clearly dictates that the offenders "shall surely be put to death." The death penalty is prescribed for other sexual offenses in the immediate context of these verses as well. Second, these verses label homosexual behavior as an abomination (*tōēbāh*). This term was often used to describe ritual impurity related to idolatry, but it can also refer to "activities that are morally offensive to God."[55] There is no doubt that such behavior is condemned.

Proponents of homosexuality take two approaches in undermining the applicability of these verses. First, some argue that the label of *abomination* means that God is condemning only homosexual activity connected to idolatry. John Boswell argues: "The Hebrew word 'toevah' . . . does not usually signify something intrinsically evil, like rape or theft (discussed elsewhere in Leviticus), but something which is ritually unclean for Jews, like eating pork or engaging in intercourse during menstruation, both of which are prohibited in these same chapters. It is used throughout the Old Testament to designate those Jewish sins which involve ethnic contamination or idolatry."[56] The problem with this interpretation is that other activities that most would consider intrinsically evil are also labeled as abominations in the immediate context of these verses—incest (Lev. 18:6–18), adultery (v. 20), and bestiality (v. 23).[57]

The other approach that proponents of homosexuality use to invalidate these verses is to claim that the Holiness Code does not apply in a new covenant context. Most Christians believe that at least part of the Holiness Code no longer applies to believers (e.g., the dietary restrictions); this prohibition against homosexuality, however, falls within the same large set of regulations. Parker argues: "May we pick and choose among the verses in these two chapters? All the behaviors listed are equally condemned. . . . If the verses on homosexual acts are cited as bearing on church policies, then the verses on adultery and intercourse during menstruation, for example, must surely also be cited as having the same impact on church policies."[58]

Such an argument accuses New Testament believers of being inconsistent in their application of the moral regulations and even punishments for such offenses

---

55. Köstenberger with Jones, *God, Marriage, and Family*, 207.
56. Boswell, *Christianity, Social Tolerance, and Homosexuality*, 100.
57. Köstenberger with Jones, *God, Marriage, and Family*, 207.
58. Parker, "Hebrew Bible and Homosexuality," 15.

(i.e., the death penalty). In response, we recognize that some components of the Holiness Code do not apply in a New Testament context (e.g., Peter's vision in Acts 10 opening the gospel to the Gentiles and releasing him from Jewish dietary restrictions) because of the nature of the laws. As we noted in our discussion of proper biblical interpretation in chapter 5, judicial (or civil) laws have underlying moral laws that reflect the abiding nature of God.[59] In this particular case, the Holiness Code includes moral laws prohibiting homosexuality and judicial laws that regulated civil application of the moral law in ancient Israel. Because the civil portion of these verses in the Holiness Code relates directly to that particular cultural time and context, it is a misunderstanding of the nature of judicial law to ask whether the command to put someone engaging in homosexual behavior to death should be applied in a modern context. Yet the underlying moral law, because it reflects the abiding nature of God, endures beyond the particulars of context and time. As David Jones explains, "While God's moral standards do not change, their application (and penalty for violation) in each time and culture is unique and ever changing."[60] In addition, the underlying moral principle is repeated in the New Testament, offering further confirmation of its abiding adherence to God's nature.

Romans 1:26–27

The most significant New Testament passage on the issue of homosexuality is found in Romans 1:26–27. Within the larger scope of Romans 1:18–32, Paul condemns the depravity of man and lists some specific sins that give evidence of just how bad the sinfulness is. In verses 26–27, Paul confronts the sin of homosexuality:

> For this reason God gave them over to degrading passions; for their women exchanged the natural function for that which is unnatural, and in the same way also the men abandoned the natural function of the woman and burned in their desire toward one another, men with men committing indecent acts and receiving in their own persons the due penalty of their error.

Romans 1:26 represents the second of three times that Paul uses the phrase "God gave them over" (cf. Rom. 1:24, 28) to describe how God sees the sin of those who refuse to worship him. In fact, the entire passage turns on the words of verses 22–23: "Professing to be wise, they became fools, and exchanged the glory of the incorruptible God for an image in the form of corruptible man and of birds and four-footed animals and crawling creatures." In light of their refusal to

---

59. See the section on "Threefold Division of the Law" in chapter 5.
60. Jones, *Introduction to Biblical Ethics*, 59.

worship him, God gave them over to their various forms of depravity. It is in this context that Paul's condemnation of homosexuality comes.

This passage is important for a couple of reasons. First, it is the only explicit mention of lesbianism in all of Scripture. While some of the other prohibitions against homosexual behavior could be applied to lesbianism, they all technically address male homosexual behavior. But Romans 1:26–27 directly connects the two. Second, this passage describes homosexual behavior as an unnatural desire. Paul's appeal to the creation order earlier in this chapter (v. 20) makes the description of homosexuality as "unnatural" important. Paul points his readers back to God's self-revelation in creation and infers that we should know God by his creation. By contrast, exchanging the natural for something unnatural is a departure from the creation-order design—in this case, he refers to sexuality.[61] The overall prohibition is fairly straightforward. When we keep in mind what we have discussed above that God created male and female as sexual complements, then it is simple to surmise that Paul's prohibition here is calling us back to God's design for sexuality.

Proponents of homosexuality attempt to reinterpret this passage in two primary ways. First, some believe that the prohibition against homosexuality is simply part of a larger prohibition against idolatry as described in Romans 1:18–32.[62] The basis for this interpretation comes from verses 18–19, which read, "For the wrath of God is revealed from heaven against all ungodliness and unrighteousness of men who suppress the truth in unrighteousness, because that which is known about God is evident within them; for God made it evident to them." Thus, the homosexuality forbidden here is merely that which results from an idolatrous expression of one's suppressing the truth of God. It is not homosexuality expressed within a "God-honoring" relationship or atmosphere; rather, it is an action expressed as a result of rebelling against God. The problem with this interpretation of the passage is that it dismisses the plain reading of Scripture for a more circuitous interpretation that may be equally valid, yet is not the direct

61. We deal with this issue at more length in the following pages, but Richard Hays offers an excellent perspective on why Paul points to the creation-order design as that which is "natural." He writes: "In the same way, the charge that these fallen humans have 'exchanged natural relations for unnatural' means nothing more nor less than that human beings, created for heterosexual companionship as the Genesis story bears witness, have distorted even so basic a truth as their sexual identity by rejecting the male and female roles which are 'naturally' theirs in God's created order. The charge is a corporate indictment of pagan society, not a narrative about the 'rake's progress' of particular individuals. Boswell's misinterpretation of this passage shares with much of the history of Western interpretation of Paul an unfortunate tendency to suppose that Paul is primarily concerned with developing a soteriological account of the fate of individuals before God." Richard B. Hays, "Relations Natural and Unnatural: A Response to John Boswell's Exegesis of Romans 1," *Journal of Religious Ethics* 14, no. 1 (1986): 200.

62. See Dale B. Martin, "Heterosexism and the Interpretation of Romans 1:18–32," *Biblical Interpretation* 3, no. 3 (January 1995): 332–55. For interaction with Martin's view, see Gagnon, *The Bible and Homosexual Practice*, 284–89.

intention of the text. While idolatry is in view in the larger context of Romans 1, it should be viewed as the root of the problem of human sin that is manifested in various ways, including homosexual behavior.

The second, and more significant, alternative interpretation offered for this passage and its relation to homosexuality is the matter of homosexual orientation. Some interpreters believe that when Paul condemned those who exchanged the "natural function" for the "unnatural," he was speaking to heterosexual individuals who participated in homosexual acts, rather than homosexually oriented individuals. Paul, it is argued, could not have known that certain individuals had a "natural" homosexual orientation. Arland Hultgren writes: "In 1:27 Paul is not speaking of homosexual attraction on the part of males. The concept of sexual orientation, including homosexual orientation, had to wait another nineteen centuries to be formulated."[63] Since Paul was incapable of understanding sexual orientation, according to this interpretation, he could not have condemned homosexuals who were acting according to their nature. Instead, Boswell states that "the persons Paul condemns are manifestly not homosexual: what he derogates are homosexual acts committed by apparently heterosexual persons. The whole point of Romans 1, in fact, is to stigmatize persons who have rejected their calling, gotten off the true path they were once on."[64] This view presupposes that anyone who has a homosexual orientation and acts on it is acting in a natural way. Therefore, the conclusion is made, Paul's condemnation of homosexual behavior as "unnatural" would not apply in such circumstances.

There are two primary problems with this view—one is theological and the other is historical. Theologically speaking, this view implies that not only was Paul incapable of understanding the nature of sexual orientation, but the Holy Spirit was incapable of communicating through Paul in such a way that would not condemn those who argue that their sexual orientation is "natural" and created by God. This view suggests that a chasm exists between what Paul communicated through the inspiration of the Holy Spirit and what people claim to know now about sexuality. As we discussed in chapter 5, however, Scripture is infallible, inerrant, immutable, and clear.[65] Scripture is reflective of God's nature and character. If we call into question the nature of Scripture on this point, there is no limit to how else we might question the authority of Scripture. In fact, one proponent of homosexuality even warns against this very approach. James Brownson argues, "Because revisionist arguments emphasize so strongly the historical distance

---

63. Arland J. Hultgren, "Being Faithful to the Scriptures: Romans 1:26–27 as a Case in Point," *Word & World* 14, no. 3 (Summer 1994): 319.

64. Boswell, *Christianity, Social Tolerance, and Homosexuality*, 109.

65. See "What Is the Nature and Character of Scripture as It Relates to Understanding Ethics as Worship?" in chapter 5.

between the Bible and contemporary experience, this interpretative strategy may implicitly call into question whether the Bible can speak directly, with sufficient specificity and power, to any issues of sexual ethics more broadly considered in contemporary life."[66] While we disagree with Brownson's ultimate conclusion regarding homosexual relationships, we agree with his warning about undermining the nature and authority of Scripture.

The second problem with this view is historical in nature. We believe that Paul was highly educated, as he attested in Acts 22:3 ("educated under Gamaliel"), and well versed in Greek and Roman philosophy (Acts 17:16–31). Centuries before Paul, Plato had proposed the idea of sexual orientation that would have made homosexuality one of the possible options.[67] For Paul to have been unaware of sexual orientation, he would have had to be unaware of the most influential Greek philosopher in history. Certainly, Paul's education could have bypassed Plato's work, but the question at least needs to be raised in relation to this interpretation.

In the end, Romans 1:26–27 provides a straightforward condemnation of homosexuality. Any attempt to offer an alternative interpretation suffers from a convoluted hermeneutic that cannot bear up under the weight of further scrutiny. Paul views all homosexual activity as a violation of God's creation-order design and a refusal to worship the Creator. Thus, Romans 1:26–27 stands as the clearest biblical statement against homosexuality.[68] True worship of the Creator results in following the guidelines he has instituted for human sexuality so that we may experience flourishing and his blessing.

1 Corinthians 6:9–11 and 1 Timothy 1:8–11

We group the last two passages together because they place homosexuality within the context of vice lists. In both these vice lists, Paul identifies homosexual behavior as sinful activity deserving of the judgment of God. Both passages also include other sins alongside homosexuality.

> Or do you not know that the unrighteous will not inherit the kingdom of God? Do not be deceived; neither fornicators, nor idolaters, nor adulterers, nor effeminate, nor homosexuals, nor thieves, nor the covetous, nor drunkards, nor revilers, nor

---

66. James V. Brownson, *Bible, Gender, Sexuality: Reframing the Church's Debate on Same-Sex Relationships* (Grand Rapids: Eerdmans, 2013), 41.

67. See Plato, *Symposium*, in *A Plato Reader: Eight Essential Dialogues*, ed. C. D. C. Reeve (Indianapolis: Hackett, 2012), 189d–193d.

68. For a more extensive treatment of Romans 1:26–27 and its various interpretations, see Evan Lenow, "Exchanging the Natural for the Unnatural: Homosexuality's Distortion of God's Design," *SWJT* 49, no. 1 (Fall 2006): 31–47; Gagnon, *The Bible and Homosexual Practice*, 229–303; Kevin DeYoung, *What Does the Bible Really Teach about Homosexuality?* (Wheaton, IL: Crossway, 2015), 49–57.

swindlers, will inherit the kingdom of God. Such were some of you; but you were washed, but you were sanctified, but you were justified in the name of the Lord Jesus Christ and in the Spirit of our God. (1 Cor. 6:9–11)

But we know that the Law is good, if one uses it lawfully, realizing the fact that law is not made for a righteous person, but for those who are lawless and rebellious, for the ungodly and sinners, for the unholy and profane, for those who kill their fathers or mothers, for murderers, and immoral men and homosexuals and kidnappers and liars and perjurers, and whatever else is contrary to sound teaching, according to the glorious gospel of the blessed God, with which I have been entrusted. (1 Tim. 1:8–11)

In both of these passages, Paul identifies homosexual behavior as unrighteous and contrary to the kingdom of God.

The significance of these passages revolves around the appearance of two unusual Greek words—*malakoi* (found only in 1 Corinthians 6:9) and *arsenokoitai* (found in both passages). In 1 Corinthians 6:9, *malakoi* is translated as "effeminate." The only three other occurrences of the root in the New Testament all refer to soft clothing (Matt. 11:8, twice; Luke 7:25). In this occurrence, it cannot refer to softness in the sense of clothing; instead, it most likely refers to a man's being soft or effeminate. David Malick suggests that the term "is thus not a technical term to describe being effeminate. It often had a more general sense of 'soft' or 'mild.' When it is employed in reference to sexual relationships of men with men, however, it is also not a technical term for male call-boys in a pederastic setting. The term may mean effeminate with respect to boys or men who take the role of a woman in homosexual relationships."[69] We should be careful in the use of this term to definitively condemn homosexuality because it is an obscure term; yet the presence of *arsenokoitai* immediately following *malakoi* in 1 Corinthians 6:9 and the reappearance of *arsenokoitai* in 1 Timothy 1:10 shed more light on Paul's description of the sin.

Arsenokoitai presents its own set of challenges because there is no evidence of its use before Paul's writing.[70] Since it appears that Paul coined this term, we have little more than his context to provide the background for its usage. The term literally means "men who lie with males" (Greek, *arsēn* "male," *koitē* "bed"). The NASB translates the term as "homosexuals" in both passages, but Gagnon argues that such a narrow translation may miss the point. He suggests that the term focuses

69. David E. Malick, "The Condemnation of Homosexuality in 1 Corinthians 6:9," *BibSac* 150, no. 600 (October 1993): 490.
70. Gagnon, *The Bible and Homosexual Practice*, 312–13.

on the action and should not be confused with attraction or supposed orientation. A narrow translation such as "homosexuals" may exclude from consideration those who claim a heterosexual or bisexual orientation yet still participate in homosexual behavior because the term "homosexuals" may lead one to think that Paul is addressing only those who are attracted to members of the same biological sex. Gagnon believes that all such behavior is condemned here and that the focus should be on behavior rather than attraction.[71] What is especially interesting to note is that the term is likely coined from the Septuagint translation of Leviticus 18:22 and 20:13. In those passages, the Greek terms *arsēn* and *koitē* are employed to translate the Mosaic prohibition against a man lying with another man as one lies with a woman.[72] In fact, the two words are side by side in Leviticus 20:13. As a result, it becomes clear that Paul is communicating the same prohibition in 1 Corinthians 6:9 and 1 Timothy 1:10 as Moses communicated in Leviticus.

Taking these two terms together, *malakoi* and *arsenokoitai* function to cover all aspects of homosexual relationships with a focus on prohibiting the sexual act between members of the same sex. While the focus in these passages is on male homosexual behavior, the assumption is that lesbian behavior is also condemned on the basis that Paul equates the two in Romans 1:26–27. The condemnation is strong in both passages as Paul equates homosexual behavior with the "lawless and rebellious," "the ungodly and sinners," and "the unholy and profane" in 1 Timothy 1 and the unrighteous who "will [not] inherit the kingdom of God" in 1 Corinthians 6. Neither description is desirable, and Paul makes it clear with the inclusion of other vices—fornication, adultery, idolatry, theft, covetousness, drunkenness, reviling, swindling, murder, kidnapping, lying, perjury—that such behavior is beyond the scope of Christian practice.

Despite the overwhelming textual evidence, some proponents of homosexuality seek to interpret these terms in ways that focus on exploitative behavior. Matthew Vines argues that *malakoi* refers to those who are weak and lack self-control even to the point of excess. This could include a lack of control sexually so that one does not practice moderation in any form of sexual encounter.[73] Dealing

---

71. Gagnon further argues: "'Homosexuals' alone is problematic because the focus of *aresnokoitēs* is on the act of having sex with other males. Experiencing desires for intercourse with people of the same sex is not in itself sin, though like all impulses it can become sin if such thoughts are embraced and nurtured (even apart from action—the Spirit is to be Lord over one's thought life as well as behavior). In other respects, 'homosexuals' is too narrow a translation since it does not encompass heterosexuals or bisexuals who have intercourse with members of the same sex." Gagnon, *The Bible and Homosexual Practice*, 312–13n99.

72. Lev. 18:22—*kai meta arsenos ou koimēthēsē koitēn gynaikeian*; Lev. 20:13—*kai hos an koimēthē meta arsenos koitēn gynaikos*, accessed April 20, 2020, https://www.septuagint.bible/leviticus.

73. Matthew Vines, *God and the Gay Christian: The Biblical Case in Support of Same-Sex Relationships* (New York: Convergent, 2014), 119–22. Although Vines is not a formally trained biblical scholar or text critic, he has become a well-respected popularizer of arguments in support of homosexuality.

with *arsenokoitai*, Vines acknowledges the evident connection to the Septuagint but dismisses it in favor of a limited application to economic exploitation that may have included the practice of pederasty.[74] While there is no doubt that some forms of homosexual behavior in the ancient world could have included exploitation, it is not a fair treatment of these terms to limit them in such a way here. Gagnon offers a couple of examples of other similar condemnations in Paul's writing that cannot be limited merely to exploitation. In 1 Corinthians 5, Paul condemns incest in keeping with Old Testament law, but it is not limited to exploitative incest. In 1 Corinthians 6:12–20, Paul forbids prostitution, but he does not make a case for allowing prostitution in cases that do not involve exploitation—all prostitution is forbidden. Since Paul's prohibitions of other sexual sins are all-inclusive, it makes sense that his prohibition of same-sex intercourse forbids all types.[75]

Before we depart from these passages, one point needs to be made that can be applied to all condemnations of homosexual behavior. Paul concludes his vice list in 1 Corinthians 6 with an admonition to the believers in Corinth. After listing all the sins and declaring that such people will not inherit the kingdom of God, he writes, "Such were some of you; but you were washed, but you were sanctified, but you were justified in the name of the Lord Jesus Christ and in the Spirit of our God" (1 Cor. 6:11). Paul makes it clear that the believers in Corinth had once been characterized by such behavior. They had been murderers, swindlers, idolaters, and those who participated in homosexual behavior. Now they were no longer characterized by such behavior. Their lives had been transformed by the power of Christ and the work of the Holy Spirit. This is indeed good news for all of us because all of us are impacted by the fall in one way or another. Just as with any of the disordered sexual behaviors we have included in this chapter, homosexuality can be cleansed by the blood of Jesus Christ.

Homosexuality and Marriage

The final connection we need to make between homosexuality and the biblical understanding of sexuality is the challenge that homosexuality presents to marriage. Specifically, homosexuality poses three direct challenges to marriage, each of which connects to one or more of our guiding theological principles for sexuality. These challenges present the most direct attack against a biblical definition of *marriage*.[76]

First, homosexuality rejects the complementary nature of sex. As we noted

---

74. Vines, *God and the Gay Christian*, 122–26.

75. Gagnon, *The Bible and Homosexual Practice*, 325.

76. Much of the following paragraphs on the challenges that homosexuality presents to marriage are drawn from Evan Lenow, "The Challenge of Homosexuality for Gender Roles," *JBMW* 17, no. 2 (Fall 2012): 28–35. Used by permission.

above, sexual intercourse is designed to take place between two individuals who are fully human, yet exhibit different, complementary characteristics that allow them to be united in a physical relationship. By contrast, homosexuality rejects the complementary nature of sex through the union of two identical partners. We can see this more clearly by considering the three biblical purposes of sex—procreation, unity, and sexual purity—and how they relate to the complementary relationship between a man and a woman. Homosexuality, in both orientation and behavior, violates these three purposes. Sexual relationships within a homosexual context violate this first purpose of sex because it is impossible for them to procreate. Biological sameness prevents procreation because the necessary biological components are not present in homosexual intercourse. Homosexual relationships also violate the second purpose of sex—unity—because the type of intercourse in which they participate does not depict the marriage covenant portrayed in Genesis 1–2. Extending marriage rights to homosexual couples does not address the issue because the problem is with the nature of marriage, not its legality. In addition, the spiritual unity that a married couple develops is designed by God to come from the complementary roles expressed by a man and a woman in marriage. God's design for this unity is far superior to anything that can be experienced by a same-sex couple. Finally, homosexuality violates the purpose of sexual purity on two levels. Homosexual behavior violates the idea of purity because Scripture labels such activity as "degrading passions," "unnatural," and "indecent acts" (Rom. 1:26–27). If sexual purity is a God-given purpose of sex, then the sexual activity itself must be free from sin. Homosexual marriages also violate the idea of purity because they tend to be nonmonogamous. In spite of the attempts to legalize same-sex marriage, such relationships do not generally exhibit the sexual purity required in Scripture. Studies indicate that the level of open sexual relationships in homosexual couples is much higher than in heterosexual couples.[77]

Second, homosexuality subverts the complementary nature of marriage. Roles in marriage are intrinsically connected to biological sex. As we identified earlier, we believe that husbands and wives have particular roles in marriage. We believe that men and women are ontologically equal—being, personhood, value, and so forth—but that God has established different roles for them to exhibit based on their biological genders. Homosexual relationships, by contrast, create a real challenge for gender roles in a committed marriage relationship. If God designed the marriage relationship to exhibit these complementary roles defined by biological sex and gender, then homosexual relationships subvert this ideal. Sometimes homosexual couples act out a distorted version of traditional gender

---

77. Scott James, "Many Successful Gay Marriages Share an Open Secret," *New York Times*, January 28, 2010, accessed April 20, 2020, http://www.nytimes.com/2010/01/29/us/29sfmetro.html.

roles when individuals within these same-sex relationships exhibit roles contrary to their gender. As Andreas Köstenberger and David Jones note, "Although same-sex couples cannot participate in God's complementary design for gender roles in marriage, one partner almost always adopts the leadership role (assigned by God to the husband), while the other adopts that of helper assigned by God to the wife."[78]

Third, the legalization of same-sex marriage undermines the very definition of *biblical marriage*. When we think back to the creation-order design for marriage, we realize that God made it clear that marriage is designed as a comprehensive, covenantal relationship between one man and one woman. No same-sex relationship is ever described as *marriage* in the pages of Scripture, and every mention of homosexual behavior is condemned. Therefore, so-called same-sex marriage is not actually marriage. Piper communicates the problem this way:

> *There is no such thing as so called same-sex marriage, and it would be wise not to call it that.* The point here is not only that so-called same-sex marriage shouldn't exist, but that it doesn't exist and it can't. Those who believe that God has spoken to us truthfully in the Bible should not concede that the committed, life-long partnership and sexual relations of two men or two women is marriage. It isn't. God has created and defined marriage. And what he has joined together in the creation and that definition cannot be separated and still called marriage in God's eyes.[79]

Piper clearly points out that the language we use carries significance and that the term *marriage* does not apply to same-sex relationships. While such is the common description today (as we have employed it even in this chapter), we agree with Piper that such relationships by definition do not constitute marriage.

These distortions of God's design for marriage further demonstrate that homosexuality is a disordered form of sexuality. Thankfully, we have clear guidance in Scripture that helps us understand God's design for sexuality and the challenge that homosexuality presents. We must be ever-vigilant to identify where support of homosexuality is creeping into the church because that is where the greatest threat will be seen in coming years.

Transgenderism

The third challenge to God's design for sexuality is *transgenderism*. Transgenderism is a distortion of God's design for sexuality through the physical body that he has created. Transgenderism is the expression of a gender identity that is

---

78. Köstenberger with Jones, *God, Marriage, and Family*, 355n9.
79. Piper, "What Does the Gospel Say?," 31 (emphasis added).

incongruent with one's biological sex. For example, a transgender male to female is a biological male who expresses gender identity as a female. A transgender female to male is a biological female who expresses gender identity as a male. Mark Yarhouse describes the term *transgender* in this way: "An umbrella term for the many ways in which people might experience and/or present and express (or live out) their gender identities differently from people whose sense of gender identity is congruent with their biological sex."[80] Such incongruence between gender identity and biological sex is generally called *gender dysphoria*. Transgenderism creates a unique challenge to biblical sexuality because it involves both the physical and psychological aspects of sexuality in a way that no other form of sexuality does.

Biblical Instructions

Unlike homosexuality, we cannot look to multiple passages that give us direction on how to think about transgenderism. The lone biblical passage that seems to address the issue is Deuteronomy 22:5. Moses writes, "A woman shall not wear man's clothing, nor shall a man put on a woman's clothing; for whoever does these things is an abomination to the LORD your God." While this verse more directly relates to cross-dressing than what we find in contemporary discussions of transgenderism, we can make a point that relates back to two of our guiding principles. The expectation from this verse is that an individual should present himself or herself in such a way that represents the appropriate gender expression of biological sex. This implies two things. First, not only is God the Creator and author of our sexuality, he designed male and female with distinct differences. God designed mankind before the fall to have specific physical, psychological, and spiritual features. Those features are readily identifiable by others in our society. Therefore, we should recognize those features and celebrate them by identifying our dress and behavior with our biological sex. Jason DeRouchie affirms this application of Deuteronomy 22:5 as he writes:

> Within Israelite culture, then, there were certain styles of dress, ornaments, or items that distinguished men and women. As such, two things appear to be at stake in this law:
>
> 1. Everyone needed to let their gender expression align with their biological sex, and
> 2. Everyone needed to guard against gender confusion, wherein others could wrongly perceive a man to be a woman and a woman to be a man based on dress.

80. Yarhouse, *Understanding Gender Dysphoria*, 20.

Whether due to pagan religious activity or to a desire to engage in roles restricted to the opposite sex, such practices opposed any form of Godliness.[81]

As we mentioned previously in our discussion of the Holiness Code, a moral principle underlies the judicial law here. Moses' regulation relates specifically to the historical context of ancient Israel, but we noted in chapter 5 that the underlying moral principle is reflective of God's nature. In this case, God's perfect design for human flourishing in relationships is promoted through presenting oneself in accord with the cultural expectations of gender.[82]

The second guiding principle at play in this verse is that physical sexuality is part of God's good creation. Hiding one's biological gender through dress or behavior is to deny the goodness of God's creation. We are made in God's image, and our physical being is good. The fall has corrupted our physical nature to a certain degree, but our physical being is still a good creation. Denying this goodness is a denial of God's design for sexuality. These distinctions are part of God's good creation and should be celebrated rather than confused. As even our preliminary discussion indicates, Deuteronomy 22:5 gives us a biblical admonition to maintain such gender differences in our outward expressions to society.

Transgenderism and Theological Principles

Without further biblical instruction regarding transgenderism, we turn our attention to an explanation of how the theological principles of sexuality shape our thinking on the topic. First, we need to acknowledge that those who suffer from gender dysphoria and who desire to change their gender are loved by God and bear his image. Transgenderism is not a status that undermines the value of the image-bearer. In many respects, it is the product of the corruption of the fall that impacts each of us in slightly different ways. Many people who experience gender dysphoria do not want to change genders; they simply want to determine how to deal with the incongruence they feel. We agree with Yarhouse, who acknowledges: "These concerns are real and often quite confusing and isolating. The person worries about who would believe them, what people would think about them, and so forth. This is tremendously isolating and often associated with other concerns, such as depression and anxiety."[83] We cannot dismiss the real struggle that individuals experiencing gender dysphoria face.

We also need to acknowledge that the exponential rise in popularity of transgenderism is a cultural phenomenon driven by numerous factors, including

---

81. Jason S. DeRouchie, "Confronting the Transgender Storm: New Covenant Reflections on Deuteronomy 22:5," *JBMW* 21, no. 1 (Spring 2016): 63.

82. Most of DeRouchie's article is devoted to making this very application.

83. Yarhouse, *Understanding Gender Dysphoria*, 22.

openness about sexuality, the desire for attention, and cultural normalization. It is difficult to imagine human history passing for millennia with transgenderism being relatively rare but seeing a spike in recent years unless the move from the fringes of social acceptance has created a certain level of popularity for this particular expression of sexuality. Ryan Anderson argues: "America is in the midst of what has been called a 'transgender moment.' Not long ago, most Americans had never heard of transgender identity, but within the space of a year it became a cause claiming the mantle of civil rights."[84] The difficulty of this discussion is balancing the real struggle of those who experience gender dysphoria while pushing back against a political agenda that pushes the boundaries of all traditional perspectives on sexuality.[85]

The most important principle for us to address related to transgenderism is that physical sexuality is part of God's good creation. Earlier in the chapter we focused this principle primarily on physical characteristics that led to attraction or desire. What went unsaid at that point is that every aspect of our physical being was created by God and intended to be good. Yes, the fall has corrupted our physical beings, but not to the point that we can no longer recognize their goodness. From our stature to our reproductive systems, God designed them to coordinate with the two sexes that he created. As a result, we generally see fully mature males who are taller in height, carry larger muscle mass, and have higher bone density. The male reproductive organs are carried on the outside of the body and are designed to be complementary with the female reproductive organs. By contrast, fully mature females generally have a slightly smaller stature, less muscle mass, and lower bone density. The reproductive organs are found inside their bodies and are biologically complementary to the male sexual organs. All of this is part of God's wonderful design of the human body. It is a design that God declared to be "very good" after its completion (Gen. 1:31).

Transgenderism enters the picture when an individual has a certain level of incongruence psychologically with the natural expression of physical sexuality. Despite the good design of God's creation, some individuals are conflicted over what they feel about their gender and sexuality versus what their bodies reveal. On the surface, it would seem that the solution to such a problem would be to bring one's thoughts and feelings into alignment with physical reality. In fact, such is the approach with other incongruencies between mind and body (e.g., eating disorders); this approach, however, is not what many people who identify as transgender are seeking. Instead, we see that many are choosing to bring their

---

84. Anderson, *When Harry Became Sally*, 1.

85. Anderson addresses this problem in more depth in his chapter "Our Transgender Moment," in *When Harry Became Sally*, 9–25.

bodies into alignment with the desires that they are experiencing and the sexual ideas and perspectives of themselves that they hold in their minds.

Bringing the body into alignment with the mind can take many different forms. The most extreme form is sex-reassignment surgery wherein an individual has a series of surgical procedures to remove all the typical markers of the person's biological gender, such as reproductive organs, and fashion new biological traits that make one appear as the opposite gender.[86] Yarhouse, however, notes: "Many adults who are diagnosed with Gender Dysphoria do not undergo any of these surgeries. They may not be prepared to do something as permanent and complete, or they may believe that their dysphoria is manageable without taking such steps. Some people who undergo some of the surgical procedures do not undergo all of the options available to them."[87] The individual may choose to undergo hormone treatments without any surgical procedure, dress and act as the opposite gender, or simply suppress the feelings of dysphoria. No matter the approach, we should be aware that the problem is in the mind, not the body. Paul McHugh, the University Distinguished Service Professor of Psychiatry at Johns Hopkins Medical School, warns:

> In fact, gender dysphoria—the official psychiatric term for feeling oneself to be of the opposite sex—belongs in the family of similarly disordered assumptions about the body, such as anorexia nervosa and body dysmorphic disorder. Its treatment should not be directed at the body as with surgery and hormones any more than one treats obesity-fearing anorexic patients with liposuction. The treatment should strive to correct the false, problematic nature of the assumption and to resolve the psychosocial conflicts provoking it.[88]

Recognizing the good creation of the body is the first step in treating gender dysphoria. This approach is not well received by many in the medical establishment at the moment, but it clearly fits with a biblical understanding of sexuality.[89]

Elevating the mind over the body in the treatment of gender dysphoria is what some have called a form of *Gnosticism*. Ancient Gnosticism elevated the mind and the immaterial over physical reality. Therefore, physical reality is a poor reflection

---

86. For a brief description of available surgical options, see Yarhouse, *Understanding Gender Dysphoria*, 117.

87. Yarhouse, *Understanding Gender Dysphoria*, 117.

88. Paul McHugh, "Transgenderism: A Pathogenic Meme," *Public Discourse* (June 10, 2015), accessed April 21, 2020, https://www.thepublicdiscourse.com/2015/06/15145/.

89. By contrast, Anderson sees the treatment promoted by transgender activists and many in the medical establishment as dangerous. He writes, "The course of treatment promoted by transgender activists is, in short, self reinforcing." Anderson, *When Harry Became Sally*, 125.

of who we really are in our minds. Andrew Walker writes: "Gnosticism says that there is an inherent tension between our true selves and the bodies we inhabit. The idea that our true self is different than the body we live in communicates that our body is something less than us, and can be used, shaped, and changed to match how we feel."[90] This Gnostic approach is a further denial of the goodness of God's creation.

The challenge of transgenderism is not going away anytime soon. If anything, it will continue to grow because it has massive implications for cultural norms, gender-specific public facilities and programs (e.g., bathrooms, locker rooms, and sporting events), and societal laws. We need to prepare ourselves to respond to this challenge by affirming the theological principles that guide our understanding of sexuality. God designed us to worship him, and our sexuality is part of that worship. Embracing the biological body that God has given us and expressing the concomitant gender is part of the plan for worshiping our Creator.

Polygamy, Polyamory, and Open Marriage

The fourth challenge to biblical sexuality is both an old challenge and a new one. Polygamy is an ancient issue that dates back to the sixth generation after the fall. Genesis 4:19 tells us, "Lamech took to himself two wives: the name of the one was Adah, and the name of the other, Zillah." *Polygamy* is a marriage arrangement in which one individual is married to multiple partners. Historically, this primarily meant that a man was married to multiple women, but it could include a woman's being married to multiple men. The technical terms for such relationships are *polygyny* (multiple wives) and *polyandry* (multiple husbands). *Polyamory* literally means "many loves" and describes "consensually non-monogamous relationships [wherein] there is an open agreement that one, both, or all individuals involved in a romantic relationship may also have other sexual and/or romantic partners."[91] Polyamory differs from polygamy because all partners can be in multiple marriagelike relationships. *Open marriage* is an arrangement that involves couples in the marriage being open to romantic, sexual relationships outside the context of their own marriage. In some respects, this is similar to polyamory, although the outside relationships may not be formalized as marriage. Proponents of open marriage argue that as long as both spouses agree with the arrangement, then it does not break the fidelity of the marriage bond. All these expressions of sexuality violate God's design for marriage—the union of one man and one woman—as the context for sexual activity.

---

90. Andrew T. Walker, *God and the Transgender Debate: What Does the Bible Actually Say about Gender Identity?* (Centralia, WA: Good Book Company, 2017), 25–26.

91. Rhonda N. Balzarini et al., "Perceptions of Primary and Secondary Relationships in Polyamory," *PLoS ONE* 12, no. 5 (2017), accessed April 21, 2020, https://doi.org/10.1371/journal.pone.0177841.

While these challenges to marriage and sexuality may seem less threatening, they are growing in popularity. From a legal standpoint, the groundwork for legalizing polygamy and polyamory may be found in the landmark *Obergefell v. Hodges* case legalizing same-sex marriage. In his dissent to the majority opinion, Chief Justice John Roberts wrote:

> One immediate question invited by the majority's position is whether States may retain the definition of marriage as a union of two people. . . . Although the majority randomly inserts the adjective "two" in various places, it offers no reason at all why the two-person element of the core definition of marriage may be preserved while the man-woman element may not. Indeed, from the standpoint of history and tradition, a leap from opposite-sex marriage to same-sex marriage is much greater than one from a two-person union to plural unions, which have deep roots in some cultures around the world. If the majority is willing to take the big leap, it is hard to see how it can say no to the shorter one.[92]

While the years since the *Obergefell* ruling have not led to the immediate legalization of polygamy and polyamory, supporters for such legalization are making a push to see this new step of "marriage equality" come to fruition.[93]

Biblical Instructions

The biblical instructions regarding polygamy, polyamory, and open marriage go back to the creation narrative, and we have already covered them in this chapter in our guiding theological principles. Genesis 2:24 gives us our first full affirmation of monogamy in marriage: "For this reason a man shall leave his father and his mother, and be joined to his wife; and they shall become one flesh." Notice that "a man" (singular) leaves his father and mother to be joined to "his wife" (singular). This verse is not a commentary on the first marriage in the garden because Adam and Eve did not have father and mother to leave. Instead, this verse is a

---

92. *Obergefell v. Hodges*, 576 U.S. 644, slip op. at 20 (Roberts, J., dissenting).

93. Numerous articles have appeared over the last few years promoting these different marriage arrangements. *New York* published an article promoting consensual nonmonogamy: "Lately, I'm seeing 'polyamory' everywhere. It's not a new word or concept of course, but it seems to be having a cultural moment." Drake Baer, "Maybe Monogamy Isn't the Only Way to Love," The Cut, *New York*, March 6, 2017, https://www.thecut.com/2017/03/science-of-polyamory-open-relationships-and-nonmonogamy.html. The *Chronicle of Higher Education* interviewed philosopher Carrie Jenkins about her new book *What Love Is and What It Could Be* in which she promotes polyamory: Moira Weigel, "'I Have Multiple Loves': Carrie Jenkins Makes the Philosophical Case for Polyamory," *Chronicle of Higher Education*, February 3, 2017, https://www.chronicle.com/article/I-Have-Multiple-Loves-/239077. *NPR* ran a story about the cultural moment for polyamory: Barbara J. King, "A Cultural Moment for Polyamory," NPR, March 23, 2017, accessed April 21, 2020, https://www.npr.org/sections/13.7/2017/03/23/521199308/a-cultural-moment-for-polyamory.

commentary on the institution of marriage of which Adam and Eve are the first example. Therefore, from the beginning God designed marriage to be between one man and one woman. Genesis 1–2 is the *norma normans* that determines how we view marriage. Faithful, monogamous marriage is the norm.

We also see affirmations of monogamous marriage in the New Testament teaching of Jesus and Paul on marriage. As Jesus engages the Pharisees in a conversation on marriage and divorce, he makes a clear statement that the creation-order design intended for marriage to be monogamous. Jesus stated: "But from the beginning of creation, God made them male and female. For this reason a man shall leave his father and mother, and the two shall become one flesh; so they are no longer two, but one flesh" (Mark 10:6–8; cf. Matt. 19:4–6). Using numbers to reflect the change that marriage brings ("no longer two, but one flesh") is an explicit way for Jesus to declare the creation-order design for marriage between one man and one woman.

Paul makes a similar affirmation in 1 Corinthians 7:2. He tells the church at Corinth, "But because of immoralities, each man is to have his own wife, and each woman her own husband." In this verse, Paul acknowledges that threats to sexual morality exist, and he may have even had polygamy in mind. In order to combat such threats, he tells the Corinthian believers that each man is to have his own wife, and each woman is to have her own husband. The use of the singular nouns in this verse makes it abundantly clear that God intended marriage to be a monogamous union.

These biblical instructions and other similar affirmations of monogamous marriage in Scripture are the standard by which we worship God through our sexuality. Yet there is one major obstacle to a unified message in Scripture—the presence and supposed acceptance of polygamy among major Old Testament figures. If Lamech were the only example of polygamy in the Old Testament, we could write him off as a vindictive descendant of Cain and move on. But some of the most influential figures of the Old Testament were polygamists, including Jacob, David, and Solomon. Therefore, we need to address this matter more directly.

Before we assume that the Old Testament is rife with polygamy, we need to examine the details more carefully. Lamech is the first example of polygamy, but we find him to be an evil man who inflicted vengeance on those who had wronged him (Gen. 4:19–24). The next possible appearance of polygamy appears in Genesis 6:1–7, where the sons of God "took wives for themselves, whomever they chose" (v. 2). This scenario led up to God's sorrow regarding the wickedness of man and his decision to destroy the earth by flood. Neither of these first two occurrences paints polygamy in a positive light. After the flood, we do not see polygamy again until the days of Abraham. As Walter Kaiser notes: "Abraham's brother Nahor had a concubine and Abraham was talked into having temporary sexual relations with

Sarah's handmaiden, Hagar. Esau was a profane person and took three wives, and Jacob married two sisters (even if he was deceived and lived among idolaters). At best then, during these thousands of years since the beginning we have only six examples of polygamy."[94] After the period of the patriarchs, the next set of polygamists were primarily judges and monarchs who functioned as the supreme rulers of Israel.[95] These supreme rulers, especially the kings, were in direct violation of God's command against kings' marrying multiple wives. In Deuteronomy 17:14–20, Moses makes regulations governing when a king will rule over Israel, and verse 17 gives this specific prohibition: "He shall not multiply wives for himself, or else his heart will turn away." Therefore, we see that the Old Testament did not necessarily approve of polygamy; rather, it seems to have been tolerated during those days and often reflected the depravity of those who practiced it.

Perhaps the best statement about monogamy comes from the pen of one who did not follow his own wisdom. Solomon gave the following instructions to his son, and they fit perfectly with God's ideal for monogamy in marriage:

> Drink water from your own cistern
> And fresh water from your own well.
> Should your springs be dispersed abroad,
> Streams of water in the streets?
> Let them be yours alone
> And not for strangers with you.
> Let your fountain be blessed,
> And rejoice in the wife of your youth.
> As a loving hind and a graceful doe,
> Let her breasts satisfy you at all times,
> Be exhilarated always with her love.
> For why should you, my son, be exhilarated with an adulteress
> And embrace the bosom of a foreigner?
> For the ways of a man are before the eyes of the LORD,
> And He watches all his paths. (Prov. 5:15–21)

God's ideal has always been monogamy. He intended for marriage to be a union between one man and one woman for a lifetime. As Kaiser notes, "Polygamy never was God's order of things for marriage even though it is present in the

---

94. Walter C. Kaiser Jr., *Toward Old Testament Ethics* (Grand Rapids: Zondervan, 1983), 183.

95. Kaiser lists the polygamists during this period as Gideon, Jair, Ibzan, Abdon, Samson, Elhanah (Sons of Uzzi), Saul, David, Solomon, Rehoboam, Abijah, Ahab, and Jehoram. He states that the case of Joash in 2 Chronicles 24:2–3 is inconclusive. Kaiser, *Toward Old Testament Ethics*, 183n4.

society of the Old Testament and New Testament."[96] Despite its presence in the culture, God's design for marriage and sexuality is limited to one man and one woman.

Responding to the Culture

The biggest challenge for believers today is responding to the cultural pressure to affirm these variations of marriage and sexuality. The push for polygamy, polyamory, and open marriage will continue in our permissive culture. How do we respond? The best response for Christians is to live out our sexuality in a faithful manner according to God's Word. This act of worship through sexuality is a countercultural witness that will speak with ever-increasing volume as the norms of marriage and sexuality continue to change. The biggest challenge for our churches will come when those who participate in polygamy, polyamory, or open marriage seek approval from our churches and desire to join our congregations. It is in the best interest of our churches to codify our expectations on marriage and sexuality so that such requests are not affirmed and so that we have the theological foundation to stand our ground on the issue of marriage.

Table 17.3. How Disordered Sexuality Distorts God's Design

Adultery and Fornication	Distortion of God's design for fidelity in marriage and sexuality
Homosexuality	Distortion of God's design for heterosexual expression of sexuality
Transgenderism	Distortion of God's design for sexual expression through the body God created
Polygamy, Polyamory, and Open Marriage	Distortion of God's design for monogamy in marriage and sexuality

Other Challenges

The four sets of challenges to biblical sexuality that we have discussed are not the only ones. As our culture changes, we are likely to see new challenges appearing all the time. Sexual abuse has been a topic of great discussion in recent years. Names such as Harvey Weinstein and Matt Lauer dominated secular news for a portion of the new cycle. Within Christian circles, scandals of sexual abuse within various denominations from Catholics to Baptists served to reshape the religious landscape. Perhaps no scandal grew any larger than the sexual-abuse

---

96. Kaiser, *Toward Old Testament Ethics*, 190.

scandal involving Dr. Larry Nassar and his abuse of gymnasts, including several high-profile Olympians. Pedophilia and the sexual abuse of children have also risen to prominence in recent years. While we do not address these challenges here, we want to make it clear that sexual abuse falls far outside the design of biblical sexuality. These types of abusive actions do not fit God's design for sexual expression in the context of a marriage that models the love and sacrifice of Christ for his bride. More than anything else, the model of Christ and the church in marriage (Eph. 5:22–33) should shape our understanding of healthy, worshipful sexual relationships within the context of marriage.

Conclusion

God's *revealed morality* regarding sexuality is given to us in Scripture because it points us to his best plan through the *revealed reality* of his creation. When he gives us instructions regarding our reality, he does not do so simply to keep us from sin. He wants us to maximally flourish in this aspect of our lives and worship. Christopher Yuan paints an elegant picture of holy sexuality: "Holy sexuality consists of two paths: chastity in singleness and faithfulness in marriage. Chastity is more than simply abstention from extramarital sex; it conveys purity and holiness. Faithfulness is more than merely maintaining chastity and avoiding illicit sex; it conveys covenantal commitment."[97] For those who personally struggle, or who have friends, neighbors, and family who struggle, with God's design for sexuality, the call to "holy sexuality" is not simply for the sake of doing what is right. It is a kind call because God desires for us to flourish in this aspect of our lives. If this call to holy sexuality is hard or requires much of us, this is because it is not simply "good" but "best" and not merely "right" but "loving."

Over the course of this chapter, we have considered the biblical and theological foundations of sexuality and the challenges that disordered versions of sexuality present to the biblical model. Beginning with the creation narrative, we saw that God created male and female and that they are complementary in nature. There are physical and spiritual components to sexuality, and both are part of God's good creation. We also saw that God designed marriage as the context for sexual activity and that it is within marriage that God intended for childbearing and rearing to take place. These guiding theological principles for sexuality help us to think clearly about God's design and to respond appropriately to challenges presented by disordered sexuality.

In our discussion of disordered sexuality, we addressed four sets of challenges that undermine the worshipful approach to sexuality. Adultery and fornication

---

97. Yuan, *Holy Sexuality and the Gospel*, 47.

distort God's design for fidelity in marriage and sexuality by stepping outside the properly ordered context for sexual expression. Homosexuality distorts God's design for heterosexual expression of sexuality. If God made male and female complementary in nature, then it is clear that our sexuality should be expressed in the union of a man and a woman. For this reason, so-called same-sex marriage is really no marriage at all. Transgenderism distorts God's design for sexual expression through the body that God created. We saw that physical sexuality is part of God's good creation. This means that our bodies—as God created them—are designed to participate in sexual expression with a complementary partner. Despite any incongruence that one might feel between gender identity and biological sex, we cannot deny God's good creation of the human body for sexual expression. Finally, the disordered sexuality of polygamy, polyamory, and open marriage distorts God's design for monogamy in marriage and sexuality. These distortions intentionally bring multiple partners into the marriage relationship and fail to reflect the unity of the covenant of marriage.

Before we conclude, we want to encourage our readers to engage conversations related to sexuality in a constructive manner. As we mentioned in the introduction, there is a tendency to talk past one another rather than with one another on matters of sexuality. We can take three steps to avoid such a problem. First, we need to ask for definitions. Rather than assuming how one is using certain terms, we should ask the other person in the conversation to define them. As we showed in our section on key terms, defining what we mean by these terms is crucial to a proper understanding of sexuality. If we do not clarify terms at the outset, then the likelihood of misunderstanding increases substantially. Second, we must listen. Since matters of sexuality are so personal, we have a tendency to want to be heard instead of slowing down to listen to the person on the other side. When we listen, we can take note of areas of agreement and fully understand the nature of disagreements. Finally, we need to humbly demonstrate rightly ordered biblical sexuality. No matter how strong our arguments for biblical sexuality are, they will be completely undermined if we do not live out a faithfully biblical sexuality that points others to worship the One who created us. At the end of the day, our lives will speak much more loudly than our words on matters of sexuality.

As we conclude, we need to remember that each of us is sexually broken in some way and that all of us are in desperate need of the grace of God to transform us more completely into his image every day. Sin has tragically marred God's design for sexuality. Thus, we must remember that ethics as worship is grounded in God's created order but it is set aflame by the redeeming and restoring work of Jesus Christ. God's goodness, mercy, and grace make it possible for us to love and minister to others in light of the fact that all of us have so much to be forgiven for and have so much in our own lives that we need God to repair. Real people who are really hurting need the real grace of God to give real healing and hope. Ethics as worship recognizes that because God is God and because God is good, he is worthy of a complete rearranging of all aspects of our lives—even in the area of human sexuality.

Key Terms and Concepts

adultery

biological sex

cisgender

disordered sexuality

fornication

gender dysphoria

gender identity

homosexuality

intersex

open marriage

polyamory

polygamy

sex

sexuality

sexual orientation

transgenderism

Key Scriptures

Genesis 1–2

Exodus 20:14

Leviticus 18:22; 20:10, 13

Deuteronomy 22:22; 23:17–18

Proverbs 5:1–6; 6:23–35

Song of Solomon

Matthew 5:27–28

Romans 1:18–27

1 Corinthians 6:9–10, 18

1 Corinthians 7:8–9, 25–35

Galatians 5:19–21

Ephesians 5:22–33

1 Timothy 4:8

Hebrews 13:4

Study Questions

1. In Genesis 1 and 2, we learn that God created bodies, sex, and marriage. What should this communicate to us about God's view on human sexuality and human sexual pleasure?

2. What are the differences between biological sex, gender, gender identity, and sexual orientation? How do the definitions of these different terms impact the contemporary conversation regarding sexuality?

3. What alternative marriagelike relationships are gaining increasing acceptance in the world today? What biblical principles can we use to evaluate those relationships?

4. How can we best minister to an individual experiencing gender dysphoria? Is there a danger in affirming someone's gender identity if it does not align with his or her biological sex?

5. What other challenges to biblical sexuality are present in the world today? How might we best address those challenges within the framework of ethics as worship?

For Further Reading

Allberry, Sam. *Is God Anti-Gay? And Other Questions about Homosexuality, the Bible and Same-Sex Attraction.* Purcellville, VA: Good Book Company, 2013.

Anderson, Ryan T. *When Harry Became Sally: Responding to the Transgender Moment.* New York: Encounter, 2018.

Budziszewski, J. *On the Meaning of Sex.* Wilmington, DE: ISI, 2012.

Burk, Denny. *What Is the Meaning of Sex?* Wheaton, IL: Crossway, 2013.

Gagnon, Robert A. J. *The Bible and Homosexual Practice: Texts and Hermeneutics.* Nashville: Abingdon, 2001.

Heimbach, Daniel R. *True Sexual Morality: Recovering Biblical Standards for a Culture in Crisis.* Wheaton, IL: Crossway, 2004.

_____. *Why Not Same-Sex Marriage? A Manual for Defending Marriage against Radical Deconstruction.* Sisters, OR: Trusted Books, 2014.

Hollinger, Dennis P. *The Meaning of Sex: Christian Ethics and the Moral Life.* Grand Rapids: Baker, 2009.

Moore, Russell D., and Andrew T. Walker, eds. *The Gospel and Same-Sex Marriage.* Nashville: B&H Academic, 2016.

Pearcey, Nancy R. *Love Thy Body: Answering Hard Questions about Life and Sexuality.* Grand Rapids: Baker, 2018.

Walker, Andrew T. *God and the Transgender Debate: What Does the Bible Actually Say about Gender Identity?* Centralia, WA: Good Book Company, 2017.

Yarhouse, Mark A. *Understanding Gender Dysphoria: Navigating Transgender Issues in a Changing Culture.* Downers Grove, IL: IVP Academic, 2015.

Yuan, Christopher. *Holy Sexuality and the Gospel: Sex, Desire, and Relationships Shaped by God's Grand Story.* New York: Multnomah, 2018.

to the norm for married couples, divorce has become a
life experience. This does not mean that those who h
an easier time adjusting to their new reality, but sh
carries the social stigma it once did.

For much of human history, the meani
been taken for granted. It was assumed t
raise a family, and live together until de
in recent years have married. This lo
as individuals wait longer to get
lation marries.[3] In addition, the
years, which has led to an un
moving back and forth be
divorce seem to show a
divorce in the 1980s
stantial changes in
There have
challenges co
polyamor
some o
divo
ou

WITH D...

Introduction

In my (Evan's) classes, I open my lectures on the topic of marriage and divorce by taking an informal poll of my students. I first have them raise their hands if they, their parents, or any of their siblings have experienced a divorce. Generally speaking, more than half of every class affirms this reality. I then expand the circle to include grandparents, aunts, uncles, and cousins, which also expands the number of hands to more than three-quarters of the students. Once I add close friends and other relatives, almost every hand in the classroom is raised. This anecdotal evidence confirms what many studies have established about the increase in divorce in our society over the last hundred years.[2] Once an exception

1. Andreas J. Köstenberger with David W. Jones, *Marriage and the Family: Biblical Essentials* (Wheaton, IL: Crossway, 2012), 9.

2. See National Vital Statistics System, "100 Years of Marriage and Divorce Statistics United States, 1867–1967," U.S. Department of Health, Education, and Welfare, 1973, https://www.cdc.gov/nchs/data/series /sr_21/sr21_024.pdf; Julissa Cruz, "Marriage: More than a Century of Change," National Center for Family

generally accepted part of
ave experienced divorce have
ows that divorce itself no longer

ng and permanence of marriage had
hat a man and a woman would marry,
ath. In fact, the majority of all adults even
ng-standing trend is currently on the decline
narried and a smaller percentage of the popu-
rates of divorce have ballooned over the last fifty
precedented number of broken families and children
ween parents. Even though current statistics related to
gradual decline and leveling off since the highest rates of
divorce rates are still higher than ever recorded before sub-
divorce laws in the 1970s.

lso been recent challenges to the very meaning of *marriage*. These
me from proponents of so-called same-sex marriage, polygamy, and
. Such challenges will continue to increase, and we have dealt with
these in the previous chapter. Yet these challenges and the challenge of
ce demonstrate the need to capture a biblical vision of marriage and prepare
rselves to answer the challenges that come from many different directions.

The place of marriage in the biblical narrative is one of great importance. The most foundational verse regarding marriage is found in the opening pages of the Bible. Genesis 2:24 sets the tone for all subsequent biblical teaching on marriage: "For this reason a man shall leave his father and his mother, and be joined to his wife; and they shall become one flesh."

Jesus and Paul both use this verse as a crucial part of their extensive teaching on marriage. God uses the analogy of marriage to speak of his own relationship to his people in both the Old and New Testaments. Violations of this relationship by God's people are also spoken of in terms of adultery. While marriage is not the point of the biblical metanarrative, it plays a key role in depicting the way in which God relates to his people. Therefore, it is vitally important for us to

and Marriage Research, 2013, https://www.bgsu.edu/content/dam/BGSU/college-of-arts-and-sciences/NCFMR/documents/FP/FP-13-13.pdf. Divorce rates appear to have leveled off in recent years. See Valerie J. Schweizer, "Marriage to Divorce Ratio in the U.S.: Geographic Variation, 2018," National Center for Family and Marriage Research, 2019, https://www.bgsu.edu/content/dam/BGSU/college-of-arts-and-sciences/NCFMR/documents/FP/fp-19-24-mar-div-ratio.pdf.

3. Kim Parker and Renee Stepler, "As U.S. Marriage Rate Hovers at 50%, Education Gap in Marital Status Widens," Pew Research Center, September 14, 2017, https://www.pewresearch.org/fact-tank/2017/09/14/as-u-s-marriage-rate-hovers-at-50-education-gap-in-marital-status-widens/.

understand the meaning of marriage as we address the most common challenge to marriage.

The purpose of this chapter, then, is to demonstrate not only that marriage is best understood as a means of worship, but also that properly ordered marriages that reflect the relationship between God and his people are one way to maximize God's glory. In order to accomplish this purpose, we first survey the main passages about marriage given in Scripture in order to define and explain the nature of marriage. Next, we explore how understanding marriage as a covenant that depicts the relationship of Christ with the church ought to shape the way that being married can be a means of worshiping God. Once we have made these elements clear, in the third part of the chapter we engage the discussion of divorce and remarriage by surveying the main passages in both the Old and New Testaments that speak to these issues. Following this, we identify and explain three of the most prominently held views regarding divorce and remarriage by evangelicals in contemporary culture. Finally, we conclude the chapter by making a case for what we believe to be an appropriate perspective on and biblical response to the problem of marriage and divorce.

Defining and Explaining the Nature of Marriage

Marriage . . . In the Beginning

Marriage enters the conversation of Scripture very early. The first two chapters of Genesis set the tone for all future teaching on marriage and family throughout the rest of Scripture. In Genesis 1:26–28, we are introduced to the first humans, who also participate in the first marriage. These two individuals created in the image of God are given the task of ruling over and subduing the rest of creation. In addition to this mandate, we discover that they are instructed to "be fruitful and multiply, and fill the earth" (v. 28). No other context for this command is given to us in the opening chapter of Genesis, but we find more details in the next chapter that place this fruitful multiplication within the context of marriage.

Genesis 2 provides more information related to the creation of the first man and woman. God formed the man out of the dust of the ground and breathed life into him (v. 7). This man, whom we know as Adam, was given instructions to cultivate and keep the garden in which he was placed (v. 15). As we have seen in chapter 2, this language of cultivation and keeping the garden relates to the man's worshipful obedience of God as well. Up to this point, there is still no woman in the garden, but God rectifies this situation after he declares, "It is not good for the man to be alone" (v. 18). God causes Adam to fall into a deep sleep and takes one of his ribs to fashion a woman, who was also made in God's image just like the man. Finally, God brings her to the man, and Adam responds, "This is now bone of my bones, and flesh of my flesh; she shall be called Woman, because she was taken out of Man" (v. 23). With these words, we begin to see the inauguration of a new relationship—marriage.

Genesis 2:24 completes the description of marriage by stating, "For this reason a man shall leave his father and his mother, and be joined to his wife; and they shall become one flesh." This verse serves as the foundation for future biblical teaching on marriage, especially in the New Testament as both Jesus (Matt. 19:5; Mark 10:7) and Paul (Eph. 5:31) quote Genesis 2:24 as part of their teaching on marriage. This verse depicts a context in which a man and woman enter into a new relationship that entails establishing a new household together. Thus, the vision of fruitful multiplication in Genesis 1:28 is to take place within the context of the marriage relationship described in 2:24.

The vast majority of societies throughout human history would have affirmed something similar to this basic concept of marriage up until recently. That is why we need to develop a fuller definition of *marriage* that more accurately reflects the biblical vision for marriage that we have rudimentarily rehearsed in the preceding paragraphs.

A Biblical Definition of *Marriage*

The definition of *marriage* has been a controversial subject for many years now. In the court of public opinion, one will find great passion on both sides of the debate. Some will vociferously argue that marriage is a traditional union between one man and one woman that often leads to children and is recognized by the government. Such a traditional definition calls on centuries of human history to bear witness to the unchanging nature of marriage across time and culture. On the other hand, many will vehemently disagree and propose that marriage is merely the most intimate relationship that an individual can have and that such an arrangement is entered into for mutual benefit. For the first decade or so of the twenty-first century, proponents of a new definition sought government recognition for their partnerships in different forms. In June 2015, the Supreme Court of the United States handed down a decision in *Obergefell v. Hodges*[4] that legalized marriage between same-sex couples. This decision, however, did not settle the cultural discussion; instead, it exacerbated the divide between traditionalists and revisionists.[5] In addition, the definition of *marriage* upheld by the Supreme Court has ramifications far beyond the debate over same-sex marriage.[6]

---

4. 576 U.S. 644 (2015).

5. Girgis, Anderson, and George use the terms *conjugal* and *revisionist* to describe the two different sides of the debate over marriage. See Sherif Girgis, Ryan T. Anderson, and Robert P. George, *What Is Marriage? Man and Woman: A Defense* (New York: Encounter, 2012), 1–2.

6. This chapter will not address same-sex marriage in detail. That topic is addressed more specifically in

While we believe that the traditional definition of *marriage* is on the right track, we want to offer a more robust, biblically grounded definition that we believe comes directly from the text of Genesis 1–2. This definition has far-reaching ramifications for the marriage relationship and divorce. Further implications of this definition for same-sex marriage, polygamy, and polyamory have been explored in chapter 17.

> *Marriage is designed by God to be a comprehensive, covenantal union between one man and one woman intended to endure for a lifetime and proximally directed toward the rearing of the next generation.*[7]

Comprehensive, Covenantal Union

The first two components of this definition of *marriage* declare it to be a comprehensive and covenantal union. First, it is *comprehensive* because marriage is designed to encompass all aspects of life. It is not simply a union that brings individuals into a sexual union or union of proximity. Instead, it brings two individuals together in such a way that they become one. This is a significant component of the statement in Genesis 2:24 that the husband and wife "shall become one flesh." This specific phrase connotes two distinct but related ideas. It certainly applies to the sexual union of a husband and wife as they give expression to the closeness of their marriage bond. But it also goes beyond the sexual union to describe the comprehensive nature of the relationship. In all aspects of life, the two are joined together in such a way that they are one.[8]

A simple way to illustrate this concept is through a lesson that my wife and I (Evan) use in premarital counseling sessions with couples. As part of our counseling, we spend a session talking about the finances of a married couple. While many young couples have little to their names from a financial standpoint, we encourage them to combine their finances through the simple act of opening joint bank

---

chapter 17. We must acknowledge, however, that even offering a definition of *marriage* opens the door for such a discussion.

7. This definition is heavily influenced by the historic emphasis within the early church that identified three primary purposes of marriage: the establishment of a "sacramental bond" that depicts Christ's relationship with the church, the procreation of children, and the union and companionship between a husband and wife that served to limit sexual sin. See, e.g., Augustine, *De Bono Coniugali* ("On the Good of Marriage"), in *The Fathers of the Church: A New Translation*, translated by Charles T. Wilcox, vol. 27 (New York: Fathers of the Church, 1955).

8. Craig Blomberg notes: "'Becoming one flesh' then focuses on the sexual union of marriage but is by no means limited to it. It incorporates every aspect of intimacy and interdependence which should ideally render the married couple a unified entity at the deepest levels of interpersonal communication." Craig L. Blomberg, "Marriage, Divorce, Remarriage, and Celibacy: An Exegesis of Matthew 19:3–12," *Trinity Journal* 11, no. 2 (Fall 1990): 167.

accounts after they marry. In the daze of wedding-planning bliss, many couples nod in agreement, but they do not always follow through. This is sometimes the result of financial planners' warning against merging finances to protect against disputes when a marriage dissolves. Precisely at this point we see a challenge that divorce brings to the discussion of a biblical definition of *marriage*. Well-meaning finance professionals may assume that a marriage will end in divorce and attempt to protect the assets of the individual over developing a comprehensive "oneness" type of relationship.

The financial illustration is just one example of the comprehensive union. Paul speaks of the comprehensive union in his statements about the sexual relationship in marriage in 1 Corinthians 7:4 as he writes, "The wife does not have authority over her own body, but the husband does; and likewise also the husband does not have authority over his own body, but the wife does." When the lives of two individuals are so intertwined in marriage that their unity permeates every facet of their relationship, then we see the comprehensive nature of the union at the forefront.

Second, and related to the comprehensive nature of the union, marriage is best understood not as a *contractual relationship* but as a *covenantal union*. In a contractual understanding of marriage, the two persons entering the relationship build the foundations of marriage on the civil laws of society. The two parties involved enter a two-sided contract that is voluntarily formed, maintained, or dissolved as they see fit. The focus is on the human-centered decision-making and the ability of each partner to live up to the agreed-upon contractual obligations. In such an understanding of marriage, the security of the relationship rests on the ability of either partner to not fail in fulfilling the contract obligations.

In contrast to this, Scripture uses covenantal language to describe the marriage relationship. Proverbs 2:17 describes the adulteress as one "that leaves the companion of her youth and forgets the covenant of her God." Malachi 2:14 decries the sins of Israel and says that "the Lord has been a witness between you and the wife of your youth, against whom you have dealt treacherously, though she is your companion and your wife by covenant." In both these verses, the term "covenant" is explicitly used to label the marriage relationship. Scripture also employs implicit references to marriage as a covenant by describing with marital language the relationships between God and Israel (e.g., Isa. 54:4–8; Jer. 2:32; 31:31–32) and Christ and the church (e.g., Matt. 9:15; 22:1–14; Mark 2:19–20; Luke 5:34–35; John 3:29; Rom. 7:1–4; 2 Cor. 11:2; Eph. 5:22–33; Rev. 19:7; 22:17). Scripture also depicts unfaithfulness to the covenant between God and his people as adultery (e.g., Isa. 1:21; Jer. 3:1–10; Ezek. 16:15–43; Hos. 4:13–14; James 4:4; Rev. 2:22).

This covenantal understanding of marriage was assumed in the writings of the church fathers and was the prevailing model in the early church. It was later affirmed by the Protestant Reformers and was the dominant model in Western culture before the development of the modern contractual understanding of marriage that dominates today. The covenantal model views marriage as a creation ordinance that was designed by God to picture his own relationship with his people and that, when entered, creates a lifelong bond between the couple before the face of God and in the eyes of the church. Its foundational strength and endurance rests not on the part of individuals who may or may not be able to abide by the agreements, but on the nature and character of an always-faithful God, who not only created the institution, but also partners with the husband and wife to enable them to become "one flesh."

By implication, this means that marriage is designed and established by God as the most intimate relationship that two humans can experience, and it points us toward an understanding of God's relationship with his people. Craig Blomberg captures the idea nicely:

> Marriage is thus seen as two-fold: a commitment to one's fundamental allegiance and an interpersonal relationship culminating in sexual intimacy. The best term to describe this two-fold enterprise is that of a covenant.[9]

A Union between One Man and One Woman

In our current cultural milieu, the idea that marriage is designed by God to be a union between one man and one woman is perhaps the most controversial part of our given definition of *marriage*. This part of the definition addresses two key aspects of the nature of marriage—monogamy and heterosexuality. These two characteristics of marriage were almost uniformly accepted across cultures until recently.

Monogamy dictates that marriage is designed by God to be a relationship between two individuals, thus precluding polygamy and polyamory. When we look to Genesis 2, we find several affirmations of the monogamous nature of marriage. In Genesis 2:18, we read God's proclamation of Adam's state of aloneness: "It is not good for the man to be alone; I will make him a helper suitable for him." God does not determine that he will make multiple women for Adam. Surely the mandate to "be fruitful and multiply" from Genesis 1:28 could have been more quickly accomplished had Adam been provided with multiple wives. But God makes it clear in the subsequent verses of chapter 2 that he made one

---

9. Blomberg, "Marriage, Divorce, Remarriage, and Celibacy," 167. There is some debate over whether marriage is actually a covenant. While we do not have space to explore this controversy, we want to acknowledge that not everyone agrees with our conclusion. Andreas Köstenberger and David Jones discuss some of the debate in their chapter "The Nature of Marriage." See Andreas J. Köstenberger with David W. Jones, *God, Marriage, and Family: Rebuilding the Biblical Foundation*, 2nd ed. (Wheaton, IL: Crossway, 2010), 69–84.

woman and brought her to Adam, and that they were joined together (2:21–23). As we continue into verse 24, we see another affirmation of the monogamous nature of marriage. The text portrays marriage as "a man" (singular) leaving his father and mother to be joined to "his wife" (singular). Then those two "shall become one flesh."

We also see affirmations of monogamy in the New Testament. In Matthew 19:3–9, Jesus interacts with the Pharisees regarding divorce. Jesus points them back to the nature of marriage in the garden of Eden and makes an explicit statement regarding monogamous marriage. After quoting Genesis 2:24, he states: "So they are no longer two, but one flesh. What therefore God has joined together, let no man separate" (Matt. 19:6). Here Jesus makes it clear that marriage was designed by God to be between one man and one woman. Paul also affirms this teaching in his discussions on marriage. Specifically, Paul addresses multiple questions related to marriage in 1 Corinthians 7, but his statement in verse 2 is the clearest affirmation of monogamy. He writes, "But because of immoralities, each man is to have his own wife, and each woman is to have her own husband."

The primary challenge to the monogamous nature of marriage comes from the lives of Old Testament figures who had multiple wives. We discussed this in more detail in the previous chapter, so it will suffice to say here that the polygamous individuals that we find in Scripture (e.g., Lamech, Jacob, David, and Solomon) are exceptions to the norm and that the polygamous kings were actually in violation of a direct command from God (Deut. 17:17). Polyamory—the practice of multiple men's and women's entering into a marriagelike relationship with one another—further departs from the standard that we find in Scripture.

The other component of marriage found in this part of the definition is the heterosexual nature of marriage. This aspect of marriage was a foregone conclusion at the turn of the twenty-first century, but steady cultural pressure resulted in the 2015 Supreme Court decision in *Obergefell v. Hodges* that legalized same-sex marriage across the United States. Again, when we look to Scripture, we find that marriage is specifically described as a relationship between a man and a woman, not two men or two women. As we have already seen in Genesis 1–2, the inauguration of the first marriage is clearly between God's special creation of man and woman. God created male and female and gave them instructions to "be fruitful and multiply" (Gen. 1:26–28). This is the first biblical statement about the heterosexual nature of marriage. Without a man and a woman, procreation cannot happen. Andreas Köstenberger and David Jones state, "Since homosexuality involves same-sex intercourse that cannot lead to procreation, it is unnatural and cannot logically entail the possibility of marriage."[10]

10. Köstenberger with Jones, *God, Marriage, and Family*, 36.

An added affirmation of the heterosexual nature of marriage is often overlooked in Genesis 2:24. While we focus on the man and his wife's becoming one flesh, we skip over the fact that the man is leaving his father and mother. So even at the first marriage when there was no father or mother yet, Genesis tells us that the new heterosexual relationship springs from the previous heterosexual relationship. The expected norm generationally is uniquely heterosexual.

Another biblical affirmation of the heterosexual nature of marriage is that all marriages in Scripture are heterosexual. There are no examples of same-sex marriage throughout Scripture, and the clear direction of all New Testament teaching on marriage assumes that marriage involves a man and a woman. For example, Paul spends most of 1 Corinthians 7 addressing matters of marriage. At the beginning of the chapter, he says, "But because of immoralities, each man is to have his own wife, and each woman is to have her own husband" (1 Cor. 7:2). If Paul had intended to include same-sex marriage as part of God's design for marriage, he could have done so at this point. Instead, he clearly eliminates same-sex marriage from consideration.

The various distortions of this part of our definition of *marriage* were explored in the previous chapter, but we must still recognize the gravity of the challenge to our definition that these distortions pose in our current culture. Polygamy, at the very least, can be understood as a tragic distortion of God's institution of marriage, while polyamorous "marriages" and so-called same-sex marriages do not even fall within the category of marriage from a biblical point of view. That is, to the degree that they are unions of people of the same sex, they do not meet the basic standard of what a biblical marriage requires. The fact that the U.S. Supreme Court has ruled that the word *marriage* can be used to describe these unions does not mean that they actually qualify as the kind of relationship that God describes as a marriage. Therefore, this part of the definition is crucial to the full definition of *marriage*. Without this part, the rest of the definition breaks down.

Intended to Endure for a Lifetime

The next component of the definition of *marriage* connects to the second half of this chapter—the matter of divorce. When marriage is introduced in the garden of Eden, there is no mechanism for ending the relationship. Therefore, marriage was designed by God to endure for a lifetime, exhibiting durability that is often lost today. The question comes after the fall whether Scripture makes allowance for divorce. This question will be the focus of the latter half of this chapter, but we want to make it clear that God's original design for marriage was that it would be permanent.

The best commentary of God's original intent for marriage permanence is found in Jesus' discussion with the Pharisees in Matthew 19:3–9 (cf. Mark 10:2–9). The Pharisees ask Jesus about allowances for divorce, but Jesus points them back to the original creation-order design for marriage. He states:

> Have you not read that He who created them from the beginning made them male and female, and said, "For this reason a man shall leave his father and mother and be joined to his wife, and the two shall become one flesh"? So they are no longer two, but one flesh. What therefore God has joined together, let no man separate. (Matt. 19:4–6)

Jesus makes it clear that God's original intent was for marriage to be lifelong—"what . . . God has joined together, let no man separate." This was Jesus' simple response to the Pharisees' direct question, "Is it lawful for a man to divorce his wife for any reason at all?" (Matt. 19:3). Jesus could have given many possible answers to this question, but his answer was simple and direct. God intended marriage to endure.

After the Pharisees press a little harder, Jesus answers their original question less directly. Jesus concedes:

> Because of your hardness of heart Moses permitted you to divorce your wives; but from the beginning it has not been this way. And I say to you, whoever divorces his wife, except for immorality, and marries another woman commits adultery. (Matt. 19:8–9)

The middle phrase of verse 9 has generated much discussion and disagreement regarding allowances for divorce, and we will discuss that at length later in this chapter. The point that Jesus made in verse 6, however, still holds true in his expanded answer. Moses permitted divorce because of the hardness of the Israelites' hearts. Had their hearts not been hard, Jesus implies, then there would be no need for divorce. Köstenberger and Jones note: "According to Jesus, however, the Mosaic statutes were interposed not to replace the Creator's original intent but merely in recognition of the reality of human hardness of heart (Matt. 19:7–8; Mark 10:5; cf. 5:31–32). In fact, marriage was *intended as a lifelong, faithful union of a man and a woman*."[11]

The *exception clauses* found in Matthew 5:32 and 19:9 create consternation on this particular component of our definition because they appear to open the door for another perspective on marriage. Even if God's original design for marriage was that of a "lifelong, faithful union," Jesus' words at least open the possibility

11. Köstenberger with Jones, *God, Marriage, and Family*, 226.

of God's plan to include the undesirable, but possible, outcome of divorce. Yet we need to be careful not to set up Jesus' words against the original creation-order design. René Gehring writes, "Jesus is not playing the Edenic ideal off against the Mosaic instruction, he rather reveals the original idea behind it, which was covered up by the custom of Judaism in Jesus' times (particularly Pharisaism, as the introduction to the debate on divorce may demonstrate), and reaffirms the lasting validity and significance of the first and only divine, biblical 'marriage pattern' given in Gen 2:24."[12] As we explore the implications of the exception clauses later in the chapter, it is important for us to remember that the Edenic ideal is the original design for marriage. No matter what we conclude on allowances for divorce or remarriage, the creation-order design is for each marriage to endure for a lifetime—"until death do us part."

Proximally Directed toward the Rearing of the Next Generation

The final component to our definition of *marriage* is one that was also regularly assumed until recently. The general expectation for marriage throughout most of human history has been that such a union would ultimately result in children. Then the parents would rear their children until they were grown and started the process over on their own. A number of challenges to the traditional view of marriage have made this component of our definition of *marriage* less than universally accepted: same-sex marriage, intentional childlessness, abortion rights, and the like. But we firmly believe that God's design for marriage includes a component that looks ahead to the next generation.

In Genesis 1:28, we read, "God blessed them; and God said to them, 'Be fruitful and multiply, and fill the earth, and subdue it.'" These instructions from God come on the heels of what we read about God's creating man and woman in his image. Taken together with the expanded narrative of the first marriage in Genesis 2, we surmise that God saw marriage—and the sexual relationship within marriage—as the means for bringing forth children to fill the earth. On the basis of the creation order alone, we ascertain that God's plan for marriage includes its being directed toward the rearing of the next generation. Yet we can look beyond just the creation narrative to see further support.

The Old Testament places great emphasis on children as part of the family. "Though originally two individual persons, husband and wife become 'one flesh' (Gen. 2:24) in their marital union, which is given visible expression by the children resulting from that union. Consequently, barrenness was regularly seen in Old Testament times as the result of divine disfavor (e.g., Gen. 29:31), while

---

12. René Gehring, *The Biblical "One Flesh" Theology of Marriage as Constituted in Genesis 2:24* (Eugene, OR: Wipf & Stock, 2013), 232–33.

children were regarded as a gift and blessing from God (e.g., Gen. 13:16; 15:1–6; Ex. 23:25–26; Ps. 127:3–5; 128:3–6)."[13]

The Old Testament is replete with commendations regarding child-rearing. Two of the most famous appear in Psalms and Proverbs. In Psalm 127:3–5, Solomon writes: "Behold, children are a gift of the LORD, the fruit of the womb is a reward. Like arrows in the hand of a warrior, so are the children of one's youth. How blessed is the man whose quiver is full of them; they will not be ashamed when they speak with their enemies in the gate." These famous verses describe the value ascribed to children. Solomon's basic assumption in these verses is that a family would want children because they are a blessing from the Lord. The gift of children brings honor to the parents personally and socially. The personal honor is found in actively participating in the growth and maturity of their children until they ultimately launch out on their own. The social honor is found in the recognition that parents receive in society as their children grow in wisdom and stature and reflect the values of their parents.

By contrast, a childless couple would seem to be missing the blessings of the Lord that come through rearing children. Such a heart is on display in 1 Samuel 1 when Hannah cries out to the Lord to take away her affliction and give her a son (1 Sam. 1:9–16). Hannah desires what she does not have, but it is not envy or covetousness. Instead, she truly seeks the blessing of children from the Lord, and the priest Eli sees the anguish on her face. Therefore, the reproach of barrenness is balanced by the blessings of children.

The other famous commendation of child-rearing in the Old Testament is Proverbs 22:6, "Train up a child in the way he should go, even when he is old he will not depart from it." While this verse is often misquoted as a proof text for parenting, we cannot overlook the general promise in the proverb. Training a child in a godly manner leads to the likelihood that the child will continue in godliness after he or she is grown. Therefore, the burden is on the parents in this proverb to rear the child properly. The only context offered in the book of Proverbs for such training is the family. In fact, the opening chapters of Proverbs constantly draw the recipient's attention back to the words and instructions of his parents (Prov. 1:8; 2:1; 3:1; 4:1–4, 10–11, 20–22; 5:1–2, 7; 6:20–21; 7:1–3, 24). The church and community may come to the aid of the parents in child-rearing, but the primary responsibility is on the parents.

The emphasis on children is not as stark in the New Testament, but there are admonitions to parents and children, especially within the context of New Testament teaching on marriage. In Ephesians 6:1–4, we find one of the most well-known New Testament passages on children. Paul instructs children to "obey

---

13. Köstenberger with Jones, *God, Marriage, and Family*, 90.

your parents in the Lord, for this is right" (6:1). This is Paul's summary of the fifth commandment that instructs children to honor their father and mother (Ex. 20:12). He does not simply stop with instructions to children. Paul also admonishes fathers, "Do not provoke your children to anger, but bring them up in the discipline and instruction of the Lord" (Eph. 6:4). Such discipline and instruction fit very nicely with the instructions of Proverbs that Solomon gives to his son. Perhaps the most interesting part of this passage is that the immediate context is Paul's comparison of marriage to the relationship between Christ and the church. Therefore, instructions regarding child-rearing fit neatly within the context of a larger discussion of marriage. Thus, even after the fall, we see that God's design for marriage includes a forward-looking component that seeks to bring up the next generation in the fear and admonition of the Lord.

Before we leave this particular aspect of our definition, we want to make it clear that having children is not a necessity for maximal worship of God. In fact, marriage is not necessary either. Christians need to be careful not to so strongly affirm the importance of marriage that we make the mistake of subtly denigrating singles or, even worse, make an idol of the marriage relationship. Paul affirms the high and beautiful status of singleness as a possible path for full devotion to and worship of God. Indeed, he even encourages unmarried believers to remain unmarried (and childless) in order to devote more time to serving the Lord (1 Cor. 7:8, 32–35).

But for those whom God does lead into marriage, clearly it is the normative pattern for married couples to both have children and desire to raise godly offspring. In a world impacted by the fall, however, not all couples can have children of their own. Therefore, it is important for married couples who do not have children to recognize that there is still a way to view marriage as proximally directed toward the rearing of the next generation. Rather than focusing only on pursuits that serve one's own marriage, childless couples can invest into the discipleship of adults, children of other families, or children who do not have parents (orphans). Some of the ways that couples can do this is through adoption and foster care, mentoring children in the community, and serving other family members with children.

Marriage as Worship

Our definition of *marriage* sets the stage for us to consider how marriage fits within the overall scheme of worship. As we mentioned in the previous section, marriage is not required to worship our Creator, but he instituted marriage as a means by which we can worship him and exhibit his relationship with his people. God created us to worship him in every action and every relationship. The marriage relationship is unique in the ability to express our worship because of its analogous relationship to the covenants that God has established with his people in both the Old and New Testaments.

An Image of God's Covenant

The marriage relationship serves as a special means by which we can worship God because it is uniquely analogous to the covenants that God has established with his people. We know that God often operated through covenants at key points in salvation history (Gen. 6:18; 9:9; 12:1–3; 2 Sam. 7:12–16; Jer. 31:31–34). These covenants demonstrate how God calls a people to himself. Throughout both the Old and New Testaments, God employs the language of *marriage* to describe his covenants (Isa. 49:18; 50:1; 54:4–8; Jer. 2:2, 32; 3:14; 31:32; Ezek. 16:1–14; Hos. 1:1–3:5; Matt. 9:15; 22:1–14; 25:1–13; Mark 2:19–20; Luke 5:34–35; John 3:29; Rom. 7:1–4; 2 Cor. 11:2; Eph. 5:22–33; Rev. 19:7; 21:2, 9; 22:17) and even calls marriage a covenant (Prov. 2:16–17; Mal. 2:14). There is no doubt that as believers, we worship God within the context of a covenant; therefore, living out a marriage covenant serves as an expression of the covenant we have with God.

We have already discussed the idea that marriage is a covenant earlier in this chapter, but to summarize our earlier point, we believe that Scripture is clear through the use of explicit covenant terminology to describe marriage and implicit language of analogy that marriage is a covenant. Marriage is even a covenant when the participants do not fully recognize the magnitude of the relationship into which they have entered. Köstenberger and Jones note that the covenantal model of marriage is "a sacred bond between a man and a woman instituted by and publicly entered into before God (whether or not this is acknowledged by the married couple), normally consummated by sexual intercourse."[14] Because God ordained marriage as a covenant before the fall and gave marriage to all of humanity, then we are all subject to the covenantal aspect of marriage. Grudem builds on this idea by saying that

> biblical teaching about marriage comes from *the beginning of the human race*, the time when Adam and Eve were created. . . . God intends for the understanding of marriage as the lifelong union between one man and one woman to be the correct definition of marriage for all people on the earth, for all cultures and societies, and for all periods of history until the beginning of the new heaven and the new earth.[15]

---

14. Köstenberger with Jones, *God, Marriage, and Family*, 73.

15. Wayne Grudem, *Christian Ethics: An Introduction to Biblical Moral Reasoning* (Wheaton, IL: Crossway, 2018), 710–11.

In order to maximize our worship through marriage, it behooves us to recognize this covenant aspect and live it out faithfully before God and man. As part of his covenant with Israel, God included a stipulation regarding marriage in the covenant obligations of Israel. The seventh commandment very clearly states, "You shall not commit adultery" (Ex. 20:14). Therefore, honoring one's marriage vows is an expression of worship to God. Violating these vows is rebellion against the covenant of marriage and one's covenant with God. John Frame goes so far as to say that "adultery is covenant treason."[16] This treason is not simply against the marriage covenant, as Frame notes: "To violate marriage is to violate that covenant, and unfaithfulness to God is adultery. All sin is unfaithfulness to God, spiritual adultery. So the seventh commandment, like the others, actually covers all of life from its particular perspective."[17]

Jesus extends this covenant obligation to include a prohibition against lust in the Sermon on the Mount: "You have heard that it was said, 'You shall not commit adultery'; but I say to you that everyone who looks at a woman with lust for her has already committed adultery with her in his heart" (Matt. 5:27–28). Maximal worship in relation to this particular covenant obligation is not simply the avoidance of adultery. God calls the married individual to love his spouse so much that he turns from all temptations that might steer his allegiance away. The connection back to our love and worship for God is clear—our worship of God should also be singularly focused. As Frame noted above, unfaithfulness to God is spiritual adultery, and unfaithfulness to a spouse is unfaithfulness to God. Thus, marital fidelity is a clear part of worshiping our Creator in the way he designed us.

Living Out the Covenant

Another component of worship through marriage is to live out the analogy between marriage and the relationship between Christ and the church. Ephesians 5 gives us the most direct statement on such a life. Much of the discussion about marriage from Ephesians 5 centers on verses 22–33, where we find Paul's instructions to husbands and wives regarding how they should relate to one another. We may miss the larger context of this chapter, however, if we merely pick up at verse 22.[18] In verses 15–17, Paul gives his readers instructions on how to live. He tells us to be careful how we walk (v. 15), to make the most of our time

16. John M. Frame, *Doctrine of the Christian Life* (Phillipsburg, NJ: P&R Publishing, 2008), 750.

17. Frame, *The Doctrine of the Christian Life*, 747.

18. "Thematically and structurally, however, 5:15–6:9 form a well-knit unit. The instructions in the household code of 5:22–6:9 follow directly from the admonition of 5:21 ('Submit to one another in the fear of Christ'), which itself is a significant outworking of the exhortation to be filled by the Spirit (v. 18). There is an evident movement within the whole unit, and no sharp division should be made between each of the paragraphs." Peter T. O'Brien, *The Letter to the Ephesians*, PNTC (Grand Rapids: Eerdmans, 1999), 378.

(v. 16), to understand the will of the Lord (v. 17), to avoid drunkenness (v. 18), and to be filled with the Spirit (v. 18). The subsequent verses of this chapter and through 6:9 extrapolate what it means to live in this way, especially through the filling of the Holy Spirit. Any discussion of the relationship between husband and wife must be part of the larger context of living a Spirit-filled life.

The core section on the relationship between husband and wife features the distinct comparison to the new covenant relationship between Christ and the church. Earlier in the book (chapter 2), we developed key elements related to the nature of men and women as image-bearers and how that fundamental aspect of humanness ought to shape our understanding of the roles that men and women play both in the marriage relationship and in the creation order in general. Here, our intention is to focus on the discussion as it particularly relates to the nature of marriage and the question of divorce. Ephesians 5:22–33 reads:

> Wives, be subject to your own husbands, as to the Lord. For the husband is the head of the wife, as Christ also is the head of the church, He Himself being the Savior of the body. But as the church is subject to Christ, so also the wives ought to be to their husbands in everything.
>
> Husbands, love your wives, just as Christ also loved the church and gave Himself up for her, so that He might sanctify her, having cleansed her by the washing of water with the word, that He might present to Himself the church in all her glory, having no spot or wrinkle or any such thing; but that she would be holy and blameless. So husbands ought also to love their own wives as their own bodies. He who loves his own wife loves himself; for no one ever hated his own flesh, but nourishes and cherishes it, just as Christ also does the church, because we are members of His body. For this reason a man shall leave his father and mother and shall be joined to his wife, and the two shall become one flesh. This mystery is great; but I am speaking with reference to Christ and the church. Nevertheless, each individual among you also is to love his own wife even as himself, and the wife must see to it that she respects her husband.

Note that in Ephesians 5:22–24, wives are instructed to submit themselves to their own husbands, "as to the Lord." The analogy is then drawn out, comparing the wife's relationship to her husband as that of the church to Christ. Paul states, "But as the church is subject to Christ, so also the wives ought to be to their husbands in everything" (v. 24). Drawing on this analogy, the wife's relationship and submission to her husband is an expression of her worship of the Lord. Lest we confuse the analogy, Paul does not instruct her to worship her husband, nor does he demand blind obedience. Instead, her submission is an act of worship to her Savior, who also serves as the head of the church, of which she is a part.

Similar implications are drawn out for the husband in this passage. He is called to love his wife, "just as Christ also loved the church and gave Himself up for her" (Eph. 5:25). This is a sacrificial love that is ultimately demonstrated by Christ through his substitutionary atonement for sin. While Paul does not directly command husbands to give up their own lives for their wives, the implication is that a husband at the very least sacrifices his own desires for the love of his wife. The example that Paul uses for husbands is the action of Christ and the results of his sacrifice for the church. This does not imply that the husband sanctifies and cleanses his wife; rather, the husband's example is Christ, and the work of Christ's sacrifice is a reminder of the husband's own dependence on the Lord. Paul continues his admonition to husbands by appealing to his love for his own body as an example of how to love his wife, but the comparison does not end there. He once again draws a connection between this love and the love that Christ has for the church, his body. Since Christ cares for and nourishes his body out of love, so, too, must the husband care for his wife. The worship implication is clear once again. A husband's love for his wife is a worshipful response to the love that Christ has bestowed on him as a member of the church. Worshiping the Savior well means that a husband must love his wife well. Obviously, then, one clear implication from this point is that any form of abuse within marriage is completely unacceptable.

Just in case Paul's readers did not connect the covenant implications of his instructions, he makes it more explicit in Ephesians 5:31–32: "For this reason a man shall leave his father and mother and shall be joined to his wife, and the two shall become one flesh. This mystery is great; but I am speaking with reference to Christ and the church." From the inauguration of the first marriage in Genesis 2, God had in mind that the marriage relationship would point us to a better understanding of the relationship between Christ and the church. Therefore, we worship Christ well when we live out his design for marriage. The enduring, other-centered nature of Christ's love for the church should shape how a Christian should understand and embody his or her marital vows. Likewise, when a watching world looks at a Christian's marriage, it should be able to recognize the kind of love and commitment that Christ gives to his bride—the church. Not only does he love the church contraconditionally (even when it fails him), he promises to never leave or forsake her (Heb. 13:5).

Paul concludes his instructions by summarizing the relationship between the husband and wife as he states, "Nevertheless, each individual among you also is to love his own wife even as himself, and the wife must see to it that she respects her husband" (Eph. 5:33). As Christians contemplate how best to live out worshipful obedience to God through marriage, we can refer back to this basic summary of Paul's instructions. Worship of the Lord through marriage looks like a husband's loving his wife and a wife's respecting her husband. Even though marriage is not required for worship, those who are married have a unique way to worship God by living out the covenant of marriage in relation to the covenant that we have with our Savior.

Consider the type of couple that lives out such a marriage covenant. Their focus is not on happiness or success. Their individual personal desires are subordinate to the needs and desires of the other. Their motivation for living sacrificially in the context of their marriage is not longevity or success; instead, their motivation is found through worshiping their Savior. Such a couple brings a worshipful component to their marriage and establishes a pattern that will generally result in a lasting, healthy marriage.

In light of all that we have covered up to this point, it may seem strange to now transition into a discussion of divorce. We recognize, however, that the ideal presented in the preceding pages is difficult to maintain and that even those who start well may find themselves departing from the ideal at some point. Such departure is the result of sin and the fall. If we lived in a sinless world, then we could avoid the painful discussion of divorce that lies ahead. As noted in the opening paragraph of this chapter, however, divorce is an ever-present reality for many people, including believers seeking to follow God faithfully. Therefore, the following discussion will ask whether divorce can be a worshipful response to the difficulties of marriage. We will explore the biblical teaching about divorce and remarriage and draw conclusions on whether and when believers can pursue divorce.

The Question of Divorce and Remarriage

George and Mary had a fairy-tale romance. They were high school sweethearts who met for the first time on a youth trip with their church. They tried their best to pursue a healthy dating relationship through high school and college and married shortly after their college graduation. The fairy tale lasted for a few more years until some discontentment started creeping into their relationship. Money was tight, a newborn child refused to sleep, and the pressures of a career change started tearing at the fabric of their perfect life together. As they grew more distant over time, George started to confide in a woman at work about his marital troubles. Before long, those quiet conversations turned into an illicit romance. The romance was short-lived, and George came to Mary, confessing his sin. But the trust in their relationship was shattered. They sought counseling through their church and tried to work through the struggles that George's adultery had exposed. After a few months of counseling, however, they started to talk more seriously about divorce. Did they have biblical grounds to pursue divorce? Could they divorce and still maintain worshipful obedience to the covenant that they had with their Savior? Did George's adultery negate the marriage covenant that he had with Mary? These are the types of questions that we seek to answer in the remainder of this chapter.

The Bible addresses the matter of divorce in a few different ways. There is one explicit regulation offered by Moses, numerous references and allusions to divorce as part of God's admonitions to his people as they violated his covenant, four instances in Jesus' teaching about marriage, and one set of guidelines proffered by Paul as part of a larger discussion on marriage. None of these references are perfectly identical, but a general pattern emerges for making sense of these statements. The pattern revolves around a set of phrases known as the *exception clauses* in Matthew 5:32 and 19:9. In these two verses, Jesus offers an apparent exception to a prohibition against divorce and remarriage. The exception clauses often function as the locus of the debate regarding divorce and remarriage in Christian circles. Before we get into such a discussion, we need to address some of the highlights of the biblical evidence on divorce.

Old Testament

The primary Old Testament passage on divorce and remarriage is found in the regulation offered by Moses in Deuteronomy 24:1–4. This particular passage sets up a specific scenario and deals with the issue of remarriage primarily. Moses writes:

> When a man takes a wife and marries her, and it happens that she finds no favor in his eyes because he has found some indecency in her, and he writes her a certificate of divorce and puts it in her hand and sends her out from his house, and she leaves his house and goes and becomes another man's wife, and if the latter husband turns against her and writes her a certificate of divorce and puts it in her hand and sends her out of his house, or if the latter husband dies who took her to be his wife, then her former husband who sent her away is not allowed to take her again to be his wife, since she has been defiled; for that is an abomination before the LORD, and you shall not bring sin on the land which the LORD your God gives you as an inheritance.

Take note of the specific circumstances of Moses' regulation. First of all, it is important to see that the passage begins with "when . . . he writes her a certificate of divorce." Thus, Moses is not *instructing* them to divorce, but rather, he is *regulating* a practice that has already begun to take place in the culture contrary to God's original instruction about the permanence of marriage in Genesis 2.

Second, notice that the passage indicates that Moses is regulating a very specific kind of scenario. It is only after:

1. He divorces her because of "some indecency in her."
2. This divorce leads to remarriage on her part.
3. Her new marriage also ends, either by divorce or by the second husband's death.

At this point, Moses steps in and declares that the first husband cannot remarry the wife he previously divorced because "she has been defiled." Given the particularities of the passage, it should come as no surprise that this passage creates interpretive problems for contemporary readers.

First, we do not know the exact nature of the "indecency" that the first husband finds in his wife. It is likely that Moses had in mind some sort of sexual sin, but we cannot know for certain. One commentator notes that "it is clear that the interpretation 'something indecent, obnoxious, or shameful' is not far off the mark as an interpretative comment. Such a rendering does not communicate the terse quality of the original Hebrew expression, however, which defies concrete objective definition."[19] The idea that sexual sin is in view comes from the root meaning of the Hebrew phrase *'erwat dābār* that includes the idea of nakedness. In fact, the allusion to this particular regulation in the interaction between Jesus and the Pharisees gives the impression that at least part of Jesus' audience interpreted the regulation to refer to adultery (Matt. 19:3–9; Mark 10:2–12).[20] The biggest problem with interpreting the "indecency" as adultery is that Moses has already provided a regulation for how to address adulterous situations. In Deuteronomy 22:22, we read, "If a man is found lying with a married woman, then both of them shall die, the man who lay with the woman, and the woman; thus you shall purge the evil from Israel." Therefore, we cannot reach a conclusive position on what led to the divorce citing some "indecency" (Deut. 24:1–4) in the first place.

Second, the passage makes no moral claim about the initial divorce. In light of this problem, we can make the case that the previous problem would be a non-issue were it not for its connection to the interaction between Jesus and the Pharisees. As Köstenberger and Jones note: "Again, Moses' stipulations must not be construed as condoning such divorces but merely as regulating them. The thrust of Deuteronomy 24:1–4 is therefore *descriptive* rather than *prescriptive*, and this seems to be one thing Jesus' contemporaries had misconstrued."[21] Because Moses

---

19. Duane L. Christensen, *Deuteronomy 21:10–34:12*, Word Biblical Commentary 6B (Nashville: Thomas Nelson, 2002), 566.

20. Eugene Merrill writes, "The use of our text by Jesus suggests that in his view the 'something indecent' had to do with marital unfaithfulness, specifically adultery, for this is the only exception Jesus allowed and, apparently, the only one he addressed in his use of the Deuteronomy stipulation." Eugene H. Merrill, *Deuteronomy*, NAC 4 (Nashville: B&H, 1994), 317.

21. Köstenberger with Jones, *God, Marriage, and Family*, 225.

makes no moral claim on the initial divorce, we cannot reach a conclusion from Deuteronomy 24 regarding the morality of divorce in cases of adultery, sexual immorality, or other possible interpretations of "indecency." Instead, we must recognize that the primary command of this passage is to prohibit the original husband from remarrying the wife whom he had previously divorced and who had entered another marriage in the intermediate period.

Moses is clear in his prohibition of the first husband's taking the woman back because "she has been defiled; for that is an abomination before the LORD, and you shall not bring sin on the land which the LORD your God gives you as an inheritance" (Deut. 24:4). Again, it is not entirely clear what the abomination is. It could be the woman or her actions of remarriage after the first divorce. Either way, she has been defiled, and that is sufficient for Moses to prohibit the remarriage of the original couple.

While this passage is intriguing and offers much fodder for speculation and debate, Deuteronomy 24:1–4 does not close the book on biblical regulation of divorce. Far from offering a "blank check" permission to divorce, this passage offers neither a moral evaluation of divorce per se nor even a broad understanding of how to apply a law of divorce. Rather, it leaves us wanting more, and we are not alone—the Pharisees clearly wanted further explanation of this passage and sought Jesus' input.

Other Old Testament passages leave us with similar incomplete ideas regarding divorce and remarriage. Leviticus 21:7 and 14 prohibit priests from marrying a divorced woman, but do not make a statement about other Israelites. God invokes the language of divorce to describe his relationship with his people in Isaiah 50:1; 54:4–8; and Jeremiah 3:1–18, but those statements may not apply directly to human marriages. In Malachi 2:16, God declares that he hates divorce, but translation difficulties make this passage less certain. In all these passages, the general perspective on divorce is negative, but we do not find definitive statements prohibiting all divorce or making specific allowances for divorce. This is perhaps why most of the discussion regarding divorce and remarriage focuses on the New Testament.

New Testament

The New Testament offers us the most detailed material related to divorce and remarriage in Scripture; still, the volume of material is not particularly large. We find multiple occurrences of Jesus' teaching in the Synoptic Gospels (at least two of which are synoptic parallels) and a couple of teaching units in the Pauline Epistles (only one of which directly addresses the matter). With this in mind, we must tread carefully through these passages to reach a conclusion on what Scripture says about divorce and remarriage, acknowledging that there is not a consensus view today.

The Sermon on the Mount

In Matthew 5:31–32, we find the first occurrence of Jesus' teaching on divorce, and this is also the first appearance of the exception clause in Matthew's Gospel:

> It was said, "Whoever sends his wife away, let him give her a certificate of divorce"; but I say to you that everyone who divorces his wife, except for the reason of *unchastity*, makes her commit adultery; and whoever marries a divorced woman commits adultery.

These verses of the Sermon on the Mount are part of the section where Jesus invokes one of the Ten Commandments or other laws and then draws an application beyond the traditional interpretation. Verses 31–32 of Matthew 5 allude to Deuteronomy 24:1–4, and Jesus then draws out his application on the matter of divorce.[22] Jesus' reference to Deuteronomy notes the certificate of divorce that Moses referenced in 24:1. Leon Morris notes: "The bill of divorce was a protection for the woman; a capricious husband could not drive her from his home and afterward claim that she was still his wife. He must give her the document that set out her right to marry someone else."[23] Before we even come to the exception clauses, we must acknowledge that Jesus held marriage in high regard and that to divorce a spouse was a very serious matter. No matter one's conclusion on the meaning of the exception clauses, we must strive toward maintaining the durability of marriage. Issuing a certificate of divorce in ancient Israel or contemporary America should be something that causes one to pause and consider the tragic implications of such a certificate.

Matthew 5:32 brings us to the crux of the divorce issue for this passage. Jesus states, "But I say to you that everyone who divorces his wife, *except for the reason of unchastity*, makes her commit adultery; and whoever marries a divorced woman commits adultery." The key phrase is "except for the reason of unchastity [*parektos logou porneias*]." This phrase has been variously interpreted to mean (1) an exception allowing for divorce in cases of adultery; (2) an explanation for who is responsible for adultery after a divorce;[24] or (3) a limitation of the allowance for divorce to the betrothal period.[25]

The central term is "unchastity," which is translated from the Greek word *porneia*. This term has a broad meaning encompassing all types of sexual sin,

22. Craig L. Blomberg, *Matthew*, NAC 22 (Nashville: B&H, 1992), 110.

23. Leon Morris, *The Gospel according to Matthew*, PNTC (Grand Rapids: Eerdmans, 1992), 120.

24. Gordon J. Wenham and William A. Heth, *Jesus and Divorce*, updated ed. (Eugene, OR: Wipf & Stock, 2002), 19–72.

25. David W. Jones, "The Betrothal View of Divorce and Remarriage," *BibSac* 165, no. 657 (January 2008): 68–85.

including adultery and fornication.[26] The problem is with its use in the phrase and whether Jesus is making an allowance for divorce. We will explore this in more detail later in this chapter, but at the very least, Jesus is keeping the door relatively closed for divorce. In addition, allowance for remarriage is potentially limited or even prohibited by the way that Jesus communicates his interpretation of divorce. He states that a man who "marries a divorced woman commits adultery." Thus, Jesus may not forbid remarriage entirely, but he certainly limits it to nothing more than remarriage after a divorce that is brought about due to sexual immorality. In fact, he declares that the man who divorces his wife for a reason other than sexual immorality causes her to commit adultery on the assumption that she would remarry.

Jesus' Interactions with the Pharisees and Disciples
The other set of Jesus' teachings on divorce represents his interactions with the Pharisees and his disciples in Matthew 19:3–9, Mark 10:2–12, and Luke 16:18.

Table 18.1. Jesus' Teaching on Divorce and Remarriage

He said to them, "Because of your hardness of heart Moses permitted you to divorce your wives; but from the beginning it has not been this way. And I say to you, whoever divorces his wife, except for immorality, and marries another woman commits adultery." (Matt. 19:8–9)

And He said to them, "Whoever divorces his wife and marries another woman commits adultery against her; and if she herself divorces her husband and marries another man, she is committing adultery." (Mark 10:11–12)

"Everyone who divorces his wife and marries another commits adultery, and he who marries one who is divorced from a husband commits adultery." (Luke 16:18)

The first two passages are almost certainly synoptic parallels,[27] and we will treat them as such. The Lukan verse represents a small portion of a teaching moment that Jesus had with his disciples, but the verse lines up in content with Mark 10:11–12. Since the content is almost identical—with one key exception—we will treat these interactions as a unit. The solitary difference among these verses is the existence of the exception clause in Matthew 19:9, which is absent from the other passages.

26. Frederick William Danker et al., eds., *A Greek-English Lexicon of the New Testament and Other Early Christian Literature*, 3rd ed. (Chicago: University of Chicago Press, 2000) (BDAG), s.v. "πορνεία."
27. A synoptic parallel occurs when an identical text (in both content and context) is found in more than one of the Synoptic Gospels (Matthew, Mark, and Luke). In this case, the circumstances and message of Matthew 19:3–9 and Mark 10:2–12 demonstrate the same teaching moment recorded by two different Gospel writers; therefore, these passages are synoptic parallels.

At this teaching and healing moment, the Pharisees ask Jesus a question that begins his discussion of marriage. They ask, "Is it lawful for a man to divorce his wife for any reason at all?" (Matt. 19:3; cf. Mark 10:2). This simple question raises a much larger issue among the Pharisees related to their interpretation of Deuteronomy 24:1. Two schools of thought—Hillel and Shammai—offered different interpretations of the indecency that a husband found in his wife in Deuteronomy 24:1. The Hillel school taught that a man could divorce his wife and remarry for any reason at all, including something as insignificant as ruining his meal. The Shammai school held a stricter interpretation that allowed a man to divorce his wife and remarry only if she was found to be sexually immoral.[28] Therefore, the question posed had the possibility of creating a dispute between Jesus and a faction of the Pharisees no matter how he answered. Undeterred by this possibility, Jesus answers their question by referring back to the created order: "Have you not read that He who created them from the beginning made them male and female, and said, 'For this reason a man shall leave his father and mother and be joined to his wife, and the two shall become one flesh'? So they are no longer two, but one flesh. What therefore God has joined together, let no man separate" (Matt. 19:4–6; cf. Mark 10:6–9). Jesus' answer goes beyond the nature of the Pharisees' question and points them back to God's design for marriage. His basic answer is that marriage should not end in divorce. God intended for marriage to last, so man should not try to end it.

If this were the end of Jesus' answer, then there would be no debate about reasons for divorce. But the Pharisees did not leave the discussion there. Instead, they pressed further and asked why there was a Mosaic regulation regarding divorce (Matt. 19:7). Jesus' response still points them back to the original nature of marriage, but he incorporates the reality of the fall. Jesus states, "Because of your hardness of heart Moses permitted you to divorce your wives; but from the beginning it has not been this way" (Matt. 19:8; cf. Mark 10:5). Having appealed to Genesis 1:27 and 2:24 and the story of the fall in Genesis 3, Jesus constantly points his questioners back to the original purpose of marriage.

At this point, we enter the controversial part of Jesus' interaction with the Pharisees and disciples. Mark recounts the next part of the discussion as occurring between Jesus and his disciples. After the disciples ask him further questions about his answers to the Pharisees, Jesus responds, "Whoever divorces his wife and marries another woman commits adultery against her; and if she herself divorces her husband and marries another man, she is committing adultery" (Mark 10:11–12).

---

28. These two schools of thought derive from the teaching of two first-century B.C. rabbis named Hillel and Shammai. Their ideas developed into the primary schools of thought on divorce and remarriage during the days of Jesus. For further discussion on the schools of Hillel and Shammai, see Köstenberger with Jones, *God, Marriage, and Family*, 228–29; Blomberg, *Matthew*, 110, 289–90; Morris, *Matthew*, 120, 480.

The answer is straightforward and without apparent controversy. Jesus declares that a man who divorces his wife and marries another woman commits adultery against his wife. In addition, a woman who divorces her husband and marries another man commits adultery. Luke reports a similar statement, with one addition. He notes that a man who marries a divorced woman also commits adultery (Luke 16:18). The controversy arises in Matthew's account because he includes another version of the exception clause in Jesus' answer. According to Matthew, the further explanation is directed to the Pharisees, and the answer is generally the same as Mark's account except that Jesus adds a qualifier. Matthew reports that Jesus states, "And I say to you, whoever divorces his wife, except for immorality, and marries another woman commits adultery" (Matt. 19:9). The question is whether the exception clauses make an allowance for divorce in cases of sexual immorality, or whether Jesus is stating who is responsible for the adultery.

Jesus' interaction with his disciples concludes in Matthew's account with an unusual exchange in which the disciples appear to be perplexed by Jesus' teaching. The disciples react to his teaching by saying, "If the relationship of the man with his wife is like this, it is better not to marry" (Matt. 19:10). The disciples seem to interpret Jesus as having said that divorce and remarriage are not allowed; therefore, it would be better never to marry. Jesus responds in kind by acknowledging their concern and saying that such a life is given only to some. He then concludes with a statement about eunuchs (vv. 11–12). This final exchange is sometimes interpreted as a statement on singleness,[29] but it could also be understood as an affirmation of a previous prohibition against remarriage.

While Jesus' interaction with the Pharisees and his disciples is limited to no more than three occurrences, these passages form the core of the New Testament debate surrounding divorce and remarriage. In fact, much of the disagreement in scholarship focuses on the two appearances of the exception clauses. Despite the centrality of these Gospel accounts, we must not forget the teachings of Paul on the matter of divorce, especially since it connects back to Jesus' teaching.

Pauline Instructions on Divorce and Remarriage

Paul addresses marriage on a few different occasions in his writings, including Romans 7:1–3, 1 Corinthians 7, and Ephesians 5:22–33. As it relates specifically to divorce and remarriage, 1 Corinthians 7:10–16 is the key passage for our study:

> But to the married I give instructions, not I, but the Lord, that the wife should not leave her husband (but if she does leave, she must remain unmarried, or else be reconciled to her husband), and that the husband should not divorce his wife.

---

29. See Barry Danylak, *Redeeming Singleness* (Wheaton, IL: Crossway, 2010), 149–63.

But to the rest I say, not the Lord, that if any brother has a wife who is an unbeliever, and she consents to live with him, he must not divorce her. And a woman who has an unbelieving husband, and he consents to live with her, she must not send her husband away. For the unbelieving husband is sanctified through his wife, and the unbelieving wife is sanctified through her believing husband; for otherwise your children are unclean, but now they are holy. Yet if the unbelieving one leaves, let him leave; the brother or the sister is not under bondage in such cases, but God has called us to peace. For how do you know, O wife, whether you will save your husband? Or how do you know, O husband, whether you will save your wife?

Paul opens these verses by restating his interpretation of Jesus' teaching.[30] He writes, "But to the married I give instructions, not I, but the Lord, that the wife should not leave her husband (but if she does leave, she must remain unmarried, or else be reconciled to her husband), and that the husband should not divorce his wife" (1 Cor. 7:10–11). This introduction immediately raises an issue about what Jesus taught. For those who believe that Jesus made an allowance for divorce and remarriage in Matthew 5:32 and 19:9, Paul does not communicate the same allowance. He reports Jesus' teaching to be one of marriage permanence that could potentially be marked by separation but not divorce or remarriage. Anthony Thiselton states, "Paul is declaring that 'alienation' between a Christian husband and a Christian wife, or even the desire of the one to leave the other (the converse of καταλλάσσω), should not of itself lead to permanent separation, let alone to remarriage."[31] Paul appears to be writing to Christians in 1 Corinthians 7:10–11, so his instructions here are directed to a different audience than the subsequent verses. Paul clearly states, however, that he is repeating the instructions of the Lord. Thus, we need to take these words into account when we consider the appropriate interpretation of the exception clauses in Matthew. The controversy is especially acute for those who interpret the exception clauses to make an allowance for remarriage after divorce.

Paul then transitions to another application of his teaching on divorce by focusing on a topic that he states that Jesus did not address—interfaith marriages. The apostle writes: "But to the rest I say, not the Lord, that if any brother has a wife who is an unbeliever, and she consents to live with him, he must not divorce her. And a woman who has an unbelieving husband, and he consents to live with

---

30. Anthony Thiselton notes: "Many writers urge that the saying of Jesus to which Paul refers finds expression in Mark 10:11–12. . . . This links the principle with the Decalogue, but concerns remarriage rather than separation or divorce." Anthony C. Thiselton, *The First Epistle to the Corinthians*, New International Greek Testament Commentary (Grand Rapids: Eerdmans, 2000), 521.

31. Thiselton, *First Epistle to the Corinthians*, 521.

her, she must not send her husband away" (1 Cor. 7:12–13). The key idea in these verses and the justification that follows through verse 16 is the application of divorce in the marriages of believers united with nonbelievers. The basic assumption is still the same as the statement to believing couples—marriage is permanent. The most likely scenario in these verses is that these couples married while both were nonbelievers and one spouse has subsequently become a Christian. Yet the application of Paul's words is not limited to such an audience. Thiselton suggests: "The key controlling principle lies in the recognition of the nature of the anxiety which Paul seeks to allay. The believer asks Paul with genuine concern: if I have left behind the old life and become a new creation in Christ, does not my relation with my unbelieving, unrepentant spouse and my entire home atmosphere threaten to pollute and to corrode my purity as one who belongs to Christ?"[32] In light of the believing spouse's desire for purity, Paul dictates that the believer is to remain with the nonbelieving spouse as long as the nonbeliever consents to live with the believer. Paul justifies this arrangement in verse 14 from an evangelistic perspective. If the believing spouse lives out his or her faith in front of the nonbelieving spouse, then the nonbeliever might come to Christ. In addition, it is also good for their children.

First Corinthians 7:15 introduces a different angle on the situation. Paul addresses the other outcome contrasted with the consenting spouses of verses 12–13. In this verse, the apostle makes an allowance for separation and even possibly divorce when the unbelieving spouse abandons the believing spouse: "Yet if the unbelieving one leaves, let him leave; the brother or the sister is not under bondage in such cases, but God has called us to peace." The problem comes in defining what Paul means by "not under bondage in such cases." Some take it to mean that the believing spouse is free to remarry after the unbelieving spouse leaves. Others view this simply as the believing spouse's no longer being required ("bound") to fight to save the marriage.[33] The controversy over this passage is complicated by Paul's use of similar language in verse 39 as he speaks to widows who are free to remarry in the Lord after the death of their husbands. While their husbands are living, they are "bound," meaning that they are not free to marry someone else.

Romans 7:1–3 also comes to bear on this passage because Paul speaks to the enduring nature of marriage:

Or do you not know, brethren (for I am speaking to those who know the law), that the law has jurisdiction over a person as long as he lives? For the married woman

32. Thiselton, *First Epistle to the Corinthians*, 528.
33. For more discussion, see Köstenberger with Jones, *God, Marriage, and Family*, 234–35.

is bound by law to her husband while he is living; but if her husband dies, she is released from the law concerning the husband. So then, if while her husband is living she is joined to another man, she shall be called an adulteress; but if her husband dies, she is free from the law, so that she is not an adulteress though she is joined to another man.

Romans 7:2 affirms the basic idea of 1 Corinthians 7:39, but these verses do not align easily with 1 Corinthians 7:15 because that verse releases the believing spouse from the unbelieving spouse if the unbeliever leaves, while the other passages require the death of a spouse to be released.

The Christian Options regarding Divorce and Remarriage

Now that we have surveyed the biblical evidence on divorce and remarriage, we will lay out three possible options for interpreting the biblical evidence. These options are no divorce and no remarriage, divorce in limited circumstances but no remarriage, and divorce and remarriage in limited circumstances. At the outset of this discussion, we want to acknowledge that all Christian options affirm the importance and durability of marriage. Some of the options, however, adhere to the idea that the marriage covenant can be severed. None of these options open the door to divorce for any reason. Each of these options serves as a large category that may contain numerous variations of the view. When those variations are significant, we will point them out.

No Divorce and No Remarriage

The *no divorce and no remarriage* view holds the Edenic ideal of marriage in highest esteem and seeks to maintain that ideal as much as possible. Gehring summarizes this position well: "It may generally be asserted that the final clauses on divorce and remarriage, diverse as they are in the synoptic accounts with their differing textual witnesses, all point to one and the same feature Jesus is evidently stressing: a formal divorce, even including the βιβλίον ἀποστασίου of Deut 24:1, is worthless and trifling."[34] This position represents a group of views that all conclude that divorce and remarriage are not biblically permissible.[35]

The *no divorce and no remarriage* position generally begins with the importance of the creation-order design for marriage. Proponents of this view emphasize the "leave and cleave" component of marriage found in Genesis 2:24 and note that

---

34. Gehring, *Biblical "One Flesh" Theology of Marriage*, 229.

35. The two most common variations of this position are the *unlawful marriages* view and the *betrothal* view.

Scripture calls a married couple to leave their parents, join together in an insepa-
rable bond, and become one flesh.[36] The importance of the creation-order design
is then imported into the various teachings of the New Testament that refer to
Genesis 1–2, including Matthew 19, Mark 10, and Ephesians 5. Since this ideal is
the foundation for all subsequent teaching on marriage, proponents of this view
believe that we must view marriage as lifelong and permanent. Even in the aftermath of the fall in Genesis 3, the creation-order design does not change. This seems
apparent in Jesus' teaching as he declares: "Have you not read that He who created
them from the beginning made them male and female, and said, 'For this reason a
man shall leave his father and mother and be joined to his wife, and the two shall
become one flesh'? So they are no longer two, but one flesh. What therefore God
has joined together, *let no man separate*" (Matt. 19:4–6). This view also incorporates the Pauline instructions from Romans 7:1–3 stating that a woman is bound to
her husband as long as he lives. From the perspective of the creation-order design,
this view has much strength.

The *no divorce and no remarriage* view also emphasizes the covenantal nature
of marriage with the presumption that the marriage covenant is indissoluble.[37]
Drawing on the Old Testament depiction of marriage as a covenant (Prov. 2:17;
Mal. 2:14) as well as the analogies between marital unfaithfulness and covenant
unfaithfulness, this position deems divorce beyond the scope of divine sanction.
J. Carl Laney writes, "Finally, she was united 'by covenant,' an allusion to the marriage contract made before God and witnesses (see Prov. 2:17; Ezek. 16:8). God
does not break covenants (see Lev. 26:40–45), and since divorce violates a marriage covenant made before God, it cannot meet with his approval."[38] There is
some debate over whether covenants are indissoluble, but that debate does not
generally enter the discussion on this view.[39] Since this view sees the marriage
covenant as indissoluble, there is no allowance for remarriage except in the case
of a spouse's dying. Any remarriage before the death of a spouse would be the
equivalent of adultery. Such a position fits well with the words of Jesus in Mark
10:11–12 and Luke 16:18 and the words of Paul in 1 Corinthians 7:39. Since
remarriage is not allowed, divorce is essentially a nonissue because any divorce
would not give freedom to remarry.

36. See J. Carl Laney, "No Divorce & No Remarriage," in *Divorce and Remarriage: Four Christian Views*,
ed. H. Wayne House (Downers Grove, IL: InterVarsity Press, 1990), 16–21.

37. David W. Jones notes, "With the rise of the covenant marriage movement it seems likely that less permissive views of divorce and remarriage, such as the betrothal view, will grow in popularity." Jones, "Betrothal
View of Divorce and Remarriage," 85n52.

38. Laney, "No Divorce & No Remarriage," 30.

39. David W. Jones and John K. Tarwater, "Are Biblical Covenants Dissoluble? Toward a Theology of
Marriage," *SWJT* 47, no. 1 (Fall 2004): 1–11.

This view must now address the possible exceptions of Matthew 5:32 and 19:9 and 1 Corinthians 7:15. The exception clauses found in Matthew's Gospel create the most difficult challenge for this position. From the sixteenth-century Reformers to contemporary evangelicals, many Protestants have held that the exception clauses make an allowance for divorce in cases of adultery. The *no divorce and no remarriage* view represents a group of positions that see the exception clauses differently. The debate centers on the meaning of *porneia* and what allowance Jesus is making. Köstenberger and Jones summarize these options when they state: "Scholars who hold this position understand *porneia* to be a reference to some type of sexual sin that would have made marriage unlawful under Jewish civil law. Suggestions as to the identity of the sexual sin in view, which would have been applicable to the recipients of Matthew's Gospel, include: premarital (betrothal period) intercourse, incest, Jew/Gentile mixed spiritual marriage, or a combination of the above."[40] This position leans on the idea that Matthew wrote to a predominantly Jewish audience who would have seen any of these potential options as forbidden. The intended Jewish audience of Matthew also explains why Mark and Luke do not have such an exception in their accounts. Therefore, the Jewish audience would interpret the exception clauses to allow for annulment of marriages that were already deemed unlawful.

The other possible exception that this position needs to address is abandonment by an unbelieving spouse from 1 Corinthians 7:15. Laney depicts this exception as follows: "In verse 15 Paul is simply saying that if the unbelieving partner demands separation, then the believer is not 'under bondage' (*dedoulōtai*, literally 'enslaved') to preserve the union through legal maneuvers or by pursuing the unwilling partner all over the Roman Empire."[41] Thus, the believing spouse can accept a divorce from the spouse who abandons her and is not required to use all means possible to preserve the marriage. Köstenberger and Jones note: "According to this view, then, that to which the abandoned party is not bound is a *relational obligation* to contest an unbelieving spouse's desire to depart. Indeed, it is argued, that doing so would be un-Christlike (cf. Jer. 3:8, 14) and possibly even hinder the prospect of reconciliation."[42] Even after accepting a divorce due to abandonment, however, remarriage is not allowed for the one who was abandoned because the marriage covenant still exists.[43] The divorce is viewed as a legal separation for the sake of safety or protection but not as an actual severing of the

---

40. Köstenberger with Jones, *God, Marriage, and Family*, 230.
41. Laney, "No Divorce & No Remarriage," 43–44.
42. Köstenberger with Jones, *God, Marriage, and Family*, 235.
43. "But note carefully that Paul says nothing in the verse about a second marriage for the deserted spouse. Allowance for the deserted spouse to remarry is simply not stated here and cannot be substantiated by an exegesis of this verse [1 Cor. 7:15]." Laney, "No Divorce & No Remarriage," 45.

marital covenant. If either spouse remarries, therefore, he or she would be entering into an adulterous context.

The *no divorce and no remarriage* view attempts to maintain the creation-order design for marriage and to hold believers to God's standard. There is no doubt that these proponents take marriage seriously and desire to promote the comparison between marriage and the covenant that God has with his people.

Divorce in Limited Circumstances but No Remarriage

The position of *divorce in limited circumstances but no remarriage* seeks to establish biblical parameters for allowing divorce in cases of adultery and abandonment but prohibiting remarriage after divorce. This view is sometimes referred to as the *early-church* view or *patristic* view because it was the nearly universal position of the early church. Like the previous *no divorce and no remarriage* view, this view holds that the creation-order ideal is the standard for marriage and that God still expects this ideal to be upheld under normal circumstances.

The covenantal model of marriage is important to this position. William Heth makes the case that God's faithfulness to his people despite their unfaithfulness to him is evidence that marriage is a lasting covenant. He writes:

> The permanence of marriage is fundamentally a theological issue, rooted in the divine-human relationship to which marriage stands as an antitype (see Eph 5:31–32). At least one theological consideration ought to be drawn from the parallel between Israel's unfaithfulness to her covenant with God and a spouse's unfaithfulness to a marriage covenant. Even though Israel repeatedly violated her covenant with Yahweh, there is no indication that this dissolved or nullified the covenant relationship (see Lev 26:44–45; Judg 2:1–3; Is 50:1; Jer 3:8, 12).[44]

The enduring covenant of marriage serves as the foundation for this view's position that remarriage is not an option even after a divorce that is biblically sanctioned. This affirms the same interpretation of the *no divorce and no remarriage* view of Mark 10:11–12; Luke 16:18; and Romans 7:1–3. All these passages consider it to be adultery when someone enters a marriage after a previous marriage

---

44. William A. Heth, "Divorce, but No Remarriage," in *Divorce and Remarriage: Four Christian Views*, ed. H. Wayne House (Downers Grove, IL: InterVarsity Press, 1990), 75–76. While this particular essay is a good summary of this position, it should be noted that Heth has subsequently changed his view to allow for remarriage in limited circumstances. He noted this change in William A. Heth, "Jesus on Divorce: How My Mind Has Changed," *SBJT* 6, no. 1 (Spring 2002): 4–29. Heth's coauthor of another book espousing his previous view, Gordon Wenham, remains a proponent of divorce in limited circumstances but no remarriage. See Wenham and Heth, *Jesus and Divorce*; Gordon J. Wenham, "Does the New Testament Approve Remarriage after Divorce?," *SBJT* 6, no. 1 (Spring 2002): 30–45.

that ended in any way other than death. The circumstances of the divorce do not matter because the covenant is enduring.

The main difference between the *divorce in limited circumstances but no remarriage* view and the *no divorce and no remarriage* view focuses on whether a divorce can be biblically sanctioned. As evidenced by the name of the view, this position holds that divorce is warranted in limited circumstances—adultery and abandonment. The warrant for such a divorce, according to this view, is not necessarily found in the exception clauses of Matthew's Gospel and 1 Corinthians 7:15, but rather lies in the idea of human sinfulness. Gordon Wenham best depicts the main thrust of the exception clauses by noting:

> Within this context the exception clause simply notes that should a wife have already committed adultery herself (the most likely form of sexual immorality in this context), her husband can hardly be said to have made her commit adultery, when under current Roman and Jewish law he was compelled to divorce her for her action. There is no suggestion here that by divorcing her for sexual immorality a husband gains the right to marry again. That is simply not in the frame of discussion here.[45]

Wenham believes that the exception clauses describe when adultery takes place. If a man divorces his wife for any reason other than her own sexual immorality, then he causes her to commit adultery if she remarries for economic and social reasons. This is a very straightforward reading of Matthew 5:32.

The second appearance of the exception clause is a little more difficult, but proponents of this view believe that it also carries the same interpretation. The exception clause of Matthew 19:9 comes in the midst of a debate between Jesus and the Pharisees. Jesus' first answer is to say that marriage is permanent (Matt. 19:6). Upon further questioning about the Mosaic code regarding divorce, Jesus offers a response that blames sinful hearts for the need for such a code. When Jesus responds with the exception clause in verse 9, he is only restating a different form of 5:32 that continues the prohibition against remarriage. When the disciples react in 19:10, they appear to be surprised at Jesus' response. Had Jesus merely adopted the position of Shammai—divorce and remarriage allowed in cases of adultery— the disciples would likely not have been surprised. Instead, they respond, "If the relationship of the man with his wife is like this, it is better not to marry." Jesus then enters a discussion that not everyone can accept this statement and that some have made themselves eunuchs for the sake of the kingdom (19:11–12). The reaction of the disciples points to something Jesus said that goes beyond the generally

---

45. Wenham, "Does the New Testament Approve Remarriage after Divorce?," 35.

accepted norm of the day. Wenham and Heth note: "In particular, the disciples object to Jesus' new teaching that legal divorce does not, under any circumstances, open the door for remarriage. Jesus responds that this is indeed a difficult path to follow, but his true followers have been given the divine resources to live up to it."[46]

In like fashion, proponents of this view do not believe that 1 Corinthians 7:10–15 allows for remarriage after a divorce. Gordon Fee argues that verses 10–11 are a clear prohibition against remarriage and the clear interpretation of Jesus' teaching: "What is *not* allowed is remarriage, both because for him that presupposes the teaching of Jesus that such is adultery and because in the Christian community reconciliation is the norm."[47] Even though divorce may happen at times, it is not the norm, and it does not allow for a believer to remarry. Once again, the reason is that the marital covenant is still understood to be in place in the eyes of God. This allowance of divorce is merely a legal allowance, but not an actual severance of the marital union. Paul's statement in 1 Corinthians 7:15 about the believer's no longer being bound when the unbelieving spouse leaves is still interpreted in light of 7:39 that a wife is bound to her husband until he dies. This keeps a uniform approach to the divorce passages and a strict prohibition against remarriage while the previous spouse is living.

The end result for the *divorce in limited circumstances but no remarriage* position is that divorce in cases of adultery and abandonment is biblically sanctioned only because it prevents further damage caused by sin. Ultimately, this position makes allowances for divorce in the same way that Jesus made allowance for the Mosaic law governing divorce—because of the hardness of hearts. But this is not the desired outcome for any marriage.

Divorce and Remarriage in Limited Circumstances

Divorce and remarriage in limited circumstances is a position holding that divorce is allowed in cases of adultery and abandonment and that remarriage is allowed for the innocent spouse in both circumstances. This position is most familiar to Protestants because it was made popular by the early Reformers after Erasmus first published the view in 1519.[48] Some modern proponents of this view have sought to expand the parameters for divorce and remarriage to include other causes, including abuse and neglect.[49] Yet the most common versions of this view fall in line with what Thomas Edgar writes:

---

46. Wenham and Heth, *Jesus and Divorce*, 65.

47. Gordon D. Fee, *The First Epistle to the Corinthians*, New International Commentary on the New Testament (Grand Rapids: Eerdmans, 1987), 296.

48. Wenham and Heth, *Jesus and Divorce*, 13.

49. See David Instone-Brewer, *Divorce and Remarriage in the Church* (Downers Grove, IL: InterVarsity Press, 2003), 93–106.

The Bible specifically states that God intended for marriage to be maintained. Just as specifically, Jesus states that there is only one valid reason for which a person may properly divorce the other and subsequently marry someone else—adultery on the part of the spouse. This is clear and specific. There is no valid basis on which to reject this teaching. First Corinthians 7:15, since it does not specifically mention remarriage, is not as clear. However, the most probable meaning is that if the spouse initiates the separation, the deserted spouse may divorce and remarry.[50]

In essence, this view holds that adultery and abandonment provide a basis for dissolving a marriage and thus free a spouse to pursue divorce and enter another marriage.

While proponents of this position acknowledge the Edenic perfection of the first marriage in Genesis 2, the focus quickly transitions to the impact that the fall had on the most intimate relationship between a man and a woman and the role that the Mosaic regulation of divorce played in the culture. David Instone-Brewer notes: "When marriages failed, the woman, being more vulnerable, usually suffered most. The law of Moses limited the damage that divorce inflicts by forcing a divorcing man to give his ex-wife a certificate that would allow her to remarry."[51] The reliance on the law to provide for remarriage functions as the main starting point for this view.

Moving along in the Old Testament, proponents of divorce and remarriage in limited circumstances point to the relationship between God and Israel as the example for how human marriage functions, especially in light of divorce. We have stated earlier in the chapter that there is an analogous connection between marriage and the relationship with God and his people. By extension, the unfaithfulness of God's people is described as adultery throughout the Old Testament. The most prominent Old Testament passage that describes the adultery of God's people and invokes the language of divorce is in Jeremiah 3. In the opening verse of the chapter, Jeremiah quotes God, alluding to Deuteronomy 24:1–4. Then he describes the behavior of Israel, calling her "a harlot with many lovers" (Jer. 3:1).

Turning to Judah several verses later, the prophet describes Judah's unwillingness to learn from Israel's mistakes. The Lord says, "And I saw that for all the adulteries of faithless Israel, I had sent her away and given her a writ of divorce, yet her treacherous sister Judah did not fear; but she went and was a harlot also" (Jer. 3:8). On the basis of this passage and others that speak with similar (but not as explicit)

---

50. Thomas R. Edgar, "Divorce & Remarriage for Adultery or Desertion," in *Divorce and Remarriage: Four Christian Views*, ed. H. Wayne House (Downers Grove, IL: InterVarsity Press, 1990), 191–92. A similar position is espoused by the Westminster Confession of Faith. See WCF 24.5–6, https://www.pcaac.org/wp-content/uploads/2019/11/WCFScriptureProofs.pdf.

51. Instone-Brewer, *Divorce and Remarriage in the Church*, 31.

language, proponents of the *divorce and remarriage in limited circumstances* view build a case for divorce on the basis of God's example.[52]

When we get to the New Testament, the focus for this view lands on the Matthean accounts of the exception clauses. Since the passages in Mark and Luke do not make allowances for divorce or remarriage on the surface, proponents of this view determine that they must be interpreted through the lens of the exception clauses.[53] This view holds that *porneia* should generally be interpreted to refer to adultery, or some form of sexual immorality, and that Jesus is giving the right to divorce on the grounds that adultery has violated the marriage covenant. Jim Newheiser states: "Jesus, however, offers one qualification: 'except for immorality' (also in Matt. 5:32). He thus affirms that one sin so seriously 'violates the "one-flesh" principle underlying marriage' that it gives the innocent party grounds to divorce the adulterer."[54] Since the marriage covenant is broken, then remarriage is logically allowed under this view. Despite the controversy surrounding this passage, supporters of this view believe the interpretation is clear.[55]

The second circumstance that allows for divorce in this view is abandonment. This allowance comes from 1 Corinthians 7:15, but it is built on the same foundations above. Since the people of Israel had abandoned God and joined themselves to other gods, the Lord divorced them. In the same way, a believer who is abandoned by his or her *unbelieving* spouse may also divorce and subsequently remarry. The proponents of this view follow the line of thinking in 1 Corinthians 7 closely and state that the believer is not at liberty to leave the unbelieving spouse simply because he or she is an unbeliever. The unbeliever in this case initiates the divorce by separating, and thus, the believer can follow through with a divorce under such circumstances. There is some disagreement over whether the believing spouse can initiate the divorce proceeding after being abandoned or must merely wait for the unbeliever to follow through with the divorce.[56]

---

52. Instone-Brewer, *Divorce and Remarriage in the Church*, 38. See also Jim Newheiser, *Marriage, Divorce, and Remarriage: Critical Questions and Answers* (Phillipsburg, NJ: P&R Publishing, 2017), 210–11.

53. Thomas Edgar writes, "The two passages in Matthew (5:31–32 and 19:3–12) seem to allow an exception where divorce and remarriage are permitted. Mark 10:2–12 describes the same statement by Jesus as that quoted in Matthew 19:9; therefore, the additional details in Matthew 19:3–12 must be understood in Mark 110:2–12." Edgar, "Divorce & Remarriage for Adultery or Desertion," 153.

54. Newheiser, *Marriage, Divorce, and Remarriage*, 212.

55. Edgar argues: "Not only is this verse clear, but it is relatively simple, despite the disagreement over its interpretation. In fact, it could be said that it is the verse's clarity, rather than any complexity, which causes the problem for those interpreters whose presuppositions allow for no divorce or remarriage." Edgar, "Divorce & Remarriage for Adultery or Desertion," 156.

56. Edgar argues that the abandoned believer "may carry out the legal technicalities for divorce." Edgar, 187. Instone-Brewer intimates, however, that the believing spouse can merely accept a divorce: "Paul says further that if someone is divorced against their will, they may accept it. There is nothing they can do to reverse the divorce, and God has called them to peace." Instone-Brewer, *Divorce and Remarriage in the Church*, 79.

With slight variations, most positions would agree with the preceding position about a believing spouse's accepting a divorce from an unbelieving spouse who leaves. But the biggest contribution that the *divorce and remarriage in limited circumstances* view seeks to offer from 1 Corinthians 7 is the idea that the believing spouse is free to remarry. Paul concludes verse 15 by saying that "the brother or the sister is not under bondage in such cases, but God has called us to peace." Based on this language and its comparison to verse 39[57] and Romans 7:2–3,[58] proponents of this view argue that the believing spouse is free to remarry a believer once the divorce from the unbeliever is complete.[59]

Divorce and remarriage in limited circumstances has become the majority position among Protestants and evangelicals. In fact, each position has ardent supporters in different segments of the church at large. As evidenced by the different interpretations that we have summarized, each position has strengths and weaknesses. What we would like to offer next is a proposed alternative that we believe addresses the question of divorce and remarriage with a focus on how best to worship the God who designed marriage in the first place.

In sum, we can say that far different from the almost "anything goes" approach to marriage and divorce that has become so common in culture—even among many Christians—God desires us to highly honor and protect the covenant of marriage. Each of the three identified perspectives seeks to retain a high view of marriage, and even the most permissive view of the three that allows for some basis for both divorce and remarriage discourages the pursuit of divorce except in the most extreme contexts.

A Proposed Alternative

As we laid out earlier in the chapter, we believe that marriage is designed by God as a comprehensive, covenantal union between one man and one woman intended to endure for a lifetime and proximally directed toward the rearing of the next generation. The phrase "intended to endure for a lifetime" has the clearest application to the question of divorce and remarriage, but the entire definition plays a part in how we determine what course of action demonstrates maximal worship of God. That being said, we want to offer an alternative to the three options that we have already discussed related to divorce and remarriage.

---

57. "A wife is bound as long as her husband lives; but if her husband is dead, she is free to be married to whom she wishes, only in the Lord" (1 Cor. 7:39).

58. "For the married woman is bound by law to her husband while he is living; but if her husband dies, she is released from the law concerning the husband. So then, if while her husband is living she is joined to another man, she shall be called an adulteress; but if her husband dies, she is free from the law, so that she is not an adulteress though she is joined to another man" (Rom. 7:2–3).

59. Newheiser, *Marriage, Divorce, and Remarriage*, 221–23.

Marriage is a comprehensive, covenantal union that necessitates that all aspects of our lives be joined together. This is the thrust of the one-flesh union of Genesis 2:24. As a result, separating the one-flesh union is extremely difficult to the point of being almost impossible. Separating the one-flesh union is not similar to tearing apart two sheets of paper that have been glued together. The man and the woman have been so intertwined through marriage that there is no reasonable way to tell where one begins and the other ends. This is why marriage is described as a covenant. It is a relationship that supersedes all other relationships in intimacy and durability. Genesis 2:24 even tells us that marriage is greater than the bond between a child and his parents ("For this reason a man shall leave his father and mother . . ."). Therefore, we must not flippantly enter into the idea of breaking apart this one-flesh relationship. It is designed to be the most cohesive relationship that a human can take part in.

We also believe—along with proponents of the first two views we discussed—that the marriage covenant is indissoluble. As Ephesians 5:22–33 clearly points out, the marriage covenant is to be a reflection of Christ's covenant with the church. Thus, if Christ will never break his covenant and leave the church, on what grounds could a Christian argue that this is legitimate? Once a man and a woman have entered this indissoluble covenant, God intends that it will endure for a lifetime. This is in keeping with our understanding of covenants throughout Scripture as well as statements about the marriage covenant in Romans 7:1–3. In fact, we could say that even death does not break a covenant, but rather fulfills the terms of a covenant between a husband and wife. Since this covenant is indissoluble, we do not believe that Scripture condones remarriage unless a spouse has died. Again, we follow along with proponents of the first two views that remarriage is expressly forbidden by Jesus in Matthew 5:32; Mark 10:2–12; and Luke 16:18, as well as by Paul in 1 Corinthians 7:10–11.

When we approach the exception clauses in Matthew, first we believe that they do not allow for remarriage. Speaking of Matthew 5:32, Wenham and Heth write: "First, the statement that divorce will cause the woman to become an adulteress is simply another way of condemning the second union she will most probably be obliged to contract in her situation. Second, the 'except for unchastity' clause . . . may mean no more than the fact that divorcing an unchaste woman would not *make* her an adulteress, for she probably is *already* an adulteress, adultery being the most common type of sexual offence covered by the term 'unchastity.'"[60] Thus, the first appearance of the exception clause merely states when adultery occurs—at remarriage unless the divorce was first brought about by the sexual immorality of one spouse. Matthew 5:32b seems to make it clear that anyone who marries

---

60. Wenham and Heth, *Jesus and Divorce*, 14–15.

a divorced person commits adultery, conceivably because the original marriage covenant is still in effect. The impact of Matthew 19:9 can be seen in much the same way, especially when we look at the disciples' reaction to Jesus' statement. They were surprised to find that Jesus would rather that a man remain unmarried than to remarry after a divorce.

It is on the matter of divorce itself that we walk a middle path between those who oppose divorce and those who allow for divorce in cases of adultery and abandonment but no remarriage. The exception clause in Matthew 19:9 gives us the best context for our middle path. Jesus is not making a blanket exception to allow for divorce in cases of adultery. Instead, his initial answer—"What therefore God has joined together, let no man separate" (Matt. 19:6b)—is the main idea. The exception in verse 9 is a restatement of the exception in 5:32 whereby Jesus explains when adultery occurs (at remarriage or due to sexual immorality during the marriage).

The reason that we do not side with the *divorce in limited circumstances but no remarriage* position at this point has to do with the earlier context of Matthew's Gospel. In the previous chapter, Jesus teaches on discipline and forgiveness. In his classic formulation for discipline, Jesus instructs his disciples to confront a fellow believer in private when the person is found to be in sin. The believer is then given the opportunity to repent. If that does not work, then we are to take one or two other believers with us and confront the believer again. If the sinful believer still refuses to repent, we take it to the church. Upon confrontation by the church, if the believer still refuses to repent, he or she is to be treated as a Gentile and tax collector—or an unbeliever (Matt. 18:15–17). In the verses that follow, Peter asks Jesus about forgiving his brother. Rather than simply forgiving his brother seven times, Jesus instructs Peter, he is to forgive his brother seventy times seven (vv. 21–22). The idea that Jesus proposes is that we should not keep count of the times we have forgiven. As Morris suggests: "This, of course, is not counseling an essay in arithmetic so that the seventy-eighth offense need not be forgiven. It is a way of saying that for Jesus' followers forgiveness is to be unlimited. For them forgiveness is a way of life. Bearing in mind what they have been forgiven, they cannot withhold forgiveness from any who sin against them."[61] The parable that follows in verses 23–35 drives home the point that we forgive those who sin against us because God has forgiven us of so much more.

In light of this teaching, the believer who finds that her spouse has committed adultery should confront him and follow the steps that Jesus laid out in the previous chapter. If none of those work, then she should consider him to be an unbeliever. All along the way, forgiveness is freely offered because God has forgiven so

---

61. Morris, *Matthew*, 472.

much more. Admittedly, this is a difficult teaching, and we must recognize that Jesus' teaching on forgiveness falls within a separate section from his teaching on marriage and divorce. But because the Holy Spirit inspired Matthew in the construction of his Gospel, it is worth noting that these two difficult teachings are back-to-back in the text.

If the situation reaches the point that the guilty party refuses to repent, then the innocent spouse is to consider him an unbeliever. Now we venture into the realm of 1 Corinthians 7:12–16. In his instructions to the church at Corinth, Paul tells the believer to remain married to an unbeliever as long as the unbelieving spouse consents to remain married (vv. 12–13). If the unbelieving spouse refuses to live with the believer, then the believer can accept a divorce (v. 15). Connecting this to the matter of adultery from Matthew 19, the innocent spouse offers forgiveness and calls the offending spouse to repent, walking through the steps of discipline from Matthew 18. Once the matter reaches the most extreme level and the guilty spouse is considered an unbeliever for lack of repentance, then the innocent party may accept a divorce from the guilty spouse if he does not consent to live with her. Such a response is consistent with Paul's summary of Jesus' teaching that believers should not divorce (1 Cor. 7:10–11) but also takes into account if a believer is not repentant and under discipline from the church.

After such a divorce, neither party has biblical warrant for remarriage because the covenant remains in place. As Romans 7:1–3 clearly states, the only event that would allow for remarriage is the death of a spouse. Again, we realize that our view may seem difficult to bear for some, but we believe it best fits the idea of worship. God has called us to worship him in every aspect of our lives. Walking through both the sublime and difficult experiences of marriage should benefit the process of sanctification. Unfortunately, many in our contemporary world encourage us to pursue the sublime and escape the difficult. Wenham and Heth summarize this idea best as they write, "In both Catholic and Protestant circles today the general trend is to move too quickly from a less-than-adequate exegesis of the relevant texts to an overly humanistic concern for the temporal happiness and wellbeing of the individuals involved."[62]

We have one last caveat before we conclude this topic. Some may argue that our position could place a vulnerable spouse in danger from abuse or neglect. Yet we do believe that in light of Paul's teaching in 1 Corinthians 7, it may very well be wise for a spouse who is facing abuse or serious neglect to physically separate from the abusive spouse for the protection of himself or herself and for the protection of any children. In fact, in many (perhaps most, depending on the situation in each individual case) cases, we further encourage including the use

---

62. Wenham and Heth, *Jesus and Divorce*, 40–41.

of legal mechanisms to ensure safety. But even in such cases, to be consistent with Paul's teaching in 1 Corinthians 7, we emphasize that the goal and intent of such a separation is not to seek divorce, but rather to pursue the proper context for restoration. Certainly, repentance, healing, and a long demonstrable history of fruit in keeping with repentance as overseen by the elders of a local church as well as other professional and legal entities are key to evaluating when a reunion would be in order. But the purpose is restoration. We do not believe that the Christian should pursue divorce, nor should the Christian pursue remarriage if the eventual outcome of that separation is divorce.

Conclusion

We have covered a significant amount of ground in this chapter—the biblical definition of *marriage*, the question of divorce and remarriage, and the connection of these to worship. As we have mentioned before, our desire in laying out this vision for marriage, divorce, and remarriage is not to create a list of rules and regulations that must be followed in order to fulfill a mandate. Instead, our desire is for all believers to live out the vision of marriage that Scripture gives us in order to love our God well and worship him fully. We believe this vision of marriage produces an attitude of worship directed toward the One who created marriage.

When lived out faithfully, this vision of marriage does not mean that life will be easy or simple. Uniting two people in the most intimate relationship possible has the effect of bringing two sinners in close proximity to each other. Dave Harvey writes:

> If you are married, or soon to be married, you are discovering that your marriage is not a romance novel. Marriage is the union of two people who arrive toting the luggage of life. And that luggage always contains sin. Often it gets opened right there on the honeymoon, sometimes it waits for the week after. But the suitcases are always there, sometimes tripping their owners, sometimes popping open unexpectedly and disgorging forgotten contents. We must not ignore our sin, because it is the very context where the gospel shines brightest.[63]

Despite the sin in our lives, we can depend on the Holy Spirit to strengthen us in marriage and to lead us in sanctification. Living out this vision of marriage is the outworking of a life of worship for this aspect of our lives.

---

63. Dave Harvey, *When Sinners Say "I Do"* (Wapwallopen, PA: Shepherd Press, 2007), 15–16.

Key Terms and Concepts

comprehensive union

covenant

divorce

divorce and remarriage in limited
  circumstances view

divorce in limited circumstances
  but no remarriage view

exception clauses

heterosexuality

monogamy

no divorce and no remarriage view

Obergefell v. Hodges

one-flesh union

remarriage

Key Scriptures

Genesis 1:26–28

Genesis 2:18–25

Deuteronomy 24:1–4

Proverbs 2:17

Jeremiah 3:1, 8, 14

Malachi 2:14–16

Matthew 5:32

Matthew 19:1–12

Mark 10:1–12

Luke 16:18

Romans 7:1–3

1 Corinthians 7

Ephesians 5:18–32

Study Questions

1. What are the key elements of the biblical definition of *marriage*? How does the biblical definition differ from definitions of *marriage* found in legal cases and government regulations? What makes the biblical definition of *marriage* superior?

2. Why is Genesis 1–2 such a significant passage for understanding God's design for marriage? What other passages are important for knowing and abiding by God's design for marriage?

3. What are the primary differences between the *divorce and remarriage in limited circumstances* view, the *divorce in limited circumstances but no remarriage* view, and the *no divorce and no remarriage* view?

4. What did Jesus teach about allowances for divorce and remarriage? What are the exception clauses? Why is one's interpretation of the exception clauses significant?

5. After studying the possible Christian views of divorce and remarriage, describe the view that best fits your understanding of the biblical passages.

For Further Reading

Ash, Christopher. *Married for God: Making Your Marriage the Best It Can Be.* Wheaton, IL: Crossway, 2016.

Gehring, René. *The Biblical "One Flesh" Theology of Marriage as Constituted in Genesis 2:24.* Eugene, OR: Wipf & Stock, 2013.

House, H. Wayne, ed. *Divorce and Remarriage: Four Christian Views.* Downers Grove, IL: InterVarsity Press, 1990.

Instone-Brewer, David. *Divorce and Remarriage in the Church.* Downers Grove, IL: InterVarsity Press, 2003.

Keller, Timothy. *The Meaning of Marriage: Facing the Complexities of Commitment with the Wisdom of God.* New York: Penguin, 2013.

Köstenberger, Andreas J., with David W. Jones. *God, Marriage, and Family: Rebuilding the Biblical Foundation.* 2nd ed. Wheaton, IL: Crossway, 2010.

Newheiser, Jim. *Marriage, Divorce, and Remarriage: Critical Questions and Answers.* Phillipsburg, NJ: P&R Publishing, 2017.

Piper, John. *This Momentary Marriage: A Parable of Permanence.* Wheaton, IL: Crossway, 2009.

Strauss, Mark L., ed. *Remarriage after Divorce in Today's Church: Three Views.* Grand Rapids: Zondervan, 2006.

Wenham, Gordon J., and William A. Heth. *Jesus and Divorce.* Updated ed. Eugene, OR: Wipf & Stock, 2002.

19

Contraception, Birth Control, and Reproductive Technologies

*"Behold, children are a gift of the Lord, the fruit of the womb is a reward.
Like arrows in the hand of a warrior, so are the children of one's youth.
How blessed is the man whose quiver is full of them; they will not be
ashamed when they speak with their enemies in the gate."*
—Psalm 127:3–5

*"The transmission of human life is a most serious role in which
married people collaborate freely and responsibly with God the Creator.
It has always been a source of great joy to them, even though it
sometimes entails many difficulties and hardships."*[1]
—Pope Paul VI, Humanae Vitae

Introduction

On June 30, 2014, the United States Supreme Court handed down a landmark ruling in *Burwell v. Hobby Lobby Stores, Inc.*[2] that allowed for privately held corporations to refuse to provide healthcare coverage for birth control if doing so would violate their religious liberty. At issue in this case was the Department of Health and Human Services (HHS) mandate issued in light of the Affordable Care Act of 2010 (so-called Obamacare) that would have required the owners of Hobby Lobby to provide birth-control coverage in their insurance plans even though doing so ran contrary to their "sincerely held religious beliefs." Ultimately, the Supreme

---

1. Paul VI, *Humanae Vitae* (1968), 1, accessed June 7, 2020, http://www.vatican.va/content/paul-vi/en /encyclicals/documents/hf_p-vi_enc_25071968_humanae-vitae.html.
2. 573 U.S. 682 (2014).

Court ruling affirmed the idea that private business owners do not need to give up their religious convictions and liberties when they go into business and that forcing Hobby Lobby to provide insurance coverage for birth control or pay huge fines was an unconstitutional choice.[3]

As important as this case was regarding First Amendment rights and the protection of religious liberty, the reason that the devoutly Christian owners of Hobby Lobby, David and Barbara Green, took the case to court in the first place was their concern regarding the potentially life-terminating effects that certain forms of birth control can have on unborn children. Interestingly enough, Hobby Lobby's typical healthcare plan included coverage for many types of contraception, including sterilization procedures for both men and women. Their "sincerely held religious belief," then, was not that all contraception was wrong. Rather, their particular concern was over specific types of birth-control drugs or devices that function (at least in part) to prevent the implantation of a fertilized egg in the uterus and thereby prevent pregnancy by causing the death of the newly conceived child.

This conviction held by the Greens regarding the nature of certain birth-control methods raises significant questions about the morality of contraception and birth control that would be wise for all of us to consider. Is it permissible for Christians to practice birth control? If so, are there any types of birth control that Christians should avoid? Indeed, if Scripture teaches that human life is sacred (the sanctity of human life) from the moment of conception, what are the implications of such teaching for issues related not only to contraception and birth control, but also to the many forms of reproductive technologies that require the manipulation of human gametes (eggs and sperm) and human embryos at the very beginning stages of life?

It goes without saying that matters of procreation and the various medical procedures related to topics such as contraception, birth control, and the use of reproductive technologies have a deeply personal element and can generate countless emotional responses. Nonetheless, because, in his loving-kindness, God desires all areas of our life to be shaped by his wise and good counsel both for his glory and for our good, it is important to seek the wisdom of Scripture and thereby shape our character and worship even (or especially) in these arenas of life. Our loving Father—the One who invented sex and who seeks to fill the world with worshipers—has what is best for us in his mind and on his heart. Thankfully, he has revealed his good moral wisdom to us through his Word.

It is our goal in this chapter, then, to explore the rich wisdom of Scripture and beseech the Holy Spirit to guide us in how we ought to worship God in spirit and

---

3. For further information on this case, see https://caselaw.findlaw.com/us-supreme-court/13-354.html.

truth in regard to the topics of contraception, birth control, and reproductive technologies. In order to do so, we begin by highlighting key terms and concepts to shape the basic framework of the conversation. Next, we will consider the relevant scriptural passages that ought to shape the theological and normative elements of our discussion. Finally, we then explore the ethical implications of these concepts and principles as they relate specifically to various forms of contraception, birth control, and humanly devised methods of combating infertility through the use of various forms of reproductive technology.

Key Terms and Definitions

As is the case with all other ethical topics, it is important to define our terms at the beginning of this conversation so as to provide both clarity and precision when discussing sensitive matters and thereby avoid unnecessary misunderstandings. We begin, then, by defining four separate terms. The first two, *contraception* and *birth control*, are related to the prevention of procreation, while the other two, *infertility* and *assisted reproductive technology*, are terms closely associated with pursuing procreation.

Contraception and Birth Control

The terms *contraception* and *birth control* are often used synonymously, but they are not identical. *Birth control* is a much larger category than *contraception*. In fact, it can be said that all forms of contraception are birth control, but not all forms of birth control are contraception. This will be an important distinction later in this chapter as we seek to apply biblical principles to the ethical issues surrounding contraception and birth control.

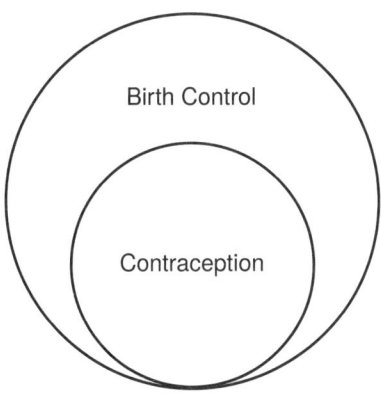

Fig. 19.1. Birth Control and Contraception

Contraception derives from the Latin prefix *contra*, meaning "against," and the term *conception*. Therefore, the basic idea of the term is the prevention of fertilization that could lead to a pregnancy. When we consider contraceptive measures, we should note that contraception works exclusively toward the end of inhibiting conception from taking place. We will go into more detail in the pages that follow, but contraception includes measures such as abstinence, the rhythm or calendar method, and any action that prevents sperm from coming into contact with eggs.

By contrast, *birth control* is any means that seeks to prevent birth from occurring. Since all forms of contraception attempt to prevent birth by impeding conception, contraception is by definition birth control. Yet there are methods of birth control that do not prevent pregnancy by preventing conception, but rather that cause *postconception effects* that directly lead to the death of an otherwise healthy and growing conceived child. Specifically, these forms of birth control function either to prevent a fertilized egg (a living, conceived child) from implanting in the uterine wall of the mother, thereby causing its death, or to cause the fertilized egg (a living, conceived child) to be expelled from the mother's womb after it has implanted in the uterine wall (pregnancy), thereby causing its death. Thus, while contraception works only to prevent conception, some forms of birth control prevent birth through the death of the conceived child. Abortion, for example, clearly "controls birth," but it does so by directly and intentionally causing the death of the conceived child after it has implanted in the uterine wall. Likewise, a major moral question is raised regarding certain other forms of birth control (such as IUDs and all chemical versions of "the pill") because of their potential to prevent a living, conceived child from implanting in the uterine wall. We will return to a discussion of these topics as the chapter progresses. At this point, we reiterate that in light of these concerns, Christians are wise to not use the terms *contraception* and *birth control* as though they were synonyms.

Infertility

Having looked at the key terms related to preventing conception and birth, we now turn our attention to the terms associated with the pursuit of conception.

Infertility is the inability to conceive after twelve or more months of regular sexual intercourse that is not impeded by contraceptive means or measures. As women age and fertility is known to decline, some medical professionals may diagnose infertility after only six months of inability to conceive if the woman is over the age of thirty-five.[4] Infertility is a relatively common problem in the

---

4. Centers for Disease Control and Prevention (CDC), "Infertility FAQs," accessed June 8, 2020, https://www.cdc.gov/reproductivehealth/infertility/index.htm. See also World Health Organization, "Infertility Definitions and Terminology," accessed June 8, 2020, https://www.who.int/reproductivehealth/topics/infertility/definitions/en/.

United States. The Centers for Disease Control and Prevention (CDC) reports: "About 6% of married women aged 15 to 44 years in the United States are unable to get pregnant after one year of trying (infertility). Also, about 12% of women aged 15 to 44 years in the United States have difficulty getting pregnant or carrying a pregnancy to term, regardless of marital status (impaired fecundity)."[5]

Among women, infertility is generally linked to a disruption to the proper function of the ovaries, fallopian tubes, or uterus. Disruption to the ovaries can include failure to ovulate regularly (or at all), a diminished reserve of available eggs, improper function of the hypothalamus and pituitary glands, and menopause. When the ovaries do not function properly, then an egg is not released, preventing sperm from fertilizing an egg. An obstruction of the fallopian tubes can also prevent egg and sperm from coming into contact. Abnormalities in the uterus, including fibroids, may also prevent conception.[6] The disruption to proper function of the ovaries, fallopian tubes, or uterus can be the result of medical conditions, genetic factors, or choices and behaviors that impact the body's ability to reproduce. Even though infertility is the inability to conceive, women may also have difficulty carrying a pregnancy to term. Such difficulty is called *impaired fecundity*.[7]

While many people may believe that infertility is primarily a problem that women face, men can also experience infertility. The CDC notes:

> Many couples struggle with infertility and seek help to become pregnant, but it is often thought of as only a woman's condition. However, in about 35% of couples with infertility, a male factor is identified along with a female factor. In about 8% of couples with infertility, a male factor is the only identifiable cause. Almost 9% of men aged 25 to 44 years in the United States reported that they or their partner saw a doctor for advice, testing, or treatment for infertility during their lifetime.[8]

Male infertility is generally linked to testicular disruption, hormonal disorders, or genetic disorders.[9] Just like female infertility, male infertility can be brought on by medical conditions, genetic factors, or choices and behavior that have an adverse impact on one's ability to reproduce.

Biblically speaking, Scripture is clear that like all other human infirmities (diabetes, cancer, and so forth), the ultimate causal element of infertility is human rebellion against God and the resulting "groaning" of creation that we read about

5. CDC, "Infertility FAQs."
6. CDC, "Infertility FAQs."
7. CDC, "Infertility FAQs."
8. CDC, "Infertility FAQs."
9. CDC, "Infertility FAQs."

in both Genesis 3 and Romans 8:22. That is, *infertility is a product of the fall.* Sin breaks the world, and this reality has implications for all areas of human existence. Now, certainly, in some cases personal moral choices may contribute to or cause a person's inability to naturally reproduce. But in the vast majority of cases in which an individual or a couple experiences issues of infertility, the inability of a person's body to contribute to the birth of a biologically related child is a natural by-product of living in a fallen world.

In addition to this physical "breaking" of the creation and its resulting impact on our ability to physically procreate, the emotional toll of infertility can also be staggering. This is especially so for couples who long to fulfill the biblical mandate to "be fruitful and multiply" (Gen. 1:28), yet find themselves unable to conceive a child of their own. The most poignant biblical example of this emotional struggle is found in 1 Samuel 1:1–18 as Hannah pours out her soul to the Lord in the face of the mistreatment she has received from her husband's other wife. In verses 6–7, we read: "Her rival, however, would provoke her bitterly to irritate her, because the LORD had closed her womb. It happened year after year, as often as she went up to the house of the LORD, she would provoke her; so she wept and would not eat." On this particular trip to offer sacrifices, Hannah cries out to God with such emotion that Eli the priest thinks she is drunk. In the face of Eli's accusation of drunkenness, she replies: "No, my lord, I am a woman oppressed in spirit; I have drunk neither wine nor strong drink, but I have poured out my soul before the LORD. Do not consider your maidservant as a worthless woman, for I have spoken until now out of my great concern and provocation" (vv. 15–16). Even in this brief interaction between Hannah and Eli brought about by the provocation of Peninnah, we can see the great heartache that infertility can bring when someone truly longs to have a child but cannot do so.

In light of both the physical and emotional struggles related to infertility, it is extremely important that we take care to love well and show compassion toward those who may be experiencing this unfortunate reality. At the very least, we must be extremely careful not to jump to the conclusion that a person's inability to conceive a child naturally is somehow tied to personal choices, the repercussions of sinful acts, or God's disfavor. More positively, Christians must learn to be sensitive, show discernment, and consider positive ways to address and speak to these issues in the church so as to help those struggling with these issues. It is important that the church seek to minister to those struggling in this area in such a way as to help individuals and couples:

1. Remain biblically grounded;
2. Find their ultimate hope not in childbirth but in God's tender care for the broken and downhearted;

3. Explore the beautiful means of growing a family through adoption;
4. Learn what biblically and morally acceptable means and methods of reproductive technologies are available within a Christian worldview; and
5. Know that God's love for them is never-ceasing.

With these thoughts in mind, then, as is the case with all other forms of medical treatment, we as Christians can also positively affirm both the desire for a person to seek medical assistance in overcoming infertility and many of the means to do so as long as those means or methods do not transgress God's moral instruction regarding the sanctity of life or the sacred nature of Christian marriage. Indeed, generally speaking, we applaud the development of medical treatments in all areas, including the treatment of infertility. As Wayne Grudem states: "God put resources in the earth for us to discover and develop, including resources that are useful for medicinal purposes, and he gave us the wisdom and the desire to do this. . . . Therefore, it seems morally right to support and welcome advances in medicine that today can bring health to people with various diseases and disabilities, including infertility."[10]

As is the case with all other medical advances, there is always the potential for negative consequences or applications associated with their development or use. Thus, our affirmation of reproductive technologies *in general* must not be taken to mean a total endorsement of all medical use. Rather, we affirm the good grace of God to enable medical technology to mitigate human suffering that results from the fall. But as is the case with all human technologies, biblical principles must be employed to guide their proper and moral application. Once again, we will address several of these points of concern later in the chapter.

Assisted Reproductive Technology[11]

The field of *assisted reproductive technology (ART)* is a realm of human ingenuity and medical treatment that is not only rapidly changing and advancing, but also fraught with many ethical questions and concerns. Most Christians are only vaguely familiar with the many and varied methods of assisted reproduction, and likewise few have adequately wrestled through all the relevant ethical questions and implications related to them. Indeed, most trained ethicists can barely keep up with the frenzied pace of technological development and the broad scope of related moral questions.

The CDC defines *ART* as follows:

10. Wayne Grudem, *Christian Ethics: An Introduction to Biblical Moral Reasoning* (Wheaton, IL: Crossway, 2018), 764–65.

11. This section is adapted from Evan Lenow, "Is It Adultery? The Use of Third-Party Gametes in Assisted Reproductive Technology," *SWJT* 59, no. 1 (Fall 2016): 43–44. Used by permission.

ART includes all fertility treatments in which both eggs and sperm are handled. In general, ART procedures involve surgically removing eggs from a woman's ovaries, combining them with sperm in the laboratory, and returning them to the woman's body or donating them to another woman. They do NOT include treatments in which only sperm are handled (i.e., intrauterine—or artificial—insemination) or procedures in which a woman takes medicine only to stimulate egg production without the intention of having eggs retrieved.[12]

Despite the limitation placed on the definition of *ART* by the CDC, we will employ this term to include reproductive technologies that involve the use of sperm as well as those that involve the use of both egg and sperm. The most common forms of ART are intrauterine insemination (IUI), gamete intrafallopian transfer (GIFT), in vitro fertilization (IVF), and surrogacy.[13] We will briefly discuss each in turn.

Intrauterine insemination (IUI), which is also known as *artificial insemination (AI)*, is usually the first option chosen by infertile couples when the problem of infertility resides chiefly in the male. The usual problem is either low sperm count or, for whatever reason, defective sperm. Relatively simple in nature, this procedure involves the collection and accumulation of male sperm and then the injection of that sperm (usually with a needle-less syringe) into the female uterus during the most fertile part of a woman's cycle. The hope, then, is that the reproductive process would proceed from that point along "natural" lines. This procedure can take place with either the husband's sperm (AIH: artificial insemination husband) or a donor's sperm (AID: artificial insemination donor). Ethically speaking, there are far fewer problems with AIH than AID (see discussion below).

Gamete intrafallopian transfer (GIFT) is the procedure by which female eggs are harvested through the use of superovulatory hormonal drugs stimulating the maturation and release of several eggs. These eggs are then harvested by means of a minor surgical procedure utilizing ultrasound guidance in the vagina. The male semen is also collected and then treated to make it less viscous, facilitating the conception process. These gametes are then placed together in a single catheter, separated only by a tiny air bubble, and placed together in the woman's fallopian tubes. The procedure facilitates the reproductive process by ensuring

---

12. CDC, "What Is Assisted Reproductive Technology?," accessed June 8, 2020, http://www.cdc.gov/art/whatis.html. In addition to the technologies involving the manipulation of both egg and sperm, our discussion on assisted reproductive technology will also encompass technologies wherein only sperm are handled. We will explore the various technologies in more detail later in the chapter.

13. The following descriptions are adapted from Mark Liederbach, "Artificial Reproductive Technologies," in *God, Marriage, and Family*, by Andreas J. Köstenberger with David W. Jones, 2nd ed. (Wheaton, IL: Crossway, 2010), 130–31.

contact between egg and sperm and thus raising the probability that conception will occur and pregnancy begin.

In vitro fertilization (IVF) is very similar to GIFT in technical procedure but has one major distinction. While in the GIFT procedure fertilization and conception take place within a woman's body, in the case of IVF fertilization takes place in an artificial environment (*in vitro* literally means "in glass," referring to the "test tube" or petri dish where conception occurs). As with GIFT, the woman receives hormonal treatments in order to stimulate the release of multiple eggs, which are then harvested for use in the procedure. Male sperm is also collected, and these gametes (eggs and sperm) are then placed in the same petri dish, in hopes that as many conceptions as possible will take place. The reproductive technician will then screen the newly formed embryos and, via embryo transfer (ET), will attempt to implant as many as four of the embryos into the woman's uterus, in hopes that she will become pregnant with at least one. The remaining embryos will then be either destroyed or frozen for use in future birthing attempts. Studies indicate that survival rates for frozen embryos range from 69 to 88 percent based on the stage at which they were frozen but that only 14 to 15 percent of embryos that survive thawing actually implant in the uterus.[14]

Surrogacy or *surrogate motherhood* refers to the procedure in which the gestation and birth of a baby occur in either a woman who is not the child's biological mother or a woman who is willing to donate her egg and carry a child but relinquishes parenting rights to those contracting with her to carry the child. Thus, *genetic surrogacy* results from an IUI procedure whereby the husband of a given couple donates his sperm in order for the surrogate to conceive, carry the child through gestation, and then give birth. While genetically related to the surrogate mother, this baby "belongs" to the couple that contracted with her to carry and birth the child. *Gestational surrogacy* differs from genetic surrogacy in that the conception of the child takes place via GIFT or IVF and the embryo is then placed by way of ET into the surrogate mother. The role of the surrogate in this case is to carry and give birth to the child, not to conceive or donate her egg. In both forms of surrogacy, it is often the case that the surrogate mother, in exchange for a fee, will enter a contract and agree to release all rights to parent the child once it is born.[15]

---

14. Mary Ellen Pavone et al., "Comparing Thaw Survival, Implantation and Live Birth Rates from Cryopreserved Zygotes, Embryos and Blastocysts," *Journal of Human Reproductive Sciences* 4, no. 1 (January–April 2011): 23–28, accessed June 15, 2020, https://www.ncbi.nlm.nih.gov/pmc/articles/PMC3136065/#.

15. Scott B. Rae, *Moral Choices: An Introduction to Ethics*, 4th ed. (Grand Rapids: Zondervan, 2018), 169–70. For additional information on intrauterine insemination, in vitro fertilization, and related issues, see Gary P. Stewart, John F. Kilner, and William R. Cutrer, eds., *Basic Questions on Sexuality and Reproductive Technology: When Is It Right to Intervene?* (Grand Rapids: Kregel, 1998); John F. Kilner, Paige C. Cunningham, and W. David

When taken into consideration, these reproductive technologies can raise numerous ethical questions that ought to be addressed. Unfortunately, our experience has been that many Christians accept these advances in medical science uncritically without using biblical and theological guidelines to help discern whether these technologies are at the very least morally allowable and can ultimately be affirmed as means by which we can maximally worship God and fully flourish in the way that God designed. For this reason, we now turn to consider the biblical and theological principles related to contraception, birth control, and infertility.

<h2 style="text-align:center">Biblical and Theological Principles Related to
Contraception, Birth Control, and Infertility</h2>

As we seek to worship God fully through the challenges brought on by contraception, birth control, and infertility, we must consider the principles that will guide us through the difficult conversations. We are not left to our own devices to navigate the world of technology or to ask whether we are morally permitted to interfere with the procreative process. Four guiding principles will help us to discern how best to worship our Creator in relation to these issues.

Sanctity of Human Life

The first guiding principle for theological reflection on matters of contraception, birth control, and reproductive technologies is the *sanctity of human life*. We have discussed this principle at length in previous chapters (13–16 on capital punishment, war, abortion, and euthanasia), but a brief review of this principle is warranted here. The principle of the sanctity of human life holds that human life is sacred because all humans are made in the image of God (Gen. 1:26–27). Biblical passages such as Genesis 1:26–27; 9:6; Psalm 8:3–8; and James 3:9 all indicate that God places a high and unique value on human life because human beings carry the special status of *image-bearers*.

For this reason, Scripture also clearly prohibits the taking of innocent human life. The commandment "You shall not murder" (Ex. 20:13) applies to all human beings who have not relinquished their right to life through ungodly or immoral behavior as specified in Scripture. As we noted in the previous chapters on issues related to life and death, the Hebrew word in this verse that is translated into English as "murder" is *ratsakh*. While the closest word we have in English to

---

Hager, eds., *The Reproduction Revolution: A Christian Appraisal of Sexuality, Reproductive Technologies, and the Family* (Grand Rapids: Eerdmans, 2000); and John F. Kilner and C. Ben Mitchell, *Does God Need Our Help? Cloning, Assisted Suicide, and Other Challenges in Bioethics*, ed. Daniel Taylor (Wheaton, IL: Tyndale, 2003).

rutsukh is *murder*, the word actually carries a meaning that not only includes the unjust killing of innocent human beings, but also includes "negligent homicide," in which death results from a failure to take adequate precautions to guard and protect human life.[16] This unique and protected status as image-bearer, therefore, begins from the moment that the life of a human being begins—conception—and extends to the point of death.[17]

This guiding principle is important in discussions of contraception and reproductive technologies because many of the methods and technologies related to these issues not only run the risk of directly causing the death of conceived children, but also create the adverse conditions within a mother's body that make survival of the child after conception perilous.

The Sacred Nature of Marriage and God's Design for Childbearing within the Context of Marriage

The second guiding principle that must shape our understanding of these issues relates to the *sacred nature of marriage* and its place as the God-ordained context for procreation and child-rearing. As we discussed in our earlier chapters on sexuality (chapter 17) and marriage (chapter 18), God designed childbearing to take place within the context of marriage. We will not repeat the full extent of the arguments that we made in those earlier chapters, but we want to remind our readers of the basic contours of those arguments.

First, we noted in our biblical definition of *marriage* that God designed marriage to be a comprehensive, covenantal union between one man and one woman intended to endure for a lifetime and proximally *directed toward the rearing of the next generation*. From the earliest record of God's creation of mankind (Gen. 1.26–28), we see that God intended for humans to populate the earth with worshipers who would bear his image and flourish in God's creation. The context for childbearing is further described in Genesis 2, where God instituted marriage as the relationship through which man and woman would "become one flesh" (2:24).

Second, we noted in our earlier discussion on marriage that God designed the marriage relationship with three good ends in mind—the procreation of children, the unity between the husband and wife, and the sacramental element that orders the marriage relationship toward God as an act of worship.[18] That is, the marriage

---

16. John M. Frame, *The Doctrine of the Christian Life* (Phillipsburg, NJ: P&R Publishing, 2008), 686–87, 687n2. See our discussion in chapter 16.

17. For a detailed argument on the value of life beginning at conception, see our sections "Personhood Objections" and "Autonomy Objections" in chapter 16. For a discussion on the definition of *death*, see our discussion in chapter 16.

18. In his work *De Bono Coniugali* ("On the Good of Marriage"), Augustine notes three goods of marriage—offspring, fidelity (or faith in chastity), and sacrament. The three purposes of sex as developed from

relationship is meant to provide a beautiful picture of Christ's relationship with the church (Eph. 5:18–33). These three ends of marriage, in turn, relate directly to the three primary purposes for which God created sex—procreation, unity, and sexual purity.[19] Building on these ideas, we also see that God designed childbearing to take place within the context of marriage.

This guiding principle is important in discussions of reproductive technologies because advancements in these procedures now allow for the introduction of a person outside the context of marriage to be part of the procreative process. For example, surrogate motherhood introduces the possibility of a woman's functioning as a gestational carrier for a child to whom she has no biological connection. The use of donor sperm, eggs, or both allows for a couple to bring a child into the world by intentionally introducing another biological parent who may not have any parental responsibilities for rearing that child. The use of nonmarital contributors in the procreative process raises several questions that we will address later in the chapter.

Children Are a Blessing from the Lord

A third guiding principle that should shape our view on these issues relates to God's pronouncement regarding *children as a blessing*. From the earliest pages of the Bible, we learn that children are a part of God's blessing to Adam and Eve. Genesis 1:28 tells us that "God blessed them; and God said to them, 'Be fruitful and multiply, and fill the earth.'" Psalm 127:3 reinforces this idea when it teaches us that "children are a gift of the LORD, the fruit of the womb is a reward."

Therefore, one of the initial questions that Christians should ask themselves when considering the use of contraception and birth control is why one would want to prevent having children in the first place. Indeed, in our contemporary Western society, there is a growing trend to view children as a burden that must

---

Augustine are procreation (offspring), sexual purity (fidelity), and unity (sacrament). Although we do not take the sacramental language of Augustine's formulation to have any soteriological significance in our discussion of the purposes of sex and marriage, it should be noted that a sacramental understanding of marriage developed from Augustine's formulation as the Roman Catholic Church developed its sacramental theology. Most, however, believe that Augustine was not using the Latin term *sacramentum* in the technical sense of a sacrament in this specific work. See Augustine, *De Bono Coniugali*, in *The Fathers of the Church: A New Translation*, trans. Charles T. Wilcox, vol. 27 (New York: Fathers of the Church, 1955), 24–32.

19. There is healthy discussion on what the purposes of sex are. Dennis Hollinger has proposed four purposes of sex—consummation of marriage, procreation, love, and pleasure. John and Paul Feinberg suggest six purposes of sex—procreation, companionship, unity, pleasure, to raise up a godly seed, and curbing fornication and adultery. J. Budziszewski proposes only two purposes of sex—procreation and union. While we consider all three contributions to be useful, we lean on the goods of marriage developed by Augustine to form the foundation for the purposes we propose. See Dennis P. Hollinger, *The Meaning of Sex: Christian Ethics and the Moral Life* (Grand Rapids: Baker, 2009), 93–115; John S. Feinberg and Paul D. Feinberg, *Ethics for a Brave New World*, 2nd ed. (Wheaton, IL: Crossway, 2010), 300–302; J. Budziszewski, *On the Meaning of Sex* (Wilmington, DE: ISI, 2012), 24–33.

be endured rather than a blessing to be welcomed and treasured. Our very language used to describe even our sexual relationships within marriage betrays this inverted view of children when we speak of "safe sex" or "protected sex." Do we mean by this as Christians that we want to be "saved" from God's blessings? Do we mean that we want to be "protected" from God's blessing us?

This does not automatically lead to the conclusion that the use of contraceptive measures to limit a family size is necessarily wrong or immoral. This is not our point here, nor is it the conclusion that we will reach about the use of contraception in this chapter. But we do believe that a consideration of God's pronouncement about the good blessings he desires to give us from having and raising children within a marriage context ought to at least make us pause and consider whether our value systems regarding the having and rearing of children have been unwittingly compromised (or even inverted). Is it possible that our perspectives on having and raising kids reflect a deeper underlying belief that children are more a burden than a blessing? Could it be that our attitudes about "protecting" our sex lives from children reflect the underlying belief that having more money or having less responsibility for others is of higher value than raising godly offspring? While we are unwilling to lay such a conclusion on any given couple, it is worthwhile for us to ask such questions in light of God's clear teaching about the value of children.

Consider the further teaching of Psalm 127:3–5:

> Behold, children are a gift of the LORD,
> The fruit of the womb is a reward.
> Like arrows in the hand of a warrior,
> So are the children of one's youth.
> How blessed is the man whose quiver is full of them;
> They will not be ashamed
> When they speak with their enemies in the gate.

Notice, first, how the psalmist describes children in this passage. They are to be understood and received as a "gift" with inherent value in their own right. The having and rearing of children itself is a part of God's grace to humans.

Second, notice how the psalmist describes children as arrows in the hand of a warrior and ascribes a special blessing to those whose quivers are full. There are two ways to look at children as "arrows." One way is to see that they are to be shot out from the parent's bow to further the legacy and mission of the parent. In this line of thinking, a warrior would work diligently to ensure that his arrows were straight and flew effectively from his bow in order to accomplish the task he set out for them. In the same way, parents are to work diligently to shape and mold their children so that they can be sent out to accomplish the purposes of their training. In the Old Testament, children were viewed as a blessing or gift because they would continue the family's heritage through the inheritance of the land.[20] The specific emphasis on godly children further fulfills the idea that God commanded the first man and woman to fill the earth with godly worshipers. Not having children, then, was a problem in ancient Israel because in that specific context, lack of children would constitute a failure to fulfill God's command to be fruitful and multiply. In this sense, then, God designed marriage to be a missional endeavor and a part of God's means for filling the earth with worshipers.

Another way that we can view children as arrows in the hand of a warrior is in the sense that they will protect their parents in their old age. Such care for an elderly parent fits the psalmist's description in Psalm 127:5 that the parent will not be ashamed before the enemies at the gate because his or her children will be there to offer a defense. One of the many struggles that childless individuals have is finding people to care for them when they cannot care for themselves. But children function in that role naturally to return the care to their parents that they received as children. Paul further emphasizes this point as he writes to Timothy, "Honor widows who are widows indeed; but if any widow has children or grandchildren, they must first learn to practice piety in regard to their own family and to make some return to their parents; for this is acceptable in the sight of God. . . . But if anyone does not provide for his own, and especially for those of his household, he has denied the faith and is worse than an unbeliever" (1 Tim. 5:3–4, 8). Paul makes it clear that if a child has an elderly parent who cannot care for himself or herself, it is the child's responsibility to care for that parent. Failure to do so is a denial of the faith.

As we can see from this passage and the overall perspective from Scripture, children are a blessing from the Lord. They are to be treasured and sent out with a purpose. Therefore, as we discuss matters related to contraception, birth control, and reproductive technologies, we need to keep in mind that children are a blessing, not a burden. Also, we need to remember that the fruit of the womb is a reward from God, not merely a commodity that we can decide to decline or receive based on our own felt needs or desires.

God's Sovereign Providence over Procreation

Finally, a fourth principle that ought to be considered when evaluating the moral use of contraception, birth control, and reproductive technology has to do

---

20. Willem A. VanGemeren, "Psalms," in *Psalms, Proverbs, Ecclesiastes, Song of Songs*, ed. Frank E. Gaebelein, Expositor's Bible Commentary 5 (Grand Rapids: Zondervan, 1991), 794. VanGemeren states, "The concern of the Israelite was not only that he would have children but particularly that he would have sons, and more particularly that they would be godly sons."

with keeping a right perspective on God's *sovereign control* over the process of the creation and taking of human life.

Medical technology has allowed us unprecedented insight into the processes of procreation. From understanding how eggs are fertilized to being able to observe a child in the womb, we have never before known more about the development of a child from conception to birth than we know now. With this knowledge and medical technology, we may also reach the conclusion that we can control every aspect of the procreation process, especially when the process does not work as it ought to. The unfortunate component of this perspective is that we may lose sight of the fact that God is the One who opens and closes the womb. Yes, we are now able to prevent conception more effectively than ever before, and we are able to address matters of infertility in ways that were unimaginable fifty years ago. Scripture still assures us, however, that God is the sovereign Ruler over all aspects of creation and that through his divine providence, he determines how and when conception will take place (Ps. 139:13–16).

Consider a few examples of individuals whose journeys through infertility and childbirth involved direct action on the part of the Lord. Scattered throughout the biblical narrative of the marriage of Abraham and Sarah (Gen. 11:29–23:2) are numerous promises regarding a child who will be an heir to Abraham and the seed of a great people (12:1–3; 15:1–6; 17:1–22; 18:9–15), but the problem was that Sarah "was barren; she had no child" (11:30; cf. 16:1). Sarah even went so far as to say, "Now behold, the LORD has prevented me from bearing children" (16:2). As the years progressed, Sarah had still not borne a child, and Abraham had fathered a child with Sarah's maid Hagar. Yet God still planned to keep his promise to Abraham to make him a great nation and to give him an heir through his wife. Finally, when Abraham was ninety-nine and Sarah was eighty-nine years old, the Lord appeared to them along with three angelic visitors and made a promise to them that Sarah would bear a child the next year (18:9–15). The Lord fulfilled his promise to Abraham and Sarah in Genesis 21:1–2, where we read, "Then the LORD took note of Sarah as He had said, and the LORD did for Sarah as He had promised. So Sarah conceived and bore a son to Abraham in his old age, at the appointed time of which God had spoken to him." The son born to Abraham and Sarah was Isaac, and he was the heir through whom God would begin to fulfill his promise to Abraham. Throughout the process, Scripture makes it clear that God was at work in preventing Sarah from conceiving and then allowing her to conceive.

We find a similar description in 1 Samuel 1 of the struggle that Hannah had in bearing a child. In verse 5, we see that "the LORD had closed her womb." Hannah endured ridicule from her rival, the other wife of her husband, because she had no children. Through the priest Eli, God made a promise to her that he would fulfill her prayer for a son. Upon Hannah's returning to their home after offering

668   *The Application of Ethics as Worship*

a sacrifice, "the LORD remembered her" (v. 19), and she conceived a son with her husband, Elkanah. This son was Samuel, who served as both priest and judge over Israel and anointed Saul and David as king. Once again, we see God's handiwork in the process of both closing and opening the womb.

One further example, which we see from the New Testament, is the life of Zacharias and Elizabeth (Luke 1:5–80). When Luke introduces us to this couple, he tells us that "they had no child, because Elizabeth was barren, and they were both advanced in years" (v. 7). As Zacharias performed his priestly function, he was chosen to enter the temple. It was here that an angel of the Lord appeared to him and promised that God had heard their prayers and that Elizabeth would bear a son. The angel also gave him further instructions to name the child John (vv. 11–13). We eventually come to know this child as John the Baptist, the one who prepared the way for Jesus' earthly ministry.

In each of these cases, God was gracious and allowed these women to conceive and bear children who would in due course play major roles in his redemptive plan. Arguably, however, God does not always act through miraculous means to overcome a couple's infertility. In recent years, advances in modern reproductive technology have paved the way for otherwise infertile couples to give birth to children of their own. In light of these advances, how should Christians respond? Is it appropriate to take advantage of these new technologies? There are those who would argue that prayer and faith alone are the proper response of Christians in the face of infertility.[21] Most Christians, however, relying on the fact that God created human beings with the ability to reason and gave them dominion over the earth (Gen. 1:28–31), do not reject the use of medical intervention as long as the type of intervention does not violate other clear principles of Scripture (e.g., the sanctity of human life).[22]

What we must remember is that God is still providentially in control over all his creation. While advances in medical technology allow us to more effectively subdue and rule over creation, God is still the One who opens and closes the womb. Therefore, we must encourage those who desire to overcome infertility and those who seek to prevent pregnancy not only to cast their cares on the Lord because it is he who opens and closes the womb, but also to approach the process with a humble posture of prayer and willing obedience, lest a desire to have or prevent children be pursued by means contrary to the commands of God.

---

21. This is hardly satisfactory, however, since, to be consistent, the proponents of this kind of argument would also have to conclude that the use of any medical intervention for a medical problem is likewise inappropriate.

22. Thus, while different in nature from the direct and gracious intervention of God on behalf of Sarah, Hannah, and Elizabeth, these new medical procedures are nonetheless wondrous in their own right.

Table 19.1. Four Principles That Ought to Shape Our Perspectives on Contraception, Birth Control, and Reproductive Technologies

Table 19.1. Four Principles That Ought to Shape Our Perspectives on Contraception, Birth Control, and Reproductive Technologies

1. The Sanctity of Human Life
2. The Sacredness of Marriage
3. Children as a Blessing
4. The Sovereign Providence of God

Ethical Implications Related to Contraception, Birth Control, and Reproductive Technologies

A number of ethical issues and concerns are related to the use of contraception, birth control, and reproductive technologies. Our exploration of these issues would be simpler if Scripture addressed them directly, but most of these matters were not conceivable to the biblical writers. As a result, we must rely on the biblical principles identified in the previous section to help us navigate the contemporary context.

Contraception and Birth Control[23]

The Bible does not use the term *contraception*, nor are there any biblical texts that specifically and directly address whether it might be appropriate to use contraceptive measures. Despite this lack of direct instruction, one should not assume that Scripture is completely silent on the matter. The task at hand is to identify the appropriate moral principles (as we have done above) and then seek to apply them to the questions being asked in the modern context.

The Question of the Legitimacy of Contraception in General

Historically speaking, Christians from across the denominational landscape initially stood in opposition to the use of contraception. Beginning with the Lambeth Conference in 1930, however, Anglicans opened the door to acceptance of contraception, and most other Protestants followed suit, concluding with a complete acceptance of the birth-control pill shortly after its release.[24] A case in point is the trajectory that Southern Baptists took on the issue. In 1934, Southern Baptists passed the "Resolution on Birth Control" that urged Congress to reject pending legislation that would allow for the dissemination of information

---

23. Portions of this section are adapted from Mark Liederbach, "Contraception," in *God, Marriage, and Family*, by Andreas J. Köstenberger with David W. Jones, 2nd ed. (Wheaton, IL: Crossway, 2010), 121–29.

24. Mary Eberstadt, *Adam and Eve after the Pill: Paradoxes of the Sexual Revolution* (San Francisco: Ignatius, 2012), 149–56.

concerning contraceptives and birth control because, they argued, "whatever the intent and motive of such proposal we cannot but believe that such legislation would be vicious in character and would prove seriously detrimental to the morals of our nation."[25]

Forty years later, however, Southern Baptists changed their stance from one that viewed birth control as detrimental to the nation as a whole to opposing only the distribution of contraceptives and birth control to minors at school without parental consent.[26] Many other Protestant denominations (e.g., United Methodist Church, Assemblies of God, Presbyterian Church [U.S.A.], Evangelical Lutheran Church in America) followed a similar trajectory. Eventually, most mainline Protestant denominations expressed direct or implicit support for the moral use of contraception for various reasons, including family planning and to fight the spread of sexually transmitted disease. Many did so with "little theological reflection."[27]

As noted earlier in the chapter, Genesis 1:28 identifies procreation as one of God's designed purposes of sexual intercourse within the context of marriage, and Psalm 127 describes children as a blessing from the Lord. When considering the question whether to use contraception, one must start from the perspective that having children is the expected norm in marriage and that children are a gift from a loving heavenly Father. Children are a blessing to be enjoyed rather than a burden to be carried. Therefore, we need to start our conversation about the legitimacy of contraception in general by noting that intentional childlessness within marriage is not God's creation-order design.

In light of the theological connection between sexual expression and childbearing, however, is it necessary that every act of sexual intercourse must "be open" to conception? Those who answer this question in the affirmative will often cite the account of Onan and Tamar in Genesis 38:6–10 to support their position. From the surrounding context of this passage, we learn that God put to death a man named Er, who was the older son of Judah, because he was "evil in the sight of the LORD." This death, in turn, left Er's wife, Tamar, a widow. In such a situation, the Hebrew custom known as *levirate marriage* (Deut. 25:5–10) stipulated that when a married man died without leaving offspring, his widow should marry the dead man's next closest male relative. The first child from that subsequent marriage would then take on the name of the older deceased brother and become his heir. Thus, as Scripture instructs, the name of the first husband will "not be blotted out from Israel" (Deut. 25:6).

---

25. Southern Baptist Convention, "Resolution on Birth Control," 1934, accessed June 9, 2020, http://www.sbc.net/resolutions/285/resolution-on-birth-control.

26. See Southern Baptist Convention, "Resolution on Permissiveness and Family Planning," 1977, accessed June 9, 2020, http://www.sbc.net/resolutions/796/resolution-on-permissiveness-and-family-planning.

27. Dennis P. Hollinger, "The Ethics of Contraception," *JETS* 56, no. 4 (December 2013): 683.

In this instance, Onan, as Er's next-oldest brother, was to take on the responsibility of providing Tamar with a child. Genesis 38:9 recounts that Onan did indeed have sexual intercourse with Tamar, but he prevented her from conceiving a child by withdrawing from her before ejaculation. Instead of providing her with an heir for her first husband, Scripture indicates, he "wasted his seed on the ground." The Bible then states that his action was "displeasing in the sight of the LORD." As a result, God took Onan's life as well (Gen. 38:10).

Roman Catholics typically cite this passage to suggest that what particularly displeased the Lord was the interruption of the sexual process for the purpose of preventing procreation.[28] Every act of sexual intercourse, it is argued, ought to be open to procreation. Thus, the interruption by Onan, as well as any other form of interruption or use of artificial means to prevent conception during sexual intercourse, is morally reprehensible. According to Catholic doctrine, all means of contraception that interrupt the natural process of procreation are contrary to God's will.[29]

Upon closer inspection of the passage, however, it appears that the Lord's displeasure should be equated not with the prevention of pregnancy per se but with the particularly exploitive, abusive, and wasteful way in which Onan carried out his sexual relations with Tamar.[30] The reason for reaching this conclusion hinges largely on the fact that the penalty prescribed in Deuteronomy 25:5–10 for a man who refuses to complete his "duty" to provide an offspring for his deceased brother is not death but public shaming and humiliation (Deut. 25:9–10). The severity of the punishment seems to indicate that reasons besides the refusal to provide an offspring for his deceased brother prompted God to take Onan's life. The death penalty was inflicted not because of the contraceptive choice, but because Onan wickedly took advantage of Tamar sexually and performed a sexual act contrary to God's design.[31]

The traditional Catholic interpretation of the passage notwithstanding, this means that no passage in the Bible specifically and directly prohibits the use of contraceptive measures within marriage. How ought one to reason biblically with regard to contraception? We must explore other closely related biblical principles that directly shape our understanding of how God wants us to apply the purposes of marriage and sex. In this regard, as we have already pointed out, Scripture indicates

---

28. See, e.g., Brian Harrison, "The Real Sin of Onan," *Catholic Answers*, March 1, 2017, https://www.catholic.com/magazine/print-edition/the-real-sin-of-onan.

29. Paul VI, *Humanae Vitae*, 14–17.

30. For related "crimes" and punishments, see Deuteronomy 22.

31. There is interesting similarity in this passage to the instruction and the death penalty warranted for rape that is described in Deuteronomy 22:25–27. There is also an interesting overlap with the fact that homosexual "intercourse" also was to be met with the death penalty (Lev. 18:22; 20:13).

that in addition to procreation, God created marriage to meet other ends as well. Unity (Gen. 2:18, 24) and marital fidelity (1 Cor. 7:1–9)—in addition to procreation—are both biblically appropriate purposes for which God created the marital sexual union. Therefore, while it seems clear that over the course of their marriage a couple ought to seek to have children (perhaps even many; see Ps. 127:5), it does not follow that *in every particular sexual encounter* the couple need to refrain from the use of contraception. The sexual encounter in marriage can retain its high value and goodness even when contraception is used in particular instances precisely because it facilitates the unitive bond between a husband and wife, which in turn can facilitate the beautiful display of a healthy marriage lived for the glory of God.[32]

Having reached this conclusion about the general permissibility of contraception within the context of a marriage that seeks to honor the end of procreation as a general rule, we now turn to a consideration of which forms of contraception are morally permissible in light of the principles and commands that we have highlighted above. With this in mind, we divide the use of contraception and birth control into three broad categories—morally permissible forms of contraception, morally impermissible forms of birth control, and forms of contraception and birth control requiring further moral consideration.

Morally Permissible Forms of Contraception

Our previous assertion that the use of contraception is morally permissible *in general* does not mean that *any and every* particular form of birth control is morally acceptable. Indeed, because passages such as Exodus 20:13 specifically prohibit the taking of innocent life, the guiding principle of the sanctity of human life, which is a significant principle in ethics as worship, must also influence one's perspective on which form of birth control is biblically permissible.

Which forms of birth control are morally acceptable? In short, the answer is that *only forms of birth control that are contraceptive in nature—exclusively prohibiting conception—are morally permissible*. Resting on this foundational principle, one can decipher which methods are acceptable to use in limiting the number of children in one's family.

Acceptable forms include natural methods such as *abstinence* and the *rhythm or calendar method* (in its various forms, such as relying on body temperature cycles or timing of ovulation and fertility periods).[33] Both these methods rely

---

32. Further resources on the issue of contraception in general include Oliver O'Donovan, *Begotten or Made?* (Oxford: Clarendon/Oxford University Press, 2002); and Brent Waters, *Reproductive Technology: Towards a Theology of Procreative Stewardship* (Cleveland: Pilgrim Press, 2001) (chapter 3 deals more specifically with the issue of childlessness and ethics).

33. The most popular form of the rhythm method (calendar method) is called the Billings Method, which is explained in Evelyn Billings and Ann Westmore, *The Billings Method*, updated ed. (Melbourne: Penguin, 2003).

exclusively on avoiding intercourse completely (abstinence) or limiting intercourse to times in which a woman is least likely to conceive (rhythm or calendar method). Natural methods do not involve any other action or mechanism to prevent conception.

In addition to the natural options, artificial methods that exclusively seek to prevent conception are also morally acceptable. Such artificial forms of contraception include *barrier methods*, such as diaphragms, cervical caps, condoms, and spermicides such as foams, creams, sponges, or vaginal suppositories. Use of these artificial methods does not require a couple to time their intercourse to the rhythms of the wife's body. With the exception of abstinence, none of these methods are 100 percent effective in preventing conception, but they all avoid the risk of violating the principle of the sanctity of human life.

One caveat that applies to these morally permissible options (and to every other form of contraception) is that even if these methods are deemed morally permissible in principle, the final moral evaluation of their use also depends on the other relevant ethical domains of assessment. The act must be rightly ordered toward seeking to maximally glorify God, reflective of godly character, permissible in light of God's commands, and appropriately determined in light of any relevant contextual factors. Thus, the interior heart motivations and reasons for their use are vitally important factors to consider before making a decision whether to use contraception. Improper motivations can cause a couple to sin even though they are using an otherwise morally permissible form of contraception. For example, if the primary reason for employing one of these methods of contraception rests on the belief that children are an expensive burden, then an otherwise permissible choice to use contraception may cross the line into an ungodly choice because it disregards God's perspective on children.

Morally Impermissible Forms of Birth Control

As noted in the category heading, we have moved from exclusively evaluating contraceptive measures to the larger category of birth control. Unacceptable forms of birth control include all forms of induced *abortion* (which we discussed in chapter 15). Abortion takes the life of a living human being made in the image of God, therefore violating the principle of the sanctity of human life. Along the same lines, certain types of *intrauterine devices* are also morally unacceptable means of birth control. There are two basic types of IUDs: copper (Paragard) and hormonal (Mirena, Kyleena, Liletta, Skyla). The copper IUD is a small T-shaped piece of plastic covered by coiled copper. It is a hormone-free device that is placed within a woman's uterus. Because it is hormone-free, it does not influence the natural menstrual cycle of a woman or prevent her from ovulating. The copper on the device, however, produces an inflammatory reaction in the woman's body that is toxic to sperm and eggs (ova).[34] Thus, while it can have the contraceptive effect of preventing sperm from reaching the egg, its primary function is to create an unstable environment for a newly conceived child (fertilized egg) to implant in the uterine wall because it functions to deplete the endometrial lining, making it incapable of supporting the life of the child. This is obviously problematic for those who hold to the moral principle of the sanctity of human life from the moment of conception. We will return to a discussion of hormonal IUDs in the next section below.

In addition, so-called *emergency contraceptives*, also known as the *morning-after pills*, *abortion pills*, or *medication abortion*, are likewise morally unacceptable, since their primary function is either to prevent the implantation of a newly conceived and living child in the uterine wall or to cause the pregnancy to terminate by inducing a miscarriage by means of the two different chemicals taken in pill form (mifepristone and misoprostol). This birth-control measure is actually mislabeled as an *emergency contraceptive* because its primary function is not to prevent conception but rather to end a pregnancy.

Forms of Contraception or Birth Control Requiring Further Moral Consideration
The final category of contraception and birth-control methods that we address require special moral consideration because even though they are widely practiced by Christians and non-Christians alike, there are significant concerns related to each. We begin with a discussion of both male and female sterilization and then consider hormonally based birth-control pills and devices most commonly referred to as some version of "the pill."

Sterilization is a method of contraception that involves a surgical procedure designed to permanently terminate an individual's fertility. For the male, a vasectomy blocks the *vas deferens* (ejaculatory duct), which prevents the sperm from leaving the body during ejaculation. For the female, a tubal occlusion or tubal ligation can be performed to block or cut off a woman's fallopian tubes in order to prevent sperm from coming into contact with the woman's eggs, thereby preventing fertilization.

Although sterilization is widely practiced, the procedure is not free from potential moral problems. By its very nature, sterilization is an elective procedure that involves the intentional and permanent setting aside or inactivation of a bodily function by a willful act of self-maiming.[35] This raises the question whether

34. See the Mayo Clinic description, "Copper IUD," accessed November 19, 2020, https://www.mayoclinic.org/tests-procedures/paragard/about/pac-20391270#:~:text=It's%20sometimes%20referred%20to%20as,(ova)%2C%20preventing%20pregnancy.
35. While this term may appear to some as an overstatement or unnecessarily harsh description of the sterilization procedure, it is reflective of the historic view prevalent in much of church history regarding voluntary self-sterilization.

it is ever ethical to remove a part of one's body (cf. Lev. 21:20; Deut. 23:1; Matt. 19:12) for the sake of convenience.[36] Suggesting that a vasectomy is the same thing as using a condom is simply not a good moral argument for the same reason that putting on a blindfold is not the same thing as cutting the nerve endings that enable the eye to see. The former involves elective *limitation* of a normal bodily function; the latter involves the elective *elimination* of a bodily function, which in turn raises questions whether this is an appropriate manner to honor the "temple of the Holy Spirit" (1 Cor. 6:19).

Both the Old and New Testaments indicate that our physical bodies should be treated with great honor and respect. For example, recall the idea we discussed earlier in the book that God created the person as an "embodied self" (chapter 2). This means that our body is an integral part of our humanity. Intentionally causing a bodily function that is otherwise functioning as it was designed to cease working is an attack on the way that God created us. In addition, Paul discusses in 1 Corinthians 6:12–20 that the body is to be honored and respected in a way that is meant to glorify God. While this text does not make a clear prohibitive statement against sterilization, it is part of the scripturally based tradition in Christianity that has long resisted the marring of the physical body with which we are otherwise commanded to glorify God.

This, in turn, makes one wonder whether sterilization through the "disabling" of a function of the body is a proper way to treat the body that God has given to us and that is the "temple of the Holy Spirit" (1 Cor. 6:19). As John Jefferson Davis comments:

> The apostle's point is that the believer does not have the right to exercise unlimited dominion over his or her body but should view the body as a trust from the Lord, to be cared for in ways that are glorifying to God. And surgical operation—such as sterilization—is not merely a personal "choice," but a decision that needs to be seen within the biblical framework of stewardship of the human body. Given the fact that our human bodies are a trust from God, and in light of the positive valuation placed on human procreative powers and large families in the Old Testament, these powers should not be rejected or surgically destroyed without compelling justification.[37]

Based on this logic, it appears that sterilization—at least at first glance—runs contrary to proper care for the *imago Dei* in that it involves the intentional marring

---

36. Matthew 5:29–30 is not relevant here, since Jesus' reference to gouging out an eye or cutting off a hand is hyperbolic in nature and relates not to parts of the body that are functioning normally but are inconvenient, but to those that are "causing" people to sin.

37. John Jefferson Davis, "Theologically Sound," in *The Sterilization Option: A Guide for Christians*, ed. David B. Biebel (Grand Rapids: Baker, 1995), 72.

of the "temple of the Holy Spirit." It seems, then, that a proper moral conclusion regarding a Christian's perspective on sterilization is that unless there are significantly compelling (e.g., life-threatening or serious-medical-need) reasons for disabling the body in this way, a Christian should avoid this form of contraception.

Having reached this conclusion, however, we want to be careful to refrain from absolute dogmatism on the topic of sterilization as a form of contraception. We want to be careful not to create a new legalism where the Scripture is largely silent. In addition, we recognize that not every Christian will reach the same conclusion regarding the proper treatment of the body as the temple of the Holy Spirit. We know of couples who have sought the Lord in prayer, submitted to godly counsel, and decided to proceed with a sterilization procedure. We also know couples who have proceeded with sterilization, later deeply regretted their decision, and sought medical procedures attempting to reverse the process. All of this points us to both encourage and provoke Christians to think carefully and deeply about this issue before proceeding. As with all other areas of life and practice, we must be willing to submit our personal desires to the Lord in prayerful consideration, look to the Scripture for guidance, and seek out godly counsel before making this decision. Ultimately, seeing ethics as an act of worship should press us to ask not whether a procedure of sterilization may be merely permissible, but whether it would most fully honor the Lord in regard to the way that each of us honors the body we have been given to steward. In light of this, we recommend against sterilization.

Another birth-control method requiring special moral consideration is what is popularly known as *the pill* but should more accurately be described as *hormonal methods of birth control*. Whether they are administered as a pill, patch, shot, implant, or ring, all these methods are similar in that they rely on manufactured forms of hormones to prevent pregnancy and control birth. Because of its wide acceptance in the culture, some Christians may be surprised to learn that the moral acceptability of the pill (and the many other various applications of the same basic chemical products) is under question. While the convenience and effectiveness of these forms of birth control have certainly commended them to many, serious moral questions must be addressed before one makes a decision whether the pill and all other forms of hormonal methods qualify as an acceptable form of contraception or birth control.

There are two basic categories of this hormone-based chemical birth control: combination and progestin-only. *Combination contraceptives* (containing both estrogen and progestin) come in both an oral form (usually referred to as COCs—combination oral contraceptives—such as Ortho Tri-Cyclen, Loestrin, Nor-Qd, and Dsogen) and an injectable form (CICs—combined injectable contraceptives—such as Cyclofem and Mesigyna). *Progestin-only contraceptives* are likewise produced in oral and injectable form. Progestin-only pills (POPs) contain the hormone progestin and are taken daily, while progestin-only injectable contraceptives (PICs) such as Depo-Provera require an injection roughly once every two to three months. At this point, there is no clinically approved hormone-based birth-control product for men.[38]

Hormonal IUDs work in a fashion very similar to the pill and other chemical forms of hormonally based forms of birth control. Like the copper IUD mentioned in the previous section, a hormonal IUD is a small T-shaped piece of plastic that is placed within a woman's uterus. It differs from the copper IUD in that instead of being covered in coiled copper, this device is designed to release a small amount of progestin into the body in order to create conditions that prohibit pregnancy.

According to Prescribers' Digital Reference, an online resource based on the *Physicians' Desk Reference*, all versions of both combined contraceptives and progestin-only contraceptives (including hormonal IUDs) work by employing the same three basic mechanisms of action. The first of these is to prevent ovulation (a contraceptive mechanism). The second is the thickening of the cervical mucus buildup, which, in turn, increases the difficulty of sperm's entering the uterus and thereby fertilizing the egg (a contraceptive mechanism). The third mechanism—in all forms of both combined contraceptives and progestin-only contraceptives—is to alter the *endometrium* (uterine lining), thereby making it less suitable for implantation and creating adverse conditions for supporting the life of a newly conceived child if fertilization takes place.[39] This third mechanism is not a contraceptive measure but rather a birth-control mechanism that works as a "fail-safe" means to control birth if the other two mechanisms do not prevent conception.[40]

In short, the central moral question of concern with all hormonal methods (so-called combined contraceptives, progestin-only contraceptives, and hormonal IUDs) is whether the use of hormonal birth control can have negative postconception effects that result in the harm or death of the child. More specifically, the

38. Some products (such as RISUG and Vasalgel) are receiving much attention and are possible forerunners of effective treatments for men. These products, if they ever become available, will not be subject to the same moral questions related to their effect on the life of a child. By preventing sperm from entering into a man's ejaculate, they would function solely as contraceptive measures.

39. See drug summaries, accessed June 9, 2020, at https://www.pdr.net/drug-summary/Ortho-Tri-Cyclen -Lo-ethinyl-estradiol-norgestimate-1363.4038; https://www.pdr.net/drug-summary/Depo-Provera-Sterile -Aqueous-Suspension-medroxyprogesterone-acetate-2875.8223#15.

40. Statistically speaking, when taken as designed, these various types of hormone-based birth-control methods are effective 99.5 percent of the time, meaning that even when taken as directed, one out of every two hundred acts of sexual intercourse (on average) will result in a pregnancy. From this fact, one can know for certain that while the pill is effective in preventing ovulation and preventing fertilization, it does not prevent all fertilization. While there are no statistical data to indicate how many births are terminated by the third mechanism, one can be assured that it does occur.

main moral problem occurs when the first and second mechanisms of action fail (prevention of ovulation and of fertilization due to mucus buildup) and fertilization of an egg takes place. At this point, these various hormonal methods cease to function as contraceptives. The third function of all of them is to create an environment in the uterus that is averse to the implantation and subsequent growth of the conceived child. In other words, the third mechanism now functions as birth control and potentially as an *abortifacient*.

Morally and ethically speaking, then, while admittedly the likelihood that the first two functions of hormonal methods will fail is considered to be statistically low (the ability to quantify specific numbers is currently beyond the ability of modern science), a high respect for the *imago Dei* in all humans and a proper regard for the principle of the sanctity of human life should cause any Christian to be seriously concerned about the use of these hormonal methods of birth control. In fact, recalling our discussion of the sixth commandment, the Bible clearly gives us a moral imperative not only to avoid the killing of innocent human life but also to take "adequate precautions to guard and protect human life." Given this understanding of the sixth commandment, it would seem that any uncertainty regarding this third function of hormonal birth-control methods should lead us to reevaluate whether a low chance of causing the death of one's own newly conceived child is worth the risk at all. From the point of view of a Christian, when the life of a baby is in doubt, the benefit of the doubt should go toward protecting life.

Before drawing this discussion to a conclusion, we offer first a word of advice and second a word of caution. Regarding the advice, for those who rightly desire to seek counsel on this issue from a medical professional such as a primary-care physician or OB/GYN, it is important to ask questions with an accurate and careful understanding of medical terminology. Indeed, precision of terminology is vitally important if one is to get at the heart of the moral problem. Specifically, it is important to have clarity on the technical and medical meanings of the words *pregnancy* and *abortion*. Medically, a *pregnancy* does not actually begin until the conceived child implants in the uterine lining. This may not take place for several days after the child is conceived. An *abortion* is defined as the termination of a pregnancy. The key element of moral concern, then, is not only what happens after a pregnancy technically begins but also what takes place *after* the child is conceived but also *before* it has implanted in the uterine wall. For while the third function of all the hormonal methods may not technically cause an *abortion* (in light of the medical definition of *pregnancy*), it may very well lead to the death of the conceived child. For example, if a young couple asks their doctor whether a particular form of birth control runs the risk of causing an abortion, the doctor may say "no" because he or she is thinking in terms of these technical definitions.

In fact, this is exactly how some of the manufacturers of hormonal birth control market their product. For example, consider the website for the PLAN B® morning-after pill. The site reads:

> Plan B® comes in a one-pill dose. If taken within 72 hours (3 days) and preferably within 12 hours after a contraceptive accident or unprotected sex, it can prevent pregnancy by doing one of three things: temporarily stops the release of an egg from the ovary, prevents fertilization, *prevents a fertilized egg from attaching to the uterus. Plan B® is not an abortion pill—if you take Plan B®, you will not be terminating a pregnancy.*[41]

Thus, while not technically terminating a pregnancy, it very specifically is targeting the proper implantation of a conceived human child.

Depending on how the medical profession defines *abortion* and *pregnancy*, then, the answer to whether these forms of birth control cause abortion may vary. If, however, this couple were to ask the question "is there a real possibility that the hormonal birth control we are considering will have postconception effects that may prevent the baby from attaching to the uterus?," based on all the available information, a knowledgeable and truthful doctor would answer "yes." For this reason, instead of inquiring whether a certain form of hormonal birth control can "cause an abortion," the wise couple should ask whether the hormonal birth control can deplete or thin the lining of the uterus, making it harder for a conceived child to implant and allow a "pregnancy" to begin.

Regarding a word of caution, because all three of the functions of hormonal birth control are known and intended effects of the medications, it would be unwise to dismiss the possible third effect as merely collateral damage or something morally insignificant. While it is true that all of life's choices have an element of danger, the difference here is that in taking these hormones, the effect is both known and designed, and therefore an intended result. For example, while it is true that driving one's children to the grocery store involves some risk that they may get hurt in an unforeseen accident, such a comparison is not actually equivalent to what is taking place when a couple uses hormonal birth control. The equivalent illustration would be a parent's driving a child to the grocery store and then, once they arrive, leaving the child unattended in a hot car. The moral question is not merely about the potential risk, but also about the chosen environment that we are willing to place our children in so that we can best honor and protect their lives.

41. Plan B, "How It Works," accessed June 11, 2020, https://planb.ca/how-it-works.html#:~:text=If%20taken%20within%2072%20hours,from%20attaching%20to%20the%20uterus (emphasis added).

Table 19.2. Methods of Contraception and Birth Control

Morally Permissible	Morally Impermissible	Needing Special Consideration
Methods that are unquestionably contraceptive in nature and function	Methods that directly and unambiguously aim to threaten the life of a conceived child	Methods that are morally problematic and require greater ethical care
Abstinence Natural family planning: rhythm methods Barrier methods: condom (male or female) diaphragm spermicide cervical cap contraceptive sponge	Abortion Emergency contraceptives Copper IUD	Sterilization (male and female) Hormonal methods (combined and progestin-only treatments): the pill the patch the ring the shot hormonal IUD

By way of summary and conclusion to this discussion on birth-control methods requiring special consideration, it is important to reiterate the need to take great care in avoiding dogmatism on matters to which Scripture does not directly speak. The Bible does not address or prohibit sterilization. It is the principle of honoring "the temple of the Holy Spirit" that one must seriously consider before deciding whether to employ such a method. With regard to use of hormonal birth-control methods, moral justification for its use is much more tenuous because of the simple fact that the principle of the sanctity of life and the moral instruction of the sixth commandment directly applies. In both cases, it is our conviction that consideration of scriptural principles ought to lead one away from employing sterilization or the pill with its many variations as a means of family planning.[42]

42. Our readers may be interested to note the scientific statement posted by the Christian Medical & Dental Associations (CMDA) on the possible postconception effects on hormonal birth control. The statement reads in part: "Christian Medical & Dental Associations (CMDA) holds firmly that God is the Creator of life, that life begins at conception, and that all human life is of infinite value. We support measures to protect life from its earliest beginnings. CMDA recognizes that there are differing viewpoints among Christians regarding the broad issue of birth control and the use of contraceptives. The issue at hand, however, is whether or not hormonal birth control methods have post-conceptional effects (i.e., cause abortion). CMDA has consulted many experts in the field of reproduction who have reviewed the scientific literature. *While there are data that cause concern, our current scientific knowledge does not establish a definitive causal link between the routine use of hormonal birth control and abortion. However, neither are there data to deny a post-conceptional effect.* Because this issue cannot be resolved with our current understanding, CMDA calls upon researchers to further investigate the mechanisms of action of hormonal birth control. Additionally,

Assisted Reproductive Technology[43]

Modern medicine now provides infertile couples with a wide range of options for aiding the fight against infertility. These medical advances include something as simple and nontechnical as encouraging a man to increase his sperm count simply by changing his wardrobe and activity levels to something as technologically dependent as procedures of intrauterine insemination, in vitro fertilization, or even cloning for reproductive purposes.[44] While all the available reproductive technologies require at least some level of ethical evaluation, the more complicated and technologically dependent ones also tend to be more ethically tenuous.

As in the case of contraception, it is important to recognize that simply because a technology is available or popularly practiced does not necessarily mean that employing it is ethically permissible. Rather, it is imperative to explore the available options with regard to how they align with biblical principles that ought to guide the decision-making process. In the matter of reproductive technologies, four principles are particularly germane and will be briefly highlighted below.

First, as in the case of contraception, respect for the *sanctity of human life* directly relates to the issue of reproductive technologies. Some forms of reproductive technology, such as cloning for reproduction, pose a direct threat to the life of the child because of the inexact nature and development of the technology. Other forms of reproductive technology may not directly threaten life, but the manner in which they are employed does. For example, it is common practice in certain methods of in vitro fertilization to fertilize multiple eggs at a time. Each of the resulting conceptions is a child waiting to be placed into a woman's uterus in order to grow toward birth. Unfortunately, it is also common practice for the doctors to select only one or two of these conceived children for implantation, leaving the others to be frozen for storage or destroyed.

Another way in which a technology is employed that threatens the sanctity of life occurs when the technique used (such as intrauterine insemination, in vitro fertilization, or the use of fertility drugs) results in a multichild pregnancy. In such cases, multiple fertilized eggs may implant in a woman's uterus, generating increased risk for her pregnancy. In such cases, reproductive specialists will often recommend a procedure known as *selective reduction*. While described as a means

---

because the possibility of abortive effects cannot be ruled out, prescribers of hormonal birth control should consider informing patients of this potential factor." CMDA, "Scientific Statement: Possible Post-conceptional Effects of Hormonal Birth Control," accessed June 11, 2020, https://cmda.org/wp-content/uploads/2018/04/Hormonalbirthcontrol-1.pdf (emphasis added).

43. Portions of this section are adapted from Liederbach, "Artificial Reproductive Technologies," 129–34.

44. See further the description below. While the topic of cloning is beyond the scope of this chapter, see the following resources for some helpful discussion of the topic: Rae, *Moral Choices*, 201–29; Glen H. Stassen and David P. Gushee, *Kingdom Ethics: Following Jesus in Contemporary Context* (Downers Grove, IL: InterVarsity Press, 2003), 262–64; Grudem, *Christian Ethics*, 777–79.

to increase the chances that some of the babies may be born alive, selective reduction is in reality nothing more than a form of abortion in which one or more of the children are killed in order to increase the odds of the others' proceeding to live birth.

In such situations, the most worshipful response is for a couple to proceed with all conceptions implanted and carried to full term in order for the use of such technology to meet the biblical standards with regard to the sanctity of life. As John Van Regenmorter advises, "*Do not allow more embryos to be formed than the number of children you are willing to parent.*"[45] Likewise, those using fertility drugs must recognize ahead of time that a multiple-child birth is a possibility and that selective reduction is not a biblically legitimate option.

A second biblical principle that must be considered is *respect for all human beings as image-bearers.* Because all humans bear the image of God (Gen. 1:27), it is immoral to use or treat others as a means to an end only or purposely to put them in harm's way when they have not incurred guilt. Once again, in the case of some forms of reproductive technologies, it is common practice to fertilize several eggs and then freeze these children for an indefinite amount of time, only to discard them if the parents opt to forgo having any more children. Christians must pause over such practices and be willing to ask important and challenging questions such as these: When did it become okay to freeze living human beings? When did it become okay to suspend the life and growth of a human being without his or her consent? When did it become okay to treat human beings like commodities that we pull out of the freezer when we are ready to take care of them? When did it become okay to leave people indefinitely in the freezer because we don't want to take care of them? By most estimates, there are likely as many as a million "surplus" frozen embryos in the United States.[46] A recent news article published by NBC News suggested that in the United States alone, there are likely over one hundred thousand of these frozen embryos that have been abandoned by their parents.[47] Such practices are inherently disrespectful to God's image-bearers. In many cases, they lead to a form of dehumanization that considers the moral status of unborn children as little more than commodities to be used or merely as a means to the parents' chosen goals. The abandonment of these "snowflake babies" also directly runs contrary to the sixth commandment and the principle of the sanctity of human life.

45. John Van Regenmorter, "Frozen Out: What to Do with Those Extra Embryos," *Christianity Today*, July 2004, 33.

46. National Embryo Donation Center, https://www.embryodonation.org/.

47. Mary Pflum, "Nation's Fertility Clinics Struggle with a Growing Number of Abandoned Embryos," NBC News, August 12, 2019, accessed June 11, 2020, https://www.nbcnews.com/health/features/nation-s -fertility-clinics-struggle-growing-number-abandoned-embryos-n1040806.

Surrogacy and the use of third-party gametes also raise problems in light of the respect for all human beings as image-bearers. The role of the surrogate is to function as a gestational carrier to give birth to a child who is generally not biologically related to her. While this can take place voluntarily among family members, such as a case in which a sister or a mother may carry a child for a sibling or child, in many cases the surrogate arrangement is a paid arrangement whereby a woman is contracted for the use of her womb. After giving birth, she then turns the baby over to the care of the couple that initiated the contractual arrangement with her. This transaction is a form of human commodification that utilizes the body of the surrogate without taking into account the biological and emotional components of pregnancy and giving birth.

The use of third-party gametes violates this principle in a similar fashion. Sperm, eggs, or both provided by "donors" can be purchased for use in intra-uterine insemination and in vitro fertilization. The gametes are selected on the basis of a physical, emotional, and intellectual profile of the donors. A couple may choose gametes because the donor exhibits certain physical characteristics that align with the husband or wife, or a couple may choose gametes because they hope that a child may have intellectual or physical advantages. In either case, the donors and the child born from the third-party gametes are often being treated as commodities who are selected based on genetic traits and who then serve as a means to an end rather than as image-bearers valuable in their own right regardless of genetic makeup.

A third guiding principle for determining the moral value of a given reproductive technology is *respect for the fidelity of the marital bond*. We addressed this idea earlier in the book when we discussed that God designed marriage to be the context for childbearing. Genesis 2:24 states that a man is to "leave his father and his mother, and be joined to his wife; and they shall become one flesh." It is within the context of this one-flesh relationship of husband and wife that God gave the command to be fruitful and multiply. Likewise, Scripture elsewhere not only condemns adulterous relationships (Ex. 20:14; Deut. 5:18; Rom. 13:9) but also affirms the exclusive nature of the marital bond (Matt. 19:5; 1 Cor. 7; Eph. 5:28–31). This biblical emphasis on the unity and exclusivity of the marital bond has direct implications for the use of reproductive technologies, particularly those methods that utilize the genetic material (donor eggs or donor sperm) from someone other than the husband or wife. Because the use of donor egg or sperm introduces into the marriage (specifically the sexual reproduction process) sexually related genetic material of a third person, there is considerable doubt with regard to the morality of such a practice.

While one would be hard pressed to place this in the exact category of what society has historically understood to be adultery, one could easily argue that using donor egg or sperm is tantamount to adultery or at the very least an inappropriate intrusion on the exclusive nature of marital fidelity and sexuality.[48] As Scott Rae rightly points out: "The weight of biblical teaching suggests that third-party contributors are not the norm for procreation. Scripture looks skeptically on any reproductive intervention that goes outside the married couple for genetic material. That would mean that technologies such as donor insemination, egg donation, and surrogate motherhood raise troubling issues and would appear to be outside the moral parameters of biblical teaching."[49]

A fourth and final principle that ought to guide the evaluation whether to use reproductive technologies relates not so much to the *form of technology* but to the *heart of the one wanting to use it*. While the desire to have and raise genetically related children is grounded in the created norms and cemented in God's imperative for us to "be fruitful and multiply," it is nonetheless important not to place one's hope or sense of worth directly on one's ability to have genetically related children. The final hope of the Christian lies neither in the ability to manipulate human reproductive systems nor in the ability to have children at all. Whether it be through direct miraculous intervention (as in Hannah's case) or through the technological advancements made possible through the minds that God has given us, children are a gift from the Lord. Beyond this, Scripture indicates that our ultimate hope lies not in our ability to have children but rather in our Savior, Jesus Christ.

Indeed, given the great crisis of orphaned children and the pandemic of abortion that afflicts us worldwide, it is more than appropriate here to emphasize the goodness of adoption not only as an amazing demonstration of neighbor love, but also as a beautiful depiction of God's saving grace toward sinners. Frozen children, abandoned children, and others who are placed up for adoption for any

---

48. A possible analogy is provided by the Old Testament practice of men's seeking offspring from women other than their wives in the case of their wives' infertility, often with their wives' consent (e.g., Abraham and Hagar, at Sarah's prompting, Gen. 16:1–4). To be sure, the analogy breaks down in that in the modern context sexual intercourse with a person other than one's spouse is not required to secure an offspring if one spouse is unable to have children. Nevertheless, in both cases an effort is made to have children through the involvement of someone outside the marriage bond. In Scripture, at least in Abraham's case, this is viewed as resulting from a lack of faith. Trusting God to remove barrenness, if possible, or adoption may therefore seem to be a preferable alternative. For a more extensive discussion of the use of third-party gametes and its connection to adultery, see Lenow, "Is it Adultery?," 41–57.

49. Rae, *Moral Choices*, 178. Some have suggested that the Old Testament practice of levirate marriage (Deut. 25:5–10) legitimizes the use of donor sperm from a family member other than one's spouse. It would seem wise, however, not to draw too close a parallel, for there are notable and important differences between the two practices. To begin with, the close relative of the deceased husband actually married the woman, which is very different from accepting donor sperm from someone other than one's husband. Also, in the case of levirate marriage, no provisions were made to assist a *living* spouse in having children. The purpose was rather to provide an inheritance and material security when a wife's husband had passed away.

number of other reasons are a gift and treasure from the Lord. Blessed are those who choose the route of adoption to raise up godly children for the glory of God and good of the nations.[50]

In sum, while the use of reproductive technology may be *generally* permissible, one should not make the further assumption that *every form* of reproductive technology is therefore biblically and morally acceptable. Concerns for the respect for human life, human dignity, and fidelity to the marital bond need to govern one's evaluation of any particular form of reproductive technology. Indeed, once one considers the broad ethical uncertainty and "gray areas" regarding many of these technologies, perhaps wisdom would suggest limiting one's efforts in this direction in favor of pursuing adoption.

Conclusion

There is no doubt that the matters of contraception, birth control, and reproductive technologies concern some of the most sensitive personal questions that a couple may have in their marriage. Such sensitivity, however, should not dissuade us from addressing these matters in our own lives, the church, and the culture at large. We are abundantly grateful for the advances of modern medicine, and we have no desire to return to the days of rudimentary medical treatments. At the same time, we need to acknowledge that the medical advances in the realm of procreation often create additional moral questions.

As we have attempted to demonstrate throughout the book, our goal is to maximize the worship of our heavenly Father. He has called us to a relationship with him that will ultimately be a restoration of the relationship he designed and created for us to enjoy with him "in the beginning." In many respects, the procreative process reflects the relationship of God with his image-bearers. Procreation is the closest we ever get to God's creative capacity. In all of this, however, God is still the One creating. He opens and closes the womb and superintends the miracle of new life. May we respect the end goal (*telos*) and the parameters and instructions that God has revealed to us regarding our character and behaviors as we seek to worship him through our role in the procreation process and the creation of life.

Key Terms and Concepts

abortifacient	abstinence
abortion	adultery

---

50. For more information regarding the adoption of frozen embryos, see https://www.embryodonation .org/.

assisted reproductive technology (ART)
barrier methods
birth control
combination contraceptives
contraception
emergency contraceptives
gamete intrafallopian transfer (GIFT)
hormonal methods of birth control
infertility

intrauterine device (IUD)
intrauterine insemination (IUI)
in vitro fertilization (IVF)
pill, the
pregnancy
progestin-only contraceptives
rhythm or calendar method
snowflake babies
sterilization
surrogacy
third-party gametes

Key Scriptures

Genesis 1–2
1 Samuel 1:1–18
Psalm 127:3–5

Psalm 139:13–16
Luke 1:5–80
1 Corinthians 6:12–20

Study Questions

1. What is the difference between contraception and birth control? Why is this difference significant? How does this difference influence our ethical decision-making?
2. What implications does God's design for childbearing to take place within the context of marriage have on decisions about the use of reproductive technologies?
3. In what ways might various forms of contraception, birth control, and reproductive technologies violate the principle of the sanctity of human life? Why should this influence our decision to use these methods?
4. Should the use of third-party gametes be considered adultery? How is the use of third-party gametes similar to and different from our cultural understanding of adultery?
5. How is adoption an illustration of salvation by grace through faith?

For Further Reading

Alcorn, Randy. *Does the Birth Control Pill Cause Abortions?* 10th ed. Sandy, OR: Eternal Perspective Ministries, 2011.

Carlson, Allan. *Godly Seed: American Evangelicals Confront Birth Control, 1872–1973.* New Brunswick, NJ: Transaction, 2012.

Cutrer, William R., and Sandra L. Glahn. *The Contraception Guidebook: Options, Risks, and Answers for Christian Couples.* Grand Rapids: Zondervan, 2005.

Eberstadt, Mary. *Adam and Eve after the Pill: Paradoxes of the Sexual Revolution.* San Francisco: Ignatius, 2012.

Hollinger, Dennis P. "The Ethics of Contraception." *JETS* 56, no. 4 (December 2013): 683–96.

Kilner, John F., Paige C. Cunningham, and W. David Hager, eds. *The Reproduction Revolution: A Christian Appraisal of Sexuality, Reproductive Technologies, and the Family.* Grand Rapids: Eerdmans, 2000.

Lenow, Evan. "Is It Adultery? The Use of Third-Party Gametes in Assisted Reproductive Technology." *SWJT* 59, no. 1 (Fall 2016): 41–57.

O'Donovan, Oliver. *Begotten or Made?* Oxford: Clarendon/Oxford University Press, 2002.

Paul VI. *Humanae Vitae.* 1968. http://www.vatican.va/content/paul-vi/en/encyclicals /documents/hf_p-vi_enc_25071968_humanae-vitae.html.

Waters, Brent. *Reproductive Technology: Towards a Theology of Procreative Stewardship.* Cleveland: Pilgrim Press, 2001.

Glossary

THIS GLOSSARY OFFERS brief definitions of some of the important terms used throughout the book. Most of these terms come from the lists of Key Terms and Concepts found at the conclusion of each chapter, but not all of those key terms and concepts are included in this glossary. The number in parentheses indicates the chapter (or chapters) where the term is discussed. If no number is present, the term appears throughout the text. Words in italic are defined elsewhere in the glossary.

abolitionist (13). Position of those who desire to abolish the death penalty. Cf. *retentionist.*

abortifacient (19). A device or substance that functions to cause an *abortion.*

abortion, elective (15). Type of induced abortion that is a response to some social or personal factor(s). See *abortion, induced.*

abortion, eugenic (15). The selective termination of a pregnancy based on factors discovered in prenatal genetic screening that are related not to the viability of a child, but to whether the genetics are either "normal" or "preferred." Type of induced abortion. See *abortion, induced.*

abortion, induced (15). The intentional interruption of a pregnancy. See *abortion, elective; abortion, eugenic; abortion, therapeutic; emergency contraceptives.*

abortion, spontaneous (15). The abrupt and unplanned (spontaneous) early end of a pregnancy that takes place before the fetus is viable. Commonly called *miscarriage.*

abortion, therapeutic (15). Type of induced abortion for purposes directly related to either terminal fetal disease or the health of the mother (broadly defined by the 1973 U.S. Supreme Court case *Doe v. Bolton* [410 U.S. 179]). Most often refers to the rare situation in which a pregnancy is purposely terminated in order to save the mother's life. See *abortion, induced.*

active euthanasia (16). The act of killing someone (including the self) through a definite action intending to end a person's life (an act of commission). See *euthanasia; physician-assisted suicide.* Cf. *passive euthanasia.*

anthropocentrism (12). A human-centered ethical theory that assumes that humans are the measure of all things and should therefore enjoy the place of moral superiority over and above their environment.

anthropology (1). The consideration of what it means to be human.

antinomianism (7, 8). Moral system that holds that because there are no objective moral principles by which an issue can be judged right or wrong, the decision must be made on subjective grounds.

applied ethics (1). The application of the norms of behavior and character in the real-life situations and contexts that one faces.

ART. See *assisted reproductive technology*.

artificial insemination. See *intrauterine insemination*.

assisted reproductive technology (ART) (19). Category of fertility treatments that handle eggs, sperm, or both. The Centers for Disease Control limits the definition to only those treatments that handle both eggs and sperm.

authority, objective (5). The concept that Scripture records what God has actually said to be true. His Word has an objective meaning that is the same for all people in all times and in all places.

beatific vision (3). The blissful sight of God for a believer upon standing before God and seeing him as he is.

biocentrism (12). A life-centered ethical theory based on the notion that all living organisms (human and nonhuman) have an inherent, noninstrumental value and should be granted the highest *moral status*.

biological sex (17). The identification of maleness or femaleness on the basis of distinct biological markers that are unique to one or the other. See *cisgender*; *gender dysphoria*; *transgenderism*.

birth control (19). Any means that seeks to prevent birth from occurring. See *contraception*; *pill*.

chiasm (2). A literary structure that reverses the order of paired concepts. Two ideas A and B are paired together, and then the order is reversed to B' and A'.

cisgender (17). The alignment of gender identity with *biological sex*.

collocation (2). A grouping of words that appear together consistently and convey a greater meaning when they appear together than they might otherwise convey when the words are used separately.

complementarianism (2). A view of gender roles that holds that both men and women are created in the image of God (*imago Dei*), having equal worth before God, but that men and women are created to express differing roles.

comprehensive union (18). Description of marriage that it is designed to encompass all aspects of life.

conflicts of duty. See *moral dilemmas*.

contraception (19). The prevention of fertilization that could ultimately lead to a pregnancy. See *birth control*; *emergency contraception*; *intrauterine device*; *pill*; *sterilization*.

covenant (18). A solemn, binding, formal agreement between two or more parties that is often considered indissoluble. Applied to marriage, it speaks to the permanent nature of marriage in the same way that Christ's relationship is with the church.

creation care (12). Term employed by Christians for environmental ethics.

creation grace (3). God's design and ordering of the entire universe and causing it to exist. Also called *first grace*.

crusade (14). Position that holds that there are no moral limits in war because war is viewed as an unconditional effort of good versus evil. Also called *jihad*.

culturally embedded sin patterns (10). The idea that because sinful people create cultures and build societies, the foundational ideas, patterns, and structures they put in place to run these societies will also be tainted by sin.

cultural mandate (2). Based on the *imago Dei*, the idea that humans were created by God to fill the earth and exercise dominion over creation. See *subdue and rule*; *worship mandate*.

death, cardiopulmonary (16). Irreversible loss of circulatory and respiratory functions (heart and lungs).

death, higher brain (16). Irreversible loss of higher brain functions (governed by the neocortex, or only those areas responsible for consciousness and motor control).

death, whole brain (16). Irreversible loss of all functions of the entire brain: cerebrum, cerebellum, brain stem ("total brain failure," "flatline EEG").

Decalogue (3). The Ten Commandments. See *moral dilemmas*.

deontology (6). The study of moral obligation.

depravity (8). Sinfulness.

deterrence (13). Position of inflicting harm or even death to prevent further wrongdoing.

discrimination (10, 13, 14). Separation of the innocent from the guilty in the process of making a judgment. Related to criminal punishment, discrimination seeks to avoid punishing the innocent. Related to war, discrimination is one of the *jus in bello* principles that refuses to engage noncombatants in war.

disordered worship (3). Offering *worship* to the wrong god or in the wrong manner.

domains of ethical assessment (6). Categories for prioritizing how to evaluate a moral question: *telos*, agent, act, circumstances, consequences, and *relational responses*. See *moral weightiness*.

doxology (1). The good and virtuous life of a disciple who lives out his or her life in God-glorifying thanksgiving and praise. Rightly formed and ordered beliefs (*orthodoxy*) give rise to rightly formed and ordered principles of life and practice (*orthopraxy*), which then result in doxology.

dualism (2). The philosophical idea that recognizes not only two distinct substances (material and immaterial) but also an affirmation of relationship of these parts as opposed or divided fundamentally from one another.

dualistic holism (2). The view that the body and soul are integrated into a unified whole. Also called *embodied self*; *psychosomatic unity*.

ecocentric (6). Relating to the metaethical view that the environment as a whole has ultimate *moral status*.

ecocentrism (12). View of environmental ethics in which the entire biosphere and its ecosystems as a whole should be equally granted the same (and highest) level of *moral status*.

ecology (12). The branch of biological studies that has to do with the relationship between living organisms and their physical surroundings or environment.

ectopic pregnancy (15). Pregnancy in which the fertilized egg attaches outside the uterus (normally in the fallopian tube). Commonly called *tubal pregnancy*.

egocentric (6). Relating to the metaethical view that the self has ultimate *moral status*.

embedded headship (2). Loving dominion of humans over the rest of creation based on the *imago Dei*.

embodied self. See *dualistic holism*.

emergency contraceptives (19). Measure of *birth control* that functions either to prevent the implantation of a newly conceived and living child in the uterine wall or to cause the pregnancy to terminate by inducing a miscarriage by means of the two different chemicals taken in pill form (mifepristone and misoprostol). Mislabeled as a contraceptive measure. See *abortion*; *contraception*.

ensoulment (15). The point at which a soul inhabits a human body.

epistemology (1). The study of the theory of knowledge.

ethnicity (10). Category for grouping people primarily based on physical differences within the human *race*.

eudaimonia (4). Greek term depicting the objective observable state of something that is fulfilling that which it is designed or created to be.

euthanasia (16). Literally, "good death." Broadly speaking, it has to do with the intentional hastening of death for the purpose of ending suffering. See *active euthanasia*; *involuntary euthanasia*; *nonvoluntary euthanasia*; *passive euthanasia*; *voluntary euthanasia*.

exception clauses (18). Found in the teaching of Jesus in Matthew 5:32 and 19:9, variously interpreted to include possible exceptions for allowing divorce.

exitus et reditus (2). Latin, "exit and return." The theological idea that God created all things and designed all things to find their highest *flourishing* in him and to return to him all the glory he is due. This theological concept is most often attributed to Thomas Aquinas.

fall, the (3). The entrance of sin into God's perfect creation through the disobedience of the first man and woman to God's command not to eat of the Tree of Knowledge of Good and Evil (Gen. 3). See *metanarrative*.

first grace. See *creation grace*.

flourishing (1, 3, 4). Living according to God's creation design for mankind. See *exitus et reditus*; *makarios*; *perfect*.

formal principle of justice (9). The idea that justice requires equals to be treated equally, and unequals to be treated unequally (Aristotle).

functionalism (15). The view that not all humans have equal moral status because some do not currently possess (or have not developed) the ability to function at a level deemed necessary to qualify for the full moral status of a "person." See *personhood*.

gamete intrafallopian transfer (GIFT) (19). Fertility procedure involving the collection of eggs and sperm. Eggs and sperm are placed into a catheter and injected into a woman's fallopian tubes, where fertilization is intended to take place.

gender dysphoria (17). Incongruence between gender identity and *biological sex*.

generalism (8). Ethical approach to the question of moral dilemmas that asserts that there are no universally binding moral laws, only guidelines that govern moral behavior generally.

GIFT. See *gamete intrafallopian transfer*.

God-breathed (5). From Greek, *theopneustos*. Relating to the idea of the inspiration of Scripture.

graded absolutism (8). Ethical approach to the question of *moral dilemmas* that holds that there are many *moral absolutes* that sometimes conflict, but that higher laws must be followed when there is a conflict. Also called *hierarchicalism*.

"greatest happiness" principle. See *principle of utility*.

hermeneutics (5). The discipline of understanding and interpreting Scripture.

hierarchicalism. See *graded absolutism*.

Holy Spirit, filling of (4). The theological concept of the Holy Spirit's taking over all aspects of a believer's life.

Holy Spirit, indwelling of (4). The theological concept of the Holy Spirit's living with and in a believer.

homosexuality (17). Disordered sexuality in which an individual is attracted to members of the same sex.

humble absolutism (8). Ethical approach to the question of *moral dilemmas* that affirms that when a regenerate believer faces what appears to be a moral dilemma, he or she must realize that the dilemma may feel very real but is in actuality only apparent. With this truth in mind, the moral agent must call on the Holy Spirit to give wisdom and grace to guide the person's interpretation of the situation, seek counsel, and reason wisely. Then the believer must decide in a manner that most clearly obeys the commands relevant to the situation regardless of perceived consequences.

ideal absolutism (8). Ethical approach to the question of *moral dilemmas* that holds that there are many *moral absolutes* that sometimes conflict in a fallen world. In such situations, the moral agent must choose to break one law in order to keep the other. In so doing, the person incurs moral guilt while at the same time attaining the highest moral accomplishment possible.

illumination (5). The doctrine that the Holy Spirit works in the life of a believer to provide both a greater mental/cognitive understanding of Scripture and the willingness to receive the teachings and abide by them.

imago Dei (2). Latin, "image of God." See *complementarianism*; *cultural mandate*; *embedded headship*; *sanctification, personal*.

imputation (3). Ascribing righteousness or guilt of one person to another. In theology, the term refers to humans' sin being placed on Christ and Christ's righteousness being placed on believers.

individualist definition of *racism* (10). The idea that the main sin of *racism* is located in the category of an individual person's sinful attitudes or actions.

inerrant (5). Without error. *Inerrancy* is a doctrine referring to Scripture. Cf. *infallible*.

infallible (5). Incapable of being wrong. *Infallibility* is a doctrine referring to Scripture. Cf. *inerrant*.

infertility (19). The inability to conceive after twelve or more months of regular sexual intercourse that is not impeded by contraceptive means or measures.

inherent value. See *intrinsic value*.

instrumental value (12). The view that something has value only insofar as it is useful to serve human ends.

intersex (17). Descriptive of conditions in which an individual does not present clear biological markers to determine whether the individual is male or female.

intrauterine device (IUD) (19). Method of *birth control* whereby either a copper or a hormonal device is placed into a woman's uterus to prevent conception or implantation of a fertilized egg. See *contraception*.

intrauterine insemination (IUI) (19). Fertility procedure involving the collection and accumulation of male sperm and then the injection of that sperm (usually with a needle-less syringe) into the female uterus during the most fertile part of a woman's cycle. Also called *artificial insemination*.

intrinsic value (12). Something's having value in its being. Also called *inherent value.*

in vitro fertilization (IVF) (19). Fertility procedure involving the collection of eggs and sperm. The eggs and sperm are placed in a petri dish to facilitate fertilization. Fertilized eggs are then injected into the uterus of the woman.

involuntary euthanasia (16). Type of *euthanasia* for which a patient has neither given consent nor left instructions. Cf. *nonvoluntary euthanasia; voluntary euthanasia.*

IUD. See *intrauterine device.*

IUI. See *intrauterine insemination.*

IVF. See *in vitro fertilization.*

jihad. See *crusade.*

jus ad bellum (14). Latin, "justice to war." Set of moral principles in just-war theory that must be met before waging war.

jus in bello (14). Latin, "justice in war." Set of moral principles in just-war theory that must be maintained while conducting war. See *discrimination.*

just cause (14). Principle of just-war theory whereby the reasons for going to war must be focused on *justice.*

just deserts (13). The concept that someone receives something that the person *deserves* in light of what he or she has done.

justice (9, 13). One of the cardinal virtues, variously defined as what one is due (classical justice) or the standard of God's holiness and righteousness that requires actions meant to reflect God's desired outcomes (biblical justice). See *just cause.*

justification (3). The declaration by God of a believer as reconciled to himself and through the righteousness he imputes to those who call on his name in faith.

just-war criteria (14). Set of criteria within just-war theory that govern whether war can be engaged and how war is conducted.

lex talionis (13). Latin, "law of retaliation or retribution." Often described as "life for life, eye for eye."

makarios (4). Greek, often translated as "blessed" or "happy." Meant to depict or describe, based on observation, the *flourishing* of a human life as a result of how one is living.

mala in se (14). Latin, "evil in itself." Used in just-war theory regarding the avoidance of evil means, which are inherently evil.

maldistribution (13). Inequitable application of punishment.

material principle of justice (9). The principle that provides specific, guiding criteria to inform how one determines what "just treatment" is in a specific context.

metaethics (1). The subfield in the discipline of ethics that focuses on the question "why?" It is foundational and thus the most important subfield of ethics because it seeks to discover and establish the origin and basis by which one might assess something as right or wrong, good or evil. It is concerned with discovering or establishing the basic grounding or justification for claiming that one's view of morality should be accepted as superior to (or at least preferred over) another view.

metanarrative (2). An overarching story line. When applied to Scripture, it includes the paradigm of creation, *fall*, *redemption*, and *restoration*.

metaphysics (1). The inquiry into the nature of reality.

miscarriage. See *abortion, spontaneous*.

missional worshiper (2). A human who expresses proper *worship* of God in the context of human society and throughout all creation.

moral absolutes (8). Binding moral principles that do not change. See *graded absolutism*; *ideal absolutism*; *nonconflicting absolutism*.

moral dilemmas (6, 8). Those complicated moral situations that occur in a broken and fallen world such that it appears that in order to obey the Lord, one must also simultaneously disobey one of his commandments. Also called *conflicts of duty*; *tragic moral choices*. See *Decalogue*; *generalism*; *graded absolutism*; *humble absolutism*; *ideal absolutism*; *nonconflicting absolutism*; *progressive transformation*; *situationalism*.

moral relativism (7). Ethical system in which right and wrong are determined by each individual or culture, with no objective standards.

moral status (6, 15). A consideration of who or what should be considered valuable and what level of value should be attributed. See *biocentrism*; *ecocentric*; *ecocentrism*; *egocentric*; *functionalism*.

moral traces (8, 13). Sense of regret after breaking a moral principle.

moral vertigo (3). A metaphor to explain what happens to human moral perception because of the darkening effects of sin on human minds and hearts.

moral weightiness (6). Significance of a moral rule or *domain of ethical assessment*.

natural law (5). The set of moral principles that are woven into the fabric of the universe by God's design and to which all humans are accountable—whether they discover them or not, or whether they attribute them to God or not.

natural man (4). One who does not accept the teachings given by the Spirit of God that relate to the spiritual realities of God and his created universe.

natural theology (5). Study of the extent of God's general revelation that can be perceived by sinners apart from the Bible. See *revelation, general*.

nonconflicting absolutism (8). Ethical approach to the question of *moral dilemmas* that holds that many moral absolutes exist, none of which ever really conflict and therefore can never be transgressed. Also called *unqualified absolutism*.

noncontingent Being (2). God, who does not depend on anything for existence.

nonvoluntary euthanasia (16). Type of *euthanasia* for which a patient is unable to give consent and has not left prior instructions. Cf. *involuntary euthanasia*; *voluntary euthanasia*.

normative ethics (1, 6). The subfield of ethics that is concerned primarily with the systematic identification and development of the virtues and norms necessary to shape morally good character and guide morally right decision-making in light of the circumstances, consequences, and relationships present in a given context.

norming norm (5). The standard by which all others are measured. Descriptive of Scripture.

Obergefell v. Hodges (18). 2015 U.S. Supreme Court opinion (576 U.S. 644) legalizing same-sex marriage.

orthodoxy (1). Rightly formed and ordered beliefs. Generally refers to beliefs about God, his Word, and his creation. See *doxology*; *orthopraxy*.

orthopraxy (1). Rightly formed and ordered principles of life and practice. See *doxology*; *orthodoxy*.

pacifism (14). Position that war and violence are never justified.

palliative care (16). Treatment focusing on providing relief from symptoms to improve a patient's quality of life.

Paraclete, first (4). Jesus Christ.

Paraclete, second (4). The Holy Spirit.

passive euthanasia (16). Type of *euthanasia* that occurs when a person refuses or forgoes life-sustaining treatments (an act of omission). Cf. *active euthanasia*.

penal substitutionary atonement (1). Jesus Christ's paying the penalty for humankind's sin through his death on the cross.

perfect (4). Complete, *flourishing*. See *teleios*.

personhood (15). Status as a person. In *abortion* debate, personhood includes the question whether one is worthy of the *sanctity of human life*.

perspicuity of Scripture (5). Clarity of Scripture; the claim that the Bible is written in a way such that it is understandable.

physician-assisted suicide (16). Type of *active euthanasia* for which a patient enlists the help of a physician to take the person's life.

pill, the (19). Hormonal method of *birth control* delivered commonly in pill form, but also by other methods (such as patch, shot, implant, and ring).

polyamory (17). The practice of multiple men's and women's entering into a marriagelike relationship with one another.

polygamy (17). A marriage arrangement whereby one individual is married to multiple partners.

positional truth (3). Foundational reality about mankind as revealed in Scripture.

poverty (11). The absence of sufficient wealth to meet the basic necessities of life. See *principle of subsidiarity*.

principle of double effect (15). Moral principle that helps determine when it is morally permissible to choose a course of action that will result in both good and bad effects.

principle of subsidiarity (11). The idea that smaller, simpler, and more local organizations should accomplish tasks rather than larger, more complex organizations. Specifically applied to alleviation of *poverty*.

principle of utility (7). Central premise of *utilitarianism* that "holds that actions are right in proportion as they tend to promote happiness, and wrong as they tend to produce the reverse of happiness" (John Stuart Mill). Also called *"greatest happiness" principle*.

principles, absolute (6). Moral rules that are always binding.

principles, *prima facie* (6, 8). Moral rules that appear binding on the surface.

progressive transformation (8). Continual renewal of the mind that leads a believer to view what once appeared as actual *moral dilemmas* (to the unregenerate) as morally complex situations that do not necessitate the transgression of absolute commands.

proportionality (14). Principle of just-war theory that deems the type of military force selected to be the least force possible commensurate with achieving the action's primary goal.

psychosomatic unity. See *dualistic holism*.

race (10). Term often used to describe various divisions within the human species. More accurately, a term that describes all of humanity—the human race. See *ethnicity*.

racism (10). A firmly held belief that the primary traits and/or tendencies of one particular people group are superior to that of another and that can lead to social, political, economic, or even religious doctrines and practices that favor the group believed to be superior. See *individualist definition of racism*; *structuralist definition of racism*.

recidivism (13). The tendency of a person who has been convicted of a crime to repeat a similar criminal behavior after having been arrested and serving a sentence of punishment.

redemption (3). The act of buying back something. Applied to theology, it is saving of mankind from the consequences of sin. See *metanarrative*.

redemptive suffering (16). The theological concept that suffering is described as a tool God uses to shape humans into the kind of people that he wants them to be.

regeneration (4). The application to one's life of the atoning work of Christ by bringing the person from spiritual death to spiritual life.

rehabilitation (11, 13). A motivation of a penal justice system to "repair" or "restore" an individual in some way such that he or she can make a successful reentry into society and the workforce at the end of a prison sentence.

relational response (7). *Domain of ethical assessment* that is concerned with understanding how caring for relationships ought to shape one's moral choices, acts, and behaviors.

restitution (13). A motivation for punishment that refers to the idea of the criminal's returning to the victim that which was stolen or taken away.

restoration (3). The return to the abundant life that God designed. See *metanarrative*.

retentionist (13, 14). Position of those who want to retain the death penalty as a viable option for governments. Cf. *abolitionist*.

revealed morality (1, 2, 12). The function of Scripture whereby God reveals the norms, principles, rules, guidelines, and moral examples for humans to become the kind of people that he designed and created them to be, and then to act in accord not only with their designed nature but also with the original design of the world as God created it.

revealed reality (1, 2, 12). The foundational understanding of the nature of reality and the way things are as revealed in Scripture.

revelation, divine (5). God's disclosure of himself.

revelation, general (5). The knowledge that God reveals about himself and that is available to be discovered "generally" by God's image-bearers—be they his disciples or not. See *natural theology*.

revelation, natural (5). Knowledge that God has revealed about himself through creation.

revelation, special (5). God's revelation of himself to particular persons at specific times and places that can lead to salvation.

Roe v. Wade (15). 1973 U.S. Supreme Court decision (410 U.S. 113) legalizing *abortion*.

rules, objective (6). Rules that exist and stand independent of someone's opinion about them.

rules, subjective (6). Rules that are derived from or heavily influenced by one's own beliefs or feelings rather than being based on facts or commands that arise external to oneself.

sanctification (4). The work of the Holy Spirit that helps Christ's disciples to become in character and practice what God has declared them to be in truth.

sanctification, final. See *sanctification, perfect*.

sanctification, future. See *sanctification, perfect*.

sanctification, perfect (3). The final experience of believers' transformation in the presence of God when their practices and attitudes fully align with God's moral law and created design and that is possible only based on the finished work of Christ. Also called *final sanctification*; *future sanctification*.

sanctification, personal (9). The process of an individual's being conformed to the image of God (*imago Dei*).

sanctification, progressive (3). The ongoing process of believers' experiencing in their daily practices and attitudes the truth of what God has declared about them because of the finished work of Christ.

sanctity of human life (13, 15, 16). Principle deriving from Genesis 1:27–28 and Exodus 20:13 that affirms that God made human beings unique among all creation when he created them in his image. For this reason, human life is to be honored and protected both individually and corporately. See *personhood*.

sexual orientation (17). The psychosexual attraction of one person toward someone else.

shalom (4, 14). Hebrew term relating to the inner harmony, wholeness, or sense of completeness of the human being that results from living a life rightly ordered to God in the manner that he designed.

situationalism (8). Ethical approach to the question of *moral dilemmas* that claims that only one absolute moral law (either "do the most loving thing" or "greatest good to the greatest number of people") governs all behavior. All other moral considerations should be determined in light of this rule. A form of *utilitarianism*.

snowflake babies (19). Frozen embryos.

social justice (9). The moral formation and lawful ordering of society.

spiritual formation (4). Growing in faith and maturity as a disciple of Jesus Christ.

sterilization (19). A method of *contraception* that involves a surgical procedure designed to permanently terminate an individual's fertility.

stewardship (11, 12). The management of resources by one individual on behalf of the owner whereby both the owner and the manager benefit.

structuralist definition of *racism* (10). The idea that there are patterns of *racism* in society even when individuals do not have racial intentions or act in racist ways.

subdue and rule (12). Mandate given by God to exercise over creation in Genesis 1:28. See *cultural mandate*; *worship mandate*.

surrogacy (19). The procedure in which the gestation and birth of a baby occur in a woman who either is not the child's biological mother or is willing to donate her egg and carry a child but who relinquishes parenting rights to those contracting with her to carry the child. Also called *surrogate motherhood*.

surrogate motherhood. See *surrogacy*.

teleios (4). Greek, *perfect*. Embodies a whole-life devotion to the things of God in character, disposition, and action such that someone is mature, complete, lacking in nothing spiritually.

teleological ethics (6). System of ethics that is concerned not so much with the consequences or results of a moral choice, but with one's intention to act toward a final goal.

telos (2). Final goal or purpose. See *domains of ethical assessment*.

third-party gametes (19). Donor eggs or sperm.

three divisions of the law (5). Civil, ceremonial, and moral.

three uses of the law (5). Condemning, restraining, guiding.

tragic moral choices. See *moral dilemmas*.

transgenderism (17). The expression of a gender identity that is incongruent with one's *biological sex*.

tubal pregnancy. See *ectopic pregnancy*.

tyranny of the majority (7). Result of consequentialism when minority perspectives are trampled for the gain of the majority because the good of the many was determined to be worthy of the sacrifices of the fewer.

uncreation (3). The sinful state of moving contrary to God's design in favor of moral degradation and everlasting death.

unqualified absolutism. See *nonconflicting absolutism*.

utilitarianism (7). Ethical theory that places a consideration of consequences as the primary domain of ethical assessment. Historically, it was developed in ancient Greece by Epicurus (341–270 B.C.); later in the Enlightenment, it was revived and reformulated by Jeremy Bentham (1748–1832) and, most famously, by John Stuart Mill (1806–73). See *principle of utility*; *situationalism*.

virtues, moral (6). Qualities that form one's character.

virtues, theological (6). Faith, hope, and love.

voluntary euthanasia (16). Type of *euthanasia* for which a patient gives consent or has left prior instructions and those instructions are followed. Cf. *involuntary euthanasia*; *nonvoluntary euthanasia*.

wealth (11). The accumulation of property and possessions that have value. See *poverty*.

wealth creation (11). Using various methods and policies to generate *wealth*. May apply to individuals and governments.

wealth gap (11). The difference in accumulated *wealth* between those at the top end of the wealth spectrum and those at the bottom end.

worldview (1). A conceptual framework made up of one's fundamental beliefs and loves that then functions as the means by which the person perceives, interprets, and judges reality and that also drives how he or she behaves in it.

worship. Giving to the right God (the one true God) all the praise, honor, and glory he is due from the heart, as he instructs, in every aspect of believers' existence, both by themselves and corporately with all other people created in his image. See *disordered worship*; *missional worshiper*; *worship mandate*.

worship mandate (2). The *worship* component of Genesis 1:27–28 whereby mankind is instructed to fill the earth with worshipers and exercise dominion over the rest of creation. See *cultural mandate*; *subdue and rule*.

Year of Jubilee (11). Old Testament practice every fiftieth year of relieving debts and allowing land to return to the family of inheritance.

Bibliography

Abort73. "U.S. Abortion Statistics." Accessed January 23, 2020. https://abort73.com/abortion_facts/us_abortion_statistics/.

———. "Worldwide Abortion Statistics." Accessed January 23, 2020. https://abort73.com/abortion_facts/worldwide_abortion_statistics/.

Agency for Health Care Administration. "Reported Induced Terminations of Pregnancy (ITOP) by Reason, by Trimester: 2019." Accessed April 7, 2020. https://ahca.myflorida.com/MCHQ/Central_Services/Training_Support/docs/TrimesterByReason_2019.pdf.

Alcorn, Randy. *Does the Birth Control Pill Cause Abortions?* 10th ed. Sandy, OR: Eternal Perspective Ministries, 2004.

———. *Managing God's Money: A Biblical Guide.* Carol Stream, IL: Tyndale, 2011.

———. *Money, Possessions, and Eternity.* Carol Stream, IL: Tyndale, 2003.

———. *ProLife Answers to ProChoice Arguments.* Expanded and updated ed. Colorado Springs: Multnomah, 2000.

———. *Why Pro-Life? Caring for the Unborn and Their Mothers.* Rev. and updated ed. Peabody, MA: Hendrickson, 2012.

Alexander, T. Desmond. *From Eden to the New Jerusalem: An Introduction to Biblical Theology.* Grand Rapids: Kregel Academic, 2008.

Allberry, Sam. *Is God Anti-Gay? And Other Questions about Homosexuality, the Bible and Same-Sex Attraction.* Purcellville, VA: Good Book Company, 2013.

Allman, Mark J. *Who Would Jesus Kill? War, Peace, and the Christian Tradition.* Winona, MN: St. Mary's, 2008.

Alper, Mariel, Matthew R. Durose, and Joshua Markman. "2018 Update on Prisoner Recidivism: A 9-Year Follow-Up Period (2005–2014)." Bureau of Justice Statistics, May 2018. Accessed January 7, 2020. https://www.bjs.gov/index.cfm?ty=pbdetail&iid=6266.

American Psychological Association. "Answers to Your Questions for a Better Understanding of Sexual Orientation and Homosexuality," 2008. Accessed April 30, 2020. http://www.apa.org/topics/lgbt/orientation.

Amnesty International. "Death Sentences and Executions 2018." Accessed March 30, 2020. https://www.amnesty.org/download/Documents/ACT5098 702019ENGLISH.PDF.

Anderson, Ryan T. *When Harry Became Sally: Responding to the Transgender Moment*. New York: Encounter, 2018.

"Answers to Your Questions for a Better Understanding of Sexual Orientation and Homosexuality." American Psychological Association, 2008. Accessed April 30, 2020. http://www.apa.org/topics/lgbt/orientation.

Anyabwile, Thabiti. "The Glory and Supremacy of Jesus Christ in Ethnic Distinction and over Ethnic Identities." In *For the Fame of God's Name: Essays in Honor of John Piper*, edited by Sam Storms and Justin Taylor, 293–307. Wheaton, IL: Crossway, 2010.

Aquinas, Thomas. *Commentary on the Sentences*. Translated by Ralph McInerny. Accessed June 23, 2020. https://isidore.co/aquinas/english/Sentences.htm.

———. *A Summa of the Summa*. Edited by Peter Kreeft. San Francisco: Ignatius, 1990.

———. *Summa Theologica*. Translated by Fathers of the English Dominican Province. Notre Dame, IN: Christian Classics, 1981.

Arichea, Daniel C., Jr. "Peace in the New Testament." *Practical Papers for the Bible Translator* 38, no. 2 (April 1987): 201–6. Accessed January 17, 2020. http://www.ubs-translations.org/tbt/1987/02/TBT198702.html?seq=3.

Aristotle. *Nicomachean Ethics*. Translated by Terence Irwin. 2nd ed. Indianapolis: Hackett, 1999.

Ash, Christopher. *Marriage: Sex in the Service of God*. Vancouver, BC: Regent College Publishing, 2003.

———. *Married for God: Making Your Marriage the Best It Can Be*. Wheaton, IL: Crossway, 2016.

Athenagoras. "A Plea for the Christians." In *Fathers of the Second Century: Hermas, Tatian, Athenagoras, Theophilus, and Clement of Alexandria (Entire)*, edited by Alexander Roberts, James Donaldson, and A. Cleveland Coxe, 129–48. Translated by B. P. Pratten. Ante-Nicene Fathers 2. Buffalo: Christian Literature, 1885.

Augustine. *City of God*. Translated by Marcus Dods. New York: Modern Library, 1993.

———. *Contra Faustum*. Accessed January 19, 2020. http://www.newadvent.org/fathers/140622.htm.

———. *De Bono Coniugali*. In *The Fathers of the Church: A New Translation*. Translated by Charles T. Wilcox. Vol. 27. New York: Fathers of the Church, 1955.

———. *The Enchiridion on Faith, Hope, and Love*. Washington, DC: Regnery Gateway, 1961.

———. *Letter: From Augustine to Jerome.* Accessed January 11, 2019. http://www
.newadvent.org/fathers/1102082.htm.

———. *On Christian Doctrine.* Accessed January 11, 2019. https://www.ccel.org
/ccel/schaff/npnf102.v.v.ix.html.

Baer, Drake. "Maybe Monogamy Isn't the Only Way to Love." The Cut. *New York,*
March 6, 2017. https://www.thecut.com/2017/03/science-of-polyamory-open
-relationships-and-nonmonogamy.html.

Bailey, Derrick Sherwin. *Homosexuality and the Western Christian Tradition.*
London: Longmans, Green and Co., 1955.

Bainton, Roland H. *Christian Attitudes toward War and Peace: A Historical Survey
and Critical Re-Evaluation.* New York: Abingdon, 1960.

Balzarini, Rhonda N., Lorne Campbell, Taylor Kohut, Bjarne M. Holmes, Justin J.
Lehmiller, Jennifer J. Harman, and Nicole Atkins. "Perceptions of Primary
and Secondary Relationships in Polyamory." *PLoS ONE* 12, no. 5 (2017).
Accessed April 21, 2020. https://doi.org/10.1371/journal.pone.0177841.

Baron, Harold M. "The Web of Urban Racism." In *Institutional Racism in America,*
edited by Louis L. Knowles and Kenneth Prewitt, 134–76. Englewood Cliffs,
NJ: Prentice-Hall, 1969.

Barth, Karl. *The Doctrine of Creation.* Edited by G. W. Bromiley and T. F. Torrance.
Translated by A. T. Mackay, T. H. L. Parker, H. Knight, H. A. Kennedy, and
J. Marks. Vol. 3.4 of *Church Dogmatics.* London: T. & T. Clark, 2004.

Bass, Gary J. "Jus Post Bellum." *Philosophy & Public Affairs* 32, no. 4 (October
2004): 384–412.

Batty, Michael, Jesse Bricker, Joseph Briggs, Elizabeth Holmquist, Susan McIn-
tosh, Kevin Moore, Eric Nielsen, Sarah Reber, Molly Shatto, Kamila Sommer,
Tom Sweeney, and Alice Henriques Volz. "Introducing the Distributional
Financial Accounts of the United States." Finance and Economic Discussion
Series 2019–017, Board of Governors of the Federal Reserve System, 2019.
https://www.federalreserve.gov/econres/feds/files/2019017pap.pdf.

Bauckham, Richard. *The Bible and Ecology: Rediscovering the Community of Creation.* Waco, TX: Baylor University Press, 2010.

Bavinck, Herman. *Reformed Dogmatics.* Vol. 1, *Prolegomena.* Grand Rapids: Baker
Academic, 2003.

Beach, Waldo. "A Theological Analysis of Race Relations." In *Faith and Ethics: The
Theology of H. Richard Niebuhr,* edited by Paul Ramsey, 205–24. New York:
Harper & Brothers, 1957.

Beach, Waldo, and H. Richard Niebuhr, eds. *Christian Ethics: Sources of the Living
Tradition.* 2nd ed. New York: John Wiley & Sons, 1973.

Beale, G. K. *The Temple and the Church's Mission.* Downers Grove, IL: InterVarsity
Press, 2004.

Beauchamp, Tom L., and James F. Childress. *Principles of Biomedical Ethics*. 4th ed. New York: Oxford University Press, 1994.

———. *Principles of Biomedical Ethics*. 6th ed. New York: Oxford University Press, 2009.

———. *Principles of Biomedical Ethics*. 8th ed. New York: Oxford University Press, 2019.

Beaumont, Douglas. "Aquinas on Abortion," March 1, 2012. Accessed January 25, 2020. https://douglasbeaumont.com/2012/03/01/aquinas-on-abortion/.

Beck, James R., and Bruce Demarest. *The Human Person in Theology and Psychology: A Biblical Anthropology for the Twenty-First Century*. Grand Rapids: Kregel, 2005.

Beckwith, Francis J. *Defending Life: A Moral and Legal Case against Abortion Choice*. Cambridge: Cambridge University Press, 2007.

———. *Politically Correct Death: Answering the Arguments for Abortion Rights*. Grand Rapids: Baker, 1993.

Bedau, Hugo Adam, ed. *The Death Penalty in America: Current Controversies*. New York: Oxford University Press, 1997.

Bedau, Hugo Adam, and Paul G. Cassell. *Debating the Death Penalty: Should America Have Capital Punishment? The Experts on Both Sides Make Their Best Case*. New York: Oxford University Press, 2004.

Beisner, E. Calvin. *Where Garden Meets Wilderness: Evangelical Entry into the Environmental Debate*. Grand Rapids: Acton Institute/Eerdmans, 1997.

Bell, Daniel M., Jr. *Just War as Christian Discipleship: Recentering the Tradition in the Church Rather than the State*. Grand Rapids: Brazos, 2009.

Bernardin, Joseph Cardinal. *Consistent Ethic of Life*. Kansas City, MO: Sheed & Ward, 1988.

Bernardin, Joseph L. *The Seamless Garment: Writings on the Consistent Ethics of Life*. Edited by Thomas A. Nairn. New York: Orbis, 2008.

Best, Harold. *Unceasing Worship*. Downers Grove, IL: InterVarsity Press, 2003.

Beville, Kieran. *Dying to Kill: A Christian Perspective on Euthanasia and Assisted Suicide*. Cambridge, OH: Christian Publishing House, 2014.

Bible, Seth A. "Pursuing Ecological Virtue: A Critical Analysis of the Environmental Virtue Ethics Models of Ronald Sandler, Louke Van Wensveen, and Philip Cafaro." PhD diss., Southeastern Baptist Theological Seminary, 2011.

Billings, Evelyn, and Ann Westmore. *The Billings Method*. Updated ed. Melbourne: Penguin, 2003.

Block, Daniel I. *For the Glory of God: Recovering a Biblical Theology of Worship*. Grand Rapids: Baker, 2014.

Blomberg, Craig L. *Christians in an Age of Wealth: A Biblical Theology of Stewardship*. Grand Rapids: Zondervan, 2013.

———. "Marriage, Divorce, Remarriage, and Celibacy: An Exegesis of Matthew 19:3–12." *Trinity Journal* 11, no. 2 (Fall 1990): 161–96.

———. *Matthew.* NAC 22. Nashville: B&H, 1992.

Blum, Edward J., and Paul Harvey. *The Color of Christ: The Son of God and the Saga of Race in America.* Chapel Hill: University of North Carolina Press, 2012.

Bonhoeffer, Dietrich. *Christology.* London: Collins, 1971.

Bonilla-Silva, Eduardo. *Racism without Racists: Color-Blind Racism and the Persistence of Racial Inequality in America.* 5th ed. Lanham, MD: Rowman & Littlefield, 2018.

Bosnich, David A. "The Principle of Subsidiarity." *Religion & Liberty* 6, no. 4 (1996): 9–10.

Boswell, John. *Christianity, Social Tolerance, and Homosexuality.* Chicago: University of Chicago Press, 1980.

Bouma-Prediger, Steven. "Doesn't Creation Care Confuse Nature with God?" In *A Faith Encompassing All Creation: Addressing Commonly Asked Questions about Christian Care for the Environment,* edited by Tripp York and Andy Alexis-Baker, 18–28. Eugene, OR: Cascade, 2014.

———. *For the Beauty of the Earth: A Christian Vision for Creation Care.* 2nd ed. Grand Rapids: Baker, 2010.

Bradley, Anne R., and Art Lindsley, eds. *For the Least of These: A Biblical Answer to Poverty.* Grand Rapids: Zondervan, 2014.

Bradley, Anthony B. *Liberating Black Theology: The Bible and the Black Experience in America.* Wheaton, IL: Crossway, 2010.

Brenan, Megan. "Americans' Strong Support for Euthanasia Persists." Gallup, May 31, 2018. Accessed February 7, 2020. https://news.gallup.com/poll/235145/americans-strong-support-euthanasia-persists.aspx.

Bridges, Jerry. *The Pursuit of Holiness.* Colorado Springs: NavPress, 2001.

Bright, Bill. *The Journey Home: Finishing with Joy.* Nashville: Thomas Nelson, 2003.

Brown, Jeannine K. *Scripture as Communication.* Grand Rapids: Baker, 2007.

Brownson, James V. *Bible, Gender, Sexuality: Reframing the Church's Debate on Same-Sex Relationships.* Grand Rapids: Eerdmans, 2013.

Brunner, Frederick Dale. *The Gospel of John: A Commentary.* Grand Rapids: Eerdmans, 2012.

Buber, Martin. *I and Thou.* Translated by Ronald Gregor Smith. New York: Scribner Classics, 2000.

Budziszewski, J. *On the Meaning of Sex.* Wilmington, DE: ISI, 2012.

———. *Written on the Heart: The Case for Natural Law.* Downers Grove, IL: InterVarsity Press, 1997.

Burk, Denny. *What Is the Meaning of Sex?* Wheaton, IL: Crossway, 2013.

Bush, George W. "Remarks by President Bush on McVeigh Execution." June 11,

2001. Accessed January 7, 2020. https://georgewbush-whitehouse.archives
.gov/news/releases/2001/06/20010611.html.

Butterfield, Rosaria. Foreword to *Holy Sexuality and the Gospel: Sex, Desire, and Relationships Shaped by God's Grand Story*, by Christopher Yuan, xiii–xv. New York: Multnomah, 2018.

Cahill, Lisa Sowle. *Love Your Enemies: Discipleship, Pacifism, and Just War Theory*. Minneapolis: Augsburg, 1994.

Calvin, John. *Commentary on the First Book of Moses Called Genesis*. Grand Rapids: Baker, 2005.

———. *Institutes of the Christian Religion*. Edited by John T. McNeill. Translated by Ford Lewis Battles. 2 vols. Library of Christian Classics 20–21. Philadelphia: Westminster Press, 1960.

Carlson, Allan. *Godly Seed: American Evangelicals Confront Birth Control, 1872–1973*. New Brunswick, NJ: Transaction, 2012.

Carson, D. A. *Christ and Culture Revisited*. Grand Rapids: Eerdmans, 2008.

———. *The Gospel according to John*. PNTC. Grand Rapids: Eerdmans, 1991.

———. "Matthew." In *Matthew, Mark, Luke*, edited by Frank E. Gaebelein, 3–599. Expositor's Bible Commentary 8. Grand Rapids: Zondervan, 1984.

———. "Worship under the Word." In *Worship by the Book*, edited by D. A. Carson, 11–63. Grand Rapids: Zondervan, 2002.

Carson, Rachel. *Silent Spring*. New York: Houghton-Mifflin, 1962.

Cassuto, Umberto. *A Commentary on the Book of Genesis*. Jerusalem: Magnes, 1978.

Centers for Disease Control and Prevention. "Infertility FAQs." Accessed June 8, 2020. https://www.cdc.gov/reproductivehealth/infertility/index.htm.

———. "What Is Assisted Reproductive Technology?" Accessed June 8, 2020. http://www.cdc.gov/art/whatis.html.

Chandler, Matt. *Mingling of Souls: Love, Marriage, Redemption, and Sex in the Song of Solomon*. Colorado Springs: David C. Cook, 2015.

Charles, J. Daryl. *Between Pacifism and Jihad: Just War and the Christian Tradition*. Downers Grove, IL: InterVarsity Press, 2005.

Charles, J. Daryl, and Timothy J. Demy. *War, Peace, and Christianity: Questions and Answers from a Just-War Perspective*. Wheaton, IL: Crossway, 2010.

Chester, Tim. *Good News to the Poor: Social Involvement and the Gospel*. Wheaton, IL: Crossway, 2013.

Childress, James F. "Just-War Theories: The Bases, Interrelations, Priorities, and Functions of Their Criteria." *MCR* (Fall 1982): 19–36.

———. "Pacifism." In *Encyclopedia of Political Theory*, edited by Mark Bevir, 1003–5. Thousand Oaks, CA: SAGE, 2010.

Chou, Vivian. "How Science and Genetics Are Reshaping the Race Debate of the

21st Century." Science in the News, Harvard University, Graduate School of Arts and Sciences, April 17, 2017. Accessed June 4, 2020. http://sitn.hms .harvard.edu/flash/2017/science-genetics-reshaping-race-debate-21st -century/.

Christensen, Duane L. *Deuteronomy 21:10–34:12*. Word Biblical Commentary 6B. Nashville: Thomas Nelson, 2002.

Christian Medical & Dental Associations. "Artificially-Administered Nutrition and Hydration." https://cmda.org/wp-content/uploads/2018/04/Artificial -Hydration-and-Nutrition.pdf.

———. "Christian Medical & Dental Associations Scientific Statement: Possible Post-conceptional Effects of Hormonal Birth Control." Accessed June 11, 2020. https://cmda.org/wp-content/uploads/2018/04/Hormonalbirthcontrol -1.pdf.

Christopher, Paul. *The Ethics of War and Peace*. Upper Saddle River, NJ: Prentice Hall, 1999.

Claar, Victor V., and Robin J. Klay. *Economics in Christian Perspective: Theory, Policy and Life Choices*. Downers Grove, IL: IVP Academic, 2007.

Clark, David K., and Robert V. Rakestraw. "Moral Dilemmas." In *Theory and Method*, edited by David K. Clark and Robert V. Rakestraw, 113–17. Vol. 1 of *Readings in Christian Ethics*. Grand Rapids: Baker, 1994.

Clay, Nolan, Penny Owen, and Ed Godfrey. "McVEIGH EXECUTED: Bomber Silenced Forever; Handwritten Final Statement Quotes Poem." *Oklahoman*, June 12, 2001. Accessed January 7, 2020. https://oklahoman.com/article /2744588/mcveigh-executed-bomber-silenced-forever-handwritten-final -statement-quotes-poem.

Clouse, Robert G., ed. *War: Four Christian Views*. Downers Grove, IL: InterVarsity Press, 1991.

Coates, A. J. *The Ethics of War*. Manchester, UK: Manchester University Press, 1997.

Cole, Graham A. *He Who Gives Life: The Doctrine of the Holy Spirit*. Wheaton, IL: Crossway, 2007.

Coleman, Robert. *The Master Plan of Evangelism*. Old Tappan, NJ: Spire, 1963.

Collinson, Sylvia Wilkey. *Making Disciples: The Significance of Jesus' Educational Methods for Today's Church*. Eugene, OR: Wipf & Stock, 2004.

Copan, Paul. *Is God a Moral Monster? Making Sense of the Old Testament God*. Grand Rapids: Baker, 2011.

Corbett, Steve, and Brian Fikkert. *When Helping Hurts: How to Alleviate Poverty without Hurting the Poor . . . and Yourself*. Chicago: Moody, 2012.

Cornwall, Susannah. *Theology and Sexuality*. London: SCM, 2013.

Cortines, John, and Gregory Baumer. *God and Money: How We Discovered True Riches at Harvard Business School*. Carson, CA: Rose Publishing, 2016.

——. *True Riches: What Jesus Really Said about Money and Your Heart*. Nashville: Thomas Nelson, 2019.

Cottrell, Jack W. "Abortion and the Mosaic Law." In *Issues and Applications*, edited by David K. Clark and Robert V. Rakestraw, 32–35. Vol. 2 of *Readings in Christian Ethics*. Grand Rapids: Baker, 1996.

——. *Gender Roles and the Bible: Creation, the Fall, and Redemption: A Critique of Feminist Biblical Interpretation*. Joplin, MO: College Press, 1994.

Council for Biblical Manhood and Womanhood. "The Danvers Statement," 1987. https://cbmw.org/about/danvers-statement/.

Council of Economic Advisors. "Returns on Investment in Recidivism Reducing Programs," May 2018. Accessed January 7, 2020. https://www.whitehouse.gov/wp-content/uploads/2018/05/Returns-on-Investments-in-Recidivism-Reducing-Programs.pdf.

Cowles, C. S., ed. *Show Them No Mercy: 4 Views on God and Canaanite Genocide*. Grand Rapids: Zondervan, 2003.

Credit Suisse. *Global Wealth Report 2018*. Zurich: Credit Suisse Research Institute, 2018. https://www.credit-suisse.com/corporate/en/research/research-institute/global-wealth-report.html.

Cruz, Julissa. "Marriage: More than a Century of Change." National Center for Family and Marriage Research, 2013. https://www.bgsu.edu/content/dam/BGSU/college-of-arts-and-sciences/NCFMR/documents/FP/FP-13-13.pdf.

Cutrer, William R., and Sandra L. Glahn. *The Contraception Guidebook: Options, Risks, and Answers for Christian Couples*. Grand Rapids: Zondervan, 2005.

Dallas, Joe. *Speaking of Homosexuality: Discussing the Issues with Kindness and Clarity*. Grand Rapids: Baker, 2016.

Danker, Frederick William, Walter Bauer, and William Arndt, eds. *A Greek-English Lexicon of the New Testament and Other Early Christian Literature*. 3rd ed. Chicago: University of Chicago Press, 2000.

Davis, John Jefferson. *Evangelical Ethics: Issues Facing the Church Today*. 4th ed. Phillipsburg, NJ: P&R Publishing, 2015.

——. "Theologically Sound." In *The Sterilization Option: A Guide for Christians*, edited by David B. Biebel, 63–76. Grand Rapids: Baker, 1995.

Death Penalty Information Center. "Constitutionality of the Death Penalty in America." Accessed January 3, 2020. https://deathpenaltyinfo.org/facts-and-research/history-of-the-death-penalty/constitutionality-of-the-death-penalty-in-america.

——. "Facts about the Death Penalty." Accessed November 13, 2020. https://files.deathpenaltyinfo.org/documents/pdf/FactSheet.f1601652961.pdf.

——. "Murder Rate of Death Penalty States Compared to Non-Death Penalty States." Accessed January 7, 2020. https://deathpenaltyinfo.org/facts-and

-research/murder-rates/murder-rate-of-death-penalty-states-compared-to
-non-death-penalty-states.

"Death with Dignity Advocate Brittany Maynard Dies in Oregon." NBC News, November 3, 2014. Accessed February 7, 2020. https://www.nbcnews.com /health/health-news/death-dignity-advocate-brittany-maynard-dies-oregon -n235091.

de Gobineau, Arthur. *The Inequality of Human Races*. Translated by Adrian Collins. London: William Heinemann, 1915. Accessed June 7, 2019. https:// archive.org/details/inequalityofhuma00gobi.

Delgado, Richard, and Jean Stefancic. *Critical Race Theory: An Introduction*. 3rd ed. New York: New York University Press, 2017.

Demarest, Bruce A. *General Revelation: Historical Views and Contemporary Issues*. Grand Rapids: Zondervan, 1982.

Department of Health and Human Services. "Annual Update of the HHS Poverty Guidelines." *Federal Register* 85 (January 17, 2020): 3060. https://www.gov info.gov/content/pkg/FR-2020-01-17/pdf/2020-00858.pdf.

DeRouchie, Jason S. "Confronting the Transgender Storm: New Covenant Reflections on Deuteronomy 22:5." *JBMW* 21, no. 1 (Spring 2016): 58–69.

Derr, Thomas Sieger, with James A. Nash and Richard John Neuhaus. *Environmental Ethics and Christian Humanism*. Nashville: Abingdon, 1996.

DesJardins, Joseph R. *Environmental Ethics: An Introduction to Environmental Philosophy*. 5th ed. Boston: Wadsworth, 2013.

DeWitt, Calvin B. *Earth-Wise: A Biblical Response to Environmental Issues*. 2nd ed. Grand Rapids: Faith Alive, 2005.

———. *The Environment and the Christian: What Does the New Testament Say about the Environment?* Grand Rapids: Baker, 1991.

DeYoung, Kevin. *What Does the Bible Really Teach about Homosexuality?* Wheaton, IL: Crossway, 2015.

DeYoung, Kevin, and Greg Gilbert. *What Is the Mission of the Church? Making Sense of Social Justice, Shalom, and the Great Commission*. Wheaton, IL: Crossway, 2011.

DeYoung, Rebecca Konyndyk. *Glittering Vices: A New Look at the Seven Deadly Sins and Their Remedies*. Grand Rapids: Brazos, 2009.

Didache. Edited by Alexander Roberts, James Donaldson, and A. Cleveland Coxe. Translated by M. B. Riddle. Ante-Nicene Fathers 7. Buffalo: Christian Literature, 1886. Accessed January 25, 2020. http://www.newadvent.org/fathers /0714.htm.

Dockery, David S. "The Environment, Ethics, and Exposition." In *The Earth Is the Lord's: Christians and the Environment*, edited by Richard D. Land and Louis A. Moore, 113–25. Nashville: Broadman Press, 1992.

Douma, J. *Responsible Conduct: Principles of Christian Ethics.* Phillipsburg, NJ: P&R Publishing, 2003.

———. *The Ten Commandments.* Phillipsburg, NJ: P&R Publishing, 1996.

Due, Noel. *Created for Worship: From Genesis to Revelation to You.* Fearn, Ross-shire, Scotland: Christian Focus, 2005.

Dumbrell, William J. *Covenant and Creation.* Flemington Markets, New South Wales, Australia: Paternoster, 1984.

Earls, Aaron. "Most Protestant Pastors See Human Activity behind Global Warming." *Baptist Press*, April 21, 2020. Accessed May 27, 2020. http://www.bpnews .net/54678/most-protestant-pastors-see-human-activity-behind-global -warming.

Eberstadt, Mary. *Adam and Eve after the Pill: Paradoxes of the Sexual Revolution.* San Francisco: Ignatius, 2012.

Edelstein, Ludwig. *The Hippocratic Oath: Text, Translation, and Interpretation.* Baltimore: Johns Hopkins University Press, 1943.

Edgar, Thomas R. "Divorce & Remarriage for Adultery or Desertion." In *Divorce and Remarriage: Four Christian Views*, edited by H. Wayne House, 151–96. Downers Grove, IL: InterVarsity Press, 1990.

Edwards, Jonathan. *A Treatise concerning Religious Affections.* Accessed May 8, 2020. http://www.jonathan-edwards.org/ReligiousAffections.pdf.

Ellis, Carl F., Jr. *Free at Last? The Gospel in the African-American Experience.* Downers Grove, IL: InterVarsity Press, 1996.

Emerson, Michael O., and Christian Smith. *Divided by Faith: Evangelical Religion and the Problem of Race in America.* Oxford: Oxford University Press, 2000.

Encyclopedia of Hebrew Language and Linguistics. Accessed May 24, 2018. http:// referenceworks.brillonline.com/entries/encyclopedia-of-hebrew-language -and-linguistics/collocation-modern-hebrew-EHLL_COM_00000796#d47 60123e68.

Engelhardt, H. Tristram, Jr. *The Foundations of Bioethics.* 2nd ed. New York: Oxford University Press, 1996.

Epistle of Barnabas. Edited by Alexander Roberts, James Donaldson, and A. Cleveland Coxe. Translated by Alexander Roberts and James Donaldson. Ante-Nicene Fathers 1. Buffalo: Christian Literature, 1885. Accessed January 25, 2020. http://www.newadvent.org/fathers/0124.htm.

Erickson, Millard J. *Christian Theology.* 3rd ed. Grand Rapids: Baker Academic, 2013.

Evans, Tony. *Oneness Embraced.* Chicago: Moody, 2011.

"The Fathers on Abortion." Accessed April 8, 2020. https://catholicism.org/fathers -abortion.html.

Fedler, Kyle D. *Exploring Christian Ethics: Biblical Foundations for Morality*. Louisville: Westminster John Knox, 2006.

Fee, Gordon D. *The First Epistle to the Corinthians*. New International Commentary on the New Testament. Grand Rapids: Eerdmans, 1987.

Fee, Gordon D., and Douglas Stuart. *How to Read the Bible for All Its Worth*. 3rd ed. Grand Rapids: Zondervan, 2003.

Feinberg, John S. *No One like Him: The Doctrine of God*. Wheaton, IL: Crossway, 2001.

Feinberg, John S., and Paul D. Feinberg. *Ethics for a Brave New World*. 2nd ed. Wheaton, IL: Crossway, 2010.

Feinberg, Paul. "Bible, Inerrancy and Infallibility of." In *Evangelical Dictionary of Theology*, edited by W. A. Elwell, 156–59. 2nd ed. Grand Rapids: Baker, 1984.

Feldahn, Shaunti. *The Good News about Marriage: Debunking Discouraging Myths about Marriage and Divorce*. Colorado Springs: Multnomah, 2014.

Ferguson, Sinclair B. "How Does the Bible Look at Itself?" In *Inerrancy and Hermeneutic: A Tradition, A Challenge, A Debate*, edited by Harvie M. Conn, 47–66. Grand Rapids: Baker, 1988.

Fields, Karen E., and Barbara J. Fields. *Racecraft: The Soul of Inequality in American Life*. Brooklyn, NY: Verso, 2012.

Fieser, James. *Metaethics, Normative Ethics, and Applied Ethics: Historical and Contemporary Readings*. Belmont, CA: Wadsworth, 2000.

Fikkert, Brian, and Russell Mask. *From Dependence to Dignity: How to Alleviate Poverty through Church-Centered Microfinance*. Grand Rapids: Zondervan, 2015.

Finer, Lawrence B., Lori F. Frowirth, Lindsay A. Dauphinee, Susheela Singh, and Ann M. Moore. "Reasons U.S. Women Have Abortions: Quantitative and Qualitative Perspectives." *Perspectives on Sexual and Reproductive Health* 37, no. 3 (2005): 112–14.

Fletcher, Joseph. "Ethics and Euthanasia." In *To Live and to Die: When, Why, and How*, edited by Robert H. Williams, 113–22. New York: Springer-Verlag, 1973.

———. *Morals and Medicine: The Moral Problems of the Patient's Right to Know the Truth, Contraception, Artificial Insemination, Sterilization, Euthanasia*. Princeton, NJ: Princeton University Press, 1979.

———. *Situation Ethics: The New Morality*. Philadelphia: Westminster Press, 1966.

Foley, Kathleen, and Herbert Hendin. *The Case against Assisted Suicide*. Baltimore: Johns Hopkins University Press, 2002.

Forster, Greg. *Joy for the World: How Christianity Lost Its Cultural Influence and Can Begin Rebuilding It*. Wheaton, IL: Crossway, 2014.

Frame, John M. *Apologetics to the Glory of God*. Phillipsburg, NJ: P&R Publishing, 1994.

———. *The Doctrine of God.* Phillipsburg, NJ: P&R Publishing, 2002.

———. *The Doctrine of the Christian Life.* Phillipsburg, NJ: P&R Publishing, 2008.

———. *Medical Ethics: Principles, Persons, and Problems.* Phillipsburg, NJ: Presbyterian and Reformed, 1988.

Fuller, Daniel P. "The Holy Spirit's Role in Biblical Interpretation." In *Scripture, Tradition and Interpretation,* edited by W. Ward Gasque and William Sanford LaSor, 189–98. Grand Rapids: Eerdmans, 1979.

———. "The Holy Spirit's Role in Biblical Interpretation." *International Journal of Frontier Missions* 14, no. 2 (April–June 1997): 91–95. Accessed February 15, 2019. https://ijfm.org/PDFs_IJFM/14_2_PDFs/14_2%20Fuller%20Holy%20 Spirit.pdf.

Gagnon, Robert A. J. *The Bible and Homosexual Practice: Texts and Hermeneutics.* Nashville: Abingdon, 2001.

Gehring, René. *The Biblical "One Flesh" Theology of Marriage as Constituted in Genesis 2:24.* Eugene, OR: Wipf & Stock, 2013.

Geisler, Norman L. *Christian Ethics: Contemporary Issues and Options.* 2nd ed. Grand Rapids: Baker Academic, 2010.

Gentry, Peter J. "The Meaning of 'Holy' in the Old Testament." *BibSac* 170, no. 680 (2013): 400–417. https://eds.a.ebscohost.com/eds/pdfviewer/pdfviewer?vid =1&sid=97513828-b4e4–4dab-a5ab-f708ba519074%40sdc-v-sessmgr01.

Gentry, Peter J., and Stephen J. Wellum. *Kingdom through Covenant: A Biblical-Theological Understanding of the Covenants.* Wheaton, IL: Crossway, 2012.

George, Robert P., and Christopher Tollefsen. *Embryo: A Defense of Human Life.* 2nd ed. Princeton, NJ: Witherspoon Institute, 2011.

Gilligan, Carol. *In a Different Voice.* Cambridge, MA: Harvard University Press, 1982.

———. "Moral Orientation and Moral Development." In *Justice and Care: Essential Readings in Feminist Ethics,* edited by Virginia Held, 31–46. Boulder, CO: Westview, 1995.

Girgis, Sherif, Ryan T. Anderson, and Robert P. George. *What Is Marriage? Man and Woman: A Defense.* New York: Encounter, 2012.

Goldsworthy, Graeme. *Gospel-Centered Hermeneutics: Foundations and Principles of Evangelical Biblical Interpretation.* Downers Grove, IL: IVP Academic, 2006.

González, Justo L. *Faith and Wealth: A History of Early Christian Ideas on the Origin, Significance, and Use of Money.* San Francisco: Harper & Row, 1990.

Granberg-Michaelson, Wesley. *Ecology and Life.* Waco, TX: Word, 1998.

———. *Worldly Spirituality.* San Francisco: Harper & Row, 1984.

Grenz, Stanley J. *The Moral Quest: Foundations of Christian Ethics.* Downers Grove, IL: InterVarsity Press, 1997.

———. *Sexual Ethics: An Evangelical Perspective*. Louisville: Westminster John Knox, 1990.

———. *The Social God and the Relational Self: A Trinitarian Theology of the Imago Dei*. Louisville: Westminster John Knox, 2001.

———. *Welcoming but Not Affirming: An Evangelical Response to Homosexuality*. Louisville: Westminster John Knox, 1998.

Groothuis, Rebecca Merrill. *Women Caught in the Conflict*. Grand Rapids: Baker, 1994.

Grudem, Wayne. *Christian Ethics: An Introduction to Biblical Moral Reasoning*. Wheaton, IL: Crossway, 2018.

———. *Systematic Theology: An Introduction to Biblical Doctrine*. Grand Rapids: Zondervan, 1994.

Grudem, Wayne, and Barry Ausmus. *The Poverty of Nations: A Sustainable Solution*. Wheaton, IL: Crossway, 2013.

"Guidelines for the Determination of Death." *JAMA* 246, no. 19 (1981): 2184–86.

Gustafson, James M. "Christian Ethics." In *Religion*, edited by Paul Ramsey, 285–354. Englewood Cliffs, NJ: Prentice-Hall, 1965.

———. "The Place of Scripture in Christian Ethics: A Methodological Study." *Interpretation* 24, no. 4 (1970): 430–55. https://eds.b.ebscohost.com/eds /pdfviewer/pdfviewer?vid=3&sid=c56ac038–83ab-435b-89f2-a050d6d a61a4%40sessionmgr101.

———. *Theology and Christian Ethics*. Philadelphia: Pilgrim, 1974.

Guttmacher Institute. "Induced Abortion in the United States." Accessed April 7, 2020. https://www.guttmacher.org/fact-sheet/induced-abortion-united-states.

Hammett, John S. "Human Nature." In *A Theology for the Church*, edited by Daniel L. Akin, 285–336. Rev. ed. Nashville: B&H Academic, 2014.

Haney López, Ian F. "The Social Construction of Race." In *Critical Race Theory: The Cutting Edge*, edited by Richard Delgado and Jean Stefancic, 238–48. 3rd ed. Philadelphia: Temple University Press, 2013.

Harrison, Brian. "The Real Sin of Onan." Catholic Answers, March 1, 2017. https:// www.catholic.com/magazine/print-edition/the-real-sin-of-onan.

Harvey, Dave. *When Sinners Say "I Do."* Wapwallopen, PA: Shepherd Press, 2007.

Hawkins, J. Russell, and Phillip Luke Sinitiere. *Christians and the Color Line: Race and Religion after* Divided by Faith. Oxford: Oxford University Press, 2014.

Hays, J. Daniel. *From Every People and Nation: A Biblical Theology of Race*. Downers Grove, IL: InterVarsity Press, 2003.

Hays, Richard B. "Relations Natural and Unnatural: A Response to John Boswell's Exegesis of Romans 1." *Journal of Religious Ethics* 14, no. 1 (1986): 184–215.

Heimbach, Daniel R. *True Sexual Morality: Recovering Biblical Standards for a Culture in Crisis*. Wheaton, IL: Crossway, 2004.

———. *Why Not Same-Sex Marriage? A Manual for Defending Marriage against Radical Deconstruction.* Sisters, OR: Trusted Books, 2014.

Held, Virginia. *The Ethics of Care: Personal, Political, and Global.* New York: Oxford University Press, 2006.

———, ed. *Justice and Care: Essential Readings in Feminist Ethics.* Boulder, CO: Westview, 1995.

Helm, P. "Situational Ethics." In *Encyclopedia of Biblical and Christian Ethics*, edited by R. K. Harrison, 384–85. Rev. ed. Nashville: Thomas Nelson, 1992.

Hemez, P., and W. D. Manning. "Thirty Years of Change in Women's Premarital Cohabitation Experience." Family Profiles, FP-17-05, National Center for Family & Marriage Research. Accessed April 17, 2020. https://www.bgsu.edu/ncfmr/resources/data/family-profiles/hemez-manning-30-yrs-change-women-premarital-cohab-fp-17-05.html.

Henderson, R. D. "How Abraham Kuyper Became a Kuyperian." *Christian Scholar's Review* 22, no. 1 (1992): 22–35.

Henry, Carl F. H. *Christian Personal Ethics.* Grand Rapids: Baker, 1957.

———. *God, Revelation, and Authority.* 6 vols. Waco, TX: Word, 1976–83.

Heth, William A. "Divorce, but No Remarriage." In *Divorce and Remarriage: Four Christian Views*, edited by H. Wayne House, 73–129. Downers Grove, IL: InterVarsity Press, 1990.

———. "Jesus on Divorce: How My Mind Has Changed." *SBJT* 6, no. 1 (Spring 2002): 4–29.

Hiebert, Ted. *The Yahwist's Landscape.* New Haven, CT: Yale University Press, 1996.

Hoang, Bethany Hanke, and Kristen Deede Johnson. *The Justice Calling: Where Passion Meets Perseverance.* Grand Rapids: Brazos, 2016.

Hodge, Charles. *Systematic Theology.* 3 vols. Grand Rapids: Hendrickson, 2003.

Hollinger, Dennis P. "The Ethics of Contraception." *JETS* 56, no. 4 (December 2013): 683–96.

———. *The Meaning of Sex: Christian Ethics and the Moral Life.* Grand Rapids: Baker, 2009.

Holmes, Arthur F., ed. *War and Christian Ethics: Classic and Contemporary Readings on the Morality of War.* 2nd ed. Grand Rapids: Baker, 2005.

Horn, Trent. *Persuasive Pro-Life: How to Talk about Our Culture's Toughest Issue.* El Cajon, CA: Catholic Answers, 2014.

House, H. Wayne, ed. *Divorce and Remarriage: Four Christian Views.* Downers Grove, IL: InterVarsity Press, 1990.

House, H. Wayne, and John Howard Yoder, eds. *The Death Penalty Debate: Two Opposing Views of Capital Punishment.* Waco, TX: Word, 1991.

Hsu, Albert Y. *Singles at the Crossroads: A Fresh Perspective on Christian Singleness.* Downers Grove, IL: InterVarsity Press, 1997.

Huebner, Harry J. *An Introduction to Christian Ethics: History, Movements, People.* Waco, TX: Baylor University Press, 2012.

Hull, Bill. *The Complete Book of Discipleship: On Being and Making Followers of Christ.* Colorado Springs: NavPress, 2006.

Hultgren, Arland J. "Being Faithful to the Scriptures: Romans 1:26–27 as a Case in Point." *Word & World* 14, no. 3 (Summer 1994): 315–25.

Instone-Brewer, David. *Divorce and Remarriage in the Church.* Downers Grove, IL: InterVarsity Press, 2003.

International Council on Biblical Inerrancy. "The Chicago Statement on Biblical Inerrancy." Accessed June 1, 2020. https://library.dts.edu/Pages/TL/Special /ICBI_1.pdf.

Intersex Society of North America. "How Common Is Intersex?" Accessed April 30, 2020. https://isna.org/faq/frequency/.

James, Scott. "Many Successful Gay Marriages Share an Open Secret." *New York Times*, January 28, 2010. Accessed April 20, 2020. http://www.nytimes.com /2010/01/29/us/29sfmetro.html.

Jamieson, Robert, A. R. Fausset, and David Brown. *Commentary Critical and Explanatory on the Whole Bible.* Oak Harbor, WA: Logos Research Systems, 1998.

Jeffery, Steve, Michael Ovey, and Andrew Sach. *Pierced for Our Transgressions: Rediscovering the Glory of Penal Substitution.* Wheaton, IL: Crossway, 2007.

Jenni, Ernst, and Claus Westermann. *Theological Lexicon of the Old Testament.* Peabody, MA: Hendrickson, 1997.

John Paul II. *Evangelium Vitae* ("The Gospel of Life"), March 25, 1996.

Johnson, Eric. "Born to Cheat? Tempers Meet Testimony at Debate on Adultery." ABC News, September 24, 2009. Accessed April 17, 2020. https://abcnews .go.com/Nightline/10Commandments/affairs-cheating-nightline-face-off -debate-adultery-infidelity/story?id=8645026.

Johnson, James Turner. *The Quest for Peace: Three Moral Traditions in Western Cultural History.* Princeton, NJ: Princeton University Press, 1987.

Jones, David Clyde. *Biblical Christian Ethics.* Grand Rapids: Baker, 1994.

Jones, David W. "The Betrothal View of Divorce and Remarriage." *BibSac* 165, no. 657 (January 2008): 68–85.

———. *An Introduction to Biblical Ethics.* Nashville: B&H Academic, 2013.

Jones, David W., and John K. Tarwater. "Are Biblical Covenants Dissoluble? Toward a Theology of Marriage." *SWJT* 47, no. 1 (Fall 2004): 1–11.

Jones, David W., and Russell S. Woodbridge. *Health, Wealth and Happiness: Has the Prosperity Gospel Overshadowed the Gospel of Christ?* Grand Rapids: Kregel, 2011.

Jones, Stanton L., and Mark A. Yarhouse. *Homosexuality: The Use of Scientific*

Research in the Church's Moral Debate. Downers Grove, IL: InterVarsity Press, 2000.

Kaiser, Walter C., Jr. "Poverty and the Poor in the Old Testament." In *For the Least of These: A Biblical Answer to Poverty*, edited by Anne R. Bradley and Art Lindsley, 39–56. Grand Rapids: Zondervan, 2014.

———. *Toward Old Testament Ethics*. Grand Rapids: Zondervan, 1983.

Kant, Immanuel. *Critique of Judgment: Including the First Introduction*. Translated with an introduction by Werner S. Pluhar. Indianapolis: Hackett, 1987.

———. *Grounding for the Metaphysics of Morals*. In *Ethical Philosophy*, edited by Warner A. Wick, 1–62. Translated by James W. Ellington. 2nd ed. Indianapolis: Hackett, 1994.

Karkazis, Katrina. *Fixing Sex: Intersex, Medical Authority, and Lived Experience*. Durham, NC: Duke University Press, 2008.

Keener, Craig S. *The Gospel of John: A Commentary*. Vol. 1. Grand Rapids: Baker Academic, 2003.

Keller, Timothy. *Center Church: Doing Balanced, Gospel-Centered Ministry in Your Church*. Grand Rapids: Zondervan, 2012.

———. *Generous Justice: How God's Grace Makes Us Just*. New York: Riverhead Books, 2012.

———. *The Meaning of Marriage: Facing the Complexities of Commitment with the Wisdom of God*. New York: Penguin, 2013.

Kilner, John F. *Why the Church Needs Bioethics: A Guide to Wise Engagement with Life's Challenges*. Grand Rapids: Zondervan, 2011.

Kilner, John F., Paige C. Cunningham, and W. David Hager, eds. *The Reproduction Revolution: A Christian Appraisal of Sexuality, Reproductive Technologies, and the Family*. Grand Rapids: Eerdmans, 2000.

Kilner, John F., and C. Ben Mitchell. *Does God Need Our Help? Cloning, Assisted Suicide, and Other Challenges in Bioethics*. Edited by Daniel Taylor. Wheaton, IL: Tyndale, 2003.

King, Barbara J. "A Cultural Moment for Polyamory." NPR, March 23, 2017. Accessed April 21, 2020. https://www.npr.org/sections/13.7/2017/03/23/521 199308/a-cultural-moment-for-polyamory.

King, Martin Luther, Jr. "I Have a Dream." In *A Testament of Hope: The Essential Writings and Speeches of Martin Luther King, Jr.*, edited by James M. Washington, 217–20. New York: HarperOne, 1986.

———. "Letter from Birmingham City Jail." In *A Testament of Hope: The Essential Writings and Speeches of Martin Luther King, Jr.*, edited by James M. Washington, 289–302. New York: HarperOne, 1986.

Kirkman, Maggie, Heather Rowe, Annarella Hardiman, Shelley Mallett, and Doreen Rosenthal. "Reasons Women Give for Abortion: A Review of the

Literature." *Archives of Women's Mental Health* 12, no. 6 (December 2009): 365–78.

Kittel, Gerhard, and Gerhard Friedrich, eds. *Theological Dictionary of the New Testament*. Translated by Geoffrey W. Bromiley. Grand Rapids: Eerdmans, 1968.

Kline, Meredith G. "Creation in the Image of the Glory-Spirit." *Westminster Theological Journal* 39, no. 2 (Spring 1977): 250–72.

———. *Images of the Spirit*. Grand Rapids: Baker, 1980.

Klusendorf, Scott. *The Case for Life: Equipping Christians to Engage the Culture*. Wheaton, IL: Crossway, 2009.

Köstenberger, Andreas J. *John*. Edited by Clinton E. Arnold. Zondervan Illustrated Bible Backgrounds Commentary. Grand Rapids: Zondervan, 2002.

Köstenberger, Andreas J., with David W. Jones. *God, Marriage, and Family: Rebuilding the Biblical Foundation*. 2nd ed. Wheaton, IL: Crossway, 2010.

———. *Marriage and the Family: Biblical Essentials*. Wheaton, IL: Crossway, 2012.

Köstenberger, Andreas J., and Margaret E. Köstenberger. *God's Design for Man and Woman: A Biblical-Theological Survey*. Wheaton, IL: Crossway, 2014.

Kotter, David. "Remember the Poor: A New Testament Perspective on the Problems of Poverty, Riches, and Redistribution." In *For the Least of These: A Biblical Answer to Poverty*, edited by Anne R. Bradley and Art Lindsley, 57–78. Grand Rapids: Zondervan, 2014.

Kreeft, Peter. *A Shorter Summa: The Most Essential Philosophical Passages of St. Thomas Aquinas' Summa*. San Francisco: Ignatius, 1990.

Kuyper, Abraham. *Lectures on Calvinism*. Grand Rapids: Eerdmans, 1931.

Laney, J. Carl "No Divorce & No Remarriage." In *Divorce and Remarriage: Four Christian Views*, edited by H. Wayne House, 15–54. Downers Grove, IL: InterVarsity Press, 1990.

Lawless, Chuck. *Discipled Warriors: Growing Healthy Churches That Are Equipped for Spiritual Warfare*. Grand Rapids: Kregel, 2002.

Lea, Thomas D., and Hayne P. Griffin Jr. *1, 2 Timothy, Titus*. NAC 34. Nashville: B&H, 1992.

Lenow, Evan. "The Challenge of Homosexuality for Gender Roles." *JBMW* 17, no. 2 (Fall 2012): 28–35.

———. "Exchanging the Natural for the Unnatural: Homosexuality's Distortion of God's Design." *SWJT* 49, no. 1 (Fall 2006): 31–47.

———. "Is It Adultery? The Use of Third-Party Gametes in Assisted Reproductive Technology." *SWJT* 59, no. 1 (Fall 2016): 41–57.

Leopold, Aldo. *A Sand County Almanac and Sketches Here and There*. Oxford: Oxford University Press, 1949.

Leo XIII. *Rerum Novarum*. Accessed November 11, 2020. http://www.vatican.va

/content/leo-xiii/en/encyclicals/documents/hf_l-xiii_enc_15051891_rerum
-novarum.html.

Lewis, C. S. "The Humanitarian Theory of Punishment." In *God in the Dock: Essays on Theology and Ethics*, edited by Walter Hooper, 224–30. Grand Rapids: Eerdmans, 1970.

———. *Mere Christianity*. New York: Touchstone, 1996.

———. *The Problem of Pain*. New York: HarperCollins, 1996.

———. *The Weight of Glory and Other Addresses*. New York: HarperOne, 2001.

Lewis, Gordon R., and Bruce A. Demarest. *Integrative Theology*. Vol. 1. Grand Rapids: Academie, 1987.

———. *Integrative Theology*. Vol. 3. Grand Rapids: Zondervan, 1994.

Liederbach, Mark. "Artificial Reproductive Technologies." In *God, Marriage, and Family*, by Andreas J. Köstenberger with David W. Jones, 129–34. 2nd ed. Wheaton, IL: Crossway, 2010.

———. *Chasing Infinity: Discipleship as the Pursuit of the Infinite Treasure*. Orlando, FL: Cru Press, 2017.

———. "Contraception." In *God, Marriage, and Family*, by Andreas J. Köstenberger with David W. Jones, 121–29. 2nd ed. Wheaton, IL: Crossway, 2010.

———. "Evaluating the 'Caiaphas Ethic' of Charles Krauthammer." https://www.firstthings.com/blogs/firstthoughts/2010/01/mark-liederbach-on-torture.

———. "'What Is Sexy?' Exploring the Question of How a Biblical Ethic of Worship Shapes One's View of Sex and Sexuality." *Southeastern Theological Review* 7, no. 1 (Summer 2016): 43–62.

Liederbach, Mark, and Seth Bible. *True North: Christ, the Gospel, and Creation Care*. Nashville: B&H Academic, 2012.

Liederbach, Mark D., and Alvin L. Reid. *The Convergent Church: Missional Worshipers in an Emerging Culture*. Grand Rapids: Kregel, 2009.

Longman, Tremper, III, and Daniel G. Reid. *God Is a Warrior*. Grand Rapids: Zondervan, 2010.

Loritts, Bryan. *Insider Outsider: My Journey as a Stranger in White Evangelicalism and My Hope for Us All*. Grand Rapids: Zondervan, 2018.

Louw, Johannes P., and Eugene A. Nida. *Greek-English Lexicon of the New Testament Based on Semantic Domains*. Vol. 1. New York: United Bible Societies, 1989.

Lu, Mathew. "Defusing the Violinist Analogy." *Human Life Review* 39, no. 1 (Winter 2013): 46–62. https://www.humanlifereview.com/wp-content/uploads/2015/11/2013-winter.pdf.

Luck, William F. "Moral Conflicts and Evangelical Ethics." *Grace Theological Journal* 8, no. 1 (Spring 1987): 19–34.

MacIntyre, Alasdair. *After Virtue: A Study in Moral Theory*. 3rd ed. Notre Dame, IN: University of Notre Dame Press, 2007.

———. *Whose Justice? Which Rationality?* Notre Dame, IN: University of Notre Dame Press, 1988.

Magnuson, Ken. *Invitation to Christian Ethics: Moral Reasoning and Contemporary Issues*. Grand Rapids: Kregel, 2020.

Malick, David E. "The Condemnation of Homosexuality in 1 Corinthians 6:9." *BibSac* 150, no. 600 (October 1993): 479–92.

Martin, Dale B. "Heterosexism and the Interpretation of Romans 1:18–32." *Biblical Interpretation* 3, no. 3 (January 1995): 332–55.

Mason, Eric. *Woke Church: An Urgent Call for Christians in America to Confront Racism and Injustice*. Chicago: Moody, 2018.

Maxwell, John. *The Difference Maker*. Nashville: Thomas Nelson, 2006.

Mayo Clinic. "Copper IUD." Accessed November 19, 2020. https://www.mayo clinic.org/tests-procedures/paragard/about/pac-20391270#:~:text–It's%20 sometimes%20referred%20to%20as,(ova)%2C%20preventing%20pregnancy.

McDaniel, Donald R., Jr. "Becoming Good Shepherds: A New Model of Creation Care for Evangelical Christians." PhD diss., Southeastern Baptist Theological Seminary, 2011.

McDowell, Josh, and Norman Geisler. *Love Is Always Right: A Defense of the One Moral Absolute*. Dallas: Word, 1996.

McGrath, Alister. *The Reenchantment of Nature: The Denial of Religion and the Ecological Crisis*. New York: Doubleday, 2002.

McHugh, Paul. "Transgenderism: A Pathogenic Meme." *Public Discourse* (June 10, 2015). Accessed April 21, 2020. https://www.thepublicdiscourse.com/2015 /06/15145/.

McLanahan, Sara, and Gary Sandefur. *Growing Up with a Single Parent: What Hurts, What Helps*. Cambridge, MA: Harvard University Press, 1994.

McNeill, John J. *The Church and the Homosexual*. Kansas City, MO: Sheed, Andrews, and McMeel, 1976.

McQuilkin, Robertson, and Paul Copan. *An Introduction to Biblical Ethics: Walking in the Way of Wisdom*. 3rd ed. Downers Grove, IL: IVP Academic, 2014.

Meilaender, Gilbert. "The First Institutions." *Pro Ecclesia* 6, no. 4 (1997): 444–55.

Merrill, Eugene H. *Deuteronomy*. NAC 4. Nashville: B&H, 1994.

Mill, John Stuart. *On Liberty*. New York: Penguin, 1974.

———. *Utilitarianism*. London: Longmans, Green, 1897.

Mitchell, C. Ben. *Ethics and Moral Reasoning: A Student's Guide*. Wheaton, IL: Crossway, 2013.

Mitchell, C. Ben, and D. Joy Riley. *Christian Bioethics: A Guide for Pastors, Health Care Professionals, and Families*. Nashville: B&H Academic, 2014.

Montagu, Ashley. *Man's Most Dangerous Myth: The Fallacy of Race*. 6th ed. Walnut Creek, CA: AltaMira Press, 1997.

Moo, Douglas J., and Jonathan A. Moo. *Creation Care: A Biblical Theology for the World*. Grand Rapids: Zondervan, 2018.

Moore, Russell D. "Heaven and Nature Sing: How Evangelical Theology Can Inform the Task of Environmental Protection (and Vice Versa)." *JETS* 57, no. 3 (September 2014): 571–88.

Moore, Russell D., and Andrew T. Walker, eds. *The Gospel and Same-Sex Marriage*. Nashville: B&H Academic, 2016.

Moreland, J. P. *Kingdom Triangle: Recover the Christian Mind, Renovate the Soul, Restore the Spirit's Power*. Grand Rapids: Zondervan, 2007.

———. *Love Your God with All Your Mind*. Colorado Springs: NavPress, 1997.

Moreland, J. P., and Norman L. Geisler. *The Life and Death Debate: Moral Issues of Our Time*. New York: Greenwood, 1990.

Moreland, J. P., and Scott Rae. *Body and Soul: Human Nature and the Crisis in Ethics*. Downers Grove, IL: InterVarsity Press, 2000.

Morris, Leon. *The Gospel according to Matthew*. PNTC. Grand Rapids: Eerdmans, 1992.

Murray, John. *Divorce*. Philadelphia: Presbyterian and Reformed, 1961.

———. *Principles of Conduct: Aspects of Biblical Ethics*. Grand Rapids: Eerdmans, 1957.

Nagin, Daniel S., and John V. Pepper, eds. *Deterrence and the Death Penalty*. Washington, DC: National Academies Press, 2012. Accessed March 30, 2020. https://www.nap.edu/read/13363/chapter/2#2.

Nash, James A. *Loving Nature: Ecological Integrity and Christian Responsibility*. Nashville: Abingdon, 1991.

Nash, Ronald H. *Life's Ultimate Questions: An Introduction to Philosophy*. Grand Rapids: Zondervan, 1999.

———. *Poverty and Wealth: Why Socialism Doesn't Work*. Richardson, TX: Probe, 1986.

———. *Worldviews in Conflict: Choosing Christianity in a World of Ideas*. Grand Rapids: Zondervan, 1992.

National Embryo Donation Center. https://www.embryodonation.org/.

National Vital Statistics System. "100 Years of Marriage and Divorce Statistics United States, 1867–1967." U.S. Department of Health, Education, and Welfare, 1973. https://www.cdc.gov/nchs/data/series/sr_21/sr21_024.pdf.

Naugle, David K. "Worldview: Definitions, History, and the Importance of the Topic." http://www3.dbu.edu/naugle/pdf/Worldview_defhistconceptlect.pdf.

———. "Worldview: History, Theology, Implications." http://www3.dbu.edu/naugle/pdf/WV-HistyTheolImplications.pdf.

———. *Worldview: The History of the Concept*. Grand Rapids: Eerdmans, 2002.

Newheiser, Jim. *Marriage, Divorce, and Remarriage: Critical Questions and Answers*. Phillipsburg, NJ: P&R Publishing, 2017.

Niebuhr, H. Richard. *Christ and Culture*. San Francisco: HarperCollins, 2001.

Noddings, Nel. "Caring." In *Justice and Care: Essential Readings in Feminist Ethics*, edited by Virginia Held, 7–30. Boulder, CO: Westview, 1995.

Northcott, Michael S. *The Environment and Christian Ethics*. New York: Cambridge University Press, 1996.

———. "The Spirit of Environmentalism." In *The Care of Creation*, edited by R. J. Berry, 167–74. Leicester, UK: Inter-Varsity Press, 2000.

Nyquist, J. Paul. *Is Justice Possible? The Elusive Pursuit of What Is Right*. Chicago: Moody, 2017.

O'Brien, Peter T. *The Letter to the Ephesians*. PNTC. Grand Rapids: Eerdmans, 1999.

Oden, Thomas C. *The Living God*. Vol. 1 of *Systematic Theology*. Peabody, MA: Hendriksen, 2008.

O'Donovan, Oliver. *Begotten or Made?* Oxford: Clarendon/Oxford University Press, 2002.

———. *The Just War Revisited*. Cambridge: Cambridge University Press, 2003.

———. *Resurrection and Moral Order: An Outline for Evangelical Ethics*. 2nd ed. Grand Rapids: Eerdmans, 1994.

Olasky, Marvin N. *Abortion Rites: A Social History of Abortion in America*. Wheaton, IL: Crossway, 1992.

Orr, James. *The Christian View of God and the World as Centering in the Incarnation*. Edinburgh: Andrew Eliot, 1893.

Orr, Robert D., and Susan Salladay. "Wisdom from Health Care." In *Why the Church Needs Bioethics: A Guide to Wise Engagement with Life's Challenges*, edited by John F. Kilner, 206–22. Grand Rapids: Zondervan, 2011.

Osborne, Grant R. *The Hermeneutical Spiral: A Comprehensive Introduction to Biblical Interpretation*. 2nd ed. Downers Grove, IL: InterVarsity Press, 2006.

Outka, Gene. *Agape: An Ethical Analysis*. New Haven, CT: Yale University Press, 1972.

Outler, Albert C. "The Wesleyan Quadrilateral in Wesley." *Wesleyan Theological Journal* 20, no. 1 (1985): 7–18.

Owens, Erik C., John D. Carlson, and Eric P. Elshtain, eds. *Religion and the Death Penalty: A Call for Reckoning*. Grand Rapids: Eerdmans, 2004.

Packer, J. I. *Concise Theology*. Wheaton, IL: Tyndale, 1993.

———. *Keep in Step with the Spirit: Finding Fullness in Our Walk with God*. 2nd ed. Grand Rapids: Baker, 2005.

———. *Knowing God*. Downers Grove, IL: InterVarsity Press, 1973.

Panicola, Michael R., David M. Belde, John Paul Slosar, and Mark F. Repenshek. *Health Care Ethics: Theological Foundations, Contemporary Issues, and Controversial Cases*. Winona, MN: Anselm Academic, 2011.

Parker, Kim, and Renee Stepler. "As U.S. Marriage Rate Hovers at 50%, Education Gap in Marital Status Widens." Pew Research Center, September 14, 2017. https://www.pewresearch.org/fact-tank/2017/09/14/as-u-s-marriage-rate-hovers-at-50-education-gap-in-marital-status-widens/.

Parker, Simon B. "The Hebrew Bible and Homosexuality." *Quarterly Review* 11, no. 3 (Fall 1991): 4–19.

Patterson, Eric. *Just American Wars: Ethical Dilemmas in U.S. Military History*. New York: Routledge, 2019.

Paul, Maureen, E. Steve Lichtenberg, Lynn Borgatta, David A. Grimes, Phillip G. Stubblefield, and Mitchell D. Creinin. *Management of Unintended and Abnormal Pregnancy: Comprehensive Abortion Care*. West Sussex, UK: Wiley-Blackwell, 2009.

Paul VI. *Humanae Vitae*. 1968. http://www.vatican.va/content/paul-vi/en/encyclicals/documents/hf_p-vi_enc_25071968_humanae-vitae.html.

Pavone, Mary Ellen, Joy Innes, Jennifer Hirshfeld-Cytron, Ralph Kazer, and John Zhang. "Comparing Thaw Survival, Implantation and Live Birth Rates from Cryopreserved Zygotes, Embryos and Blastocysts." *Journal of Human Reproductive Sciences* 4, no. 1 (January–April 2011): 23–28. Accessed June 15, 2020. https://www.ncbi.nlm.nih.gov/pmc/articles/PMC3136065/#.

PDR. "Ethinyl estradiol/norgestimate—Drug Summary." Accessed June 9, 2020. https://www.pdr.net/drug-summary/Ortho-Tri-Cyclen-Lo-ethinyl-estradiol-norgestimate-1363.4038.

———. "Medroxyprogesterone acetate—Drug Summary." Accessed June 9, 2020. https://www.pdr.net/drug-summary/Depo-Provera-Sterile-Aqueous-Suspension-medroxyprogesterone-acetate-2875.8223#15.

Pearcey, Nancy R. *Love Thy Body: Answering Hard Questions about Life and Sexuality*. Grand Rapids: Baker, 2018.

Peart, Norman Anthony. *Separate No More: Understanding and Developing Racial Reconciliation in Your Church*. Grand Rapids: Baker, 2000.

Pellegrino, Edmund D. "The False Promise of Beneficent Killing." In *Regulating How We Die: The Ethical, Medical, and Legal Issues Surrounding Physician-Assisted Suicide*, edited by Linda L. Emanuel, 71–91. Cambridge, MA: Harvard University Press, 1998.

Pennington, Jonathan T. *The Sermon on the Mount and Human Flourishing: A Theological Commentary*. Grand Rapids: Baker, 2016.

Perkins, John M. *Beyond Charity: The Call to Christian Community Development*. Grand Rapids: Baker, 1993.

———. *Dream with Me: Race, Love, and the Struggle We Must Win*. Grand Rapids: Baker, 2017.

———. *One Blood: Parting Words to the Church on Race and Love*. Chicago: Moody, 2018.

Peterson, David. *Engaging with God: A Biblical Theology of Worship*. Downers Grove, IL: InterVarsity Press, 1992.

Pflum, Mary. "Nation's Fertility Clinics Struggle with a Growing Number of Abandoned Embryos." NBC News, August 12, 2019. Accessed June 11, 2020. https://www.nbcnews.com/health/features/nation-s-fertility-clinics-struggle-growing-number-abandoned-embryos-n1040806.

Piper, John. *Bloodlines: Race, Cross, and the Christian*. Wheaton, IL: Crossway, 2011.

———. "How the Spirit Helps Us Understand," May 20, 1984. Accessed February 15, 2019. https://www.desiringgod.org/messages/how-the-spirit-helps-us-understand.

———. *This Momentary Marriage: A Parable of Permanence*. Wheaton, IL: Crossway, 2009.

———. "What Does the Gospel Say?" In *The Gospel and Same-Sex Marriage*, edited by Russell D. Moore and Andrew T. Walker, 27–40. Nashville: B&H Academic, 2016.

Plan B. "How It Works." Accessed June 11, 2020. https://planb.ca/how-it-works.html#:~:text=If%20taken%20within%2072%20hours,from%20attaching%20to%20the%2()uterus.

Plato. *Apology*. In *A Plato Reader: Eight Essential Dialogues*, edited by C. D. C. Reeve, 21–46. Indianapolis: Hackett, 2012.

———. *Republic*. In *A Plato Reader: Eight Essential Dialogues*, edited by C. D. C. Reeve, 267–573. Indianapolis: Hackett, 2012.

———. *Symposium*. In *A Plato Reader: Eight Essential Dialogues*, edited by C. D. C. Reeve, 153–208. Indianapolis: Hackett, 2012.

Platt, David. *Counter Culture: A Compassionate Call to Counter Culture in a World of Poverty, Same-Sex Marriage, Racism, Sex Slavery, Immigration, Abortion, Persecution, Orphans, and Pornography*. Carol Stream, IL: Tyndale, 2015.

———. *Radical: Taking Back Your Faith from the American Dream*. Colorado Springs: Multnomah, 2010.

Plummer, Robert L. *40 Questions about Interpreting the Bible*. Grand Rapids: Kregel, 2010.

Pojman, Louis P. *Ethics: Discovering Right and Wrong*. Belmont, CA: Wadsworth, 1990.

———. *Life and Death: Grappling with the Moral Dilemmas of Our Time*. Belmont, CA: Wadsworth, 2000.

Pojman, Louis P., Paul Pojman, and Katie McShane, eds. *Environmental Ethics: Readings in Theory and Application*. 7th ed. Boston: Wadsworth, 2016.

Ponder, Douglas B. "Thanks Be to God: Exploring the Nature and Place of Gratitude in Christian Ethics." ThM thesis, Southeastern Baptist Theological Seminary, 2020.

Poythress, Vern S. *Redeeming Science*. Wheaton, IL: Crossway, 2006.

Quigley, William P. "The Living Wage and Catholic Social Teaching." *America: The Jesuit Review of Faith & Culture*, August 28, 2006. Accessed November 11, 2020. https://www.americamagazine.org/issue/581/article/living-wage-and -catholic-social-teaching.

Quill, Timothy E. "Death and Dignity: A Case of Individualized Decision-Making." *NEJM* 324 (March 7, 1991): 691–94.

Quill, Timothy E., and Margaret E. Battin. *Physician-Assisted Dying: The Case for Palliative Care and Patient Choice*. Baltimore: Johns Hopkins University Press, 2004.

Quinones, Julian, and Arijeta Lajka. "What Kind of Society Do You Want to Live In? Inside the Country Where Down Syndrome Is Disappearing." CBS News, August 14, 2017. Accessed April 7, 2020. https://www.cbsnews.com/news /down-syndrome-iceland/.

Rachels, James. "Active and Passive Euthanasia." *NEJM* 292, no. 2 (January 9, 1975): 78–80.

Rachels, James, and Stuart Rachels. *The Elements of Moral Philosophy*. 9th ed. New York: McGraw-Hill Education, 2019.

Rae, Scott B. *Moral Choices: An Introduction to Ethics*. 4th ed. Grand Rapids: Zondervan, 2018.

Rakestraw, Robert V. "Ethical Choices: A Case for Non-Conflicting Absolutism." *Criswell Theological Review* 2, no. 2 (1988): 239–67.

———. "Ethical Choices: A Case for Non-Conflicting Absolutism." In *Theory and Method*, edited by David K. Clark and Robert V. Rakestraw, 118–24. Vol. 1 of *Readings in Christian Ethics*. Grand Rapids: Baker, 1994.

Ramsey, Paul. *Basic Christian Ethics*. New York: Charles Scribner's Sons, 1951.

———. "'Euthanasia' and Dying Well Enough." *Linacre Quarterly* 44, no. 1 (February 1977): 37–46. Accessed February 5, 2020. https://epublications.marquette .edu/lnq/vol44/iss1/7/.

———. "The Indignity of 'Death with Dignity.'" *Hastings Center Studies* 2, no. 2 (May 1974): 47–62.

———. *The Just War: Force and Political Responsibility*. Lanham, MD: Rowman & Littlefield, 1983.

———. "Military Service as a Moral System." *MCR* 2, no. 1 (January 1973): 8–21.

———. *War and the Christian Conscience: How Shall Modern War Be Conducted Justly?* Durham, NC: Duke University Press, 1961.

Ratzinger, Joseph. "Instruction on Certain Aspects of the 'Theology of Liberation.'" Congregation for the Doctrine of Faith, August 6, 1984. http://www.vatican.va/roman_curia/congregations/cfaith/documents/rc_con_cfaith_doc_19840806_theology-liberation_en.html.

Rawls, John. *Justice as Fairness: A Restatement.* Cambridge, MA: Harvard University Press, 2001.

———. *A Theory of Justice.* Cambridge, MA: Harvard University Press, 1971.

Reeves, Michael. *Delighting in the Trinity: An Introduction to the Christian Faith.* Downers Grove, IL: InterVarsity Press, 2012.

Regan, Richard J. *Just War: Principles and Cases.* Washington, DC: Catholic University of America Press, 1996.

Reiman, Jeffrey. *Critical Moral Liberalism.* Lanham, MD: Rowman & Littlefield, 1997.

Reinhart, R. J. "George H. W. Bush Retrospective." Gallup, December 1, 2018. Accessed April 3, 2020. https://news.gallup.com/opinion/gallup/234971/george-bush-retrospective.aspx.

Reuschling, Wyndy Corbin. *Reviving Evangelical Ethics: The Promises and Pitfalls of Classic Models of Morality.* Grand Rapids: Brazos, 2008.

Rhodes, Michael, and Robby Holt with Brian Fikkert. *Practicing the King's Economy: Honoring Jesus in How We Work, Earn, Spend, Save, and Give.* Grand Rapids: Baker, 2018.

Richards, Jay W. *Money, Greed, and God: Why Capitalism Is the Solution and Not the Problem.* New York: HarperOne, 2009.

Ricucci, Gary, and Betsy Ricucci. *Love That Lasts: When Marriage Meets Grace.* Wheaton, IL: Crossway, 2006.

Roberts, J. Deotis. *Liberation and Reconciliation: A Black Theology.* 2nd ed. Louisville: Westminster John Knox, 2005.

Rooker, Mark F. *The Ten Commandments: Ethics for the Twenty-First Century.* Nashville: B&H Academic, 2010.

Ross, Allen P. *Recalling the Hope of Glory: Biblical Worship from the Garden to the New Creation.* Grand Rapids: Kregel, 2006.

Ross, W. D. *The Right and the Good.* Oxford: Oxford University Press, 1930.

Ryan, George. "An Address on the Death Penalty." University of Chicago Divinity School, June 3, 2002. Accessed January 10, 2020. https://www.pewforum.org/2002/06/03/governor-george-ryan-an-address-on-the-death-penalty/.

Ryrie, Charles C. *Basic Theology.* Wheaton, IL: Victor, 1986.

Sailhamer, John H. "Genesis." In *Genesis, Exodus, Leviticus, Numbers,* edited by

Frank E. Gaebelein, 3–284. Expositor's Bible Commentary 2. Grand Rapids: Zondervan, 1990.

Sanders, Fred. *The Deep Things of God: How the Trinity Changes Everything.* 2nd ed. Wheaton, IL: Crossway, 2017.

Schaeffer, Francis. *A Christian Manifesto.* Westchester, IL: Crossway, 1981.

———. *Pollution and the Death of Man.* Wheaton, IL: Crossway, 1970.

Schaeffer, Francis, and Udo W. Middelmann. *Pollution and the Death of Man.* Wheaton, IL: Crossway, 2011.

Schweizer, Valerie J. "Marriage to Divorce Ratio in the U.S.: Geographic Variation, 2018." National Center for Family and Marriage Research, 2019. https://www.bgsu.edu/content/dam/BGSU/college-of-arts-and-sciences/NCFMR/documents/FP/fp-19-24-mar-div-ratio.pdf.

Sedgh, Gilda, Jonathan Bearak, Susheela Singh, Akinrinola Bankole, Anna Popinchalk, Bela Ganatra, Clémentine Rossier, Caitlin Gerdts, Özge Tunçalp, Brooke Ronald Johnson Jr., Heidi Bart Johnston, and Leontine Alkema. "Abortion Incidence between 1990 and 2014: Global, Regional, and Subregional Levels and Trends." *Lancet* 388, no. 10041 (July 16, 2016): 258–67. Accessed April 7, 2020. https://www.thelancet.com/journals/lancet/article/PIIS0140–6736(16)30380–4/fulltext.

Semega, Jessica, Melissa Kollar, Emily A. Shrider, and John F. Creamer. *Income and Poverty in the United States: 2019.* Washington, DC: U.S. Census Bureau, 2019. Accessed November 6, 2020. https://www.census.gov/content/dam/Census/library/publications/2020/demo/p60-270.pdf.

Sider, Ronald J., ed. *The Early Church on Killing: A Comprehensive Sourcebook on War, Abortion, and Capital Punishment.* Grand Rapids: Baker Academic, 2012.

———. *Rich Christians in an Age of Hunger.* Rev. ed. Dallas: Word, 1997.

Singer, Peter. *Animal Liberation.* New York: HarperCollins, 2009.

———. *Practical Ethics.* 3rd ed. Cambridge: Cambridge University Press, 2011.

Sire, James. *The Universe Next Door: A Basic Worldview Catalog.* 4th ed. Downers Grove, IL: InterVarsity Press, 2004.

Sleeth, J. Matthew. *Serve God, Save the Planet: A Christian Call to Action.* Grand Rapids: Zondervan, 2006.

Sleeth, Nancy. "Isn't It All Going to Burn Anyway? Finding Common Ground with Creation Care Skeptics." In *A Faith Encompassing All Creation*, edited by Tripp York and Andy Alexis-Baker, 111–19. Eugene, OR: Cascade, 2014.

Smith, Harmon L., and Louis W. Hodges. *The Christian and His Decisions: An Introduction to Christian Ethics.* Nashville: Abingdon, 1969.

Smith, James K. A. *Desiring the Kingdom.* Grand Rapids: Baker, 2009.

Southern Baptist Convention. "Resolution on Birth Control," 1934. Accessed June 9, 2020. http://www.sbc.net/resolutions/285/resolution-on-birth-control.

———. "Resolution on Permissiveness and Family Planning," 1977. Accessed June 9, 2020. http://www.sbc.net/resolutions/796/resolution-on-permissiveness-and-family-planning.

Sprinkle, Preston. *People to Be Loved: Why Homosexuality Is Not Just an Issue.* Grand Rapids: Zondervan, 2016.

Sproul, R. C. *The Mystery of the Holy Spirit.* Fearn, Ross-shire, Scotland: Christian Focus, 1990.

Stanford School of Medicine. "Where Do Americans Die?" Accessed February 4, 2020. https://palliative.stanford.edu/home-hospice-home-care-of-the-dying-patient/where-do-americans-die/.

Stassen, Glen H., and David P. Gushee. *Kingdom Ethics: Following Jesus in Contemporary Context.* Downers Grove, IL: InterVarsity Press, 2003.

Stewart, Gary P., John F. Kilner, and William R. Cutrer, eds. *Basic Questions on Sexuality and Reproductive Technology: When Is It Right to Intervene?* Grand Rapids: Kregel, 1998.

Stott, John. *Issues Facing Christians Today.* 4th ed. Grand Rapids: Zondervan, 2006.

Strauss, Mark L. *Remarriage after Divorce in Today's Church: Three Views.* Grand Rapids: Zondervan, 2006.

Strickland, Walter R., II, and Dayton Hartman. *For God So Loved the World.* Nashville: B&H Academic, 2020.

Stuart, Douglas K. *Exodus.* NAC 2. Nashville: B&H, 2006.

Sunshine, Glenn. "Who Are the Poor?" In *For the Least of These: A Biblical Answer to Poverty*, edited by Anne R. Bradley and Art Lindsley, 17–38. Grand Rapids: Zondervan, 2014.

Taylor, Paul. *Respect for Nature: A Theory of Environmental Ethics.* Princeton, NJ: Princeton University Press, 1986.

Teno, Joan M., Pedro L. Gozalo, Julie P. W. Bynum, Natalie E. Leland, Susan C. Miller, Nancy E. Morden, Thomas Scupp, David C. Goodman, and Vincent Mor. "Change in End-of-Life Care for Medicare Beneficiaries." *JAMA* 309, no. 5 (2013): 470–77. Accessed February 4, 2020. https://jamanetwork.com/journals/jama/fullarticle/1568250.

Tertullian. *On Idolatry.* Edited by Alexander Roberts, James Donaldson, and A. Cleveland Coxe. Translated by S. Thelwall. Ante-Nicene Fathers 3. Buffalo: Christian Literature, 1885. Accessed April 3, 2020. http://www.newadvent.org/fathers/0302.htm.

Theology of Work Project. "Gleaning (Leviticus 19:9–10)." *Leviticus and Work*, 2014. https://www.theologyofwork.org/old-testament/leviticus-and-work/holiness-leviticus-1727/gleaning-leviticus-19910.

Thielicke, Helmut. "The Borderline Situation of Extreme Conflict." In *Theology* and Method, edited by David K. Clark and Robert V. Rakestraw, 125–30. Vol. 1 of *Readings in Christian Ethics*. Grand Rapids: Baker, 1994.

———. *Foundations*. Vol. 1 of *Theological Ethics*. Edited by William H. Lazareth. Philadelphia: Fortress Press, 1966.

Thiselton, Anthony C. *The First Epistle to the Corinthians*. New International Greek Testament Commentary. Grand Rapids: Eerdmans, 2000.

Thomas, Gary. *Sacred Marriage*. Rev. ed. Grand Rapids: Zondervan, 2015.

Thomson, Judith Jarvis. "A Defense of Abortion." *Philosophy & Public Affairs* 1, no. 1 (Fall 1971): 47–66.

Thorsen, Donald A. D. *The Wesleyan Quadrilateral*. Grand Rapids: Zondervan, 1990. Reprint, Lexington, KY: Emeth, 2005.

Tolkien, J. R. R. *The Return of the King: Being the Third Part of the Lord of the Rings*. New York: Ballantine, 2012.

Tollefson, Christopher. "Torture: What It Is, and Why It Is Wrong." Real Clear Politics, April 28, 2009. https://www.realclearpolitics.com/articles/2009/04/28/torture_what_it_is_and_why_it_is_wrong_96216.html.

Tooley, Michael. "Abortion and Infanticide." In *Rights and Wrongs of Abortion*, edited by Marshall Cohen, Thomas Nagel, and Thomas Scanlon, 52–84. Princeton, NJ: Princeton University Press, 1974.

Torrance, Andrew B., and Thomas H. McCall, eds. *Christ and the Created Order: Perspectives from Theology, Philosophy, and Science*. Grand Rapids: Zondervan, 2018.

Tozer, A. W. *The Knowledge of the Holy*. San Francisco: HarperCollins, 1961.

Tripp, Paul David. *What Did You Expect? Redeeming the Realities of Marriage*. Wheaton, IL: Crossway, 2010.

2018 SBC Annual Meeting. "Annual Meeting Resolutions," June 12–13, 2018. Accessed January 29, 2020. http://sbcannualmeeting.net/sbc18/resolutions/.

Unander, Dave. *Shattering the Myth of Race: Genetic Realities and Biblical Truths*. Valley Forge, PA: Judson, 2000.

United Nations. *World Population Policies 2017: Abortion Laws and Policies (2020)*. Accessed April 7, 2020. https://www.un.org/en/development/desa/population/publications/pdf/policy/WPP2017/WPP2017_Report.pdf.

VanDrunen, David. *Bioethics and the Christian Life: A Guide to Making Difficult Decisions*. Wheaton, IL: Crossway, 2009.

VanGemeren, Willem A. "Psalms." In *Psalms, Proverbs, Ecclesiastes, Song of Songs*, edited by Frank E. Gaebelein, 3–880. Expositor's Bible Commentary 5. Grand Rapids: Zondervan, 1991.

Vanhoozer, Kevin J. "Holy Scripture." In *Christian Dogmatics: Reformed Theology for the Church Catholic*, edited by Michael Allen and Scott R. Swain, 30–56. Grand Rapids: Baker, 2016.

Van Regenmorter, John. "Frozen Out: What to Do with Those Extra Embryos." *Christianity Today*, July 2004, 32–33.

Van Til, Cornelius. *Christian Theistic Ethics*. Phillipsburg, NJ: Presbyterian and Reformed, 1980.

Verhey, Allen. *The Christian Art of Dying: Learning from Jesus*. Grand Rapids: Eerdmans, 2011.

Vines, Matthew. *God and the Gay Christian: The Biblical Case in Support of Same-Sex Relationships*. New York: Convergent, 2014.

Walker, Andrew T. *God and the Transgender Debate: What Does the Bible Actually Say about Gender Identity?* Centralia, WA: Good Book Company, 2017.

Walvoord, John F., and Roy B. Zuck. *The Bible Knowledge Commentary, New Testament Edition*. Colorado Springs: David C. Cook, 1983.

Walzer, Michael. *Just and Unjust Wars: A Moral Argument with Historical Illustrations*. 5th ed. New York: Basic, 2015.

Wang, Wendy. "A Portrait of Contemporary Family Living Arrangements for U.S. Children." Institute for Family Studies, April 14, 2020. Accessed April 16, 2020. https://ifstudies.org/blog/a-portrait-of-contemporary-family-living-arrangements-for-us-children.

Warfield, B. B. "The Real Problem of Inspiration." In *Revelation and Inspiration*, 169–228. Vol. 1 of *The Works of Benjamin B. Warfield*. Grand Rapids: Baker, 2003.

Waters, Brent. *Reproductive Technology: Towards a Theology of Procreative Stewardship*. Cleveland: Pilgrim Press, 2001.

Weaver, Richard M. *Ideas Have Consequences*. Chicago: University of Chicago Press, 1948.

Weigel, Moira. "'I Have Multiple Loves': Carrie Jenkins Makes the Philosophical Case for Polyamory." Chronicle of Higher Education, February 3, 2017. https://www.chronicle.com/article/I-Have-Multiple-Loves-/239077.

Wenham, Gordon J. "Does the New Testament Approve Remarriage after Divorce?" *SBJT* 6, no. 1 (Spring 2002): 30–45.

———. "Sanctuary Symbolism in the Garden of Eden Story." In *Proceedings of the Ninth World Congress of Jewish Studies, Division A: The Period of the Bible*, 19–25. Jerusalem: World Union of Jewish Studies, 1986.

———. *Story as Torah*. Grand Rapids: Baker Academic, 2000.

Wenham, Gordon J., and William A. Heth. *Jesus and Divorce*. Updated ed. Eugene, OR: Wipf & Stock, 2002.

White, Lynn, Jr. "The Historical Roots of Our Ecological Crisis." *Science* 155 (March 10, 1967): 1203–7.

White, R. E. O. *Christian Ethics*. Macon, GA: Mercer University Press, 1994.

Wiker, Benjamin. *Moral Darwinism: How We Became Hedonists*. Downers Grove, IL: InterVarsity Press, 2002.

Wilcox, W. Bradford. "The Marriage Divide: How and Why Working-Class Families Are More Fragile Today." Institute for Family Studies, September 25, 2017. Accessed May 15, 2020. https://ifstudies.org/blog/the-marriage-divide-how-and-why-working-class-families-are-more-fragile-today.

——. "Married Parents: One Way to Reduce Child Poverty." Institute for Family Studies, June 21, 2017. Accessed May 15, 2020. https://ifstudies.org/blog/married-parents-one-way-to-reduce-child-poverty.

Wilgoren, Jodi. "Citing Issue of Fairness, Governor Clears Out Death Row in Illinois." *New York Times*, January 12, 2003. Accessed March 31, 2020. https://www.nytimes.com/2003/01/12/us/citing-issue-of-fairness-governor-clears-out-death-row-in-illinois.html.

Williams, Jarvis J. *One New Man: The Cross and Racial Reconciliation in Pauline Theology*. Nashville: B&H Academic, 2010.

Williams, John R. *Medical Ethics Manual*. 3rd ed. Ferney-Voltaire Cedex, France: World Medical Association, 2015. Accessed February 14, 2020. https://www.wma.net/wpcontent/uploads/2016/11/Ethics_manual_3rd_Nov2015_en_1x1.pdf#page=38.

Wirzba, Norman. *From Nature to Creation: A Christian Vision for Understanding and Loving Our World*. Grand Rapids: Baker, 2015.

Wolters, Albert M. *Creation Regained: Biblical Basics for a Reformational Worldview*. 2nd ed. Grand Rapids: Eerdmans, 2005.

World Bank. "Poverty Overview." Accessed November 12, 2020. http://www.worldbank.org/en/topic/poverty/overview.

World Health Organization. "Infertility Definitions and Terminology." Accessed June 8, 2020. https://www.who.int/reproductivehealth/topics/infertility/definitions/en/.

Wright, Christopher J. H. *The Mission of God*. Downers Grove, IL: IVP Academic, 2006.

——. *Old Testament Ethics for the People of God*. Downers Grove, IL: IVP Academic, 2004.

Wright, N. T. *After You Believe: Why Christian Character Matters*. New York: HarperOne, 2010.

Yancey, George. *Beyond Racial Gridlock: Embracing Mutual Responsibility*. Downers Grove, IL: InterVarsity Press, 2006.

Yarhouse, Mark A. *Understanding Gender Dysphoria: Navigating Transgender Issues in a Changing Culture*. Downers Grove, IL: IVP Academic, 2015.

Yoder, John Howard. *The Politics of Jesus: Victi Agnus Noster*. Grand Rapids: Eerdmans, 1972.

York, Tripp, and Andy Alexis-Baker, eds. *A Faith Encompassing All Creation.* Eugene, OR: Cascade, 2014.

Young, Richard A. *Healing the Earth: A Theocentric Perspective on Environmental Problems and Their Solutions.* Nashville: B&H, 1994.

Yuan, Christopher. *Holy Sexuality and the Gospel: Sex, Desire, and Relationships Shaped by God's Grand Story.* New York: Multnomah, 2018.

Yuill, Kevin. *Assisted Suicide: The Liberal, Humanist Case against Legalization.* New York: Palgrave Macmillan, 2013.

Zill, Nicholas. "Family Still Matters for Key Indicators of Student Performance." Institute for Family Studies, April 6, 2020. Accessed April 16, 2020. https://ifstudies.org/blog/family-still-matters-for-key-indicators-of-student-performance.

Index of Scripture

Index of Subjects and Names

P&R Academic

Reliable. Relevant. Reformed.

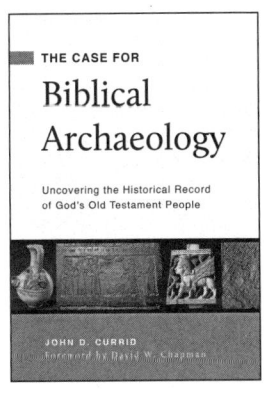

"I strongly recommend this."
—**H. Wayne House**

"Fills an important gap."
—**Michael Horton**

"[An] outstanding achievement."
—**J. I. Packer**

"Refreshingly insightful,
profoundly biblical."
—**Wayne Grudem**

"[A] magnificent work."
—**Eugene H. Merrill**

"Accessible and user-friendly."
—**Timothy Keller**

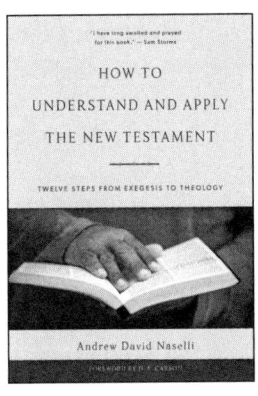

Discover our wide-ranging academic resources at www.prpbooks.com.
We offer desk, examination, and personal copies of textbooks to qualifying
professors. See www.prpbooks.com/academic-copies.

Did you find this book helpful?
Consider leaving a review online.
The authors appreciate your feedback!

Or write to P&R at editorial@prpbooks.com
with your comments. We'd love to hear from you.